HUMAN THOUGHT

for
Bob Chandreas
with
best regards,

Joe Mendola

PHILOSOPHICAL STUDIES SERIES

VOLUME 70

Founded by Wilfrid S. Sellars and Keith Lehrer

The titles published in this series are listed at the end of this volume.

HUMAN THOUGHT

JOSEPH MENDOLA
University of Nebraska-Lincoln, U.S.A.

KLUWER ACADEMIC PUBLISHERS
DORDRECHT / BOSTON / LONDON

A C.I.P. Catalogue record for this book is available from the Library of Congress.

ISBN 0-7923-4401-4 (Hb)
ISBN 0-7923-4402-2 (Pb)

Published by Kluwer Academic Publishers,
P.O. Box 17, 3300 AA Dordrecht, The Netherlands.

Kluwer Academic Publishers incorporates
the publishing programmes of
D. Reidel, Martinus Nijhoff, Dr W. Junk and MTP Press.

Sold and distributed in the U.S.A. and Canada
by Kluwer Academic Publishers,
101 Philip Drive, Norwell, MA 02061, U.S.A.

In all other countries, sold and distributed
by Kluwer Academic Publishers Group,
P.O. Box 322, 3300 AH Dordrecht, The Netherlands.

Printed on acid-free paper

Printed in the Netherlands

For Mom, Dad, Gary, and Pam

ACKNOWLEDGMENTS

I am grateful for help from Jean Griffin, Robert Audi, David Austin, Bob Batterman, Ed Becker, Bryan Belknap, Hugh Benson, Mike Bishop, Tim Black, Nancy Brahm, A B Carter, Al Casullo, Mark Cullison, Maja de Keijzer, Jonathan Evans, Kit Fine, Pat Francken, Allan Gibbard, Ann Hickman, Phil Hugly, Harry Ide, Eileen John, Jim Joyce, Jaegwon Kim, Keith Lehrer, Mary Klucas, Heidi Malm, Ross Mandel, Sally Markowitz, Thad Metz, Alex Miller, Peter Murphy, Lex Newman, Donette Petersen, Jeff Poland, Nelson Potter, Ann Rives, Richard Rodgers, Charlie Sayward, Bill Schmitz, Dion Scott-Kakures, Larry Sklar, Mike Tonderum, Candace Upton, Sheldon Wein, Nick White, Stephen White, Jack Wilson, Cathy Wolfe, Mark van Roojen, Barbara Von Eckardt, Steve Yablo, Xiaomei Yang, and the students of Philosophy 914 in Spring 1992.

CONTENTS

CHAPTER ONE

INTRODUCTION

Worms, dogs, and bats, if they think anything, cannot think about evolutionary biology and quantum mechanics. I believe that we humans are also bound by our form, a form due to some mixture of evolutionary pressure and chance.[1] There are significant limits to what we can think, rooted in the limits of our capacity for experience. And the limits of our capacity for experience are themselves rooted in the very contingent form of our sense organs, our muscles and limbs, and the neurophysiology which links them. These limits place significant restrictions on our ability to understand how we think what we do[2] and the nature of the world.[3]

This book is about what humans can think, about how they think it, and about whether any of it is true. It has three parts: Part One develops a theory of content for human thought. It delineates the things which humans can think. Part Two develops a coherent and humanly conceivable account of the "realization" of such thought, of how thoughts with that range of contents might be constituted, of how there might be people with such thoughts. Part Three argues that no coherent and humanly conceivable account of the realization of our thought is plausible, in particular because no coherently conceivable account of how we have our experience is plausible. How we can think that we think what we think is not how we do think what we think. This is for reasons which also suggest that no positive human conception of anything contingent is true.

This chapter elaborates some elements of this very compressed outline. It approaches the material along a particular axis, as an attempt to answer a recent and rather dramatic skeptical problem. You may be in trouble. Consider this argument:

Premise One:	You are so deeply an agent, and agents so crucially have thoughts with representational content, that if there were no such thoughts you would not exist.
Premise Two:	But there are no thoughts with representational content, and in fact they may be even impossible.

Hence you do not exist, and may be even impossible.

This is a peculiar argument in many ways.[4] Whether such an argument can succeed is at best an open question. But its conclusion is certainly surprising, and there is a case to be made for each of its premises. That case is the focus of the following two sections.

1

Consider this venerable picture: Unlike a wind-blown tree or thunderstorm, you are an *agent*. You *act*, and your actions are explained and constrained by psychological states behind them, by wants, desires, drives, will, appetite, or lust and by perceptions, beliefs, or knowledge of the world. Among the psychological states which underwrite human agency, so the story goes, are states which are about other things under certain of those things' descriptions, which have *representational content*.[5] These psychological states with representational content are the central, crucial examples of what I will call "thoughts".[6] According to our tradition, thoughts with representational content, agency, and action come all together.[7]

Consider an example: Hearing the woods rustle and feeling the wind, seeing the sky darken, you fear a storm. Wanting to stay dry, believing there's a cave nearby on a hill, you run off, hopping over a rotting orange you see in the path. But the sky clears, and you stop. Here you run and hop and stop because of your fears and beliefs and perceptions. In fact, the things you do would not *be* what they are if you lacked the psychological states that lie behind them. Your incomplete run to the hill to keep dry *is* that because it is informed by your beliefs that a storm is coming and that there is a cave to keep you dry, and by your desire to stay dry. Something that looked just like the run could be something very different, say merely romping in the woods, if different states lay behind it.

Consider those perceptions, fears, wants, and beliefs. They are about or of things other than themselves; they have objects. You have a sensation of or a belief about *the orange*. Not all of these objects are real. You fear the coming of the rain, but it never happens. But many psychological states have some object, actual or imagined, happening or not. Call this property their "intentionality".

You saw the orange and believed that it was rotten. But you didn't see the worms crawling around inside. While the rot was in fact a complicated chemical development in an elegant microstructure, while it looked at the properly tiny scale like the coming of the storm, you didn't believe that all *that* was going on. Your psychological states are about things, but sometimes only about them in regard to certain of their features, under certain of their descriptions. The worms and the storm-like appearance are not part of the representational content of your belief in or perception of the rottenness of the orange. They don't enter into your consideration of the orange, your reasoning and inference and action regarding it. Call this feature, this partial blindness and opacity of at least some of your psychological states, their "intensionality".

Whatever elaborations and subtleties distinguish your own picture of ourselves from those favored by others in our ancient tradition, we all share allegiance to this core of doctrine: We and our fellows have thoughts, and of the central and paradigmatic sort we have been discussing. These are psychological states which exhibit intentionality and intensionality, which have "representational content". But, further, with such thoughts come actions. Our thoughts with representational content influence what actions we perform and help determine that they *are* the particular sorts of action they are, runnings to the cave and not merely rompings in the woods.

Of course, not all psychological states are thoughts with representational content. Many of the traditional psychological states do have objects, and they are at least sometimes about objects under some descriptions rather than others. But thoughts with representational content are not the only psychological states which are recognized in our tradition. And there are in fact many different kinds of thoughts which have been recognized. Still, as we will see, only thoughts with representational content, not any particular kind and not any other sort of psychological state, are really central to our self-conception.

You are an agent with thoughts with representational contents, or at least that is the deep traditional core of your conception of yourself. So basic is that conception to what you are taken to be, by yourself and by others, that if there were no such things as such thoughts it could only be in a strained sense that *you* exist. That lends some support to the first premise of our peculiar argument.

2

You may be in trouble and at risk, because there may be no thoughts with representational content, and hence no agents. They may be even impossible. Philosophers have questioned the commonsense conception of agency in a number of ways, have puzzled about our freedom, persistence over time, or identity at a moment. But agency seems to be now more directly and radically in question, since a number of recent authors have argued that there are not, and even *cannot* be, such things as thoughts with representational content.

Arguments with the conclusion that there are no thoughts may hardly seem credible, even given the skeptical heritage of philosophy. In fact that heritage may make such arguments particularly incredible. Descartes, it is said, revolutionized philosophy by bringing epistemological questions, questions about knowledge and the justification of belief, to the center of philosophical discourse.[8] By asking himself in his solitude what he knew *for sure*, whether he could *prove* he wasn't mad or dreaming or misled by a malevolent deity, he gave impetus to epistemic skepticisms which tormented his philosophical descendants. Some became convinced that they could not know if other minds existed, or if there were material things such as they seemed to perceive, or even if they had a past. But most remained convinced that they could know for *certain* that they existed in the moment with the thoughts they took themselves to have. The very thing that is now in question once seemed the one indubitable certainty.

But, so the story goes, philosophy more recently underwent another revolution. Beginning with Frege and Russell and Wittgenstein and Moore, or Brentano and Husserl and Heidegger, or maybe with Nietzsche, philosophers became more than usually obsessed with questions about language and its meaning. The linguistic turn superseded the epistemic one. Philosophy of language, not epistemology, became the central philosophical discipline.[9] And philosophy of language has bred a new sort of skepticism, a skepticism about meaning. The meaning of language had been traditionally thought to be a kind of representational content. But some philosophers turned against such a picture. Wittgenstein suggested that we not study unreflectively the putative representational content of language. He suggested we observe instead how it is used in our complex forms of life.[10] And Kripke has recently read Wittgenstein as having raised a deep skepticism about even the possibility of meaning.[11] Representational content involves intension and intention, but Quine has argued that a scientific philosophy should take flight from talk of intension, and that even the intention of linguistic items is indeterminate. There is, he thinks, no meaning for sentences or theories but one relativized to a scheme of translation arbitrarily chosen from among a group of distinct candidates.[12] And, in a very different tradition, Derrida suggests that to consider texts as primarily bearers of determinate meaning and representational content is to fall prey to an ancient philosophical folly.[13]

This recent skepticism is primarily a skepticism about the meaning of language and not about the representational content of thoughts. Words and not thoughts are its primary concern. But skeptics about the representational content of sentences may also take the representational content of thoughts to be dependent on that of words. Or they may think their arguments apply not merely to language but also directly to thoughts. If there is, as some writers suggest, *nothing* with determinate representational content, then there is no such thing as you take yourself to be. In addition, there have been a number of recent arguments rooted in the development of cognitive science or neuroscience, for instance those of Stephen Stich and Paul Churchland, which suggest more directly that there are no thoughts with representational content.[14]

All of these arguments, those of Wittgenstein, Quine, and Derrida, and those rooted in cognitive science and neuroscience, deserve careful examination, and they will be discussed in detail in later chapters. But none are *obviously* mistaken. They give some support to the thought that there are in fact no thoughts. Indeed, as we shall see, some of them even suggest that thoughts are impossible. Hence these arguments lend some plausibility to the second premise of our troubling argument.

Reasonable arguments against the existence of thoughts with representational content present two dangers. First, the mere prevalence of such arguments raises the disturbing possibility that it may come to be thought that there are no such agents as you take yourself to be. That this *is* a danger is the concern of the next section. A second danger is that those who argue that there are no such thoughts are right. Most immediately this is the focus of the remaining sections of this chapter. But it is also the concern of the rest of this book.

3

Some would say that if there are no agents with representational attitudes you need not be disturbed, for if we came to abandon that picture nothing much would change. Perhaps the picture, if ancient, is a commitment only of philosophers, of Plato and Descartes but not Euripides and your cousins and your aunts. Common sense does not, they say, presuppose thoughts with representational content. It is merely that common discourse includes a certain activity involving psychological terminology. Philosophers mistakenly took this as presupposing both intentionality and intensionality, but life would go on the same if we abandoned the old philosophers' error. And so Wittgenstein teaches us that representational content is not a commitment of our way of talking about ourselves and others. And Davidson tells us how the interpretation of others might go on even if Quine is right about representational content, how in that condition we might legitimately speak of the truth of beliefs, the inferences of reasoners, and the actions of agents.[15]

If you were to insist that belief or inference without representational content is not belief or inference, that truth without the correspondence of representational content to the facts is not truth, that interpretation without the assignment of unrelativized meaning is not interpretation, the friends of this strategy would suggest therapy or translate what you say into something unexpected. They use an old ploy. Like Berkeley, they claim to be revolutionizing only philosophy, to be getting back to common sense. They either try not to allow you the words to state a philosophical view differing from their own, or they allow you the difference but interpret your commonsense examples so that your view conflicts with those examples. But these interpreters beyond representational content face a problem: They must maintain, as the price of consistency, that the apparatus they do admit, beyond representational content, does not presuppose the existence of thoughts with representational content. Consistency demands that if, for instance, they speak of the "truth" of uttered sentences or the play of psychological language in forms of life, then language and sentences are things which can exist when there are no psychological states with representational content. We will see in Chapter Ten that the half-way position of the interpreters fails on this ground. There would be no language of the sort they presume, nothing like ordinary human language, if there were no thoughts with representational content. There can be no consistent salvaging of your commonsense psychological discourse if representational content is lost. There would be no such discourse if there were no thoughts.

Still, some may consistently hunker down into a deeper skepticism. Surely *something* happens in ordinary life, involving what we perhaps mistakenly take to be psychological *vocabulary* and *sentences*, even if there are no thoughts. Some air gets moved by mouths and caught by ears, and ink gets on the page. Even if the commonsense understanding of these phenomena is radically mistaken, that doesn't mean the phenomena don't exist. But it is worth reflecting on how dramatic this suggestion is. For instance, it is far from clear that our ordinary life could survive our recognition that our common understanding is as radically mistaken as skeptics about thoughts with representational content must consistently presume.[16]

Imagine a city street on a summer Saturday. You walk down the sidewalk, dodging passersby. People shop at stands, argue, listen to a sax player. Someone cranks down an awning. Someone sells a newspaper. You hear a loud car radio, and a child crying. A friend rounds the corner, and you stop to talk. Now imagine, if you can, another city, buried in that one of your old experience, in which everything goes on the same but there are no agents. Those hagglers and friends and strollers have no psychological states with representational content, and they don't pretend. They don't consider that others have them either. They all "agree" that they have no beliefs about the street or the stock market or the weather. They don't want food, have no frustrated desires for self-respect. They aren't running to catch the bus, nor putting down the awning to shade the window and not to interrupt a certain chemical reaction. They don't know you. When they look in your direction they don't see your face as opposed to the atomic structure beneath. For all their gesticulations and all the sounds that come out of their mouths, they aren't telling anyone anything in particular nor treating them as agents. They aren't, at least in the common understanding of those things, reasoning, or inferring, or criticizing, or justifying. It may be hard to imagine this, but think it repeatedly, as you might repeat a word until its sense is lost to you.

That would be how things would seem if you and other people abandoned belief in thoughts with representational content and the other things which rest on them. That would be your vision of the world in a life after content. Now ask yourself if it in any way resembles the particular form our life after content would take. Would things really go on the same? Would people gesticulate and make sounds and hand over fruit for metal coins if they didn't think the others were agents? Doesn't it *matter* that people think of other people as having beliefs which are true or false and desires which may be satisfied or frustrated, good or bad? Can people get on without doing so? Doesn't our ethical discourse, don't our institutions, don't all our forms of social life, presuppose that there are agents who believe and desire and act and see and need? Would life after belief in representational content, and so after our ethics and politics and institutions, really be even remotely the same? Maybe you could think that no one else is an agent and survive that peculiar loneliness. Maybe you'd be lucky and after content people would go on behaving as if they were agents, and as if they thought they were. But now think of yourself. Can you even imagine that you are not an agent? What would it be like to treat *yourself* as if you had no thoughts, as if you no longer reasoned and inferred and acted? Wouldn't life after content be almost unimaginably different than our own? Wouldn't people after content, without a conception of themselves and others as agents, cease to interact as persons?

Some may grant all this, but claim that change might be for the best. Certainly human lives are not now in the form they should be, few intellectual revolutions have been obvious disasters, and hope may be taken from the fact that skepticism about content, especially in its continental varieties, is often allied with progressive politics.[17] But we have as yet no coherent understanding of a politics without people, of a liberation which is not a liberation of persons, of agents. If some social life could survive the death of content, the brave new idiom of that life which would replace our psychological talk might simply serve to disguise some of the bad things which happen to people. And it is far from clear that any social life could survive that change. There is some evidence that the autistic have a specific neurological deficit which makes them unable to form a conception of others' agency.[18] Their disabilities may be our best clue about what it would be like not to think of others as agents. And if there's a model for failing to think of oneself as an agent, it may be some extreme schizophrenia.[19]

Of course, no one really takes philosophy as seriously as this suggests. The streets didn't ring with cries when Quine abandoned determinate representational content. It is unlikely that philosophers could overturn a conception of ourselves as basic as this one. Even philosophers themselves who reach skeptical conclusions in this area hardly act as if they believe them. They may hasten to proclaim that common life ought go on unchanged if a mere philosophical interpretation of common sense is destroyed, or they may just go on with their lives and leave their philosophical positions behind in the study. But a small chance of horror may still be a bad risk.

4

And even if no one takes philosophy that seriously, there is still a danger. If the arguments of those who would abandon belief in representational thoughts are correct, if there aren't in fact any such things, then that's the way things are. There may be no agents such as you take yourself to be whether you admit it or not, whether it's horrible or mad or inconvenient to think so or not. Even if those who in theory eschew belief in representational content are insincere or only half believe what they say, maybe the truth on these matters is something people can only insincerely half-believe. Maybe the ancient picture is fortunate or innate, but nonetheless an error. Maybe that root of our sociality, institutions, and morality is a mistake. There are *two* dangers we face. One is that people will come to abandon the notion that there are agents with thoughts with representational content. The other is that the notion is false.

Are there agents? There may seem to be easy roads to a certain and affirmative answer to this question. Descartes would have said so. The foundation of all your knowledge, he held, must be your knowledge that you exist and have the thoughts you do. You may be radically deceived about the world or your past, but you know with surety the contents of your present mind. Nothing, surely not the premises of arguments against your thoughts, is known more certainly than they are.

This cartesian story no longer seems fully convincing. Introspection no longer seems so infinitely reliable, nor even more reliable than all our other sources of knowledge. When people sincerely report introspected beliefs, desires, and emotions, cynical or suspicious or freudian observers may now reasonably retain their doubts. Even if in fact introspection is our most reliable source of knowledge, we are no longer in possession of confidence that it is. It seems to us the sort of thing that other evidence could defeat.

But even if Descartes was wrong in thinking that your thoughts provide an epistemic foundation, it still may seem that to question the representational content of your thoughts is to try to pull the floor out from under yourself while at the same time you try to stand on it. After all, you can't have a thought that there are no thoughts with representational content if that thought is true. And this may seem to provide another sort of quick and easy remedy against skepticism about such thoughts. Such skepticism, which I will label "thought skepticism", may seem oddly self-defeating.

There are various types of self-defeat arguments against thought skepticism which have some currency. First of all, there are what have been called "pragmatic incoherence" arguments.[20] These arguments try to reveal a contradiction not *within* thought skepticism but *between* it and the conditions required for its assertion or consideration. They presume that thought skepticism is a bit like the sentence "There are no sentences." Though we can conceive of conditions which would make that sentence true, they are not conditions in which the sentence itself exists. There are two kinds of pragmatic incoherence arguments, which focus respectively on psychological attitudes towards thought skepticism and on assertion of it.

One might argue in this way: Belief is a kind of thought. Hence if there were no thoughts, no one would believe anything. So if some skeptic believes thought skepticism, then that belief is false. Alternatively, one might favor a line defended by Lynne Rudder Baker against Paul Churchland:[21]

P1) If there are no thoughts, then no one ever means anything when uttering words.

P2) There are meaningful sentences only if people sometimes mean something when uttering words.

P3) If thought skepticism is asserted, then there are meaningful sentences which assert that theory.

P4) If thought skepticism is true, then there are no thoughts.

Hence thought skepticism can be asserted only if it isn't true. It cannot be truly asserted.

Yet another sort of self-defeat argument would maintain that thought skepticism harbors an *internal* contradiction. Such an argument might be modelled on Paul Boghossian's argument that the position of those who would assert that no sentence is true is incoherent:[22] Whatever such a skeptic's controversial philosophical conception of what it is to call a sentence "true", they seem committed to accepting the commonsense "disquotational" principle for the use of that word, that declarative sentence P is properly assertible just in case it is properly assertible that "P" is true. And such a skeptic does not deny that there are sentences. Hence they seem committed to two premises:

P1) "Every sentence is not true" is a sentence.

P2) Every sentence is not true if and only if "Every sentence is not true" is true.

But these two premises entail that it is false that every sentence is not true. They entail that what such a skeptic maintains is false.[23]

Still, the quick remedy of a self-defeat argument is not enough. A good self-defeat argument will cut very deep; it will show that something we take to be absolutely crucial to our cognitive lives, speech or argument or reason-giving or truth, requires thoughts with representational content. But, as I suggested in section 3, no such argument can cut deep enough to touch the really determined skeptic. Those skeptical about thoughts can always insist that there really is no speech or argument or reason-giving or truth, and still not be forced by consistency into silence. Even if the commonsense account of what we are doing now adverts to language and argument and truth, that account need not be correct. Even if in fact we aren't now using language or considering evidence, still we're doing *something*, if only in the sense that trees do things. Still we're moving ink and air around. And, so the skeptic might insist, it is the wonderful behavioral or physical mesh of this movement that really matters. And if none of it is true and none of it false, well then still some of it might have some sort of positive quasi-cognitive value and some of it might lack it. Perhaps this mesh cannot be expressed in English without "false" talk of language and thought, and perhaps its value cannot be expressed without talk of the true and the false, but still the mesh and the value exist.[24] Even if in fact there are no thoughts, that part of our lives which we (so to speak) *call* "cognitive" surely exists. Perhaps, as we have seen, it could not survive (to speak with the vulgar) the *recognition* that there are no thoughts. Perhaps we cannot help but (pardon the phrase) *believe* that it involves thoughts. But that doesn't entail there really are any.

Self-defeat arguments are not sufficient by themselves to conclusively establish that there are thoughts. But they can serve to reinforce our sense of the depth of our commitment to thoughts, a commitment so deep that even those who have denied that there are thoughts have presupposed it. And they can give us a good deal of motivation to examine with a critical eye the arguments of the skeptics. This in fact locates the second problem with the self-defeat arguments, that they cannot alone suffice. Whatever the status of the self-defeat arguments, the *arguments* of the skeptics would need to be defeated for a proper vindication of thoughts and representational content. We need to examine the premises of those arguments, and see which we are prepared to abandon. The arguments may show that there are problems with some of the details of current commonsense psychology or even the ancient tradition of which it is heir. And they may show that the existence of thoughts with representational content is inconsistent with other things we'd like to believe. Representational content and agency may have a cost, and that cost is worth identifying.

It may be that the price is too high. Good skeptical arguments against thoughts often have the following form: There are limited resources, in behavior or neurons or whatever, which could plausibly constitute thoughts, but those limited resources do not suffice. It may be that the conditions required for agency are simply implausible.

That would be bad enough, but there are worse possibilities. Each of the classical arguments against representational content, arguments to be examined in detail in Part Two, arose within a distinguished tradition attempting to make sense of how there *could* be a thought with representational content or a sentence with meaning. Each is a kind of internal criticism of such a tradition. Wittgenstein's alleged skepticism arises out of criticism of his own positive account of meaningfulness in the *Tractatus*.[25] Quine's skeptical *Word and Object* is deeply indebted to Carnap's attempt at empirical semantics.[26] Derrida's skepticism is rooted in internal criticism of Husserl.[27] It may be, if the skeptical arguments succeed as *reductiones* of the most plausible attempts to explain how meaning or representational content *could* be, that there is evidence that such a task cannot be discharged. And this in turn may be evidence that agents are in some sense impossible, that no possible conditions would suffice for agency. Perhaps the project of making sense of agency and thought cannot be carried out. And if thought cannot be made sense of, if we cannot come to understand even how such a thing *could* be, then our agency may well be suspect.

This book attempts another strategy against thought skepticism than the quick remedies we have just dismissed, a strategy which answers the arguments of the thought skeptics. It attempts to overcome the two difficulties just articulated, to establish that agency can be made sense of, and that the conditions which are required for agency are plausible. We will see that even this strategy will to some degree fail, but in a way which reveals that thoughts with representational content are no more suspect than anything else we might be tempted to favor over them, neurons and molecules for instance.

5

For the moment, lay aside the question of whether thoughts and agents are plausible. Does agency even make sense? That question suggests another: What would be required to show that agency makes sense, to show that there are appropriately possible conditions which would suffice for thoughts?

The task might seem easy. Isn't it enough to say that agency requires agency? Certainly that is something we understand, and it is expressible in meaningful language. At the very most, isn't it enough to say that there would be agents if there were thoughts, and thoughts if there were psychological states with representational content?

Certainly these stories are in some weak sense meaningful, and we certainly do, in some similarly weak sense, understand them. But that in itself is not enough. Consider the following two stories: There would be round squares if there were triangular half-moons arranged in the right way. There would be jabberwocks if there were snackersnicks on, but not in, snickersnacks. Such stories do not suffice to make sense of round squares and jabberwocks; they don't really show us how such things could be. But these stories are in some weak sense meaningful and understandable. We know *something* even about jabberwocks.

Of course these two stories might not be meaningful or understandable in the same way as those we need to assess. The first suffers from a kind of inconsistency, and the second from an overabundance of nonsense words, and certainly it doesn't seem likely that stories about agents have *these* problems. But the stories about round squares and jabberwocks do show that the mere fact that we manage to use the words "agent" and "thought" is not enough. It doesn't in itself show that agency makes sense. It is a philosophical discovery at least as old as Socrates that what people say and think often doesn't make sense, and the skeptical arguments show there is at least some danger that talk and thought of agency suffer this problem.

If we are to see whether agency makes sense, then it is clear that we will need an account of what it is to make sense. For now, I will say that a notion or conception, or a story expressing one, makes sense just in case it has "coherent" content. I will say that something makes sense if and only if the conditions it requires are "coherently conceivable". But clearly these are placeholder phrases;

they must be filled in. This will require a theory of coherent content, of coherent conceivability, but the place-holding phrases themselves should be unobjectionable. Even so, some may object that I have slipped in a focus primarily on the content of thoughts rather than on the meaning of sentences. They may claim that the latter place is where making sense occurs. But recall that our concern is primarily to make plausible sense of our *conception* of our own agency.

To make sense of agency, we will need, in addition to a theory of coherent conceivability, an account showing that agency in particular is coherently conceivable in the requisite sense. This will require a general theory of content, not merely of coherent content, though in an indirect way: Agents are things with thoughts, and thoughts have content. Consider the range of those contents. Even if some things agents think are incoherent or senseless or inconsistent or confused, still the range of possible contents of their thoughts includes coherent contents.[28] But a theory of coherent content would be merely a part of a general theory of content. And this general theory of conceivability, this account of the whole range of contents agents' thoughts can have, is crucial to a full understanding of agency and the conditions it may require. After all, thoughts with particular contents require particular conditions.

One might reasonably complain that what is conceivable by one creature need not be conceivable by another, so that there is no single general account of conceivability to be given. This seems to me correct, and requires a qualification. If our goal is to vindicate our self-conception, to make sense of ordinary adult human agency to ordinary adult humans like us, we need be concerned only with a general theory of conceivability for ordinary adult humans, assuming there is such a thing. The project of making sense of agency turns such a theory of representational content back upon itself. It explains how ordinary adult people's thinking is thought by such people, what you are conceiving when you imagine yourself to have psychological states with representational content.

The first two parts of this book attempt to execute this project; they try to make sense of agency. Part One will develop an account of what is conceivable in general by normal adult humans, and coherently conceivable in particular. This will serve both to determine the resources allowed in the construction of a coherent conception of agents, and to fix the range of contents which the agents think. Part Two will construct, in a kind of rigorous imagination, a coherent conception of an agent who can have thoughts with all of the contents recognized by the theory of conceivability articulated in Part One.

Part Two will presume a homely and familiar picture of our world. It is a picture which, even independently of the particular commitments of the content theory I favor, should suffice to demonstrate that thoughts of many familiar sorts can be realized in a world of a rather mundane and familiar sort. Even independently of that content theory, our discussion in Part Two will seem relevant to the issues we face. But in the context of the content theory sketched in Part One, the account developed in Part Two can be seen as a proof that all thoughts of which humans are capable are thoughts whose realization we can at least coherently conceive.

The double constraint which a theory of conceivability places on coherent conceptions of agency is mirrored by two elements in many skeptical arguments. Such arguments purport to demonstrate that i) a certain range of thoughts, involving a certain range of contents, cannot be constructed from ii) a certain range of available resources, in behavior or neurons or whatever. The novelty here is that a general account of content plays a crucial role in generating both constraints on a coherent conception of agency.

This novelty may seem to make for an easy project, without much importance. How could it turn out that we humans can't even coherently *conceive* agents such as we take ourselves to be? But, as we shall see, the arguments of the skeptics about content have significant bite when conjoined with a plausible content theory. The particular double bind placed on coherent conceptions of agency by a plausible content theory will allow us to make sense of our agency. But it will put considerable strain on the *plausibility* of any humanly conceivable and coherent conception of ourselves. The mundane resources which Part Two will deploy to constitute our thoughts are in fact not available in the world we inhabit, no matter how homey and platitudinous they may seem.

6

Consider again not the mere possibility, but rather the plausibility of agency. If plausible agency must be coherently conceivable, it will turn out that the plausibility of agency is in serious doubt. Part Three concerns this problem.

There may be routes around it. Could agency be plausible and *not* coherently conceivable? Perhaps. Perhaps agents could exist and not be coherently conceivably by people, just as balloons exist and are not conceivable by earthworms. Perhaps in such a situation we might even have evidence that agency exists and has a nature which we cannot coherently understand, evidence which makes agency plausible. Perhaps in such a condition we might even have words for agency and its nature. Alternatively, perhaps we can coherently conceive agency, but not as it actually is. Perhaps the few coherent human conceptions of agency don't match the nature which actual agency exhibits, and somehow we still have evidence which makes that incomprehensible nature plausible. But even if these are possibilities, they are dark routes of last resort. They leave all the features of human life which rest on agency beyond our real comprehension. I will try to go the other way. I will try to argue that coherently conceivable agency is also plausible.

I will fail. Or at least I will fail aside from a desperate maneuver I attempt in Chapter Nineteen, which may save familiar thoughts by giving up on our ability to understand their realization in any detail, by abandoning any hope of truly making sense of them, of coherently conceiving them in the full manner articulated in Part One. But I fail in a way which I hope puts thoughts in the proper light.

Part One will develop a theory of conceivability. Part Two will construct, on the basis of that theory of conceivability, a coherent conception of agency, a way that agents might be. At a certain level of generality, this will be the only way an agent can be coherently conceived within the strictures of Part One. But it will turn out to be very hard to fit both i) the conditions which this picture will demand as the price of agency and ii) other conditions in which we have good reason to believe, into a single comprehensible and plausible world. This problem will be the focus of Part Three. In the face of this difficulty, my strategy will be to up the ante. I will argue that the problematic conditions required for coherently conceivable agency are also required for the truth of a whole range of ordinary platitudes (and for plausible scientific refinements of those platitudes), including those on which skeptics about content rely. My strategy will be to show that if we have difficulties in vindicating our agency, still we would have these difficulties in any case. This will not in itself solve the problem, of course, but it will show that our talk and thought about our own agency is no worse off than lots of other seemingly indispensable talk and thought. And it will help to indicate our few, and rather breathtaking, options.

Some contemporary thought skeptics make much of difficulties apparently set by such alleged phenomena as the normativity and infinity of thought. In Part Two, we will see that such highfalutin difficulties can be met within a rather homey and ordinary conception of the world, which contains merely mundane and familiar things. So Part Two argues in effect that these ordinary skeptical worries about thoughts are misplaced. Thoughts are not *specially* problematic things, worrisome because of their highfalutin features. However, in Part Three we will see that there is another problem. Our capacity for thoughts with the full range of human contents seems clearly to rest on our capacity for certain sorts of experience. It is customary among contemporary philosophers of mind who haven't fallen prey to skepticism to distinguish between the supposedly tractable problem of thought content and the seemingly intractable problem presented by the introspectible features of our experience.[29] But as we will see, these problems are in fact quite closely connected. It is the difficulty we will have in solving the second problem in a plausible and coherently conceivable way which makes our thoughts most genuinely problematic. And it will turn out that we can make coherently conceivable and plausible sense of our capacity for our introspectible experience, that we can understand that capacity, only if it is plausible that there are in fact things of the ordinary sorts our experience seems to reveal. These ordinary sorts of things are some of the mundane and familiar resources deployed in Part Two, but they also play a crucial role in grounding the truth of all kinds of commonsense beliefs. This is the link between the existence of coherently conceivable thoughts and the truth of even more ordinary and indispensable claims. This link may seem to present no great difficulty in our attempt to vindicate agency. It may seem that if agency stands or falls with even more platitudinous things, so much the better for agency. But the link does create grounds for worry, because there are grounds for worry about those apparently more obvious things. Such things are problematic. They are not plausible.

The real difficulties with thoughts are tied up with another set of philosophical problems which philosophers have faced in one form or another ever since modern physics and modern philosophy were born together, ever since Galileo. Our experience is misleading in many ways. This creates the real problem we have in understanding how thoughts such as ours can fit into a world such as this one, but it is no more a problem for the existence of thoughts than for the existence of anything else we can coherently conceive. That's what allows me to up the ante. Things of the sort our experience seems to reveal play a crucial role in grounding the truth of all kinds of commonsense beliefs.

The resources deployed in Part Two are mundane and familiar resources, of the sort we experience the world to contain. If they are unavailable, then thoughts are problematic. Under those conditions, thoughts may not exist. But neither may things even more platitudinous than thoughts. In fact, the conditions we will face in Part Three imply that all positive human conceptions of anything contingent are false. Thoughts are no worse off than anything else which we humans can coherently conceive. Thought skeptics who think that we can retain neurons or sentences or causal-functional states even if the conditions required for thoughts do not obtain are living in a false paradise. If thoughts are in trouble, they aren't in special trouble.

Let me elaborate just a bit more. Among platitudes, the following two seem even more trivial and obvious than any which involve thoughts:

1) There are rocks, dogs, balloons, and stars, among other things. They continue to exist even when we aren't looking at them, and they remain then much the same as when we are looking on.

2) These things have the commonsense properties they display in our experience, for instance colors. Some dogs are brown and some stars are blue.

We believe these platitudes, just as we believe the platitudes that there are thoughts and meaningful sentences, but there is some reason to think that all of these platitudes are false. The problem is not merely the familiar litany of epistemic skepticism, Descartes' suggestion that for all we know *for sure* we *may* be deceived by an evil demon so that our apparent perceptions of sentences and rocks and dogs are really illusions. The problem is not that our evidence may be misleading or inconclusive, but rather that there is evidence *against* all of the platitudes. The worry is that the view which it is rational to hold on the basis of all our evidence, our very best theory, entails that all the platitudes are false.[30]

We are the inheritors of a spectacularly successful scientific program, which may be credited to Galileo as well as anyone and called "physicalism" as well as anything. It holds that the true physics would be the arbiter of what there is, that everything there *really* is is constituted by entities which that proper physics would recognize. And it holds that the true physics would have an appropriately post-galilean form, that it would eschew some properties which our experience of things suggests that they have, for instance color, in favor of others which are in some appropriate way like those Galileo's physics employed, which are in the requisite way objective, or basic, or causal, or mathematizable, or tied to extension, or *somehow* similar to paradigms like mass and velocity and force.

Galilean physicalism deserves the respect it enjoys on the basis of its striking intellectual and practical achievements, including twentieth-century physics and evolutionary and molecular biology among other things. But there is some reason to think it conflicts with each of our trivial platitudes:

It may conflict with the platitudes about minds and meanings we canvassed earlier in the chapter. Descartes' own dualism of mutually irreducible minds and bodies testifies to an early suspicion that mental phenomena and agency cannot be captured in a galilean net, but there has been a proliferation of attempts to make physicalist sense of minds and their thoughts and experiences, and sentences and their meanings as well. It is now far from clear that these physicalist attempts can succeed. So some, as we've already seen, more committed to physicalism than to minds or meanings, have come to argue that there are no persons or meaningful sentences.

But physicalism may conflict even with our two new platitudes. Galilean science was born in the denigration of the reality of colors, which Galileo called "mere names".[31] While some contemporary fans of physicalism believe that colors can be identified with physically acceptable properties of objects, still others follow Galileo. They argue that while there may be illusory *experiences* of color, nothing in fact *is* red.[32] If they are right, then even platitude (2) is in question.

Since Galileo, it has been recognized to be hard to fit phenomenal properties like color, or, as we will see, even our experience of such properties, into the world which physicists describe. This "problem of qualia" is deeply troubling in its own right. But the problem turns out to have important analogies to certain other problems which bedevil our understanding of physics itself. Galileo's physics privileged some of the commonsense properties of objects, like weight and length and motion, over others, like color, which it denigrated as *merely* phenomenal, as merely appearing in our experience of objects rather than really being in the objects. But as galilean physics has developed, it has come to have a very troubled and ambiguous relation to even classical physical properties like length and weight and motion. Sometimes it seems to suggest that they are little less merely artifacts of our experience than color itself.

Even platitude (1), that stars exist when we aren't looking on, may be put in doubt by physicalism, for instance because of the notorious interpretation problems which attend quantum mechanics. There are some who argue, in the face of these difficulties, that physical objects *aren't* there when we aren't looking on, and others who argue that, while they *are* there, they lack the sort of spatio-temporal form arguably essential to rocks and stars.[33] Our experience may be even more seriously misleading than Galileo presumed.

Of course, it will take much more argument than this to show that there really is a conflict between physicalism and each of the platitudes. And it will take still more argument to show that the conflict is of a serious and radical sort, that galilean science excludes even refined modifications of the commonsense platitudes with which we began. Some of the burden of this book is an examination of those arguments, but at least the threat of inconsistency is real.

What if the platitudes *are* inconsistent with physicalism? So much the worse for the platitudes, some might say. But it is important to remember that the authority of galilean science is rooted in its capacity to explain ordinary phenomena like litmus paper turning blue, or at the very least to explain our *experience* of such things. Perhaps a plausible science should modify in some way our initial, naive, commonsense characterizations of those phenomena and that experience, perhaps it should abandon some ordinary platitudes, but if it excludes those phenomena and even our experience of them in some radical way, then it may well seem to lack intellectual authority. Certainly one might have reasonable concern about the situation of a physicalist who believes that there are no beliefs. Worse, we will see by the end of Part One that there is reason to believe that our human thought cannot get very far beyond platitudes at least roughly like these, that human thought cannot encompass a world too different from that we seem to experience.

So much the worse for physicalism, some might say. But it is important also to remember that we have no plausible alternative. For instance, it seems clear that we who think and experience are flesh and blood, that we are parts of nature who have evolved. We, for all our thinking and sensing, seem to be biological organisms, and, like other biological organisms, we seem to be composed of the same sorts of physical particles as stars and rocks. And these stars and rocks at least seem to be insentient and mind-independent. Neither some idealism holding that rocks and stars are sentient or mind-dependent, nor some cartesian dualism of mutually irreducible minds and bodies, constitutes a particularly plausible alternative to physicalism. And we will soon see that there are lots of good reasons to believe that physicalism pushes us out beyond our human capacity for understanding, that it points toward a world out beyond the limits of human thought.

Under the pressure of *our* evidence, it is hard to construct a plausible view which makes coherent sense, at least to us. Certainly we can talk about the conditions suggested by all our evidence. But we can also talk about round squares. It is far from clear that we humans can form a *coherent* conception of the world suggested by our evidence, which meets all plausible constraints and yet which we can understand. As I will say, it is far from clear that we humans can "coherently conceive" the world we inhabit.

This problem is one that future developments in each of the particular sciences are unlikely to entirely dissolve. It is not merely our current sciences, but the *phenomena* with which they deal, which present a problem. For instance, as we shall see, any successor of current physics will probably inherit some analogue of the interpretation problems which plague current physics and threaten commonsense conceptions of physical objects. Nor will it be easy for such a physics to allow a plausible and coherently conceivable account of even our experience of commonsense physical objects. But, despite the seriousness and difficulty of our problem, it is to a large degree hidden by the organization of our intellectual life. Specialization yields us many benefits, but it also allows us largely to ignore problems of integration, problems which in our current intellectual situation are extreme. We have physicalist and eliminativist philosophers of mind, and idealist physicists. We root our understanding of everything in our understanding of physics, and we have what some physicists proclaim to be an incomprehensible physics. If consistency is a problem, then we have a problem.

If we are to have a coherent intellectual life expressing a consistent and plausible understanding, however partial, of the world, then it is crucial that we think about all these matters together at least long enough to sort things out better. And if we are to sort things out, then there is a specific set of concerns which must engage us more than they have. These are issues regarding what is conceivable or thinkable by us, and in particular regarding what is coherently conceivable by us, the issues of Part One.

One way to see this is to note another difference between our problem and that which faced Descartes. His invocation of epistemic skepticism may have been an appropriate, or at least comprehensible, philosophical response to the initial rise of a new galilean science, a science which expelled color from the world and claimed our experience of that color to be systematically misleading. But as that science has developed, it suggests a different problem: It is not, as the epistemic skeptic worries, that we have a bunch of different theories of the general nature of things each of which fits all our available evidence perfectly well. Rather the problem is that we seem to lack even a single consistent and coherent theory of such matters which fits all the constraints our evidence suggests. We lack a single such theory which is both plausible and makes coherent sense to us. Our problem isn't merely that we can't *know* the truth, know which things, of the many things we might think, are true. Rather the problem is that it is far from clear that we can even *think* the truth, let alone make coherent sense of it. Our problem may not be that we have too little evidence to have knowledge, but too little imagination. The true theory may be a theory we humans cannot entertain, or at least of which we cannot make coherent sense. It is not merely our own agency which may not be coherently conceivable by us. The very most general features of the world which is suggested by our evidence may be beyond our coherent comprehension. If the platitudes we have been discussing are false, then it is far from clear that we can understand anything.

A serious consideration of what we can think, and above all coherently conceive, may help us in our predicament in two different ways: First, there is an optimistic alternative. In charting the range of contents our thoughts can have, it may be that we will discover the resources to construct a coherent conception of the world which meets all the constraints our evidence suggests. If we are self-conscious about what we can imagine, it may aid our imagination. Through a close inventory of our resources, we may find what we need. Alternatively, there is pessimism. It may be that we will determine that there are fixed limits to what we, evolved and constituted as we contingently are, can think and can make coherent sense of, limits which explain why our predicament arises and why, for us, it is irresolvable. It is this pessimistic option that we will be forced to embrace.

The contents of human thoughts are rooted in, but not exhausted by, experience. In the end, we will be unable to make coherent and plausible sense of our capacity for thoughts, because we will be unable to make plausible and coherent sense of our capacity for experience. And this will be because the world is not as we experience it to be, because it does not contain things of the sort our experience seems to reveal. But then even platitudes (1) and (2) will be in question. In fact, all of the positive thoughts of which we humans are capable, all of our thoughts that things *are* such and so rather than merely *not* such and so, are false. The existence of our thoughts is in no greater doubt than the existence of stars, colored balls, neurons, and anything else we can coherently conceive. I will call this a "vindication" of thoughts.

NOTES

1. Stephen Stich, *The Fragmentation of Reason* (Cambridge, MA: MIT Press, 1990) argues that the principles of reasoning which we have evolved to follow are not truth-tracking. Kathleen Akins, "On Piranhas, Narcissism and Mental Representation" (University of Michigan Dissertation, 1989) and Paul Thomson, "Evolutionary Epistemology and Anti-Realism" (Princeton University Dissertation, 1990) explore some related implications of evolution for the nature of cognition.

2. Colin McGinn has argued that we cannot form a proper conception of how we have the experience we do. See the papers collected in *The Problem of Consciousness* (Oxford: Blackwell, 1991).

3. The position to be developed here is thus analogous to Kant's, though some commentators avoid these elements of his work. But it is shorn of his transcendental concerns. I believe that it is our very contingent limitations which leave us unable to understand certain very contingent features of the world.

4. For instance, it may be that its first premise cannot be true unless you exist, since it refers to you. Hence it may be that the truth of that first premise would guarantee the falsity of the argument's conclusion. Likewise it may be that that conclusion itself cannot be true unless you

exist, hence unless it is false. And of course the argument is addressed to you who it says do not exist, and claims that you are a certain way while not existing. Indeed, the argument may have even greater difficulties, which will be the concern of later sections of this chapter. The second-person singular pronoun is itself interesting in several ways. For instance, the "you" of the first sentence may refer to different people each time it is read. And while inanimate objects or the dead can be so addressed, its written use seems generally to suppose that some person, indeed some sighted person literate in English, will read it.

5. According to some ears, seeing and hearing things, as opposed to seeing and hearing things *as* such and so, are psychological states which do not possess intensionality in the sense to be noted below, which are "transparent". See G.J. Warnock, "On What is Seen", in *Perception: A Philosophical Symposium*, edited by F.N. Sibley (London: Methuen, 1971), 1-12, and the first chapter of Fred Dretske, *Seeing and Knowing* (London: Routledge & Kegan Paul, 1969). If "perceiving" were just a generic word for such transparent states, it too would not possess intensionality. But it seems to me that it is consistent with at least some ordinary usage to say that we see and hear things that do not in fact exist, and this, as we will see, suggests intensionality.

6. This admittedly involves some deviation from common usage, but so would the application of any ordinary term to this general category, and my use is sanctioned by the customary translations of Descartes. I will ignore the other, deviant examples of thoughts until the next chapter.

7. Some philosophers, Frege and Peacocke among them, write "thoughts" where I would write "contents of thoughts". That is a legitimate usage, sanctioned by common speech and philosophical tradition. But so is mine.

8. Rene Descartes, *Meditations on First Philosophy*, translated by Elizabeth Haldane and G.R.T. Ross, in Haldane and Ross (editors), *The Philosophical Works of Descartes* (Cambridge: Cambridge University Press, 1911), 131-200.

9. Many of the major disputes of twentieth century philosophy have been about questions in the philosophy of language: Should philosophy attend carefully to the detailed usages of ordinary language or construct ideal scientific languages? Is the meaning of sentences their representational content, or is it an error to consider language primarily as the bearer of representational content? Is the primary determinant of linguistic meaning either the play of differences between terms of a language or rather the things in the world those terms name? Are there important historical and social determinants of the meanings of sentences? What is prior, the intentionality of mental states or linguistic items? What are the primary bearers of linguistic meaning, words or sentences or theories or languages or texts? Is speech or writing the primary linguistic mode? Is the primary linguistic phenomenon the language or the idiolect, is it *la langue*, the articulated system of a language belonging to a group, or *la parole*, speech?

10. Ludwig Wittgenstein, *Philosophical Investigations*, third edition, translated by G.E.M. Anscombe (New York: Macmillan, 1968).

11. Saul A. Kripke, *Wittgenstein on Rules and Private Language* (Cambridge, MA: Harvard University Press, 1982).

12. Willard Van Orman Quine, *Word and Object* (Cambridge, MA: The MIT Press, 1960). Quine's doctrine of the indeterminacy of translation is an indeterminacy of intension, and his doctrine of the inscrutability of reference is an inscrutability of intention.

13. Jacques Derrida, *Of Grammatology*, translated by Gayatri Spivak (Baltimore: Johns Hopkins University Press, 1976).

14. Stephen P. Stich, *From Folk Psychology to Cognitive Science* (Cambridge, MA: The MIT Press, 1983). Paul M. Churchland, "Eliminative Materialism and Propositional Attitudes", *Journal of Philosophy* 78, 1981, 67-90.

15. Donald Davidson, *Inquiries into Truth and Interpretation* (Oxford: Oxford University Press, 1984) and *Essays on Actions and Events* (Oxford: Oxford University Press, 1980).

16. Some of the following rhetoric is overblown if there might be psychological states with content which is not representational and yet which possesses intentionality. This possibility is addressed in the following chapter.
17. Though it certainly isn't always so allied.
18. Uta Frith, *Autism: Explaining the Enigma* (Oxford: Blackwell, 1989). Simon Baron-Cohen, Helen Tager-Flusberg, and Donald J. Cohen (editors), *Understanding Other Minds: Perspectives from Autism* (Oxford: Oxford University Press, 1993).
19. When considering the disadvantages of life after belief in representational content is abandoned, some add to horror inconvenience. Fodor, among many others, has stressed the enormous predictive-explanatory capacity of ordinary "folk psychology", with its apparatus of beliefs and desires and representational content. He has also stressed the lack of any alternative theory with anything like the same capacity. Folk psychology provides us with very useful, indeed indispensable, predictions of how people will behave in the wide range of ordinary circumstances. The astonishing success of these predictions is evidenced by how little surprise we really encounter in our social lives, how much we can foresee what others will do from what they say and what we know of them. See, for instance, Jerry A. Fodor, *Psychosemantics* (Cambridge, MA: The MIT Press, 1987), 8-10. Perhaps "inconvenience" is a mild word for what Fodor, on his page xii, holds the loss of folk psychology to entail: "[I]f commonsense intentional psychology really were to collapse, that would be, beyond comparison, the greatest intellectual catastrophe in the history of our species." My own view is that any causal-explanatory role played by thoughts could by mimicked by things without representational content. But I commend this point to your consideration.
20. Norman Malcolm, "The Conceivability of Mechanism", in Gary Watson (editor), *Free Will* (Oxford: Oxford University Press, 1982), 127-149, introduces such an argument to show that we could not be neurophysiological mechanisms. This would, he argues, entail we perform no behaviors as a result of intentions. There are a number of analogous arguments stemming from Kant and attempting to show that determinism is somehow pragmatically incoherent.
21. Lynne Rudder Baker, "Cognitive Suicide?", a paper presented to the Oberlin Colloquium in Philosophy, April 12-14 1985, 22-27, and *Saving Belief* (Princeton: Princeton University Press, 1987). Churchland, "Eliminative Materialism and Propositional Attitudes".
22. Paul Boghossian, "The Status of Content", *The Philosophical Review* XCIX, 1990, 157-184. Boghossian is only discussing intentional, not intensional content. And his argument is focussed on sentences in particular, though he thinks that any good argument for skepticism about truth-apt thoughts would also be a good argument for skepticism about truth-apt sentences, that these issues are linked.
23. Check it out:

1 Assumption	(x)(if Sx then not Tx)
2 (Premise 1)	Sa
3 (Premise 2)	Ta iff (x)(if Sx then not Tx)
4 (from 1,2)	not Ta
5 (from 3,4)	not (x)(if Sx then not Tx)

I owe this compressed exposition of Boghossian to Phil Hugly.
24. Boghossian in effect mentions this response. See also Michael Devitt, "Transcendentalism About Content", *Pacific Philosophical Quarterly* 71, 1990, 247-263.
25. Ludwig Wittgenstein, *Tractatus Logico-Philosophicus*, translated by D.F. Pears and B.F. McGuinness (London: Routledge & Kegan Paul, 1961).
26. Quine, *Word and Object*, 35. Rudolf Carnap, *Meaning and Necessity*, second edition (Chicago: University of Chicago Press, 1956), Suppl. D.
27. Jacques Derrida, *Speech and Phenomena and Other Essays on Husserl's Theory of Signs*, translated by David B. Allison and Newton Garver (Evanston, IL: Northwestern University Press, 1973).

28. Someone might be pessimistic enough to deny this, but it is supported by the content theory in Part One.
29. But see Keith Lehrer, *Metamind* (Oxford: Oxford University Press, 1990), 2-4 and 271-294.
30. Some features of this worry are nicely articulated in Wilfrid Sellars, "Philosophy and the Scientific Image of Man", in *Science, Perception and Reality* (London: Routledge & Kegan Paul, 1963), 1-40.
31. Galileo, "Excerpts from The Assayer", in Drake (editor), *Discoveries and Opinions of Galileo* (Garden City, NY: Doubleday, 1957), 274. Galileo was referring to color in the guise of an objective property of material objects.
32. See for instance C. L. Hardin, *Color for Philosophers* (Indianapolis: Hackett, 1988).
33. One introduction to some of this is N. David Mermin, "Quantum Mysteries for Anyone", *Journal of Philosophy* 78, 1981, 397-408.

Part One

CONTENT

CHAPTER TWO

FROM CONTENT TO REPRESENTATIONAL CONTENT

Part One is an account of the range of contents which human thoughts can have. This is not the only way to focus a theory of content, and it is not unproblematic. It is not unproblematic even if our human form is relevant to what we can think. Even if there is some single paradigm of normal adult human neurophysiology, still other humans differ from that paradigm in relevant ways. At best, we can hope only to provide an account of content for "normal" adult humans. And even "normal" adult humans may relevantly differ, so that some idealization unavoidably infects our account. Also, any biological constraints we humans now suffer may one day be broken by technological advance, which will allow us to alter our form. Despite the legitimacy of these worries, the account which follows will show that normal adult human capacities are, at least for now, at least enough alike to make a focus on "human" content reasonable.

Some may deny that there are interesting limits to what humans even with our current form can think. Certainly human cognitive life has included an enormous range of thoughts, spanning a huge variation across individuals, places, and times. And human thought does seem capable of development without obvious limit, as the histories of math and physics and even philosophy show. Indeed, if there are limits to what *particular* individuals can think, such limits seem set precisely by the contingent historical and cultural position of those individuals and by the accidents of their education and development, *not* by their humanity, not for instance by some transculturally and (so far) transtemporally invariant human biology.

This is a serious objection, and it requires that our theory of content take a certain form. That theory holds that there are a number of operations by which contents can be generated or constructed or derived from other contents. It also holds that the full range of human contents can be derived, in some cases only by a series of operations, from a certain concrete core of underived content, which I call "basic content".[1] These generation operations are *semantic* operations, not psychological processes; they exhibit dependencies in the *contents* of thought, not the history of the development of thought in individuals or cultures. Nevertheless, they are helpful in dissolving the objection we face.

While there is a limited range of basic content, and a limited number of different operations which can generate other contents from that basic content, still iterations and combinations of those operations may generate new contents in a way which is potentially endless. This makes the range of human thought limitless in just the particular way the history of our intellectual endeavor and cognitive variation suggests. But it does not make the range of our thoughts limitless in every sense. It does not, for instance, ensure that humans can think everything which is true, since there may be no route from basic content through the operations allowed to some truths. Also, while at least something reasonably akin to the full range of basic contents and content generation operations is required if we are to deliver the contents of the thoughts of each normal adult human, still it is very unlikely that without training the thought of any given human would duplicate on its own the historical developments required to come to a thought with some particular highly-derived content. Training, enculturation, and accidents of individual development are crucial to which particular contents from the full human range will in fact be exhibited in the thought of any particular individual, and it is in this way that culture and contingency limits thought.

Basic content is content from which the full range of human thought can be derived, by a specific series of operations to be characterized in the next chapter. It is basic in that sense, basic in what I will call "generation", above all.

But basic content is basic in another sense; it is also basic in *truth.* Barring a few complications to which I have already alluded and to which we will return, its truth or falsity serves to fix the truth or falsity of all human thoughts, whether their content is merely basic or not.[2] Because of the way in which it does this, basic content will turn out to be the *coherent* content which we seek. It is from basic content that a conception of human agency must be constructed if we are to make proper sense of ourselves, if we are to coherently articulate what would need to be true for there to be such agents as we take ourselves to be. Let me elaborate these two claims, though for now just a bit and without argument:

There is a specific set of basic contents. Depending on the way the world happens to be, each particular basic content either "matches" the world, or it doesn't. What is match? One intuitive understanding of the vague but intuitive notion of truth by correspondence.[3] The content expressed by "there are at least three red spheres" matches any world where there really are three such red, spherical things, and fails to match any world where there aren't.[4] If a basic content matches the world, it is true.[5] If it doesn't, it is false.[6]

There are various complex ways in which contents are dependent for their truth on other contents, and hence ultimately on basic contents. But, as we will see, the truth or falsity of any thought is fixed by i) the content it has, ii) the truth dependencies among contents, and iii) which basic contents are true and which false.[7] More exactly, I should say that it is fixed by no more than these. If there are any analogues of traditional analytic truths, then truth dependencies alone will serve to fix their truth.[8] To make "coherent" sense of something in my sense, to show that it can be coherently conceived, is to exhibit some basic contents, each of which would make it true that there is such a thing.[9]

Basic content is basic in generation and truth. Barring some qualifications which will become evident as we proceed, it is also basic in yet a third sense, basic in what I will call "realization": The capacity for a particular thought with a particular less than basic content requires capacities for thoughts with the more basic contents from which that less basic content is derived.[10] Though the content generation operations are *semantic* and not *psychological* operations, they mirror this particular sort of psychological dependency.

Parts Two and Three discuss at length the realization of thoughts with the contents recognized by the content theory to be presented here, what capacities are required of agents capable of thoughts with the range of contents this part articulates. Though the history of philosophy reveals a number of distinct content theories, each organized around some fixation of the day, of Aristotle and Plato on the good, of Medieval philosophers on the attributes of god, and of post-cartesian philosophers on epistemology,[11] a concern with realization has been prominent in philosophy since modern philosophy began. Indeed, the skeptical developments sketched in the last chapter are one indication of this. It seems to me that this is a fruitful focus. Our understanding of our neurophysiology has only recently advanced sufficiently to allow a reasonably fine-grained understanding of the realization of our thought, and I pursue such an understanding in later parts. But even in this part we will see that the account of human content to be proposed fits in a natural way with some obvious commonsense platitudes about our nature and capacities. We will see that basic content is a sort of concrete content rooted in experience, an experience of concrete objects, with phenomenal and causal properties and located in space and time. We will also see that possession of such an experience, with both phenomenal and causal components, is natural for creatures who *sense* things and *do* things, that phenomenal experience is tied to sensation, and causal experience to action. Other contents are generated from basic content, in the account to be proposed, by operations including abstraction and various machinations with words, and the conditions required for thoughts with those derived sorts of content will turn out to be obviously parasitic on the more "primitive" capacities required for experience. But despite my concern with realization, and despite the attention which we will eventually pay it, I will begin by articulating the content theory independently of much concern about the *details* of its realization. Guided by at most quite general platitudes about our capacities, and by commonsense views about our thoughts, we can develop a plausible account of content quite directly. But this should not be misunderstood. I do not claim that we can *infallibly* introspect either that we have thoughts with the contents to be noted here or that those contents can be generated as I specify. After Freud we lack sufficient confidence in our introspective capacities to be happy with that sort of methodology. And if we could infallibly introspect that we have thoughts with a certain range of contents, then my whole indirect project of conceiving agents to vindicate our agency would be unnecessary. Rather, I merely propose that in Part One we grant our sometimes introspective but never infallible beliefs that we have thoughts with something like the commonsense range of contents I will specify here, and also all the commonsense platitudes and scientific refinements of those platitudes I will cite here in support of my account of those contents, an initial but not indefeasible authority. Later on we will consider whether such a refinement of our commonsense conception of our thoughts can meet two important tests, can make rigorous and coherent sense of its own possibility, and eventually of its own plausibility in a world such as we inhabit.

Let me forestall certain other misunderstandings before we begin, even if they take us a bit beyond our immediate concerns: My talk here of the nature of contents should not be taken to endorse the first side of the debate between i) those who think that the world contains *contents* as distinct and independent entities and ii) those who think that it merely contains *people* with thoughts with such contents. It should not be taken to imply that contents are more like the chairs in which we can sit than the vehemence with which we can speak. Some may wonder what makes it the case that particular contents are dependent on particular others, say for truth, in the ways I will describe here. The answer is that they wouldn't be the contents they are if they weren't so dependent, that their dependencies are "essential" to them. But again, this shouldn't necessarily be taken to imply that contents are strange distinct platonic entities standing in strange essential relations. In the same sense in which there are essential relations among contents, the vehemence with which we speak may be essentially more heated than indifference. There is of course a legitimate question here: How can there be people with thoughts with contents exhibiting such dependencies? But the proper answer to this question may not involve any platonic beasts, and, in any case, is primarily a matter for Parts Two and Three.[12]

The remaining chapters of Part One are an account of the content of human thoughts. The next chapter sketches the "content generation" operations by which contents can be derived from other contents, and hence ultimately from basic contents. Chapter Four does some stage-setting for the account of basic content to be presented in the following three chapters, in particular by articulating more clearly the relation between basic contents and experience. The remaining chapters provide an account of basic contents. Basic contents consist of point-instant property-exemplifications, which I call "microevents". These microevents stand in certain sorts of spatio-temporal relations and exhibit either "phenomenal" properties, say a certain shade of red as we experience it to be, or causal properties. Chapter Five sketches a metaphysics for basic contents, characterizing microevents and their spatial relations. Chapter Six concerns their phenomenal properties, and Chapter Seven their causal properties.

This chapter clarifies the kind of content which we will pursue here. It is perhaps more accurate to say not that I seek an account of thought content in general, but of *representational* content in particular. Thoughts with representational content possess *intentionality*. They are about things. And they also possess *intensionality*. They are about things only under certain aspects or modes of presentation rather than others. The thought "there's a red apple" may be about a particular decaying piece of fruit in the guise merely of a red apple; it need not present it in the guise of the wormiest thing in miles, even if it is. But there is more than a little ambiguity in these terms and phrases. This chapter more adequately characterizes representational contents, by distinguishing them from other things. Section 1 concerns the implications of a certain understanding of intentionality. Then I turn to a clarification of what I mean by "intensionality", and to the implications of that clarification. Our discussion will show that while there are contents other than representational contents which thoughts have, still those contents are rooted, in at least a limited sense, in representational content, and hence ultimately in basic content. So this chapter sketches how, in the same limited sense, the account of representational content in the following chapters could be extended into a full account of thought content.

1

Representational contents possess intentionality; they are about things. In at least the central and paradigmatic cases, this means that we say that they are true or false. If we say that contents[13] are true or false, I will call them "cognitive contents". My understanding of the intentionality of representational contents is that they are cognitive contents.

Notice how cheaply this appellation comes, how it is rooted merely in our ordinary ways of talking, of calling things true or false. Some philosophers have marked a deeper and more theoretical distinction, between thoughts *really* about the world, for instance thoughts that cherries are red, and others, say mathematical or normative thoughts, that 2+2=4 or that stealing is morally problematic, that are supposed to not *really* be about the world, but to play some other sort of role, say in inference or commendation. Whatever the plausibility of such a distinction or such a treatment of these examples, I am beginning more superficially and less theoretically. Since we call thoughts about mathematics and ethics true and false, that's enough for them to have cognitive content in my cheap sense.

Despite the fact that cognitive content is so cheap, this understanding of the intentionality of representational contents exacts a price, which the rest of this section surveys. Many things we are tempted to call thoughts pretty clearly have cognitive contents. But there are problem cases. I will treat the problem cases in three different ways. First of all, there are things at least a lot like thoughts which lack cognitive content, and which I want to largely set aside. Second, there are thoughts which *appear* to lack cognitive content and yet which in fact possess it. Third, there are things which I intend to call "thoughts" which yet lack cognitive, and hence representational, contents. This last set of thoughts has a kind of content which is in an important way rooted in cognitive, and ultimately representational, content. Let me treat these three sets of cases in that order.

1) First, consider some cases which, in the production of a theory of content, I will largely ignore. These are cases of knowledge *how* to do something rather than knowledge *that* something is the case.[14] While we may know *that* there's a break in the fence, we know *how* to walk through it. We know *how* to untie a knot; we know *that* it is tied. Such know how might be said by someone to have a content of some sort, which distinguishes one bit of it from another, knowledge how to speak English from knowledge how to fly a balloon. But while know how may be more or less graceful or expert, more or less useful or sufficient in this or that circumstance, still it doesn't seem liable to evaluation as true or false. It doesn't have cognitive content in my sense.

Psychological states like know how are not, at least on the surface, all the psychological states that there are. But some may object when I ignore them while developing an account of thought content. And even if common sense recognizes some thoughts *that*, some may object that such things aren't really central to psychologies, or even that the commonsense understanding which posits them is mistaken. People do things. They differ in their capacities to do things, and in what they do in particular circumstances. An objector may grant that there are psychological differences between agents, that individual psychologies mediate between sensory input and particular behavioral output. But, such an objector may insist, it is far from clear that what mediates in such cases is primarily thoughts *that*. And certainly it isn't exclusively thoughts *that*.[15]

My defense of the existence and importance of thoughts *that* is a long story to come. As that story unfolds, we will see that intuitive cases of know *how* count as psychological phenomena only because they are deeply entwined with our capacities for thought *that* of certain kinds. Still, some elements of the proper defense of thoughts *that* can be evident even now: There are some reasons to think that the proper classification of people's know *how* rests on their thoughts *that*. Two behaviors which look just alike may be different sorts of behaviors in one crucial sense. Some guards may scribble on some paper in the same way if trying to add or to doodle; they may make the same noises if singing a nonsense song or clearing their throats. The intentions, and hence cognitive thoughts, which lie behind those physical motions seem crucial to their intuitive classification as particular behaviors, as adding, or doodling, or singing, and so on. In this way, the "content" of even know *how* may be bound by the account of cognitive content to follow.

On the other hand, some people may in some sense know *how* to do things they don't or can't think about. Even in the intuitive examples of *this* sort, say those involving young children, at least *other* people not only know *how* to do the thing in question, but can think *that* it has been done. The "content" of even these states is within the bounds of the following account of human cognitive content. Still, there may be a sense in which people can "know *how*" to do something which no human can think *that* people have done. If such states have a kind of "content", then that content cannot be captured by the content theory to follow. But of course it is beyond our human comprehension anyway, ineffable.

2) The next set of cases we need to treat involve thoughts which *seem* to lack cognitive content, and yet in fact really possess it. Some cognitive contents, for instance those of thoughts that snow is white or that air is clear, have *components* which seem neither true nor false, and yet which seem also to be the exhaustive contents of some thoughts. Consider thought merely of snow, or merely of the property white. Such thoughts may intuitively possess representational content. They are about things, and at least sometimes about them under some of their aspects rather than others. But they seem ruled out of our consideration by my focus on *cognitive* contents, capable of truth or falsity.

Still, I'm going to give such contents no special consideration here. That is really for two reasons: It turns out that in giving an account of *cognitive* representational contents in the following chapters, we will develop also the resources to provide an account of these other contents as well. We will get them as a kind of side benefit. Even if we don't say that certain thoughts with such contents are true or false, we say that other thoughts, which we will see to have the same contents as the problematic cases, *are* true or false.[16] This will in turn suggest a more interesting reason to ignore these problem cases. We will see in Chapter Five that the failure of ordinary speech to call certain thoughts true or false lacks the deep implications which philosophers often presume. There is less difference here than meets the eye of many metaphysicians.

3) A third set of cases are psychological states which do not possess cognitive and hence representational contents, and yet which are to be considered thoughts in my sense. They involve some of our machinations with words. We speak and write; we utter words with meaning. Also, at least after training in deceit and etiquette, we sometimes speak not out loud but to ourselves, in our mind's ear. This inner speech, and outer speech as well, seems to be one of the many forms our thought can take. The meaning of speech seems sometimes to be the content of a thought, or at least something closely analogous. Some things we say, for instance "There's a red balloon moored in the next field", seem to have representational content. But some do not. Some sentences we utter don't, it seems, even *purport* to say anything about how the world is or might be. They don't seem liable to evaluation as true or false, and hence lack what I have called cognitive content. Yet they still seem to possess what is sometimes called a "noncognitive" content. In speaking these words we may have a thought which yet lacks representational content. Some examples: As philosophers have noted, Wittgenstein perhaps most vehemently,[17] we do a lot more with words than assert that the world is thus and so. We question: "Will you help me steal the balloon?" We command: "Cut that rope!" We coordinate: "1, 2, 3, go!" We express emotion: "Hurrah." And we perform in other ways: "Goodbye." "I promise to write." Inner or outer speech of phrases like these may sometimes make for thoughts with merely noncognitive content.

Why consider these cases to be thoughts at all? Because they are so like the word-mediated thoughts we do call true and false and will discuss in Chapter Three. And because we cannot just ignore noncognitive content anyway. Inner and outer speech even of declarative sentences we call true or false may sometimes involve something a lot like the noncognitive contents introduced by these problem cases. But while noncognitive content is to be distinguished from the representational and hence cognitive content, apt for truth or falsity, which we will explore in the following chapters, still there are at least some reasons to think that an account of cognitive content would be the crucial core of an account of noncognitive content.[18]

Our meaningful words must do *something* characteristic in the world, must have *some* characteristic use. And there is at least some reason to believe that what they do must be within the range of cognitive contents of human thoughts.

Consider the first claim of the last paragraph first. If our words do something characteristic which constitutes or helps constitute their meaning, then a full account of the meaning of those words must invoke ways the world might be in at least two places. Rather trivially, it must specify the conditions in the world which would make for the existence of those words. But also, it must specify what in the world those particular words do, that they assert and in particular what, or that they choreograph and in particular choreograph what, or even that they merely serve as a proper response to other particular words.

To invoke ways the world might be is not in itself to invoke cognitive content, true of ways the world might be *thought* to be. But there are assumptions about word-meaning which would close this gap, and give human cognitive content a crucial role in any account of human noncognitive content and word-meaning.

First of all, we might invoke certain realization dependencies. There is a *kind* of noncognitive content which accrues to words which mediate thought in a manner I will sketch in Chapters Three and Ten, and which involves a capacity of the speaker for thoughts about the words it utters, indeed for thoughts that there are such words, and also a capacity for thought about whatever it is the words mean. In that sort of case, the meanings can be for the speaker the object of various sorts of thought with cognitive content, subject to truth or falsity.[19]

This isn't, of course, the only sort of possible case. In learning a language, we may simply become initiated into a practice, in which we do things which constitute utterances with meanings we do not necessarily understand, or perhaps "understand" only in some way not constituting, involving, or invoking cognitive thought, or even a capacity for cognitive thought, of the sort I will deploy in my account. So another sort of word-mediated thought may be possible. Still, that sort of case would be very different from the case of thoughts which are *not* mediated by words.

In thought that isn't mediated by words, for instance certain perceptual episodes, to have a thought with a content is to think directly into that content. To think there's a balloon flying by is to think of a balloon flying by. In thoughts mediated by words, however, to think something may be to have the words which mean it, and not what the words mean, most immediately in mind. When one says words to oneself, it is the words and not their meaning which one hears in one's mind's ear. When such thought involves word-meanings which are reflected in the speaker's cognitive thought in the way I will propose, then there is a linking of capacities which at least mimics unmediated thought. The agent's inner speech invokes capacities of word-understanding which involve thought with relevant cognitive content, or at least would involve that thought under appropriate conditions. It is this kind of word-mediation which is most closely analogous to other sorts of thought. So it is only inner and outer speech of this particular kind which I will call a "thought".

Still, an objector may insist, one might understand *how* to use a word, without an understanding of the sort I will presume. Or one might speak without any sort of understanding, and still in so doing have at least some close analogue of a thought. Stipulation alone is not enough. But there's another point. There's another set of considerations which suggest that whatever human words do that is relevant to their meaning or content is within the range of human cognitive content.

If our words have meanings humans as a species *cannot* think about, and *cannot* think that a word has, then these might seem irrelevant even to our objector. Perhaps in stumbling around in the world we might ignorantly "utter" some word in a language not cognitively comprehensible by humans, perhaps a Martian language whose words and meanings no human could even be taught to cognitively recognize or comprehend, and perhaps someone would insist that this constitutes a thought. But this is an ineffable possibility I think we can reasonably ignore. Barring noncognitive contents of a sort no human could understand in a cognitive way, contents no human could think that a word has, and barring words no human could so recognize or distinguish, words no human could think to exist, then an account of cognitive content could be the core of a full account of even noncognitive content and meaning. The range of elements, of words and their meanings, noted in an account of human noncognitive meaning would be limited by the range of human cognitive contents. One might well wonder what possible significance this very remote and convoluted limitation of noncognitive content and meaning by cognitive content might have. But by Chapter Nineteen we will be in position to see that in our peculiar circumstances this limitation is very significant indeed. This point is setup.

2

I believe that all thoughts with cognitive content, apt to be called true or false, have representational content. Or perhaps it is more accurate to say that I stipulate that, as a constraint on my use of "thought". Representational content possesses not only intentionality, but intensionality. It is about things under certain of their aspects rather than others.

I have been brief and vague about what I mean by "intensionality", and the first thing this section does is clear that up. Once I clear it up, my focus on intensional content may seem controversial or inept. For instance, then it will be evident that there is another sort of content which cognitive thoughts have. And this other sort of content may seem, in light of some of the most interesting work in recent philosophy of language and mind, work associated with Kripke, Putnam, and Burge, to be where our focus ought to be. In actual fact, the account which follows is consistent with the lion's share of the claims made by those authors. It even provides a way to underwrite many of their claims. But at first glance, it may not seem that way. After I clear up what I mean by "intensionality", I will explore the implications of that understanding by considering objections which the recent literature might suggest to someone.

Intensionality of the sort we will pursue is closely linked to introspectibility. Descartes was wrong, it seems, in thinking that introspection is infallible and indefeasible, that it can serve as some sort of indubitable foundation for our knowledge. And yet introspection, even if it is fallible and sensitive to training, can play an important semantic role. The intensionality of representational contents lies in their being about things under certain aspects rather than others. Which aspects? Those that are "present to the mind". What is it to be present to the mind? It is to be introspectible, at least to a first approximation. A person can introspect the aspects under which things are presented to them in their thoughts about those things.

This characterization is still imprecise. First, there is some vagueness in the notion of introspection. I will more fully discuss introspection in Chapter Eight, but here are two cases I want to include: We can at least normally introspect in a quite immediate way the content of our sense experience, which will turn out to be thought of a peculiar kind.[20] But we can also introspect in a much more tortured way the content, though perhaps not the meaning, carried by words in our word-mediated thought, sometimes only after long struggle and the consideration of all sorts of hypothetical cases which it would be very unlikely that the unimaginative would dream up on their own. These two kinds of introspection on the surface have little in common except that they both can be performed in an armchair, at least after suitable training. And yet this account of content and the proper account of the realization of thought show, I think, that they belong together. They access what is in an important sense the same kind of content, as we will see in the rest of Part One. And the realization of thoughts with such contents, and of the capacities to introspect those contents, requires at least roughly the same kinds of resources, as we will see in Part Two.

There is another important imprecision in my claim that people can introspect the aspects under which things are presented to them in their thoughts. We can in fact introspect the intensional content of some of our thoughts, but not necessarily all. For that matter, there seems to be no necessity even that beings with intensional thoughts be capable of any sort of introspection. Consider for instance some "primitive" animals, or young children. So let me try to be a little more precise about the link between intensionality and introspectibility: The kind of content we will consider here is that which we adult humans happen to be able to introspect in certain particular cases, for instance experience and word-mediated thought. But it seems at least conceivable that that kind of content may also be had by thoughts whose contents we cannot introspect. For instance, perhaps we have unconscious memories, or perhaps certain unconscious thoughts which play an important role in the calculations required to catch fly balls. It may be not only that we *do* not but that we *cannot* introspect the contents of these thoughts. And still these thoughts may have contents of the representational sort we will soon consider. Still things may be "present to the mind" in such thoughts under some aspects rather than others. If these complications seem to leave it unclear what kind of content I am talking about, the following several chapters will help clear things up.[21]

This characterization of intensionality may seem to suggest yet another feature of representational content, but this suggestion is an illusion. Some may confuse my claims here with another claim which they find objectionable, because they have a certain view about what introspectibility requires, and which I'm not necessarily endorsing.[22] "Internalism" is the view that only the internal states of an agent, what's inside its skin, constitute it[23] as having the thoughts with the representational contents that it does. "Externalists" deny this. They hold that the representational content of one's thoughts may depend on more than one's internal states, so that one's exact *internal* twin, *internally* identical down to the last microphysical particle or sense datum, will have, if in a different *external* context, thoughts with different representational contents. Externalists may find my claim that representational content is introspectible suspicious. But they shouldn't. Issues about what *constitutes* thoughts are the concern of Part Two, not this part. And representational content has not been characterized here in such a way as to entail in itself that externalism is false.

Even our rough initial characterization of the intensionality of representational content puts us in position to consider some implications and objections. First of all, given that characterization, it is easy to see that there is another kind of content which at least some thoughts with representational content also possess: Hesperus, the evening star, and Phosphorus, the morning star, were not always known to be one thing, Venus. Frege said that the names "Hesperus" and "Phosphorus" differ in sense, but have the same reference.[24] They present one thing, Venus, under two different aspects or "modes of presentation", as the first star in the evening and as the last star in the morning. So it might be that the word-mediated thoughts "Hesperus has risen" and "Phosphorus has risen" differ in introspectible representational content. But they seem to share a kind of content we might call "referential content". There may also be examples which run in the other direction, though they are more controversial: Two people are flying in balloons on opposite sides of the earth. Each balloon passes over a small town, and the towns are identical-looking but otherwise unknown to the observers. The two people say to themselves "The little town below is picturesque". Those word-mediated thoughts might, it seems, share introspectible and hence representational content.[25] The introspectible aspects under which one town is present in the thought of one balloonist might be the same as those under which the other town is present in the thought of the other balloonist. And yet the referential contents of their thoughts are distinct. There may be legitimate objections to my treatment of this second case, though it is in accord with suggestions of the recent literature. But even the first case alone is sufficient to underwrite the distinction at issue, and this model:

First, all thoughts with cognitive content, thoughts about the world and liable to truth and falsity, have representational content. Second, at least some cognitive thoughts, for instance true ones, have referential content. To put this in a slightly different way, all cognitive thought, even about Santa Claus and his reindeer, is thought about certain "objects of thought" under certain modes of presentation, thought of certain of the "notional objects" of Dennett or the "intensional objects" of Brentano.[26] In having representational content, it possesses intentionality in that weak sense. And sometimes, for instance when a thought is true, then it has in addition referential content. It is then about some particular bit of the world.

Let me forestall one possible misunderstanding of this by reminding you how cheap intentionality in my sense comes. It may be unlikely that all thoughts which are cognitive in that weak sense, which we call true or false, are really about the world in the same deep philosophical sense in which a thought that there are rocks is about the world. Consider for instance what would be the case if mathematical truth were provability. But I am talking about objects of thought and objects in the world in the same cheap sense in which I talked about intentionality. The objectual form of true inner speech about numbers would be sufficient to grant it objects of thought and reference in the world in my perhaps debased and devalued sense, even if mathematical truth *were* provability.

In light of recent work on reference, this picture may seem quite obtuse. There are a number of objections which may suggest themselves, but let me begin with only one: Some cognitive thoughts, if they have representational content at all, seem to have representational content which "covers" only a bit of their referential content. That is to say, only a bit of their referential content is presented under some particular aspect within their representational content. For instance, while the predicate terms of certain word-mediated thoughts may well carry representational content, still their subject terms seem not to.[27] The subject terms seem merely to refer to an entity, and not to present it under one aspect or another. Some cases:

Quine distinguished between belief *de dicto*, belief that a certain (nonsingular) proposition is true, and belief *de re*, belief of an object that it is such and so.[28]

One might believe *of* a certain spy seen on the ground that he looks suspicious, and have no idea that he is a spy. On the other hand, one might say to oneself, "that spy looks suspicious." The first belief, Quine would say, is a belief *de re*, and the second a belief *de dicto*. Notice that the belief *de re* refers to the spy despite the fact that the spy is apparently not presented in one's thought under any particular aspect which one might introspect. However, it is plausible to insist that the *de re* characterization of the belief simply ignores some aspects which one might introspect. One experiences the spy in one way or another, and that might be the aspect under which the spy is present in one's thought. There may be different ways of reporting beliefs, which capture more or less of its introspectible content, but there aren't obviously two kinds of beliefs here.

This response relies heavily on perceptual acquaintance with the spy, and there are other kinds of cases where such a resource is unavailable. Putnam has argued that "elm" and "beech" differ in reference even if a speaker has no difference in meaning in mind between them.[29] So one might infer that the word-mediated thoughts "elms are trees" and "beeches are trees" may have "uncovered" subject terms. Kripke has argued that one may refer to Richard Feynman by using his name even if one knows almost nothing about him.[30] This too may provide the opportunity for a word-mediated thought with an uncovered term. In cases of this sort, however, there is at least a "metalinguistic" aspect which one might introspect. One knows of elms at least that they are called "elms", of beeches that they are called "beeches", of Richard Feynman that he's called that.[31] Various standard objections to this treatment of these cases may suggest themselves. But let me delay consideration of objections for a moment, until after we have surveyed the range of possible hard cases. Here's another case:

Two different people in different years and on opposite sides of the earth say to themselves "I am here now". Their word-mediated thoughts differ in referential content. Is there a representational and hence introspectible content which they might share? Yes, it seems. They also might share something metalinguistic, rooted in an understanding of how words like "I", "here", and "now" function, namely to pick out the person who utters them or the place or time of their utterance.[32]

It might seem plausible to insist that surely there must be *some* cases in which someone utters words in inner speech which bear no content present to their mind and yet which do refer, say because they are words of some public language. But remember that if there are such cases, then they aren't thoughts in my sense. And there are reasons to think there are no such cases. The very words which mediate such thoughts provide an aspect under which their referents may be present to the mind.

I have discussed several cases in which some crucial part of the referential content of a thought may initially appear to be uncovered by any intensional content. These cases involve perceptual acquaintance and word-mediation, as do all the standard cases, and it was those features of the cases which allowed the treatment I deployed. One might wonder if there are other sorts of cases, which cannot be treated in such a way. It seems to me that there are general reasons to think that there cannot be a kind of case which involves no aspect present to the mind. It is only because they have aspects present to the mind that we intuitively take referents to be elements of the content of thoughts. But let me try to press the opposing worry anyway:

Perhaps psychologies and agency need not involve intensionality at all. If there were a creature whose behavior was directed towards various things in the world, which pursued or fled or hung around things in a way which suggested that it had particular beliefs about them or desires for them, then it could be an agent with a psychology. But such a creature need not have thoughts with *intensional* content. Psychological states with intensionality are partially blind or opaque, are about things in the world under some descriptions of those things rather than others. But perhaps this is not essential to agency and to a psychology. And even intensionality of a kind might be rooted in something other than introspectibility. For word-mediated thought, the practices of some community of language users which are not "present to the mind" of the speaker or even any speaker, might help fix the relevant aspects. In thoughts which are not mediated by words, perhaps evolutionary or divinely-commanded functions might play a similar role.

Let me admit that it is conceivable that there be cases like these, which bear at least a distant analogy to the thoughts I have been discussing. Let me even grant that someone might reasonably call them "thoughts". That word no doubt has a vague enough meaning in ordinary speech to allow a variety of reasonable refinements. For now, I insist only that we be aware of the differences between these cases and those I have been discussing, in which the relevant aspects of referents are present to the mind. I don't want to fight about the word "thought". But let me also hint at other considerations which we won't be in a position to fully evaluate until Part Three.

If the commonsense conception of our psychologies is at all right, then there are thoughts of the kind I have been presuming, with intensionality linked at least indirectly to introspectibility. This is for a somewhat involved reason: Many psychological states seem to be about nothing in the world at all. Consider a daydream about a non-actualized possibility, or a radically false belief. There are two ways in which such states still possess a kind of intentionality. They are not about real objects, but are about mere objects of thought. And they are in some sense false thoughts about *the world*. But both of those sorts of intentionality involve intensionality also. Such states have *particular* objects of thought just by having certain contents of a representational and hence intensional sort. And if they are thoughts about the world, still they are thoughts that it be certain *specific* ways that in fact it isn't. Not all false thoughts have the same content in simply being about the world, and the differences between those thoughts are differences in intensional content, specifying different conditions which would make them true, even though they aren't true.

It might seem that false thoughts are a secondary case, that their intensionality might be parasitic on that of true thoughts. But we will eventually see that this is a problematic response, problematic in a way which suggests that intensionality should be linked to introspectibility in the way I have specified. Descartes thought that we could know with certainty the contents of our thoughts about the world, even if the world is not at all like we think it to be, even if we are radically deceived about the world by some evil genie. Descartes would have insisted that the introspectible aspects of such thoughts are a crucial feature of them, which they might retain even if they were radically false. Whatever the plausibility of Descartes' epistemic claims and of his view of the resources which realize thought, we will see in Part Three that our actual situation is in fact not too relevantly different from the implausible and wildly hypothetical scenarios involving genii which Descartes considers. While it is massively unlikely that we are deceived by evil genii, still our experience, and all our thought rooted in that experience, is in radical error about the world. As we will see in Part Three, all of our positive contingent thoughts, with familiar contents of the sorts articulated in Part One, are false. So if we are to have psychological states with such familiar contents, intensionality of a sort linked to introspectibility must play a crucial role. It might be thought that social practices or evolutionary or theological functions can generate intensionality of a reasonably intuitive form even in our wild situation. But I argue later that even those strategies aren't very helpful.[33] The crucial point is the one I just deployed. The friends of reference without intensionality-qua-introspectibility forget that while our thoughts are familiar, the world itself may be very strange. If the world is very strange, then only introspectible contents of thoughts can be at all familiar ones.[34]

Let me turn now to some specific objections suggested by my treatment of the cases with which we began. One might worry that all of my maneuvers have a cost. They may leave representational content suspiciously unlike content of any ordinary and commonsense sort, despite my rhetoric. This worry may come upon us from several angles.

Objection: It may be possible, in treating cases such as those with which we began, to specify "covering" aspects present to the mind, if we drag everything a thinker believes or perceives regarding an object, unconsciously or implicitly or not, into the content of the thoughts in question. But surely not all of that belongs there. It would violate our sense of how our thoughts are to be distinguished from one another.[35] Reply: Questions about thought-individuation are much more tangled than common sense recognizes. These are matters we will discuss in Part Two, but it is sometimes far from clear what is part of the content of our thought, and what is rather merely background presumed by that thought. At the very least, we should *hesitate* before insisting that some part of our conception of an object is not part of the content of a particular thought we have regarding that object.

But this objection can be pressed in a more specific way. For instance, the metalinguistic differences between our thoughts about elms and beeches are not reflected in the meanings of those words.[36] Those "aspects" of elms and beeches aren't anything we would attempt to preserve in translation of English sentences including "elm" and "beech" into German or Italian. But we would try to preserve meaning. Reply: But this only implies that we cannot quite identify the intuitive meaning of words with the content of word-mediated thoughts. Still the introspectible *contents* are relevant to a speaker's understanding of elms. This understanding is somewhat different for those who speak only English or German or Italian.

That reply may seem to just make matters worse. For instance, there are probably quite significant differences in the understandings different people have of any given object. Perhaps it is only because they share a *reference* to objects that they can manage to communicate or think about the same things at all.[37] Perhaps it is at the level of shared *referential* content that commonsense talk of shared content is pitched. Let me reply to this important objection with a bit of defense, and a bit of offense. First, the defense: While there probably *are* significant differences between the representational contents of different people's thoughts about the objects regarding which they communicate, still there will be some relatively abstract and inexact characterizations of those representational contents which our commonsense talk of shared contents captures. It does matter that representational contents be *contents* of more or less intuitive sorts, if we are to vindicate anything like the commonsense conception of our psychologies. Proof that they are awaits the details to come. But this doesn't imply that we must individuate contents in quite exactly the rough and ready way common sense does. Surely people who have beliefs about one object under different aspects do have significant psychological differences, which may even show in their behavior. When trying to understand someone, we often are happy to stop when we've determined enough about what they're thinking to determine whether we should assent to what they say, or disagree. But clearly there is often much more to what they are thinking than that. Any plausible account of content must involve some refinement of commonsense views. But as we will see the account presented here will only involve refinement, not replacement.

Now the offense, which will deploy some familiar hints about what's coming: It isn't clear that ordinary communication really involves shared referential content at all, or at least any reference more particular than the world itself. Let me start with hypothetical cases: If all humans shared a certain perceptual illusion, say that there was a large golden mountain of a certain sort in a certain place, then they might well communicate about, point at, think about, something which doesn't exist. If a cartesian evil demon perpetrated a universal but coordinated set of perceptual delusions on people (except perhaps regarding the words they utter) then they might communicate about and think about a world which was largely illusory. These are hypothetical cases. But, as I've hinted, we will see in Part Three that our actual situation is closely analogous. If there is any communication or shared thought among humans, shared reference to real objects has in fact little to do with it.

So I believe that all cognitive thoughts have representational contents which "cover" their referential contents. This does not imply that representational content "determines" referential content in any of the standard ways, but it may seem to. Let me now defuse objections which that mistaken worry would invite.

Russell thought that the sense of names determined their reference in the following way:[38] The sense of a name is captured by a definite description, something of the form "the unique so and so". For instance, the sense of "Hesperus" might be "the unique first star in the evening". The reference of a name, when it has one, is whatever thing in the world satisfies the relevant definite description. Similarly, one might think that the referential content of a thought must be determined solely by its representational content, which picks out its referential content from everything else in the world.

But representational content does *not* always determine referential content in this sense. This is apparent from some of the cases we have discussed. The thoughts about the small towns, and the thoughts that "I am here now", differ in referential content while sharing representational content. Such thoughts are "aimed" at the world. Their reference[39] depends not only on what their representational content is, but who has them, and where, and facing what direction.[40] Such thoughts must be aimed to refer.

There are various ways in which thoughts might be aimed. Consider for instance thoughts mediated by words. Kripke has suggested that the historical chain of transmission of a name, say "Richard Feynman", from an initial baptism, through a chain of users who intend to use the name in the same way as the person from whom they got it, to a current use, plays a crucial role in linking that current speech to its particular referent.[41] If that history had been different, someone else might be tagged by that speech. Hilary Putnam has argued that the reference of natural kind terms like "water" is sensitive to the particular stuff in the neighborhood, in the following way:[42] Imagine that there is a planet we might call "Twin Earth", which is just like Earth, right down to the presence of a language much like English, except that all the so-called "water" on the planet is XYZ rather than H-O-H. XYZ looks, smells, tastes, feels, and reacts under ordinary conditions just like H-O-H, but it has a different chemical constitution. Now imagine a time in the history of Earth and Twin Earth when the chemical constitutions of things had not yet been discovered. Putnam claims that in saying "water is wet", residents of the two planets would be referring only to the kind of stuff found on their own planet. Residents of the different planets would refer to different things, even if the aspects they had present to mind were the same. Even if a Twin Earthling hopped on a spaceship and flew off to observe liquid on Earth, in talking about "water" that person would, Putnam claims, be referring to the stuff on their home planet. They would be mistaken if they said upon landing here, "There is water about." Putnam also maintains that there is a "linguistic division of labor" governing the use of natural kind terms like "elm", "beech", and "gold", so that expert opinion plays a crucial role in fixing their reference within a given language community. If expert opinion were different, so too might be the reference of one's natural kind terms. Tyler Burge has argued on the basis of similar examples that the referents of all sorts of terms may depend on more than what's present to one's mind. Reference generally depends, he thinks, on the particular linguistic practices of one's community.[43] People often have a very incomplete understanding of what their words mean, and two people with the same incomplete understanding may mean different things by a word, if they are part of linguistic communities with relevantly different practices.

I think that a speaker's thoughts would not plausibly be aimed in these ways unless speakers were prepared to accept the authority of experts and language communities and chains of historical transmission, in a way reflected in their psychologies and even recoverable by introspection. All the purported facts about how we use words on which Kripke, Burge, and Putnam rely are, it seems, discoverable by introspection, in the armchair.[44] This may show that there is more present to the mind in these cases than one might initially assume. But still even the simple cases we have already considered[45] show that Russell's claim is in general too strong. In some cases, representational content can at best determine referential content only when it is aimed.

The next section develops such a limited claim. It may seem like a completely empty one. After all, the letter "c" is such that there is *some* function from contexts in which it might appear, say in certain positions in certain sentences which mean certain things and which are true in some particular way, to facts. When "aimed" in a complex enough way, even it has a referential content. But the existence of such a function is not sufficient to ascribe a representational content, or a content of any kind, to "c". Representational content must be, recognizably, *content*.[46] However, representational content *is* recognizably content in the following way: It characterizes a way the world might be in which it need not be aimed to be true. We will return to this point in Chapter Four.

3

Consider the following hypothesis: A thought with representational content can have only a referential content which the representational content matches. The representational content of a thought may ignore many aspects of the referential content, but it can be about something only when the aspects under which that thing is presented in the thought are veridical, get the thing right. Moreover, such a thought can be true only when it gets things right in that way.

Even this hypothesis, much weaker than Russell's in at least one respect, is too strong. For one thing, it presumes that there are facts of the matter about something which the last section of Chapter Three will make us skeptical about, a clean distinction between an object and its environment. But more to the immediate point, we have succeeded in finding intensional contents for certain word-mediated thoughts only by dragging in just about everything a speaker has in mind which might be remotely relevant to the content of his or her word-mediated thought. But if we drag just about everything one thinks about some object into its mode of presentation in one's thought, some of those things will probably not be true, even if we ignore our old worries about radical error. For instance, as Kripke has claimed, if one believes that Gödel discovered the undecidability of arithmetic, but really he stole it from Schmidt, still one thinks of Gödel when deploying that name in inner speech. One's thought that Gödel wore glasses doesn't lack referential content because the world fails to include something which meets one's full conception of him.[47] Or, to vary Keith Donnellan's case, if one looks at a man drinking what one falsely takes to be champagne, and says to oneself "that man is a spy", one's thought may refer, and even be true, despite the fact that he's really drinking water.[48] These cases are related to another important problem which I have so far ignored. False belief about real objects always involves thoughts which somehow manage to be about certain objects despite possessing representational contents which fail to match the world in all respects. Yet such thoughts surely refer.

Despite these objections, a modification of the hypothesis we are considering may still articulate a plausible role for intensional content in helping to fix reference and truth. It is this modification which I would defend. But let me first make a methodological point. "Truth" and "reference" are just words, though important and dear ones. They no doubt suffer from enough vagueness in ordinary speech to underwrite a variety of more refined uses, deployed in different philosophical accounts of truth and reference. Still, the sketch I will provide here captures a central commitment of ordinary talk of truth and reference, central enough so that if our thoughts lack truth and reference in this sense then it would be false consciousness to claim we don't care.

The central commitment of our ordinary thinking on which I'm focussing has been expressed by philosophers through the claim that true thoughts correspond to the world, in a sense which makes some prone to the postulation of what seem to be bizarre and implausible entities as truth-makers for sentences like "2+2=4" and "Pegasus has wings", even though reasonably refined semantic analyses of such sentences might show such an ontological extravagance unnecessary. We seem to want a certain sort of robust correspondence between true contents and robust objects really in the world, at least in central and paradigm cases. We want it so badly that we are prone to presume it even in cases where we should know better.

The following account, I believe, is the proper response to the conflicting pressures present in the preceding paragraph, against semantic and ontological naivete, but for a robust conception of truth by correspondence. It is also supported by the discussion of truth dependency in the following chapters: There are complicated dependencies among contents which distinguish some representational contents from others in regard to the matters under consideration: First, *basic* contents, an important but somewhat unusual subclass of representational contents, either match the world (or the bit of the world at which they are aimed) perfectly, are veridical in every detail, or they don't so match. Thoughts with basic contents are, at least in the primary sense, true if and only if their contents completely match, are veridical in all details. They are false otherwise.[49] Likewise, thoughts with basic contents can refer only to things which they get just right. But second, most thoughts with representational contents are not thoughts with some particular basic content. The contents of most thoughts are generated from basic contents in the ways sketched in the next chapter, ways which leave their truth and reference dependent on the truth of basic contents.

Consider first truth dependency. There are various truth dependencies among contents, which we will discuss quite soon. They leave the truth of all contents, or rather all contents which are not analogous to traditional analytic truths, dependent in some way on the truth of basic contents. While the truth of basic contents plays some role in the truth of thoughts with other sorts of contents, it may be a complicated and indirect one. For instance, consider some word-mediated thoughts. If I say to myself "my table is flat", there are difficult issues about what basic contents accrue to such an utterance, and how they accrue. For instance, it's hard to see whether the utterance means on the one hand that the table is *absolutely* flat, so that my table's scratches make the word-mediated thought literally false, though a close enough approximation of the truth to be usefully dubbed "true" in our daily lives, or whether it means on the other hand something a little less severe.[50] And it may be hard to see whether it's actually a part of the introspectible content of such an utterance and hence my thought, or rather some distinct background *presumption*, that there is more than one table in the world. And perhaps basic contents merely presumed as background conditions in the utterance of such a sentence would be relevant to its truth, even if they weren't quite a part of its introspectible content. Many such issues need to be sorted out before we can understand what complex relations to basic contents the representational content expressed by such a sentence would have, and how those basic contents and relations would determine its truth. Adequate consideration of these issues awaits at least the discussion of how content accrues to sentences in Part Two and of issues regarding complexity and vagueness in the next chapter. But whatever the detailed form that truth-dependence takes, there is, as we will soon see, some sort of dependence of the truth of other contents ultimately on the truth of basic contents. If the truth of basic contents is fixed, so too is the truth of all thoughts.

What about reference? There must be some particular conditions under which a thought succeeds in referring, if it does. But since humans understand their word "reference", it seems that humans can understand in a representational way the conditions which reference requires, and that those conditions can ultimately be cashed out in terms of basic content. One way to see this is to consider one of Kripke's objections to a significant role for introspectible content which we haven't yet discussed. It focusses on the need for a *non-circular* account of reference. For instance, if the aspect under which an object is present in our thought is merely metalinguistic, if it is present merely as a thing called "elm", we should notice that "called" is a term implying reference. But nothing we need to conclude about the cases at hand implies any vicious circularity. There are at least three ways to make the necessary point:

First of all, there must be at least the possibility of some concrete human understanding of the conditions which make for reference, of the sort which Kripke for instance attempts to provide. And those conditions must obtain for reference to succeed. For instance, if no basic content matches the world, then there is no reference of any sort we humans can coherently conceive. Under those conditions, any metalinguistic mode of presentation of the sort we have been discussing would be false. It is not implausible to insist that any reference of human thoughts must be a kind of reference which humans can cognitively understand, so that under the dramatic quasi-cartesian conditions we have been contemplating it would be proper to conclude that no human thought refers.

Second, ordinary people do manage to discriminate between concrete cases in which reference succeeds and in which reference fails, and apparently do so on the basis of the concrete differences between those cases. So not only are there particular concrete criteria for reference which must be met for reference to occur, but also ordinary people who can make judgments about reference must have some sense of those criteria, no matter how hard they would find it to articulate any theory of reference.

Third, reference seems attributed subject to the following particular constraint: Thoughts with other than basic contents can refer to things (even when they are false) only if some portion of their content[51] is true. Let me put this first more theoretically, and then more concretely: Because true basic contents need not include every detail of the truth, more than one basic content may be true at once. So the basic contents which suffice for the truth of a dependent content will characteristically each be true only if less detailed basic contents are true also. A thought refers, I think, only when certain (relatively less detailed) basic contents, which would be true if the thought were true but do not suffice for its truth, are themselves true (perhaps when aimed in the way appropriate for that thought). To put this more concretely: If there were no man of the sort he perceives and takes to be drinking champagne, then Donnellan's thought wouldn't refer.

Furthermore, all this seems to be something one might introspect, in one's armchair. Reference seems to require the truth of various concrete basic contents. And it seems that one might introspect which contents are relevant, though perhaps only in a complex and tortured way led by examples like those which Kripke and Putnam deploy. After all, what else is their methodology?

The correct story about how the contents of some word-mediated thoughts are dependent in truth on basic contents may leave the truth of such word-mediated thoughts quite indeterminate, or a matter of degree. But I think that the facts about the truth of thoughts may be relatively harder and cleaner than facts about reference. Some clearly false thoughts may not clearly refer or clearly fail to refer. Various social pressures to attribute some reference even in pretty marginal cases, which are perhaps underwritten by the linguistic division of labor or "normative" pressures to maximize the rationality we ascribe to the people we interact with, may infect which basic contents it is whose truth would be taken to suffice for the reference of some thoughts. And it may be that the referential dependencies are more sensitive to social pressures. It may be that they are, unlike the truth dependencies, not essential to the nature of the contents involved, but rather that they represent a kind of selection among various possibilities allowed by the essential semantic relations.[52] Social pressures *are* important. In fact, they may even make us prone to speak of the debased "truth" of thoughts with merely basic contents when that truth is not constituted as I have suggested, by match. But it would seem that even cases like that, if they involve conditions for debased truth which humans can recognize, involve the match of other basic contents to the world.

Before I conclude, I should at least note that there is another set of examples which has been deployed in support of the new theory of reference of Kripke and Putnam, which may seem relevant here, and which I haven't yet discussed. These are "modal" examples, examples regarding reference "across possible worlds". But we will not be in position to deal properly with these examples until section 6 of the next chapter.[53] So let me ignore those cases for a little while longer.

The central claim of this section has been that referential content and truth accrues to thoughts only through the perfect match of certain basic and hence representational contents to the world.[54] This is, I think, a plausible model. Of course it ideally demands closer inspection and more discussion, but it will become important only at the very end of Part Three. If the model is correct, then the range of our representational contents in a very weak sense sets the range of our referential contents.[55] Later on, in the final chapter, this may well seem more significant than it does now. It is another piece of setup.

Note that this model does not imply that the referential content of a thought is *exhausted* by its representational content, for even if we can only refer to things which we can also accurately represent, still they may have features we cannot accurately represent. On the other hand, if our referential contents do have features we cannot represent, we will not be giving any *account* of those features. But to bring things more securely home: However reference works, and whatever the plausibility of the model I have sketched in this section, the features of referential contents which we cannot represent are not relevant to making a sense we can understand of the existence of agents with thoughts like we take ours to be.

NOTES

1. There may be other sorts of derivational operations and another sort of underived content which can generate all human content. My only claim here is that all the contents of our thoughts can be specified in the way I will sketch, not that they cannot be derived in some other way.
2. Another set of contents, other than the set of basic contents I will isolate, might also serve to fix truth, so another set might also be basic in truth. My claim here is only that my set is.
3. I say "match" rather than "correspond" in part because the second word is used by different philosophers in a variety of different ways.
4. Why "*really* are"? To distinguish this case from others introduced at the beginning of section 1. This characterization is only a first approximation of something which will become clearer as we proceed.
5. More than one basic content may be true, as we will see.
6. In a certain primary sense. It may be that thoughts with merely basic content might be considered "true" in another sense we will consider later in the chapter, via various semantic relations to other basic contents, even if they don't match the world.
7. This ignores complications to which we will return at the end of the chapter.
8. Indeed, more precision would require still more explanation. For instance, the truth of something like "nothing is all red and all green" is fixed by truth dependencies and the nature of all the basic contents.
9. Perhaps there is a stronger sort of "making sense" which requires exhibiting *all* the basic contents which would make it true. In any case, this is just the first approximation of an account of coherent sense. It is for instance only applicable to contingent things, like us. And it will turn out that even in the case of certain sorts of contingent thoughts, for instance those mediated by words, there are two kinds of sense one can make of something. Further conditions must be met if things are to make *literal* sense. We will return to this point in Chapter Three.
10. It may be that there are dependencies which run the other way, that capacities for thoughts with more basic contents also require the presence of certain capacities for thoughts with less basic contents. For instance, maybe a capacity for thoughts with abstracted thoughts is required if someone is to be capable of experience. I do not mean to foreclose this possibility. Also, note that it will turn out that the three different roles it plays put some strain on the notion of basic content, since for instance along the axis of realization-dependency there is a sort of seed content which is yet more basic than even most basic contents. But for now I will ignore this complication.
11. Aside from classic empiricists--Locke, Berkeley, and Hume--see Alfred Jules Ayer, *Language, Truth and Logic* (New York: Dover, 1952), and Rudolf Carnap, *The Logical Structure of the World*, translated by Rolf A. George (Berkeley: University of California Press, 1967). For older examples, see Frances A. Yates, "Essays on the Art of Ramon Lull", in her *Lull & Bruno: Collected Essays, volume 1* (London: Routledge & Kegan Paul, 1982), 3-121. James Knowlson, *Universal Language Schemes in England and France 1600-1800* (Toronto: University of Toronto Press, 1975). Descartes to Mersenne, 20 Nov 1629, in Anthony Kenny (editor), *Descartes' Philosophical Letters* (Minneapolis: University of Minnesota Press, 1981), 3-6. Walter O'Briant (translator), *Gottfried Wilhelm Leibniz's General Investigations Concerning the Analysis of Concepts and Truth* (Athens, GA: University of

Georgia Press, 1968), 28-34.
12. Some may object that if analytic truths are true merely because of content dependencies, then this threatens to make their truth contingent on the existence of agents with thoughts with such contents. But this is a mistake. That the content dependencies give such a thought its truth does not imply that they are among its truth-conditions, that such thoughts are true in virtue of those dependencies does not imply that they are about such dependencies. To make an analogy, even synthetic sentences are true in part in virtue of the meanings they have, but they aren't about their having those meanings. Some may of course object to the claim that there are analytic truths. But I'm only concerned here with how they would be true, if there were any.
13. Of course, analogous things can be said about thoughts with such contents, or sentences asserting such contents.
14. This is Ryle's terminology, but the most resolute development may be Martin Heidegger, *Being and Time*, translated by J. Macquarrie and E. Robinson (New York: Harper, 1962). A good short introduction to this aspect of Heidegger is the discussion by Hubert Dreyfuss in Bryan Magee, *The Great Philosophers* (Oxford: Oxford University Press, 1988), 257-275.
15. Let me put this worry in another way: Some maintain that to know Italian is to know some facts about Italian, about its grammar and lexicon, and to make inferences with this knowledge. But others maintain that to know Italian is merely to have a certain capacity, to possess a certain ability for operating with Italian, independent of much knowledge *about* it. They may object to my treating thoughts with cognitive contents as central psychological phenomena, and note that even their opponents seem committed to some sort of know *how*--inferential capacities. Lewis Carroll's tortoise and hare seem to show us that not all knowledge can be knowledge *that*, since they seem to show that every argument must use a principle of inference which does not appear in the argument as a premise.
16. It is more accurate to say that any differences in these contents are what I will call in Chapter Three "mere artifacts of the approach apparatus".
17. Ludwig Wittgenstein, *Philosophical Investigations*.
18. Many have insisted that the sentences "Turn up the flame", "Will the flame be turned up?", and "The flame will be turned up" have much in common, in meaning and not just in component words. Frege would say they share sense but not force, at least in the translation suggested by Dummett. See Michael Dummett, *Frege: Philosophy of Language*, second edition (Cambridge, MA: Harvard University Press, 1981), 1-3, 83-84, 327-339. Searle following Austin would claim they are used to perform different illocutionary acts but have the same propositional content. See J. L. Austin, *How to Do Things with Words*, second edition (Cambridge, MA: Harvard University Press, 1975), and John R. Searle, *Speech Acts* (Cambridge: Cambridge University Press, 1969). Others would say they share a single sentence radical but not a mood, or a phrastic but not a neustic. See Erik Stenius, "Mood and Language Game", *Synthese* 17, 1967, 254-274, and R.M. Hare, *The Language of Morals* (Oxford: Oxford University Press, 1952). Sentences may be used to question or command or promise rather than assert that the world is a certain way, but in doing those things they seem to invoke a kind of content which is true to a way the world is commanded or promised or questioned but not asserted to be. On the other hand, some psychological states mix cognitive and noncognitive elements in complex ways which make sense and force hard to disentangle. And some things we do with words suggest meanings that do not easily fit the sense-force model at all. Consider what happens when we say "Goodbye", or count to choreograph something like a liftoff, or play ring-around-the-rosie. And the standard model utilizes distinctions, for instance between asserting, expressing, and presuming something, which may be too clean-edged to capture the messy facts of ordinary speech.
19. Young children may tempt us to resist this model. They have no abstract understanding of the categories of words or meanings or questionings, surely. And yet they meaningfully speak and question. There are a number of ambiguities which this objection deploys, and we aren't yet in a position to properly expose. One ambiguity is revealed by the discussion of introspection in the next section. Another is the ambiguity of "thinking about what the words mean", which can mean thinking something with the content of those words, or thinking that it is a content had by certain words. Still, we will see in Chapter Ten that plausible stories about the realization even of children's speech invoke

certain sorts of capacities for perceptual thoughts about words and for certain sorts of intentions to questioning behaviors, though not necessarily under the quite adult and abstract descriptions which my ways of characterizing those thoughts here have presumed. We will see that it may well be that an individual who may be properly said to understand a word in fact lacks explicit unconscious thought of the meaning of that word, but still we will see that they should be *capable* of explicit thought with content closely allied to that meaning.

20. In claiming that experience is a kind of thought with representational content, I put myself at odds with a tradition which holds that experience is not apt for truth and falsity. For instance, Descartes may be in this tradition. But Part Three will provide more than enough evidence for holding that experience is apt for truth and falsity. I believe that ordinary speech would call experience true and false in light of this evidence.

21. There is another way to initially characterize the content at issue which may be helpful: It is content of a kind that common sense recognizes. We might expect this, since in some cases we can introspect it. But even this characterization has its problems. As we will see, my account of content clearly involves some refinement of commonsense conceptions. And even some recalcitrant elements of common sense may suggest that if a field is full of grubs, whether or not that is "present to your mind", it still makes a good deal of difference to whether you act so as to spit at such a thing when you spit at the field, or see such a thing when you see it. That characterization of the field, even if not present to your mind, may be relevant to some commonsense characterizations of the "content" of your action and thought. But still, there is *another* commonsense mode of characterization of your thoughts and action, in which you reason and act towards the field, in such a case, in exactly the same way whether it's full of grubs or not. Representational content is what is invoked by *this* commonsense mode of individuation of thoughts and actions.

22. Donald Davidson, for instance, has sometimes favored an alternative.

23. As opposed, say, to causing it to have the thoughts that it does.

24. Gottlob Frege, "On Sense and Reference", translated by M. Black, in P. Geach and M. Black (editors), *Translations from the Philosophical Writings of Gottlob Frege*, second edition (Oxford: Blackwell, 1960), 56-78.

25. In fact, this case presumes that the contents of the various thoughts of each balloonist are easily disentwined, and as we will see this may be an implausible assumption. And there is another way to individuate even introspectible contents which implies that these thoughts differ in such content, irrespective of worries about the entanglement of thought contents. See for instance John Searle, *Intentionality* (Cambridge: Cambridge University Press, 1983). Searle's treatment of these issues is admirable in many respects, but the kind of content he attributes to thoughts in accord with this maneuver is unfortunately too complex to be deployed in all the cases we need to consider, in particular in the case of some thoughts with primarily basic contents.

26. Daniel C. Dennett, "Beyond Belief", in A. Woodfield (editor), *Thought and Object* (Oxford: Oxford University Press, 1982), 1-96, 6.

27. Certainly some aspects of anything might not be present in the thought of people about it. So in light of Chapter Five's discussion of the "difference" between facts, objects, and properties, it may seem that there is another way to dispose of these troublesome cases than that I pursue here.

28. W.V.O. Quine, "Quantifiers and Propositional Attitudes", in *Ways of Paradox* (New York: Random House, 1966), 183-194.

29. Hilary Putnam, "The Meaning of 'Meaning'", *Philosophical Papers*, vol. 2 (Cambridge: Cambridge University Press, 1975), 215-271.

30. Saul Kripke, *Naming and Necessity* (Cambridge, MA: Harvard University Press, 1980).

31. This move is attributed by Kripke to Robert Nozick. See also Searle, *Intentionality*.

32. The capacity to introspect such metalinguistic aspects in precisely that guise is quite a sophisticated capacity, which for instance young children lack. And yet even children who are capable of the kinds of speech which require this treatment have in some sense learned how to use the words. This learning, as I have suggested and will develop in Part Two, is reflected in their psychologies in ways which they may not be able to abstractly characterize. But still it is in the relevant sense "present

to mind".
33. What I do not explicitly consider later is a mixed view, some seed intensionality generated by introspectibility which in turn constrains a kind of intensionality allowed by social practice. The second component of such a view is, however, implicitly treated in the rest of this section.
34. Externalists who worried before that I was assuming something inimical to their position may reasonably suspect my claims here. These are properly matters for later. But for now let me at least hint that this argument will be underwritten later on.
35. It would also surely tarnish my treatment of the "picturesque" case in section 2.
36. Hilary Putnam, *Representation and Reality* (Cambridge, MA: The MIT Press, 1988), 27.
37. Some aspects of this are well developed by Gareth Evans, in *The Varieties of Reference* (Oxford: Oxford University Press, 1982), chapter 9. This also parallels Frege's famous argument, in "The Thought", translated by A. and M. Quinton, in P. F. Strawson (editor), *Philosophical Logic* (Oxford: Oxford University Press, 1967), for something different.
38. Bertrand Russell, "Descriptions", in *Introduction to Mathematical Philosophy* (London: George Allen & Unwin, 1919).
39. And hence at least sometimes their truth.
40. Some may reject my treatment of those cases, a treatment which is in accord with intuitions fostered by the recent literature. But, in any case, we will see in the following chapters that the basic content of many experiences *does* need to be aimed.
41. Kripke, *Naming and Necessity*.
42. Putnam, "The Meaning of 'Meaning'".
43. Tyler Burge, "Individualism and the Mental", *Midwest Studies in Philosophy* IV, 1979, 73-121.
44. This point is made by Ned Block, "Advertisement for a Semantics for Psychology", *Midwest Studies in Philosophy* X, 1986, 615-678.
45. Or at the very least the forthcoming cases, involving the content of experiences, to which I have alluded.
46. I owe something like this point to Pat Francken. It has also been deployed by Loewer and Lepore. For this reason also, certain forms of "short-armed" conceptual role semantics are not in themselves sufficient. See Block, "Advertisement for a Semantics for Psychology".
47. The other way Kripke uses examples like this is defused by what has gone before. It isn't that something other than Gödel meets your full conception of Gödel, because part of that conception is that he is tagged by "Gödel".
48. Keith Donnellan, "Reference and Definite Descriptions", *Philosophical Review* 55, 1966, 281-304.
49. But there may be complications. For instance, given the various relations among contents we will sketch, in particular of various basic contents to abstract contents above them, it may be that there are reasons to call "true" in a lesser sense even thoughts with basic contents which don't match the world, but which approximate basic contents which do get it right. But let me for the moment ignore this complication.
50. Peter Unger, *Philosophical Relativity* (Minneapolis: University of Minnesota Press, 1984).
51. Not necessarily of their meaning.
52. On the other hand, the treatment I have adopted for the components of cognitive thoughts which we do not call true or false may suggest limits on the appropriate selections.
53. Questions about reference across possible worlds are what I will call "artifacts of the approach apparatus".
54. For analogues of analytic truths, truth dependencies alone may suffice to underwrite truth, and even reference of a sort.
55. It would do this in a way which lets me explain a distinction I introduced earlier. If a (non-analytic) thought has a reference, then either it is a "concrete" reference, which can be matched by some basic content, or it is a "cheap" reference to a cheap object of the sort introduced in section 2. And even in the second case, the conditions required for reference can be matched by some basic content.

CHAPTER THREE

FROM REPRESENTATIONAL CONTENT TO BASIC CONTENT

This chapter concerns the content generation operations, by which representational contents can be derived from other representational contents, and hence ultimately from basic contents. As well as these semantic dependencies, we will briefly note some allied dependencies in realization, and relevant truth-dependencies.

I have said that the content generation operations are semantic operations which "generate" other contents, but this may be obscure. So let me explain. Imagine that all the contents sanctioned by Part One are present.[1] Those contents bear certain semantic relations to each other, of which the most familiar are logical relations. We, the content theorists, want to chart all of the contents. So we start somewhere, with basic contents, which happen also to be basic in truth. The basic contents have interesting "horizontal" relations to each other, to which we will return in the next chapter, but for the moment our interest lies elsewhere. We want to move "up" from the basic contents to contents progressively less basic in truth, in a way which will eventually bring us to all of the contents. So we pick a set of semantic relations which can yield together such routes to all of the contents, and a corresponding set of operations. Each operation takes us from one content to another content which is dependent in truth on the first, along a certain sort of semantic relation. Having isolated basic contents and that set of semantic operations, we can provide an account which can generate characterizations of all the contents. That's all I mean when I say that contents are "generated" from others.

My account of content involves some idealization across human differences. It will also "generate" some contents which in fact will never be the content of any human thought. That is because some contents it delivers are simply too big, detailed, and complicated. These big contents are human contents only in the attenuated sense that they bear the kinds of semantic relations to the contents of actual human thoughts which those actual contents bear to each other. But at least we will succeed in getting all of the contents of actual thoughts of normal adult humans aboard.

1

Let me begin with the most familiar sort of content generation operation. Representational contents can be generated from other contents, which I will call their "components", by quasi-logical operations, which mirror traditional logical operations performed on propositions. In particular, we should admit at least:[2]

i) "conjoining", whereby the component contents A and B yield a single content "A *and* B",
ii) "disjoining", whereby our two contents may yield the content "A *or* B",
and
iii) "negation", whereby a content can yield its denial. Unlike the analogous logical operations, disjoining and conjoining may be performed on more than two components at once.

Some of these operations come in different flavors, which involve different sorts of truth dependency and realization. Disjoining comes in two flavors: An *inclusive* disjunction over components A and B, which we might express as "A or B or maybe both", is true in case at least one of A and B are true, and false otherwise. The *exclusive* disjunction "A or B but not both" is true in case either just A is true or just B is true, but is false when both or neither are true.[3] "A and B" is true just in case A is true and B is true. In at least the most straightforward cases, where the components are each either determinately true or determinately false, "A and B" will be false otherwise. But there are complications introduced by certain vague or word-mediated components, which may be neither determinately true nor false, and which I will ignore for now. Negation also involves complications. First of all, at least when the contents involved are not realized through the mediation of words, repeated iterations of negation may yield no new contents. More important, there are two sorts of dependency in truth which correspond to different flavors of negation. Sometimes the denial of a component will be true just in case that component is false, and false when that component is true. This is *external* negation. But there is also *internal* negation, in which the truth of the denial of some component requires not merely that the component be false, but also that something in some range of positive alternatives to that component be true. For instance, sometimes when we say that a balloon isn't red, we imply that it is some other color. This distinction will be important later on.

Some of the thoughts with contents yielded by these quasi-logical operations are mediated by words. But there are also thoughts with contents derived by these operations which are not mediated by words. That second set of cases introduces another complication. The realization of such thoughts with contents derived by internal negation is unproblematic. But I think that the best we can deliver in the manner of such thoughts with contents derived by external negation are vague negative contents, which are indeterminate between internal and external negations of their components. In any case, the capacity to entertain a denial, as well as a disjunction or conjunction, seems clearly dependent on the capacity to conceive its component or components.

2

This section characterizes abstraction, an operation by which certain representational contents, which I will call "abstracted contents", can be generated from others, which I will call their "abstraction basis". Here's an example: Up in your balloon, you might see planes fly by, perhaps even one peddled furiously. Birds might soar about, and a fly might escape from your lunch bucket. Having thought about all of these flying things, you might notice that they all share a certain form, a body stretching aft and fore with symmetrical wings stretching out on either side. They each have the form of a symmetrical cross with its legs of no particular lengths and joined at no particular angles, despite the fact that they are shaped in detail quite differently. You might wonder why such a form is suited to flight, though your balloon lacks it, and why people with their arms extended have it but still can't fly unassisted. That form can be an object of your thought. It can enter into representational contents separately from the particular flying things which have it. The various flying things are among the things from which that form can be abstracted. A content into which that form enters is an abstracted content, semantically dependent on the less abstract contents, involving for instance particularly shaped things, from which it is abstracted. In fact, there is more than one kind of abstraction present in the case at hand. You can think of the shape of each of the flying machines independently of the other properties of that thing, for instance its color and size. You can also think of what is shared by all those particular shapes, and of shape in general.

Let me stress that abstraction is a *semantic* and not a *psychological* operation. It captures something analogous to a logical relation between contents, not the history by which some particular person comes to think of certain contents. *Each* of the representational contents which could constitute realizations, instantiations, examples, or values of an abstracted content are a legitimate component of its semantic abstraction basis. It is because of the kind of objects of thought which color-in-general and red are that red is an instance of color, because of the semantic dependency of color-in-general on red. And color has a similar semantic dependency on all particular colors, regardless of whether they were implicated in the particular psychological history of someone's coming to the thought of color.

No one, short of denial of the commonsense conception of our thought contents, can plausibly deny that we can think of at least some such abstracted things, that they constitute objects of our thought and enter representational contents. It may seem as if some philosophers *have* denied that abstracted entities can constitute objects of our thought, perhaps Berkeley most notoriously. But even *he* did not deny that meaningful thought and discourse about such things as shape-in-general occurs.[4] He only denied certain explanations of that phenomena, certain accounts of the realization of abstracted thought. Nor did he even deny that shape in general is an "object of thought" in the particular cheap sense I've given that phrase. People talk meaningfully of such forms. That talk of forms is capable of truth, in at least the debased and devalued sense I have adopted. Such truth-capable talk of forms is all that is required if they are to be objects of thought in my weak sense.

Some may insist that these supposedly abstracted contents are really something which can be delivered in some other way than by a special operation of abstraction. For instance, at least some abstracted contents seem analogous to disjunctions. There is a range of contents in which a balloon has the range of possible shades of red. Then there is the abstracted content which represents the balloon as being merely red. Maybe that is just a disjunction across the range of original contents.[5] But this strategy seems to involve some misrepresentation of the abstracted content. Abstracted "red" no longer bears the full marks of all its particular instances, as the disjunctive property rooted in all of those instances would. Admittedly, this is a relatively subtle difference, but it is intuitive, and if we want to generate the full range of contents recognized by common sense, we'll need to grant this distinction some play. Also, we will see in Chapter Thirteen that there is an intuitive difference between the realization of abstracted and disjunctive thoughts, indeed a difference which explains one complication I intend to largely ignore for the moment: Not any random set of contents can form together the abstraction basis for an abstracted content. Members of an abstraction basis must have some natural similarity, and include all coherently conceivable elements which do so.

There are some controversial examples of abstraction which should be endorsed. For instance, Kit Fine has renewed interest in "arbitrary objects", where an arbitrary object of a certain type has just those properties common to individual objects of that type. "[A]n arbitrary number is odd or even, an arbitrary man is mortal, since each individual number is odd or even, each individual man is mortal. On the other hand, an arbitrary number fails to be prime, an arbitrary man fails to be a philosopher, since some individual number is not prime, some individual man is not a philosopher."[6] These *are* objects of thought, but they present some difficulties. Let "A" name the arbitrary whole number. Then "either A is odd or A is even" is true, since for each whole number "either that number is odd or that number is even" is true. But neither "A is odd" nor "A is even" are true. The logic appropriate for arbitrary objects must be different than that appropriate for ordinary objects, or for basic contents.[7] Also, since the arbitrary whole number is an arbitrary number rather than an individual number, it is only *some* properties of the individual whole numbers, properties Fine calls "generic", which the arbitrary whole number can be properly said to have. It may be that only in thought mediated by words are these complications possible, and it may even be that they are undesirable complications, that we'd be better off not thinking about arbitrary numbers. But such talk is possible for us, and seems capable of "truth" in my cheap sense. It can give us at least word-mediated thought about such objects, "objects" of my cheap sort. So I think we should admit that arbitrary objects can enter representational contents.

Much abstracted thought is word-mediated, but some is not. For instance, we seem able to abstract spatial patterns from perceptual experience in a manner which is not mediated by words. The semantic dependency of abstracted contents on their abstraction basis suggests some dependency in realization. The capacity to entertain the notion of shape-in-general seems dependent on the capacity to entertain notions of particular shapes. One may be tempted to object that the colorblind cannot form the conception of the full range of particular colors, but can still form the conception of color-in-general. But such a colorblind notion of color is in fact a somewhat different notion than that of normal humans, though similar enough to be expressed by the same word. The notion of color is complex, consisting of at least two sorts of components, one derived by abstraction on instances, and another generated in more devious ways, via word-mediated thought of "the perceptual properties sensed through a certain sort of physically characterizable perceptual system". The colorblind may share the second with normals, while not the former.

More important for the moment is truth-dependency. How are abstracted contents true? Through semantic connections with their abstraction basis, it seems. A simple story goes this way: The truth of an abstracted content is fixed when the truth of its instantiations is fixed. But there are some complications. For instance, as in the case of negation and disjoining, there may be different flavors of abstraction, in which truth dependency takes different forms. If a balloon is colored, then it is because it has some particular color. But if the arbitrary number is odd or even, then that is because each individual number is odd or even. There may be intermediate cases as well, which require the truth of most or a few of the relevant instances.

And there is another complication. Some contents seem to mix levels of abstraction, and in such cases the semantic relations themselves may serve to constitute truth, independent of the truth of any basic content. For instance, color is more abstract than red, and if red is a color, then it is because of the range of hues that count as colors. And there are other relations among abstracted contents which mirror traditional "analytic" connections between word-meanings which were supposed to constitute "analytic" truths. Consider for instance the claim that red is not identical to blue. Perhaps it shouldn't be a surprise that these cases introduce some of the traditional difficulties which afflict analytic "truths". For instance, there can be word-mediated thought that red is a color, but it isn't obvious that we are capable of such thoughts independently of the mediation of words. Or perhaps it is more accurate to say that there would be no clear distinction between the possession of such a general belief and certain inferential propensities. Note also that the contents of these quasi-analytic thoughts are not delivered directly by abstraction operating on other contents in the way I have presumed. Rather, abstraction delivers a structure of contents whose span encompasses the quasi-analytic "contents" we are now discussing.

In any case, the truth of at least non-analytic abstracted thoughts seems to require the truth of at least some instance. Some will eventually be tempted to dissent even from this claim, to insist that there are contents which are generated in my account by abstraction, and which are not analytic, and yet which may be true independently of the truth of any of their instances, or at least true independently of the truth of any of their instances which we can conceive.[8] This is a mistake. It is essential to the particular contents which can be abstracted in the way I have sketched here that they have exactly the truth dependencies sketched. But this is a point to which we will return in Chapter Nineteen. Barring such possibilities, our agency, which is itself something of an abstraction, and other coherent abstracted entities, must be instantiable in less abstract content, and ultimately in the least abstract content, basic content.[9]

3

Some of the contents of our thoughts are less than ideal, and not just because they are false. It will be useful to canvass these other ways in which contents fail, though only one will introduce a new content-generation operation. The canvass will be useful because basic content is ideal in corresponding ways, and we will need to see how this account can nevertheless generate less than ideal contents of each sort.

Our thoughts are sometimes inconsistent. Sometimes this is because we have two thoughts which are not consistent with one another: We may quite honestly say we're sure that balloon flight is safe, but act in a way which indicates we suspect otherwise. But sometimes the inconsistency seems internal to the content of a thought: We may spend time considering round squares.

But even if many of our thoughts are internally inconsistent in this way, their contents can be generated from consistent contents, among which basic contents are found. All inconsistent contents have internally consistent parts which don't fit consistently together. For instance, a round square is round and a square. In all cases, the elements which serve to generate the inconsistency in a content must have enough content to do so. Perhaps the elements themselves are inconsistent, but then they too have inconsistent elements. Might those elements in turn be internally inconsistent? Perhaps, but this can't go on forever. There wouldn't be enough content in the elements to generate an inconsistency if it did.

So if a content is to be inconsistent, it must ultimately consist of internally consistent elements. Inconsistent contents can be generated out of internally consistent elements in this way.

In fact, we already have the resources by which to generate the inconsistent from the consistent: the quasi-logical operations introduced in section 1. From the content P one can generate the content not-P, and also the inconsistent content P *and* not-P. Of course, there aren't merely inconsistent propositions, but inconsistent objects, like round-squares. But we will see in Chapter Five that the difference between objects and facts is largely illusory. The logical operations can generate a round-square as an object of thought as easily as they can generate the content that something is round and is a square.[10]

What of our other dependencies? Inconsistent contents aren't true, though their components may be. And thoughts with inconsistent contents are, like other thoughts with contents generated by the quasi-logical operations, apparently dependent in realization on the capacity for thoughts of their components.

Our thoughts may be less than ideal in another way, which does demand a new content generation operation. Our thoughts may be vague. Our admiration for balloons may neither clearly exclude nor clearly include dirigibles. When we believe there's a city off over the horizon in some direction, there will be some places where a city might be that won't clearly make our belief true, nor clearly make it false.

We have vague thoughts, and basic content is merely precise. But there is reason to believe that vague contents are semantically dependent on relatively precise ones, that we might generate vague contents from precise ones, and hence ultimately from basic contents. Someone's conception of balloons may vaguely include dirigibles, and vaguely not. Certainly we can *represent* such a vague content as one which includes, more or less vaguely, various relatively precise ones. And this natural method of representation indicates a semantic dependency. A vague content is one which vaguely resolves into various relatively precise contents. There is some structure in the way it does this. Take the vague conception of a balloon. Certain more precise conceptions clearly fall within its range, for instance the conception of a child's balloon. But there are other more precise conceptions, say that of a dirigible, which it only vaguely or fuzzily includes. And there may be different degrees of fuzziness with which a relatively precise conception falls within its range. But, it seems, one can understand such vague contents as generated out of relatively precise ones.[11] Vagueness is merely vagueness.

Notice that on this account contents are vague relative to other contents. But vague contents may be vague in another way, fall short of a precision provided not by other *contents* but by the world. For instance, perhaps even basic contents, at the bottom of any chains of relative precision provided by my account of content, are imprecise in this way. But still, basic contents give us our sense of what even absolute precision *could* be. They represent to us, from the inside of our structure of thought, a paradigm of precision. We may come to believe that the world has a precision, say in color, which is beyond the capacity of our experience or thought to capture, though there are serious limits to our capacity to coherently conceive that. But, in any case, basic contents, concrete contents rooted in our experience, including objects with precise shades of the color we *can* experience, do represent to us ways the world *might* precisely be.

Still, there might be two kinds of vagueness. So let me a bit more precise: What I call "relatively vague" contents are in some sense semantically dependent on relatively precise ones, and ultimately on the most relatively-precise contents, among which basic contents are found. If relatively vague contents are to be generated from relatively precise ones, a new content generation operation, or rather a new class of such operations, is required. Vague contents include some precise contents quite clearly, and others less clearly. There are *degrees* (and not necessarily precise numerical degrees) to which various relatively precise contents fall within the range of a relatively vague one. Those precise contents are something analogous to the instantiations or disjuncts of the vague contents, but they are instantiations or disjuncts in greater or lesser degrees. To put this in another way, the operations introducing vagueness are really not distinct new operations, but rather a peculiar sort of generalization of disjunction and abstraction.

What of the other dependencies we're tracking? It seems that the capacity to entertain a relatively vague content depends on the capacity for thoughts with the relatively precise contents into which it resolves. Also, such relatively vague contents are apparently dependent in truth. If some vague content is true, then it is because of the truth of some one of the relatively precise contents from which it is generated.[12]

Even true thoughts may fall short in other ways than vagueness or inconsistency. Some thoughts are gappy and incomplete. Our thought of a balloon may completely ignore its distance to Polaris or the details of its construction. This incompleteness may be of two sorts: Some true thoughts simply leave some truth uncaptured, but their contents do not themselves proclaim this. But also some thoughts have contents, for instance disjunctive contents, which mark them from the inside as incomplete.

Even some *basic* contents will be obviously incomplete in the first sense, and thoughts which are incomplete in the second sense can be generated from complete contents by operations already introduced, in particular by disjunction and abstraction. So the account proposed here can deliver the requisite incomplete contents. Nevertheless, as basic contents represent a paradigm of precision, they also represent a paradigm of completeness in even the first sense. Each basic content corresponds to a complete way the world might be, a "possible world", which it exhaustively characterizes. Each basic content might also be true if it were incomplete, if the world contained more details than it captures. But it does specify a way that the world might completely be.

4

The next set of content generation operations involve some of the machinations of words in word-mediated thought. Word-mediation itself is, properly speaking, a way in which thoughts may be realized, not a content generation operation. For instance, it is one way in which thoughts with the contents discussed in the three previous sections and in section 6 can be realized, and a way in which inner speech can possess non-cognitive content. But word-mediation can also realize thoughts with representational contents of a new sort, which must be generated by special operations. It is these contents which are the crucial focus of this section, and which, for lack of a better phrase, I will say are generated by "word-mediation". Still, since word-mediation is a crucial means by which thoughts are realized, it is also useful for us to get some initial general sense of how word-mediation works. Part Two provides a fuller account, and Chapter Nineteen will review its most important implications. But this brief sketch should serve to allay certain initial objections.

Any thought which is mediated by words has a certain abstract form suggested in the last chapter. Words one speaks, to oneself or out loud, sometimes have an introspectible content, rooted in one's individual psychology. This is crucial for the realization of thoughts whose contents possess certain complex semantic dependencies. If one is capable of thought with a certain content, that content can be taken up also by a certain form of words. And that form of words may bunch together more than one such bit of content, bits which would otherwise have had nothing much to do with one another. It may be that so various are the kinds of content collected by that word, and so various are the historical contingencies which clumped *that* collection together rather than a slightly or wildly different one, that there is no very deep or necessary reason that all of those kinds be united, that no particular one of the contents clumped together by a word is essential to the content of all thought about more or less the same subject matter invoked by that word. Furthermore, syntax may collect content in very different ways. It may be that a bit of content accrues as a unit to an individual word, or a phrase, or a sentence, or a group of sentences, or even a set of interrelated terms. It may be that a bit of content accrues to a certain word directly, or only via the mediation of other words collected by the first. It may be that some bit of content quite clearly and determinately is collected by a word, or there may be different degrees of indeterminacy about that. And words may collect content in various roles, so that it is relevant in different ways to the truth of those words. For instance, one content may characterize not what a form of words asserts but what it presumes, so that when that content is false the words may not be false but rather nonsensical.

It is because of the different ways in which words can collect contents that new sorts of content are introduced by word-mediation. But first let me say a word about mechanisms, about realization. There is, within the psychology of a speaker of a language, a certain interanimation or association of words and contents. Generally speaking, a normal adult speaker can introspect the contents which a form of words collects for them. Perhaps they cannot do this in the immediate way they can introspect the content of their experience, but still they can do it while sitting in an armchair, by considering all sorts of hypothetical situations and what they would or might say under those conditions, and what they would think or do if various things were said. It is important not to confuse the intuitive meaning of a sentence with the introspectible contents it collects in the psychology of some speaker, and it is also important not to presume that even all those collected contents are representational contents of thoughts mediated by that sentence. As we saw in the last chapter, other things than the contents of a sentence which its speaker can introspect may be relevant to the intuitive meaning of those words. Remember, for instance, the linguistic division of labor. More to our immediate point, words may not intuitively be *about* all or even any of their collected content, may not *represent* such things. Remember that words can do all sorts of things besides say that the world is thus and so. For instance, they can commend and promise. When we do not say that some commending or promising sentence is true or false, it lacks cognitive and hence representational content. And yet it may collect content. And even sentences with representational content, which we say are true or false, may not be *about* contents which they collect. Here is where the new representational contents come in, the central focus of this section.

For instance, in being appropriate responses to certain other words, sentences may be called true under conditions which they are not intuitively about. Consider the relation between mathematical sentences and proofs. Even if we pretend for the moment that the truth of a mathematical sentence consists of its provability, still it is not intuitively about its proofs. Word-mediated thought which we call true or false has cognitive and representational content. But while, as I argue in Part Two, the contents collected by words play a crucial role in constituting them to have the representational content and more generally the meaning they do, those collected contents are not always to be identified with that meaning or even that representational content.

Let me elaborate a bit. I focus here not on the intuitive meaning of words but on a particular kind of content they bear, by which they may mediate thought. This is a kind of introspectible representational content which a form of words bears in the particular idiolect of their particular speaker. While not all psychologically associated contents are representational contents, this particular sort of introspectible representational content is fixed by, though not necessarily identified with, the introspectible contents collected by that form of words and the introspectible roles in which it collects them. Because it is introspectible, it is this content of the word-mediated thought of the speaker which is most analogous to the representational contents of those thoughts of the speaker which are not mediated by words, the other contents we chart in this part. If one's words have a kind of representational content which one cannot introspect, in the admittedly tortured and complicated way in which we can introspect what each of us as individuals mean by our words, then it is sufficiently unlike the content of thoughts which are not mediated by words to be beyond our immediate concern. And when we introspect what we mean by our words we merely introspect what contents are associated with those words and in what roles.

But even if I do not insist that intuitive *meaning* is introspectible, this model of word-mediated thought exacts a certain cognitive cost: Each bit of the introspectible content of a form of words is something of which its speaker may think, independently of the mediation of that particular form of words. For instance, if some word is an appropriate response to certain words or is for doing certain things (in the idiolect of a particular speaker), then that speaker can conceive concrete inscriptions of those words or performances of those actions. Because of this limit on the content which can accrue to human words in the idiolects of their speakers, words can extend our capacity for thought in only certain ways. They can only bundle together contents which can be delivered by other content generation operations, or by the mediation of other words whose content does not itself crucially involve the very words in question. The ultimate dependence on basic contents of all the contents delivered by the other content generation operations hence assures that no human words are capable of asserting consistent and positive and contingent things about the concrete world which are not within the range of basic contents.

This claim may seem objectionable. Some may worry that speech which is an appropriate response to other speech or evidence can allow us to extend our conceptions of even the concrete out beyond the limits of basic contents. So let me elaborate still more, to defuse this objection. At least characteristically, there is a certain range of contents specifying conditions under which at least a declarative sentence is appropriately assertible and appropriately called "true",[13] and which its speaker might introspect. The speaker can introspect the conditions under which they would assert the sentence, not correct the assertion, call the sentence "true", and not correct such a claim. These we might call the "truth-conditions" of the sentence. More exactly, of course, we should say that they are its truth-conditions in the individual idiolect of the speaker. In at least the most characteristic cases, these truth-conditions must obtain for the word-mediated thought which is an inner or outer utterance of that sentence (if perhaps not the sentence itself) to be true, and the truth of that word-mediated thought is dependent on the truth of those contents. After all, it is what *the speaker* thinks through that utterance which is our primary concern here. In at least the most straightforward cases, when those conditions do not obtain the thought is false.[14]

There is some ambiguity in this model which plasters over some complexity. For instance, there may be a range of distinct truth-conditions for a sentence, each of which would be sufficient for the truth of the sentence. A thought mediated by such a sentence would be false only if none of those conditions were true. But this simple model does suggest that no relevant content can accrue to words which outruns basic content in a certain important sense. All the conditions which the speaker can introspect as making the words appropriate are conditions which the speaker can think of in some other way, which are basic contents or delivered up by the mediation of other words or the other content generation operations. This suggests that, at least if they are positive and contingent conditions, they can obtain only if some basic content is true.

Still, sometimes the truth-conditions of word-mediated thoughts yield a "truth" for such thoughts which is significantly unlike the truth of thoughts which are not mediated by words. Imagine once again that the truth of mathematical sentences consists in their being provable in certain ways. Still mathematical sentences are not intuitively about their conditions of provability. Or imagine that the conditions which make the assertion of a certain sentence appropriate for one person do not make its assertion appropriate for all, and not because of some disguised indexicality. In both these cases, it would perhaps be better to call the relevant conditions "assertion conditions" rather than truth-conditions. But in situations like these there is still the dependency of word-mediated contents on other contents which I have suggested. The dependency of all contents on basic contents still suggests that we cannot form thoughts, even thoughts mediated by words, which allow us to think of a *world* which outruns basic contents. Word-mediation may allow us to think of "objects of thought" of a new variety, say certain numbers, but none which are found out in the real world which grounds the truth of basic contents. There are inscriptions of proofs in the world. If mathematical truth is provability, then still thoughts about numbers are not intuitively about proofs. The proofs are assertion conditions but not ordinary truth-conditions for those thoughts. The thoughts are about numbers, but not about numbers out in the real world. Here are new contents, generated by word-mediation.

This development requires a qualification in our account of coherent sense. Certain forms of speech may be dubbed "true" under conditions which do not imply that there literally are things in the world of which they truly speak. Such forms may make sense, but not "literal" sense. To make *literal* sense of something said by a sentence is to exhibit particular conditions, hence ultimately conditions in basic content, in which that sentence would be properly asserted and called "true" by all, and which that sentence is intuitively about. It is important to make *literal* sense of talk of our agency, if we are to vindicate that talk for all of us, and if such talk is to really be about agents in the world.

Even in the face of my treatment of this set of cases, and even given my plausible insistence that what words mean to a speaker is most relevant to mediating what *they* think through inner utterance of those words, and even in light of my promissory notes referring to discussions in Part Two and Chapter Nineteen, you may dissent from this rough model. So let me remind you that no intuitive cases which support the linguistic division of labor suggest that humans as a whole cannot think about the conditions which would make a human sentence true. And indeed they do not support the suggestion that humans cannot think about those conditions even independently of the mediation of the words in question. The representational content of word-mediated thought, as well as its content generally, seems limited to elements which can be delivered by the other content generation operations or the mediation of other words, even if the particular psychologically-based story about the realization of word-mediated thought which I have been telling is false. Many are impressed by possible worlds semantics, and conceive of possible worlds in a rather concrete way. But any humanly relevant contents must be limited to possible worlds which humans can conceive. Identify the account of basic contents to follow as my account of these conceivable possible worlds.

Word-mediated contents are in general dependent in truth on other contents, and hence ultimately on basic contents, though let me note a complication which may already be evident from what has come before. Contents delivered by some flavors of negation, and those whose truth is assured simply by certain content dependencies, may also be born by words, for instance by sentences involving negation or by analytic sentences. Still all *positive* and *contingent* word-mediated thoughts, which say something positive and informative about the world, would be false if all basic contents were false.

5

There are other sorts of mediation than word-mediation, and they may allow for the generation of subtly different sorts of contents. For instance, sensory images may sometimes collect contents as words do, though the images have a kind of content-analogue in themselves, independently of what they collect, that words do not.[15] They picture certain things. Also unlike words, they lack intuitive syntax.

Metaphors may also mediate thought. Capable of thought of oceans and air, balloons and floating buoys, you may come to think also that the air is (but not *really*) an ocean, and the balloon (though not *actually*) a buoy. Tracing your route over a map with colored circles and lines, you may think that some mark is (but not *literally*) a certain city. You think of the ocean, the buoy, and the mark as metaphors for other things. You think about those other things via the mediation of the metaphor.

In these cases, there is some abstract form that the metaphor shares with what it is a metaphor for, and which it in some way conveys. This constitutes it as an appropriate metaphor. You might abstract out these forms, and think abstractly about them, but in cases such as these you don't. Rather than think about something and its abstract form in a straightforward way, you instead pick some (often familiar or concrete) entity which shares the relevant form of the first thing, and think about it instead. But you think about it in a peculiar way, as an analogy or metaphor or likeness of the original thing. Perhaps the second entity is merely simpler or more comprehensible than the first. Then it is a *model* of that thing. In any case, you somehow manage to think about one thing via the mediation of the other. You might think of that mediating thing in itself, as you might think of a word in itself, but you can also think *through* it, into the content it collects.

Sometimes metaphors for things can become very deeply entrenched in our thought, but still retain some of their force as metaphors, not become mere dead metaphors. In such cases, part of the content of one's thought about something may be carried quite centrally by metaphors and models and analogies for that thing, and the metaphors may govern and organize that cognition. Argument becomes (but not really) war, with strategy, defense, and victory. Time becomes (but not actually) money, spent and saved.[16]

Note that this suggestion about thought content bears a close relation to a traditional view of the meaning of metaphoric language, a view which holds that words, when used in successful metaphors, convey something in addition to their ordinary meaning, something that successfully captures some form of the thing of which they are said.[17] That traditional view of metaphoric language is controversial. Davidson, for instance, claims that in metaphors words have their ordinary meanings only, but that successful metaphors are useful forms of false speech.[18] But it is important to remember that we are centrally concerned with thought contents, not the meanings of words, and that in the last chapter we already saw reason to distinguish between the meaning and the content of even inner speech. And it does seem that metaphors and sensory images may mediate our thought in much the manner of words, with the additional complexity that images only appropriately picture, and metaphors only appropriately express, certain things.

So far, we have only clearly managed to characterize other ways in which thoughts may be realized, not necessarily a new content generation operation, an operation which can deliver new contents, contents which for instance word-mediation cannot provide. But I include metaphoric and imagistic mediation here because it may be that the artificial and conventional way in which our words carry content may make them incapable of the particular subtle shades of content which metaphors and images carry.

Like word-mediated thought, it seems that thought mediated by images and metaphors is dependent in realization. It depends on the capacity to conceive the image or the metaphor itself, and also what it is an image or metaphor for. Such thought seems also dependent in truth in the complex manner of word-mediated thought. If the commonsense conception of agency is merely some metaphor or image of the truth, then to vindicate that conception is to refine it into something which gets things quite literally right, to reveal the literal truth mediated by that image or metaphor.

6

There is one last set of content generation operations which we have to consider. These are operations which *organize* contents, which create organized contents from relatively unorganized ones. For instance, they include an operation by which certain bits of a basic content are clumped or bundled together in such a way as to constitute a *single* object, with a unity in space and over time, *one* object distinct from its environment.

The particular organization of contents which accrues in the thought of a particular agent is in some sense an arbitrary matter. No particular organization is mandated by *the world*, no more than the world mandates that a particular language, English or Italian, be spoken. The same world, the same true basic content, is captured by a content regardless of the way in which it is organized; differences in the organization of a content are not really differences in the basic content which grounds the truth of that content, just as the basic content which makes a particular Italian sentence true may also make an English sentence true. But the particular organization of contents in our thoughts can be quite deeply entrenched. It can seem so natural and inevitable to us that we may come to feel that there *is* an issue of truth between us and those who have another form of content organization. Since differences in organization introduce what we *call* differences in truth, and since I am committed to a rather cheap understanding of what is required for the truth of a content, I will grant that there is a kind of representational content which includes the artifacts which the organization of a content can produce. I will grant that one unorganized, or as I shall say "raw", representational content can generate a number of distinct organized, "cooked" representational contents.[19] But I will continue to insist that there is no difference of truth of a certain important kind between them, that any (contingent) cooked content is made true by the same basic contents which would also make true the raw content from which it is cooked, and also other contents which might be cooked from that raw content in different ways. The apparent differences in truth are merely apparent, mere artifacts of what I will call "the approach apparatus", the specific way in which contents are organized in people's thoughts.

My discussion of cooked content should serve to forestall some objections to the relatively austere conception of basic content to be outlined in the following chapters, in particular to the way it ignores certain "metaphysical" issues. I hold these issues to involve artifacts of the approach apparatus. Classical empiricism was sometimes anti-metaphysical; it sometimes held that certain traditional metaphysical debates were simply meaningless. On the other hand, some philosophers held that at least some of the traditional debates could be resolved, not dissolved, by appeals to ordinary ways of speaking, in effect by recourse to something a lot like analyticities. It has now become hard to believe that analyticities and appeals to ordinary language can resolve issues which very much divide competent and sensitive speakers of languages, but while contemporary analytic philosophy has returned again to a discussion of the full panoply of traditional, indeed medieval, metaphysical issues, it lacks a clear and generally accepted account of what it is doing when it addresses such issues, of what is supposed to ground the truth which might resolve various metaphysical debates which now rage again. My account of content suggests that such metaphysical debates are not meaningless, but rather that they involve content organization, the form of the approach apparatus. There are two ways in which they might do this. Insofar as putatively metaphysical debates are, covertly, issues about what our rather contingent form of organization of content happens to be or perhaps ought to be, there may well be a real issue of real truth in those debates, just as there may be a fact of the matter about what language we speak. Insofar as sentences in some speaker's idiolect have "truth-conditions" which make their "truth" sensitive to our form of organization, then those sentences may possess truth of a kind. But if this is so, it must be pretty covert. Metaphysical debates are not intuitively *about* some of our cognitive quirks, and metaphysicians may insist on that point. Just as the world doesn't mandate that it be expressed in English rather than Italian, so too alternative forms of content organization, and hence different metaphysical positions, are sometimes such that the world itself does not mandate that we adopt one rather than the other. There is sometimes not that kind of issue of truth between them. And yet sometimes metaphysicians act like there is. In that case, there are artifacts of the approach apparatus.

To understand raw and cooked contents, consider first the distinction which some classic empiricists would have drawn between what is *given* in experience, and the contingent manner in which that material is organized by language and in judgment. Balloon connoisseurs may be able to identify 47 varieties of what I would call simply "red silk". It's not that my sense experience fails to provide the raw material for such distinctions. It's just that I lack the vocabulary to easily express the same discriminations. My experience and an expert's experience of a given bit of silk is quite the same. We just conceptualize things differently; we differ in our approach apparatus.[20] Now consider this example:

You are up in a balloon, looking out over the sunny countryside. You have the language and conceptualization capacities you now possess. You think about the green fields. Now imagine a comparison case. You are up on just such a day, are having just such experiences. You have most of the same beliefs you've always had. You think the world of the countryside is really just a vast structure of microphysical particles. You think that food is grown below. The only difference with the original case is this: You have been taught not to speak and think of familiar things like fields and of corn, but of odd patterns of unusual slices of plant-parts, perhaps all the slices at a single height spread all about the field. All your thoughts in the second case are just as in the first, except where these conceptual differences require a revision.

Such an example involves machinations of an approach apparatus which may create artifacts. The particular judgments one makes, involving one's particular conceptualization, can come to seem reflected in the very world about which they are made. It can come to seem a matter of truth whether the fields are really single objects or not. The person who fails to speak of pieces of corn or of fields may seem to have for that very reason false beliefs. One might suspect that an unusual form of content organization would lead to some false belief in some other sphere, say some misconceptions about the best science. But the person who fails to speak of pieces of corn, and speaks instead of the odd agglomerations of slices, may seem to *us* to have false beliefs even if they have a *more* successful science, even if their form of content organization doesn't yield some falsehood elsewhere among their thoughts. That would be a genuine artifact.

It is as if the same raw situation were given to you in both of the cases, and you cut it up differently. In one case you cut it up into fields, and in the other situation into what seem odd patterns. The raw situation allows finer discriminations than any you make in either case, or grosser ones. While not necessarily arbitrary, it is at least contingent and unrequired by the world that one cook the raw material in one way rather than the other. But still the two differently cooked contents can seem like different contents. So it can seem as if there is an issue of truth about which objects, the corn or the odd agglomerations of slices, are really present in the world.

Objection: Even in our *experience*, the things we take to be unified objects present themselves as continuous and unified objects, raised up from the ground of their surroundings. Looking far off into the distance, you'd literally *see* the field as a unit. So there are features of our experience which grant even a basic content rooted in that experience the wherewithal to represent the unity of objects. No machinations of an approach apparatus are required. We can think that the world really contains certain objectively unified objects, which match this unity in experience. Reply: Granted. We can conceive basic contents which include such unity, and hence these issues *may* be matters of, as we might say, real truth. However, we may come to think that the unity of objects in our experience is a mere artifact of that experience, like the fact that distant objects look smaller. We may come to entertain basic contents which eschew that unity, contents we can share with other creatures who have different conceptions of the unity of objects. It has seemed to some that if one person believes that a balloon is *one* thing and if someone else believes that the balloon is a collection of undetached balloon parts, then there *must* be a significant difference between their beliefs, that it *must* be that one may be true while the other is false. So it has seemed to some that there *must* be some deep metaphysical fact of the matter here, that certain things of which one might speak are really single things and others are not, that there are certain magic boundaries in the world which only one of the beliefs noted can get right. But there is no necessity that our talk of the unity of objects invokes magic boundaries. And the most charitable reading of our ordinary talk of such unities is that it does not. Admittedly, *some* basic contents, even those closely rooted in features of our experience of objects, show ways the world might be which would include such magic boundaries. But for *some* basic contents, in fact the most plausible ones, only the approach apparatus contributes the requisite unity of objects. And certainly it is a way which such unity *could* be provided.

Perhaps because of the misleading suggestions of our experience, some continue to dicker about the unity of objects in contents in which it is clearly and merely due to the machinations of an approach apparatus, as if it could still be a matter mandated by truth, and yet is not a matter *about* our approach apparatus, nor even a matter legitimated by the form of our approach apparatus in the way in which a mathematical sentence may be legitimated by a proof. For instance, many believe that fields aren't big irreducible entities, but rather consist of dirt, and ultimately of microphysical particles arranged in certain ways. An arrangement of microphysical particles such as is taken to constitute a field could be taken to constitute an agglomeration of undetached field-parts with no plausible error, no more error than preferring English to Italian. But some metaphysicians may still worry about the "truth" of the issue even while accepting this reductionist view of things like fields, and even while insisting that they are not merely concerned with charting or reflecting the contingent form which happens to be taken by our approach apparatus. This would be a mistake. It is not as if the boundaries between field and field are necessarily more significant physically than those between a part of a field with one sort of soil and another. Rather, it seems, we speak of fields in such a case, we draw their boundaries where we do, for all sorts of contingent psychological and social reasons, because the things are registered and owned as units, because it's hard to divide labor and recompense over units not separated by fences or tree-lines, because we like regular shapes, and so on. And we need not be covertly denying physicalism to do so. In speaking of fields rather than field-parts we may become committed to certain social practices, but not obviously to anything having anything to do with real truth. It isn't insignificant that even current metaphysicians who believe, perhaps misled by experience, that there are magic boundaries in the world, characteristically appeal not to experience but to our linguistic practice, for instance our talk of identity, as their evidence about where such boundaries are to be found. But while our talk of identity is not intuitively about our practices, still certainly such evidence is not obviously evidence about magic boundaries in the world, nor even evidence that we believe that there are such. Our practice of individuation seems completely oblivious to any magic boundaries except when that practice is rooted in the (plausibly misleading) features of our experience. There *can* be an issue of real truth here which the metaphysicians address, since some basic contents include magic boundaries and there is a truth about our practices. But such disputes often involve mere artifacts of the approach apparatus.[21]

There is a temporal analogue of the phenomena we are discussing: The field on which one gazes may be thought of as a moment-field, which lasts but a moment until it is replaced by a similar moment-field, or alternatively as persisting through some time. It might be thought to be destroyed only by the next plowing, or as lasting throughout the season. Metaphysicians often debate questions about numerical identity over *time*, about what sorts of continuity in properties or matter or whatever are required for a thing to continue to exist through time as one and the same thing, to persist even despite undergoing some changes. They propound puzzles about it: Take a balloon made of 100 parts. Replace one part a day, putting the replaced part in the garage. After 100 days, reassemble a balloon from the parts in the garage. Which is the balloon you started out with, that now in the garage, made out of exactly the same parts as the original, or that not now in the garage, which is otherwise continuous with the original? Note that no experience we might have of what goes on here, even if we could watch everything from all sides at all times, would resolve this puzzle. That suggests that the issue might be an artifact of the approach apparatus, at least if only the concrete content which is rooted in experience can be basic in truth.

There are various theories about identity over time which bear on puzzle cases like these. Some maintain, with Chisholm and Butler, that nothing which changes its parts persists over time in the strict and philosophical sense, though one may speak loosely and popularly as if it did, so that the balloon does not strictly speaking survive the change of a single part. Some maintain, with Locke, that a continuous organization of matter fulfilling a particular function, with parts replaced in a slow enough fashion, is sufficient for the identity over time of something like a balloon. Some fans of authentic parts insist that the original balloon gradually migrates into the garage. In each case, with enough ingenuity these metaphysicians can probably defend the internal coherence of speaking of identity over time in the way they prefer. When evidence beyond coherence is cited for the "truth" of such theories, it is their fit with intuitions about what to say and our ordinary ways of talking. Nobody suggests going out and examining real balloons. It is then plausible to take such disputes either to be about or to be resolved by what our contingent form of approach apparatus happens to be, which of course might not unambiguously resolve puzzle cases, or to be rooted in mere artifacts of the approach apparatus. Since such disputes are not intuitively about or resolved by our approach apparatus, which might suffer from obvious indeterminacies the disputants seem rarely to consider possible, the second option may well be most plausible.[22]

There is a second cluster of "metaphysical" issues which in recent decades have received a good deal of philosophical attention, after a period of neglect. These are *modal* matters, issues about possibility and necessity. Debates about many such modal issues seem not to appeal to any evidence rooted in the contingent course of our concrete experience, but rather to modal "intuitions", which may merely be intuitions about how to speak, as if in English rather than Italian. So it is natural to propose that these too are matters of the approach apparatus. Metaphysicians who discuss such issues may be doing something important, figuring out the form of our approach apparatus or different forms an approach apparatus can take. But there need be no issue of real truth, rooted in basic content, between two alternative forms of approach apparatus used by different people, forms supporting different modal claims. Apparent differences in truth may be mere artifacts of the approach apparatus. This view is in effect the "conventionalism" about modal truth suggested by Nathan Salmon, Paul Coppock, and Alan Sidelle.[23]

The first set of modal issues which may be artifacts of the approach apparatus are analogous to the issues about identity over time which we've just discussed. Perhaps one's practice of individuating a thing over time recognizes some properties of the thing as privileged in a certain way, such that if the object loses those properties it will be held to go out of existence. Such properties are seen as essential to the persistence of that thing. But perhaps one recognizes questions about the identity of objects not merely at a moment or across time, but across situations that it doesn't and won't but *might* have inhabited. Perhaps one recognizes issues about identity across such merely possible situations, "across possible worlds". That raises questions about another sort of essential property: Is this balloon in front of you such that there is some possible world in which it might have existed without ever having that basket? Could it have been made of plastic entirely rather than of silk, or of the very bits of silk which actually make up that other balloon now off on the horizon? Does it have any properties without which it couldn't exist and which it doesn't share with all entities, any interesting modally essential properties?

Here again it seems possible to imagine different coherent practices of modal talk, none of which conflict with any concrete facts. One might hold that "trans-world identity" requires preservation of one set of properties or another. One might hold that it requires that a majority of matter be preserved, at the cost of making trans-world identity intransitive. Or one might hold that there is no trans-world identity properly so called, that an object has counterparts in certain other worlds which resemble it in various ways, but that *it* cannot strictly speaking be any different than it is. In this last case, it would be something's counterparts about which one is really thinking when one thinks how things would have been had *that* thing been different.

When such alternative practices are internally coherent, and when the only additional evidence that is taken as relevant to their "truth" is their fit with our practice of individuation, and when that practice is not in any obvious way responsive to anything in the world which grounds its particular claims, then it is not unreasonable to conclude that such "truth" as one such form of speech or thought can enjoy and another lack is merely a fit with our more or less contingent practice of modal speech, and not with any deep metaphysical facts written into the world itself. Again, the differences between such practices may merely be differences in the form of organization of content for thought and speech provided by the approach apparatus. If there seems a *deep* issue of truth here, if debates about such issues are not intuitively about our approach apparatus, nor resolved by it as mathematical disputes are by proofs, then that may generate another sort of artifact of the approach apparatus.

Consider another modal issue: Some are troubled by the issue of whether there are any contingent identities, or only necessary identities, between named entities. For instance, "Hesperus" and "Phosphorus" name one thing, Venus. Given that, could there be a possible world in which Hesperus and Phosphorus were different things? Some hold that the meaning of names is determined by descriptions which give their sense, and that this shows that there can be contingent identities involving names. For instance, if "Hesperus" means the same as "the last star in the morning" and "Phosphorus" means the same as "the first star in the evening", and if while those two descriptions are in fact both true of one thing they could have been true of two different things, then the identity of Hesperus and Phosphorus seems contingent. But this view of names is thought by many, influenced by Kripke's important work, to be mistaken. The meaning of a name is thought by these to be its reference. In that case, Hesperus is of necessity identical to Phosphorus, since both names mean Venus and Venus is of necessity identical to itself. And indeed it would appear then that all identities between two named entities are necessary. But consider Allan Gibbard's case:[24] Let "Goliath" be used to baptize a certain statue and "Lumpl" be used to baptize the lump of clay of which Goliath happens to be made. Assume that in fact the two things come into existence and go out of existence at the same time, that they are created and destroyed together. Then it is plausible to say that they are identical. But Lumpl *might* have continued to persist after Goliath was destroyed by squashing. And then clearly they wouldn't have been the same thing, since they would have lasted for different periods of time. So it seems that Lumpl and Goliath are in fact identical but might have been distinct, that they are merely contingently identical. Names seem to refer to things only relative to a kind, in the guise of a statue or in the guise of a piece of clay.

The fan of necessary identity may reply that there is no identity between Lumpl and Goliath, since identical things have identical properties, and Lumpl and Goliath have different modal properties and belong to different kinds. Rather, such a partisan may insist, there is a special *constitution* relation that Lumpl bears to Goliath. Lumpl *constitutes* Goliath, but isn't identical to it. Then the aficionado of contingent identity may reply that modal properties and sortal properties aren't properties of the sort that identical things must share, that such so-called properties are not relevant to the identity of things, and that constitution really is identity.

Perhaps this exchange could continue. But even this much should convince us, I think, that each of these ways of talking has its own internal integrity. Note also that there is nothing in the account of content proposed here which rules on these issues one way or another. The introspectible *content* of a name need not constrain its reference "across possible worlds" in any specific way, even if the *meaning* of a name might. I believe, in fact, that one might speak a language in which names were disguised descriptions, or merely tagged objects, or made reference only relative to a sortal, and then in consistency speak a language which endorsed different claims about the contingency of identity. Given the internal coherence of all such practices, still one may be preferred as our own, or more familiar, or more economical. But it is implausible to think that one of the practices is really truer to the world than another. It may be that those who argue about whether identities are contingent or necessary are really arguing about the form of our practices of naming and identification. Certainly the evidence they cite, the appeals to intuition and linguistic usage they make, makes this suggestion a charitable one. But we have no particular reason to believe that they are arguing about how our practice must be to be true to deep metaphysical facts written into the world. Some metaphysicians may insist that modal truths are not about our practices, nor even legitimated by them. But supposed modal "truths" of such a deep sort are merely artifacts of the approach apparatus.[25]

Objection: In the account of basic content to follow, various properties and relations which are exhibited by microevents may be found in more than one basic content. And in each basic content in which they are found, each of those properties and relations has the same nature. They possess the same higher-order properties and relations to be characterized in the following chapters, which are subsumed into the very language we will use to characterize basic contents. These higher-order properties and relations are essential properties and relations of the properties and relations exhibited by microevents. Hence there are some issues of modality which are not artifacts of the approach apparatus. For instance, phenomenal red is essentially more similar to phenomenal orange than to phenomenal blue. Reply: This is indeed the case. But still the other "modal" issues we have discussed here remain artifacts. One might wonder what grounds the truth of the legitimate modal truths. But it is simply the nature of the properties exhibited in basic contents. The question then to ask is how we have thoughts with contents involving properties with such natures, how we can think of phenomenal red and orange and blue. And that is an issue for Parts Two and Three.

There are other noteworthy machinations of the approach apparatus,[26] but that exhausts those which we need to consider before developing a clear account of basic content. Let me end by reviewing our three sorts of dependencies. To the degree to which cooked contents are *new* contents, distinct from the raw contents from which they are generated, they may be said to be generated from raw contents by the machinations of the approach apparatus, in a manner paralleling the other content generation operations. Because of the semantic dependency of cooked on raw contents, we have reason to expect a parallel dependency in realization.[27] What about truth dependency? Two differently cooked contents derived from the same raw content convey the same real truth, rooted in basic content. This is a truth they share with each other and with the raw content. In this sense, whatever truth they have is dependent on that of the raw content. It makes no more sense to say that one form of organization of a content is truer to the world than another than it does to say that one natural language is truer than another. If there are certain things which *seem* true to the world in one form of organization and false in the other, then they are mere artifacts of the approach apparatus.

So to make sense of agency is to show that there are raw contents which include the conditions it requires. The conception of a particular agent may involve an organized, cooked content, but there must be a difference in raw content when agency is present and when it is not. If agency is to make the sort of coherent sense we hope, then it cannot merely be an artifact of the approach apparatus.

NOTES

1. This may not be a coherently conceivable possibility, but it is at least an expositionally convenient and familiar fiction.
2. Because of differences in the way in which thoughts with variously derived contents are realized, it will be useful to specify more than a minimal complete set. Maybe for that very reason I should include operations analogous to the Sheffer stroke and the like, but I will ignore this possible complication.
3. There may be cases where the truth relations between a content and what *appear* to be its quasi-logical components do not mirror the standard rules of inference for propositional connectives. Consider, for instance, the difficulties introduced by arbitrary objects in the next section. But such cases, for instance the problematic "disjunctive" content involving the arbitrary number introduced there, are not in fact contents directly generated by quasi-logical operations, but rather by other operations, in that instance by abstraction on disjunctions involving particular numbers.
4. George Berkeley, *A Treatise concerning the Principles of Human Knowledge* and *Three Dialogues between Hylas and Philonous* (Peru, IL: Open Court, 1986). Julius R. Weinberg, *Abstraction, Relation and Induction* (Milwaukee: University of Wisconsin Press, 1965.)
5. There are other sorts of cases, which we will discuss below, which are more like conjunctions.
6. Kit Fine, *Reasoning With Arbitrary Objects* (Oxford: Blackwell, 1985), 5.
7. Fine, 11. See note 3.
8. I mean which we can conceive in some direct way, unmediated by devious modes of presentation like "something we can't conceive".
9. Of course some very abstracted entities may be instantiable in all basic contents.
10. It may be that both of these require more than quasi-logical operations on basic contents, that we also need to deploy some of the resources noted in section 6 to get a content in which a *single thing* is both round and a square.
11. A nice device for representing a vague content is a fuzzy set.

12. Remember that we are discussing only the vagueness that would be a defect in a thought. Some may claim that *the world* can be vague in some way that basic content cannot capture. But that seems to me a possibility which is not coherently conceivable.
13. Rather than say 'call it "true"', I should perhaps more precisely say 'call it by a word which plays the role which "true" plays in English.'
14. There are other sorts of cases, which will be introduced in the next chapter.
15. Of course, some sensory images are images of words. And written words may picture themselves, though that is not part of their intuitive content.
16. George Lakoff and Mark Johnson, "Conceptual Metaphor in Everyday Language", *Journal of Philosophy* 77, 1980, 453-486, and *Metaphors We Live By* (Chicago: University of Chicago Press, 1980). George Lakoff, *Women, Fire, and Dangerous Things* (Chicago: University of Chicago Press, 1987).
17. M. Black, "Metaphor", in *Models and Metaphors* (Ithaca: Cornell University Press, 1962), chapter 3.
18. Donald Davidson, "What Metaphors Mean", *Inquiries into Truth and Interpretation*), 245-264.
19. Some cooked contents are generated only from more than one raw content, but for the most part we can ignore this complication in what follows.
20. This traditional empiricist example carries some controversial baggage. Some think that perception is theoretically infected, so that there is no pure experience prior to conceptualization, that one's language and judgment very much infect what one sees. There are, I think, limits to the plausibility of this objection. See Michael Bishop, "Theory-Ladenness of Perception Arguments", *PSA 1992* vol. 1, 287-299. But, in any case, let me only insist that what is recognizably the same experience can *sometimes* be conceptualized in different ways. The distinction between experience and judgment isn't easy to draw, and may not have been drawn correctly by the empiricist tradition. Consider the difference in experience as you change your attitude regarding the foreground of a Necker cube. And certainly the beliefs we have may causally affect our experience to some degree. But there is still a way to draw a distinction between experience and judgment, in fact a way which is implicit in the account of basic content in the following chapters. Still, some may be tempted to resist. Traditional empiricism neglected to recognize that not all ways of grouping hues, for instance, are equally salient. There are natural ways to group hues, and important cross-cultural similarities in color languages due to these natural resemblances. The various shades of red belong together, in a way that the blue-greens and the green-blues do not. Certain ways of grouping hues are "truer" than others, better reflect facts about hues. But I reply that the example under discussion should not be taken to suggest the contrary. Some features of the ways we categorize visual colors are merely matters of the approach apparatus, but some are not. We will return to the categorization of colors in Chapter Six.
21. Some, when presented with cases like that of the dirt field constituted entirely by its microphysical bits, are tempted to claim that there can be in such a content no thing *the field*, but only the bits. But there is no particularly convincing reason to believe this claim, because the alternative account provided by the approach apparatus is already available to us.
22. This discussion puts us in position to consider one final objection, rooted in some very suggestive work of Immanuel Kant. See *The Critique of Pure Reason*, translated by Norman Kemp Smith (New York: Macmillan, 1929), 244. It is difficult to give an account of how we come to the conception of an objective world, persisting through time independently of our experience, an experience which weaves fitfully through it. It might be that our very conception of a world independent of our experience is mediated by our conception of the world as organized into particular objects, persisting beyond our momentary view of them, with backs and sides we do not see. So to claim that the real world might not be organized into particular persisting and unified objects may seem incoherent. Reply: I grant that the history of our cognitive development as individuals is such that we come to the conception of an objective, experience-independent world only through the conception of particular objects unified and persisting over time in particular ways. Certainly in even our experience there is some reflection of this, in the magic boundaries which our experience presents. If our experience of the world didn't exhibit the sort of regularity and stability which leads us to make the particular

judgments about the identity of objects we in fact make, we might never come to the conception of a world independent of the vagaries of our experience. Particularly important, perhaps, is our conception of ourselves as persisting entities. But still, many issues about identity over time and at a moment, for instance those regarding the balloon with the 100 parts, could obviously be resolved in various ways or not at all with no effect on our capacity to conceive an objective world. In general, a conception of the world need not be mediated by any *particular* conception of the unity of objects. So there still seems no issue of real truth here, even if some conception of the identity of objects is implicated in the cognitive history of each individual.

23. Nathan Salmon, *Referene and Essence* (Princeton, NJ: Princeton University Press, 1981), Appendix 2. Paul Coppock, "Review of *Reference and Essence*", *Journal of Philosophy* 81, 1984, 261-270. Alan Sidelle, *Necessity, Essence, and Individuation* (Ithaca: Cornell University Press, 1989).

24. Allan Gibbard, "Contingent Identity", *Journal of Philosophical Logic* 4, 1975, 187-221.

25. Some may be tempted to hold that modal properties depend on things other than the approach apparatus, because for instance whether water is essentially H-O-H or not depends on what it is, and not on what our concept of it is. But such claims seem underwritten by a concept of water which assures it has essentially whatever constitution it turns out to have, a concept which generates a function from the way the world is to the relevant modal property. Still the approach apparatus is doing the real modal work here. See Salmon, Coppock, and Sidelle.

26. Consider for instance disputes about human categorization, whether it takes the classic form suggested by Socrates and Plato, in which kinds of things have sharply defined borders, and are sharply definable, or that championed by Wittgenstein and Eleanor Rosch, in which a particular kind of thing exhibits a family-likeness, criss-crossing patterns of resemblance that leave some things more and some things less paradigmatic members of the kind but provide no clear boundaries. See Eleanor Rosch and Carolyn B. Mervis, "Family Resemblances: Studies in the Internal Structure of Categories", *Cognitive Psychology* 7, 1975, 573-605; and Eleanor Rosch, et. al., "Basic Objects in Natural Categories", *Cognitive Science* 8, 1976, 382-439. Or consider a number of debates which have arisen in cognitive science about the higher-order organization of content, whether it involves schemes or scripts, Minsky's frames, Fauconnier's mental spaces, or Lakoff's cognitive models (which invoke metaphoric organization). Or consider certain debates about the "logical form" of sentences which are supposed not be resolved by the surfaces of the sentences.

27. On the other hand, it is quite likely that there are some realization dependencies which run here in the other direction as well.

CHAPTER FOUR

BASIC CONTENT AND EXPERIENCE

Basic content is concrete content rooted in experience. This suggests a form of empiricism. But it is a severely chastened form. This account deploys an enriched conception of experience, and the expansive list of content generation operations surveyed in the last chapter. Still, there are important similarities between my view and traditional empiricism. Traditional empiricism held that experience plays a crucial role in generating thought contents, but nevertheless that we can think of more concrete things than those we in fact experience. Likewise, I believe that while all content is rooted in experience, even basic content is not exhausted by it. Basic contents consist solely of the *sorts* of elements we *can* experience, but not merely of those we *do* experience.

There are, among basic contents, "seed" contents. Seed contents are the contents which a moment of one's experience might have. They are in certain ways even more basic than the rest of basic contents. This chapter discusses seed contents, the ways in which other basic contents are rooted in seed contents, and the relations of these issues to a proper conception of truth. Traditional empiricism, and any doctrine which roots content in our experience, invokes the specter of certain controversial doctrines: verificationism, anti-realism, relativism, and idealism. This chapter gives these issues some brief, necessary attention.

1

The account of basic content to be presented in the following chapters maintains that basic contents are *concrete*, by which I mean that they are constituted primarily by causal and phenomenal elements of the sort we can experience. Falling towards the ground, you might feel the rush of air, vertigo, your flailing limbs, and fear. You might see the ground rush up, buildings grow from nubs to towers. Finally you might see the pavement, threatening a more vivid experience than the catch in your throat. Let's suspend you in that moment, your nose an inch from the ground, your arms stretched forward in optimistic resistance. There are a number of things present in your experience of that moment: the look of the street, the feel of your fear, the tightness in your chest and throat, the position of your limbs, the acrid smell of the city, a taste of blood and the city air, the ragged surface of the asphalt. These are what I will later call "phenomenal" elements. I believe that there are also some causal elements present in your experience: The wind is experienced putting up resistance, as having that causal property, though not enough of it. The ground threatens to present a ruder and more certain resistance. All these sorts of things are what the following chapters will characterize as bits of basic content.

While basic contents do not consist solely of the particular things you do in fact experience, they do consist of the kinds of things you can experience. It is in this sense that basic contents are rooted in but not exhausted by experience. We need to become clearer about exactly what this means, and we will do so slowly during this chapter, in several steps. Here's the first:

What, someone might reasonably ask, is meant by "experience"? If you experience a balloon crash, one might call the balloon crash itself your "experience", and be in accord with some sorts of ordinary usage. But I use the word in a different way, to refer to your state. I mean to focus on your experience of the balloon, your perception of it. That is, I think, a kind of thought. Your experience has, I claim, representational content. It is capable of truth and falsity, and possesses intensionality. Your experience is about the crash under certain introspectible aspects rather than others.

There have been philosophers who would dissent from these claims. Descartes thought that sense experience itself is neither true nor false, that it is beyond that sort of evaluation. And many philosophers have thought that intensionality enters into cognition only with the judgments which we make on the basis of experience, not with perceptual experience itself. However, it is quite evident that experience presents things as being one introspectible way or another. Hence it at least potentially misrepresents those things. Indeed, Part Three will present abundant evidence that experience has an often false representational content, that it often presents the world as being ways that it is not.

There are less and more expansive conceptions of what human experience includes. On the one hand, there are conceptions which treat some obvious artifacts of our experience as not a part of the content of experience itself, but rather as a part of our way of viewing that experience. On the other hand, there are conceptions which treat some of our complex reactions to our experience as part of the content of that experience. I will try to include everything which might reasonably be taken to contribute an element of representational content.

2

Why think that basic contents are rooted in our experience at all? Because basic contents are basic along three axes, and for each axis there is reason to think that a correspondingly basic content would be rooted in experience.

First, consider content generation. An intuitive sense of the introspectible contents of our thoughts, together with the account of content generation provided by the last chapter, points to a basic content which is plausibly experience-rooted. While we can think of sophisticated derived contents, for instance abstracted and word-mediated contents, still the concrete seems plausibly the ultimate basis of abstraction and of the other operations of content generation. And our sense of the concrete seems to be that we can experience it, that we can see it and smell it and feel its resistance when we kick it. Content rooted in experience is, I think, intuitively basic in generation. And this is underwritten by the overall plausibility of the complete account of content developed here, an account which generates, I think, all the contents anyone could plausibly insist on.

Basic content is also basic in realization, and there is reason to think that it should be rooted in experience along this axis as well. Consider the kinds of creatures who are capable of thoughts with contents which are *not* concrete, which are *not* closely tied to experience. While we may dream of those who can understand higher mathematics or other forms of abstract human thought but lack any sensory experience, we don't really know of any beings like that. Our own "higher" capacities are obviously parasitic on our "lower" and older capacities, older in the history of biological evolution and of the development of thought in each particular group and the growth of each individual. Our particular understanding of calculus is obviously parasitic on our capacities to count concrete objects and trace their edges, and this on our capacity to experience such things. Tigers and babies plausibly think merely of the concrete things which they experience, and we don't know of any creatures who think merely of abstract mathematical entities. Any plausible understanding of our form seems to underwrite this suggestion of our "history". Our "higher" mental capacities seem layered over our "lower" capacities for sense experience and motor action. The higher capacities seem a matter of ever more complex processing between what comes in and what goes out, of ever more complex neural convolutions between eye and muscle, while the less complex convolutions in tigers would suffice for experience.

Basic content is also basic in truth. But there is reason to think that concrete content rooted in experience is basic in truth. We saw in the preceding chapters that the truth of derived contents seems ultimately dependent on the match of contents which are basic in generation to the world.[1] And, as I've suggested, the contents which are basic in generation seem to be concrete contents rooted in experience. If basic contents rooted in experience don't match the world, then there is no way for contents generated from those contents to be true.

There is another and more direct argument to this conclusion: If the truth of derived contents must ultimately be rooted in the match of contents to the world, then it is important that our very sense of the world itself seems to be our sense of what we might experience. Let me elaborate this point, which will serve to reveal a kind of qualified verificationism which is latent in my account of content. That will in turn put us in position to attain a clearer understanding of how basic contents are not exhausted by experience.

3

Why think that our human sense of a world which could root the truth of our thoughts must be our sense of the concrete, of what we might experience? Because of considerations involving realization, considerations regarding what it would be for us to have an attitude of the requisite kind towards our thoughts, considerations which link the second and third concerns of the last section.

The concrete things we might experience seem to be the things which creatures such as we, with our particular input and output capacities, can respond to and act upon in a reasonably direct way. Or rather, I should say, they are the things we could so respond to and act upon if we were in the right situation, say projected into the past, and if the things we believed in were in fact about. Concrete things are, it seems, the things we can interact with, the things which can be revealed in our sensation and affected by our muscle action. And this is significant and relevant. For to *believe* something, to hold it implicitly or explicitly to be *true* and not merely some idle imagination, seems to be in part to have some tendency to act on that belief, to respond to the world and act in the world in some appropriate way. Certainly it involves other things also, if the content of the belief is to be introspectible in the way that at least representational content characteristically is, and it may be that the kinds of action by which a particular belief is manifest depend on one's desires. But some tendency to act on a belief seems to be a necessary condition for its existence. And it seems that only concrete things which might be manifest in experience can be responded to and acted upon in any reasonably direct way. We can't *get at* anything else.

One might reasonably object that the response and action which manifests a belief might be other than a direct response to or action upon the object of the belief itself. For one thing, we manifest beliefs which fail of reference, or which concern the inaccessible past. And one may act so as to manifest a belief by speaking or responding to speech, and not by directly interacting with the object of the belief in any way. Still, the sorts of things which we *cannot* interact with in the direct manner of concrete things, which we *couldn't* interact with even if they existed, or which we *can* only hear about or talk about, seem for that very reason good candidates for contents whose truth is dependent in the ways noted in the preceding chapter, if they are good candidates for truth at all. Belief with *basic* content must be manifestable in quite direct ways, by direct action in response to direct experience. Merely chanting the word "true" in the presence of the relevant sentences, or confidently asserting those sentences, would not alone be sufficient in such cases.

This argument in effect makes two claims: What we can successfully take to be true in the full and basic sense is closely bound by what we could more or less directly respond to and act upon. And that is limited to concrete things of the sort revealed by our experience, and which we might get at by sensation and muscle action. Let me proceed by considering objections to these two claims.

Even those who hold that we have access to mathematical objects or the oneness of the universe via other than the concrete mediation of ordinary experience, for instance via some mystical faculty rather than the mediation of eyes and muscles, still may accept the first claim of the argument, still may accept that we can take to be true in the full sense only facts of the sort we have access to, which we might get at. They merely dissent from the second claim, regarding the form of our input and output capacities. But they are at least fighting surface plausibility. We seem to be concrete biological creatures, with sensory input and motor output. Even those who hold that the experience and basic contents I will characterize in the following chapters are a veil of illusion hiding a reality which they understand seem to exhibit that understanding in part by concrete action, if only by speech or smiling enigmatically. And at least a part of their access to such insight seems mediated by concrete things like feelings of joy or the words of texts. Their thought seems manifest in concrete interaction with the world. They still concretely talk and respond to talk, whether they deny it or not, or so it seems. They continue to treat the concrete world which is supposed to be a veil of illusion in pretty much the same way as everyone else, and it is only in doing so that they manage by small perturbations in speech or other action to manifest their transcendent "beliefs".

But even if the second claim of the argument seems plausible enough to pass at least initial muster, the first claim shared with these mystics may not. Isn't it plausible to insist that we can take things to be basic in truth which we know quite well we *can't* get at, which we can't "directly" access? Indeed, in some senses this insistence seems to me quite plausible. But the insistence is ambiguous, and the plausible senses do not cut against the argument, at least barring certain rather radical possibilities. To understand this, it is useful to consider "verificationism". This is a traditional empiricist thesis, which maintains that our (coherent) thoughts are exhausted by what we might have evidence about, and that our only evidence about the concrete world is rooted in sense experience. It maintains that all our (coherent) thoughts must be confirmable or disconfirmable, in the relevant cases through experience. One might take this as another, clearer way of saying that we cannot think about what we cannot get at, and one may then object. Verificationism certainly *seems* implausible. Can't we, for instance, at least make hunches about the past on which no current evidence can bear? But there is a good deal of ambiguity in what verificationism entails. To claim that all thoughts must be confirm*able* or disconfirm*able*, must be *capable* of confirmation or disconfirmation under certain hypothetical conditions, is not to claim anything particularly restrictive. Under hypothetical *enough* conditions, for instance if we were omniscient gods, then we might be capable of confirming any truth. But this is a trivial claim. Verificationism becomes an *interesting* thesis only to the degree that it is closely specified what is meant by "confirmable" and "disconfirmable", to the degree that it is specified what sorts of hypothetical conditions may legitimately be considered in determining that something is properly tagged "confirmable" because it would be confirmed under those particular conditions.

Not all contents are basic contents, but this account of content will in effect suggest a sense in which a severely qualified verificationism is true of at least basic contents. Basic contents have elements which are the sorts of things which might appear in an experience like ours. They are elements we *might* experience and hence, at least on a plausible and traditional understanding of confirmation, which we might confirm under certain hypothetical conditions. But the relevant hypothetical conditions are quite particular ones. In one quite specific sense, but that sense only, my account is verificationist. In that sense, but that sense only, basic contents can include only elements which we can directly access, which we can get directly at. But this turn outs to involve neither a very interesting, nor a particularly troubling, form of verificationism.

In what sense do basic contents include elements which we might experience? Let me restrict our consideration for the moment to a world which is concrete and in which our experience is generally veridical. Then, first, basic contents will *not* include elements which could only appear in our experience if we had a different form, say radically different sense organs. But, second, basic contents may include elements which don't appear to us, but merely *would* appear to us *if* we moved around the world in certain ways, back in time or off to the far side of the moon, or down to smaller scales.

The second, expansive aspect of this conception requires elaboration, which will help to specify yet more clearly in what way basic contents are rooted in but not exhausted by our experience. We'll turn to that issue in section 5. But the first, restrictive aspect of the conception may seem immediately objectionable, and in a number of ways. Aren't there concrete things which we might hear about, from articulate bats or Martians, which are true but which we *can't* experience? Aren't there things basic in truth which creatures with our sense and motor capacities couldn't access, even by hypothetical motion around the world?

Perhaps. But, as we will see in Part Three, it is far from clear that we humans can succeed in even *thinking* what such truths would be. What *we* can think may be too limited to encompass some truths. Still, some will insist, isn't it clear that at least some philosophers do manifest belief that the world itself contains more than merely concrete things of the sort we humans can experience? Don't some people hold that even what is basic in truth includes, for instance, abstract platonic entities, things which will play no role in my account of basic contents?

Well, they may say words to that effect. But it isn't obvious that this is a coherent thought, given what content their talk of abstract contents can possess. Our legitimate conceptions of "abstract" entities seem to be conceptions of abstract*ed* things, dependent in truth on their more concrete abstraction basis. Furthermore, it isn't plausible to think that these philosophers can manifest belief in their claims by any action except speech. (Or response to speech. If you believe in platonic entities, tap three times.) When speech alone can manifest a belief, we may reasonably suspect that it is insufficient to realize an acceptance that the speech has the full sort of truth required of contents which are to be basic in truth. We may reasonably suggest that it is a word-mediated belief whose content is dependent in the manner of the essentially word-mediated content discussed in Chapter Three.

I have in fact given this argument in a more confident way than is justified. I have presumed that the world is at least in part, at least more or less, as we experience it to be, that it does consist of the sorts of things we could experience there to be if only we moved around in the right ways. But, as we will see, this is false; there are no things of the sort we experience there to be. My account of content is in fact verificationist only if we restrict consideration to worlds in which our experience is generally veridical, and this is in a certain sense to say that it isn't verificationist at all. Still, to the degree that we humans can manage to understand how we do take things to be true, the argument I have given retains its force. It is an argument underwritten from the inside, by the very structure of our thought, and by the dependence of all human content on basic content. The failure of the argument would require a quite general failure of our thought, a that failure would imply, I think, that belief is in fact impossible.[2]

Belief with representational content ordinarily involves at least two elements, capacities for introspection of that content, and action or tendency for action in accord with belief with that content. Clearly action in accord with belief need not require that the belief be veridical. Possessed by cartesian demons, I might lunge around the room exhibiting belief in all sorts of hallucinations. But still, such familiar cases of manifestation of beliefs which are false in the suitably basic sense involve actions which would be interactions with the appropriate objects, if only those objects were around and our possession over. In familiar cases of this sort, the concrete world contains spots where the appropriate concrete objects would in fact fit in rather nicely, where our senses might access them and our muscles manipulate them. This is all my argument really requires; introspection and action would then still be in accord in the relevant sense. But if action and introspection were to come *radically* apart, or if either were absent, then there would be a lot of pressure on our ordinary notion of belief. If you were to act just like Descartes acted when he soldiered one day, but while introspecting what you now introspect, the ordinary conditions for ascribing to you either Descartes' beliefs about battle or your own current beliefs would not be satisfied. You might have the *thoughts* you do now, but they wouldn't, I think, be beliefs in anything like the full sense. Still, you might take yourself to be acting in certain ways you are not, and this might lead us to ascribe something reasonably called "a belief" to you, such as we might also ascribe to a dreamer. But, on the other hand, if your experience is *radically* misleading in the way we will eventually consider, you aren't capable of waking up, in the manner of a dreamer, to interaction of the right sort. And it isn't obvious that there is anything that is present to your introspection which could differentiate your so-called "belief" from some very vivid day-dream or imagining. Nor may there be anything helpful in your true "external" action, if our experience of your body and motions is radically misleading. While it might be relevant that you *take* yourself to be acting in one way rather than another, still it isn't obvious what the difference between taking yourself to be acting and merely day-dreaming about acting might be in such a case. Perhaps vividness or coherence with your continuing experience play a role here of the sort traditional empiricists favored to distinguish between perception and imagination or dreams and reality, or maybe there is some relevant tendency for memories of what's "believed" not to extinguish. But it seems to me that we are far enough away from ordinary conditions of belief-ascription in a situation such as we are considering to conclude that these things are really insufficient to distinguish belief from other sorts of thoughts in that situation. If our experience is radically misleading about the world, then not enough of the usual conditions for belief obtain.

In conditions in which we were capable of belief, the argument sketched earlier in this section would succeed. And even in conditions in which we are not, still the nature of our capacity for thoughts, rooted in our introspectible experience, assures that if we hypothetically were capable of belief then it would be belief in things grounded in a concrete world captured by basic contents rooted in that experience.

4

Traditional empiricism is not only sometimes a form of verificationism, a view that we can only (coherently) think things which are confirmable or disconfirmable. It is also sometimes a kind of anti-realism, a view that *truth* is rooted in confirmation, and falsehood in disconfirmation. According to anti-realism, there may be thoughts which fail to be either confirmable or disconfirmable, but they fail to be either true or false. Any thought or sentence which is "undecidable", neither confirmable nor disconfirmable, is neither true nor false, and so "bivalence" fails for such a sentence or thought, even if it appears coherent.

Sometimes anti-realism purports to be not merely a semantic doctrine, a doctrine about which of our thoughts are true and how they are true, but also to imply that the world itself is limited in corresponding ways. To this degree anti-realism is in effect a species of idealism. So perhaps it is worth noting that my account of content has no implications one way or the other on that topic. Some basic contents characterize worlds of which some idealists dream. But while a basic content consists of elements of the sort which can appear in our experience, it doesn't follow that all such elements in that content appear in experience, so there are non-idealist basic contents. And indeed I believe that idealism of any interesting sort is false, for familiar reasons. It would be absurd cosmic hubris to maintain that the world depends on us for its existence.

The bite exacted by anti-realism as a semantic doctrine is not necessarily more ferocious or less ambiguous than that of verificationism. To be confirmable is not necessarily to be confirmed, and it is open to nicely latitudinarian conceptions, involving for instance what we'd know if we were omniscient gods, which rule nothing interesting out as undecidable, and hence as neither true nor false. Even if we restrict ourselves to forms of anti-realism which insist that bivalence fails for some interesting set of sentences, say about mathematical entities or material objects or the past, there are more and less radical forms. To identify the truth of a sentence with its being confirmable leaves open the possibility that the confirmation conditions of that sentence, the conditions which constitute it as confirmed (for instance states of present experience) are determinately the way they are, and such that sentences about those confirmation conditions (about that experience) are either determinately true or determinately false. One may be an anti-realist about certain things, but a realist about their confirmation conditions (for instance states of experience).

Basic contents, including seed contents, and the sentences which express them, are bivalent, either true or false. And their truth is constituted not by their confirmation, but by match, even if in fact they are verifiable. Or at least that is the possibility suggested from the inside, by the structure of our thought. But this is consistent with semantic anti-realism about things other than those present in basic contents, and with a failure of bivalence for sentences about those other things. Just as my account is consistent with a certain sort of verificationism, it is also consistent with certain kinds of anti-realism. Dummett and Putnam have presented a variety of interesting arguments for anti-realism which are in effect realization arguments, arguments that plausible conditions do not suffice to make someone capable of true thought or speech beyond the range of confirmation or disconfirmation. When we turn in the next part to consideration of the realization of thoughts, these arguments will be defused for certain crucial cases. But, as I said, my position is consistent with at least a certain degree of success for the arguments, consistent with certain sorts of anti-realism, for instance regarding numbers. And indeed my argument in section 3 bears more than a little affinity to Dummett's and Putnam's realization arguments.

Sometimes, however, Dummett and Putnam have suggested a radical anti-realism, "soft on truth all the way down", which holds that no set even of confirmation conditions is determinately the way it is and such that there is a set of sentences characterizing those conditions which are either determinately true or false. No argument for anti-realism which I know underwrites this radical a suggestion.[3] But one might wonder if it is a coherent possibility.

A *radical* anti-realist must hold that *all* content of sentences is deferred in the following way: For a sentence about some class of entities to be true is for certain confirmation conditions to obtain. But for those confirmation conditions to obtain, for sentences characterizing those conditions to be true, is just for other and different confirmation conditions to obtain. Likewise, for those other confirmation conditions to obtain is simply for further confirmation conditions to obtain, and so on. Since the content of any set of sentences characterizing a class of entities is dependent on the content of another set characterizing the confirmation conditions for those entities, and plausible semantic dependencies cannot go in a circle, there must be, if radical anti-realism is true, an infinite regress of content dependencies. But it is plausible to insist that there cannot be an infinite regress of such dependencies if there is to be content at all. Not all content can be dependent on other contents in the way that radical anti-realism requires. One way to see this is to consider dependencies in realization. If there were an infinite regress of content dependencies, then so, it seems, there would have to be an infinite regress of dependencies in realization, of capacities to conceive contents on other capacities to conceive contents. And this seems impossible. Of course, regress arguments have a long and suspicious lineage, but it is also relevant that our capacity for experience clearly provides us with a capacity for thought with a content which is not dependent in these ways. So radical anti-realism as a semantic doctrine seems implausible. And it seems incoherent to insist that there is no determinate way the world is, as radical anti-realism sometimes suggests, no world which could be characterized by at least *some* set of sentences[4] which are either determinately true or false.[5]

5

Before we turn to a discussion of relativism, let me be more precise about the ways in which basic contents are not exhausted by experience. As I have said, not merely things one *actually* experiences, but the range of things one *can* experience, help generate basic contents. By "things one can experience" I mean things one might experience with the sorts of sense and motor capacities one now possesses, if one were in the right place, time, and orientation, and not merely after some hypothetical transformation to another form of perception and experience. It includes colors unseen and tones unheard, but not things we might experience only if we became bats with sonar. And basic contents outrun experience in yet a second way. Certainly one can think a thought at some moment with a basic content which one cannot exhaustively experience all at once in that moment. The concrete basic contents one can entertain include pasts no longer seen, objects with backs and fronts and sides which can't be experienced all at once, and several peoples' experience of things.

Let me elaborate. In section 1 we left you suspended in the moment, your nose an inch from the ground. Review that situation: There were present in your experience of that moment a number of things which are plausible elements of basic content. There were things with phenomenal properties commonly associated with perception, for instance buildings and cars and pavement with colors and tastes and feels and shapes. There were not merely external objects but also internal feelings, for instance your painful vertigo. Some things seemed to have phenomenal properties from more than one class, as a building might have both a color and a felt texture. And some things, like the wind you felt and the pavement you were threatened with feeling, seemed also to have causal properties, powers to bend and shape and resist. Also, the things you experienced in that moment seemed to be arranged spatially, as in your visual sensation of the pavement between your hands.

Your experience of a moment exhibits elements with causal and phenomenal properties and in spatial relations. But however complex the form of your experience seems when it is viewed frozen in the moment, the complexities ramify when the experience is flowing in its usual way. Should the wind gust and a car materialize racing driverless down the street such that you slide neatly in place behind the wheel, to find yourself careening down the street around slow trucks and yellow cabs, rounding corners and buildings rather than smashed into the pavement, then your experience and the things in it would unfold in complex ways. A cab in front might grow, then move to the side, then be seen in side relief, and finally just be glimpsed behind in the mirror. So far the moral is merely that experience is not static, that it exhibits not only spatial but also temporal relations. But, further, the experience of any moment is present in a now that in the next moment will have fallen into the past, and as you lurch around a cab or a building you may think of its unseen side, in anticipation or memory. The unseen side of the building may be conceived as continuous with its seen front, though not at the moment present in your experience. As you drive down the street, the massive causal and phenomenal structures, the structures of power and color and shape and taste and smell and feeling that unfold in your experience, leave some residue in your thought of the succeeding moment, so that some even think that the immediate past continues to be experienced, at least in a very faint way. But even if the immediate past is present in experience in this faint way, it is presented *as* past and not merely as a dim present. And certainly we can think of a concrete past not even faintly experienced, a past which is no longer experienced as it was. This involves concrete content beyond present experience. Further, you can think of the *simultaneous* but unexperienced back sides of things you see. These are things you might have experienced if you were on the other side, though you aren't on that other side. There are other cases like this, in which you manage to think of things, say trees falling in an unoccupied forest, which no one is around to experience, and of things too small for us with our large eyes to see. Moreover, you might round a corner wildly only to just miss a pedestrian, have a pointed look cast your way, and see yourself for a moment in your mind's eye as the other sees you, as an object in someone else's experience.

Basic content has elements which are the *sorts* of things which can match elements in your experience. This is the way that basic content is rooted in experience. But this rootedness does not entail that basic content is exhausted by experience, that it cannot outrun your experience in the ways noted in the preceding paragraph. There are basic contents which contain elements which are not present in your experience. But they consist of elements which are the *kinds* of things which *could* be present in your experience.

This rootedness of all basic content in experience is reflected in various dependencies *among* basic contents. One can think of concrete pasts or inexperienced objects or things seen by another only like those one might presently experience. So we might isolate seed contents, contents which match and exhaust what might be present in one's experience in a moment, from which we might generate by special operations all basic contents, much as representational contents in general are generated from basic contents.

We humans not only experience, we come to think of a concrete and stable world which we and our experience weave through, an historically and spatially extended world which is the same for all of us despite the fact that we live at different times and places, a third-person world specially centered on no particular time or place and the experience of no particular person, a world which we all can share, living people and dead Martians. This too constitutes a basic content, but it in a certain sense remains rooted in our experience. It consists of the kinds of things we might experience.

Of course, in our experience of a moment, and hence in seed contents, there are certain features of certain objects which a plausible third-person world would eschew. Some things are a greater focus of our attention from one moment to the next, and the change in our experience as our attention passes first from one to another seems usually not to infect our conception of the concrete objects we are attending to. In fact, there are many things which we come over our lives to recognize as mere artifacts of our experience. We come to thoughts with concrete and hence basic contents which leave the artifacts out, which leave out the highlights on a glass or the pain we might naively feel as a property on the edge of a knife. Under the spell of Galileo or a recognition of biological diversity, we may even come to think of color as such an artifact. Our conception of the concrete world as it really is, formed under the pressure for stability exerted by our need to act, under the pressure for commensurability with the world of other people exerted by our social lives, even under the pressure for consistency with the world of dolphins or a god or Martians exerted by a reasonable modesty, must leave out what we come to take to be the mere artifacts of our experience, and add in things which are not present in our experience, though they might have been. Hence our thought comes to have other than seed content. By somehow deleting and transforming features of seed contents, somehow including features not present in the actual experience of a moment but before or beyond or beneath it, we form our conception of the concrete world, a thought with a plausible basic content whose truth might ground the truth of all we think. We might form the conception of a very limited world, exhausted merely by our experience of a moment. So seed contents are among the basic contents. But *plausible* basic contents outrun experience and hence seed contents, and they eschew some artifacts of experience and hence of seed contents. Yet they are still rooted in experience; they can be generated from seed contents which capture what we might in fact experience.

Seed contents are among the basic contents, and yet there are various content dependencies among seed contents and other basic contents, and hence among basic contents generally. There are various sorts of "horizontal" relations among basic contents, beyond the "vertical" content relations discussed in the last chapter. Some we will discuss in the next chapter. But now we'll focus on those which help reveal how basic content in general is rooted in experience and its seed content.

Along two of the axes which concern us, seed content, whose range exhausts the range of one's possible experience of a moment, is even more basic than the rest of basic content. Seed contents are, as we have seen, in some sense more basic in generation. Our conception of the past color of some object seems derivative of our conception of that color as it might be present in experience. In fact, it may even seem as if we already possess the operations necessary to generate all basic contents from seed contents. We might abstract out the features of a seed content which are not involved in thought of the unseen past of something, for instance a focus of attention present in experience, and then deploy a quasi-logical operation like conjoining to tack that past on to our conception of the present. But this doesn't quite work. In the first place, to think of something as past requires not merely tacking it on to one's thought of the present, but somehow transforming, for instance, a thought of a color into the thought of the color as past. In the second place, it isn't quite abstraction as so far characterized which is involved in generating contents without artifacts of experience, for the latter are in no intuitive sense instantiations or examples of the former. Truth dependency does not flow here in the way *abstraction* requires. This is, as so often for content generation operations, a rather subtle distinction, but there is this difference. Despite all this, there are content generation operations at least in many ways analogous to those we've already seen which could serve to generate the full range of basic contents from seed contents. Their novelty is that, unlike the content generation operations we have so far surveyed, they can introduce new semantic elements into basic contents. For instance, they can introduce certain temporal relations.

Seed contents are not merely in some sense more basic in generation, they also at least seem more basic in realization than the rest of basic content. For instance, the capacity to entertain a content as of the past or as involving another's experience seems dependent on a more primitive capacity, to conceive of similar things present in experience. If tigers are free of the past or an objective conception of the world, still they have capacities which capacities for third-person thought and nostalgia presume.

Since basic content was introduced as basic in generation and realization, these two dependencies of the rest of basic contents on seed contents may trouble our sense of what basic contents are. Exactly what basic contents are will be clear after the next several chapters, but in any case basic contents remain more basic in generation than the contents noted in the last chapter. Basic contents *include* the seed contents, so all contents which can be generated from seed contents by the operations noted in the last chapter can be also generated from basic contents. Basic content is basic in generation, even if it isn't a *minimal* base. And some contents noted in the last chapter, for instance some abstractions and conjunctions over merely third-person states of affairs, cannot be generated directly from seed contents except via the generation of basic contents which are not seed contents. Analogous points hold for realization dependencies.

Still, there is a sense in which seed contents *are* more basic in generation and realization than basic contents which are not seed contents. I don't take advantage of this to provide more economy in my account of content simply because, if basic content is to be the coherent content relevant to making sense of agency, it must be basic in truth. My specification of basic content enacts a certain compromise among the axes of our interest. Basic content is basic in generation and realization to a degree and in a sense, and it is flat out basic in truth.

Why aren't seed contents more basic in truth than other basic contents? Because the truth of any particular seed content does not serve to fix the truth of all basic contents. We can have the conception of a concrete world which outruns our immediate experience of it. It might outrun it in extent, or in the tiny details within. A seed content which does not capture the full extent of the world or leaves out some of its tiny details may still be true, but only when a more exhaustive basic content is also true.[6] The truth of any seed content is fixed by the truth of the basic content which captures all the details of the world, plus perhaps some considerations which serve to aim that seed content at the world.

Further, it is worthy of note that such "truth" as is actually had by the seed contents of at least our *visual* experience is not likely to be match. Our visual experience not merely leaves things out, but gets things wrong. For instance, in our experience distant things look smaller, but they really aren't. And our experience exhibits a focus of attention which the world itself does not. Perhaps we can conceive of seed contents which get things exactly right (at least up to a point), but the seed contents of our actual experiences in the actual world are, plausibly, misleading. At best there is some sort of distorting projection from visual experience to the world, eliminating artifacts of that experience, like the fact that distant objects look smaller, stretching things to their proper size. More exactly, there is a projection of the seed content of that experience onto another basic content which does match the world, and underwrites such "truth" as the experience possesses.

6

There is another distinction between types of basic contents which reveals an interesting set of horizontal truth dependencies, and which will bring us back finally to relativism. As we have seen, you can form the conception of basic contents which have elements which are not present in your moment's experience, which are "absent" from that experience in a way in which none of the elements of the seed contents of that experience would be. You can conceive a world which outruns your experience of a moment.

But there are two sorts of basic content which outrun experience, centered and uncentered: You can form the conception of a world which outruns your experience of a moment, and yet remains "centered" on your experience of a moment, in which you are located at one particular point and time, in which certain events are now and here. To such a world there corresponds a "centered" basic content.[7]

But basic contents like this, in which some elements are "present" to experience and some not, plausibly involve some artifacts. Probably the world itself is not centered on your experience of a particular moment. It is a third-person world, shared by all, that not only outruns your experience but is not centered on it. We seem capable of the conception of uncentered basic contents, which capture such a third-person world.

Let me elaborate. Some basic contents are, while not exhausted by experience, centered on the position of someone's experience of a moment. Such contents remain a kind of basic content. They suggest a way the world might be, a heritage from our ignorant past as individuals and groups and a species. We can at least *think* that some strange solipsism is true, that the world really is centered on ourselves here, or perhaps more plausibly on now, that other places or at least the past and future are not real in the same way as what is present. It is just that this sort of thing can come to seem very implausible. The centered basic contents seem plausibly dependent in truth on yet others, which aren't centered.

While centered contents do describe a way the world *might* be, which they would match, a world with a center on *now* and/or *here*, such a peculiar solipsism is hard to believe. There are other people than oneself, and such people conceive a world centered differently, at least on a different place. None of these spatial centers seems worth taking too seriously. And we will see in Part Three reasons to believe that we cannot easily disentangle spatial and temporal centering in quite the way a different treatment of centering on now would require. So it seems that there is a third-person world, a world without a center on a particular place and a particular time, which exhausts the basic truth which grounds whatever derived truth is possessed by these differently centered contents.

A basic content centered on a particular here and now will be expressed, in the account of content to follow, through special indexical phrases. Such a centered content may be true in and of itself, though as I said this is implausible. It may match a centered world. More plausibly, it is true merely *relative* to the particular center at which it is thought. For instance, if a basic content is centered in particular on the self at a time, then its truth or falsity may be relative to the self who has a thought with that content and the time of the thought. If you see a fish bowl now and say so, and if on the T.V. beneath there is concurrently a videotape of someone else saying yesterday "I don't see a fish bowl now", what you both say may be true. This isn't in itself all that radical or interesting. It is another instance of the aiming we discussed in Chapter Two. Despite the relative truth of some contents, there is still a way the world is, not relative to anything. It includes non-relative facts regarding what thoughts with what indexical-infested basic contents are thought at which centers. It also fixes in a non-relative manner which of those thoughts and contents are true. To make an analogy: If various people are looking out various windows at a park, with variously colored glasses on, still there are non-relative facts about who has what glasses on and how the park is and how the park will look to people at various angles and wearing variously colored glasses.

A centered basic content is plausibly dependent in truth, dependent on the truth of a third-person content that decrees that it is thought at a certain specific center, and horizontal content dependencies which entail that such a thought at such a center is true. But, as I said, there is a second way in which a centered basic content *might* be true, in which it would not be dependent in truth. It might be true straightforwardly, by directly matching a centered world. It is just implausible to think the world really is so centered. The indexicality of centered but basic contents gives them an unusual double nature. They can match implausible worlds directly, or they can be aimed in a world which lacks indexicality and still match. They can depend on other basic contents for their truth, but they need not. This double possibility of truth for indexical contents isn't so surprising when we remember the history and the pressures under which our conception of concrete truth is formed.

There is yet a third way in which some think that centered contents can be true. It involves *radical* relativism. Radical relativism *denies* the following platitudinous manifesto, which I have presumed but is worth elaborating: The world is some way absolutely, not merely relative to someone's thought.[8] Among the features of this absolute world are non-relative facts about who is thinking what thought with what contents at what center and aimed in what way, so that horizontal content dependencies determine what centered basic contents are true when thought at which centers and aimed in particular ways and false when thought elsewhere.[9] This non-relative base grounds the truth of whatever centered or uncentered contents are thought in such a world. If a certain centered or aimed basic content when thought at one center or aimed in one way is false, and if that same basic content when thought at another center or aimed in another way is true, then that must not be inconsistent with the existence of such a non-relative base. There really can be no *conflict* involved when one basic content is true for someone but false for someone else. True contents must be "commensurable". Indeed, which basic contents would be true when thought at which centers and aimed in which ways must be projectible from the non-relative nature of the world.

While the picture of the preceding paragraph is consistent with a fair degree of relativism about truth, there are radical relativisms which it forbids, and which some propound. But relativisms inconsistent with this picture are incoherent. Nelson Goodman may propose one such radical relativism. He holds that there are a number of different "versions" of the world, versions which are either different descriptions of the world as in various scientific theories or different depictions of it as in various artistic works. So far this is obvious. But Goodman in addition holds that sometimes two such versions are irreconcilable, that they cannot both be seen as parts of one larger and more inclusive version, and at the same time are such that both are right.[10] Even that claim can be read so as to be compatible with the manifesto above, if versions differ merely in their manner of expression of some non-relative base of truth, as a painting and a T.V. picture might capture in a different manner even the same aspects of a park. But if Goodman or someone else does deny the constraints outlined, then they deny precisely that there is a way things are, that there is a world. A radical goodmanian must insist on conditions which deny truth not merely to human thoughts, but to any thoughts whatsoever, even those of a hypothetical god. And this fails to be a coherent possibility. It fails not merely to be coherently conceivable, but to be coherent in any sense. In Part Three we will see that the truth may elude human thought, but radical relativism is the claim that there is no truth, no world, and that is a much more radical and implausible claim.

Let me put this another way: A radical relativist of the sort who both denies the constraints I noted and holds that some thoughts are true relative to a center must hold that there is no non-relative base of truth whose truth grounds the relative truth of those thoughts. They must think that truth is infinitely deferred, each truth true only relative to some centers, even regarding who is thinking what in what centers or what in what centers would be true. And this infinite deferral of truth would yield no world at all.

NOTES

1. Let me for the moment ignore special cases like external negation.
2. At least belief in the positive and contingent.
3. Here are some candidates. First, consider a radical construal of Dummett's "manifestation" argument, from "What is a Theory of Meaning? (II)", in G. Evans and J. McDowell (editors), *Truth and Meaning* (Oxford: Oxford University Press, 1976), 67-137:

P1) There is, for each sentence one *understands* (knows the meaning of), a specific practical ability one possesses, a particular "semantic ability".

P2) Practical abilities must be manifestable in behavior.

P3) Assent and dissent to a sentence upon presentation of evidence is the only behavior which can manifest a semantic ability.

P4) If P2 and P3, then the only practical semantic abilities one possesses are knowledge of verification conditions, conditions under which sentences are confirmed or disconfirmed.

Hence any sentence that is understood by one has only verification conditions.

P5) But if any sentence one understands has merely verification conditions, then no class of sentences possesses bivalent truth.

This a serious argument, rooted in a legitimate concern about realization. But it has problems. The second and third premises of this argument are at best problematic: For instance, it is far from clear that one cannot manifest an understanding of a sentence like "grass is in pain" which is not verifiable in the suitably strict sense, for instance by acting so as not to step on the grass and so on while asserting the sentence. So it is far from clear that this argument even succeeds in showing that all sentences which are understood have verification conditions in the suitably strict sense. But P5 is the real problem. Before we uncover its difficulties, it will be useful to sketch the other candidate arguments for radical anti-realism, since both deploy the offending P5 or a close analogue. Here's a generalization of Dummett's "learning" argument, from "The Reality of the Past", *Truth and Other Enigmas* (Cambridge, MA: Harvard University Press, 1978), 358-374:

P1) There is, for each sentence one understands, a meaning one has learned.

P2) The only meanings for sentences one can learn are those evidential conditions under which it is proper to assent or dissent to the sentences.

P3) If P2, then the only meanings one can learn are verification conditions.

Hence any sentence one can understand has merely verification conditions.

P4) P5 above.

Hence, no class of sentences possesses bivalent truth.

A specific difficulty with this argument is that it is far from clear that the compositionality of language, it's consisting of recombinable words, does not allow one to learn, through learning the meanings of verifiable sentences, the meanings of sentence fragments, for instance words which make up such sentences, and that one cannot recombine those fragments into sentences which lack verification-conditions in the strict sense, but which one can still understand. For instance, consider "grass is in pain" again. But the last premise is again the central difficulty.

One last argument is a generalization of Hilary Putnam's "model-theoretic" argument. See "Models and Reality", *Philosophical Papers* vol.3 (Cambridge: Cambridge University Press, 1983), 1-25; *Reason, Truth and History* (Cambridge: Cambridge University Press, 1981); "Realism and Reason", in *Meaning and the Moral Sciences* (London: Routledge & Kegan Paul, 1978). My reconstruction follows David Lewis, "Putnam's Paradox", *Australasian Journal of Philosophy* 62, 1984, 221-236.

P1) The meaning of a set of sentences is their correct interpretation.

P2) An interpretation of a set of sentences assigns to their parts certain extensions, certain entities to which they apply.

P3) An interpretation of a set of one's sentences is correct if it is one's intended interpretation.

P4) What fixes an interpretation as one's intended interpretation is i) the verification conditions of the sentences interpreted and ii) which sentences one does and does not accept.

P5) If P1-P4 are true, then global descriptivism is true, which is the view that the correct interpretation of a set of sentences is an assignment to their parts of extensions determined by the verification conditions possessed by the sentences and the truth-values one accepts the sentences to have.

P6) But global descriptivism entails an *indeterminacy* of extensions for terms in sentences which do not possess verification conditions.

Hence either sentences possess verification conditions or an indeterminate meaning.

P7) But if so then radical anti-realism is true.

It is far from clear that there could be distinct extensions and interpretations for sentences only indeterminately to capture if the argument succeeds, at least any one could have in mind. It is hard to see how the sentences of the argument itself can be understood by one if one cannot bear these different interpretations in mind *as* different. But, again, the real problem is the last premise.

These arguments fail in their guise as arguments for *radical* anti-realism. Each works by arguing that all determinately meaningful sentences possess verification conditions, by attempting to establish a rather strict brand of verificationism for such sentences. But this in itself cannot establish radical anti-realism, without the additional and implausible final premises. Even if such a strict verificationism were true of all sentences, that would not entail that all classes of sentences characterizing all classes of entities would lack bivalent truth-conditions. If there were any set of sentences which characterized just some basic verification conditions, sentences of a sense data language for instance, they would possess bivalent truth. Radical anti-realism rests firmly on that sole unsupported premise that there cannot be such a characterization.

4. Not necessarily human ones.

5. In light of these considerations, it might be instructive to consider the actual example of a quite radical anti-realism which Dummett discusses, in Michael Dummett, *The Logical Basis of Metaphysics* (Cambridge, MA: Harvard University Press, 1991), 301-351. It involves no infinite regress of the sort just described, and hence is less radical than it appears. Dummett considers that it might be that at any moment there is a determinate way that experience is, which can be characterized by a set of sentences about present experience which are either determinately true or false. The "radical" nature of this particular sort of anti-realism lies merely in a certain deployment of anti-realism about the past and future. Sentences about past experience are supposed to be true only to the degree that they are capable of confirmation now. Hence, sentences about this moment's present experience, which for now possess bivalent truth, may come to lack it in the future. This particular sort of anti-realism may be coherent, at least for all the regress argument suggests, but it isn't all that radical. It is not in fact inconsistent with bivalence for basic contents of the sort I will presume. This is because, as we will shortly see, some basic contents are centered on a moment of time. One way such a basic content might be true involves matching a world similarly centered, perhaps only momentarily, at that point. And other basic contents consist only of a moment of time. One might think the world merely is the present moment, and that in a while it will be a different one. I have difficulties with anti-realism of this sort, but they are merely that it either involves a rather implausible view of the world or the kind of incoherent relativism which we will dismiss in section 6. But at least in the moment it isn't "soft on truth all the way down".

6. Unless the details are not coherently conceivable.

7. For an introduction to these issues see David Lewis, "Attitudes De Dicto and De Se", *Philosophical Review* 88, 1979, 513-543.

8. Perhaps it is, implausibly, absolutely centered on one person at one moment, but still that is a fact for all.

9. Of course if there are no thoughts, I should put this in a different way.

10. Nelson Goodman, *Ways of Worldmaking* (Indianapolis: Hackett, 1978). See especially the chapter "The Fabrication of Facts".

CHAPTER FIVE

MICROEVENTS

This and the following two chapters characterize basic content. That concrete content rooted in experience has three significant features: It is spatial and temporal. It includes elements with phenomenal properties, for instance blue and sweet as they appear in our experience. And it includes elements with causal properties, with powers. Each of these chapters is centered on one of those three features, and in that order.

This chapter develops an ontology for basic contents, sketching in a general way their constitution and spatio-temporal form. It argues that basic contents consist of *microevents*, property-exemplifications without spatio-temporal parts, standing in spatio-temporal relations. There are two sorts of microevents: those with phenomenal properties, and those with causal properties. The peculiarities of these two sorts of microevents are the concern of Chapters Six and Seven. We will advance to a full understanding of microevents by first sketching an outline of the general features of basic contents, and then gradually filling it in.

These chapters provide an account of the range of basic contents by characterizing a "language of conceivability", which I'll call "C" for short. Each "story" in that rather artificial and regimented language exhaustively expresses, expresses in full detail, one basic content. And each basic content is exhaustively expressed by one such story, at least if we treat logically equivalent stories as the same. Of course, it isn't necessary that C be spoken or understood by everyone who is capable of thoughts with the full range of basic contents it expresses, but it is one means to capture what they can think.

C will have the form of a fragment of a standard "first-order" fregean language. The stories of C are existentially quantified sentences, which quantify over microevents, and specify their characteristic intrinsic properties, spatio-temporal relations, and a few other features. These stories say that *there are* microevents with various properties and relations.

It is important that C is just a fragment of an ordinary first-order language. It will include most of the apparatus familiar from standard first-order predicate logic: quantifiers, individual variables, attributive constants, and certain truth-functional connectives. But it will *not* include individual constants, names for individual microevents. And though it will be capable of saying that certain microevents are distinct, it will not be capable of saying that microevents are identical to one another.

This may make us suspect that a fregean language is not an ideal idiom for my purposes. Some may reasonably prefer an alternative. Sommers has claimed that aristotelian term languages have been underdeveloped, and it may be that such a language could serve our purposes just as well as C.[1] And a strawsonian feature-placing language might be especially appropriate for our task.[2] I adopt a language with a fregean form simply because that sort of language is most familiar to philosophers. But we will need to remember that the truncated form I will deploy dampens some of the customary resonance of such a language.

The stories of C are bound by the grammar of their standard fregean form. They are well-formed formulas of C. In addition, since basic content is consistent, the *stories* of C must be logically consistent. But even some grammatical and logically consistent formulations in C do not express basic contents, and are hence not stories of C. The stories of C must in addition meet certain "extra-logical combinatorial constraints", which rule out the problematic formulations. I will introduce these constraints gradually as we proceed.

To develop a better understanding of C, we need to consider what it says. In particular, we need to understand the things of which it speaks and the properties and relations which it says that they have. Let me begin by sketching their general ontology.

1

C speaks of things. It quantifies over them and predicates properties and relations of them. But they are things of a peculiar sort. Chapter Three argued that the things we think about are often polluted by artifacts of the approach apparatus, artifacts irrelevant to basic content. But the things of which C speaks are not things of this cooked sort. They are raw. And they are also *thin* things, wholly characterized by the particular story of C in which they appear.[3] To get a better view of these raw, thin things, it will be useful to first consider a bit of standard metaphysical typography.

Ordinary declarative English sentences, for instance "The balloon burst" and "The brown building is next to the grey one", express *propositions*, and when true express *facts*. The subject term of a paradigmatic sentence refers to an *object*, for instance the balloon or the brown building, and the rest of such a sentence predicates of that object some *property*, or some *relation* to another *object*. The *fact* expressed by a paradigmatic true English sentence seems to consist of an *object* having a *property*, or standing in a *relation* to some other *object* or *objects*. We have here what seem to be three distinct metaphysical categories of entities: i) objects, ii) properties and relations, and iii) facts and false propositions.

Properties and relations on the one hand and objects on the other seem to be different kinds of things. Properties seem characteristically able to be wholly present at two different places at the same time. They can, it seems, be had by two different objects at the same time. Two balloons can have the same color. And something analogous seems true of relations. But objects seem quite different. They seem incapable of being wholly present at two different places at the same time. Properties seem to be "multiply instantiable", while objects seem not to be.

And propositions and facts seem to be different kinds of things than either objects or properties. Facts and propositions seem capable of truth or falsity. But neither properties alone nor objects alone seem capable of those things.

Despite these apparent differences, paradigmatic facts seem to consist of objects having, "instantiating", properties, or standing in relations to other objects. On the other hand, it doesn't seem quite right to say that facts are constituted *solely* by objects and properties, since those things are tied together in a fact by "instantiation", and instantiation doesn't seem like an ordinary relation. For instance, F.H. Bradley argued that if instantiation were an ordinary relation, then it would have to be tied together with the objects and properties it ties together by some further relation of instantiation, and it has seemed to many that the infinite regress this suggests is implausible.[4] There are a variety of ways we might attempt to avoid this regress, which aren't necessarily all distinct. How should we deal with it? Frege suggested that properties were "unsaturated" things, incomplete except when joined to an object. But in fact we will soon see reason to believe that many properties are in fact saturated, while some objects are not. So I will adopt another route. Wittgenstein has been taken to claim in the *Tractatus* that instantiation can be *shown* by a language, through the concatenation of symbols for objects and symbols for properties, but that it cannot be *said*. It is, as it were, inexpressible. And indeed it is arguable that in at least C it is shown and not said. Gustav Bergman suggested that instantiation be considered not an ordinary relation but a "nexus", a metaphysical element of another sort. This seems to me a plausible suggestion, which C adopts and shows. In any case, however this particular matter turns out, many facts seem to include both objects and properties or relations as crucial constituents.

But perhaps not all. Properties can have properties. Properties are referred to by the subject terms of sentences like "Grey is my favorite color". The subjects of some sentences are apparently not the properties of any object, while the subjects of some are properties of other objects. We might call the first sort of subject "first-order" entities. And we might call these two sorts of sentences respectively "first-order" and "higher-order" discourse.

This standard typography suggests some questions about basic contents. But before we consider them, it is important to remind ourselves that basic contents and the elements which constitute them are mere objects (or propositions or properties) of thought, which may match real bits of the world but aren't themselves necessarily real bits of the world, floating around in some empyrean realm.

Are the thin things over which C quantifies objects, facts, or properties? On the surface, there are some conflicting indications. I've already hinted that C quantifies over microevents, property-exemplifications without spatio-temporal parts. Microevents seem to be little, fast-living objects, which have properties and enter relations but aren't predicated of anything. But they are events, and events seem suspiciously fact-like. For instance, we might think that events are instantiations of a property at some place and time or by some object. And since a particular microevent is captured by an existentially quantified story of C, it might match the world twice over. The sentence "there is a brown microevent" (just like the claim that there is a brown cow) might be made true by more than one bit of the world at the same time. So microevents may well be multiply instantiable, in the manner supposedly characteristic of properties.

Similar ambiguities infect the notion of a basic content. On the surface, it would seem that a basic content must be fact-like, since it is capable of truth and falsehood. But, on the other hand, a basic content seems to be an object of which we might predicate properties. It also seems to correspond to a way the world might be, a vast property which the world might instantiate.

These conflicting indications seem to me to point towards something important. There is, I think, less to the standard distinction among objects, facts, and properties than meets the eye of many a metaphysician. I initially motivated the distinction between objects and properties by the standard observation that properties are multiply instantiable while objects are not. But it is worth noting that some things which are intuitively properties, for instance the property of being identical to Napoleon, can intuitively be had by only one object. They seem not multiply instantiable. And some intuitive objects, for instance the play *Hamlet*, have many intuitive instances.[5] *Hamlet* might be found on various shelves and boards all at the same time. What of the intuitive distinction between facts on the one hand, and objects and properties on the other? We noted that fact-like entities seem to differ from objects and properties in being capable of truth or falsehood. But, on the other hand, we saw that they seem to consist at least largely of objects and properties. And certainly the *existence* of objects and the *instantiation* of properties are at least close analogues of the *truth* of propositions. We might think that they all come down to the same thing, at least for basic contents, that they all are match. There might be no real difference between truth, instantiation, and existence.

In fact, I believe that there is no concrete difference, no difference relevant to basic contents, between certain objects, facts, and properties. I believe that microevents might plausibly be put in all of those categories. I've just cited some considerations which cast doubt on the standard motivations for the standard typography, motivations which I deployed earlier. Let me now make a positive case that there is no distinction, and then consider objections.

We'll start with some general considerations, and then move on to some examples. One sort of paradigm fact is an object having a property. But an object is always something with a character, something which has properties. Any object is an object having properties. So some facts and some objects seem not really to be distinct. Likewise, a particular instantiation of a property might be a particular object having that property. So we might conclude that certain facts, objects and instantiations of properties are not really to be distinguished. Further, many philosophers have held that properties exist only in being instantiated. It might be, then, that there is no difference between there being a property and its being instantiated. And some properties have only a single instantiation. There might be no difference between such a property and its single instantiation. All this together suggests that there might be no difference between certain facts, objects, and properties.

Some parts of this sketchy argument are underwritten by certain traditional analyses of objects. Objects are supposed by some to be bundles of properties (including relational properties, the properties which they have by bearing certain relations to other things). There are certain traditional difficulties with the bundle theory. Some we will return to, but let me consider a key one now. We might be tempted to restrict the bundle of properties which constitutes an object to only those properties which are essential to the object, since intuitively the object could exist without the other properties. And this might not yield enough properties to differentiate one object from another. So we might worry about the plausibility of the bundle theory. But remember that thin things have no modal properties. A particular microevent is not found in more than one story of C. So we might identify microevents with the bundle of all of their properties. Take all those properties and conjoin them into a vast conjunctive property. It seems that such an object exists just when that property is instantiated, and that that would also constitute the truth of a certain proposition. Indeed, I think that the object which so exists, the property which is so instantiated, and the fact which so obtains are the same thing, characterized in three different ways, by three different phrases.

There is, I think, some ambiguity in the notion of an instantiation, which we must clear up to see all of this as clearly as we should. But before I turn to a consideration of clarifications and objections, let me appeal to a concrete example, which makes the positive case in a more vivid way. Quine formed the verb "to pegasize" to capture the property one would have in being Pegasus. But there seems to be no concrete difference in the content of the thought of Pegasus, the thought of Pegasus existing, and the thought of pegasizing. Likewise, it would seem that there would be no difference in experiencing any of those things. So at least some thoughts with these supposedly "different" contents would seem to be realized in exactly the same way.

This concludes my initial and positive case. But the distinction among facts, objects, and properties is dear to many philosophers, and objections will seem pressing. First, there is a class of objections which I believe are rooted in certain artifacts of our ordinary speech and language.

Objection One: Only complete sentences constitute complete utterances, complete moves in a language game. And complete sentences express facts, rather than name objects or properties. This suggests a significant difference.

Reply: Aren't complete sentences really a grammarian's, and more to the point a professor's, fetish? Don't students make complete if inelegant moves all the time which are not complete sentences? Despite what some philosophers have said, facts can be named. Call your favorite fact "Sam". So certainly uttering a name could constitute a complete move in a language game. And why think that such an utterance can be a complete move only if it names something other than an object or property?

Objection Two: While it is true that we think of objects and of properties, and not merely think that various propositions obtain, still certain psychological attitudes are had only towards fact-like entities. For instance, we can only predict or expect that certain things are the case.

Reply: Can't we predict or expect snow or Armageddon or Rome?

Objection Three: We say that facts *obtain* or are *true*, but that objects *exist*, and that properties are *instantiated*.

Reply: But, as I've already suggested, this is merely an artifact of ordinary speech, marking no real distinction. Exactly the same sort of match constitutes each of these things, at least for basic contents. An object of thought matches a world in which it exists. A proposition matches a world in which it is true. A property matches a world in which it is instantiated. And in any case, ordinary speech does not mark quite the difference between existence and truth that philosophers would like. We do sometimes say that we expect snow or Armageddon (rather than that snow will fall or that Armageddon will come), and still call such an expectation true or false. The evidence of ordinary language should not, I think, be treated as decisive, but at least it should all be treated with equal respect. For instance, we cannot say in standard fregean languages that Pegasus exists without turning the name into a predicate, but this is taken as no objection to fregean languages. That is the proper response, I think, and so much the worse for ordinary language. I must admit that C is a fregean language, and incorporates the traditional philosophical difference between existence and truth. But this doesn't matter, because the thin things over which C quantifies cannot be disentangled from the facts which contain them. They are just as the story in which they appear says they are, and do not appear in other stories. What a story of C quantifies over and what it expresses are not really distinct.

This brings us to a second and more metaphysical set of objections. Objection Four: Consider the fact that my balloon is deflated. Perhaps that particular instantiation of deflation crucially involves that object and hence is to be identified with that fact, but certainly there is a distinction between *my balloon* and that instantiation and fact. My balloon's nature isn't exhausted by its being deflated. Nor does its *nature* in any interesting sense even really involve that, for my balloon could exist inflated. It seems quite distinct from that instantiation and fact.

Reply: Whatever the plausibility of this objection for the objects of ordinary speech, it has no significance for the peculiar objects captured by stories of C.

They are thin things. The nature of an object referred to by a story in C is exhausted by that story. There is nothing to it beyond what that story expresses, and nothing less. That story expresses its complete nature. And thin things are *raw*, unpolluted by artifacts of the approach apparatus which generate modal identity claims. C does not include individual constants, names for microevents, which allow speech of the same individual object in two different stories. It expresses the nature of basic contents solely by existential quantifications over microevents with such and such natures expressible in C, things with various properties and related in various ways to other thin things.

Objection Five: Clearly, certain *properties* and *relations* are found in more than one basic content.

Reply: Yes, there are these facts about recombination. And as I said, they do introduce some modal facts which are not artifacts of the approach apparatus. But other modal facts are mere artifacts.[6]

Objection Six: There are some properties of things referred to by stories of C which are not expressed in that story, for instance that they are nameable in English. Or that they are microevents.

Reply: The nature of a thin thing *relevant to its contribution to basic content*, all with which we are properly concerned here, excludes properties like being nameable in English, properties *external* to the basic content itself. And C shows rather than says certain things, for instance that it quantifies over microevents.

Objection Seven: It's very implausible that two thin things could be distinguished even *within* a basic content by their properties and relations only.

Reply: Let me sketch how they are so distinguished. This sketch requires a bit of background. Some properties are quite like relations. They are what we have called "relational" properties. For Frege to have been a son is for Frege to have had certain relations to other individuals. Let an "intrinsic" property be a property which is not covertly relational in this way. The thin things constituting basic contents have phenomenal or causal intrinsic properties,[7] and spatio-temporal relations to other thin things. While two thin things might not be distinguished by their intrinsic properties alone, their spatial and temporal relations to other thin things will often turn the trick. This picture may seem to beg important questions about the nature of time and space and location, about whether for instance space is constituted by spatial relations among concrete entities. And to distinguish thin things by their spatio-temporal relations to other thin things generates the possibility of a vicious circularity or impredicativity, since the identity of those other thin things might rest on that of the original one, directly or in some indirect way. But let this serve as a sketch of the metaphysics of thin things which I will need to more fully elaborate and defend as we proceed.

Objection Eight: We have been focussing on the distinction between objects and facts, but there are other metaphysical distinctions to consider. Even if there is no distinction between certain *instantiations* of properties on the one hand and objects and facts on the other, still there is a real distinction between *properties* and the other two metaphysical categories. The argument above that the instantiations of certain properties are the same as the properties was unconvincing. And it certainly didn't show that such a distinction fails for microevents' properties in particular.

Reply: Recall that some properties, say being identical to Napoleon, are not necessarily multiply instantiable. And recall that some objects, say the play Hamlet, and some facts, say that there is a brown cow, are. The elements of C, the properties, objects, and facts it expresses, are all multiply instantiable. This is the primary reason why there is no distinction relevant to basic content between properties and members of other ontological categories. But there is an ambiguity in what is said when it is said that something is instantiated, which may suggest this objection. To see this, first consider an entire basic content. It characterizes a way the world might be. But that content might match a world which contains more than is captured in that content, and even a world which contains two or more regions each of which is matched by that content. Basic contents are expressed by stories which claim that *there are* such and such sorts of thin things, not that there are *unique* thin things of that sort. Basic contents are expressed by existentially quantified statements, and hence may be true twice or many times over. While basic contents represent to us a paradigm of possible completeness, they do not say that they are a complete characterization of the world. That additional stipulation would require something not available within the resources of basic content, I think. Since a basic content can match, even within a single world, two different regions, it can be "instantiated" twice, in one sense of that phrase. In that sense, it seems rather more like a property than an instantiation of a property. But in another sense, it fully characterizes, it *is*, a particular *instantiation* of a way the world might be. It is an *object* of thought, which might match and exhaust the world, another object. That second sort of "instantiation" *is* a property in the most interesting sense. It is multiply exemplifiable, capable of matching two or more different regions of the world. Basic contents and thin things exhibit a kind of generality thought to be specially characteristic of properties. Of course, two different thin things *within* a basic content may be different instantiations, in one sense, of the same, say intrinsic, property. And there is a sense in which the two microevents are particular instantiations of that property, as it were within the basic content. But such a story, as we've seen, specifies "instantiations" which are themselves multiply instantiable, and hence not in any interesting way distinct from properties. Those instantiations in one sense *have* instantiations in the other.

Objection Nine: How is the thought of unique things available to us then? How do we manage to think that some property or thing has a single instance in the real world if this account of content is correct?

Reply: Through thoughts with contents generated by negation and conjunction from basic contents. We can think that there is (at least) one red microevent and that there are not (at least) two red microevents. Hence we can think that there is just exactly one red microevent.

Objection Ten: Chapter Four introduced some indexical elements into basic contents. We can think of microevents which are present here and now. This indexicality introduces singularity into basic contents, and this must be expressed in some way other than by existential quantification.

Reply: Indexicality is not the same as singularity. Many basic contents include indexical features of the sort Chapter Four introduced. But if the way in which those contents are aimed at the world goes awry, then even a particular centered basic content may match more than one bit of the world. We might invert David Austin's case to get an example of how this might happen.[8] Suppose you look through what you take to be a binocular microscope at what you take to be an image of a single red spot, which in fact is an overlapping image of two qualitatively identical red spots created through some miracle of fiber optics. Mightn't your in some sense "singular" thought "That's red" be about two spots? Isn't this a case where one object of thought matches two spots in the world? Indexicality doesn't really alter anything. Just as you might point at an object of hallucination and in so doing point at a mere object of thought, so you can point at one object of thought which is really two objects in the world. This response requires taking the sentences of C to be existentially quantified sentences, rather than statements that there are unique things which are thus and so, and this may seem like a relatively soft feature of C. But it is important to remember that basic contents are rooted in experience, and experience doesn't reveal anything as unique.

Objection Eleven: It reveals what's uniquely *here*. And it wouldn't be entirely implausible to claim in the variant of Austin's case that the thought in question is false.

Reply: Is that really plausible? Would it be plausible if the world itself were so doubled and fed to our eyes and other senses? Would all our thoughts be false just because they matched twice over? They'd be true if one half of the dual world existed alone, and true if the other half existed alone, but not true if both halves did. This seems wrong. "True" of course is just a word, and it can be used in different ways. But the usages suggested by this objection aren't, I think, our usages, and in any case they don't track anything like a natural phenomena on the order of match. Basic contents can generally match twice over, and it would be something of a modification of the intuitive and natural sense of match if indexical thoughts don't also do so in a case like Austin's. Match is enough for truth in ordinary cases, and doubled match is fine in those cases, but with the centered cases it is supposed to be insufficient. This seems to me strained. But if we do withhold the designation "true" in such cases, we should be clear about exactly what we are merely doing. No deep metaphysical fact could turn on such an accident of convention.

Objection Twelve: Even if all this works for thin things and basic contents, still earlier chapters claimed something more. They claimed that *in general* the distinction between objects, facts, and properties breaks down. But we have seen here no good reason to believe that general claim.

Reply: All contents are generated from basic contents and dependent in truth on basic contents in the way preceding chapters specified. So if the three-way distinction between objects, facts, and properties can be generated for other than basic contents, we already have the resources to do so. I suggest that the differences are often mere artifacts of the approach apparatus. This need not imply that all contents or objects are multiply instantiable, for not all properties may be. And as I said, a content may be other than multiply exemplifiable by *excluding* certain basic contents. But metaphysicians have been misled by the contingent form of our language when they claimed that there was a deep and significant difference between objects, facts, and properties.

Objection Thirteen: Properties, as Frege held, are unsaturated, while objects and facts are saturated. There is at least *that* difference.

Reply: In effect, this account will show that certain properties are saturated. They can be instantiated independently of others, just as certain objects can exist independently of others. And certain objects, for instance the play *Hamlet*, are not saturated. Could it exist without paper or actors or the like? The distinction between the saturated and the unsaturated may be metaphysically significant, but it is not the same as any of the distinctions we are now concerned with.

Perhaps I've missed some objections, though I think this surveys the major contenders. Now let me turn from defense to offense. There are other accounts of content possible, which would allow that we can think of objects in basic contents which possess genuine individuality of a sort that would require more apparatus than C deploys. But alternative accounts face certain difficulties: i) They could not, I believe, be underwritten by a plausible story about the realization of thoughts with such introspectible content, as this account will be. ii) They are accompanied by all sorts of traditional puzzles about how we can be aware of the presence of the genuine individuality they deploy. It might be supposed to be present in our experience of individual objects, but our inversion of David Austin's case seems to cast doubt on this. iii) We are in possession of an error theory, which explains away the thought that there is such genuine individuality as a mere artifact of the approach apparatus. English contains names for entities, which allow us to tell stories about Napoleon escaping from Elba in a balloon, and other lies. So there is little obvious motivation to prefer a singularist account to our own. We are now in a position to see, I think, that the thin things over which C quantifies are not really to be distinguished from the propositions it expresses or the masses of properties and relations which it says are instanced.

Our initial typography of facts, objects, and properties introduced the issue of *first-order* discourse, speech of objects which are not themselves properties. It may have suggested the question of whether C is first- or higher-order discourse. The considerations noted above suggest that there are no true first-order objects, at least in basic contents. Still, at least an *analogue* of the relevant question still arises. C will have an obvious higher-order extension whose resources it will eschew, and we should see why. The stories of C quantify over certain thin things and predicate of them certain properties. But one may well wonder why those stories do not speak of the properties of those properties.

Certainly the properties predicated of thin things by stories in C do have properties. In fact, much of the following two chapters will be a discussion of the properties of the properties and relations expressed in C. But while my account of C will speak in such a higher-order way, C itself does not. While C will speak of things having colors like red and orange and yellow, it will not itself be capable of saying that orange is more like red than yellow is.

But this is appropriate: C is a language designed to generate stories which express each basic content. It is attuned to the combinatorial needs of that task. And all basic contents are constrained by the crucial properties and relations had by the properties and relations C invokes and which the next two chapters will discuss, for instance by the fact that red is more like orange then yellow. There are no basic contents in which *that* constraint is violated. There are no basic contents in which properties and relations lack those higher-order natures, so the stories of C need not mention that constraint. Those stories can concern themselves merely with the *differences* among basic contents.

The crucial higher-order properties and relations are the essential properties and relations of the properties and relations expressed by the stories of C, which the following account of C will characterize at least to a degree. They are not, as I've said, mere modal artifacts of the approach apparatus. Certainly such higher-order properties and relations are present in a world matched by a basic content, and they are present in the basic contents themselves. But they are implicit in the very properties and relations which C explicitly deploys. The stories of C need not *express* such constraints explicitly, since those constraints are implicit in the very language they employ.[9] To deploy the familiar wittgensteinian distinction, we might hope to fix things up so that they are shown but not said by that language.[10]

There may be other, "contingent" higher-order properties and relations present in basic contents, but they are fixed by the essential natures of the properties and relations expressed by C and the "first-order" facts expressed by C. So I will ignore them also. Let me finally note that to possess thoughts with basic contents characterizable in C is to possess thoughts with contents in which higher-order properties and relations are properly deployed, so accounts of the realization of the one must automatically be accounts of the realization of the other.

2

This and the following section develop a trio of propositions, i) that C need only express a kind of reductive basis for concrete contents, ii) that such a basis consists of simple, elementless objects with a basic set of properties and relations, and iii) that those simple things are microevents in particular, that they are concrete-intrinsic-property exemplifications without spatio-temporal parts, standing in spatio-temporal relations. I have deployed the last point in our discussion, but have not yet argued for it. Now is the time.

This section in particular discusses reduction or constitution. I hold that the relation between something and what makes it up, what constitutes it, what it is reducible to, is a semantic relation. Some contemporary philosophical discussions distinguish between reduction and constitution, partly because of concerns about modal issues that we know to be mere artifacts of the approach apparatus, and partly because some people want to treat abstracted things with very many or an infinity of possible realizations differently from those with a few. But I will use the words interchangeably.

Philosophy has been intermittently concerned with *semantic* analysis, the reduction of notions into their semantic parts. Consider for instance the empiricist attempt to decompose all ideas into elements which can be traced back to experience, or the traditional view that to be a bachelor is to be an unmarried male. In counterpoint to such *semantic* reductions, underwritten by meaning relations, philosophers have also sought what might be called *metaphysical* reductions. These are reductions of entities to whatever elements in fact constitute them, and they seem quite independent of meaning relations, to be quite different than semantic reductions. One good example of metaphysical reduction is physical microreduction, the reduction of physical things to their microphysical parts, of biology to chemistry and chemistry to physics, of animals to configurations of molecules and of molecules to complexes of quarks. And this seems to have little to do with semantic relations. Progress in physical microreduction certainly doesn't occur by meaning analysis.

Semantic reductions seem uncovered by *a priori* meaning analysis, which reveals semantic necessities rooted in the essential dependency of certain contents on others.[11] Bachelors for instance must be unmarried males. But at least some metaphysical reductions seem uncovered by *a posteriori* investigation. And at least to a past generation they seemed to be contingent matters, regarding what merely happened to constitute what, not what had to constitute it.

Despite these apparent differences between semantic and metaphysical reductions, we can turn certain metaphysical reductions to our semantic advantage here. That is because, despite appearances, the relation between something and what metaphysically reduces it, what constitutes it, is a semantic relation, or, perhaps it is more accurate to say, reflects one. But to see this requires some background.

Let a "supervenience base" of a concrete content consist of some minimal class of objects possessing whatever minimal class of intrinsic properties and relations to each other are required i) to fix that concrete content as it is in all internal detail relevant to its semantic role as a content, and ii) to fix it in particular by specifying its reductive elements, the elements which reduce it or constitute it in the metaphysical sense.[12]

A story of C must express exhaustively a basic content. But to do so, it need merely express exhaustively a supervenience base for that basic content. That supervenience base will fix all the relevant semantic features of that basic content.

Of course, to express something which fixes or determines something else is not necessarily to express that second thing. For instance, to express A is not necessarily to express everything A entails, though all that would be fixed as true if A were true. But the particular relation of supervenience which I've invoked is a special kind, tighter than mere entailment. It involves fixing by constituting. A basic content *is* in some sense its supervenience base. In talking about microevents, C will speak merely of the supervenience base of each basic content. But each basic content is its supervenience base.

This may seem at odds with other things I've said about basic contents. I've claimed that basic contents are concrete contents, rooted in experience. But the thoughts that water is flowing by and that a red balloon is about seem to have concrete content, such as could appear in experience. And it seems that the content of those thoughts cannot be captured by talk of the elements which constitute or reduce water or the balloon, on which the water and the balloon supervene. For instance, H_2O constitutes water, but the thought that water is flowing by and the thought that H_2O is flowing by don't seem to have the same representational content. And while some congeries of molecules presumably constitutes the balloon, the thoughts that there is such a balloon and that there is such a complex of balloon-constituting microparticles seem to differ in representational content.

But still, *fully* concrete contents have concrete details. There are other contents which we call "concrete", but which in fact are a bit abstract, rooted in abstraction. For instance, if I say a balloon is red but don't specify a shade, I express what is in fact to some degree an abstracted thought. Likewise, the claim that there's a red balloon, since red balloons might be constituted by lots of different little details other than the particular configuration of particles which happens to constitute some particular balloon, can be itself covertly abstracted or disjunctive. There would be a semantic and truth dependency running up from the supervenience base of a basic content to some particular configuration of molecules which that base is one way to constitute, and then another running up from such molecules to such a red balloon. It would be a kind of semantic necessity that such a configuration of the supervenience base would count as that sort of molecular configuration, and another semantic necessity that such a molecular configuration would count as such a balloon. Hence there would be something analogous to a pair of analyticities underwriting this reduction. It would *not* be a semantic necessity that such a balloon be realized in that configuration of molecules in particular, that if something be such a red balloon then it have that particular microstructure of all the different alternatives which might constitute a red balloon. It would be merely contingent that that is the way any particular red balloon happens to be constituted. But it would be necessary that if something had that structure, then it would be such a red balloon.

Generally, I think that if something X constitutes Y, then it is a semantic necessity that it would do so. For something, say some configuration of molecules, to count as something else, say water or a red balloon, it must meet whatever semantic criteria we deploy for something to be water or a red balloon. And that particular configurations of molecules would meet those semantic criteria seems a matter of semantic necessity.

Of course, I presume a lot when I deploy these examples. For instance, I assume that the molecules are governed by laws of the ordinary sort. But I hope that this can serve as at least an initial and motivating case, before we turn to a discussion of the full range of possible objections. My claims may seem objectionable in a number of ways even beyond those already mentioned.

Objection One: We found out that water is constituted by H_2O through empirical research, not by meaning analysis.

Reply: In itself, this merely implies that thought about water is covertly disjunctive or abstracted. What we found out empirically might be which particular disjunct or abstraction basis of water obtains around here. We found out empirically which of the many conditions which would of necessity have sufficed for water in fact is realized in our world.

Objection Two: Water is *identical* to H_2O, and identity is to be distinguished from the sort of constitution we've just discussed. For instance, a particular red balloon which is constituted by certain parts might have been constituted by others. But water *must* be H_2O.

Reply: This sort of modal difference is merely an artifact of the approach apparatus. So is any motivation for distinguishing between constitution and identity in these cases.

Objection Three: Are you suggesting that water might have been constituted by, or been identical to, lots of different things? Haven't you read your Kripke and Putnam?[13] Water is *necessarily* identical to H_2O. Water, the stuff we have around here in oceans and lakes, which is potable and transparent and such, couldn't be constituted but as it is.

Reply: We may have a notion of something, call it "water", which is the stuff around here, whatever it is, that happens to be potable and transparent and found in lakes. That is, we may have the notion of a natural kind which is indexical in this way. But it is important to remember that a thought with the same indexical content "water is wet" (=the stuff around here which is potable and so on is wet) might have been made true by a range of different conditions in the world, if only those conditions had happened to constitute the potable stuff around here. Indexical thoughts can be aimed at different conditions and retain their truth.

Objection Four: This misconstrues the point. Two such indexical thoughts aimed at different stuffs with different constitutions have different contents. The stuff itself is part of the content of the thought about it.

Reply: Remember that we are discussing representational content, which is characteristically introspectible. We are not talking about referential content. And it is important to remember that issues about the contingency and necessity of identity for such things as water are mere artifacts of the approach apparatus.

Objection Five: Surely the claims about modal truth that Kripke and Putnam make are coherently conceivable.

Reply: One might adopt or have a convention to the effect that water is essentially whatever stuff it happens to be. But of course this is merely a convention, though one which might generate an artifact of the approach apparatus.

Objection Six: Sometimes things are constituted by, literally contain as parts, only some of the conditions which are necessary for their existence. For instance, what makes something a balloon is not only its concrete parts, but that it is used in certain ways.

Reply: This context then is a part of what constitutes it. Since modal facts are generally artifacts of the approach apparatus, we need not worry much about the ordinary distinction between concrete conditions which help make something what it is and those which literally constitute it.

Objection Seven: Our ancestors had thoughts with contents which were perfectly precise and concrete, when they thought that red balloons were about. They conceived such things as things which looked as such things do, with just the level of detail revealed by our experience. There was nothing vague or disjunctive or abstracted about such thoughts. The ordinary, naive conception of things is closely tied to experience. Once it has been corrected for certain obvious artifacts, we can take quite directly from that experience a naive but *veridical* conception of at least a bit of the world, a conception which doesn't specify much detail but is correct as far as it goes. In contrast, the account sketched here would suggest that we can only directly take from our experience a content which makes devastatingly false claims about the constitutions of all objects, as if they had merely the parts we experience. Such an account cannot explain how our naive concrete conceptions, directly rooted in our experience, can be true. But at least plausibly they are true.

Reply: This objection presupposes a mistaken conception of what the truth of a basic content would require. A particular basic content, potentially characterizing a complete world, may be true even if it leaves out some features of the world which are beyond the purview of that basic content. It may match just a bit of the world. It may specify the nature of concrete objects in only some particular locale, leaving out certain brown hoofed herbivores on the fourth planet of Polaris, and still be true. But, by the same token, a basic content may be true even if it matches some region of the world only at a sort of macro-level, even if it leaves out some detail of the world *internal* to the objects matched by the content. Microevents are without spatio-temporal parts *within* the content in which they appear. Such a partless microevent may still match something which *really* does have parts. There is a range of possible "completions" of any basic content which leaves out true (and coherently conceivable) details in either of these ways. The completions consist of more internally-detailed or more extended basic contents. A relatively undetailed basic content has an important semantic relation to a disjunction or abstraction across its possible completions. But the content and disjunctions or abstractions across its possible completions are distinct contents. For instance, the basic content itself might be immediately rooted in experience, while the disjunction is not.[14] This all implies that if any basic content is true, more than one is true. But there is still only one which captures the complete truth.[15] The relation between a basic content and its completions involves an important horizontal truth-dependency. The basic content is true if any of its completions is true. The horizontal relation between a basic content and its more extended completions is a logical relation which is clearly revealed by the syntactic structure of C. But the horizontal relation between a basic content and its more internally detailed completions is unfortunately obscured by the syntax of C. It is a bit like the relation between an abstraction and its abstraction basis, though a basic content can be true independently of the truth of any of its completions. This objection does establish that there are many ways to think of red balloons, and that some thoughts of red balloons do *not* require in the basic contents which might root their truth anything like the full detail of constitution that red balloons actually have, which may have been misleadingly suggested by my earlier remarks.

Objection Eight: Basic contents can't be parts of other basic contents in quite the way which all this suggests. For instance, a basic content including "just a red balloon" would really also include an empty space which cannot be variously filled with other objects without denying that content.

Reply: In such an example, the spatial structure of the original content is highly developed in a particular way in which the spatial structure of many basic contents is not. Consider for instance a seed content which matches merely one's immediate experience. Such a basic content can literally be imbedded in another basic content which reaches out beyond that experience. What is present in experience does not foreclose such an extension.

Objection Nine: Our ancestors truly thought that there were red balloons. But they had a completely *false* conception of their constitution. How is this possible according to this account of content?

Reply: There are limits to how wrong they might have been and still thought that there were red balloons. If they thought the "balloons" were grey pachyderms, and if they had no other conception of the lighter-than-air craft, then they simply failed to think that there were red balloons in any relevant sense. If they had some partial but veridical notion of balloons, and thought that there were such things, then those notions would have been true. If in addition they thought that balloons were constituted in some false way, then perhaps that thought, but not the first, was false. More likely, the content of each of their thoughts about balloons was some mixture of accuracy and error. This is a common case. Some have come to think of water in terms of its micro-causal structure only, so that even if nothing has the phenomenal properties which water appears to have in our experience, still they would say that there is water. So they may maintain that their ancestors' notion of water, which includes the misleading phenomenal bits, is partially erroneous. Such cases introduce complex questions about the individuation of thoughts and partial truth noted in Chapter Two, and which I will continue to ignore here in detail as irrelevant to *basic* content.[16]

There may be still other objections to the claim that constitution is a semantic relation, but this should serve to defuse the obvious worries. One piece of offense: Let me suggest that if constitution is not a semantic relation as I have suggested, then we are owed some other account of what it is supposed to be. I think that no other plausible account is available.

3

Where are we? We know that the stories of C express basic contents by quantifying over, characterizing, and expressing certain thin things, by saying there are such things. And we know that the relevant thin things are a supervenience base for basic contents. Finally, we know that basic contents are concrete and spatio-temporal. Let me draw out some implications of all this.

Basic contents are whatever constitutes them. And constitution is a transitive relation. Sometimes the constituents of something themselves have constituents, as a gear which helps make up a watch in turn consists of molecules. In consisting in part of the gear, the watch consists in part of those molecules. If there were *simple* constituents of all basic contents, constituents which themselves had no constituents but which sufficed themselves to constitute the basic contents, then each basic content might consist merely of such simple constituents. To express basic contents, C might speak merely of these simples. Such simples might be the thin things we seek.

Since basic contents have a spatio-temporal form, likely simple constituents for such contents would be spatio-temporally simple, without spatio-temporal constituents. Point-instants seem plausible such simple constituents. Indeed, the stories of C will quantify over simple event-like objects, which have no spatio-temporal components within the content. The stories will predicate of those objects a basic set of properties and relations which fix their thin nature, and which are hence sufficient to fix the relevant semantic features of basic contents.

Basic contents consist of *microevents*. These are instantiations, without spatio-temporal parts, of basic concrete intrinsic properties of either a phenomenal or causal sort, in certain positions characterized largely by the spatio-temporal relations of such microevents to one another. They are, in a certain significantly qualified sense to which we will return, "point-instant" property-exemplifications. The stories of C quantify over microevents, and express their nature by characterizing their intrinsic properties and spatio-temporal relations. They are existential quantifications which express those natures. The rest of this chapter concerns certain details of this proposal, but let's begin with some obvious objections.

Objection One: There are no absolute constituents or simples. Everything is composite in some sense. For instance, microevents consist of certain points, instants, and properties in a kind of nexus.

Reply: There may be no *absolute* simples, but there are still simples of certain particular sorts, for instance spatio-temporal simples. And that is all we require.

Objection Two: In Chapter Three, issues about identity over time were dismissed as mere artifacts of the approach apparatus, but now we hear that the true constituents of concrete things are microevents. There cannot be a true ontology of microevents for concrete basic contents if there are no facts of the matter about how long objects persist over time.

Reply: There are a variety of ways to express basic contents. They can be expressed by languages employing speech of microevents, which have no spatio-temporal parts. But they can also be expressed by languages which recognize only single entities corresponding to entire basic contents, with very fussily described properties, and languages which speak of smaller entities which yet persist over time. C is only one means to express basic contents, not the only way. But there are certain difficulties that would attend the other options; to develop the alternative options properly would be a more difficult and more complicated task in certain ways. There is a sense in which the stories of C, quantifying over microevents, express something which might be expressed by sentences which say there is a world which has one big property. But that property would have to characterize the spatio-temporal detail present in the content even if the sentence didn't directly quantify over spatio-temporal bits, and that would be a complex and inefficient matter. Languages which employ speech of smaller but persisting objects would need to be strictly and complexly regimented if they weren't to introduce different descriptions of the same concrete content, something we need to avoid. There will be some arbitrariness in the way in which C expresses basic contents, for instance in the particular basic spatio-temporal relations which it deploys to express the myriad of spatial and temporal relations in such contents, and even in its quantification over spatio-temporally simple objects. But C is *one* way to capture basic contents. There may be other ways, but these are merely notational warrants, which capture the same basic contents. And there are distinct disadvantages for languages which do not quantify over microevents.

Objection Three: There are no simple constituents of even a spatio-temporal sort. Everything has an infinity of spatio-temporal parts.

Reply: To claim that there are spatio-temporally simple constituents of basic contents is not to deny that ordinary concrete objects of thought have an infinity of parts. Even if each tiny particle, each quark or atom, consists of an infinity of parts, it could consist of parts which are themselves partless points.

Objection Four: Seed contents are pitched at the scale of our ordinary experience, an experience which leaves out some of the tiny detail of things. And yet such contents are supposed to be true by matching the world. Certainly they can't be constituted by point-instants. Their elements must be grainier.

Reply: Remember that it is in fact in only a very regimented and unusual sense that microevents are point-instants. They have no spatio-temporal parts *within* their basic content, within the content which is expressed by the story in which they figure. It is not that they must correspond to partless parts of the real world for that story and content to be true. It is merely that those stories simply don't say that there are such parts. Indeed, it might even be that microevents could correspond to bits of the world which have constituents which we cannot coherently conceive, just as basic contents might be true though they leave out some things on the fourth planet of Polaris which we cannot coherently conceive. But it seems to me that it is at least necessary that those constituents be *spatio-temporal* parts.

Objection Five: No concrete intrinsic property can be instantiated at a point-instant, and all microevents are the instantiation of such a phenomenal or causal property.

Reply: Again, microevents are point-instants in only a qualified sense. They are the smallest units which possess such concrete intrinsic properties within the content in which they are found.

Objection Six: Not even concrete contents consist only of elements with intrinsic properties. Certainly there are points of void between concrete objects in certain basic contents.

Reply: We'll address these issues in the next two chapters, but the intrinsic properties which we will recognize include certain null properties which will defuse this objection. To forestall a parallel objection, let me also say that there are basic contents which consist of a single microevent, without any spatial or temporal relations within its basic content.

Objection Seven: No number of infinitesimal entities like point-instants can constitute concrete objects with finite sizes.

Reply: They might, if the relations among the infinitesimal entities possessed the kind of metric structure which we will soon deploy. But it is important to remember that microevents are not necessarily infinitesimal. As I keep repeating, microevents are point-instants only in a very regimented sense. They have no spatio-temporal parts within the basic content in which they are found. This does not exclude, as I said, that they can match things with spatio-temporal parts. And while current talk at least in intellectual circles of points and instants often carries implications regarding density and continuity, microevents do not necessarily enter into such spatio-temporal structure. In at least seed contents, there are presumably a finite number of microevents between any two microevents. There are, I think, other basic contents as well, which are at least potentially dense (in which there are microevents between any microevents) or even continuous. But microevents are not always located in continuous or dense or even infinite structures. The notion of something without spatio-temporal parts may seem a quite complex, sophisticated, and temporally recent development, beyond anything which should infect the basic contents of all human thought. But remember that the language of C need not be understood by everyone capable of thoughts with the contents which it expresses. And C doesn't always deploy quite so much sophisticated baggage as this paragraph may suggest. Microevents have no spatio-temporal parts within the content in which they are found. That is all I mean when I say that they are point-instants.

4

To gain a better understanding of microevents and their general ontology, we need a better understanding of the spatio-temporal structure of basic contents. This section characterizes such structure at the level of intermediate detail required. The following chapters provide still more detail. We will begin with seed contents which match and capture immediate experience, and then move on to complications introduced by basic contents which are not seed contents. In fact, we will begin merely with seed contents suggested by a somewhat simplified *model* of immediate experience.

Consider one's visual field of a moment, one's momentary experience of seen shapes and colors. One might at least model that field as composed of tiny color elements, the smallest discernible bits of color, arranged in a finite two-dimensional visual space, a space with edges. A seed content which matches such an experience would consist of microevents, in this case something like *color*-exemplifications without spatio-temporal parts, standing in spatial relations to each other. To capture to at least a first approximation those spatial relations, we might specify which microevents are "to the left of" (that is, to the left of some imaginary perpendicular axis running through) which others, and which are (in a similar sense) "above" which others. Some observations about this model: The *spatial* nature of such a content and its elements ensures that the "intrinsic" properties of such elements are *spatially* intrinsic, literally *within* the elements which have them. Two distinct microevents within the same such content, and two distinct elements within the momentary field it matches, may possess the same color. So those properties must be capable of being wholly instantiated in two different locations at the same time. Yet, at least in this example, the properties exist only in being instantiated.[17] They are "immanent" but not "transcendent" universals.[18] Similarly, the microevents of such contents stand in spatial relations which are themselves universals, which different pairs of microevents in the contents can have at the same time.

Note also that while we have adopted a certain way of specifying the spatial relations of the microevents making up such a content, by speech of "to the left of" and "above", still there are obvious alternatives with the same expressive capacity, for instance speech of "to the right of" and "below". While C will inevitably exhibit some arbitrariness in the particular language with which it captures spatial relations, we need to be wary of introducing extraneous or foreign content through the associations of that language, and we need to be aware of the way in which our particular language does involve arbitrary choice.

Also note that what distinguishes two microevents within the content which share the same intrinsic property is their position in the space of that content. And this, at least in our model, is determined by the spatial *relations* of those microevents to other microevents. We can "individuate" those microevents within the content (which is all that is relevant for such thin things) by their spatial relations.

This feature of our simple model may well seem problematic, and it will certainly become so under the pressure of the more complex contents we will soon consider. But we should see how it is supposed to work at least in this simple case: The visual field has edges, at least in our simple model, and so do corresponding seed contents. To individuate each of the microevents within such a basic content, first identify, by their colors and their spatial relations and lack of spatial relations to other color microevents, those on the edge of the field in various positions. Identify "landmarks" which have unique such characterizations. Then pick out the rest of the microevents by their spatial relations to one another and to those landmarks. In our simple model, for instance, there might be a yellow microevent out on the left edge and above any other yellow microevents which happened to be as far left. And this might serve as a landmark by relation to which other microevents might be individuated.[19]

A more realistic model of the spatial relations within the visual field would complicate things a good bit. But I will ignore these particular complexities until the next chapter. For the moment we will be occupied enough with the complexities introduced when we move beyond the immediate experience of a single sense. There is more to even our experience of a moment than the visual field. Our experience comes organized into what are, at least *prima facie*, many distinct sensory fields, with different sorts of spatial organization. There is not only a visual field, but a tactile field, an auditory field, and so on. And while one's visual field has elements with a rich and relatively dense spatial structure, one's field of auditory sensation seems less rich in spatial detail.

On the other hand, elements of different fields seem capable of being *fused*, in the sense that we may *experience* a correspondence, for instance, between points in visual and tactile space. The spatial structure of one field can in this way infect another. For instance, an internally two-dimensional visual field may inherit some sort of indirect three-dimensional structure by the fusion of its elements and those of a 3-D tactile field. This fusion within experience must be matched by some feature of seed contents. The fusing of two or more microevents is expressed in C by a special relational predicate.

This introduces some complexities. A single microevent of one field may sometimes be fused to more than one microevent of another field. There can be many-one fusing, for instance of many contiguous visual microevents to a single tactile element in its own simpler and less dense tactile field.[20] Coherently conceivable fusion is bound by a complicated set of extra-logical combinatorial constraints: For instance, two microevents in distinct parts of the same field cannot be fused, though we will see in the next chapter reason to think that there can be fusion of certain distinct microevents even within a particular sense field. And microevents cannot be fused so as to generate a linkage of fields with contradictory, as opposed to merely more and less detailed, spatial structure.[21]

There is yet more spatio-temporal structure present in some basic contents. First of all, experience flows from one moment to the next. There is a temporal relation which moments of experience may have in experience, albeit not in the experience of a moment. C must be able to express a relation which captures this temporality, perhaps by speaking of how one microevent may be "before" another.

Second, we saw in the last chapter that some basic contents[22] are centered on the here and now. This too introduces complexities: We can coherently conceive that the present simultaneous moment of the whole world, the now, has a certain metaphysical priority, while not claiming that the here does. So we must deploy distinct indexical phrases in C to capture here and now. Being now is a property which can be possessed by groups of simultaneous microevents. Let me note some relevant disanalogies between here and now. We experience the world at a present center which is now. But while the here is also present, it is present in a slightly different way: We experience even at a moment, and even when located in a particular place, more than a spatial point.[23] But we seem able in our experience of that moment to fixate on a spatial center which is a more precise here than our bodily location, a spatial center for the world. There is thus a way in which spatial centering appears in experience and temporal centering does not.

The center of a centered content which outruns immediate experience may provide a useful landmark relative to which the microevents of that content may be individuated. But the third thing to note is that some basic contents outrun experience and have no center, and they may include no obvious landmarks. Max

Black described a world which consisted solely of two identical black balls in eternal rotation about each other.[24] Each, it seems, has identical spatial relations to the same sort of thing. And each has the same intrinsic nature. It seems then that the two balls differ without a difference we can capture in C as so far characterized. There are in fact certain complications involved in this example, which we won't be in position to see for a while, but it is the most familiar example of a general kind of case which should be available within the full resources of C. Such cases require the introduction into C of a way to express "relative haecceities" for microevents. Let me explain.

In the face of apparently distinct individuals which apparently share all the same properties and relations, some philosophers have proposed that objects are more than mere bundles of their properties in a nexus, that they are constituted as well by a bare individuality or "haecceity". Haecceities, bare thisnesses, might serve a pair of related functions. They might serve to distinguish entities, and to identify them. Two individuals with different haecceities are hence different, and only one and the self-same individual can have a particular haecceity. There are at least three grades of commitment to haecceities which one might adopt. The first level shuns haecceities altogether. A theory of content of that sort would hold that there are no basic contents containing distinct but qualitatively indistinguishable microevents, individuals with the same concrete properties and relations expressible in C, and also that there are no two distinct contents which are qualitatively indistinguishable. The second level of commitment involves what I will call "relative haecceities". A theory of content deploying relative haecceities would allow that there are particular basic contents which contain distinct but qualitatively indistinguishable microevents within, but that there are no two distinct basic contents which are qualitatively indistinguishable. The third level of commitment involves "absolute haecceities". A theory of content deploying absolute haecceities would allow that there is a basic content containing qualitatively indistinguishable microevents and that there are also at least two distinct but qualitatively indistinguishable basic contents. This third level would allow modal claims which are inappropriate for basic contents given that microevents are thin things. But the troubles we face regarding the individuation of microevents in some basic contents suggest that we should accept at least *relative* haecceities, relations which serve to distinguish otherwise qualitatively indistinguishable but distinct microevents within a basic content. But they do not allow us to distinguish *basic contents* except on qualitative grounds. Unlike theories of the first grade, those of the second can admit that there is a basic content consisting solely of two otherwise qualitatively identical but still distinct black balls in rotation about each other. Unlike theories of the third grade, those of the second forbid that there be more than one content containing just one of the balls and nothing more.[25] Individual constants allow expression of absolute haecceities. Hence we should shun that feature of ordinary first-order fregean languages. But we must find some way to express relative haecceities. C will do this by speaking of the non-identity of otherwise qualitatively identical microevents within a particular story of C. To put this another way, it will introduce a special relation. Hence really microevents still consist merely of a bunch of properties and relations in a nexus. We still have a kind of bundle theory for microevents.

There is yet more spatio-temporal structure in basic contents. There are not merely extensions of basic content out beyond experience to bigger things, but also down within it to finer detail, to a finer level of spatio-temporal structure than is revealed in our experience of things. It seems to me that we can even conceive potentially *dense* basic contents, which are such that between any two microevents there is a third, and even potentially *continuous* ones, in which microevents are point-instants in the *full* sense, which have the cardinality of the continuum. But I will return to this issue in a bit.

There is indeed yet another sort of spatio-temporal structure which microevents can have. The spatial form of the experience of a moment may encode certain spatial information in a disguised or indirect way. Via perspective, the relative size in immediate experience of the visual images of two objects, say of two balloons known to be of the same size, may carry information about their relative distance. More generally, one's immediate visual experience of something has a place in a continuum of the visual experiences of that thing one *would* have if one moved in various ways. From one's knowledge of the spatial structure of the world, one can form on the basis of the experience of a moment an expectation about how that experience would change if one moved about. To each object, with a particular shape and size and orientation, and with a particular spatial relation to one, at a certain distance and in a certain direction, there corresponds a series of visual experiences one would have of the object if one moved in various ways, along various paths in the world. This is so even if the object is not within one's immediate experience, assuming that the object itself is stable and unmoving over the relevant temporal internal. And there is a different series of experiences which one would have of the object if it itself were moving along some path. One's sense of the *paths* which one or these objects might take through the world is, at least in ordinary cases, constituted by two different sorts of things, and the second introduces a kind of spatio-temporal relation which we have yet to consider. Such paths of objects through the world may appear in phenomenal experience from various vantage points, as continuous spatial paths traversed by objects over time. But one's sense of such paths is also one's sense of how one or an object would travel if one or it *did* various things (or simply coasted along).[26] For instance, one's sense of a particular path forward from where one is is in part one's sense of what would happen if one performed a series of motor operations, running forward and turning slightly left. And this is a sense of a path by which causal influence can pass through the world, of the trajectory an object like a balloon might take. C predicates causal powers of microevents. It will also speak of paths by which causal influence propagates, of for instance what a particular power instantiation can immediately act upon, without causal intermediaries, and also chains of such immediate influence. In doing so, it will be capable of generating more spatial-temporal structure than the relations of the sort which we have so far surveyed would allow.

This should serve as an initial orientation regarding the kinds of spatio-temporal structure present in basic contents. These matters will be developed at greater length in the following two chapters. Of course, we will eventually need to turn to a consideration of the realization of thought with content with this sort of structure, but that is a matter for Part Two. Let me for now merely summarize what we know about the stories of C so far.

1) All microevents instantiate either a causal power or one of the intrinsic phenomenal properties.

2) These microevents possess various sorts of spatio-temporal relations, and are sometimes fused.

3) Some microevents are here, or now, or here and now. These odd properties are closely bound by extra-logical consistency constraints.

4) Some microevents which cannot be distinguished within their content by the resources already noted possess relative haecceities. These signify that the two otherwise qualitatively-identical microevents are distinct. C will say that such microevents are not identical.

5) To each basic content there corresponds a story of C. That story of C begins with a string of existentially quantified variables, one for each of the microevents in the basic content. It expresses the nature of each microevent as suggested by 1 to 4 above. It is in effect a Ramsey sentence, which characterizes each microevent by saying that there is something with such intrinsic concrete properties, spatio-temporal relations, and (possibly) centeredness and relative haecceities, as constitute its nature.

We might worry that some basic contents consist of an infinity or even a continuum of microevents, while stories of C cannot have that many quantifiers. My own view is that it is far from obvious that there cannot be sentences of C with even nondenumerably many quantifiers. C is not a language to be spoken by finite humans, but merely a device to capture each basic content. But even if C cannot capture all basic contents, then still C can express at least all the finite basic contents, and we will merely need some additional apparatus to capture the others.

6) The stories of C are well-formed formulas of C, which are also logically consistent, and which obey the extra-logical combinatorial constraints.

NOTES

1. Fred Sommers, *The Logic of Natural Language* (Oxford: Oxford University Press, 1982).

2. P.F. Strawson, *Individuals* (London: Methuen, 1959), 202. See also W.V.O. Quine, *The roots of reference* (La Salle, IL: Open Court, 1973).
3. That is, qua object of thought. It is consistent with this claim that more than one basic content may be true, and in such a way that the bit of the world which is matched by one microevent in one basic content is matched by something with more structure in another basic content.
4. F.H. Bradley, *Appearance and Reality*, second edition (Oxford: Oxford University Press, 1897).
5. This example is drawn from W.R. Carter, *The Elements of Metaphysics* (New York: McGraw-Hill, 1990).
6. It is important to recall that microevents are mere objects of thought. Two microevents in different basic contents, one for instance which encompasses the other, may match the same bit of world. There seem to me to plausibly be no modal facts buried in that particular bit of the world, but in any case it may include things we can't capture in any basic content. For instance, some metaphysicians believe that there are bare haecceities in things, which can serve to constitute their individuality, but which are not concrete properties. My claim is only that we have no coherent notion of such things, not that there is nothing we cannot conceive. Such haecceities are not concrete, and do not appear in experience or basic contents rooted in experience. In so far as we talk about bare haecceities, it is just talk, which introduces artifacts of the approach apparatus. There may be features out there which help constitute things other than those of their concrete features which we can understand. It's just that no one has given an account of how we might plausibly think of them.
7. That causal properties may be intrinsic is an issue for Chapter Seven.
8. David Austin, *What is the Meaning of 'This'?* (Ithaca: Cornell University Press, 1990).
9. This is also why stories in C need not *say* that they quantify over microevents. All stories in C do.
10. Actually, the fregean form of that language may be said to show certain things, like a difference between truth and existence, which are misleading. But, as I said, I am suppressing certain features of standard fregean languages.
11. Such necessities are not mere artifacts of the approach apparatus.
12. These objects are clearly objects of *thought*. There are complicated debates regarding varieties of supervenience. See Jaegwon Kim, *Supervenience and Mind* (Cambridge: Cambridge University Press, 1993).
13. Hilary Putnam, "The Meaning of 'Meaning'". Saul Kripke, *Naming and Necessity*.
14. And an abstraction is incapable of independent truth, unlike a less-detailed basic content, as I shortly note.
15. So such contents as our experience suggests are *analogous* to abstractions. But they are not abstractions. They are perfectly concrete.
16. There are pressures which we articulated there which might even lead us to think that even basic contents are true in some lesser sense when they don't match, but still the match of some basic contents underwrites this lesser truth
17. In one of the senses noted above.
18. For an introduction to these issues, see David Armstrong, *Nominalism and Realism* (Cambridge: Cambridge University Press, 1978).
19. A story in C would not *say* that a microevent lacked certain spatial relations, but it would show that it lacked them *within the content at question*.
20. So microevents are sometimes partless only within their own field, even internal to their content.
21. That in our experience a color and a sound can have the same location suggests that we might, rather than speak of the fusing of two microevents each of which is the instantiation of a simple intrinsic property, each of which is visual or aural but not both, alternatively speak of a microevent with a more complex intrinsic property. This again suggests that C may not be the only way to capture the range of basic contents. But it is a way.
22. Though not necessarily seed contents.
23. Maybe past experience hangs about reverberating in present experience, but not in a semantically relevant way. And so maybe one's experience over time is centered on the present even in experience, though not in the same way that through attention spatial experience may be centered on a point.

24. Max Black, "The Identity of Indiscernibles", *Mind* 61, 1952, 153-164.
25. Let me ignore the fact that the ball might be constituted in more than one way.
26. This involves some analogue of the persistence of objects, but it is one which can be reconstructed without recourse to artifacts of the approach apparatus. When I speak of one's continuing to execute a plan over time, that has basic content, even if my way of expressing it carries some artifacts.

CHAPTER SIX

PHENOMENAL ELEMENTS

Humans sense things and do things. This, we will see, is reflected in the form of our experience, and in the two sorts of elements found in basic contents, phenomenal and causal microevents. We have phenomenal experience in particular because we sense things. This chapter concerns phenomenal microevents, which capture that experience.

1

Phenomenal microevents possess phenomenal intrinsic properties: colors such as blue, tastes such as sweet, smells, painfulness, and the like, properties rooted in our form of sensation and feeling. By "phenomenal" properties I mean properties such as red and sweet as they appear in our experience, and yet properties which might be had by coherently conceivable balloons and sugar cubes even while we are not experiencing them.

Before Galileo, this would have required little explanation. But we have fallen from the grace of that simplicity. Galileo helped develop a hugely successful science, which was rooted at least initially in the denial that color really is a property of balloons and balls and sugar cubes. The colors we perceive such objects to have seemed to Galileo to be at least as much a function of our own state as that of the objects themselves, to be mere artifacts of our experience. Properly "physical" properties employed and sanctioned by the new galilean physics, properties like mass and velocity, came to seem the only real and objective properties of material objects. While Galileo himself denied that balloons and stars had colors,[1] later writers deployed a subtler strategy. They saved color for the new physics by identifying particular colors with particular physical properties of objects, for instance dispositions to reflect certain wavelengths of light. Such identifications imply that certain features a color presents in our experience are not really features of that color, that our experience of color is misleading in certain ways. For instance, certain reds and blues are experienced to be quite similar, but red and blue light are on the opposite ends of the visual spectrum.

The point of this history is this: By "phenomenal" colors I mean colors just as they appear in our experience, not colors as they have been reconceived by post-galilean philosophers. I believe that in our unreflective moments, we, like our ancestors, take such phenomenal colors to be true and objective properties of objects. To understand what I mean here, it is important to maintain that naivete.

It will also be important to be clear that phenomenal properties cannot be identified with causal properties. There is more than a little reason to identify "galilean" properties like mass and charge with causal properties, powers to deflect particles and move oil drops. So some post-galileans identify colors as they appear in our experience not merely with "physical" properties, but in particular with powers, the intrinsic properties exhibited by causal microevents. But, as we have just seen in the case of red and blue, *phenomenal* color, color just as it appears within our experience, cannot be identified with any available causal candidates, because of the kinds of similarities which those candidates in fact possess. Any reduction of color must be revisionist, must claim that some features which color seems to have within our experience are not features it really has. And hence it cannot be a reduction of *phenomenal* color.

And there are additional reasons to resist the identification of the causal and the phenomenal. First of all, we can certainly *imagine* concrete contents consisting of microevents with merely phenomenal intrinsic properties, with no causal intrinsic properties, even if such contents are false. Humean phenomenalism may be quite wrong about the world, but it represents a coherently conceivable concrete possibility. In at least *some* basic contents, there are phenomenal intrinsic properties but no causal intrinsic properties. Those who think that conceivability arguments can reveal real distinctions between things may conclude that this shows that in no basic contents are phenomenal and causal intrinsic properties to be identified.

If you are skeptical about such arguments, still there is yet another reason to believe that in no basic content is there an identity between the phenomenal properties under consideration and causal powers. These phenomenal properties present themselves as intrinsic properties of objects, and any admissible reduction of the phenomenal properties of objects as they present themselves in experience, to causal properties or anything else, would need to heed this restriction. What's more, phenomenal properties present themselves as intrinsic properties of a certain kind. An object with such a phenomenal property sits there, exhibiting that property. But to do so, to be phenomenal blue or yellow or green, is not to do anything that involves a restriction on the rest of the world in quite the way characteristic of causal properties. If some microevent is phenomenal yellow, that does not, beyond the demands of certain extra-logical combinatorial constraints, restrict the rest of the basic content in which it exists to be anyway in particular. On the other hand, we will see that it is the very nature of causal microevents to make such restrictions. The yellow microevent could be replaced by a green one, or a red one, and it wouldn't make any difference to the rest of its content. But causal microevents aren't like this. They reach out of themselves in such a way that any difference in the particular power instantiated by a certain microevent would involve a difference in a restriction made on the rest of the content.[2] Phenomenal properties present themselves in our experience in at least as different a way from causal properties as do phenomenal colors from phenomenal smells. As we will see, these differences are rooted in the different ways in which various sorts of experience are realized. In this light, we should no more expect an identification of the phenomenal and causal elements of basic contents than of one sort of phenomenal property, say a color, with another, say a smell.

A parable may help make this vivid: One might plausibly maintain, at least to a first approximation, that galilean science privileged causal properties over phenomenal properties. Now imagine that instead of a galilean science rooted in uncovering the hidden causal structure of things, and hence at least initially banishing their color and other phenomenal properties as mere artifacts of experience, we'd developed a science based on phenomenal color. For instance, imagine that Galileo and his cronies had discovered hidden colors of things, colors only revealed under certain drugs, which provided a unified and predictively powerful theory of the world. Then today we might face the difficulty of understanding where, in the world of color, phenomenal sound could fit. Some of the lessons of this parable will be relevant only later. For instance, it may be as difficult to constitute the experience of colors out of causal entities as it might be to constitute the experience of sound out of the entities recognized by such a science of true colors. But some of the lessons are relevant now. The parable exhibits the difficulties faced by someone who would claim that in basic contents phenomenal colors and causal powers are to be identified. That claim is about as plausible as the claim that phenomenal colors and smells might be the same properties, which is to say that it is not plausible at all.

Because of the very contingent historical road through Galileo which we have traveled, some may be inclined to object to my claim that phenomenal color is had by elements of basic *contents*, on the grounds that phenomenal properties can play no significant *semantic* role. Because of the tradition which Galileo begot, the experience of red is sometimes thought to be a peculiarly inner and private affair, under one's hat and hence irrelevant to the socially shared meaning of a word like “red”. Even if the form of each person's phenomenal experience is different, so the objection runs, still we all use the same words and mean the same things by them. Content, like other semantic things, must be public, while phenomenal properties are not. Indeed, some may even be tempted by “private language” arguments, which purport to show that we cannot coherently talk about these putatively private properties.

Our history may make such arguments attractive, but it also shows that not everyone has accepted their premises. If some aristotelian thought that red as it appears in our experience was a color of material objects, then they would have denied that it was private in any way. Of course, such an aristotelian might have been wrong, but we certainly can *think* that the world includes such public phenomenal properties. Our aristotelian forbearers certainly did think that, and so do we, when we're walking down the street and not thinking too hard about these matters. The fact that we can concretely and coherently *imagine* such a possibility as objects with phenomenal colors gives phenomenal color *some* semantic relevance. It is present in the introspectible content of *that* thought. And even if phenomenal properties weren't in fact relevant to sentence meaning because too private, our thought *includes* our intensional perceptual experience. Hence it includes the perhaps merely private and phenomenal artifacts of that experience. Some place must be made for phenomenal properties in at least the basic contents which match immediate experience, even if that experience is private. And once we admit phenomenal properties into those seed contents, we have no particularly good reason to exclude them from basic contents generally.

Some may continue to insist that we cannot meaningfully talk about our putatively private phenomenal experience. But certainly the premises of their arguments are more properly controversial than our understanding of Aristotle or the psychological work on the nature of phenomenal properties which I will soon cite, even if some of those premises are motivated by our contingent historical circumstance. Fans of private language arguments owe us an explanation of what we have been doing for untold centuries as we have talked about the color which appears within our experience, and our apparent understanding of that talk. If they can provide one, then they should have no objection to my discussion here. In any case, in Parts Two and Three we will devote much attention to understanding the realization of phenomenal experience and of our talk about it.

2

Phenomenal microevents possess intrinsic phenomenal properties, and often enter into spatio-temporal relations with other microevents. Section 3 discusses their "characteristic" intrinsic properties, for instance redness and sweetness, and section 4 concerns their spatial and temporal properties. This section gets some less important matters quickly out of the way.

More or less arbitrarily adopting one of many terminological possibilities, the stories of C will capture the nature of a phenomenal microevent by specifying a single characteristic intrinsic property for that microevent. For instance, C will specify a single color, and not a separate hue and shade, for each color microevent. This will allow the characteristic properties expressed by C to be saturated, and it will lend itself to a certain economy of presentation. But, on the other hand, there are certain other intrinsic phenomenal properties which microevents can possess, in addition to their characteristic phenomenal properties. Since these are absent from many phenomenal microevents, and since they are not saturated, since they cannot be had by microevents which lack a characteristic intrinsic property, I will treat them distinctly from the characteristic intrinsic properties. But, again, this is a more or less arbitrary terminological choice. The characteristic intrinsic phenomenal properties and the spatio-temporal relations of phenomenal microevents are for our purposes their most interesting features, because they are the least obviously mere artifacts of our experience. But phenomenal experience includes certain other features, which allow us to conceive basic contents which include them, and temporal centering introduces yet another feature which can be present in basic contents. Whether or not any of these features yield basic contents which are plausibly basic in truth, they still require some attention in our development of C. They are the focus of the rest of this section.

First of all, as was suggested previously, some phenomenal microevents in a basic content may be *present* in a way others are not, may be marked in that basic content as here or now. C must incorporate a predicate to express now, whose use in stories is closely constrained by extra-logical combinatorial constraints. I have also already talked about here, but now let me add some refinements: As one's attention passes from place to place over a map or a painting, that may produce some phenomenal differences which cannot be characterized merely by speech of the phenomenal colors and spatio-temporal relations of microevents. Different parts of the painting may appear in experience as more highly attended to. Likewise, some microevents must present themselves as at the focus of attention in matching seed contents. So C will employ a class of predicates which express a degree of valence of attention. The proper use of these predicates is clearly closely bound by extra-logical combinatorial constraints. It will have a maximum value within any given seed content. That represents a kind of geographic center of the sense fields which are matched by that content. I take this to introduce the hereness which may infect basic contents.[3]

There is another feature which requires our brief attention. Certain entities, say within the visual field, present themselves as such, as unified entities distinct from their surroundings.[4] Certain groups of visual microevents present themselves as a unit with a sharp edge, bound by a magic boundary in experience. This phenomenon obviously introduces complex forms of phenomenal property, requiring predicates rigidly and complexly constrained by quasi-logical combinatorial constraints.

C requires resources of this general sort. But let me walk quite quickly by the features of experience we are now discussing, admitting that my sketchy model may be inadequate in many ways. These features seem absent from plausible conceptions of the world, from basic contents which are plausibly basic in truth.

3

Each phenomenal microevent has a characteristic intrinsic phenomenal property. Some phenomenal microevents have characteristic properties commonly associated not with sense perception but with emotions and feelings.

We will return to that sort of microevent in section 5. This section surveys the characteristic intrinsic properties which might capture the content of sensation.

A couple of notes about my methodology before we begin: We are discussing representational, and hence introspectible, content. So we are concerned with introspectible qualities of sensation. But I will deploy some of the long tradition of scientific study of the senses, which has been influenced not merely by expert introspection but also by other sorts of empirical data, including hypotheses about how sensation is realized. It is at best a tutored introspection which underlies my account of the characteristic intrinsic phenomenal properties, but I hope that it is in accord with your introspection. Also, in many ways these issues remain controversial, and I will ignore even some non-controversial complications. So at best this section will provide us with a rough model of the form the proper and final C should take. That should be sufficient for our later purposes.

Let's begin with a case that is in some ways the easiest and most familiar, though it is a relatively recent evolutionary development: vision. The introspectible structure of colors is quite complex.[5] Consider the familiar color wheel, rounding from red through purple and blue and green and yellow and orange and back to red, passing through all the intervening colors. Not all colors are to be found on such a child's wheel, but it captures some important phenomenal structure. Colors closer along the rim of the wheel are more similar. Colors across the wheel, say red and green, are in phenomenal opposition.

The boundaries of colors, of the ranges of specific hues we naturally call by single names like "red", are a bit vague, but there is a lot of cross-cultural evidence that they are not drawn in completely arbitrary places. And those colors exhibit some internal structure. There are, for instance, "unique" hues. There is a blue which looks neither reddish nor greenish, a red which is neither orangish nor purplish, and likewise a unique yellow and green. These seem to be phenomenal primaries.

Not all colors are found on the familiar color wheel. Consider for instance brown and black and white. And also it's important to realize that there are different kinds of colors--for instance those of the surfaces of opaque objects versus those of shiny colored lights against a dark background. There are various systems of color classification for colors of particular kinds, which reveal structure absent from the child's color wheel. For instance, the Swedish Natural Color System for surface colors organizes those colors into a finite three-dimensional space in something like the shape of a solid globe, with the fully chromatic colors, the colors on the child's color wheel, arranged along the equator, and black and white at opposing poles. In between red on the equator and white at the pole, there is a range of pinks. On the other hand, the H-B-S space, which captures colors of illumination seen against a neutral background, presents colors in a similarly shaped space, but one reaching not from the surface color black to the surface color white but from low to high luminosity.

We might attempt a grotesque amalgam: a four-dimensional finite space which has as a single three-dimensional slice the globe of the Swedish Color System, and also has another axis for luminosity, for brightness.[6] Each color might be assigned four coordinates[7] in that space, and hence might be expressed by a predicate C in our language C, with four numerical subscripts.[8]

Even if this color space succeeds in cramming together surface colors and colors of illumination, it ignores some structure of phenomenal color. For instance, something seen out of the corner of your eye presents an indistinct color, which is more or less a matter of light and dark. I will ignore this complication, though it might be that we can conceive concrete contents with merely the properties we experience out of the corners of our eyes. This is because such indistinct colors seem a mere artifact of our experience. On the other hand, I should admit that indistinct colors may help provide a way out of certain difficulties we will face in Part Three, though not I think a plausible one.

There is another complication, though, which I won't ignore. Perhaps because we can conceive basic contents which reach beyond immediate experience, perhaps because visual experience may be fused with various other sorts of experience, we can conceive of transparent points in the world, points with a sort of null color. Likewise, we can conceive of colored objects with varying degrees of translucence, say a point in a smokey room. So we need to add yet a fifth axis to our color space, running from something on the order of transparent to opaque, with the entire color space collapsing to a point at the location of the null color. We need to add a fifth numerical subscript to the predicate C.

There is a good deal known about the realization of our experience of phenomenal color, and indeed color will be our primary focus when we turn to a discussion of the realization of phenomenal experience in Part Three. For now, though, it may be useful to note that if unique red, green, blue, and yellow, and black and white for that matter, are color primaries, still they are primaries in a phenomenal sense only. For instance, there are only three sorts of sensory receptor cells responsive to chromatic light, not four as we might expect from the four unique hues of the child's color wheel. And of course we learn early that blue and yellow paint can be mixed to yield green paint. But, for the moment, we are concerned only with the *phenomenal* structure of color, not with these features of what yields our color experience.

The next sense we will consider is probably the most recent evolutionary development, and, because of the importance of speech for humans, it plays a central role in our lives. That sense, of course, is hearing. The scientific study of hearing, perhaps because of our quite ancient understanding of stringed instruments, is in many ways the oldest science of a sense. We have long had a reasonably good sense of what the physical stimuli corresponding to different phenomenal sounds might be. Paradoxically, this may have impeded the development of an adequate account of one important phenomenal feature of sounds, as we will shortly see.

There seem to be three significant features of the intrinsic phenomenal properties characteristic of hearing. The most straightforward is loudness. Phenomenal sounds range from a zero-point of quiet out to what I will presume is some finite maximum loudness. There may be reasons to think that at least word-mediation allows us to think of sounds louder than anything our senses might reveal, but I will ignore that sort of complexity here. The zero-point generates some analogue of the null color.

Sounds also differ in pitch, from low to high. I will also presume that this range is finite, but note that nowhere in the range is there an intuitive zero-point. And the range of pitches has a peculiar internal structure. For instance, certain pitches are an octave apart, or a fifth apart. This constitutes an important sort of structure in the space of sounds.

So far we have two dimensions for our sound space, but there is another important feature of phenomenal sound, though it has had less traditional investigation than might be expected, perhaps because differences in this feature have long been held to be caused by overtones, by the overlapping of sound stimuli. This feature is "timbre", or sound color. There are sometimes differences in timbre between two voices or vowels or instruments sounding at the same pitch and loudness. There have been some attempts to chart phenomenal timbre space.[9] Four-dimensional spaces seem adequate to capture most of the phenomenal similarities among vowel sounds and the sounds of musical instruments at a given pitch and loudness. The axes of such a space seem to correspond fairly well to certain verbal classifications of sounds: soft to hard (or perhaps dull to sharp), compact to scattered (or perhaps dampened to ringing, or tight to wide), empty to full, and colorless to colorful (or dim to brilliant). So we might tentatively identify a six-dimensional space for sounds, adding to the four-dimensional timbre space a dimension for loudness and a dimension for pitch, and we might generate a predicate S with six numerical subscripts for each phenomenal sound.[10]

Concrete contents seem to exhibit only one color microevent at each location. But the complex way in which we experience sounds at locations seems to allow us to conceive that more than one sound is present at a particular location, and hence more than one sound microevent, each with distinct characteristic properties.[11] Imagine, for instance, a bunch of different people talking at a party. Now imagine that that is heard through a single cheap speaker. The surface of the speaker seems to possess a complex sound of the sort at issue.[12] This may help explain why the tradition largely ignored timbre for overtones.

The first two senses we have discussed are perhaps the most characteristic human senses. They are not only evolutionarily recent, but they are senses which work well at a distance. And their phenomenal structure, except perhaps in regards to timbre, is reasonably familiar. There is more controversy about the phenomenal properties characteristic of the next two senses--taste and smell. I will proceed by recounting some of the history of that controversy.

Let's begin with taste. Taste is like smell in many ways. In fact, we know from suffering stuffy noses that much of what are called differences in food "taste" are really differences in smell. We might roughly distinguish taste from smell as the sense mediated by contact on the tongue.

There are four traditional "primary" tastes--sweet, sour, bitter, and salty. But there is quite a lot of controversy about whether these are the only primaries, and in what sense they are primaries.[13] Some of the controversy about primary tastes involves attempts to specify physical stimuli and sense receptors and neural paths which correspond to each sort of primary. We, of course, are here only interested in phenomenal structure, so we can ignore all that for now. But still there is plenty of controversy we can't ignore. For instance, Galen listed harsh, pungent, and astringent as additional primaries, and there has been a continuing controversy about whether insipid, something conceived sometimes I think as an analogue of the null-color and sometimes as an analogue of white, is another taste primary. Beginning in the nineteenth century, there was an extended debate about whether the four primary tastes correspond to different *modalities*. This would imply that even though each might scale in intensity, and even while there might be substances that have a complex taste which is composed of each of the primaries, still there aren't *intermediate* tastes, as purple is an intermediate color between the primary colors blue and red. Some have thought the taste primaries correspond to different modalities, as sounds and colors correspond to different modalities. But some have thought that there are intermediate tastes. If there are intermediate tastes, then still there is a question about what sort of structure they possess. Henning very vividly represented all tastes as on the surface of a "taste tetrahedron", with each of the four primaries at a vertex. But there might be other tastes inside, or even perhaps outside, such a tetrahedron.

If there are indeed four primary tastes, and if there are intermediate tastes, and if we can treat insipid as a matter of no taste intensity, then it seems not implausible to claim that we can locate each characteristic taste in a four-dimensional space, one dimension for intensity, and then three dimensions for a space in which the Henning tetrahedron is imbedded. So we might deploy a range of predicates T with four numerical subscripts.[14] Tastes, like sounds but unlike colors, seem things which might be complex, in the sense that there might be two taste microevents with different characteristic properties at the same location.

With smell, things are yet more complicated and controversial.[15] There is a traditional classification of smells rooted in Linnaeus which recognizes seven categories of smells. This may be a new sort of phenomenal structure, in which there aren't primaries, but rather classes. Zwaardemaker's development of Linnaeus' scheme perhaps represents the most plausible such proposal. It incorporates nine classes: 1) ethereal (the smell of ether or beeswax), 2) aromatic (of camphor, cloves, citrus, almonds, anise), 3) fragrant (of flowers, vanilla, lilac, balsam), 4) ambrosial (of amber or musk), 5) alliaceous (of onion, garlic, iodine, chlorine), 6) empyreumatic (of roasted coffee or tobacco smoke), 7) caprylic (goaty), 8) repulsive (of nightshade), and 9) nauseous (of carrion or feces).

But Amoore proposed seven primary smells as distinct modalities, with nicely corresponding chemical stimuli, receptors, and neural paths: camphoraceous, pungent, floral, ethereal, minty, musky, putrid. And Henning proposed a vivid analogue of his taste tetrahedron. He held that there were six smell primaries, with intermediate smells arranged on the surface of an odor prism: Imagine a triangle whose vertices are spicy, burned, and resinous, and another triangle placed parallel and above, with a vertex for fragrant corresponding to spicy below, with putrid over burned, and with ethereal over resinous. Now connect the corresponding vertices with edges to get the odor prism.

To make a concrete proposal, allow me to place Henning's prism in a 3-space, add a dimension for intensity, and represent odors along four dimensions, expressed by O with four numerical subscripts.[16] Presumably, there might be more than one odor at a location. And zero intensity yields a null odor.

The traditional sense of touch is now characteristically treated as a collection of senses.[17] There are skin senses, associated with at least four different types of sensory receptor cells in the skin. These are often taken to correspond to four different phenomenal primaries--pain, pressure, hot, and cold.[18] There is dispute about whether they are different modalities, or whether there are intermediate touch sensations. The feeling of wetness, for instance, might be intermediate between pressure and cold, or it might be a mixture of those. Note that cold and warmth are generally considered separate phenomenal primaries, perhaps because they seem mediated by separate sorts of sensory receptor cells, though it may be a mistake to automatically link issues in this way.

In addition to the skin senses, there is also organic sensitivity, which involves similar sorts of sensations internal to the body. Another set of "touch" sensations are associated with the class of sensory mechanisms involved in proprioception, which give us a sense of the relative position and movement of our body parts and limbs, and also provide us with phenomenal feelings of effort, apparently mediated by special sensory receptor cells in muscles and tendons. The vestibular sense, mediated by organs in the ear, responds to angular rotation and acceleration and linear acceleration. It plays a crucial role in the stabilization of our retinal images, in orientation, and in smooth locomotion, and may be associated with sensations of vertigo.

Whether or not the characteristic intrinsic properties introduced by touch are deployed in commonsense conceptions of inorganic objects, still it seems that we can conceive of at least implausible concrete circumstances deploying such properties not merely as the properties of organic entities, felt on the inside of our bodies, but even as part of fanciful inorganic objects.[19] We even sometimes seem to naively *feel* pain as on objects, say on the edge of a sharp cuisinart blade, and I think we can even conceive of a horrible world of pain.

Let me make at least a rough proposal about the characteristic phenomenal properties introduced by the class of senses under consideration:

i) There is a phenomenal sense of down, introduced by the vestibular sense, but it isn't an intrinsic property of microevents. Rather it serves to orient other sorts of microevents, to turn a three-dimensional structure of colors into something in which one direction in that space is *down* in the full traditional sense.[20] In vertigo, that direction might spin.

ii) There are three modalities introduced by the skin senses and organic sensitivity: Pain, which scales in intensity from nothing to some finite limit. Pressure, which has a similar structure. And a single modality from a finite maximum felt cold to a finite maximum felt heat, with a zero point between. There can be only one microevent of each of these modalities at a given location, and there is a distinct field for each.

What of proprioception? Perhaps it yields a sort of vague spatial structure for the phenomenal products of the skin senses and organic sensitivity, of which there are null variants. But perhaps also it introduces another modality, a feeling of effort which is distinct from both pressure and the causal experience to be discussed in the next chapter. Assume so.

Let C include the appropriate predicates. This rough proposal unquestionably ignores many interesting and unresolved issues. For instance, there is some recent work which suggests that itch is a distinct modality.[21] But it should do for our purposes.

4

This section concerns the spatio-temporal relations of phenomenal microevents. I will begin by discussing certain model basic contents, which eschew some artifacts of our experience. Then I'll move on to other cases.

We'll start with a specific sort of three-dimensional basic content, which eschews artifacts of our experience like a center on now or here and magic boundaries. To each of the various sense modalities, there corresponds a spatially three-dimensional and temporally one-dimensional field of microevents in that content, with the intrinsic properties characteristic of that modality. For instance, there is a spatially three-dimensional color field, with each point occupied by a phenomenal color, including of course the null color. Some fields, for instance the taste field, exhibit more than one microevent at a single location, fused; others, such as the color field, do not.

How might we capture the spatio-temporal structure of, for instance, this color-field? Temporal structure is easy. We might specify which microevents are before or simultaneous to which.[22] There is probably some metric structure present in the temporal relations of basic contents, so that for instance certain intervals of time are longer than others, but let me ignore that complication for the moment.

How might we capture the spatial structure of the color field? Imagine that through each color microevent there run three mutually perpendicular planes, parallel to corresponding planes running through the other color microevents. We might call one "the x plane", and the others "y" and "z". We might specify which microevents are either on the x plane running through a particular microevent or on one particular side of it. And we might repeat that specification for the other two planes through that particular microevent. And then again for each set of planes running through each particular microevent. Resources like this would fix a lot of the spatial structure in at least the model contents I am considering.

Now let me flirt with an error, because it's an error worth noticing. Call microevents on one side of the x plane running through a microevent "below" it, and others appropriately related to the y and z planes "left" and "above". These labels carry, I think, misleading suggestions of a certain orientation in a gravitational field, the feeling of down introduced by the vestibular senses, and another artifact rooted in the fact that our senses are focussed forward and we tend to move in that way. This assorted baggage may be why mirrors seem to us to reverse right to left rather than up and down. Since there appears to be no special *physical* reason for such an asymmetry, there may well be a kind of asymmetry in the way we ordinarily conceptualize those directions. And this may suggest that there are ways of conceptualizing spatial directions, ways different from our own, in which such conceptual artifacts would disappear or be altered. Perhaps if we had grown up in a world where gravity wasn't so important, but in which we were stationary creatures with a single fixed orientation and in which there was always a left to right wind, the vertical orientation would have been conceptualized by us in such a way that it would seem to reverse in mirrors. In any case, we don't want these artifacts to infect basic contents of at least the standard sort we are considering, where the sensations characteristic of the vestibular sense are ignored. Certainly we post-galileans don't want to think that the universe itself has a true down. Unfortunately, there are lots of complications which this introduces. Perhaps we can coherently conceive a situation merely different from our own in which all the matter in the universe is turned upside down in space, a world flipped over in space; perhaps that is a distinct basic content. But it may be that we cannot conceive of a basic content distinct from that which matches our own world in which space itself as well as its material contents are inverted. We *can* of course imagine a different content which is a *mirror* inversion of our world, left swapped for right. We may well want to avoid different stories for basic contents which are simply rotated in any given moment in the planes we have arbitrarily introduced; on the other hand, we may sometimes want to allow these differences. And we may also want to allow an intermediate level of structure, in which we can distinguish changes in orientation over time.

I will return to a discussion of some of this in Part Three, but the general point is that we need to be wary of creating misleading artifacts by speaking of one particular set of spatial relations characterized in some particular way, and yet we need to capture enough structure to preserve the differences in orientation created by at least mirror inversions, and maybe other differences as well. At least generally what we need to do is this: Introduce mutually perpendicular planes and corresponding "directions" into all the fields of all basic contents in some arbitrary but uniform way, and introduce complicated extra-logical combinatorial constraints so that there aren't two ways in C to express the single spatial structure within any given field. Then note how microevents of distinct fields (or within a single field in which there might be more than one microevent at a given location) are fused. Let C possess the appropriate relational predicates.[23]

There are yet more complications. Basic contents at least often possess a certain kind of metric structure. Certain distances in the contents are longer than, or even perhaps exactly twice as long as, certain others.[24] I have already hinted that we might need this sort of thing for time as well. So we need to provide C with ways to capture such structure. Let me specify that the full spatial structure of the model basic contents has a standard euclidean metric structure.[25]

Standard euclidean spaces have other features we should attend to. The model contents we are discussing extend out infinitely in all directions. C does not have the resources to say explicitly that a content is infinite in this way, and yet at least an infinitely long story of C can express such an infinite basic contents. The stories of C and hence basic contents are at least potentially infinite. But there is not merely infinity of this particular sort. We have learned to distinguish various sorts of infinite structure within a concrete thing, within a given region of a basic content. It might be that between any two points there is another, that the space is dense, so that there are in fact an infinite number of points between any two given points. To each of the points on a line through such a dense structure there corresponds a rational number. But we have also learned to distinguish between rational and irrational real numbers, and between the infinite cardinality just introduced and the larger cardinality of the continuum. There are not only dense but continuous spaces of points, we say.

There are lots of pitfalls here. The distinction between dense and continuous structures seems to be captured only by a kind of metric structure which involves the assignment of numbers to points, and distinguishes dense from continuous structures on the basis of the distinction between the cardinality of the sets of numbers which can be correlated with their points. One might well wonder if this difference is a concrete difference. But let me avoid that particular labyrinth, and simply assume a difference. C does not have the resources to say explicitly that a space of microevents is dense or continuous, but it does seem to have the resources to at least potentially characterize a basic content which is dense and even continuous. Basic contents are potentially dense and continuous in the same way that they are potentially infinite in extent. I have so far avoided explicit discussion of the complications which dense and continuous contents introduce. But, in fact, the preceding discussion has been tailored to provide some of the resources they require. That is, for instance, why I spoke of microevents being something like "above", and not rather something like "immediately above", others.

We have so far been largely talking about only the spatio-temporal structure of particular phenomenal fields within a basic content. So let me remind you of something introduced in the last chapter. We can link fields together by fusion.

As complicated as this is already, further complications are introduced by phenomenal basic contents which are not model contents. Consider for instance seed contents, which match immediate experience. The spatial structure of certain actual *sense* fields, the portions of immediate experience corresponding to single modalities, is probably two-dimensional. I think the visual sense field is like this, though that is controversial. And some fields are much more indistinct than my discussion so far might suggest. Even visual experience gets indistinct in structure out at the edges. Two-dimensional spatial structure might be captured along arbitrary axes functioning quite like our arbitrary planes. What of indistinct structure? Since some phenomenal sense fields may, absent fusing with other sense fields, be so rudimentary in form as to lack any structure but that provided by simple contiguity, I think that we have reason to admit a relational predicate into our language specifically to refer to the contiguity of microevents.

But even this apparatus does not provide enough variety of spatial structure. Consider the differences between the highly-determinate center of the visual sense field, and the vague field of temperature sensation. Much of the difference surely lies in the fact that the temperature field is less detailed, that it consists of fewer elements than the visual field. But there is still a residual difference in structure between the fields which we cannot yet express. The microevents exhaustively matching your visual sense field are arranged on straight lines in certain ways as well as at determinate distances.[26] But the microevents matching temperature sensation have a much looser spatial structure. We might omit a specification of metric structure, or express a weaker sort of metric structure than that possessed by model contents. But of course even our manner of capturing spatial orientation, through the perpendicular planes, presumed a rich euclidean structure. And yet we need something more than mere contiguity. So an adequate C would need to be complicated in certain further ways. Because these later features of sense fields are presumably mere artifacts of our experience, I will rest content with this indication of where further work is required. Note also that it may be that some distinct fields do not fuse in any way, since fusion requires a kind of spatial relation. Rather, distinct fields may include spatially-unrelated microevents which are merely simultaneous.

This rather creaky and convoluted set of resources, augmented by ferociously complicated extra-logical combinatorial constraints at which I've less than gestured, would, I think, do the trick for us. But picking any particular set of relational predicates for C would obviously involve a number of quite arbitrary choices. Nevertheless, this does not introduce any arbitrariness into what constitutes the supervenience base of basic contents, and hence basic contents themselves. It may be useful at this point to review why: A supervenience base of a basic content is a certain concrete state of affairs, a certain concrete configuration of things. Or, rather, it is such an object of thought. The first element of arbitrariness is introduced when C lays a very fine spatio-temporal grid over that concrete configuration, and speaks of point-instants. The second element of arbitrariness introduced by C is the recognition of certain numbers of microevents of various modalities at each point, fused together, and a corresponding set of characteristic intrinsic properties. Likewise, there is an arbitrary choice of the predicates deployed to capture all the spatio-temporal structure which is present among locations. What is more or less arbitrary in all of this is how the original concrete configuration is expressed, not what the concrete configuration is, though some early choices about a means of expression constrain some later ones. The stories of C are one way to express the supervenience base of a basic content, and hence the basic content. But that is all they are. There are other ways.

5

There at least seem to be other candidates for phenomenal experience, and hence other sorts of phenomenal microevents, than those associated with sensation. They demand at least a little attention.

We are clearly very adept at recognition of certain kinds of things, for instance particular kinds of faces and the particular emotions they express. This may seem to involve a new kind of phenomenal experience. Faces look smiley or grim, Abe Lincolny or no. But the so-called "experience" of a certain kind of face as smiley or Lincolny seems properly to be considered an abstracted thought, whose content can be generated by abstraction and hence requires no explicit expression in C.

On the other hand, there are other cases which may require an expansion of C. Consider for instance our experience of our feelings and emotions. It is traditional to recognize at least one dimension of affective tone, from unpleasant to pleasant. One can *feel* good or bad. And one can do so in varying degrees of intensity, it seems.[27] These feelings seem located in at least rough ways, at least within one's body, and they seem to introduce a new set of characteristic intrinsic phenomenal properties. They may well require some addition to C, though we may reasonably wonder if they are really distinct from sensations of pain.[28]

What's more, this traditional picture may well be much too simple. Perhaps emotional states like anger have phenomenal feeling components distinct from those involved in happiness and unhappiness. And various unhappy emotions, from depression to bitterness, may have quite distinct phenomenal components.

Indeed, it may be that we should go even farther afield. Maybe humorousness can be present in phenomenal experience. And one might read Heidegger's *Being and Time* as suggesting a yet more inclusive conception of phenomenal experience, in which, for instance, words may present themselves as ready-to-hand.[29]

I will not pursue these matters here. Generally accepted conceptions of the world seem to eschew such features, at least as features of concrete inorganic objects like balls and balloons. And we will understand at least roughly how the experience of such putative phenomenal feelings would fit into the world if we understand how phenomenal sensation, for instance the experience of pain, fits in. Permit me to leave this then, at least for now, a dark and unexplored corner of C.

NOTES

1. Galileo, "Excerpts from The Assayer".
2. This wouldn't necessarily require that the other microevents in the content be different.
3. It may be that the hereness of centered contents which are not seed contents is introduced in much the indirect manner that nowness is introduced, so that we really need another hereness predicate also. But I will ignore this complication.
4. This in fact was already suggested by Chapter Three.
5. C.L. Hardin, *Color for Philosophers*.
6. Such a space would have unoccupied points.
7. Given some arbitrary cartesian coordinatization of that space.
8. If we wanted the stories of the language C to *show*, in the wittgensteinian sense, more color structure, we'd need to deploy a coordinatization which gave, for instance, the unique hues some revealing characterization, and also which captured the proper metric of similarity between colors. But I will ignore these complexities.
9. Reinier Plomp, *Aspects of Tone Sensation* (London: Academic Press, 1976), ch. 6.
10. If we want the language C to *show* more of the structure of phenomenal sound, for instance metrics of similarity, a particular sort of coordinatization or even a different space would be required. A spiral may capture some octave structure that a line for rising pitch cannot.
11. I should admit that perhaps it is more accurate to say that it is arbitrary whether, on the one hand, C attributes more than one sound to a location or, on the other, admits more complexity of structure into the characteristic sound properties, but the strategy I deploy here seems the most economical way to deal with these matters.
12. In analogy with color, we might expect the speaker itself to have a null or perhaps translucent sound, and the sound to be projected back to its source. Though, on the other hand, we recognize the surface of a TV screen to have the color of what it represents.
13. See Linda Bartoshuk, "History of Taste Research", in E. Carterette and M. Friedman (editors), *Handbook of Perception, VIa* (New York: Academic Press, 1978), 3-18, and the references cited there.

14. As always, I will ignore complexities introduced by similarity metrics and attempts to show more structure.
15. See William S. Cain, "History of Research on Smell", in Carterette and Friedman, 197-229, and the references cited there. See also R.J. Christman, *Sensory Experience* (Scranton, PA: International Textbook Company, 1971).
16. As always, I'll ignore metrics.
17. See Joseph Stevens and Barry Green, "History of Research on Feeling", in E. Carterette and M. Friedman (editors), *Handbook of Perception, VIb* (New York: Academic Press, 1978), 3-23, and other readings in that volume, especially Dan Kenshalo, "Biophysics and Psychophysics of Feeling", 29-63.
18. Note that pleasure is not usually considered a skin sense. This doesn't seem that plausible to me, but let me ignore that complication.
19. Do people naively consider pain on the inside of someone else's body to be something they'd feel as pain if they reached inside the other person?
20. I am assuming that there is a *phenomenal* feeling here, only contingently connected with traditional causal associations like down-pulling gravity.
21. *Scientific American* 273:7, July 1995, 22-23.
22. If we admit contents looping in time, which I think would be a mistake, then we should separately specify which are before and which are simultaneous with which. If we can ignore such cases, then if two events are before or simultaneous with each other, they are simultaneous.
23. There are more economical ways to express all the spatio-temporal structure than this, since for instance the structure in one field may duplicate that in another with which its elements are fused, so this is a minor extravagance.
24. And certain angles are greater than certain others.
25. Some may worry that this excludes some obvious truths which twentieth century physics has uncovered. But we are now only discussing certain model basic contents consisting of phenomenal microevents. There are also merely causal basic contents, which exclude phenomenal microevents but include causal microevents of the sort we will discuss in the next chapter, and some of these fit with at least a lot of twentieth century physics. Causal basic contents can lack the familiar sort of "phenomenal" spatio-temporal structure. We will return to these issues at length in Part Three.
26. This is admittedly a controversial claim.
27. See Joseph Mendola, "Objective Value and Subjective States", *Philosophy and Phenomenological Research* L, 1990, 695-713, and C.I. Lewis, *An Analysis of Knowledge and Valuation* (La Salle, IL: Open Court, 1971), 397-431.
28. And pleasure too, if that's a sensation.
29. It may also suggest that the smiley may also be an irreducible and not abstracted feature of experience.

CHAPTER SEVEN

CAUSAL ELEMENTS

The characteristic intrinsic properties of some microevents are causal powers. This chapter concerns these causal microevents. Why think that basic contents include causal microevents? Three reasons:

First, common sense proclaims that ordinary concrete entities have causal properties. Consider the capacity of a sandy beach to stop a falling volleyball, of the ball to compress the sand, of a bench to stop a distracted runner. We can coherently conceive objects with causal powers. And if ordinary concrete entities can have causal powers, then so can individual microevents. Size shouldn't make a difference.

Second, some physicalists have held that phenomenal properties are mere artifacts of our experience, that the true and objective properties of things are physical properties, and indeed that things generally are constituted out of their microphysical bits. But the paradigmatic "physical" properties--mass, charge, velocity, and so on--seem to be causal properties. The charge of a particle seems to be its capacity to do various things, for instance to move oil drops. Whether or not such a physicalism is true, it does represent a concrete and coherently conceivable possibility.

Third, basic content is rooted in experience. And we will soon see that experience includes causal elements, rooted in our capacity to *do* things. Causal properties are the intrinsic properties of the microevents which match a causal field present in immediate experience, a field analogous to phenomenal sense fields. This final motivation suggests that causal microevents are a close analogue of phenomenal microevents, and indeed they too can possess the unsaturated intrinsic properties involved in magic boundaries and centering on here or now. They too can be fused with microevents in other sorts of fields. But we will focus here on the causal properties themselves.

All of these reasons represent only an initial case, and some of their elements certainly require further discussion. This chapter will defend at greater length two central claims, one about contents, and one about the realization of thoughts with such contents:

First, some microevents are causal microevents, whose characteristic intrinsic properties are "irreducible" causal powers. The instantiation of such a power would restrict the world in some coherently conceivable way, a way which I will say is "relatively characterizable" in C.

Second, our capacity for thoughts with contents including such powers rests on our capacity to experience powers, which in turn rests on our capacity to act in one way rather than another. While the realization of thoughts is not our immediate concern, this second claim, or rather pair of claims, will play an important role in what follows, so it is worth some attention even in this chapter.

Section 1 characterizes the powers which microevents can exhibit. Section 2 discusses certain familiar objections to this conception. Section 3 provides further defense of the conception by sketching how thoughts with such contents might be realized. Section 4 draws various threads from the preceding sections together, and adds a final level of refinement to the characterization of the powers recognized by C. Section 5 concerns the spatio-temporal relations of causal microevents.

1

The characteristic intrinsic properties of causal microevents are causal powers. These are quite familiar, but sometimes suspect in the eyes of philosophers. At our mothers' knees, we entertained at least a gross conception of the powers which particular objects exerted--of what those objects did in the world. My rattle had the power to rattle when shook, to shatter when smashed, to resist when chewed, to please me in all cases. It made a difference to what went on. And even within the relatively sophisticated sphere of particle physics, we distinguish electrons from other particles by the particular difference they make to what goes on, for instance by their particular power to affect protons and other electrons. Different kinds of objects, for instance rattles and electrons, seem to have different kinds of powers. And different individual objects, say two electrons, sometimes exhibit the same power. So we may speak of different "instantiations" of a single causal power.

But even if this general class of properties is familiar, we need to be more specific about the nature of the particular causal powers exhibited by microevents and expressed by stories of C. Since this involves lots of complications, I will proceed by characterizing powers even in this first section in four waves. Each wave adds a bit more refinement to our characterization of the causal powers of microevents. As will become evident in section 4, I will work more or less backwards in developing a characterization of powers. We will discuss the complications introduced by the most primitive and central powers last, and indeed not completely until later sections. This will make our discussion somewhat more tractable than it otherwise would be.

1.1

Let me start out by listing certain features of the powers of microevents: First, these causal powers are characteristic intrinsic properties of a peculiar sort, by which microevents somehow reach out of themselves. A causal microevent matches a bit of the world which *restricts* the world, not merely in a vacuous sense, so that the world includes the bit itself, but also in another way. It restricts to some degree the way the *rest* of the world is. It makes the world beyond it be some way rather than another. And it does this while somehow remaining an intrinsic property. Different powers are different sorts of restrictions.

Second, the causal powers invoked by C are irreducible. We'll talk more about what this involves in the next section, but the immediately relevant point is that these causal powers require explicit expression in the stories of C. They are not constituted or fixed by the other resources which C invokes.

Third, while causal powers are irreducible, we can characterize the *content* of the restrictions they make. We can "relatively characterize" a particular causal power by characterizing the particular restriction it makes on the world, by characterizing how it restricts the world to be out of the wide space of possibility. To a first approximation, coherently conceivable casual powers which causal microevents can exhibit can be relatively characterized in C.[1] The simplest sort of causal power restricts the world so that some story of C is true. Causal microevents can restrict the world to include certain sorts of causal microevents, and also to include certain sorts of phenomenal microevents. But there are other sorts of powers also. For instance, some powers restrict the world so that certain things are not true. And some powers restrict the world so that it is among some range of alternative possibilities, with a different story corresponding to each possibility.

This sketch of the characterization of powers is inadequate in more than a few ways, and we will return to many of these issues shortly. But I hope this at least conveys the general flavor of the powers recognized by C. The last chapter discussed at length the "nature" of the characteristic intrinsic phenomenal properties exhibited by phenomenal microevents, the second-order properties and relations of those properties. Here we can be briefer in at least our first pass: Since causal powers can be relatively characterized by a description of the contents of the restrictions which they make, their axes of similarity and difference are the axes of similarity and difference among the contents of those restrictions. Beyond a characterization of its content, there is something more to the characterization of a causal power, but that additional characterization is the same for all causal powers: They act to restrict a world in which they are instantiated to fit the contents of the restrictions they make. Causal powers likewise introduce only a single new extra-logical combinatorial constraint, though a very crucial one. If a power is instantiated in a basic content, then the rest of the basic content must be such as to meet the restriction the power makes.

The relative characterization of causal powers suggests a fourth relevant feature: Causal "powers" in my sense are a very broad class of properties. Some might well object that it is too broad. A pair of examples which underline this worry: First, it is often held that many of the causal powers of entities are merely *dispositional*, that they would be released only under certain hypothetical conditions. For instance, a tree in an uninhabited forest has only a *disposition* to deflect volleyballs, when there are no volleyballs about. But the causal predicates deployed by C capture such merely "dispositional" powers by speech of *actual* restrictions. If some microevent A has the dispositional power to repel electrons, a power released only when a proton is nearby, and a proton is not nearby, still it restricts the world in such a way that there could not be protons near and electrons unrepelled. The microevent A makes the same restriction regardless of what goes on around it. It's just that that actual restriction may rule out some things even in merely hypothetical circumstances. At least that much modality is not an artifact of the approach apparatus. Consider a second case, the persistence over time of a point-particle with a given momentum. That persistence can be captured by our broad notion of a power. Each moment in that particle's history restricts the world to be such that at the next moment it contains a relevantly similar moment of a particle's history in the relevant spatial location. It may seem idiosyncratic, or at least controversial, to treat persistence and dispositions in this way. However, in this particular context the broadness of my notion of a power is a strength and not a weakness. This notion can help to capture the full range of characteristic intrinsic properties other than phenomenal properties which microevents have. If you prefer not to call them all *causal* powers, then adopt an alternative terminology and make the necessary substitutions in what follows. Nothing of substance will be affected.

1.2

That was my first pass at characterizing the causal powers recognized by C. Now let me make a second pass. Take all the stories of C. There is a power which restricts the world so that:

i) Any particular such story is true.[2]
ii) Any particular such story is false.
iii) Some member of a specific set of mutually exclusive stories is true.
iv) Some member of a specific set of mutually exclusive stories is false.
v) Something like (i) or (iii), except that the relevant story is *exhaustively* true, captures all the truth.

Before we get to (vi) and (vii), let me fill in some background: Heretofore, I have ignored probabilistic restriction, but it is coherently conceivable. Entities, and in particular microevents, can instantiate powers which involve various probabilities of various restrictions on the world, rather than, for instance, the certainty of one restriction. Hence

vi) There is a power which restricts the world so that there are various non-zero probabilities that each of some range of stories of C will be true, with the probabilities of the various stories summing to 1 so that it is certain that some one of them will be true. This is a probabilistic analogue of (i).

vii) Finally, there are complicated mixed cases, for instance involving lotteries of the sort noted under (vi) within disjuncts of the sort noted under (iii). But let me stop before things get too complicated. Even if (vii) were filled out properly, this second pass would miss some important things. So let's try a third pass.

1.3

There is an intuitive distinction between powers which are exercised directly and those which are exercised indirectly, between powers exercised without, or only through, an intervening causal medium. If I light a fuse here and blow something up elsewhere, then I cause the explosion only by the mediation of the burning fuse. But the lighting of the fuse by my contiguous match involves a more "immediate" influence. And there is this related intuitive distinction: Two microevents located at different positions in a basic content might exercise what we would so far have to characterize as the same restriction, but possess intuitively different powers. If I snap my finger here and you snap yours there, and both events cause a snapping sound in my vicinity, that surely seems to involve a difference in powers.

Perhaps some coherently conceivable powers make merely general restrictions on the world, for instance when exercised anywhere create a blue lake with goldfish somewhere in the universe, but the most plausible powers aren't like that. The most plausible powers produce effects at some specific distance from and in some specific relation to what does the producing. If I drop my pen it is not just that it will cause the falling of a pen and a splashing of water somewhere in the universe, but rather that there will be a falling and a splashing right here in this vicinity.

The relative characterization of certain causal powers must capture this feature of the powers. Since any microevent degenerately restricts the world to include it, mention of such a microevent itself might be included in the descriptions which relatively characterize its power. Hence in those descriptions it might be singled out by a special predicate, "PP" (for present power), and the descriptions of the restrictions "centered" on it.[3]

Now we are in position to see that the relative characterizations of powers cannot, strictly speaking, be stories of C. That is partly because of reasons implicit in our discussion in 1.2, where we recognized contents of restrictions involving for instance *lotteries* over stories of C. But it is also because C does not include the special predicate "PP".[4]

1.4

There are more complications. More art is required in the proper characterization of powers than I've admitted so far. The relative characterization of every "centered" power will mention at least one microevent instantiating it. This would raise a kind of circularity problem if our relative characterizations of causal powers were meant as definitions, but they are not. They serve merely to *relatively* characterize the powers. But this circularity is an instance of a more general phenomena which demands some wariness on our part.

An account of basic content must introduce both the relative characterizations of powers and powers which may be mentioned in those characterizations all at once. Powers are at once characterized by their contents and mentioned in the characterizations of certain of those contents. But this is potentially dangerous, even if it isn't a vicious circularity. For instance, we cannot allow a *difference* between characterizations of powers, and hence between powers, where the only differences in the *contents* of the relevant restrictions involve the presence of instantiations of the particular powers so characterized. If the only "difference" between the contents of supposedly different powers A and B is that the content of A involves microevents with power A where the content of B involves microevents with power B, then they aren't really different powers. There are other sorts of situation which can generate this general sort of problem. For instance, the characterization of some causal power may make reference to microevents with causal powers characterized in turn by reference to it, or to powers characterized by reference to powers characterized by reference to it, and so on. We must be careful that the characterizations of powers admitted by C and the powers admitted by C fit together in the right way, and yet allow no differences between powers where there is no concrete difference. In effect, to each distinct power there corresponds a distinct pattern of restriction, perhaps characterized not only by reference to phenomenal microevents but also to causal microevents which are themselves characterized merely by reference to such patterns. To each power their corresponds a particular role in the global characterization of all powers.

In fact, even this is a serious over-simplification. Some powers are not characterized merely by such patterns. I have withheld the most important complication. So far I have ignored what we will see in the fourth section to be the most crucial and characteristic powers, rooted quite immediately in our causal experience and motor action. We can act with more or less of what I will call "force", and these restrictions may have different effects in the face of different degrees of "force" exerted by other entities. So we need to introduce more resources to characterize the contents of all causal restrictions, but I will return to this complication only when the necessary background is in place. Our discussion so far prescinds from certain important differences in the ways thoughts of different powers are realized, to which we will turn in section 3. While this has meant that we have so far focussed on less characteristic cases, there is a corresponding benefit. They are also simpler.

But one more small initial complication: In analogy with null colors, one might wonder if there is a null power. There may be reasons to resist null powers. Some may think them necessary if causal microevents are to be capable of constituting a vacuum,[5] but in fact our ordinary conception of the void is of something which restricts the world so that, absent the influence of other powers and various post-galilean complications, it will contain another bit of void in the next moment. So even a point-instant of vacuum might exhibit a non-null "causal power" of the broad sort I have characterized here. And it seems not unreasonable to claim that a null power, unlike a null color, fails to be suitably concrete. But, on the other hand, a causal field in immediate experience might exhibit a null power, as an auditory field might exhibit a null sound. And we might also reasonably wonder if there really is any concrete distinction between a null color, a null sound, and a null power, except that they are found in different sorts of fields. If we admit null sounds, then it may be that we have to admit null powers, because the distinction between null events of different types may be a mere artifact of my way of capturing basic contents in C. So, on balance, it seems most reasonable to allow that there is a null power.

This completes my initial rough sketch of the range of causal powers. There is a causal power expressible in C for each relative characterization of the sort at least vaguely described in this section. Assign each a predicate of C, which might be "P" with a complicated numerical subscript.

2

It cannot plausibly be denied that coherent concrete contents include entities, say volleyballs, with causal properties. But some may deny that we can coherently conceive the irreducible causal powers which I have described in the previous section, the characteristic intrinsic properties of causal microevents.

Objection One: Aren't we all good late empiricists who laugh at lockean causal powers, and favor regularity accounts of causation in the style of David Hume?[6] Aren't causal properties constituted by regular, law-like connections among *types* of events, so that the causal properties of particular events are constituted by their places in certain regular patterns of events. For instance, someone might insist, a particular microevent A of type A* causes a particular microevent B of type B* just in case microevents of the first type always immediately precede contiguous events of the second type, and A so precedes B.

Reply: There are a variety of standard difficulties which such regularity analyses face. Is it plausible that the only asymmetry between cause and effect is a temporal asymmetry? Can regularity accounts adequately underwrite the intuitive distinction between real law-like connections and mere accidental regularities? But let me focus on another objection, which is also relevant against other "reductive" accounts of the causal powers of microevents: All microevents have characteristic intrinsic properties. Otherwise there'd be nothing concrete present in such an event to enter into spatio-temporal relations, nothing concrete in even the way that null colors and powers are concrete. But according to a regularity account of causation, causal properties are not intrinsic properties of things. Rather, they are constituted by the place of those things in a general regularity. If basic contents are to consist of more than merely phenomenal microevents, then we need some other sort of characteristic intrinsic properties. The unsaturated properties, say valences of attention, are not adequate in themselves to introduce other sorts of microevents. The only plausible and suitably concrete candidates seem to be causal powers. Let me put it this way: A causal law cannot be a statement about regularities except when there are entities to enter into such a regular pattern. Causal properties cannot be constituted by regularities among microevents within a basic content unless those microevents are present in that basic content, and microevents cannot fail to have characteristic intrinsic properties. I'm not a good late empiricist who believes in the regularity analysis and laughs at lockean powers, because I believe that phenomenalism is false, at least in the account it would give of the range of basic contents. There is more to be dreamt of than that. This of course is not to deny that some "causal laws" are regularities; it is just to deny that regularities can constitute *all* causal properties of microevents. If phenomenalism is false as an account of basic content, then irreducible causal powers are coherently conceivable.[7]

Objection Two: Is it really clear that microevents need characteristic intrinsic properties? And of course there are null colors and sounds available. Maybe we can treat entities with causal properties and no phenomenal properties of the familiar sort as consisting of microevents with null phenomenal properties as their characteristic intrinsic properties. The differences between the powers of such microevents might be treated as differences in their relations.

Reply: There may be ways to do this which are merely notational variants of C, which capture the same contents in a different way. But note that we need to be able to talk about the instantiation of the same power in different contents, where there might not be the same sorts of other microevents around to have the same relations to. Any proper characterization of the differences of the powers of microevents by reference to differences in their relations would need to deploy relations to merely possible entities, which a microevent with a certain power might have independently of whether other specific microevents are present in its basic content.[8] These are in effect intrinsic properties, though I think somewhat awkwardly characterized. The traditional physicalist story cited at the beginning of this chapter shows, it seems, that we can at least coherently conceive contents which include entities with causal properties but without standard phenomenal properties. These must be captured by appeal to microevents with causal powers of the sort I will characterize or a mere notational variant. The "phenomenalist" resources deployed in the last chapter and in orthodox regularity accounts of causation are not enough.

Objection Three: There are other "reductive" accounts of causation to consider. For instance, David Lewis has proposed a counterfactual analysis, according to which an event B causally depends on an event A just in case A and B occur and a certain conditional with a false antecedent, a certain "counterfactual conditional", is true: If A had not occurred, then B would not have occurred.[9]

Reply: This analysis is also subject to a variety of special difficulties,[10] but for our purposes the following difficulty is sufficient: What in a basic content could make such a counterfactual true? The instantiation of some intrinsic causal power might ground the truth of the counterfactual, but then we wouldn't have a reductive account of causal powers. Perhaps some may suggest that there is an irreducible true counterfactual proposition present in a basic content, but such a thing is too abstract to be an element of basic content. Lewis holds that the relevant counterfactual is true of a "possible world" (we might substitute "basic content") just in case there is another possible world in which the antecedent of the conditional is true and the consequent is also true, and which is more similar to the original world than is any other in which the antecedent is true but the consequent false.[11] There are various ways to understand these claims, depending in what way and with what seriousness we take the references to possible worlds and their relations of similarity, and what sorts of similarity we take to be relevant. But again, we face a dilemma. Either this sort of account turns out to be an awkward notational variant of the view that there are causal powers, or it implies that causal properties are not suitably intrinsic. Like regularity accounts which invoke relations to merely possible entities, these claims might be a complicated way of expressing the presence of intrinsic causal powers. But if they aren't, then they also don't provide us with an appropriate way to capture all the differences between basic contents, which do possess the differences which C expresses by speech of intrinsic causal powers. The same purely phenomenal basic content cannot differ in its relations of "similarity" to other purely phenomenal basic contents, and we need to be able to capture differences in the powers instantiated in worlds which are phenomenally identical. Phenomenalism cannot capture the range of basic contents or "possible worlds".

Objection Four: Some hold that causation is a special irreducible *relation* between *actual* events, or perhaps between properties exhibited by events.

Reply: It might be a relational fact that some specific event causes some specific other. But still the powers which microevents can exhibit are intrinsic in the specific way I have suggested in the preceding replies.

Objection Five: Even some who accept *intrinsic* causal powers may quarrel with their irreducibility. Sometimes it is thought that to have a certain causal power is to have a certain physical micro-structure which underwrites that power.

Reply: But what could such a structure be but a configuration of smaller entities with causal powers of their own? And one cannot reduce all powers exhibited in basic contents to lower level structure in this way; microevents are spatio-temporal *simples*, which may be parts of other concrete entities but which have no spatio-temporal parts themselves.[12] If microevents have intrinsic causal powers, then they must have irreducible causal powers.

Objection Six: Chapter Three proposed that modal claims, claims about possibility and necessity, are mere artifacts of the approach apparatus, and that basic contents were unpolluted by such artifacts. But causal powers introduce modality and necessity into basic contents. If a power is instantiated in the world, it *necessitates* that the rest of the world be some way rather than another.

Reply: *This* sort of modality and real necessity is not the sort which Chapter Three discusses and dismisses.

Objection Seven: Despite all this, the traditional skepticism of empiricism regarding irreducible causal powers is well-motivated, particularly under the shadow thrown by the traditional empiricist account of the realization of our thought. If content is rooted in experience, and if experience is merely phenomenal, then there may be no room for the coherent conception of irreducible causal powers. Is it really clear that there are the other than phenomenal differences between basic contents which have been repeatedly insisted upon here?

Reply: As I've said, classical empiricism labored under an unduly constricted conception of experience. It failed to recognize that we experience certain things not because we *sense* things but because we *do* things. To adequately defuse empiricist objections to the intrinsic causal powers which C deploys, we will need to develop a better sense of how causal thought is realized in us. Though this is more properly a matter for Parts Two and Three, let me hazard an initial sketch in the following section, which will also set us up to complete, in section 4, the characterization of the powers recognized by C.

3

This section concerns the realization of thoughts with causal contents. Our capacity to conceive causal phenomena is, in the first instance, rooted in our capacity to *experience* causal phenomena. And this in turn is rooted in our capacity to *do* things. Hit a ball, push up against a bench or tree, walk or row into the wind, swim in a lake, and you'll experience causal powers. But it is important to distinguish the experience of causal powers from two other things in its near vicinity:

First, one might experience a change in one's phenomenal experience while swimming into the wind, a dynamic trajectory of phenomenal experience in the presence of such a wind away from one's expectation of the course that phenomenal experience would have taken in its absence. But this is not the experience of an intrinsic causal power of the sort we pursue here. A power might act to change the course of phenomenal experience, but it isn't that experience changing.

Second, we saw in the last chapter that there are a variety of tactile sense fields. They present sensations of effort and pressure, and it may be tempting to identify these with causal experience. But these are not to be identified with the causal experience which often accompanies them. A phenomenal element of experience involves a feel, a genuine passivity, which causal elements do not in fact exhibit.

How then can there be genuine causal experience? We are *agents*, who can do different things, walk or push or swim with greater or lesser force. And in striking or pushing or bracing ourselves with greater or lesser force, in doing one thing rather than another, in ourselves restricting the course of the world in one way rather than another, we perform actions which may be informed by thoughts with particular causal contents.

First of all, we can intend to do one thing rather than another, to make one restriction rather than another on the world. Second, we act into an immediate environment, of balls and water and gravity, which itself seems to exert causal powers of one sort rather than another, to make its own restrictions on things. And our action may be informed by our conception of the causal powers exhibited in that immediate environment, as we push through the water with greater force than the air, as we step lightly on the moon or tread mightily on Neptune.

Agents do things which are a function of their thoughts, in particular their intentions to act. They leap to a particular point on the ground, they reach out and grab a certain apple, or push toward a particular point in an oncoming wave. By acting into the world in a certain way, by jumping in a particular way to take advantage of a particular sort of wave, or reaching out in a particular way to meet a particular swing of a rope, an agent can act in a way informed by a thought that the world beyond it has one causal structure or another. It can exhibit the intention, in that situation, to exert one causal power of its own rather than another, to make or be itself a particular kind of restriction on the world.

This view of the realization of causal content is in some ways quite traditional. While empiricists since Hume have been skeptical about powers, even that arch-empiricist Berkeley recognized that we have a capacity for thought with causal contents which is rooted in a familiarity with our own powers.[13] Hume argued that we cannot *perceive* such powers, that they do not appear in our sense experience, but of course we and Berkeley might agree to *that*. As was suggested by some discussion in Chapter Four, it seems to me that the central idea of empiricism is that our thought is rooted in experience, and that we experience what we (take ourselves to) concretely interact with, and that this includes what we act on as well as what we sense. So I'm inclined to speak of causal experience, and think that Locke and Berkeley were better empiricists than Hume might have allowed. But, of course, it isn't worth fighting over labels. If you don't like my way of putting this, feel free to put the point in another way. Certainly it seems that we have some concrete intercourse with the causal, through our motor activity, which gives us a capacity for certain sorts of thought we otherwise would lack.

Obviously, this account of the realization of causal thought requires more adequate development. But there is one question, regarding what *sort* of causal content thought can have in this way, which we should immediately address. You will act towards a wave in exactly the same way regardless of your beliefs about its tiny causal details. And your beliefs about the causal structure of things not present in immediate experience, say the far side of the moon, are not so directly revealed in your immediate behavior as are beliefs about the gross causal structure of an oncoming wave. Further, we can understand causal powers which, it seems, *cannot* be had by anything in our immediate environment, for instance those exerted at the surface of the sun. The puzzle is how we can have thoughts with causal contents which are not present in immediate experience.

One solution to *part* of the puzzle is obviously suggested by a necessary parallel treatment of phenomenal contents. Causal elements which *might* be present in experience but are not so present are no harder to conceive than similar colors. There are some causal elements present in immediate experience. *That* experience is realized through immediate action in the way we have just considered. But we can also entertain the thought of other forms of immediate causal experience through our sense of what our immediate action and causal experience might have been. Just as we can think of phenomenal microevents which do not match our immediate experience, but our past experience, or objects unseen, or another's experience, so too we can think of causal microevents like those we might presently experience but which are at points unseen, or in the past, or experienced by others. By imagining ourselves much smaller or larger or in a different place in the world, we can entertain causal contents which would otherwise be unavailable to us, including details of molecular structure and the far side of the moon. We are in fact capable of experiencing causal powers quite similar to those we believe to be exhibited at the center of the sun, though on a perhaps unexpected axis of similarity. We can experience analogues of the powers of the sun on a different spatial or temporal scale. For instance, we actually might experience concrete entities which model the powers of the sun quite well, say a luminous foot-round globe tugging to scale on a circling planet-colored pea. And we can certainly experience things which model the powers of the small particles which constitute the conflagration at the center of the sun. So causal powers which outrun our experience in the manner of those on the sun may be conceived in something like the same way we conceive of colored objects too small or large to really see, though our ordinary ways of thinking about the similarities of causal powers may hide this.

Clearly our capacity to conceive these additional causal contents is still bound in some sense by our contingent constitution as animals, just as our capacities to conceive the analogous phenomenal contents are bound. We cannot come in the ways I have already discussed to thoughts of causal microevents which have powers sufficiently unlike those which might appear in our experience. Still, there are yet coherently conceivable powers even more foreign to our experience than those found on the surface of the sun, for instance powers which work backwards in time or over great distances. There are similarities and differences between even these powers and the powers we *can* experience which we can understand, because we can understand the similarities and differences between the contents of the restrictions they make. And this understanding is sufficient to constitute for us the sense of those sorts of powers as something which might concretely be. Our capacity to entertain these causal elements which cannot be present in our immediate experience is rooted in the fact that we can relatively characterize causal powers by noting the contents of the restrictions they make. We can come to the conception of a power by deploying our understanding of the *content* of its causal restriction.

I am telling a story with distinct steps. We can think of causal restrictions in the first place because we can perform them. But we can come to see particular restrictions as relatively characterizable in one way rather than another. We can understand the relative characterizations of powers which we cannot immediately experience. And so we can come to the thought of those other powers. It is not an accident that causal notions can be extended and refined in this way. It is rooted in the very nature of powers as restrictions that there be some way to relatively characterize those restrictions. Since C generates an account of the coherently conceivable, it naturally generates an analogous account of coherently conceivable powers, and it is this account which we have deployed so far. There is a real disanalogy between the causal powers of microevents and the intrinsic phenomenal properties characteristic of sense fields. It lies in the fact that powers are restrictions and hence can be relatively characterized by the contents of those restrictions. This makes the conception of powers subject to a kind of refinement and development unavailable in our conception of phenomenal properties. But that follows quite naturally from the notion of a power.

Of course, we haven't yet considered the promised modification of our manner of relatively characterizing powers required by the most primitive powers, the powers which we can experience. But let me for the moment turn to other pressing objections and questions.

Objection One: Chapter Four argued that basic content must be rooted in experience, because what we might experience closely limits our sense of what the world might be, and governs what we can coherently and sincerely take to be basic in truth. But now it seems we've admitted to C causal powers which are not very directly rooted in experience.

Reply: In fact, *all* the causal powers invoked by C are rooted in experience. C is rooted in experience, and it limits quite severely the powers we can relatively characterize. It's just that the manner in which all causal contents are rooted in experience is not quite the same as that in which phenomenal contents are so rooted.

Objection Two: Still, there is a quite significant disanalogy between phenomenal and causal experience. There are artifacts of sense experience; our sense experience is misleading in certain ways. For instance, we may experience color when there is no color. But if we act into the world in one way rather than another, then that's that. There are no artifacts of causal experience. And this in turn makes it hard to see how our own introspectible *sense* of our powers, relatively characterizable and refinable in the way we have developed here, is much relevant to the causal contents of intentions we exhibit by *in fact* doing one thing rather than another.

My complete reply to this objection will be a long time in coming. In fact, it involves the central issue of Part Three. But my answer eventually will be that there is a quite significant and disturbing analogy between our situations as sensers and doers in this respect, that there may well be artifacts of even our causal experience. When I say that the phenomenal is what we can sense, the unwary may take this to imply that the phenomenal, say color, is really there for us to sense, that it is a part of the world. Philosophers are unlikely to make this mistake. But I am using "do" in a closely analogous way, and let me now at least hint at something we will eventually confront: The things we seem able to get at by action, in the sense invoked at the beginning of Chapter Four, may be as contaminated by illusory artifacts of experience as the things we seem to get at through perception. There are, in fact, artifactual modes of manipulation as well as artifactual modes of sense presentation of objects. Because of the peculiarities of our motor capacities, we "do" things, concrete things we experience in the manner of causal contents, which aren't really there to be done. Making sense of this will be a tall order, but the need will be thrust upon us in a while. For now let me simply say that the discussion of realization in this part is meant merely to motivate as intuitive and initially plausible the account of basic content provided here. That account will in the end be subject to pressures of various sorts, when we see how unintuitive the world really is. Now let me turn to some questions:

Question One: There are a number of phenomenal fields present in momentary experience. Is there only one causal field present in experience?

Reply: It seems to me that there is only one, and that this is rooted in another aspect of the analogy between phenomenal and causal contents. There are a number of distinct sensory organs, but really only one motor organ. While we have distinct hands and legs, still we seem able to manipulate all of them to do roughly the same sorts of things. We can exert pressure and manipulate things by jaw or hand or leg in at least roughly the same way, and even, by moving around, in at least roughly the same places. A creature who *could* act in two radically different ways on the same objects, say in our ordinary way and also by telepathy, or acted into two radically different arenas, say on one side of the earth and the other, might be a creature with two causal fields in immediate experience. But we seem not to be like that. On the other hand, there are at least some not entirely unreasonable candidates for distinct output organs in humans, which might suggest to some the presence of distinct causal fields. Perhaps by speaking, or by releasing hormones or smells in a way which has emotional influence on ourselves or others, or by walking upright in a gravitational field, or by acting mentally, we exert causal influence in a radically different way than we do by the manipulation of our hands. Indeed, there will be reason to consider the first of these particular possibilities again, in Part Two. Perhaps this might even be ground for an expansion of C, though I think that it isn't.

Question Two: Since thoughts with causal contents are realized through our motor capacities, does this mean that training and extending our motor capacities can extend our capacity for thought? Can athletes, pianists, dancers, and practitioners of yoga think things which the more awkward cannot?

Reply: These sorts of training seem to create no radical discontinuity of capacity, at least no more than the analogous training of the sense capacities of painters and wine-tasters. I assume that neither sort of training requires a modification of C, at least given our usual idealization, which ignores small individual differences. In any case, all normal adult humans can refine their conceptions of causal contents by considering the contents of restrictions, and that should take up any remaining slack. Still, if a development of our capacities were radical enough, and of the right sort, then there might well be a genuine expansion of thought content. This will become evident in Part Three.

Question Three: What about tools? Do they extend our capacity to think things, by extending our capacity to do things?

Reply: Note that tools too have a sensory analogue, in instruments which extend vision and such. Some *hypothetical* instruments and tools, attached to us in such a manner that radically new motor or sensory capacities are wired into us and our cognition, instruments and tools we don't manipulate via our ordinary sense and motor capacities but directly instead, might require an extension of C, just as any radical development in our motor capacities might. But ordinary tools, like ordinary instruments, do not require such an extension. They are manipulated via our ordinary motor and sensory capacities. We can, by the action of actual instruments and tools, extend in some intuitive sense what we can do. Through such tools we can act at a distance and possess powers beyond our unaided capacity. But, on the other hand, it seems that we need some independent capacity to understand what such an instrument or tool does to allow us to use it in a way which can reveal our thought. So such an instrument or tool cannot really extend the contents we can entertain beyond those we antecedently understand. Perhaps in learning to use a tool we "learn", in some intuitive sense, to conceive more contents, but no more than in other forms of learning. No more than other forms of learning does this sort suggest that the account of basic contents should be relativized to times in individual lives. The education of normal people still traces a trajectory through things which all normal human adults *can* think, in the sense relevant to basic content.

4

Let me now draw some threads together. Recall that my account of causal elements makes two key commitments. First, some microevents are causal microevents, whose intrinsic properties are irreducible causal powers which are relatively characterizable in the way we have sketched. Second, our capacity to entertain contents involving causal powers rests on our capacity to experience such powers, which occurs when we act in one way rather than another.

Consider a contrasting, Hume-style account. According to this competitor, the only characteristic intrinsic properties of microevents are phenomenal. When phenomenal events exhibit a certain regularity, when events of two types are constantly conjoined, we form an association of ideas, a habit which leads us to expect an event of the second type whenever we experience an event of the first type. We then say "the first event causes the second", but that does nothing more than report the regularity and gild the world with our expectation.

Note that there are two claims such a humean makes, one about contents, and another about realization. First, there are only phenomenal microevents. When they exhibit a certain regularity, then there is the objective basis for a causal claim. Second, the realization of our causal thought, which is in fact speech about causation, is rooted merely in our phenomenal experience and our habitual expectations. On this view, causal properties are not intrinsic irreducible powers, and the realization of causal thought involves no causal experience of the sort I have invoked.

Now let me present a case which motivates my view against Hume's. I claim that we can coherently imagine two concrete situations which are "phenomenally identical", which have similar phenomenal microevents in similar locations and in which similar people have similar phenomenal experiences, but in which the powers exhibited are distinct. For instance, imagine someone stepping into a wave, and then imagine a phenomenal twin of that someone stepping into a wave which is twice as forceful, but with a correspondingly more powerful step.

Imagine that in the second circumstance all the waves and winds are twice as forceful, but that so are all the people.

It seems to me that these are different circumstances, so that the humean account of what we can coherently imagine is incorrect. It also seems to me that the phenomenal twins think different things, and that this underwrites my account of the realization of causal thought over the humean account. To change our motor capacities would be to change the causal contents we entertain. For instance, the much stronger twin has a different conception of the power of his wave than the weaker twin has of his wave, and a different intention when he steps. This would be dramatically revealed if he were suddenly transported into the world of the weaker twin, to face the weaker wave. Now let me consider some objections.

Objection One: The twins think the same things in their allegedly different circumstances.

Reply: But a third party, who experienced both circumstances, would experience a difference in the force of the waves and the stepping of the twins. A concrete difference between two levels of force might show up *within* a particular content, so it is legitimate to postulate a concrete difference in levels of force *between* contents.[14] And if these two scenarios are indeed different, it does seem that the twins have different intentions.

Objection Two: This is too quick. Recall the phenomenal experience of pressure. The two circumstances we imagined were supposed to be phenomenally identical, so that the phenomenal pressure each twin feels must be the same. But we might reasonably wonder if the difference in the experience of the third party might be a difference in phenomenal pressure.

Reply: Phenomenal pressure need not vary with the causal experience of pressure, as in fact the phenomenal similarity of the twins, or even our own habituation to pressure, can reveal. So there might be a third party whose phenomenal experience of the two waves was identical, and yet had a different causal experience of them. Imagine for instance someone with two sets of limbs, one set twice as strong as another and habituated to a more forceful environment. If that person variously deployed the two sets of limbs to walk into the two waves, the differences between their intentions in deploying the alternative limbs, and the differences between the waves, would be revealed.

Objection Three: We might concede that the twin case involves two different coherently conceivable scenarios, and still try to capture that difference other than by appeal to irreducible forces. For instance, we might deploy counterfactual conditionals. It's true in the more forceful circumstance that if the weaker twin had stepped into the wave, then he would have been brushed aside. It's true in the less forceful scenario that if the stronger twin had stepped into the wave, then he would have tripped because he was over-rambunctious.

Reply: But what about the two scenarios is supposed to ground the truth of those counterfactuals? Some difference between the two scenarios is required, and it must be a concrete difference relevant to basic content. What else but powers can do the trick?

Objection Four: We might grant that these are different scenarios and that the difference involves irreducible causal powers, and yet maintain that we come to a conception of those powers in a different way than has been proposed here. Perhaps we can *experience* only phenomenal contents, but there is some way that content generation operations can yield the coherent concrete conception of powers.

Reply: Until we have a more complete story than this, we should be skeptical of claims that there is another sort of content generation operation, or that any of those introduced in Chapter Three can do the trick. For instance, word-mediation could not *introduce* the conception of concrete powers, if the account of word-mediation which was suggested in Chapter Three is at all correct. And in any case, thoughts with such dependent contents would be realized in a way which leaves them too internal to a psychology, too far removed from the peripheral motor intentions which most obviously bear causal contents. It is hard to see how such a neo-humean account could provide for the difference in the thoughts of our phenomenal twins.

Objection Five: The two twins have the same *introspectible* experience. So how can they then differ in introspectible thought content, which is supposed to be rooted in experience.

Reply: In fact, we *will* need to develop an account of introspectible causal experience which denies that the twins have the same such experience. But this constitutes no objection. In the end, we will see that is only in the false light of a misleading but introspectible mode of manipulation that there seems to be the sort of structure in the world which these scenarios presume. It is only because we introspect such a structure in our experience that we "act" in the relevant ways. This, again, is an issue which will be joined in Part Three.

Objection Six: One might question the coherence of the twin case. For instance, think of all the complicated adjustments which would be required if there were to be a world phenomenally identical to this one, but in which people stepped twice as hard into waves twice as forceful. Wouldn't everything need to be twice as forceful? But of course force as it is conceived in our physics is related to all sorts of other quantities. For instance, people in the more forceful world would hit volleyballs twice as hard, and if those volleyballs weren't to go farther, they'd need greater mass, or to be in a stronger gravitational field.

Reply: It seems that, with the appropriate modification of all the causal properties of the other entities in the world, this could be worked out coherently and still generate an intuitively distinct scenario. But even if it couldn't be, still it is important to see that post-galilean "force", force as conceived in our physics and tied to various other properties, is a kind of sophisticated elaboration of a more primitive conception present in our experience and not necessarily mathematically characterized in exactly the traditional physical manner. There is a primitive sort of restriction which we can "perform" (in the same perhaps illusory sense that we "sense" color), which involves a dynamical power of a very primitive sort, and which post-galilean conceptions of force refine in various ways. Our capacity for causal experience is quite limited, limited to differences in the force of this primitive sort with which we can pursue various manipulations of objects. It is very much restricted by our kinds of muscles and joints and the motor action we can perform. It is this very primitive sort of power which I mentioned briefly at the end of section 1, as the central sort of power which I would only characterize last. The centrality of these sorts of primitive powers explains why, I think, we have a physics that would occur naturally to baseball players and pool sharks.

Let me elaborate. It seems quite crucial to the powers we can experience, to the causal contents our motor intentions can exhibit, that we have musculature and joints and motor control systems of certain sorts. For instance, keeping our shoulders straight, we can move our hands by controlling three joints--at shoulder, elbow, and wrist--through respectively three, one, and three degrees of freedom. By our motor intentions, we can project a hand into a position and orientation in a familiar space of three dimensions. These motor intentions control antagonist muscles at each of the joints, muscles with little rowing spindles.[15] And the muscles allow us to exert a kind of mechanical force in that space of our movement. We can move our limbs with more or less force and speed and in various directions. With these more or less solid limbs, we can push or pull with more or less force at solid, resisting, sometimes moving things. The solidity and resistance of our limbs and these things seem themselves to be a kind of force. There are here forces exerted in space and over time, and causing certain movements through space in light of other forces. A physics of mechanical force in three spatial dimensions is just what creatures such as we might be expected to come to, once we had become convinced of the illusory nature of our phenomenal experience.[16] If we had other sorts of output capacities than we do, say capacities to change phenomenal colors directly and at will, and with different degrees of force or insistence, and if things in our environment possessed similar powers, then very different sorts of powers might have been present in our causal experience. Very different sorts of primitive powers would be present in basic contents.[17]

We have admittedly very ancient notions of powers, for instance powers of persistence and to burn and to perform mental activities, which are different than the primitive dynamical powers, but even these seem to exhibit some sophistication, to be secondary and dependent. They too depend on our ability to understand a power by understanding the content of its restriction, which I freely deployed in my initial characterization of powers. That initial characterization was in a certain way misleading, because it left the really central and primitive powers to come in as an afterthought.

The full story of the realization of our causal thought must be complex. But let me elaborate at least a bit on some of the hints we have collected. We can distinguish two steps.

First step: By motor experience we become capable of thought with a certain sort of causal content, involving a certain kind of mechanical force in three-space. This introduces causal contents of a very particular kind. These contents include forces which differently *move* objects through time and space depending on various forces of resistance, forces that are specially connected to the spatial and temporal structure we experience. They are a kind of force by which a particular sort of spatial and temporal circumstance, say a certain trajectory of a limb, can be pursued, which then, given the presence of various sorts of resisting forces, can lead to one trajectory of a volleyball or one sort of locomotion rather than another. Some of the effects of such forces seem to be phenomenal. Volleyballs can be conceived to have phenomenal colors, so that hitting a volleyball can move a white thing. But, of course, even merely causal experience has a spatial structure, and the purest form of these powers seem to be powers which restrict a kind of mechanical world, where the things restricted at least most directly are themselves characterized by their forces and spatial trajectories. Maybe they have phenomenal properties too, but on the side, so that it doesn't directly matter whether they are red or blue or colorless. The primitive powers are powers to affect the spatial and temporal trajectories of entities, and in particular to do that in the face of other such forces. The contents of these restrictions are tied to no particular intrinsic phenomenal properties.

Second step: To conceive such a primitive force is to conceive something with a content, which restricts the world in one way rather than another. Given our capacity to understand other sorts of contents, we hence naturally come to the conception of other powers, for instance of the power of fire to cause pain. We come to see the pain which accompanies falling into the fire as more than a mere regularity in the world; we come to see it as caused. Likewise, by the mediation of words and abstract thought we can come to conceive the contents of powers, and hence powers, with an even greater refinement. All these new powers enter into basic contents, and hence lead to still further contents and hence further restrictions, so that we end up with something like the complicated structure of powers articulated in section 1, but with a special place for the primitive powers which we experience. So let those primitive sorts of powers be expressible in C.

While this two-step story might seem to give human thought of powers a certain limitless extent, certainly less limited than our thought of the phenomenal, still coherently conceivable powers are restrictions with coherently conceivable contents. And we will see in Part Three that the kind of asymmetrical restriction involved in causation, combined with the spatio-temporality constraining all basic contents, exacts a significant cognitive price. It places a significant limit on our capacity to understand the world.

5

What sorts of spatio-temporal relations can causal microevents possess? First of all, causal microevents can exhibit all the spatio-temporal structure possessed by phenomenal microevents and discussed in the previous chapter.[18] In effect, there may be a causal field in a basic content analogous to the various sorts of phenomenal fields.[19] But, causal microevents[20] may also possess an additional sort of spatio-temporal structure.

This additional structure is provided by the paths by which causal influence can pass through the world. Let me elaborate. A causal microevent may "immediately restrict" another microevent, causal or phenomenal. This happens when the first causally restricts the world to include the second without some intervening causal chain.

We can also conceive basic contents with a dense causal structure, in which between any two causal microevents on some path by which causal influence passes through the world there is yet a third intervening causal microevent. In such contents there is no "immediate restriction", yet there is an analogue. And this analogue can also serve to fix relations of immediate restriction when they do happen to be present. Certain microevents lie along certain causal paths in dense and even continuous contents, with some between others on a particular causal route, a particular route which causal influence could travel. Let C recognize ordered relations had by sets of microevents along a causal path in that order.[21] Call these the "O" (for *order*) relations.

O relations help to constitute a crucial sort of spatio-temporal structure. For instance, when all the O-relations in a content are fixed, so too, at least to a first approximation, are the continuous causal paths or curves in that content, the paths which particles or observers might traverse. And these in turn fix a good deal of spatio-temporal structure. We will return to these matters at greater length in Part Three, but here for instance is Larry Sklar reporting a result of David Malament regarding the spacetimes of general relativity: "Given any two spacetimes (taken to be four-dimensional manifolds with pseudo-Riemannian metrics of Lorentzian signature) any bijection which takes continuous causal curves into continuous causal curves will be a homeomorphism! In other words, the full topology of the spacetime will be fixed by its class of continuous causal curves."[22]

For the Malament reduction to succeed, not only those causal curves which causal influence actually traverses, but those curves it *can* traverse, must be fixed. But the notion of causal power invoked by C is so broad that when the O relations of causal microevents in a content are fixed, so too are these "merely possible" paths. It is important to recall that C's notion of causal restriction is so broad that even bits of the void are causal microevents, which "restrict" other bits of it. And what in common parlance are merely "possible" causal chains involve actual restrictions as characterized by C.

The topology of a spacetime isn't its full spatio-temporal structure. For instance, other resources must be deployed to fix metrics within such a spacetime if we abandon the kind of metrical structure present in phenomenal fields, perhaps a specification of conventional rigid measuring rods and clocks or their like.[23] And we will need to take special care to capture the *chirality*, the handedness, of spatio-temporal relations. Distinctions between spacetimes which are left and right mirror-images of one another are not fixed when the continuous causal curves of those contents are fixed unless those curves are chirally oriented in the appropriate way. C must have some capacity to express this difference by expressing the chiral orientation of order relations. Indeed, it must be capable of expressing all the flavors of chirality we noted in section 4 of Chapter Six.

We will return to some of these issues in Part Three. But this completes our rather rough and ready initial characterization of basic contents, and the language C which captures them.

NOTES

1. There are certain qualifications to this, which will emerge shortly.
2. This might imply that others are true as well.
3. Note that this isn't a centering of the sort which we have already seen that some basic contents exhibit.
4. Note also that hence not all stories of C will generate power descriptions, since for instance some include no causal microevents at all.
5. These might be fused to other causal microevents if there is a substantival space, a space which is distinct from the material entities it contains.
6. David Hume, *A Treatise of Human Nature*, L.A. Selby-Bigge and P.H. Nidditch (editors) (Oxford: Clarendon Press, 1985); *Enquiry Concerning Human Understanding*, in David Hume, *Enquiries*, L.A. Selby-Bigge and P.H. Nidditch (editors) (Oxford: Clarendon Press, 1975).
7. There are alternative, pretty implausible but coherently conceivable, sorts of laws: Laws might be ghostly things which themselves exercise causal powers, either somehow reading how the events of the world are and then acting alone on that information, or acting along with those worldly events. But in any case these alternatives provide no grounds for objection to this argument.
8. Except, of course, that the world in which a power is instantiated must meet the content of that restriction.
9. David Lewis, "Causation", *Journal of Philosophy* 70, 1973, 556-567.
10. Jaegwon Kim, "Causes and Counterfactuals", *Journal of Philosophy* 70, 1973, 570-572.
11. David Lewis, *Counterfactuals* (Oxford: Oxford University Press, 1973).
12. At least within their home content.
13. George Berkeley, *Three Dialogues Between Hylas and Philonous*, Dialogue Three.
14. This seems like a reasonable inference for a case involving ordinary concrete properties, but not for a case involving the mere bare dissimilarity introduced by relative haecceities. This is because of the very different ways in which thoughts with the first pair of features would be realized.
15. Eye-hand coordination which constitutes merely know how, and also direct feedback and reflex arcs, are no doubt involved in the execution of motor action, but still there seem to be motor intentions of this sort as well.

16. We were lucky that a plausible and coherent theory was there to be adopted, but we will see that in the end it isn't all that plausible, and up to some point we had good luck with phenomenal colors as well.
17. We will return to these issues in Chapter Sixteen.
18. More than one causal microevent may be found at the same location, I think, and this may help underwrite our capacity to distinguish between concrete material entities and occupied locations in a containing substantival space.
19. For reasons which will become relevant in Part Three, it may be important to distinguish between two kinds of metrical structure which may be present in a causal field. The "affine structure" of a field is fixed when it is fixed which paths between points are the geodesics, the locally shortest paths. On the other hand, there might be a fuller and more familiar sort of metrical structure.
20. And phenomenal microevents which are fused to or caused by those causal microevents.
21. Such a relation isn't necessarily symmetric. Consider for instance situations in which there is a finite upper speed by which causal influence can spread, and in which event A can causally influence B but B cannot influence A.
22. Lawrence Sklar, "What Might be Right about the Causal Theory of Spacetime", *Synthese* 77, 155-171, 161.
23. On the definition of the metric in this way see Hans Reichenbach, *The Philosophy of Space and Time* (New York: Dover, 1958), 14.

Part Two

CONCEIVING AGENTS

CHAPTER EIGHT

THOUGHTS

Part One surveyed what humans can think. Parts Two and Three concern *how* they think it, the *realization* of human thought. They concern the nature of creatures capable of the range of thoughts articulated in Part One. When Galileo watched a red ball drop by his window, his experience was a thought in our broad sense. When he said to himself that the ball wasn't *really* red, that too was a thought. Our question now is what it is to have such thoughts, what resources of firing neurons, flapping tongues in the surrounding streets, or machinations of dubious spiritual substance, might constitute that.

Part Two in particular concerns the mere coherent possibility of thoughts, how we can coherently conceive that we think what we do. Our thoughts *are* coherently conceivable; there *are* coherently conceivable conditions which could serve to realize all the thoughts recognized by Part One. This part will sketch at least *hypothetical* conditions in basic content which would suffice for the existence of people with the capacity for such thoughts. They are conditions which are homey and familiar.

On the other hand, the *plausibility* of any coherently conceivable account of the realization of our thoughts is at best in serious doubt. That is the message of Part Three. How we can coherently conceive that we think what we do is not in fact how we do think what we do, because what we think is generally false. The basic contents which might ground the truth of human thoughts are rooted in experience. But our experience is, as we will see in Part Three, seriously misleading. Bluntly put, it is false. So our thoughts in general are false. And we will also see that coherently conceivable accounts of our experience must presume that it is veridical. Since it isn't veridical, there is no account of our experience which is at once plausible and coherently conceivable. And because our capacities for thought in general are rooted in our capacities for experience, likewise there is no plausible and coherently conceivable account of the realization of our thought in general.[1]

Still, if we ignore the difficulties introduced by our experience, if we simply and unreflectively assume a capacity for experience such as we seem to have, then we might make coherently conceivable *and* plausible sense of the rest of the conditions required for our thoughts.[2] In fact, the coherently conceivable account of our capacities for thoughts beyond experience which is constructed in this part will be to that degree also plausible. Our science has shown, Part Three argues, that our experience is very misleading. But it is only quite particular and (in one sense) relatively localized developments in our science which show our experience to be misleading. Even most of the psychologically relevant findings of that science may be grafted in a coherent way onto a commonsense understanding of the world, which takes it pretty much as our experience suggests. And if Galileo and the red ball had been roughly as humans saw and heard and felt them to be, if even their tiny and hidden details had been such as most human experiments and instruments would suggest, if for instance the fantastically complicated neural machinery behind Galileo's eyes had been more or less what some demonic but human vivisectionist would have uncovered, then we could coherently conceive the way his thought was realized.

In this part we will assume a fleshy, mundane world, which fits both commonsense conceptions rooted in our experience and plausible refinements of common sense suggested, for instance, by neuroscience and nineteenth century physics. Our thoughts will fit nicely into such a world. Only in the next part will we slip away from this happy compromise of our science and common sense. While this part concerns the mere coherent conceivability of our thought, I will assume here a world which grafts together suggestions of our experience, common sense, and science in a way which is also plausible in most respects. We will presume a concrete world in which phenomenal properties like phenomenal color are splashed onto concrete objects like tables, balls, and neurons. Aside from twentieth century physics, most of our post-galilean science fits quite nicely into that pre-galilean conception of things. Neurophysiology provides an especially important set of resources. In a world such as we seem to experience, but with the findings of our neurophysiology grafted on, the realization of our thought would be quite straightforward. Our science has shown us some things about neurons which can remove certain traditional worries about the realization of our thought by concrete and familiar resources, and also defuse certain contemporary philosophical worries rooted in rather highfalutin features of our thoughts. This can help focus us on what I take to be the real problem, the problem of Part Three.

A number of contemporary philosophers worry that concrete, mundane resources of the sort we will deploy in this part can't underwrite certain exotic features of our thought. For instance, some have raised concerns about what they consider the "normativity" or the infinity of that thought. And others worry about non-confirmable thoughts about the inaccessible past. I think that these rather highfalutin worries can be dissolved, in the manner I will suggest over this part. I worry about a much more mundane feature of our thoughts, how they are rooted in thoughts of the concrete objects which we experience. On the other hand, I think that we should be no more skeptical or mystical about thoughts than about all that familiar stuff. Thoughts aren't a *special* problem. The problem with thoughts is a problem we would have in any case.

Such a fleshy, concrete world as we presume here is what I later call the "forensic truth", or at least closely related to that. It is matched by a basic content which consists of both phenomenal and causal microevents, standing in both sorts of spatio-temporal structure introduced in Part One. It is coherently conceivable.

This world is a kind of cognitive paradise for humans. It roots the truth of many ordinary human conceptions, particularly the natural human conception of our own thought. It is a false paradise, but we'll stay there until forced out in Part Three.

A brief map of this part may be useful. This chapter constitutes an introduction to this part, and indeed the next as well. It reviews the nature of the thoughts whose realization we seek, considers some objections to a focus on thoughts, and sketches, in a rough initial way, various accounts of their realization. Chapter Nine concerns the arguments of those who are skeptical about the existence of thoughts. Most of those arguments were conceived in the first instance as arguments against the existence of meaningful speech, and Chapter Ten responds to this meaning skepticism by developing a positive account of meaningful language which will support our later account of word-mediated thought. Chapter Eleven sketches the primary plausible resources for the realization of our thoughts, which are neural resources. Chapter Twelve sketches a coherently conceivable and somewhat plausible, although as we will see in Part Three not *fully* plausible, account of the realization of our experience. It also discusses the important faculty I call the "primary imagination". Chapter Thirteen sketches an apparently plausible and coherently conceivable account of how we might have capacities for all the thoughts beyond experience which Part One suggests, if we had capacities of the sort discussed in Chapter Twelve. That will discharge the task of this part. We will have a coherently conceivable account of the realization of our thoughts. We will even have an account of our capacities for thought beyond experience which would mesh with the more plausible account of experience which we pursue, but don't catch, in Part Three.

1

What are thoughts? At least to a first approximation, they are just what Descartes would have indicated. To have thoughts is to think, and a thinking thing is "a thing that doubts, understands, affirms, denies, is willing, is unwilling, and which also imagines and has sensory perceptions."[3] But let me be a little more precise. Thoughts have two key features:

First of all, thoughts are psychological states. They intervene between the environment we perceive and the actions we perform in some way relevant to the explanation of that behavior. We experience things in our environment, and we do things. Our sensory experiences and intentions to act are thoughts in my sense, which mediate the effect of our environment on our behavior. Perhaps other thoughts intervene between our sensory experiences and motor intentions.

The second crucial feature of thoughts is that they have contents. In fact, the central and paradigmatic instances of thoughts, indeed all thoughts except word-mediated noncognitive thoughts, have *representational* contents, and hence possess intentionality and intensionality. They are about things, and under certain aspects rather than others. Content of the sort we seek is closely linked to introspectibility. We are attempting to vindicate thoughts with the intuitive range of contents articulated in Part One, with the kind of contents which, at least in the case of some of our thoughts, we can introspect.

I have already given reasons for thinking that intensional content is important. But it is symptomatic of current thinking that Kripke's seminal *Naming and Necessity* suggests an alternative to that traditional view without discussing either of its two central and traditional motivations, the intuitive differences in sense of some co-referential names, and the intuitive meaningfulness of non-referring names.[4] They become, respectively, a "puzzle" about belief, and a detail left to other authors.[5] What once seemed quite central phenomena now seem parasitic and secondary. But, as I've promised, by Part Three we will be in position to see that such phenomena are indeed central, because the world is not at all the way we conceive it to be.

Still, there may be other objections to my focus on thoughts here. I believe that our talk of thoughts is important talk. I believe that the primary feature of our self-conception is that we take ourselves to be agents, with psychologies which crucially involve a trajectory of thoughts with representational content. But even those who admit that thoughts with intentionality and intensionality are an important feature of our psychologies, may object to my focus on thoughts above all.

Objection One: Even if thoughts are a crucial component of our psychologies, other things are crucial as well. For instance, feelings and emotions and arousal of various kinds are central psychological phenomena, as are various states of character. And we shouldn't neglect those bits of our know how which aren't to be identified with knowledge that, for instance the inferential capacities of those who aren't self-conscious about logic. None of these states are thoughts. And yet they are clearly important psychological phenomena. To focus on thoughts as if they were the primary commitment of our self-conception is an error.

Let me reply to this objection in stages. First of all, some of the psychological states just mentioned are or involve thoughts, in ways which may not be immediately evident. For instance, not all of the states which might be called "emotions and feelings" are alike, but some of them are thoughts, or consist in part of thoughts. Sometimes a part of what it is to possess certain emotions and feelings is to have certain desires or to make certain judgments with representational content. These are thoughts in my broad sense. And part of what it is to have certain emotions and feelings is to have certain experiences. The experience of pain counts in ordinary discourse as both a sensation and a feeling, and other feelings seem to have similar experiential components. These experiences, like sensory experiences, are also thoughts in my broad sense.[6]

If we subtract thoughts from emotions and feelings, there *is* something left over, so my reply requires a second stage. For instance, when someone is anxious they are more apt to burst into tears and jump to conclusions. When someone is angry, they are more apt to yell at slight provocation. But some of the crucial effects of such states are clearly effects on thoughts, say jumping to conclusions. And in so far as they affect behavior, they often do so by affecting intentions to act. Such states are generally exhibited by their effects on the sequence of one's thoughts; they are dispositions to have particular thoughts in the presence of other particular thoughts. They cause perturbations in the sequence of one's thoughts. We should conclude that psychologies include such dispositions for thoughts as well as thoughts, but that is more a refinement than a rejection of the conception of a psychology we are pursuing here.

Of course, there may be some features of an emotion which bypass our psychology of thought entirely. For instance, some emotion-inducing smells may release hormones which make our hands shake without perturbing our thoughts, even our experience of smells. So there's a third stage of my reply: *These* features of an emotion are in only a very derivative and secondary way psychological phenomena. It is only because they afflict a creature capable of thoughts and hence intentional behavior, and because they are realized by conditions which are bound up in the realization of that creature's thoughts, that they count as psychological phenomena in even an extended sense.

I've so far spoken only about emotions and feelings, but similar things clearly could be said about arousal, if indeed that doesn't count as an emotion or feeling, and about character differences. And if our inference involves know how, still it will be realized in the particular sequence which our thoughts exhibit as we infer. Know how of all intuitive sorts must involve or affect some transition of our thoughts, somewhere between perception and motor intention.

Objection Two: Not merely thoughts, but particular *kinds* of thoughts, are crucial to our agency. And the conditions which realize the various kinds of thoughts are quite distinct. To lump the whole class of thoughts together, to focus on the realization of thoughts as a group, is to invite mistake. For instance, memories are crucially distinct from thoughts of the present, beliefs are very different from imaginings, judgment is quite unlike sensation, and cognitive attitudes, like belief and knowledge, are very different from conative attitudes, like desire, want, and fear. Beliefs and desires are realized in *radically* different ways, so that very different accounts of their realization are required. To pursue one account of the realization of all thoughts is to blunder.

Reply: Let me first focus on the last case, the belief-desire case, and then apply our discussion to the other troublesome cases. I wonder about the depth of the commitment of our tradition to distinct cognitive and conative states,[7] and of course even a deep commitment of our tradition may be wrong,[8] but the main point is this: Even if in fact our psychologies involve two sorts of thoughts, cognitive and conative, for instance beliefs and desires, that need not imply that beliefs and desires are realized in *radically* different ways, that we cannot provide a unitary account of what it is to have a thought with a certain content, be it a belief or a desire. The difference between a belief and a desire with the same content may be relatively trivial. Many contemporary models of mental states suggest that what makes such thoughts the thoughts they are, what gives them their particular content, is one thing, and what makes them into beliefs or desires in particular is another. The first thing might involve, for instance, some particular sort of causal relation to objects in the world such as we will consider later in the chapter, and the second thing might involve the "functional" role of the thoughts, the other mental states to which they lead.[9] This feature of contemporary models of mentation seems to me to be laudable. I admit that it is coherently conceivable that there be two radically different sorts of thoughts, with quite distinct conditions of realization. It is a possible way thoughts could be. I just don't think it's the actual way.

The account of the realization of our thoughts which follows goes some distance towards vindicating this hunch. But even if this possibility can't be vindicated, there are only three sorts of evidence which are relevant to its assessment: First, the behavioral (and *genuine* introspective) phenomena to be explained.[10] Certainly the proper account of our psychology must explain cognitive and conative behavioral phenomena of an obvious kind, someone reasoning coolly or running about in passionate pursuit, and perhaps this requires that we recognize different types of thoughts. Second, the contingent details suggested bottom-up by our neurophysiology, or our spiritual substance, or whatever else realizes our psychology. These suggest that the really significant distinctions are, for instance, among thoughts and things which perturb the sequence of thoughts, rather than between beliefs and desires per se. Third, top-down constraints underwritten by the notion of a thought. These require that if there are human thoughts then they ought to have the contents sketched in Part One, and there may be necessary constraints on the realization of thoughts with such contents, such as the realization dependencies suggested there. Maybe there are no thoughts, but if there are, then they should have intuitive contents. Even *this* constraint on thoughts is defeasible, but we shouldn't give it up unless forced; it should have some priority. Because thoughts with the contents surveyed in Part One are a crucial semantic resource, and because the possession of such an intuitive content is a legitimate conceptual constraint on any psychology which is at all like we take ours to be, we have legitimate grounds to pursue this one relatively "conceptual" and quasi-aprioristic constraint, but we should avoid hobbling an account of the realization of our thoughts in advance by other such constraints, for instance by the demand that it treat beliefs and desires in radically different ways because of some suggestions of our familiar psychological idiom. If we come to the conclusion that beliefs and desires are radically different in their manner of realization, then it should be because of details of how they contingently happen to be constituted, and not because of some prior commitment of common sense. A psychology crucially involves a sequence of thoughts with content, which mediates between environment and action. The invocation of such states with intuitive content is the crucial commitment of our tradition of psychological explanation. Hence the three sorts of consideration just cited are the only sorts which are really relevant to determining the actual form of our psychologies. What realizes someone's psychology, the behavioral and introspective phenomena it explains, and the semantic resources it invokes and what they require, are the only legitimate constraints on what it is.[11]

That's all about the belief-desire case. Let's briefly consider the other cases. There are various resources we might deploy to distinguish between kinds of thoughts without postulating radically different sorts of realization conditions, and these resources seem generally sufficient. Some cases we can treat as many contemporary models treat beliefs and desires. For instance, the functional roles of beliefs and imaginings may be distinct. We can also sometimes appeal to differences in content. For instance, occurrent memories and occurrent beliefs about the present differ in content. And sometimes we can appeal to differences between what is a thought and what is not. Certain non-occurrent memories seem to be dispositions for thoughts rather than thoughts. The unified account of the realization of thoughts which follows in fact often treats thoughts with different contents in a significantly different way. It is this sort of difference, and the difference between thoughts and dispositions for thoughts, rather than various alleged differences between different sorts of thoughts with the same content, which seem to me most significant. But the differences we will track do underwrite some of the traditional differences between kinds of thoughts as well. They will automatically deliver some of those traditional differences, relieving us of any need to scratch around for additional details to underwrite some intuitive differences in kind. For instance, some traditional "judgments" are probably to be identified with word-mediated thoughts, which according to the account which follows not only have significantly different sorts of content from sense experiences, at least in normal cases, but are realized in a significantly different way.

Objection Three: No matter how central to our self-conception they are, thoughts are suspicious entities. They are difficult to individuate, and we should accept "no entity without identity". How can thoughts be counted?

Reply: Recall that we are not yet committed to there being distinct and detachable contents. Likewise we are not really committed to distinct and detachable thoughts, tightly individuated by specific brain locations, for instance. For people to have thoughts with contents is just for those people to be in certain states, and our goal here is to understand what those states are, whether for instance they do in fact involve the existence of distinct and separable contents or thoughts. My talk about the contents of thoughts is just an indirect way of talking about people. Nor should my talk of the intervention of thoughts between environment and behavior be misunderstood. While someone's experience may explain their intentions to act, this need not necessarily involve causal relations between spatially distinct things. There are facts about what we think. And there are facts about how our thoughts change and might change in content over time. There are some facts about the *way* in which we think what we do, perhaps whether we believe or desire something. There are also facts about the way in which our thoughts are realized. All these facts may, though again they may not, suggest some ways in which someone's thoughts may be distinguished. But these are all the facts relevant to thought-individuation, and they may leave some indeterminacy, so that there is no fact of the matter about whether some state of someone counts as one thought or two. I believe that they leave a lot of indeterminacy about that. So I believe that we shouldn't worry too much about counting thoughts, which are more like moods than pebbles on a beach.

Indeed, I also believe that it is probably too optimistic even to expect that there are always facts about what we think. Even if we can't count our thoughts, it may seem that we should be able to say when we think something, and when we do not. For instance, it may seem that we should be able to say when there are thoughts as opposed to dispositions for thoughts. There should at least be facts about what we think, as opposed to what we are disposed to think. But in some cases there are reasons to doubt that even this is true. Certainly the contingent details which happen to realize our psychologies may help determine when we have, for instance, a particular thought as opposed to a mere disposition for that thought. But all the facts about what realizes our psychologies may still leave it indeterminate whether we think certain things. This is not because of, or at least not solely because of, quinean worries about indeterminacy of content, to which we will return. The problem is with the notion of a thought. The notion of a thought, not only my notion but any notion suitably close to common sense, may be too vague to allow there to be facts about whether someone thinks or is merely disposed to think certain things in the contingent circumstances in which we happen to find ourselves, in a world where thoughts are realized in the messy and complicated way in which our thoughts are in fact realized.

Still, I think there are limits to this indeterminacy. Even without considering the details of what realizes our psychologies, I think that we can see that there are at least two clear cases of thoughts: Experiences, and word-mediated thoughts. We seem able to introspect that we have these thoughts. This claim may relieve some worries, but it does suggest in turn another objection. Introspectionist psychology is not as popular as it once was. To rest on introspection here may seem quite problematic. In fact, introspection is important to my account of the realization of thoughts in yet another way. The kind of representational content pursued in the last part is itself rooted in introspection. The aspects under which things are present in our thoughts, the aspects relevant to the intensionality of those thoughts, are those which we can introspect, at least in certain cases. If I have an experience, then I can introspect not only that I am having an experience, but the content of that thought. All this talk of introspection may seem very problematic.

Objection Four: The dual role which introspection plays in this account of thoughts, the claim that the aspects under which objects are present to us in our thoughts are introspectible, and that we can introspect that we in fact have certain paradigm thoughts, experiences and word-mediated thoughts, is objectionable. Descartes thought that we are aware of all our thoughts in some indefeasible way, but this no longer seems plausible.

Reply: There are a number of confused presumptions of this objection. First, I do not claim that introspection is indefeasible. Since at least Freud, that has seemed implausible to us. I do think it should take a pretty strong argument to convince us that we don't think what we introspect that we think. But I admit that introspection may well be defeasible, that more is required to vindicate the existence of our thoughts than merely the observation that we introspect them. Second, to say that something is introspect*ible*, that we *can* introspect it, is not to imply that we are in fact aware of it. What's more, I haven't claimed that we even *can* introspect all the thoughts we have, only that we can introspect that we have two important sorts of thoughts. Third, I don't claim that we can introspect all the contents of all our thoughts. I merely claim that the contents of all our thoughts are of the same general sort as normal adult humans can introspect in the case of their sense experiences and certain of their word-mediated thoughts. I merely claim that the contents of our thoughts are of the general sort articulated in Part One, which are ultimately rooted in introspectible features of our experience.

So I haven't said anything as deeply cartesian as this objection presumes. Nevertheless, my account is cartesian in some senses. Introspection does play a central role, indeed two central roles. So it may be helpful to consider the notion of introspection a little, before we begin sketching an account of the realization of the semi-cartesian thoughts sanctioned by Part One.

2

Let's begin by distinguishing certain ways in which we might be "aware" or "conscious" of something. In one sense, any thought *is* an awareness or consciousness. You perceive the orange. That is an awareness or consciousness, in some sense, of the orange. You intend to get to the cave, and that is a focus on getting to the cave. When you dream of some storm that never occurs, you are aware of that mere object of thought. If there is unconscious thought, then it is in some sense unconscious awareness, unconscious consciousness. So there is something we might call the "introspection" of the content of such a thought which is no different than the thought itself. The thought is an awareness of its content. Certainly an *intense* or *attentive* awareness of that content, an intense or attentive perception for instance, is sometimes called "introspection" by philosophers. As William Lyons argues in *The Disappearance of Introspection*, much which is intuitively introspection is merely such perception.[12]

There are different kinds of awareness or consciousness of an orange that a thought may involve. If a thought, even an unconscious thought, is some kind of awareness of its content, still a thinker may be aware of features of that content in different senses, in different ways. One may have different degrees of awareness of an orange, for instance. It may be one's primary concern, or merely out on the edge of sensory awareness. And one's awareness may involve actual speech about the orange or actual behaviors sorting the orange from other things, or it may merely involve a disposition to behave, say to speak in a certain way if asked to describe the orange or to place it in a certain pile if asked to sort fruit.

Perhaps introspection of any full and proper sort requires a special and specific sort of awareness. For instance, perhaps proper introspection of the content of an experience requires actual verbal characterization of the content, at least to oneself, at least in the mind's ear. But none of the forms of awareness of the content of a thought which we have just noted are especially unfamiliar or problematic. It's just that these phenomena have come to be described in a language conditioned by various cartesian presumptions about the realization of our thoughts which make the phenomena seem much more mysterious than they really are.

I have so far noted different ways in which we might be aware of the content of a thought. But there is also a somewhat more sophisticated thing that we can learn to do. We can learn to introspect that we have a certain *experience* or *desire* or word-mediated *belief*, that we are in some specific psychological state, that we have a specific sort of attitude towards a given content. And we can learn to introspect the content of such a thought as the content of such a thought.

It may be worth working through an example. So consider one specific sort of relatively simple "introspective" phenomenon which motivates that peculiar quasi-spatial tag especially well, which does suggest a looking inward and not a looking outward. It involves what I take to be a third sort of clear example of thoughts. Sometimes when we imagine something, we have a kind of quasi-perceptual awareness or experience of it, of a sort I later call "quasi-experience". We can "see" an image of some fantastic city, in our mind's eye. Some people report having no such quasi-visual images, but even they have quasi-experiences of words they speak to themselves.[13]

We can introspect the content of such an imagination much as we would that of a perception. But such instances of imagination also provide a useful contrast with perception. We can introspect not only the content of a perception or imagination, but that it is a perception or an imagination. We learn psychological words, words for perceptions and for mere imaginings. And we learn to read the cues that we have one sort of thing rather than the other. The contents of perceptions and of the instances of imagination which we are discussing are quite concrete, but certain differences, say in vividness, with which the contents of a perception and of an imagination present themselves are also quite concrete. This explains why the unwary may sometimes confuse a vivid imagination of a sound with a perception of a faint sound. Our capacity to introspect the difference between a perception and an imagination seems quite closely related to our capacity to introspect the differences between the contents of certain perceptions.

These are quite simple cases. Some others are somewhat more complex, and require somewhat more complex capacities. For instance, we may have both memory images and fantasy images, and tell the difference by the way in which those thoughts arise for us. And, as Lyons has suggested, there are also significantly more complicated cases, complicated thoughts which introduce correspondingly complicated sorts of introspection of both thoughts and their contents.

The way in which you can introspect the content of a word-mediated thought which is realized by your inner speech, and the way in which you can introspect the content of a sensory experience, are quite different. In the case of the word-mediated thought, you are most immediately aware of just the words themselves, and perhaps a bit of their content, in that faint way we can be aware of things we imagine. There are various reasons to think that you cannot introspect the intuitive meaning of your words, but that in itself does not imply that you cannot introspect their *content*. Still, you can get at the full content of the words only by a difficult and tortured introspective process of a sort I will discuss in Chapter Ten, for instance by imagining all sorts of imaginary scenarios and then judging what you would say in those various circumstances. Or perhaps "judging" is the wrong word. You consider a concrete situation in imagination and then literally feel, have a concrete quasi-experience of, what you would say in that situation. Your dispositions underwrite a kind of imaginary act in those imaginary circumstances, which you feel yourself doing, in some imaginary sense, in that imaginary situation. Of course one's sense of what one would say in such a circumstance and what in fact one would say in that circumstance may come apart to some degree. Hence the relative uncertainty of such an introspection. But it seems to me that there are limits to this divergence. If the divergence between one's sense of what one would say and what one would in fact say were too great, then the conditions required for meaningful speech would break down.[14]

Consider another case. To introspect that you have certain desires is to assess quite complex things about your psychological dispositions, quite complex things about what you would try to do and what you would feel if various things happened. After enough experience with yourself and training in psychological explanation, this assessment is something you can perform in an armchair. Given your in some sense greater experience of yourself, you can often do it better than other people, so that you can have a better sense of your psychology than other people, at least in certain respects. But this is a kind of "introspection" which is not terribly different from the psychological assessment of other people, as Ryle showed us.[15]

In all of these complex cases, quite concrete contents, the contents of experiences or quasi-experiences, constitute the *immediate* content of one's awareness. This fact meshes nicely with the account of the realization of such thoughts developed here. If there is a theater of the mind, then it is a theater of the concrete. It presents the concrete contents of certain thoughts, and not all sorts of abstract psychological states and complicated contents, most directly. But it is our medium for other and more complicated sorts of introspection.[16]

Only after achieving some degree of cognitive sophistication will one be capable of some of the advanced sorts of introspection we've been talking about, for instance of consciously introspecting words as things one says to oneself, and then reflecting upon their content as a whole. Only a certain education allows one to sit in an armchair and consider which conditions would incline one to utter a word, and which would not. And perhaps even more education is required to muse these things over to oneself, to do it quietly and "introspectively", in the mind's ear and eye.[17] Still, normal adult humans can introspect[18] in at least the ways I have noted.

This is merely a sketch of an account of introspection which is consistent with the story about thoughts and their realization which I will tell in this part, but it should do for our purposes. Our relatively indefeasible introspection of our experiences and quasi-experiences and their contents, and of the presence of our word-mediated thoughts bearing at least some elements of content, deliver to us our clearest examples of thoughts.[19] But with a better sense now of the many ways in which we may be aware of our thoughts, let's return again to the general issue of what thoughts we have.

Descartes held that we are actually aware of all of our thoughts. This claim is controversial, at best. We now know that it is ambiguous in certain ways, but certainly not all the controversy would be eliminated by removal of all the ambiguities. Let me focus for discussion on a fairly robust sort of introspection, which gives us the immediate capacity, without a moment's hesitation, to verbally characterize the nature of some thought at issue and its content, and which also involves some sort of actual concrete presence in experience or quasi-experience of at least certain elements of that thought or its content. It seems to me that such a robust sort of awareness is what at least many of the parties to this controversy presume to be at issue.

Freud held that we have repressed thoughts of which we *cannot* become aware, at least without lengthy psychoanalysis. Current cognitive science postulates all sorts of levels of unconscious cognitive processing which no one is able to introspect. And even those who are skeptical about the existence of thoughts which we cannot introspect, for instance Searle, often follow common sense in holding that we have thoughts of which we are not currently aware, but which we can become aware of, if only we try, at a moment's notice.[20] Consider for instance all the beliefs and memories regarding your family which you intuitively continue to retain even while you are entirely involved in some distinct and distracting pursuit, even while you are not aware of any of those thoughts.

On these issues, I want to maintain a kind of neutral ground. Unlike Searle, I think it is at least possible that there be thoughts which are not open to introspection, the kinds which Freud and cognitive science presume. On the other hand, I don't think that it is *obvious* that there are even the commonsense unconscious thoughts which Searle allows, which we are not aware of but would be if only we tried. The only clear and obvious examples of thoughts, I think, are our actual experiences and quasi-experiences and word-mediated thoughts, of which we are in some sense immediately aware. I think that it is only clear that there are those thoughts which we do in fact introspect, of which we are in fact aware in the relevant sense. To that degree I am a cartesian. But I admit that there may be others which we don't but could introspect. And I think there may be yet others which we cannot introspect. I believe that the proper resolution of these issues depends partly on how the details of the realization of our thoughts turn out. On the other hand, it does seem to me that current cognitive science and analytical psychology jump much too quickly to postulate thoughts when there isn't any clearly adequate reason, and that in fact it is still pretty unclear what it is to claim that there are unconscious thoughts. In our actual circumstances, there may be no fact of the matter about whether there are unconscious thoughts of some sorts that people have been tempted to postulate. And if there are facts about that, still the evidence which has been cited for their existence so far seems to me insufficient to establish it, at least if there is to be any difference in real content between claims asserting that there are unconscious thoughts and those claiming that there are the various uncontroversial dispositions for thoughts which those hostile to the unconscious prefer.

In issues of this sort, there are two sorts of questions of fact at issue. There are facts about the meaning of words like "thought", whether for instance such a word legitimately applies to neurophysiologically-rooted dispositions for memory images of certain kinds. And there are the relevant concrete facts about whatever it is that realizes our psychologies. Perhaps if dualism were true, and there were irreducible conceptions floating around in some gaseous spirit, then there would always be a fact of the matter between explanations such as those at issue in debates about the unconscious. But it may well be that the meanings of words like "thought" are simply too indeterminate to resolve some such issues in the particular contingent circumstances in which we find ourselves, in which our psychologies are realized in messy and complicated ways. There may be no real issues to resolve.

Let me consider one case that will be useful later on. Recently it has become popular to propose that Parallel Distributed Processing machines ("PDP" or "Connectionist" machines) provide a better model for the mind than do conventional computers. PDP machines involve large numbers of highly interconnected processing units working in parallel, and, also unlike conventional computers, they do not deploy distinct memory and computational units. Their units fire as a function of the firing of units connected to them and the strength of those connections, and the strength of those connections is modified over time by the firing of the various units. The units are often arranged in layers, with an initial layer receiving some broad range of inputs, and connected so as to influence the firing of the next layer, and so on until we reach a layer controlling some broad range of outputs.[21] Consider one strikingly successful PDP network, NETtalk.[22] It consists of 3 layers of interconnected units. The bottom layer receives written input, and the upper layer specifies phonetic features. Such a device can be "trained", by adjustment of its connections in response to trial and error, to "read" out loud. It does quite well in reproducing the complex situational complexity of English pronunciation, and also makes mistakes in learning that parallel human mistakes. It is of course at best controversial and at worst silly to think that this net has thoughts in anything like the full sense. But it might seem to have "representational" states of some kind, states which might be assigned representational content. It seems plausible to assign to the inner and outer layers, designed to correspond to particular written input or to particular phonetic output, particular representational contents. But the machine seems also to have a kind of knowledge of what pronunciations to make. Where and in what form is that "knowledge" located? The system when trained has a relatively stable state, involving particularly weighted connections. When it "reads" a passage it goes through a certain dynamic of firing in the intermediate layer. Some say that the pattern of firing is something analogous to a thought *that* a certain letter is to be pronounced in a certain way.[23] But on the other hand, it also seems reasonable to say that that pattern is part of the activation of a capacity for pronunciation present in the stable state of the machine, with its peculiarly weighted connections, that it is the activation of certain sorts of know *how* stably present in the machine whether it is reading that particular passage or not, rather than a momentary bit of knowledge *that*.[24] Standard discussions of NETtalk attribute to it lots of *representational* states, knowledge *that* rather than know *how*. It may even seem to retain knowledge *that* certain letters are pronounced in certain ways when it isn't pronouncing them. But to me the moral of the machine seems quite different. I think that thoughts and not just know-how are important psychological states, but if in fact we are a lot like such a machine, then there might be a lot fewer thoughts in us than conventional cognitive science presumes. Or at least there might be a good deal of indeterminacy about whether we have particular thoughts *that* rather than related know *how*, except in the clear cases which we can introspect, and in other cases where we can make out clearly that there is no difference in truth between a claim that there are particular thoughts *that* and a claim that there are particular dispositions for thoughts of which we would be aware.

Clearly, our experiences are thoughts. Clearly also we have word-mediated thoughts, when we speak to ourselves in our mind's ear, or out loud. The quasi-experiences which we will discuss later also provide, I think, some clear examples. But it might be that for the rest we merely possess various sorts of capacities and dispositions for such clear thoughts and sequences of such clear thoughts, which are sometimes activated and sometimes not.[25] These capacities and dispositions are of various sorts, and we will return to a discussion of them in a bit. But though they are capacities and dispositions entwined with and affecting the sequence of our clear thoughts in various ways, and capacities rooted in the same neural resources as our clear thoughts, still they might be merely capacities and dispositions rather than thoughts.[26] On the other hand, I hope for a little more. It may be that the contingent details of the realization of our thoughts turn out so that there are some other clear cases of thoughts, realized in a manner not entirely dissimilar from the familiar clear cases, from experiences and word-mediated thoughts. And, however those contingent details turn out, I think there are also likely to be a range of other commonsense thoughts, which are in fact nothing more than mere dispositions for clear thoughts, that some such dispositions in fact serve to constitute some such thoughts. However, there is also likely to be good deal of indeterminacy about whether there are certain other commonsense thoughts, an indeterminacy which the concrete facts which realize our psychologies are insufficient to resolve. My most detailed suggestions about what thoughts to postulate in light of all the relevant considerations are contained in Chapter Eleven.

3

There are a variety of possible views about the *realization* of thoughts, about the constitution of agents capable of psychological states with the range of contents articulated in Part One. This section provides an initial survey, before we attempt a particular account.

First of all, there is a class of views which maintain that thoughts *aren't* realized. I will call this entire class "thought skepticism", but focus on a particular instance of it. That clean and simple instance is the view that there literally but contingently are no thoughts, just as there literally but contingently are no witches or ptolemaic crystal spheres. It is the view that our talk of thoughts is false in the manner of talk of witches. In the terminology of Part One, it is the view that talk of thoughts makes "literal sense", but that the conditions which would serve to make it literally true do not obtain.

There are other sorts of skepticism. Even more radically dismissive views are possible. Some may hold that talk of thoughts is incoherent in the way that talk of round squares is incoherent, or even senseless in the way that nonsense talk is senseless. These quite radical views will be defused by this part, which provides a coherently conceivable model of the realization of our thoughts. It is also possible to think that while thoughts aren't realized, talk of thoughts is good talk. Indeed, some views of this sort are consistent with the characterization of clean and simple thought skepticism with which we began. "Instrumentalists" hold that while talk of thoughts is literally false, it is a close enough approximation of the truth to be useful in our lives. Still other views imply that, while talk of thoughts is coherent in some sense, it doesn't carry the sort of content and meaning which would allow it *literal* truth or falsity. There are a variety of models for this situation, for instance noncognitivist treatments of ethical claims. As I suggested in Chapter One, all of these alternative sorts of skepticism seem committed to the literal truth of claims about the existence of certain sentences, and, as we will see in Chapter Ten, that is not consistent with the treatment of thoughts they propound. And again, in this part we will succeed in making literal sense of thoughts. So because of these difficulties faced by the more complicated forms of thought skepticism, I will focus our discussion here on clean and simple non-instrumentalist thought skepticism, and indeed on a certain "hypothetical" formulation of that view, to skirt the problems which sentences may face: If there were sentences which spoke of thoughts, then they would be false in the literal manner.[27]

The other views which we will discuss maintain that thoughts *are* realized. But let me distinguish two classes of such views. First of all, there are what I will call "objectual accounts", in which at least part of which constitutes one's having a thought with a certain sort of content is something which the content matches.[28] For instance, one might maintain that your experience of a colorful apple is in fact partly constituted by such an apple.[29]

Second, there are what I will call "non-objectual" accounts, in which such things do not play such a role. For instance, one might maintain that Galileo's experience of a red ball might exist even if there were no red balls. Non-objectual accounts bear a close affinity to "adverbial" models of experience, according to which the claim that Galileo had a red experience is to be construed not as a claim that there is a relation between Galileo and a red object, but as a claim that Galileo was doing something, experiencing, in a certain *manner*, "redly".

This is a rough and ready typography. There are mixed views, objectual for some thoughts and non-objectual for others, or objectual in some respects and not in others. I think that non-objectual accounts of a rather radical form, which involve non-objectual accounts of the realization of all features[30] of all our thoughts, are the most plausible accounts. But the standard accounts of thought realization, and in fact the coherently conceivable account developed in this part, deploy significant objectual resources. On the other hand, the standard accounts, and the account in this part, are also in many respects non-objectual. They are mixed views, significantly more non-objectual than certain traditional accounts from which they descend, and yet more objectual than others.

If I think that a radically non-objectual account is correct, why do I bother with a detour through a partly objectual account? Because, as we will see in Part Three, the plausible radical non-objectual accounts, which include non-objectual accounts of our experience, are not coherently conceivable. This part will develop a coherently conceivable account of the realization of our thoughts, which hence must deploy some objectual resources, in particular in its account of our capacity for experience. It will be to that degree more in line with the standard mixed views than is the view which we will eventually pursue. But, again like the standard views, it deploys significant non-objectual resources, which will allow the portion of the account which deals with thought beyond experience to mesh nicely with the non-objectual account of experience pursued in Part Three.[31]

The rest of this chapter develops a short, initial brief for a non-objectual treatment of thoughts, which I hope serves to orient the remaining discussion. It is a brief both for the non-objectual features of the standard views and of the coherently conceivable view to be sketched in this part, and for the more radically non-objectual features of the strictly inconceivable view which we will pursue in Part Three. Of course, there are other important distinctions between accounts of the realization of thoughts than those I have mentioned. For instance, some views are "physicalist" in one sense or another, and some are not. Physicalist accounts eschew things like ghostly spiritual substances and nonconcrete abstracta, in favor of physicalist resources of some appropriately post-galilean sort. And some accounts are "internalist" while others are "externalist". Internalist accounts of the constitution of your thoughts advert merely to things which are found inside your skin, while externalist accounts appeal to features of your environment. But the objectual versus non-objectual debate will be our primary focus of concern, at least for the moment.

Let's begin by considering some of the motivation for a radically *objectual* account, in particular of an externalist variety. To have a thought about something, say a desire for an apple or a perception that a ball is red, is to be in a state which possesses intentionality. The state is, at least characteristically, about particular objects out in the world. So it is perhaps natural to suppose that the realization of those thoughts involves those objects. It is perhaps natural to conclude that what constitutes the difference between an experience with the content of the perception of an orange and an experience with the content of the perception of an apple is exactly the orange and the apple. This is in effect to identify the content of the experience with the object perceived, to maintain that those contents are in fact distinct and detachable bits of the world.

On the other hand, the intensionality of thoughts should give us pause here. Thoughts are about things under only certain of their aspects and features. And, of course, thoughts may be false, and may even be dreaming fantasy. Not all the aspects of objects in the world, and not merely objects really in the world, are present in the contents of our thoughts.

Nevertheless, some still feel the pull towards objectual accounts of all our thoughts. Perhaps this is because of the form of our customary psychological idiom, which reports fantasy and true belief alike in the same apparently relational form. The considerations noted in the last paragraph may move someone not to abandon relations to content-specifying objects as crucial elements in the realization of thoughts, but rather to introduce some pretty implausible and certainly unfamiliar entities. They may propose ghostly golden mountains and unicorns which "subsist" but do not "exist", as part of what constitutes thoughts of golden mountains and unicorns. Or they may propose that contents are things of a third and intermediate kind, neither psychological states of some thinker, nor the objects in the world on which the thinker's thoughts are ultimately directed, but rather abstract and intervening "propositions". All thought, true or false, is directed at a proposition, which is its content, and then the proposition is true or false of the world. These propositions are supposed to have only some of the features of the facts in the world to which they might correspond, but nevertheless they remain, I believe, recognizably "objectual" resources.

Ghostly golden mountains and abstract propositions seem to many to be quite implausible resources, and this is reasonable. Part One gives us reason to believe that such things aren't even coherently conceivable. Basic contents cannot underwrite in any obvious way a distinction between subsistence and existence. And abstract entities, for instance propositions, might best be seen as abstract*ed* entities, not as elements of basic content. In any case, in the face of false belief and fantasy and the intensionality of our thoughts, the standard accounts of thought realization, like the account we will pursue in this part, move in another direction.

They deploy an objectual account of the realization of certain plausibly veridical thoughts, for instance our perceptual experiences. While the intensionality of even these veridical thoughts may require some complicated machinations, still at least in the case of veridical perceptual experience an objectual account need not dally with imaginary golden mountains and strange abstracta. Given an objectual account of the content of perceptual states, the standard accounts then deploy some non-objectual resources. They at least gesture at a story about how thoughts which are not perceptual are somehow rooted in those that are. They provide a non-objectual account of those other thoughts. You experience pink things and squirrels, and those thoughts involve pink things and squirrels. But this then somehow gives you the capacity to think of pink squirrels, even though there are none.

The popularity of such accounts has, I think, a variety of sources. We are legitimately suspicious of the implausible resources deployed in the more flamboyantly objectual accounts favored by some of our philosophical ancestors. But even neuroscientists receive grants to search for correlations between perceptible features of the world and patterns of neural firing, so that seems okay. And such accounts of perceptual states bear some affinity with the popular, new views about reference noted briefly in Chapter Two. Another source of the popularity of the standard views is what is widely considered to be the failure of a very different sort of account. Let me sketch a bit of its history.

Physicalist philosophers, fighting a long dark tradition which held thoughts to involve some ghostly spirit substance or abstract propositions, were initially attracted to behaviorism. This, in its simplest form, is the view that to have a certain thought is to perform certain publicly observable behaviors characteristic of that state, that to feel pain, for instance, is to hop around and yell. Soon philosophers became convinced, however, that liars and actors might perform these behaviors in the absence of the appropriate thought; and that the tough and Spartan might not exhibit such behaviors even in the presence of the thought.[32] So it came to seem that feeling pain shouldn't be identified with screaming and hopping around, but rather with whatever hidden internal state of people typically causes such behavior. That was presumed to be the firing of certain neurons. So physicalist philosophers became "central state materialists". But in turn it came to seem problematic to *identify* pain with the firing of those neurons, even if it also seemed that in certain specific instances the firing of such neurons did *constitute* the pain. Those neurons cut out and firing in a jar would not plausibly be pain. Nor do those particular sorts of firing neurons really seem necessary for the existence of pain. Other sorts of neurons playing a similar role in dolphins or neurophysiologically deviant humans seem sufficient.[33] Rather, pain came to seem something properly identified with whatever it was that happened to play the causal-functional role characteristic of pain, whatever mediated between sensory input and motor output and between other mental states in the way characteristic of pain. In the human neural economy, one sort of neuron might perform that role. In dolphins, perhaps a different sort, and in Martians or robots, perhaps something wildly different, swiss cheese or transistors or hydraulic tubes. But, so the story goes, as long as that role is fulfilled, and only so long as it is fulfilled, is there pain. Physicalist philosophers became "functionalists".

In my cartoon history, let me ignore some complications presented by messy reality, and pretend that all of these accounts were *internalist* accounts. I have focussed on pain, and if there is an object "pain", it is an internal object. But behaviorism and central state materialism and functionalism exhibited at least a tendency towards internalist accounts not only of the realization of such feelings but of thoughts in general, hence even of perceptual beliefs. Still, as physicalist accounts of mental states continued to evolve, it came to seem that internalist resources were insufficient to distinguish between at least some distinct mental states with content, in particular between different beliefs and experiences. For instance, the objects of perceptual beliefs came to seem a necessary and helpful resource in distinguishing between different perceptual beliefs. Internalist resources could only go so far to distinguish between different thoughts with different contents. Externalist resources were required to fill the remaining gap, and the most plausible deployment of those resources seemed to be in the realization of perceptual experience and beliefs. Consider the case of a very simple organism: It has the capacity to internally represent its environment as in one of two broadly characterized states, p or not-p. It can respond to the situation it "believes" to be the case in either of two ways, by doing A or doing B. What it will do depends on what it "believes" is the case and on what it "desires" to do in such a case. These exhaust the creature's thoughts and the repertoire of its possible actions. The problem is that any *internal* functional structure of such a creature (and hence, if functionalism is true, any internal physical structure) which can be taken to encode the belief that p and the desire to do A if p and B if not-p could also be taken to encode the belief that not-p and the desire to do A if not-p and B if p.[34] In one case we might have a creature with systematically incorrect beliefs, constituted always to believe p when not-p and the reverse, but if beliefs are determined by internalist resources then the true state of the *external* environment cannot help to determine what thoughts are to be ascribed to the creature. The relevance of such an example might be disputed on the grounds that such a simple case in itself proves nothing. Such a creature may not be a haver of thoughts just because of its very simplicity. To have a thought with a determinate content is to have something which plays in a complicated way into the complex structure of attitudes one has. A functional characterization as complex as yours would be might be taken to rule out such permutations in attribution as afflict our creature. However, for complexity to yield determination it must be the right kind of complexity. It might be that the sorts of complexity and remote connections there are between thoughts and actions in your own case simply allow greater room for perverse but consistent permutations in content-attribution. Furthermore, even if the additional complexity of your internalist functional structure suffices to restrict the possible assignment of contents to your thoughts, if even two radically different assignments remain, functionalism fails as an internalist account of thoughts. Internal functional structure alone fails to yield unique assignments of contents to thoughts, or at least so it seems.

Because of worries like these, the standard physicalist accounts of the realization of thoughts are now externalist accounts, which mix objectual and non-objectual elements. These accounts, which I will call "correlational" accounts, have roughly the following general form:

1) Internal to someone with thoughts there are certain physical states, say certain neurophysiological states, which constitute particular thoughts with particular contents. According to one currently popular option, these are inscriptions in the language of thought "Mentalese". For instance, there may be Mentalese inscriptions within some perceptual system roughly equivalent to the English sentences "the ball is red" or "the cat is grey".

2) At least in the case of perceptual beliefs, these physical states, these internal sentences, have the contents they do because they bear some sort of physical

relation to their objects, say to the ball and its redness or to the cat and its greyness. The states have the contents they do because of their "correlations" with such things.

3) Other sorts of mental states, say Mentalese sentences which are thoughts about the effects of interest rates on inflation, possess their contents in more indirect ways, perhaps by their inferential relations to Mentalese sentences involved in perceptual beliefs.

This is an extremely crude sketch of the standard correlational accounts of the realization of thoughts.[35] For instance, correlational accounts differ about exactly what sort of correlation is involved in perceptual belief and experience. One very traditional sort of account invokes isomorphism. On such a view, a "representational state", a state with content, say a sentence of Mentalese in some perceptual processing system, refers to whatever in the world it happens to be isomorphic to.[36] But such views seem open to the objection that isomorphism is too cheap. It seems that just about anything might share some sort of form with any particular sentence of Mentalese. Pre-physicalist accounts of thoughts sometimes deployed some very special sorts of isomorphism to eliminate this difficulty, say that of pictures to what they picture or that between things which share an aristotelian perceptual form, but the standard physicalist accounts do not easily mesh with such resources. The neurons inside our heads don't look in particular like anything in our environment. So the most popular of the standard correlational accounts conceive the relevant correlation to involve a causal or counterfactual dependency relation.

Perhaps the simplest and most characteristic account holds that the content of a representational state which is a perceptual state, say a sentence of Mentalese, is its cause, so that for instance Galileo's Mentalese sentence "Fido is brown" has the content it does because it is caused by Fido being brown. An alternative simple account holds that the content of a representational state in a perceptual system is not merely its actual cause. Rather, that state would be made true by anything which *would* cause it.[37]

Such simple accounts face certain difficulties rooted in the intensionality of content. A plausible account of thought realization must find some way to distinguish between the intuitive content of a perceptual state and other things in the chain of causes which lead to it. Consider for instance a case in which Galileo strikes a match, and hence creates some light, and hence alerts a prowler, who hence scares Fido, who hence runs out, and hence leads Galileo to perceive that Fido is brown. Also, such simple accounts seem to imply that all perceptual states are veridical, and we know they aren't. Perceptual error does occur. We misidentify things at a distance or in dim light, and we suffer perceptual hallucinations.

The standard accounts have adopted various strategies to evade these kinds of difficulties. Dretske has proposed that the content of a certain sort of perceptual state is its cause during a "learning period", and that after that period another cause for such a state might hence lead to perceptual error. Fodor has plausibly wondered how the boundaries of the learning period are to be determined.[38] Does a bell ring? He has rather proposed that the content of a perceptual state is determined by "asymmetrical dependence". On this view, the content of such a state is the cause on which other causes depend.[39] If the content didn't cause it, then the other causes wouldn't cause it either. Cummins has plausibly suggested that the notorious trickiness of counterfactual conditionals and the sensitivity of their evaluation to context allows such an account to hide some unmotivated stipulations about how to evaluate the relevant counterfactuals in the complexity of the issues they raise, to lose all the interesting problems in complexity.[40] There is yet another popular set of accounts of correlation, rooted in suggestions of Gibbard, Millikan, Stampe, and one period of Dretske's work, which maintain that the content of a perceptual state is whatever it is the function of that state to be caused by, where the function of that state is somehow determined by its evolutionary history.[41] But we might reasonably wonder if evolutionary history can underwrite functions of the necessary specificity to generate intuitive perceptual contents. And the evolutionary history leading to an organism, just like its educational history, may reasonably seem irrelevant to *constituting* what it thinks *now*.

Whatever the force of these various standard criticisms, there are decisive difficulties with any variety of correlational account. The coherently conceivable account we will develop in this part will have something like the standard form. But at least by Part Three we will be in position to see that the standard accounts, and the account developed in this part, are not really very plausible, because of considerations which I will sketch in section 4, considerations which will eventually push us in another direction, towards a radically non-objectual account.

As I've said, the standard correlational accounts deploy some non-objectual resources, in the realization of thoughts which are not perceptual thoughts. *Radical* non-objectual accounts, non-objectual accounts of the realization of *all* our thoughts, abandon correlational and objectual stories about even perceptual states. They deploy an "adverbial", non-objectual account of our perceptual experience. They maintain that what constitutes us to experience what we experience does not include objects of the sort we experience, that when Galileo experienced a red ball falling by the window that was not even in part *constituted* by a real ball, that when he experienced something being red that didn't necessarily involve anything red, not even a red sense datum.

According to such a view, it is at least possible that our perceptual states, and our thoughts generally, be radically erroneous. According to such a view, not the representational states which help realize thoughts, but rather the contents of the thoughts, have a kind of strong and specific isomorphism with the world, at least when the thoughts are true. The contents match the world. What *realizes* thoughts with those contents need not. Isomorphism of some sort determines the truth of thoughts, but does not determine their content.

This part will pursue a coherently conceivable account of the realization of our thoughts which bears a close affinity to the standard correlational accounts. But in Part Three we will drive towards a more plausible, though not coherently conceivable, radically non-objectual account. When standard functionalist resources seemed insufficient to generate determinate content for thoughts, traditional physicalists looked outward for other helpful resources. It seems to me that they might have been better off looking "inward", to introspection, but even that route will not ultimately help us enough. For now, however, let me merely sketch the reasons which will eventually drive us away from the space of the standard accounts.

4

There are basically two reasons to resist standard objectual accounts of our experience. But the objections do not function in the same way. The first is straightforward and decisive. And it will also ultimately undermine the coherently conceivable objectual account of our experience developed in this part. In Part Three, this objection will wreak havoc with that account. But the second objection plays a more torturous role, or at least it will be a more torturous task to get to a form of the objection which plays a straightforward role. The simplest form of the second objection is only successful against a very crude caricature of the standard correlational accounts, though perhaps it does suggest that actual correlational accounts should be developed in a certain way, to emphasize certain resources more than they often do. This is the direction which we will adopt in this part. In fact, the resources which the second objection in its crude first form suggests should be emphasized are precisely those deployed in the internalist physicalist tradition of behaviorism, central state materialism, and functionalism, a tradition which feeds into the standard accounts, even if they ignore it. Recall how internalist physicalism seemed finally to falter in its account of the differences between certain thoughts. Some psychological differences seemed appropriately characterized by internalist, at least largely non-objectual resources, but these seemed to leave a gap where externalist objectual resources were needed, to distinguish between certain distinct thoughts. Most standard accounts of perceptual states stress these externalist elements at the expense of internalist resources, neglect their heritage of internalist physicalism a bit too much, try to deploy what merely should fill a gap to tell the whole story. But, of course, this is just a question of emphasis and detail. So the first form of the second objection is hardly decisive in itself, though it nudges us in a certain direction. And it has another role as well. When internalist resources are properly deployed, and we see precisely the gap which externalist objectual resources are needed to fill, then it will put standard physicalist accounts of thoughts, though not the variant adopted in this part, in quite a difficult position. Standard accounts will run out of objectual resources in a very embarrassing place. What's worse, even if we help ourselves to all the objectual resources required, for instance all those deployed in the account developed in this part, they still will not mesh in a plausible way with the other, internalist resources we must deploy.[42] The simple first form of the second objection can lead us eventually to quite telling objections against both standard physicalist correlational accounts and the account developed here. But it will take some work to see this. With that stage-setting, let me begin. First, the short and decisive objection.

Objection One: There aren't in fact the sorts of objects which our experience seems to reveal. No experience with the introspectible content which our experience possesses can be given a plausible objectual account. For instance, we experience objects with phenomenal color, red balls. But Galileo long ago argued that no ball in fact is red. We will see in Part Three that Galileo's pattern of argument can be extended in ways which challenge even traditional galilean properties which our experience might seem to reveal. Look around you. It's not like that at all.

As I said, in the end I think that this objection is decisive. But I intend to largely ignore it until Part Three. We are presuming in this part a concrete mundane world, consistent with most of the suggestions of our experience as well as of our science, a world including red balls and fleshy brains fed by red blood. On the other hand, the *standard* accounts of thought realization are orthodox physicalist accounts, which presume a *galilean* conception of the world, shorn of phenomenal color, but with galilean properties like charge and mass and velocity and ordinary spatial and temporal relations intact. We will see that this is a false and unstable paradise, but it is somewhat ironic that it leaves those standard physicalist accounts with no objectual resources to deploy exactly where they need them most. To see this, though, we need to work through the next objection.

Objection Two: If the content of some inner representational state, say some sentence of Mentalese, is determined by what in the world it happens to be correlated with, then there is no assurance that the content of that state is reflected appropriately in the other mental states and behaviors to which that state leads. Differences between experiences should be reflected, for instance, in different behaviors, in a way which standard correlational accounts of perceptual experience do not explain.

That's the general point, but it will take some work to get it into a proper and telling form, and in fact there are somewhat different forms which are relevant against different objectual accounts. Let me begin by phrasing it as a simple argument, and then back into one proper form of the objection by considering several sources of plausible resistance to that argument. That argument, which we might call "the causal sufficiency argument", is familiar at least in general outline.[43] It goes roughly like this: It is one of the oldest observations about animals that the primary causes of their behaviors seem to be internal. And indeed, at least the primary causes of human behavior, of for instance the wagging of our tongues and mouths which helps constitute our speech, are internal states, in particular neurophysiological states and events. Certainly our behavior is affected by changes in our environment, but those changes in the environment only cause changes in behavior when they are reflected in our nervous system, when we take the changes in. Certainly some environmental conditions, say gravitational fields, affect what we do even if we are unaware, but intuitively these are background conditions rather than anything like full-blown primary causes of our behavior. It is primarily certain internal states of an individual animal which are reflected in the wide variety of its behavior.

But, for instance, our experiences also seem to be such primary causes of our behavior. The differences between the contents of various experiences seem reflected in our behavior, in what we say for instance. Different mental states with different contents seem to make a causal difference, a difference in what we do, at least in the context of other of our mental states. If someone perceives that a cat is grey, or alternatively perceives that it is red, there are conditions under which they will behave in different ways. The failure of behaviorism may have shown us that perceiving a grey cat will not always lead to the same behavior, but still, if we presume a fixed context of other psychological states, the experience of a grey cat rather than a red ball may make a behavioral difference.

Now put these two points together: If our internal neurophysiological states are the primary causes of our behavior, and if different mental states with different contents are to be different primary causes, then our internal states must constitute those mental states with those contents. So correlations with external objects can play no role.

There are a number of things wrong with this form of our objection. Let me consider several forms of resistance in turn.

Resistance One: I've been more than a little vague about what a primary cause is, but even so there are cases which should make us worry about the treatment this argument presumes. For instance, the intuitively "primary" cause of my death may be quite sensitive to who fired a bullet and why.[44] It may not be intuitively sufficient to say that the cause of my death was a bullet entering my body, though that was nonetheless causally sufficient for that death in just the way my internal states are for my behavior. It may seem quite causally significant who fired the gun. And a perceived zinc ball may cause someone to behave in a different way than a perceived lead ball would have, even if the difference is not reflected in that person's neurophysiology. It may cause them to grab a zinc ball rather than a lead one, and that is in some sense a difference in behavior, a difference in the effect which is caused. They act into a different world, and hence in some sense act differently. In one intuitive sense of "cause" and "behavior", differences in one's environment which are not reflected in one's neurophysiology and other internal states are not relevant to one's behavior or its causes, while one's mental states are so relevant. But intuitions may differ, and we shouldn't rest too much weight on intuitions about such a slippery and interest-infected notion as cause. So there is a worry about the force of our second objection, in its crude first form. And there are other worries too.

Resistance Two: It may well be that to call the explanatory relations among environment and psychological states and behavior specifically "causal" relations is a mistake. For instance, it may be that this connotes causal powers of the sort discussed in Chapter Seven, acting between spatially distinct entities. And it may be that the relation between what we experience and what we do is an explanatory relation which is not causal in this narrow sense. For instance, we know from Part One that phenomenal properties are not causal properties, and yet it may be necessary to deploy those properties in the explanation of certain psychological states. In fact, the account developed in this part will deploy such non-causal explanations. Whatever the current rage for "causal" accounts of everything, including reference and perception, we shouldn't forget that there are apparently coherently conceivable traditional accounts of perception which deploy, for instance, migrating sensible species to explain color perception, waves of color flying off the surface of objects towards the eyes. Such a movement would be more (or other) than merely the transmission of causal influence. So it is reasonable to insist that the things which help constitute that someone has a particular thought with a particular content, say a particular experience, may at least conceivably include more than merely those things which underwrite the primary *causal* role of that thought.

I think that much of the force of our argument may survive these two forms of resistance, at least when that argument is deployed against standard correlational accounts as I have crudely characterized them. Whatever the importance of these forms of resistance, the standard objectual accounts are perversely input driven. They ignore important characteristic causal effects of different sorts of perceptual experience. Assume that Galileo's perceptual states are "correlated" with a grey cat falling by the window and a red ball under the table. Still, we may reasonably wonder about his perceptual beliefs and experience if, when he neither intends to lie or to play act, he puts out milk under the table, scratches the ball, goes off to the window to watch for the bounce, and, asked to draw what he sees falling, sketches a circular form. Of course, people sometimes act in mad or odd ways on the basis of veridical perceptions, but sometimes too they hallucinate. So as I said, I think our objection survives the first two forms of resistance. Still, there is another.

Resistance Three: The standard accounts have lots of resources to deploy in this sort of scenario. Of course, they all try in one way or another to account for hallucinations, by talking about deviant causes or the like. And they even have resources to explain the *causal* differences between the experience of a grey cat and a red ball. Perhaps it is plausible to insist that it is more than contingent that such differences are reflected in behavior in appropriate ways in those who aren't lying or acting, or at least plausible to insist that it's more than contingent that such differences are reflected somewhere in Galileo's *internal* states, for instance in some sequence of his other Mentalese sentences. But standard accounts can take over some helpful resources here from their behaviorist and functionalist ancestors. At best, this objection suggests that standard accounts be developed, not abandoned. And in fact the standard correlational accounts have been crudely caricatured here. In some of their less than crude actual forms, they actually field the helpful resources, the kinds of resources which functionalists also deployed. For instance, a given thing, say a cat, may be represented in the conceptual economy of a person or two persons in two different ways, say by two different words in the language of thought. And these words may possess two different "conceptual roles", roles reflected in the inferences and speech and behavior of those people.[45] Two different people with different experiences of a cat, say as a ball and as a cat, may represent it in two different ways, by Mentalese words possessing different conceptual roles.

I believe that this form of resistance has some legitimate force. As I've said, the account I develop in this part takes something like the direction suggested here. But unfortunately the force of this form of resistance runs out in what are for standard physicalist views some very embarrassing places. This is the final form of our second objection, which I will deploy against those standard accounts. But to see its force, it is important to distinguish various cases.

Colin McGinn has discussed the case of perceptual experience of squares and circles. He notes that the standard accounts seem to ignore the fact that we would trace such patterns with different behaviors.[46] He is too sanguine about whether or not this would be possible even if there weren't at least square and circular spatial patterns, and, as we will see in Part Three, he is too sanguine about whether there are such patterns. But such experiences do at least typically cause distinct tracing behaviors, and at least the crudest forms of the standard accounts do not take this properly into account.[47]

Still, standard physicalist accounts are well-positioned to handle cases like McGinn's, at least with a little development. They have familiar resources to deploy, which they can take over from their behaviorist and functionalist ancestors. On the other hand, McGinn's case at least first glance seems like one where behavior can reveal most or all of the difference between the two sorts of experience. The *correlated* objects, the objects of perception, don't do much if any work in a case like that.

Consider another important kind of case, however. Consider the difference between experience of a red ball and a green ball. It's an old philosophical chestnut that someone with their color experience inverted relative to the normal human form, with red exchanged for green and blue for yellow and with corresponding exchanges all around the color wheel, might in some sense behave just like us. There is a causal difference between the experience of red and green within such a person's behavior, but not between their experience of green and ours of red, at least not in the narrow sense relevant to how arms and limbs and tongues are moved. We will examine such "inverted spectrum" arguments in Part Three at length, where we will see that they have some force.

Here might be a place for correlation with objects to play an important role in constituting the difference between thoughts. What might constitute an inverted experience in such a person is that the objects they interact with are green where ours are red.[48] Ironically, though, this is just the sort of object which a standard galilean physicalist will not be in position to deploy. If there are no phenomenal red or green things, then phenomenal red and green things cannot help constitute the difference between two kinds of phenomenal experience.

And it is important also to consider a difficulty made vivid by certain mixed cases. For instance, if our perceptual experience of red and our perceptual experience of purple cause us to proclaim one a primary color and the other not, it cannot be that the sole difference between our experience of red and of purple is that they involve different Mentalese words correlated with red and with purple respectively. Not any difference in the mental words will do. There must be a difference in the causal roles of those mental words which is appropriate to the color which is assigned to them as a content. But it would be a miracle if differences in the causal roles of the relevant Mentalese words and the correlated properties fit together so snugly. Remember that phenomenal color has no causal effects, of the sort which might plausibly influence evolution, or for that matter the way our mouths move. Even if there were plausible objectual resources to deploy here, it would be a miracle if they were to mesh properly with other resources which also must be deployed. More precisely: We have inherited a reasonable post-galilean understanding of the kind of regularities which are found in our world, regularities underwritten by causal mechanisms, which make us legitimately suspicious of correlations of this sort. Perhaps to an earlier generation the necessary correlations would not have seemed miraculous, but they do now.

In this part, we will develop an account of the realization of experience which deploys some objectual resources, for instance phenomenal color, of a sort denied to the traditional galilean physicalist. But, as we will see in Part Three, these sorts of objectual resources aren't really all that plausible. And that last case should make us worry even if they were.[49]

NOTES

1. One might wonder if certain peculiarities of the model of the realization of our thoughts which I adopt in this part create our difficulty, whether there might not be other sorts of account of the realization of our thought which don't invoke the crucial presence of such an experience as we seem

to possess, and which hence are at once coherently conceivable and plausible. But this is a vain hope. First of all, some of the thoughts recognized by Part One *are* experiences. Second, as I've said, this part will underwrite the intuitive suggestions of Part One that our capacities for thoughts beyond experience are plausibly dependent on our capacities for experience.

2. Barring the success of some desperate machinations I will attempt in Chapter Nineteen, this claim would need to be qualified in certain ways. In fact, Part Three will show that, for the very reasons we cannot make coherently conceivable and plausible sense of our experience, we cannot in fact make *fully* plausible and coherently conceivable sense of *anything*. But for the moment let me ignore this complication.

3. Descartes, "Second Meditation", in John Cottingham, Robert Stoothoff, Dugal Murdoch (translators), *The Philosophical Writings of Descartes*, vol. II (Cambridge: Cambridge University Press, 1984), 19.

4. Saul Kripke, *Naming and Necessity*.

5. Saul Kripke, "A Puzzle About Belief", in A. Margalit (editor), *Meaning and Use* (Dordrecht: Reidel, 1979), 239-283. Keith Donnellan, "Speaking of Nothing", *The Philosophical Review* 83, 1974, 3-32.

6. One might worry that this implies that feelings are truth-evaluable, when it seems evident that they are not. But in the relevant sense they are. Perhaps we don't notice this just because we ordinarily take our feelings of pain to give us some sort of privileged access to things within our bodies, to pains, so that we don't even consider the possibility that such a feeling could misrepresent things, that there might be states of feeling pain and no objects which are pains even within our bodies. Or perhaps it's the other way around. Perhaps we are so used to thinking that different people have different feelings that we don't even contemplate the possibility of a thing, a pain, even within our bodies, which might correspond to our experience of pain as a blue object might correspond to our experience of blue. But just as there are states of experiencing blue which either do or do not correspond to blue objects out in the world, so too there are states of experiencing pain which either do or do not correspond to pains, say sitting in someone's sore arm.

7. Certainly our current psychological idiom makes much of the distinction between beliefs and desires, which also underlies a lot of current philosophical and psychological work. But it may be, as Adam Morton has argued in *Frames of Mind* (Oxford: Oxford University Press, 1980), 47-51, that there are different characteristic styles of psychological explanation deployed in different periods and places, styles employing different vocabularies which focus on differences between people and features of people which are in those specific periods and places particularly salient. Consider for instance the differences between how people would be described in a society in which (to use our current style of explanation) aims were generally shared and situations simple but character differences played a big role in underwriting the differences in individual actions, and how they would be described in a society where people calculated the satisfaction of idiosyncratic desires under conditions where deception and misunderstanding were widespread. It may be that talk of beliefs and desires is natural in situations which resemble our own, but it doesn't follow from this that two components are an inevitable commitment of our tradition in all sorts of circumstances. It is also worth considering cross-cultural examples. Even in a culture where there is a commitment to two components, the relevant distinction need not answer exactly to the peculiarities encoded in the current English sense of "belief" and "desire". For instance, Rodney Needham, in *Belief, Language, and Experience* (Oxford: Blackwell, 1972), has catalogued the serious difficulties missionaries faced in translating "belief" into various other tongues, difficulties which suggest that other cultures do not necessarily incorporate a notion of belief *per se* into their conceptions of agency. The Nuer appear not to have had such a notion, despite possessing a complicated vocabulary of character states and emotions and attitudinal states.

Evidence about the age of the two-component model seems mixed. There is some evidence that the Indo-European root of both English "believe" and "love" and German "glauben" and "lieben" is the same "leu bh-". See Needham, 42. Perhaps the Indo-Europeans did not clearly and decisively distinguish cognitive and conative attitudes, but made do with the generic notion of something like a thought. Or perhaps the typing of thoughts they found most salient was not into the cognitive and conative. Both what we believe and what we love we in some sense stand up for. And Richard Onians, in *The Origins of European Thought* (New York: Arno Press, 1973), has not implausibly argued that all psychological states even in Homer are tinged with both cognitive and conative features, and that the *thymos* and *noos* are not distinct faculties. Rather, he suggests, the *thymos* was held to be the basic psychological phenomena, a sort of wet wind located in the lungs, and the *noos* was supposed to be merely a sort of current in it, directing it one way or the other. But for an alternative view see Bruno Snell, *The Discovery of the Mind*, translated by R.G. Rosenmeyer (Oxford: Blackwell, 1953).

8. Contemporary commonsense does distinguish between beliefs and desires in what now seems an intuitive way. Beliefs seem more closely and specifically tied to perception, and desires to action. A particular belief may seem obviously appropriate under certain perceptual conditions, but seem to require no particular action in the absence of particular desires. A particular desire may have obvious conditions of satisfaction, but seem not to be required by any particular perceptual conditions. So it may seem that a particular action must be rooted in both particular desire and particular belief. Still, there are cases which cast doubt on this tidy picture. Some states which are intuitively beliefs, say the belief that chocolate is delicious, seem quite closely tied to particular actions. And some intuitively conative states, say hunger, seem closely tied to certain perceptual conditions in the stomach or the blood. And the supposedly distinct classes have no firm internal integrity. Certain intuitive "desires" are more like the dispositions for thoughts discussed previously than they are like any paradigm thoughts, for instance thoughts mediated by our inner speech. But so are certain background beliefs. Some desires are a lot like imagining things, and so are some beliefs about the past. Some articulate judgments about the world are more like some self-conscious desires than they are like sense experiences.

9. See for instance Jerry Fodor and Ernest Lepore, *Holism* (Oxford: Blackwell, 1992), 105-135.

10. While introspection may provide some genuine data, not anything anyone is tempted to claim about their own psychology counts as genuine evidence. Consider the homeric Greeks on the interventions of Athena in their psychological lives. We will turn to this issue again in a moment.

11. It isn't that those three things are merely *evidence* which bears on our inference to some distinct range of theoretical entities called "thoughts". Rather those three things are all that can constrain what thoughts in fact *are*.

12. William Lyons, *The Disappearance of Introspection* (Cambridge, MA: MIT Press, 1986).

13. Some deaf people report that they gesture to themselves.

14. In light of Part Three, perhaps I should say "between one's sense of what one would say and one's sense of what one was saying when one said it."

15. Gilbert Ryle, *The Concept of Mind* (London: Hutchinson, 1949), Chapter VI.

16. This may make some sorts of introspection more certain and infallible than others. One can introspect the bare presence of word-mediated thoughts quite directly, and with something approaching certainty, the same sort of certainty we can have about the content of our experience. One can hear the words in one's mind's ear. On the other hand, one's rather involved and indirect introspection of the full content of such a word-mediated thought may well be something over which one legitimately retains doubts. And there are yet more torturous and uncertain cases. Certainly one's ascription to oneself of various desires, by considering in an armchair what one imagines one would concretely do and feel under various hypothetical circumstances, and remembering what one has done and felt in the past, is a yet more easily defeasible sort of introspection than even our introspection of the contents of our word-mediated thoughts. There is, for instance, a lot more motivation for self-deception in such cases.

17. What's more, introspection is not only a sophisticated but a fragile achievement. One's sense of what one perceives, which one might verbally report, and one's other behavior in light of perception, fit nicely together in ordinary situations, and can together help underwrite the presence of introspection of an intuitive sort, but we know now that in some instances these things come apart. See Larry Weiskrantz, *Blindsight* (Oxford: Oxford University Press, 1986). And perhaps I should be

explicit again that I include motor intentions in experience. Not merely perception but action involves an awareness of content, and we can explicitly articulate the introspectible content of certain motor intentions, which help constitute our concrete experience.

18. With reasonable success.

19. Notice that introspection may not help us sufficiently to count thoughts. How many experiences are you having at this moment? Of course, word-mediated thoughts, even those realized in inner speech, may be more easily counted than experiences.

20. John Searle, *The Rediscovery of the Mind* (Cambridge, MA: MIT Press, 1992), 151-173.

21. Such PDP machines are often held to have certain large advantages over conventional computers as models of our minds. See for instance P.S. Churchland and T.J. Sejnowski, "Neural Representation and Neural Computation", in Nadel, Cooper, Culicover, and Harnish (editors), *Neural Connections, Neural Computation* (Cambridge, MA: MIT Press, 1989), 15-48. As we will see, they seem significantly more like our neural hardware. They are good at things at which we seem especially good, for instance things like perceptual recognition, which involve simultaneous satisfaction of lots of soft constraints all at once. And the capacities of such machines degrade gracefully, like our own capacities: they don't completely crash when some part of their network of units has been disturbed.

22. See Churchland and Sejnowski.

23. See again, for instance, Churchland and Sejnowski.

24. It is also worth noting about this case that we might not be able to sharply distinguish what realizes the various bits of "knowledge" present in the machine, in the way in which we might distinguish between what realizes the various bits of information stored in a conventional computer memory.

25. Of course a clear and obvious thought might also realize a disposition, but I mean dispositions which are not constituted by clear and obvious thoughts.

26. That might imply that many of the thought contents besides those I dubbed "word-mediated" are, as a matter of contingent fact, only present in thoughts mediated by words.

27. Someone may worry that the possible world closest to the actual world in which there are sentences is one in which there are also thoughts. If so, and that's the way you evaluate conditionals of this kind, then help yourself to another formulation.

28. If a content may be true but not match, then it isn't a plausible candidate to which to apply an objectual account.

29. Notice that I said "constituted", not "caused".

30. All features rooted in content differences, that is.

31. If what follows over the rest of the book bears some affinity to both objectual and non-objectual views, it also bears some affinity to thought skepticism as well. The only coherently conceivable accounts of the realization of thoughts deploy, I think, significant objectual resources. The most plausible accounts are radically non-objectual, but they aren't even coherently conceivable. Because there aren't in fact things of the sort we experience there to be, no account of our experience and hence our thought is at once plausible and coherently conceivable, at least in any detail. And this in turn suggests a kind of skepticism about thoughts, though no more about thoughts than about any of the mundane things which we experience there to be, the mundane things which might ground the truth of any human thoughts, if we can pretend for the moment there really are any. Literally speaking, any of our so-called talk of our having thoughts may be (more precisely, would be) false talk. But this would leave whatever it is we "call" our talk of thoughts no worse off than what we "call" our talk of very mundane things, say red apples. This is what I meant in Chapter One when I said my strategy would be to up the ante.

32. Hilary Putnam, "Brains and Behavior", in *Philosophical Papers* vol. 2, 325-341.

33. Hilary Putnam, "The Nature of Mental States", *Philosophical Papers* vol. 2, 429-440.

34. I owe this example to a discussion with Richard Rodgers many years ago. A similar argument is to be found in Brian Loar, *Mind and Meaning* (Cambridge: Cambridge University Press, 1981).

35. Brian Loar, *Mind and Meaning* and Fred Dretske, *Knowledge and the Flow of Information* (Cambridge, MA: MIT Press, 1981) are two early examples.

36. One possible sort of isomorphism view is internalist, and not really correlational and objectual in the way I have sketched. This is a view which holds that a representational state has a content such that it would be made true by any even merely hypothetical external things to which it was isomorphic. Let me ignore this complication in this quick sketch.
37. Depending on how broadly "would" is construed, this might represent an internalist alternative.
38. Jerry Fodor, *Psychosemantics.*
39. See Fodor, *Psychosemantics*, and also *A Theory of Content and other Essays* (Cambridge, MA: MIT Press, 1990).
40. Robert Cummins, *Meaning and Mental Representation* (Cambridge, MA: MIT Press, 1989).
41. Dennis Stampe, "Toward a Causal Theory of Linguistic Representation", *Midwest Studies in Philosophy* II, 1977, 81-102. Allan Gibbard, "Human Evolution and the Sense of Justice", *Midwest Studies in Philosophy* VII, 1982, 31-46. Ruth Garrett Millikan, *Language, Thought, and Other Biological Categories* (Cambridge, MA: MIT Press, 1984). Fred Dretske, "Misrepresentation", in Radu Bogdan (editor), *Belief: Form, Content, and Function* (Oxford: Clarendon Press, 1986), 17-36.
42. In fact, it only tells against objectual accounts of traditional perceptual experience, not of causal experience, at least in any straightforward way. If objectual accounts of causal experience fail, it will be primarily because of the first objection. In Part Three, though, I stretch for an application of the second objection to those accounts.
43. Something of the sort is deployed, for instance, by Jerry Fodor, "A Modal Argument for Narrow Content", *Journal of Philosophy* 88, 1991, 5-26.
44. See for instance Gilbert Harman, "Wide Functionalism", in Schiffer and Steele (editors), *Cognition and Representation* (Boulder, CO: Westview Press: 1988), 11-20.
45. See for instance Ned Block, "Advertisement for a Semantics for Psychology".
46. Colin McGinn, *Mental Content* (Oxford: Blackwell, 1989), 58-99.
47. McGinn's case is interesting in a number of ways. For instance, it may involve objectual resources, though not deployed in a correlational way. The tracing behavior itself may be, as it were, square-shaped. And note that at least over time the square shape may be encompassed by what are in at least one sense internalist resources, by the pattern of a finger's movement.
48. Presumably, these would be inner sense data, little colored images under the hat.
49. If there is, for instance, nothing with phenomenal color, if the two objections we have sketched succeed against standard accounts of certain sorts of perceptual experience which are crucial for the realization of thoughts with the familiar contents sketched in Part One, then note implications: First, the causal-explanatory arch which runs from environment through inner states to behavior will not closely match the psychological arch which runs from experience through other thoughts to action. If our neural states carry "information" about the environment, or have an evolutionary function to carry information, that information may be radically different from intuitive thought content. It may be that there is some sort of interesting higher-order causal structure in the brain which cognitive science of the computational variety describes, but it's not to be identified with the psychological. Second, if we are to give an account of the realization of thoughts with the familiar contents I have sketched, then we must pay special heed to exactly those features of the contents we "introspect". The contents of our experience which we introspect, as opposed say to the actual objects in the world which cause our experience, play at least one crucial semantic and psychological role. This requires at the very least that the contents of our thoughts be reflected in our behavior, and not only in the usual straightforward way, say by our running after a ball if we want a ball, or at least by our moving in the way we would run after a ball which we don't realize is a mere hallucination. Those contents should also be reflected in our reports and tracings and paintings of the contents of our thoughts. It is common for contemporary philosophers to distinguish between what they cede to be the very difficult problem of introspectible consciousness and the supposedly more tractable problem of thought content. But, as I have said, if in fact the intuitive content theory suggested in Part One is correct, then they are largely the same problem.

CHAPTER NINE

THOUGHT SKEPTICISM

This chapter reviews the arguments of the thought skeptics, who deny that there are thoughts with intuitive contents of the sorts surveyed in Part One. If thoughts are to be vindicated, then we will need to locate the failures of the arguments of thought skeptics who presume a familiar concrete world but hold that such a world does not contain sufficient resources to constitute thoughts. But this chapter has another target as well. That is *meaning* skepticism, the claim that there are no meaningful words. This second focus is appropriate for two reasons: First of all, the machinations of words are a crucial resource in the realization of some of our thoughts. To properly discharge the task of Chapter Thirteen, to see how, if we assume a capacity for experience, other sorts of thought are possible, we need to have some sense of how language operates. Second, we need to consider the thought skeptics' arguments in detail, to exhibit the full range of difficulties which must be faced if we are to vindicate our thoughts, and certain of these arguments are in the first instance arguments for meaning skepticism. They are only indirectly arguments for thought skepticism.

Certainly the two issues, thoughts with content and words with meaning, are closely entwined. Common sense maintains that we can say what we think and think what we say. It suggests that if there were no determinate meaning for sentences, then there would be no determinate content for our thought. And certainly any plausible understanding of thought and speech should recognize various interdependencies: Part One distinguished the content and the meaning of words, but those things are connected in certain ways we need to explore, and Part One also suggested that some of our thoughts are word-mediated, depend in some way on contentful words. We will see in the following chapter that capacities for contentful and meaningful speech depend in turn on capacities for certain sorts of thoughts which are not mediated by words.

There is a traditional philosophical dispute regarding the primary root of semantic phenomena. Some have thought that the meaning of sentences is dependent on the content of thoughts, for instance on the content of the intentions of speakers. On the other hand, some have claimed that the dependency runs the other way, for instance that all thought is internalized speech. I will take a middle road. Some of our thoughts are crucially mediated by words, but meaningful speech of such words depends on capacities for other sorts of thoughts. If we are to block the skeptical arguments we will consider in this chapter, then a proper understanding of the complex interdependency of thoughts and sentences can help show the way.

The next three sections present three classic arguments against the existence of words with determinate meaning, and hence indirectly against the existence of thoughts with determinate content. Each argument arose within a tradition attempting to produce an account of meaning. Logical positivism was subjected by Quine to severe internal criticism, Wittgenstein's early account of meaning was, or so at least Kripke has argued, rejected by Wittgenstein himself, and Derrida turned Husserl's phenomenological tradition against itself. Each major tradition in twentieth-century philosophy of language has yielded a characteristic skepticism. In section 4, we turn to a consideration of more direct sorts of skepticism about thoughts.

All of these arguments share a general form. They claim that the resources relevant to constituting thoughts and meaningful speech do not suffice to constitute thought or speech with appropriately specific content or meaning. As we will see, most of the arguments also share certain difficulties. They ignore certain relevant resources; they don't fully exploit the resources they do deploy; they unreasonably assume that if there isn't meaning or content of some quite specific sort then there is no contentful thought or meaningful speech at all; and they blunt the force of their skepticism by an implausible assumption that there might be certain activities involving language even if there were no thoughts or meaningful speech.

The rest of the book attempts to provide a refutation of thought and meaning skepticism. It attempts to develop a plausible and coherently conceivable account of how in fact our thoughts are constituted and our words have meaning. In this chapter, we will try only to defuse the thought and meaning skeptics' negative arguments. In the next chapter, I will sketch a seemingly plausible and coherently conceivable way in which meaningful language might be realized, at least if we allow ourselves the resource of certain thoughts which are not mediated by words. This sketch will be helpful when we turn to the issues of Chapter Thirteen, and it also points the way to a refutation of a specifically *meaning* skepticism.

1

Consider first Quine's argument in *Word and Object* that linguistic meaning is "indeterminate", that there is no fact of the matter about what certain words mean.[1] Quine dramatizes his argument by describing a situation in which an English-speaking linguist, confronting an unknown language "L" spoken in an alien though human culture, attempts to construct a translation manual for L, a mapping of L onto English, grounded in the appropriate criteria fixing such a recipe for translation as correct. He argues that two or more distinct translation manuals, assigning to words of L English words with intuitively distinct meanings, fit all the relevant criteria, hence that linguistic meaning is indeterminate. Let me decompose Quine's argument into several distinct premises:

P1) *If there is a unique and determinate assignment of linguistic meaning to L, then there is only one appropriate manual for the translation of L into English.* If there are determinate meanings then appropriate translations will have to preserve them. So P1 seems plausible, at least when we note that by distinct translation manuals Quine doesn't mean those which map a word of L onto English synonyms or near synonyms, but rather those which map that word onto English words with intuitively very different meanings.[2]

P2) *All facts about linguistic meaning in language L are constituted by facts about the dispositions possessed by speakers of L to perform behaviors of certain sorts in certain circumstances observable by translators.* Quine's best argument for this premise is found in his article "Indeterminacy of Translation Again":[3] "As long as our command of our language fits all external checkpoints, where our utterance or our reaction to someone's utterance can be appraised in the light of some shared situation, so long all is well. Our mental life between checkpoints is indifferent to our rating as a master of the language." In other words: All one needs to have to be a competent speaker of L are the right dispositions to behave in certain ways in certain humanly observable circumstances. Whether someone is a speaker of L depends on what they do or are disposed to do, not on their hidden and possibly idiosyncratic mental life, the special history of their peculiar conditioning, or the hardware in their heads. And it certainly seems plausible to claim that if there are facts about linguistic meaning in L, then they are constituted by the conditions which determine that there are competent speakers of L, for the meaning of L must be respected by its competent speakers.

The third premise of Quine's argument requires some background: Quine believes that the speakers of a language associate the sentences of that language with one another in a pattern which one might picture as a great web. Nearer sentences in the web are more closely associated by the speakers in a manner which mirrors, or perhaps constitutes, logical and other inferential connections between those sentences. At the edge of the web are sentences which are associated fairly directly with sense stimulation. On that periphery are "observation sentences", acceptance of which can be elicited from a speaker by some range of sensory stimuli relatively independently of the acceptance by the speaker of other sentences. Relatively internal to the web are sentences for which acceptance by a speaker is relatively dependent on the acceptance by the speaker of other sentences.

In addition to this picture of language, we need to understand some of Quine's terminology: To a rough first approximation, the "stimulus meaning" of a sentence S for person P at time t is the class of all sensory stimulations which would prompt P's assent to S. More precisely: "a stimulation σ belongs to the affirmative stimulus meaning of a sentence S for a given speaker if and only if there is a stimulation σ' such that if the speaker were given σ', then were asked

S, then were given σ, and then were asked S again, he would dissent the first time and assent the second. We may define the *negative* stimulus meaning similarly with 'assent' and 'dissent' interchanged, and then define the *stimulus meaning* as the ordered pair of the two."[4] Two sentences which have the same stimulus meaning for a speaker are said by Quine to have "intrasubjective stimulus synonymy". A sentence which a subject would assent to after every stimulus is said to be "stimulus-analytic". And a sentence to which a subject would dissent after every stimulus is said to be "stimulus-contradictory".[5]

Quine believes that the stimulus meaning of a sentence in L can be determined by a translator, that it depends on the dispositions of speakers of L to behave verbally in certain ways in various humanly observable circumstances. The translator simply "queries" speakers about a sentence, presents it for their assent or dissent, under various humanly observable circumstances, and hence under a certain range of easily inferable sense stimulation. This procedure requires that assent and dissent be determinable on the basis of behavior, but Quine believes this likely, since one will assent to a sentence in every situation in which one would volunteer it. And it requires that the translator be able to query the speakers of L about particular sentences. But on these assumptions, stimulus meaning would be a major resource in the construction of interpretation manuals.

One other piece of background: Quine divides sentences into various classes. Sentences are either "occasion sentences" (for instance "Lo, a rabbit!", "It is raining", and "It hurts") which command assent only if queried after an appropriate prompting sensory stimulation, or they are "standing sentences" (for instance "There is ether drift", "The Times has come", or "The crocuses are out") which may command assent unprompted by any current sensory stimulation. Among occasion sentences are the observation sentences mentioned previously, whose acceptance is mostly insensitive to the acceptance of other sentences, mostly insensitive to a speaker's possession of what Quine calls "collateral information". On the other hand, "Lo, a rabbit" is an occasion sentence which might be prompted for some speakers and not others by movement of grass or the presence of rabbit flies, depending on their prior acceptance of sentences like "rabbit flies are found near rabbits". Hence to that degree such a sentence is not observational. There is a behavioral mark of observation sentences. The more nearly the stimulus meaning of a sentence is the same for all speakers of a language, the more observational it is. This wouldn't be the case if there were certain pieces of collateral information shared by all speakers of a language, but Quine suspects that such universally shared information shouldn't be clearly distinguished from the meaning of the sentence anyway. With this background in place, let's turn to the third premise:

P3) *Facts about dispositions to perform behaviors of certain sorts in certain circumstances observable by the translator govern the construction of an appropriate translation manual according to a routine I will call "The Method".* The Method is as follows:

1) The observation sentences of L are identified, and their stimulus meanings determined. Sentences with greater and lesser degrees of observationality are also identified.

2) The truth-functional logical connectives of L (for instance those expressing negation and conjunction) are identified as meeting the standard semantic criteria for those connectives. They are revealed by queries regarding compound sentences and their components.

3) Stimulus-analytic and stimulus-contradictory sentences are identified, as well as sentences with various degrees of those properties.

4) The intrasubjective stimulus synonymy of pairs of occasion sentences is determined, and also degrees of such synonymy.

5) The sentences of L are segmented into words, then mapped onto English words, under the following constraints: The observation sentences of L map onto observation sentences of English with the same stimulus meanings. The connectives of L are mapped onto the corresponding connectives in English. Stimulus-analytic sentences of L are mapped onto stimulus-analytic sentences of English, likewise for stimulus-contradictory sentences. Pairs of intrasubjectively stimulus synonymous sentences of L are mapped onto such pairs in English. Degrees of approximation to observationality and stimulus-analyticity are likewise preserved. In constructing such a mapping, translators ought to attempt to make out the utterances of speakers of L as relatively continuous in topic, and simple and plausible in meaning. Quine calls a mapping constructed in this way a set of "analytical hypotheses".

6) This yields a translation manual for L, which is further tested by queries and pragmatic interaction based upon it, and suitably modified in their light.[6]

P4) *The Method does not yield a unique translation manual for L, since it does not yield a unique set of appropriate analytical hypotheses for L.* Quine supports this premise by presenting three sorts of examples which, in light of the fact that the primary meaning-fixing resource invoked by The Method is stimulus meaning, reveal likely indeterminacies of meaning:

a) Even for such relatively observational sentences as "Lo, a rabbit", synonymy cannot be identified with sameness of stimulus meaning, since two phrases can be synonymous in the intuitive sense and yet lack sameness of stimulus meaning. "Lo, a rabbit" may possess different stimulus meanings for different speakers who have different collateral information, for instance regarding the significance of moving grass or of the presence of rabbit flies.

b) For sentences which are further inside the web, and hence relatively less observational, like "Lo, a bachelor", this problem is even more acute.

c) The reference even of words in relatively observational sentences is not fixed by their stimulus meaning. If "Gavagai" in L is observational and has the same stimulus meaning as "Lo, a rabbit" in English, still "gavagai"[7] may refer not to rabbits, but to undetached rabbit parts, or collections of time-slices of rabbits, or instantiations of the universal rabbithood, or the rabbit fusion, which consists of the one spatio-temporally discontinuous individual which has all rabbits as parts. It might seem that a translator could query the speakers of L about the number of gavagai about and use this information to discriminate among these possibilities, many rabbits matching one fusion and very many time slices. But Quine believes that this would require that the counting and identity-expressing features of L be somehow identifiable and interpretable prior to the general translation of L, and this he claims impossible given the resources of The Method.

P2, P3, and P4 entail that there isn't a unique appropriate translation manual for L, hence with P1 they entail Quine's skeptical conclusion: *The linguistic meaning of L is indeterminate*. And so, by parity of argument, is the meaning of any language, even English.

This argument seems to have a radical and improbable conclusion, one we'd have a great deal of difficulty accepting. But there is a quinean stopgap, elaborated in the work of Donald Davidson.[8] Even if linguistic meaning is indeterminate, still we might modify our meaning talk in certain ways. We might continue to talk of meaning and synonymy being determinate *relative to* a particular translation manual.[9] And if we arbitrarily choose one manual and stick by it, we might even leave the relativization implicit, and properly talk much as we always have about linguistic meaning. Despite this stopgap, Quine's indeterminacy argument is open to the four types of objections I've already mentioned:

1) Quine's skeptical picture of language, and the Quine-Davidson strategy to blunt the impact of that skepticism in our lives by endorsing activity involving meaning-attributing sentences, both assume that there are determinate sentences, determinate syntax. But it is not clear that Quine's behaviorist resources allow an appropriate individuation of sentences, relative to one another and to things which are not sentences. If sentence identity were indeterminate, then commonsense talk of linguistic phenomena might be more radically wrong than Quine suggests. We will return to this issue in the next chapter.

2) Quine seems to ignore some crucial meaning-fixing resources. Even if we accept Quine's contention that behavioral dispositions are all the facts on which linguistic meaning supervenes, we might find the particular sorts of behaviors to which he primarily restricts his consideration, behaviors involving sentences, unnecessarily circumscribed. For instance, perhaps one important sort of constraint on what one means are the psychological attitudes one has, say one's intentions in using words. And perhaps dispositions to behavior of other than a purely linguistic sort help constitute those psychological states, since psychological states influence and underlie more than one's merely linguistic behavior.[10] Alternatively, one might plausibly object to any sort of behaviorist constraint, and insist for instance that intentions matter yet are *not* constituted solely by dispositions to publicly observable behavior. We will see in the next chapter that this *sort* of objection, though perhaps not this particular instance of it, is in fact quite telling. Thoughts are a crucial resource in the realization of linguistic meaning, and are not constituted solely by behavioral dispositions of the sort Quine invokes.

3) As I've said, skeptical arguments tend to move quite quickly from the conclusion that meaning is vague or indeterminate in some unexpected way to a

fairly radical skeptical conclusion. Quine's is no exception. Consider the reference of "gavagai". I think it's really far from clear that there isn't a way to fix its appropriate reference on the basis of behavioral dispositions, but even if there isn't, we might well wonder how important that is. If what a native means is really indeterminate in reference between rabbits and rabbit stages and rabbit fusions, maybe that should suggest that the proper notion of meaning for a language is one in which these differences which are no differences disappear. In fact, they did disappear in Part One, at least from basic contents.

Let me come at this point from another angle. Whatever the success of Quine's own examples, there are quite intuitive examples of indeterminacy, which don't depend on any suspicious behavioral presumptions. Peter Unger has distinguished *contextualism* about the meaning of a certain expression, the view that the meaning of that expression varies from one context in which it is uttered to another in the manner that the reference of "I am here now" varies depending on who says it, from *invariantism* about the meaning of that expression, the view that the meaning of that utterance does not vary from one context to the next, as the meaning of "At times in the history of the universe there were no stones" does not vary.[11] He has argued that for certain sentences--for instance "The field is flat" said of a slightly bumpy field on one occasion to croquet duffers, on another to finicky experts, and on a third to the same experts drunk and looking for amusement--there is no fact of the matter whether their meaning i) varies with the context of utterance such that each time such a sentence expresses a different proposition, or ii) stays rigid and invariant in such a way as to make each utterance of such a sentence literally false, but at the right distance from truth for everyone involved to get along nicely. Or consider such a treatment of an example of Lakoff and Johnson's: the meaning of "buttressed" in "He buttressed the wall" and "He buttressed his argument with an appeal to authority". Some may hold that the meaning of "buttressed" is the same in each sentence, that it invokes an abstract sort of buttressing which can be done both to buildings and to arguments. Some may hold that "buttress" in each sentence has a different meaning. And others may hold a sort of metaphor view, according to which the meaning of "buttress" in each sentence is the same, invoking the sort of thing literally done to buildings, so that the second sentence is literally false but still a useful metaphor. But perhaps one may more plausibly insist that there is no fact of the matter which adjudicates among these views of the meaning of the term, that there is simply an indeterminacy.

I think that there are in fact indeterminacies of these sorts. But it is certainly not obvious that such indeterminacies should lead us to be skeptical about meaning, rather than simply more sophisticated about what sort of meaning there is. Philosophers deploy various theories of meaning which incorporate various distinctions, say between the assertion and expression of attitudes, which may just be too fine-grained to capture the rough-hewn meaning of much ordinary speech. But if it is indeterminate whether someone is expressing or asserting their preferences when they say "ice cream is good", still they mean something by that. Skeptical arguments at best demonstrate particular sorts of indeterminacy of particular sorts of meaning. To establish a radically skeptical conclusion, and not just support a reformulation of our view about what sort of meaning a sentence has, one needs to argue that determinacy of the relevant sort of meaning is crucial to the existence of meaning *per se*. Examples like "gavagai", and "flat" and "buttress" for that matter, do not alone suffice to establish this. It is consistent with the presence of intuitive and introspectible meaning of the sort which we pursue here that there are some indeterminacies.

4) Quine exhibits a tendency to under-exploit the very meaning-fixing resources he deploys. Like the "gavagai" case, Quine's other examples of indeterminacy also depend on the fact that sameness of stimulus meaning does not imply intuitive synonymy. There are cases in which differences in the collateral information possessed by speakers affect the stimulus meaning of the sentence for those people without affecting its intuitive meaning. Remember rabbit flies. And there is the problem that some sentences, say logical truths and theoretical sentences, cannot be assigned any particular distinct stimulus meaning, but are still intuitively distinct in meaning.

But Quine's linguist may well have resources to help with these problems. Quine presents a certain theory of how meaning accrues to sentences, by their association in a web which impinges directly on experience only at the edges. That theory is an assumption of his indeterminacy argument. But he gives us no particular argument that the exact form of a particular person's web[12] is not determinable on behavioral evidence of a sort which he should allow. That argument is what he owes us. In fact, it seems to me very likely that the form of the web is fixed by behavioral dispositions, despite Quine's own apparent failure to consider the sort of behavioral evidence relevant to determining the inferential connections of accepted sentences.[13] As Ed Becker has suggested to me, one might go a long way by simply admitting sentences themselves into stimulus-conditions.[14] And differences between idiosyncratic collateral information and meaning might be revealed to the linguist by the *differences* in the stimulus meanings of particular sentences for *different* speakers of L. Nothing in Quine's method forbids a translator from observing more than one speaker. And socially shared collateral information might not in fact be distinct from intuitive meaning, or it might be distinguished by a consideration of how speakers would react under various hypothetical series of sensory stimulations. A better use of the very sorts of resources which Quine allows would dispose of at least some of his examples of indeterminacy, and the indeterminacy that remains may simply be an indeterminacy that there intuitively is.

Quine's method is also inadequate in other ways. For instance, he doesn't even hint at a way that the noncognitive meaning of certain terms might be determined. But some relevant suggestions may be contained in the next skeptical argument, which deploys a very different kind of example.

2

This section will concern a skeptical argument against meaning proposed by Kripke[15] as an interpretation of Wittgenstein's *Philosophical Investigations*.[16] Like Quine's argument, it suggests a sort of meaning indeterminacy. But unlike Quine's argument, it does not rest on a suspicious behaviorist premise. It admits more meaning-fixing resources. Consider a person "X" who uses the symbol "+" as English speakers do, and has in fact performed a number of additions in his or her time, though never of any numbers greater than or equal to 57.

P1) *If the symbol "+" has determinate meaning for X, then it denotes the function "plus" and not the function "quus", where plus = x+y, and where quus equals x+y if x is less than or equal to 57, and equals 5 otherwise.* Note that the argument assumes that there are determinate functions denoted by "plus" and "quus", and hence should probably be considered a *reductio*. Notice also that quus could be replaced in the argument by an infinity of other functions, for instance which when x > 57 equal 6, or 7, or so on.

P2) *Whatever meaning the symbol "+" has for X is determined by either*

a) *X's actual present or past use of the symbol, in computations public or private.*

b) *a rule that X has internalized.*

c) *a particular introspectible "qualia", a sensory image or other experience, associated with "+" by X.*

d) *X's dispositions to use the symbol in private and public computations.*

or

e) *some combination of (a) - (d) plus a constraint that requires that "+" refer to the simplest function meeting all other constraints on its meaning.*

This is a crucial premise. It is not supported in Kripke's Wittgenstein by any explicit argument.[17] Is it plausible? It considers a lot of resources which Quine simply ignores. But all of the resources it allows are "internalist" resources, available if the meaning of someone's words is constituted by their more or less *internal* states, roughly and intuitively by what's inside their skin, or perhaps only slightly outside, like their computational behavior with pencil and paper. It notably excludes certain externalist resources. Quite notably, it excludes the resources which many think Kripke invokes when he claims that the reference of a name is fixed not by the description of the referent which a user of the name has in mind, but rather by the particular historical chain of transmission of that name leading back to an initial baptism of the referent.[18] And it excludes the resources which it is often thought are deployed by Wittgenstein in the *Philosophical Investigations*, and reflected in the suggestion that the use of a term by a *social* group and not merely by a single *individual* fixes such meaning as it has. Perhaps we are supposed to conclude that arguments against the sufficiency of the internalist resources cited in P2 can be extended to dispose of their externalist cousins. For instance, if we see that individual behavior cannot fix meaning, then perhaps we are supposed to conclude that neither can the behavior of a group. However, we will soon see that the arguments do not easily generalize in this way. At the very least, P2 is a premise to keep your eye on.

P3) *X's actual past and present use of "+" in computations is consistent with its denoting either plus or quus*. This is because X is someone who has never added numbers greater than or equal to 57, and it is only out there that plus and quus diverge. One might insist that no actual individual escapes school without having added beyond 56, but for any actual individual there is some number which they haven't added beyond, and hence an analogue of this argument should be available for any actual individual.

P4) *No rule X has internalized fixes whether by "+" X means plus or quus.*

P5) *No introspectible quale which X associates with "+", no image or picture or adding experience, fixes whether by "+" X means plus or quus.*

Both of these premises are supported, by Kripke's Wittgenstein, with forms of the same argument, which might be encapsulated in the slogan "Nothing interprets itself". Here's the form of the argument relevant to P4:

i) A rule internalized by X for the use of "+" consists either of a) a set of directions for an activity involving counting[19] or b) a set of laws for addition,[20] in either case present to X's mind.

ii) These directions or laws are sentences involving words like "count" or the successor stroke.

iii) Either "count", the successor stroke, and their like can be assigned interpretations, consistent with all the facts that fix their meanings, which leave the meaning of "+" indeterminate between plus and quus, or the meaning of those words is fixed by facts other than internalized rules.

Hence P4. In other words, internalized rules for the use of a symbol are just other words present to the mind, themselves in need of interpretation. One might try to specify that interpretation in other sentences present to the mind. But all sentences present to the mind might be variously interpretable as a group in a manner which leaves the meaning of "+" indeterminate.

There is a corresponding argument for P5, since images are no more able to interpret themselves than sentences:

i) Even if there were a particular introspectible quale that constrains the meaning of "+", it would determine that "+" means plus and not quus only if the quale mandated the uses of "+" consistent with its meaning plus but not with its meaning quus, and did so independently of some interpretation.[21]

ii) But no quale can do that, since images no more interpret themselves than sentences do.

Hence P5. Now on to the next premise:

P6) *X's dispositions to use the symbol "+" in private and public computations do not determine whether X means quus or plus by "+".* This premise is supported in Kripke's version of Wittgenstein by two arguments, the "infinity argument" and the "normativity argument". The infinity argument:

i) If X's dispositions to use "+" fix its meaning, then for X to mean plus by "+" is for X to be disposed, when asked for x+y, to give the sum of x and y as the answer, where the sum is the number yielded by the plus function, and for X to mean quus is for X to be disposed, when asked for x+y, to give the quum of x and y as the answer, where that is yielded by the quus function.

ii) But X's dispositions to use "+" in this way are finite, since some numbers are just too large for X to add.

iii) It follows from this that X's dispositions underdetermine whether X means plus or quus.

Hence P6.

There is an obvious objection to this argument in this form: (iii) is ridiculous. Certainly any ordinary person X has dispositions which carry him or her at least as far as the proper addition of 58 and 58, which would rule quus out of contention. But there is also an obvious reply to this objection: Since the dispositions of an ordinary X are finite, there is *some* number which generates an analogue of quus and plus between which "+"'s meaning is indeterminate for that X, a number far enough out to be beyond X's dispositions to add. So even if the argument as stated would be unsound if applied to any actual X, there is a sound analogue of the argument available. This reply is problematic, and we will return to this issue in a moment.[22]

The second of Kripke's Wittgenstein's arguments for P6 is the normativity argument. There is some controversy about the proper interpretation of this argument. I will presume a rather down-to-earth reading for the moment, but consider alternatives soon.

i) (i) as in the preceding argument.

ii) X will have dispositions to make mistakes when adding, for instance when rushed, or distracted, or when adding large enough numbers.

iii) But such mistakes are not constitutive of what X means by "+".

Hence X's dispositions to use "+" do not determine its meaning.

One might object that we need only add a clause excluding as irrelevant to meaning those dispositions which are a source of mistakes, but Kripke's Wittgenstein's response is that this cannot be done without an independent specification of what constitutes adding, and whether that is available for X is precisely the issue at hand.

P7) *If P3 through P6 are true, then X's actual present and past use of "+ ", a rule X has internalized for its use, associated introspectible qualia, and X's dispositions to use the symbol in computations, are not sufficient together to determine whether or not X means plus or quus by "+ ".* Given P3 through P6 and the arguments which supported them, it would seem that adding these various resources together would not help much.

P8) *If P3 through P7 are true, then the addition to the resources summarized in P7 of a simplicity constraint, requiring the function denoted to be the simplest candidate meeting all other constraints, will not appropriately serve to fix that X means plus and not quus by "+ ".* Kripke's Wittgenstein appears to favor the following argument for P8: Simplicity considerations can only lead one *distinct* alternative to be preferred to another, and in this context quus and plus are not distinct alternatives. Unfortunately, that last claim is, in this context, a begging of the question at issue.[23] But Kripke's Wittgenstein might well invoke other considerations. For instance, he might claim that simplicity considerations are irrelevant and inappropriate, since even had quus been simpler than plus, X would still have meant plus by "+". One can certainly sometimes mean something which is not the simplest alternative. And it is far from clear that simplicity isn't relative or indeterminate in such a way as to leave neither plus nor quus non-relatively and determinately simpler.

From P1 through P8 we can conclude that the meaning of "+" for X is indeterminate. But the argument begs for generalization:

P9) *There is nothing about the preceding argument which blocks a generalization to other words.*

One might resist P9 with a claim that in a mathematical example the problem of infinity is specially troubling, and that such a case is also abstract in a way in which talk of tables and chairs is not. But most words are generally held to have an infinity of possible correct uses, and the abstractness of mathematics plays no obvious role in Kripke's Wittgenstein's argument. So P9 at least seems plausible. From P1 through P9 we may conclude that there is an indeterminacy of meaning for any word. Kripke's Wittgenstein concludes from this that "there is no such thing as meaning anything by any word."[24]

Kripke's Wittgenstein's argument appears to have an intolerably dramatic conclusion. But the force of the conclusion is mitigated by what Kripke calls Wittgenstein's "skeptical solution": The conclusion of the argument, if it carries the sense that philosophers perhaps illegitimately or impossibly or at least idiosyncratically intend, is true. But *ordinary* talk of meaning does not carry such a sense, and is appropriate even if the conclusion, read "philosophically", is true. The form of words of the conclusion would not be appropriate in ordinary, non-philosophical contexts.

Kripke claims that the skeptical solution is an example of a new view of meaning Wittgenstein had come to adopt in the *Philosophical Investigations*, against his older position in the *Tractatus*, a new view with two components: i) It is not that the meaning of a sentence is its *truth-condition*, the fact which would obtain if it were true and fail to obtain were it false, but rather its *assertibility conditions*, the pair of sets of conditions under which it is appropriately asserted, and denied. A single sentence with a given pair of assertibility conditions may be appropriately denied by one person in one situation while appropriately asserted by another person in another situation, but a sentence with a "truth-condition" cannot be true for one and false for another. ii) It is not that sentences consist always of names of objects concatenated in some way, but rather that sentences often include words which appear to be names but really don't function as tags of distinct and separable things. Think of "sake" in "I did it for his sake."

In this light, the "skeptical solution" is this: i) There is no distinct thing, the meaning of a sentence, to which the word "meaning" attaches as a tag. ii) Sentences "about" meaning do not have "truth-conditions" of the relevant sorts. Hence they do not assert "facts". Rather they have assertibility conditions.[25] If there is a general background of *social* agreement in linguistic and mathematical practice, without which talk of the meanings of mathematical utterances loses its point, these are the putative relevant assertibility conditions:[26] X is entitled to say "I mean plus by '+'" whenever X has a feeling of confidence that he or she can give correct responses when queried in new calculations, and he or she is entitled to judge a new response to be correct because it is the response he or she is inclined to make. However, another individual Y need not accept X's authority in these matters. Y is entitled to judge X to mean plus by "+" only if either i) Y judges that X's answers to particular calculations agree with those he or she is inclined to give or ii) if they occasionally disagree, still the disagreements aren't too radical and significant.

Why bother with talk of meanings if it fails to express facts?[27] Because when one attributes to someone the mastery of certain linguistic practices or rules, one is claiming that we can entrust them to act as one does, rather than in a bizarre way, in ordinary interactions with others. To say that someone means plus by "+" is to indicate that they will act in the way one takes to be ordinary ways. If we can presume that one is in line with the background of agreement in practice which gives meaning ascriptions their point, then they will be ordinary ways. To say that someone means quus by "+" is to indicate that they will act strangely.

Despite this skeptical solution, Kripke's Wittgenstein's argument faces a number of serious difficulties, which parallel those of Quine's argument:

First of all, the skeptical solution, like the Quine-Davidson stopgap, attempts to blunt the bite of meaning skepticism by claiming that a certain linguistic activity, involving words like "meaning", is possible and appropriate even if there literally is no such thing as meaning anything by any word. But the skeptical solution is only available if, in a world in which there is no such thing as meaning anything by any word, there are words. And it might be that any resources which can give us determinate words, determinate syntax, would be sufficient to remove the problem about meaning as well. Again, more on this in the next chapter. Also, it is worth noting that, if the picture of truth-dependencies sketched in Part One is correct, at least some thoughts must have more than mere assertibility conditions.

A second problem, of course, is P2, which limits meaning-fixing resources to the internalist buffet specifically addressed by Kripke's Wittgenstein. Were one to prefer instead irreducible states of intending to mean plus by "+", or external determinants of meaning in what is perhaps the manner of Kripke himself, then one should find P2 as difficult to swallow as Quine's behaviorist premise. In fact, there are a couple of quite specific ways in which P2 seems mistaken, which are rooted even in the standard interpretation of Wittgenstein. We'll come back to this point in a moment. In fact, let me consider both our two remaining characteristic objections at the same time as well, because all these objections interact here in an interesting way. Kripke's Wittgenstein may be criticized for failing to adequately deploy the resources he allows as well as for ignoring certain resources, and also for failing to acknowledge that if there is *some* indeterminacy of meaning that does not necessarily entail that there is no meaning. Let me make these charges more concrete:

P1, which says that if the meaning of "+" is indeterminate between plus and quus then "+" has no meaning, might be criticized on the following grounds: Even if there were an indeterminacy between plus and quus, still "+" would have a meaning which constrains its use under 57. It is just that the meaning might have a range of vagueness and indeterminacy out beyond that. If, as many think, Wittgenstein discovered the vagueness of what we mean, that does not imply that he discovered that we mean nothing.

This point seems best deployed in conjunction with a criticism which might be lodged against P6. Recall that Kripke's Wittgenstein has two arguments for P6, which is the claim that *dispositions* to use "+" underdetermine its meaning plus or quus. The first is the argument from the infinity of the applications of "+" and the finitude of the dispositions of a finite creature like X. The second is the "normativity" argument. Since both infinity and normativity are often the source of resistance to accounts of the realization of thoughts which deploy mundane resources of the sorts we will consider in this part, it is worth noting how much ambiguity such notions can hide.

First, consider infinity. It is relatively easy to imagine a finite creature with dispositions which underwrite an infinity of responses when that infinity and those responses are of certain sorts. For instance, imagine a creature which stamps the word "red" on red things it examines, and the word "yellow" on yellow things. It has what are in one sense dispositions to only two behaviors. But notice that it might hence have a disposition to stamp "red" on things with an infinity of subtly different patterns of red, without even noticing the differences, without even being capable of noticing the differences. And it is also not implausible to claim that a given human might occupy an infinity of alternative microphysical states, which might constitute an infinity of different dispositions to different hand motions, underwriting movement of the hands to one particular exact location and orientation rather than another, though again these differences might be beyond our ordinary notice. If the Kripke-Wittgenstein argument is to succeed, finitude of some plausible and particular sort must be incapable of underwriting "infinite" behaviors of another plausible and particular sort.

Why is it that a finite human is supposed to lack dispositions to perform certain additions? Apparently because addition is required to take a certain form. Apparently it isn't enough to write "+1" next to any name for a number, nor to write "+ the continuum" next to it, to have performed an addition. Rather, one must take two numbers in standard decimal notation, or something similar, and then add them together in such a way that their sum is also expressed in such a notation. Kripke's Wittgenstein is only talking about additions of one particular and canonical sort. Why don't we have enough dispositions to do this very particular sort of thing? For two related reasons, I think. Because some numbers are simply two big for us to write or read in decimal notation. And because we must be able to perform an infinity of what we would *recognize* as different behaviors to perform all possible additions in this form. To put things in this way reveals, I think, that the problems of "+" may have more to do with the specific infinity of mathematics than Kripke's Wittgenstein allows.

Consider another, more direct problem with the infinity argument. Kripke's Wittgenstein claims that the particular finitude suffered by X's dispositions implies that there is no disposition X has to reply with the addition, and not the quadition, of numbers over 57. As I said, this would be a ridiculous claim for any actual X, but recall the obvious response to this criticism: For any actual X, there is some number n such that there is an analogue of the quus/plus case available which pivots around n rather than 57, and which is beyond X's finite dispositions. Some numbers are just too damn big for us to have dispositions to add, at least in the canonical way. But there is some difficulty with this response: Kripke's Wittgenstein doesn't provide us with an actual case of meaning indeterminacy, but rather with a recipe for constructing one. In fact, there is reason to think he cannot provide us with an actual case, and this should make us suspicious. He seems to face a dilemma. On the one hand, a case involving an actual X might be such that the reader could see that ordinary addition was not indeterminate between the two alternatives it invokes. Then the ordinary reader, and likely also the actual X, would have dispositions to perform calculations which ruled out one of the alternatives. Hence the case would not demonstrate that X's dispositions failed to fix what X means by "+". On the other hand, an actual case might be such that *the reader* would fail to have dispositions to perform calculations in one of the alternative ways rather than the other. But then such a case would be one which the reader could not see as really involving an indeterminacy between the ordinary meaning of "+" and something else, hence it would fail to convince the reader that X's dispositions underdetermine the meaning of "+". In other words, a realistic case which really exceeds an ordinary X's, and the reader's, dispositions to use "+", if there is such a case, is a case in which there may be a vagueness in what the reader and X mean by "+", a vagueness in the meaning of our language which does not in itself show that "+" means nothing intuitive. Of course, some realistic Xs may lack some dispositions which a reader has. For instance, perhaps the dispositions underwriting the meaning of "+" in the seventeenth century did not determine how to add certain transfinite cardinals. But even that doesn't imply that "+" meant nothing then. It just implies that it meant something a bit more indeterminate than it does now.

One may reasonably object, on behalf of Kripke's Wittgenstein, that surely what we mean by "+" is determinate out beyond our dispositions to add in the particular canonical way which Kripke's Wittgenstein requires. This seems to me correct. But this seems to me also to put more stress on the importance of the canonical form of addition than it should be asked to bear. Perhaps the best way to see this is to consider the *other* argument which Kripke's Wittgenstein deploys to buttress P6, the normativity argument.

The normativity argument, at least as I construed it, claims that dispositions to use "+" may involve dispositions to make mistakes in calculations which are not constitutive of the meaning of "+". The obvious reply to *this* argument is that the dispositions which should be held to fix the meaning of "+" include not merely dispositions to use it in calculations of the canonical sort, but also dispositions to correct such use, to correct such corrections, and so on. Indeed, yet other dispositions, for instance to count in certain ways, to give certain proofs, to make statements of theoretical constraints on the nature of addition, to add in other than the canonical way, and so on, seem also to help determine the meaning of "+" for X. P4, for instance, may be taken to show us that all this wouldn't help much. Sentences don't interpret themselves, we are told, not even sentences about how to perform additions. But Kripke's Wittgenstein seems to me to lack a convincing argument that dispositions to *use* those other sentences would not be of at least some help.

Let me now draw all of these threads together: It seems to me that any way in which any ordinary speaker can see that some X's dispositions are insufficient to mean plus by "+" is a case where that ordinary speaker has some disposition which constrains the use of "+" beyond the way it is constrained by X's dispositions. Recall again that we are talking about a very particular sort of case, a mathematical case. Isn't our mathematical thought word-mediated in a crucial way, so that our dispositions to use words in inner and outer speech have in such a case a very special role in constituting what we think when we speak using those words? It is quite intuitive to claim that we understand how addition works even out beyond cases we can actually add explicitly, at least in the canonical way favored by Kripke's Wittgenstein. But if all *our* dispositions to talk about additions and infinities and deploy "+" in additions and to correct those additions, and all the inferences we are disposed to make between arithmetical sentences and more mundane sentences, leave the interpretation of what we mean by "+" indeterminate in some particular way, then it seems to me that we should not be so certain that it is determinate in that way. And if there is some vagueness in what we mean, that does not imply that we mean nothing.

What reason does Kripke's Wittgenstein provide us for thinking that all of X's dispositions together, not just to add but to do all the rest a plausible X would plausibly be disposed to do, underdetermine their meaning plus by "+"? None explicitly, but perhaps his claim would be that an individual's dispositions even to correct, even to correct corrections and so on, might be in error. For instance, they might not meet our community standards for what "+" means. But if X is to mean what we as a community mean by "+" in such a case, if "+" is not for X a phrase in an idiolect which *X's* dispositions alone fix, then it seems not unlikely that the dispositions not merely of X but of X's entire linguistic community should be relevant to fixing the meaning of "+". Hence externalist determination occurs, and P2 is false. It doesn't make obvious sense to say that an entire linguistic community's dispositions to use "+" and to correct such uses could underdetermine whatever meaning it has in that community.

There is one last resource Kripke's Wittgenstein could deploy at this point, which requires what I take to be a rather highfalutin reading of his normativity argument. One might take the "normativity" objection to be more than the claim that someone's dispositions to use a word might be incorrect. Rather, one might claim that meaning is "normative" in some way like the way in which goodness and rightness are supposed to be normative, and claim that the "normative" cannot be constituted by anything mundane like dispositions, even the dispositions of communities.

As with infinity, I think it is worth being very clear about what sort of normativity is supposed to be present in these cases. For instance, it is trivially true that thoughts and sentences with content or meaning can be true or false, and hence "correct" or "incorrect" in some sense. And "correct" seems like a normative word. But this kind of "normativity" would of course be assured by any account of the realization of thoughts, for instance of the very mundane sort we will develop in this part. This isn't the kind of normativity which has seemed beyond naturalistic reduction. What more might someone mean by the "normativity" of thoughts or meaning? Some say that we must attribute thoughts to persons and interpret their utterances under a constraint of "rationality", that we must assume that thinkers and speakers will rationally infer, say *P and Q* from P and from Q, and also move in a rational way from wanting P and believing that Q is a means to P to doing Q. And rationality seems to involve reasons, and reasons to introduce normativity. We'll discuss rationality constraints a bit in section 4, though I have doubts about the plausibility of such constraints in anything like their popular form. But, in any case, it is important to see that they aren't "normative" in anything like the traditional sense appropriate to the good and the right. If I think that it would have been rational, in the sense relevant to interpretation, for Hitler to invade England before he invaded the Soviet Union, I am not endorsing his invading England in any sense. Rather than infer from his premises or act on his desires, I think he should have shot himself or gone back to painting. The "normativity" of the right and the good, which some people think cannot be constituted out of mundane things like dispositions, has nothing obvious to do with the rationality which constrains interpretation.

Another way to see that is this: If some irreducible normativity is alleged to be part of what constitutes some X to mean what they do, then still we might coherently conceive a non-normative twin Y, who has all the dispositions for verbal behavior and other non-normative concrete properties of X, but who does not glow with positive value. In fact, we can even imagine another twin who burns with negative value. That this is possible is ensured by the irreducibility of the normative properties and the content theory of Part One, or at least by that theory buttressed to include those alleged normative properties. Y does all the concrete things which we do. Indeed, we would be hard put to tell whether *we* glow with the irreducible value possessed by X, which we can neither hear nor smell nor see. Y does something semantic, which we characterize in this part and can assign content and truth in the manner I sketch. Call it "mean*" if you favor the irreducible normativity of meaning itself, but it is all we need to vindicate our agency.

Perhaps, as Allan Gibbard has suggested, the claim that meaning is normative might be interpreted in another way:[28] Assume that all non-normative facts about someone, for instance those we have so far surveyed, don't fix whether we agree with them or not, perhaps because of indeterminacies and vagueness in what they think, or perhaps because what they think mixes what we take to be both truth and error. Then there's still a question about our proper behavior in the face of that indeterminacy or partial error, about whether we *should* agree with them or not, and this is a question which could be considered a question of their proper interpretation and meaning. If they utter a sentence which is indeterminate between what we take to be error and truth, or which mixes together some error and truth, do we agree or disagree? A dispute between those who think we *ought* to agree and those who think we *ought* to disagree in such a case might be a full-blown normative dispute, and yet how we interpret them might turn on its resolution. There is a variant of this way of considering the normativity of meaning according to which the central issue is the agreement of a single person with himself or herself over time. Do all the non-normative facts about oneself yesterday suffice to determine how one "should" go on today?

Let me treat both these cases at once. There is room for genuinely normative dispute of these sorts only when there is in fact an indeterminacy of one sort of content or meaning, in one's past speech or the speech of another speaker, or a mixing together of true and false content or meaning. And it is merely *that* kind of non-normative content or meaning which we pursue here. Nothing more than that is required for our particular purposes.

This has been a long negative discussion, but we've learned some things which will be helpful when we turn to a positive account of linguistic meaning in the next chapter. First, individual dispositions to linguistic and other behaviors go further, in the ways we have seen, to fix linguistic meaning than Quine or Kripke's Wittgenstein allow. Second, social resources, for instance the dispositions of an entire linguistic community, may provide further determinacy.

I believe that there is a crucial third resource which Quine and Kripke's Wittgenstein do not explicitly consider, namely thoughts which are not linguistically mediated. I believe that they are crucially implicated in the conditions which allow there to be determinate words and determinate meaning. But before we turn to a positive account of linguistic phenomena, we'll more briefly survey some other important skeptical arguments. They share many of the difficulties we've already encountered, and they won't provide an introduction to any helpful meaning-fixing resources, but we should be aware of the full range of skeptical opposition to thoughts.

3

Jacques Derrida has proposed a skeptical argument which bears some affinities to those of Quine and Kripke's Wittgenstein.[29]

P1) *Thoughts (including intentions and notions) and words (both spoken and written) are kinds of "signs".*

But what are signs?

P2) *Signs are (i) rooted in so-called "differance", and (ii) infinitely iterable in both so-called "serious" and "non-serious" contexts.*

"Differance" is neither a word nor a concept, Derrida says. It expresses two putative features of signs, which we might ordinarily call syntactic and semantic features:

i) Signs, as Saussure suggested, are constituted by their *differences* from other signs, by their relative place in a system of signs, one phoneme distinguished only relative to another, one letter only relative to another, and so forth.

ii) Signs *defer* the presence of their referent, which is almost present in them though not really so, which is really absent when merely the sign is present, but somehow not wholly so.

To say that signs are infinitely iterable is just to say that a particular sign may be found in an infinite variety of different contexts, for instance not only in the immediate utterance of a particular speaker but in later citations of that utterance. Some of the contexts in which signs are found are traditionally thought to be "serious" and central contexts, literal utterance of truths for instance. Only in such serious contexts is the meaning of the sign supposed to be revealed or constituted. (Consider Quine on the determination of meaning by assent under sensory stimulation.) The other contexts in which the same sign are found are traditionally considered less central, "non-serious", and parasitic. For instance, words may be cited in quotations or in play-acting, and may be used in joking talk of the false, the impossible, and even the senseless. They may be used in all sorts of even more playful and deviant ways, in word games for instance. And they are employed in mistakes.

P3) *If a sign is infinitely iterable in "non-serious" contexts, then it has no determinate meaning (or content) unless those uses are somehow constituted as parasitic, less privileged, non-standard or deviant, and the "serious" uses as privileged or central.* In other words, if the deviant uses of a word are part of its meaning, then it has no univocal meaning. Derrida holds that philosophy has long functioned as part of the cultural myth of the hegemony of the "standard" over the "non-standard" uses of words. Part of its attempt to underwrite that hegemony is its promulgation of the myth of an introspectible meaning of a word, present to the mind of its utterer, which constitutes some uses of the word as legitimate or central and others as non-legitimate or parasitic.

P4) *The only way in which "serious" uses might be constituted as privileged is by a governing intention or notion of proper use, wholly present to the mind of the utterer or writer of the sign (or its possessor in the case of thoughts).*

But remember that notions and intentions themselves are implied by P1 to be signs, and hence are subject to the nature of signs. And the nature of signs articulated in P2 leaves them, Derrida suggests, incapable of being wholly present to the mind.

P5) *Something which is rooted in differance cannot be wholly present to the mind, nor can something which is infinitely iterable be so present.*

Derrida's argument for the first claim of P5: A sign rooted in differance, which is, Derrida says, an "effect" of differance, cannot be wholly present to the mind, because the deference of such a sign to its object, and the manner in which such a sign is constituted by its play of differences with other signs, prevent it from being wholly present. A sign *is* something which defers beyond itself to a non-present referent, and is constituted by differences with other signs not present, hence it cannot be wholly present.

Derrida's argument that something infinitely iterable cannot be present to mind is reminiscent of Kripke's Wittgenstein: There isn't room for this infinity of content in the finite minds of speakers. Plato invented the myth of the universal which is the myth of the presence to mind of the infinitely iterable, but such universals cannot be present to finite minds, Derrida holds.

These premises entail that *words and thoughts have no determinate meaning or content.* But the argument is open to objection at a number of familiar points:

i) The resources which the argument allows to fix meaning and content do not exhaust the plausible candidates. For instance, notions are not obviously signs if signs are constituted by a play of differance, nor for that matter are all thoughts obviously infinitely iterable in non-serious contexts. The derridean argument may succeed as a *reductio* within an important tradition which invokes a certain range of resources, but a plausible account of meaningful language can deploy different resources.

ii) Derrida at best may show not that there is no meaning, but rather that the meaning of words is not such as some have assumed. Perhaps non-serious uses should be accommodated as central and legitimate by the proper account of meaning. On the other hand, if mistakes can't be excluded, then there may not be much hope for resistance along these lines.

iii) Derrida helps himself to sameness of signs across different contexts. Unlike Quine and Kripke's Wittgenstein, however, Derrida is not uncritical about such resources. He is merely prepared to help himself to a pretty implausible metaphysics to underwrite them. We will return to this issue in the next chapter, but this metaphysics certainly puts us beyond the familiar concrete resources deployed in this part, and indeed beyond anything which is coherently conceivable.

4

Skepticism about the meaning of language is an important source of skepticism about the content of thoughts. But there are several recent *direct* arguments for skepticism about thoughts. While such arguments are often explicitly directed only against the existence of specific kinds of thoughts, they may suggest generalizations which might stand against the whole class.

There are several popular forms of skepticism about thoughts of at least traditional sorts, which I will call "beliefs and desires". *Instrumentalists* believe that there are, strictly speaking, no such things as beliefs and desires, though talking as if there were is a useful fiction. *Top-down* skeptics hold that the correct psychology or cognitive science will eschew, for reasons independent of the bloody details of neurophysiology, talk of beliefs and desires. *Bottom-up* skeptics hold that since psychological phenomena are neurophysiological phenomena, the correct psychological theory will be suggested bottom-up by the correct understanding of our neurophysiology, and will have no place for beliefs and desires. Let me consider these forms of skepticism, in that order.

Dennett was, at least for a while, an instrumentalist:[30] He held that there really are no beliefs and desires, but that pretending that there are can be useful in predicting behavior. His argument for this skepticism:

P1) *If anything really had beliefs and desires, then it would fully fulfill certain principles of rationality--requiring that one believe all the entailments of one's views, not believe contradictions, act so as to maximize one's expected utility given one's beliefs and desires, and the like--which help define those states.*

P2) *But nothing is so ideally rational as to fulfill all of those constraints.*

Hence there are no beliefs and desires.

On the other hand, Dennett thinks that some things are at least intermittently close enough to ideal rationality so that adopting "the intentional stance" towards them is useful, where to do that is to pretend that they are ideally rational and hence have beliefs and desires. People and chess-playing computers are among those things. While there are no beliefs and desires, sometimes speaking as if there were is a useful fiction.

Some familiar difficulties:

i) It is far from clear that ideal rationality is really required if there are to be beliefs and desires. Less than ideally rational persons seem to have beliefs and desires, the skewed sequence of which in fact constitutes them as irrational. So Dennett may be mistaken in thinking that ideal rationality is a crucial resource in the realization of beliefs and desires. And in any case, we aim to vindicate not specifically beliefs and desires, but thoughts in general. And we will see in what follows that ideal rationality is not required for their realization.

ii) Instrumentalism requires that there be no beliefs and desires, but at the same time that there be certain practices involving linguistic syntax. That syntax is involved in the expression of attributed attitudes and predictions made from the intentional stance. But it is not obvious that this is a coherent combination. Again, more on this in the next chapter. Now let me turn to top-down skepticism.

One prominent *non-skeptical* position is Fodor's: Thoughts, say beliefs and desires, involve relations between their possessors and internal formulae in some language of thought, whose words are somehow written in the brain and somehow have content. At least one important branch of cognitive science takes all cognitive phenomena to crucially involve computations performed on syntactic structures of this kind. But some philosophers have held that while there is a language of thought, it lacks content. Hence top-down skepticism, or the "Syntactic Theory of the Mind": Our behavior is appropriately explained by a theory which postulates computational states in the brain, sentences in some language of thought and between which there are computational relations which are analogues of inferential relations. But those sentences have no meaning or content; they are syntax without a semantics.

Schiffer and Field have suggested that such a purely syntactic psychological theory should have all the explanatory resources available to a Fodor-style semantical analogue, and that when augmented with a "reliability theory", a theory about which syntactic states of which people are reliable indicators of which phenomena in the world, it should be capable of doing all that semanticized psychology can do for us.[31] Stich has argued in addition that there are things which a syntactic theory can explain that a psychology committed to content cannot, and is hence to be preferred.[32]

P1) *Psychology committed to content explains behavior by the postulation of states individuated by their content.*

P2) *Such content is the sort of content which commonsense psychological explanations invoke.*

P3) *Similarity of such commonsense content for psychological states is a function of i) shared reference of the states, ii) shared causal role of the states, and iii) ideological similarity, which is shared belief about the nature of the referent.*

P4) *But there are important phenomena which cognitive science must explain and which cannot be explained by psychological states adverting to content of this sort.* For instance, cognitive science should explain the inferences of people whose reference is so hopelessly confused that the commonsense content of their thoughts is indeterminate, and it should explain the inferences of people whose ideological similarity to us is severely limited, like poor Mrs. T, who says that McKinley was assassinated but knows nothing at all of what assassination involves. Stich alleges that a psychology committed to explaining things by reference to states with commonsense content cannot handle these cases.

A number of difficulties for Stich, Schiffer, and Field:

i) A familiar refrain: The syntactic theory postulates that there are syntactic states, the presence of sentences in some language of thought, even though that language lacks a content or meaning. But it has not been shown that there can be such sentences of determinate sorts if there is no such content or meaning. Of course, it may be that we are not to take the label "syntactic theory" too seriously. But calling a so-called psychology "syntactic" if there really is no fact of the matter about the identity of syntax may simply hide how little like a psychology it is.

ii) Schiffer and Field admit that we will need to augment a syntactic explanation of human behavior with a reliability theory, which will allow us to use people as barometers of various features of the world. But it is far from clear that the complicated reliability theory required for the use of texts and utterances and thoughts about all sorts of distant, hypothetical, and abstract matters would fail to provide sufficient resources to assign contents to psychological states. Syntactic psychology plus an adequate reliability theory might *entail* a semantic psychology. And, on the other hand, in Part Three we will see reasons to worry that reliability of the sort Schiffer and Field favor is not in fact a feature of we human barometers.

iii) Of course, even if a semantic psychological theory cannot explain some phenomena, this does not imply that it doesn't explain others. And it is noteworthy that Stich's argument that a semantic psychological theory cannot do some things which need to be done, and which a syntactic theory can do, assumes that content must be as commonsense has it, and that commonsense has it in a particular way. But to show that content or meaning of a certain narrowly circumscribed sort does not exist or is insufficient for some purposes is not show that there is no content or meaning or that content or meaning of any sort is insufficient. For instance, the theory of content sketched in Part One might treat Mrs. T's thought as involving a certain quite limited sort of word-mediated content when she says "assassinate" to herself. Presumably she says that only certain individuals are assassinated, for instance. So there are assertion conditions in her idiolect for the word. And that account of content largely ignores reference. Even if someone is so hopelessly confused that we cannot figure out what they in fact are referring to, we might attribute to them determinate thought contents of the sort sketched in Part One.

Bottom-up skepticism about thoughts, skepticism rooted in neurophysiology, is perhaps less straightforwardly implicated in commitments to meaningful speech than the two sorts we have just examined, but it's perhaps worthy of note that its primary practitioners seem confident that meaningful speech of some sort can survive their skepticism. Paul and Patricia Churchland have argued that the ancient "folk-psychological" theory of our ancestors has no more antecedent plausibility than our ancestors' implausible theories of the planets and the weather, that "folk" psychology may well be a false theory. Since our actual mental states seem realized by our neurophysiological states, by the complex of neural tissue and electrical and chemical action which intervenes in us between sensory input and motor output, the Churchlands suggest that the true psychology will be constructed bottom-up out of neurophysiology, and may involve nothing like beliefs and desires as they have been traditionally conceived.

My argument that plausible conditions like neurons constitute our thoughts is yet to come. And it is important to recall that the generic and abstract class of thoughts which I am defending, psychological states with representational contents of the sorts articulated in Part One, is not necessarily hostage to many specific commitments by folk psychology, for instance regarding the particular nature of beliefs and desires. Nevertheless, the Churchlands may plausibly complain that the account of content in Part One is quite traditional and conservative. They may grant that there are things roughly like thoughts, but nothing with the sort of "folk-content" articulated there. Cognitive and neuroscience may require a radical revision of our conception of the content of our psychological states, they may insist. The content endorsed by Part One is not only representational. Such content is, at least in paradigm cases, introspectible. But theories in cognitive science and neuroscience have postulated levels of psychological processing involving contents which are not obviously of this introspectible sort. Such theories may require a reformulation of our conception of content, and indeed may embolden someone to claim that all our thoughts have merely such unfamiliar content.[33]

Consider the Churchlands' favorite example. Work on the unconscious processing of motor movements in the cerebellum led Llinas and Pellionisz to formulate a general theory of cognitive processing, the Tensor Network Theory or "TNT", which may seem to suggest a very different account of content than that articulated in Part One.[34] Llinas and Pellionisz noted that it seems plausible that all sorts of cognitive processing can be modeled as a transformation of a vector in some n-dimensional phase space into another vector in another phase space, where the transformation is described by a mathematical entity called a tensor. For example, consider Paul Churchland's 2-dimensional Roger the Crab: Roger has two eyes which foveate on an object placed within reach, and wired to relay to his processing unit the angles they subtend. Roger reaches out to the object by a jointed arm controlled by motors which adjust the angles subtended by the arm at Roger's body and at his elbow. Roger's cognitive processing can be represented by a transformation of positions in a 2-dimensional coordinate system representing the angles subtended by his eyes, into positions in another 2-dimensional space representing the angles to be subtended by his joints. TNT has the resources to represent many different sorts of cognitive processing, and seems to closely model the workings of actual neurophysiological systems. And it may seem not to invoke states with contents of the sorts articulated in Part One.

The first part of my reply is that it isn't *obvious* that such examples introduce sorts of content which Part One cannot deliver. We should notice that the contents of Roger's representations of arm angle and eye angle,[35] either seem to be quite concrete and hence just the sort of thing which basic contents are well-situated to capture, or abstractions from such concrete contents. Roger's sensory inputs and motor outputs might be specifically angled eyes and arms, or at least specific angles for eyes and arms. TNT represents cognitive processing as a series of phase space transformations which begins with sensory input and ends with motor output. The phase spaces seem either to represent at least relatively concrete sensory inputs and motor outputs, or, when they are intermediate phase spaces in the trajectory from input to output, abstractions from such. TNT[36] seems not to be in *obvious* conflict with the account sketched in Part One.

But if we dig a bit deeper, there may well be a certain kind of conflict, though more a conflict of emphasis rather than of truth.[37] For instance, if a creature as simple as Roger the Crab had *experience*, then it might be very different from our own. It isn't clear that we could understand what Roger thought in quite the same sense that we can understand what humans think. It isn't clear that we could understand how the world would have to be if thoughts with contents rooted in *his* experience were to match that world. If TNT delivers some account of what Roger thinks, then it isn't an account of quite the same thing as we have been seeking here. Let me put it this way: We might develop a TNT-like account of the "thought" of any creature which we can cut up, for instance a bat. We note the form of their sensory and motor organs and the features of the environment to which they respond. We note levels of neural processing which connect them. And we construct the necessary phase spaces and tensors. But it is at best an open question whether we can understand what a bat thinks in anything like the sense required to understand the experience of the bat, who "hears" all sorts of things we can only imagine seeing. Hence it is at best an open question whether we can construct a content theory for the bat along the lines sketched in Part One. It is at best an open question whether we can determine how the world would have to be for the bat's "introspectible" thought to match. In a world where our experience was in radical error, and in which some aliens with very different sense organs and experiences constructed a TNT-like account of our thought, such an account might look nothing like the account in Part One. And this tells,

I think, against its being an account of the sort we seek. We will return to these issues later on, but the immediate point is that even if there is content of the sort pursued by the Churchlands, it may well be a very different kind of content than that we pursue. It may be something different rather than an alternative form of the same thing, something different rather than a competitor. TNT may simply change the subject.

NOTES

1. W.V.O. Quine, *Word and Object*, chapter 2.
2. There might be a problem about how there can be such an intuitive sense of what constitutes radical distinctness of translations if Quine's argument succeeds, but we might read his argument as a *reductio* of the opposing view. I am told that under pressure from commentators, Quine moved later to adopt Harman's formulation, that two translations are distinct when two translators might disagree about them.
3. W.V.O. Quine, "Indeterminacy of Translation Again", *Journal of Philosophy* 4, 1987, 5-10. He also deploys there another argument: "Each of us learns his language by observing other people's verbal behavior observed and reinforced or corrected by others." In other words: All one learns in learning L is to behave in certain ways in certain observable circumstances, and these behaviors must constitute the capacity to meaningfully speak L. But this argument seems to depend on a controversial, very unpopular behaviorist account of language learning.
4. Quine, *Word and Object*, 32-33.
5. Quine, *Word and Object*, 55.
6. It isn't obvious that we would behave towards those who speak L in a significantly different way depending on which of the plausible manuals we adopt. But there are other things that this constraint may be taken to encompass. Perhaps, for instance, in the manner of Davidson, Quine holds that of two alternative translations we should adopt that according to which, other things equal, the speaker thinks as we do. "Gavagai" should be taken to refer to rabbits, if we refer to rabbits.
7. Note that "gavagai" is a term, "Gavagai" a sentence.
8. Donald Davidson, *Essays on Truth and Interpretation*. Davidson differs from Quine in holding that first-order quantificational form is a constraint on interpretation, but he still supposes that some indeterminacy remains.
9. Of course, those features of meaning which are invariant across the manuals need not be relativized.
10. Quine at least sometimes suggests that there are no such helpful additional behaviorist resources to deploy, but this seems to me to be an implausible claim. See Chapter 6 of *Word and Object*.
11. Peter Unger, *Philosophical Relativity*.
12. Perhaps the "web" is a web for all speakers of the language as a group. If so, we may need to deploy social resources here.
13. Maybe degrees of observationality and stimulus analyticity are supposed to help, but if they do completely determine the web, then maybe they dispose of Quine's examples.
14. Edward Becker, "Analyticity, Indeterminacy, and Ontological Relativity", manuscript, 1989.
15. Saul A. Kripke, *Wittgenstein on Rules and Private Language*.
16. Ludwig Wittgenstein, *Philosophical Investigations*.
17. Kripke's discussion of meaning skepticism is a setting for a discussion of the possibility of a private language, but it is as a general argument against linguistic meaning that it is relevant to our present concerns.
18. Saul Kripke, *Naming and Necessity*.
19. Kripke, *Wittgenstein on Rules and Private Language*, 15.

20. Kripke, *Wittgenstein on Rules and Private Language*, 16.
21. Of course it is implausible to maintain that there is any unique quale associated with addition. But it is perhaps more plausible to claim that for other sorts of words against which Kripke's Wittgenstein will generalize his argument. So this isn't an unmotivated detour.
22. There are other possible objections to this argument, centering on (i). Some might think that not X's *actual* dispositions but the dispositions X *would have* if X had infinite capacity are relevant to determining what X means by "+". Kripke's reasonable reply is that this is unsatisfactory, since we have no idea whether X would go crazy, or mean quus, or whatever, if they had such an infinite capacity. A situation characterized as one in which X has infinite capacity is not precisely enough characterized to tell, and there is no way of more precisely specifying it without smuggling in some phrase that would impart circularity into the account. Another possible objection to (i): Some might think that the proper dispositional account embodies those dispositions in an adding machine, which X might actually construct, or embody in a machine description. But if the dispositions were embodied in an actual machine whose use constituted the meaning of "+", an analogue of the following "normativity" argument for P6 would also apparently tell against the machine alternative. And if they were merely embodied in a machine *description*, then the problems about sentences being unable to interpret themselves would again come into play.
23. This may not be fair on my part. Kripke's Wittgenstein objects that simplicity is only appropriate as an epistemic criteria for judging between two hypotheses which are already known to be distinct, and hence isn't appropriate in the case at hand. But it isn't obvious to me why someone couldn't maintain that simplicity is part of what constitutes determinate meaning. So I prefer the reading in the body of the text.
24. Kripke, *Wittgenstein on Rules and Private Language*, 55.
25. We can accept (i) but must deny (ii).
26. Kripke, *Wittgenstein on Rules and Private Language*, 90-91.
27. Kripke, *Wittgenstein on Rules and Private Language*, 92-93.
28. Allan Gibbard, untitled manuscript, 1989.
29. I have cribbed what little of this is probably right from Ross Mandel, to whom many thanks. One relevant text is Jacques Derrida, *Speech and Phenomena and Other Essays on Husserl's Theory of Signs*, which includes the essay "Differance". See also *Of Grammatology*.
30. I think that he has oscillated between holding that beliefs and desires are real entities in the same sense that the equator and centers of gravity are real, and merely fictitious, as the claim that the gravitational force between two objects acts merely between their centers of gravity is fictitious. See *The Intentional Stance* (Cambridge, MA: MIT Press, 1987).
31. Hartry Field, "Thought without Content", manuscript, 1984.
32. Stephen Stich, *From Folk Psychology to Cognitive Science, The Case Against Belief.*
33. There are also such cases rooted not primarily bottom-up in neurophysiology, but top-down in cognitive science. Various plausible cognitive scientific theories of perceptual input and motor output postulate representational states with contents which are not accessible to consciousness. For instance, consider David Marr, *Vision* (San Francisco: W.H. Freeman, 1982). This famous work on visual processing suggests that it occurs in several stages. First, from sensory input a "primal sketch" is developed by visual faculties, which makes explicit certain properties of a 2-dimensional sensory image available via sensory input to the cognizer. For instance, this primal sketch contains representations of the spatial dispositions and amounts of changes in light intensity in that image, and also of a primitive local geometry. This primal sketch is supposed to act as input to another stage of cognitive processing which produces what Marr calls the "2 ½ D sketch", which is a viewer-centered representation of the depth and orientation of visible surfaces. Finally, cognitive processing is said to construct from this sketch the "3 D sketch", which is centered on external objects rather than the viewer, and contains a representation of visual objects as hierarchical organizations of volumetric primitives. Consider also Adam Morton's discussion of motor output, in *Frames of Mind* (Oxford: Oxford University Press, 1980). Presumably when an able pianist wills the playing of a run, that occurs only if there are intermediate levels of processing, which break down the playing of the run

into the playing of particular notes and the playing of the notes into particular motor movements. A great deal of such mental processing is inaccessible to consciousness, and may involve contents which are not obviously introspectible by us.

34. Patricia Smith Churchland, *Neurophilosophy* (Cambridge, MA: MIT Press, 1986). Paul Churchland, "Some Reductive Strategies in Cognitive Neurobiology".

35. And also the contents of Marr's hidden levels of visual processing and of Morton's hidden levels of motor processing.

36. Along with the other cognitive scientific theories of content.

37. These worries look beyond the edge of the familiar concrete world we presume in this part, but it is still useful to review them now.

CHAPTER TEN

WORDS AND MEANING

This chapter develops a positive sketch of our capacity for meaningful speech, and hence of our capacity for word-mediated thought. More precisely, this chapter sketches an account of how there might be words with both content and meaning. We will soon flesh out this abstract story in coherently conceivable and apparently plausible resources, but it also fits with the alternative account of thought realization pursued in Part Three.

The main point of this sketch is simple. Meaningful speech is dependent on the existence of certain thoughts with content. Word-mediated thoughts depend crucially on the existence of other thoughts which are not mediated by words, or at least not by the same words. In the inner and outer speech which constitutes word-mediated thought, certain thoughts are knitted together in such a manner that new thoughts are realized, thoughts with some contents which would otherwise be unavailable to us.

The main resource deployed here is that knitting together, which I will call the "interanimation" of thoughts. We will not be in position for an adequate understanding of interanimation until next chapter. But, roughly, one thought "interanimates" a second within someone's psychology when it more or less immediately calls it forth, leads to it, causes it,[1] or at least has some tendency to do so. One thought "potentially interanimates" a second in someone's psychology when the first would lead to the second if the first were to occur, or at least would have some tendency to lead to it. I will speak here of the "interanimation" of two thoughts when the first either actually or potentially interanimates the second. We will consider the relationship between interanimation and the traditional "association" of ideas, and of stimuli with behavior, in the next chapter, but clearly this account is within the associationist tradition.

Still, there are other important resources deployed in this chapter as well. We are most concerned with the *content* which words bear in the individual idiolect of their speaker. It is this which is most analogous to the contents of thoughts which are not mediated by words, and it is this which is most immediately rooted in interanimation. But the *meaning* of the terms of a language is something else. It may be, for instance, some complex function of the contents of all the idiolects of the various speakers of that language, and indeed of other features of the speakers' context.

I will begin indirectly, by reviewing and amplifying certain difficulties of the meaning skeptics. I will work towards a positive account of language by extending and modifying certain resources which the skeptics deploy in their half-hearted attempts to construct accounts of how there might be meaningful language. So that positive sketch will emerge only gradually, by contrast with the views of the meaning skeptics. Section 1 concerns words. Section 2 concerns the meaning and content of words.

Two methodological points before we begin. It would be easy in a context like this to fall into idle bickering about the common use of the folk words "word" and "language". But that can't be all that important. Those words themselves are probably indeterminate enough in meaning to make such a dispute unproductive at just the point where it becomes philosophically interesting. And even if those words *were* quite definite in meaning, even if they *did* imply that some strict and particular conditions were necessary for the existence of language, that wouldn't be very interesting. Under conditions like that, if we found out that something wasn't a language, still we wouldn't necessarily know that it wasn't a lot *like* a language. Indeed, we wouldn't know that it wasn't like enough for our purposes, like enough to mediate thought. So my first concern here will not be to specify conditions which are necessary and sufficient for language in some strict and familiar folk sense. Rather, it will be to isolate conditions which are crucial for anything reasonably akin to a language like ours, anything which allows for the extension of our capacity for thought by something like word-mediation.

One other methodological point: For reasons similar to those just cited, and even though I intend to show that thoughts are crucial for meaningful speech, I will try to avoid appeals to purported necessary conditions for meaningful language when there is reasonable doubt that our own language meets such conditions. I will try to avoid conditions which are quite controversial in this way. Consider an example which will be most relevant in section 2. Some say not only that language must be meaningful, but that meaning accrues through the intentions of speakers.[2] And intentions are thoughts in my sense. But it won't do to appeal to such an intention-based semantics to *securely* demonstrate the importance of thoughts which are not mediated by words for word-mediated thought. This is because it is not unreasonable to worry that when we speak we often have no particular intentions present to mind. Perhaps when challenged we can introspect what we mean by a sentence, and say that one thing was what we "intended" by it, but that alone doesn't show that there was an intention present in mind when the sentence was uttered, which helped constitute its meaning. In fact, if word-mediation can *extend* our capacities for thought, then such intentions cannot be necessary. And we do think things through the mediation of language which we could not intend to mean without it.

1

There is a difficulty for positive accounts of meaningful language which even meaning skeptics ignore. Each prominent meaning skepticism blunts its own force by implying that, even if there is no meaning, still there are certain sorts of activity involving words. Skeptics about meaningful words are characteristically not skeptics about words. But I have already suggested that these blunted skepticisms may not be consistent.

One thing which might support this contention is a sense that any account of the distinction between language and what isn't language, and between one word and another, would rely heavily on thoughts, and that if these sorts of resources are available, determinate meaning should be forthcoming. It is this sort of picture which will be developed here. It reveals a dependency of words on thoughts which are not mediated by words. But let me begin slowly.

On the face of it, those who are committed to the existence of linguistic activity, to the existence of sentences or words, are committed to at least two things: First, that there are determinate facts of the matter regarding whether some bit of the world counts as a linguistic item, for instance whether some sound is the utterance of a word rather than merely a loud breath or a belch. Second, that there are determinate facts of the matter regarding what particular word or sentence an inscription or utterance constitutes. It seems that "speaker" and "speaker" are both inscriptions of the *same* word.

There are some grounds for thinking that skeptics about meaning might consistently claim that there are determinate sentences but no meanings. Certainly it seems possible to first specify the syntactic features of a language, complete with words and rules for combining those words into sentences, without having specified the proper semantics for that language. Not only could a given bit of syntax be assigned a variety of different meanings, it might be assigned no meaning at all.

But there are also opposing grounds. Even if there are in fact uninterpreted languages, it may be that they are parasitic. Perhaps the distinction between a spoken word and some merely guttural noise rests on the fact that the former (or at least things much like it, at least *other* words) carries meaning and the latter does not. And perhaps meaning is also implicated in the conditions which constitute two sets of marks on paper or gusts of air as instances of the *same* word. Certainly a particular material form alone is insufficient, since the same shapes or gusts might be inscriptions of different words in different languages. Some have held that words in a language are the same word only if they have the same meaning, or at least that we can only pick out syntactic units in a line of speech by making semantic assignments.[3] And if these claims are too strong, or merely point to our *evidence* about words rather than what helps *constitute* them, still it might be that two sets of marks which are inscriptions of a particular word must be two things which function at least *potentially* as bearers of the same meaning. And maybe this potential must be not quite so far removed from actualization as the arguments of the meaning skeptics would require.

These considerations seem to me to have some force, but it is in fact another line of argument which I will first pursue here. Even if meaning isn't somehow *directly* implicated in the conditions which constitute particular sentences as that, it may be that any set of resources which would suffice to constitute determinate sentences would also help provide for more determinacy of meaning than the meaning skeptics allow. As I said, we will see that determinate sentences of anything like an ordinary sort are possible only when there are certain thoughts which are not linguistically mediated. And in the next section we will see that such thoughts also provide a crucial resource to help fix meaning.

I think that the conditions for the existence of language, meaningful or not, or at least something sufficiently language-like to serve in mediating thought, are these: 1) The inscriptions or utterances of words of a speaker must be capable of being experienced and produced at will by the speaker. 2) The inscriptions must be typed in some way reflected in the psychology of that speaker, at least to the degree that the speaker responds to and produces instances of a word as a type, in the same relevant way. We will see that both these conditions require that there be thoughts which are not mediated by language.

That will be my primary point here, but there's also the other. I admit that I think that bits of language or anything relevantly like it must possess content, or at least must be related in some close way to other words which possess content, and indeed a content which is rooted in the psychology of their speaker. This, as we will see in the next section, also involves thoughts which are not mediated by words, though not necessarily in the way suggested by intention-based semantics. And it helps constitute the meaning of language.

Now consider some of the specific difficulties with words which meaning skeptics face. Derrida, unlike the other meaning skeptics, does have an account of words. His argument addresses an idealist tradition according to which all objects are objects of thought, and objects of thought are sign-like, with hidden backs which are almost present yet really absent in their visible front, as is a referent in a name. Derrida seems to assume that everything in the manifest world is a sign, an effect of "differance". And he apparently also has an account of sign-*identity*: Different marks which we might call inscriptions of the same word are really the very self-same particular thing, appearing in different guises, just as a particular person may appear in different masks or through different windows. Each element of which the world is constituted is a particular sign, and the only instance of it.[4] On Derrida's view, the world itself is a syntax.

Derrida should be commended for being one meaning skeptic with an account of words, but there are problems with his account. The world is not plausibly constituted by irreducible signs, effects of some inconceivable differance beneath. In fact, a world constituted by such irreducible signs is not even a coherently conceivable possibility. Certainly it is not an option which can help us to flesh out the realization of thoughts in basic content, and in particular in the mundane sort of basic content which is our immediate focus in this part.

Since Kripke's Wittgenstein is probably not quite Wittgenstein, we don't have any obvious resource to tap for the kripkensteinian account of words and sentences. But it is worth noting that some have thought that there can't be such an account. Paul Hoffman has argued that an analogue of the "infinity" argument of Kripke's Wittgenstein, which was supposed to help establish meaning skepticism, can also show that syntax is indeterminate. If finite resources cannot fix meaning, maybe they cannot fix the identity of words either.[5] As I said in Chapter Nine, I think the infinity argument for meaning skepticism fails. That is just another way for Kripke's Wittgenstein to be wrong, but it also makes it hard for me to endorse Hoffman's syntactic infinity argument.[6] Nevertheless, that argument does draw out what seems an interesting parallel.

Unlike Derrida, Quine eschews any metaphysical extravagance beyond the reach of the basic contents we are deploying here. But, on the other hand, there is reason to worry that Quine, like Kripke's Wittgenstein, may lack the resources for an appropriate account of what constitutes the distinction between linguistic and non-linguistic items, and of what constitutes particular inscriptions to be instances of particular words.

There is little even approximating an account of sentences or words in Quine's work. He does discuss grammaticality, suggesting that it can be determined by a translator operating under behavioristic constraints of the sort he favors, by noting "bizarreness reactions" of speakers of the language.[7] This seems a questionable account of grammaticality, since speakers of a language may have the same observable bizarreness reaction to any variety of grammatical but odd remarks as they do to the ungrammatical.[8] And in any case it is not in itself an account of when there is a sentence, and of sentence-identity. Quine does suggest that we can determine the differences between linguistic items within some stream of speech by noticing full stops within the stream. But even if this is plausible, which seems doubtful given the way we run words together in speech, it is insufficient in itself to determine when sounds which count as utterances of words count as utterances of the *same* word. Quine's account assumes a translator facing a number of speakers of the same language, without explaining adequately what that is.

Of course, even if Quine doesn't provide an explicit account of the identity of words, that doesn't imply that he couldn't provide one. But one might well wonder if it is possible to give an account of word-identity which is consistent with Quine's behaviorist constraints on translation. It might be even harder to give a behaviorist account of syntax than of semantics. Of course, we saw in the last chapter that Quine's behaviorist resources may be deployed more effectively than he deploys them, that they do not yield quite the indeterminacy of meaning he believes. But it seems to me that if they *did* yield a radical indeterminacy of meaning, then they would also plausibly yield an indeterminacy of word-identity. Such a hypothetical claim would be hard to establish. So let me merely be more specific about the difficulties which Quine would face in dealing with words. That can help set us up to see the importance of thoughts for word-identity.

Quine's own concrete example of the construction of a translation manual for an alien culture obscures some of the difficulty which translation of the *truly* alien would involve. Quine's linguist faces humans, and can assume that if a language is spoken by those people it will involve sounds uttered from mouths and heard through ears, and marks written and read in a standard human way. The translator can assume not only that the members of the alien society speak a language, in fact the same language, but that it employs linguistic inscriptions and utterances typed in familiar human ways, by shape and sound inflection.

But if Quine's linguist had faced alien enough creatures, even creatures somehow known to be speakers of a single language, that translator would have had a much harder time of it.[9] If those Martians lacked arms and eyes and ears and mouths, they might still be engaged in linguistic activity involving odors or postures. Even if they made sounds and marks in some regular way, it would be far from clear that such marks and sounds constituted a language, instead of a web in which to catch translators. And if the translator could form no idea of the content of the creatures' thoughts and of the meanings they were likely to express, then the translator might not even be able to identify the conditions which would be likely to produce linguistic activity by the aliens.

Even if our translator succeeded in identifying the linguistic items of that truly alien culture, distinguished them in some way from the Martians' analogues of sweat and burps, our linguist could not assume that those tokens were typed in the way humans would type them. Even if our linguist knew that all words of a Martian L were marks and that those marks were typed by shape, still the creatures might have strange sense organs and hence unusual notions of what constitutes sameness of shape.

I've put this in what may sound like an overly "epistemic" way, as difficulties a translator would face in *figuring out* what the words of some aliens were, when the real issue is what *constitutes* the fact that the aliens utter particular words. But this is merely so I can ape the way in which Quine the behaviorist sets things up. Dispositions to behavior are all that is supposed to *constitute* someone as a user of a language. So, it seems, the behavioral dispositions which a translator of aliens can observe must *constitute* the identity of words in their language.

How might Quine address these worries? First, he might rule this case out of bounds. He might stipulate that languages can only be spoken by humans, or at least by creatures quite like humans, so that the ordinary working assumptions of a human linguist facing humans could help constitute wordhood and word-identity. This response seems not only massively chauvinistic, but massively implausible. Can't we at least coherently conceive the aliens I've just described?

Second, Quine might prefer a "pragmatic" response: There aren't facts of the matter about whether something is a language or whether there are certain linguistic types. Rather we must be pragmatic and relativistic. Anything which can be given a translation which facilitates our getting on in the world can count as a language to us. If we can translate some feature of the aliens' life into

English in a way that facilitates our getting along with them, which serves our pragmatic interests, then it counts as a language for us. However, even if we can live with this sort of pragmatism regarding the aliens, it has a serious cost. Consider whether it could apply back to the translator, or back to us. It's hard to swallow the thought that one is only speaking relative to some translators' pragmatic interests. And Quine can't even distinguish between what counts as a translation and what doesn't, and between translations, if there isn't a fact of the matter about whether a putative translator speaks a language, and about what words a particular translation involves.[10]

Third, Quine might hunker down into a massively skeptical response: His skeptical argument is meant only as a *reductio*. It can help itself to any resources, for instance sentences, to which the friend of meaning is committed, but it does not endorse those resources. If there are no determinate sentences, then that's one *more* problem for the friends of meaning. If he takes this route, then what I have called the Quine-Davidson stopgap is unavailable to Quine. Still, he might insist, there are the behaviors which (to speak with the vulgar) we ignorantly "call" the utterance or inscription of particular sentences. But there are no linguistic facts at all. This is coherent, but much more radical than anything which traditional meaning skeptics have admitted.

Fourth, Quine might try a straight response. He might try to construct a general account of when some material item counts as the inscription of a sentence, and when two items count as inscriptions of the same sentence, which is at once applicable to aliens and humans, and consistent with his skeptical conclusion. Just conceivably, Quine might deploy more resources than behaviorist resources in such a account. For instance, perhaps word-typing is innate in some way which would make neurophysiology relevant in this case while not relevant to meaning. But Quine's most plausible *argument* for a behaviorist semantics is not a learning argument. Recall that our mental life between checkpoints is supposed to be indifferent to our rating as a master of a language. And to be a master of a language, we must be a master of its words. So Quine should probably attempt to construct a behaviorist account of word-identity. This would, I think, be difficult, unless behaviorist resources were enough to deliver thoughts with determinate content. But behaviorist resources *do* underwrite more determinacy of meaning than he allows.

That completes our negative discussion. I believe that if we attend to some obvious platitudes about language, we can develop a positive sketch of the conditions which are required for determinate words, conditions which apply even to Martians. Since we merely need to isolate conditions which are necessary for things which are roughly language-like, things which might mediate thought, a good place to start is a consideration of certain animal "languages". They aren't languages in anything like the full familiar sense, but can help reveal some crucial conditions for things which might mediate thought. They are both alien enough and familiar enough to think about clearly. Consider whales, or bees. If bees wiggle about "at will" in a variety of different ways, and if bees can "see" other bees wiggling around in those ways, and if the wiggling has a certain complex variable form, then it seems we have at least some of the rudiments required for bee words. Let me admit that I think that it is also crucial that we can translate the wiggling in some determinate way, assign it a meaning, say of distance and direction to flowers, a meaning which is reflected in the behavior of the individual bees, in their response to "communications" in that language. But note that even short of this semantic resource, the influence of bee "language" must plausibly be mediated by bee neurophysiology. The bees must *experience* the movements and *perform* them. If they merely were blown around in a complex hive in complex ways, so that they bumped into one another in such a way that fresh bees were pointed toward flowers in a certain direction when other bees flew back into the hive from that direction, that wouldn't be enough for language. The communicative influence of a language must be mediated by the sensation and action of "speakers" of the language.

Of course, bees probably don't have language in anything like the full human sense. But their case suggests that, in anything like a normal human language which might mediate thought, at least two sorts of thoughts are implicated, sensory experiences and motor intentions. These are thoughts in my sense. If aliens have a language, then we can presume that they are able to experience tokens of the language, and to produce some "at will", like the bees.[11]

But the case of the bees may itself suggest an objection. Perhaps bees wiggle and respond to wiggling in ways mediated by their neurophysiology, but not by psychologies. Perhaps their so-called "experience" isn't really experience at all, and hence isn't really a thought. Perhaps it lacks the intensionality which our capacity to introspect helps give our experience. And even if their wiggling isn't accidental, even if it is mediated by their neurophysiology, still perhaps they don't perform it under any particular characterization.

Perhaps, but then that is a point at which the bee analogy breaks down. If the bees don't have some experience of the wiggling, and don't produce it "intentionally" and under some intensional characterization, then they don't have a language relevantly like our own, a language which might mediate thought of the kind we are seeking to understand. We have seen lots of reasons to think that if a creature lacks experience and intentional action, then it lacks thoughts of anything like the sorts we are discussing here. In Part Three, we will see even more. And our primary concern is to characterize ordinary human linguistic resources, which do extend our capacity for thought. Only words enough like ordinary human words to mediate thoughts with contents of the sort sketched in Part One need concern us. So if bees lack experience and intentional action, they lack any *relevant* linguistic capacity. And certainly any words which can mediate thought for a creature which can experience and form intentions must have inscriptions it can experience and emit at will. If we perform some sort of unconscious thermal wiggling like a bee dance which only Martians can experience, then it isn't language which can mediate introspectible human thought of the sort we are discussing, even if it has some effect on other humans' behavior which is mediated by human neurophysiology. Particular inscriptions or utterances of a human word like "rabbit" are plausibly the sort of concrete entity found in basic contents, the sort of thing we can experience. Even when an utterance or inscription of a word is a mere object of thought, is heard merely in the mind's ear, still it appears in that quasi-experience as concrete, as a trajectory of phenomenal sound and throat movements.

Quine's translator may presume that Martian words are things which they can experience and produce at will.[12] That isn't much, but there are other important conditions to consider. Also like the bees, the aliens must differentially respond to and produce certain inscriptions or utterances *as* instances of a type. Some repeatable pattern of concrete movement or sound or shape or color must count as a word to which they react and which they produce in some regular way. And as we've just seen, this reaction and production must be mediated by something like a neurophysiology, something which helps to constitute in them a relatively stable psychology, an entrenched trajectory of thought. Certainly there can be change over time in the way one reacts to inscriptions of words, but if there isn't an at least momentarily entrenched and stable set of dispositions to react to inscriptions in some regular way, to respond to inscriptions of the same word in the same way, then there isn't the kind of syntactic typing rooted in one's psychology which is characteristic of ordinary human language and which might mediate the kind of introspectible word-mediated thought we pursue. Perhaps word typing of another sort is possible, underwritten by the intentions of a god or some pseudo-evolutionary selection pressure on speech. But psychologically-mediated typing is the sort relevant to a language which might extend our capacities for thought.

If an alien creature is self-conscious and sophisticated in the way in which adult humans are, then I think even more is required. They must be capable of recognizing their inscriptions as words, and as inscriptions of particular words, in an explicit way. But even short of this self-consciousness, they must be capable of recognizing or responding to the similarity between two inscriptions of one of their words, in a manner mediated by their psychology of thoughts.

We have seen that thoughts are crucially involved in the conditions required for anything at all like human language, words which could mediate thoughts. But, as I've said, there is yet another way in which thoughts are implicated in the conditions required for language. We wouldn't count alien utterance as language, or even as language-like, unless, as in the case of bee language, we had reason to believe that it had a reasonably determinate meaning. And if that language is to mediate thought, then that meaning should be itself reflected at least to a degree in the psychology of the creatures, in the interanimation of their thoughts. It is *content* that should accrue to the inscriptions as types, as instances of particular words. The regular pattern of interanimation which types the inscriptions should also underwrite their content, which in turn helps underwrite their meaning. But, as we have seen, even apart from issues about meaning, determinate words require determinate thoughts which are not mediated by words.

Do we have even a rudimentary account of syntax here, or just some crucial conditions? There is reason to think that syntax in any full sense requires more conditions. Things which aren't languages in anything like an intuitive sense may meet all the conditions which I have articulated. For instance, perhaps some subtle human postures and gestures and facial expressions are experienced by humans, and controlled by their neurophysiology in a way which suggests the presence of motor intentions. And they may even have a kind of meaning rooted in the interanimation of thoughts. Consider for instance the way they may coordinate our emotional responses. So we might plausibly demand other conditions on language, say combinatorial form, or meaning of a "non-natural" sort unlike the "natural" meaning born by smoke. Perhaps we evolved so that at least some specific facial expressions coordinate our emotions in some helpful way, while we didn't evolve to adopt any particular human language.

But even phenomena like genetically-determined facial expressions without combinatorial structure would be language-like enough for our purposes. Postures and gestures of even these kinds might mediate a kind of thought. We can smile falsely, and smile to ourselves. And that may mediate something not unlike ordinary word-mediated thought, at least if the content of those postures and gestures is something we can introspect.[13]

Still, we have yet to discuss what may seem the most striking and characteristic feature of human languages, something which demands at least cursory treatment in any discussion of human thought. While word-mediated thought does not necessarily involve this complexity, still it commands our attention. I have so far ignored the syntactical *structure* of language.

The syntax of a language isn't just a list of its words. The syntactical rules of a language allow only certain combinations of words to be sentences, and they affect the way in which the meanings of those sentences reflect the meanings of their words. Our languages have generative grammars, in Chomsky's sense.[14] Even if chomskian syntactical rules aren't innate, nor even explicitly represented in our brains, still Chomsky and his friends have developed a number of ways to characterize the syntax of languages by reference to such syntactical rules. The syntactical structure of a language is also fixed once meaning is assigned to all its linguistic items in the way I will soon suggest, but still it may be mediated in us by specific capacities, and these capacities may play a crucial role in the realization of much of our word-mediated thought. So there is reason even beyond its humanity for us to give the syntactic, combinatorial structure of our languages at least brief attention.

It is worth noting that the combinatorial nature of actual human languages is connected to a second striking feature of those languages, their "productivity".

Let me say first what that does *not* imply. Some allege that human languages are infinite. They insist that it is a crucial feature of our languages that they each include an infinity of different sentences, and perhaps even sentences which are infinitely long. I think that this is not obviously true, and even if true not obviously crucial. Is it really obvious that English has infinitely long sentences which could never be written or uttered or heard or read by humans, or even the potential for an infinity of distinct sentences? And even if a public language like English is infinite in these ways, is it obvious that the private idiolect of any particular speaker of English is infinite in this way? Galileo couldn't deploy or read infinite sentences, and yet certainly he could speak human languages. Of course, even the idiolect of a speaker, rooted in the speaker's own psychology, may include sentences which the speaker cannot read or write, in something like the way the meaning of "+" can be fixed for a speaker by their dispositions even out beyond their dispositions to add in a canonical way. But the main point is that, whatever the viability of claims about the infinity of human languages, clearly our combinatorial syntax gives us a capacity for an enormous range of thoughts. Clearly it gives us the capacity to string words together in a novel way to form word-mediated thoughts no one has had yet, which no one has explicitly learned how to express or possess. *This* is productivity.

Human languages are combinatorial in a variety of ways. Any given language deploys a specific finite set of letters or sounds that can be combined in certain ways to form longer strings of marks or trajectories of utterance. Certain relatively short strings, word roots, carry content and meaning even down beneath the level of words. They combine in systematic ways to form words with contents and meanings that are a particular function of those roots and their position in the word.[15] Consider "untie" and "unloose". And words combine systematically into phrases, for instance noun phrases, verb phrases, and prepositional phrases, whose contents and meanings are a function of the words in them and their positions in those phrases.[16] Sentences may be made up of a variety of phrases, in a certain order and possibly glued together with specific "function words" like "or" or "and", so that the content and meaning of the sentence as a whole is a function of that of the phrases and of their location in a structure which may include function words. Indeed, there are apparently specific abstract syntactic rules which all actual human languages meet, with parameters filled in by the individual peculiarities of individual languages (specifying for instance a certain order for subject, object, and verb in a sentence), so that our Martians might recognize all human languages as idiolects of one single human language.

The syntactical rules which specify the grammar of human languages may suggest yet other roles for thoughts in fixing syntax than any we have yet noted: It is of course a notorious chomskian claim that we possess innate representations of the rules of a general human grammar. And even if syntactical rules are learned, their explicit representation in us might be a certain sort of abstracted thought. On the other hand, it may be more plausible to consider a specific set of syntactic rules merely a way (not necessarily the only way) to capture a capacity which involves no explicit representation, no knowledge *that*, but merely know *how*, so we have not yet identified any non-controversial role for thoughts here. Some may alternatively suggest that there is interanimation not merely linking thoughts of words and of their content, in the manner we will discuss in the next section, but of words with other words in the same syntactic category. Or they may suggest an interanimation which links thought of the first part of a sentence and thoughts of the words which could be its grammatical continuations.[17] And whatever the fate of these various speculative claims about the way in which our grammatical capacities are realized, there may be another, firmer role for thoughts. Clearly the peculiar deployment of subjects, objects, and verbs by all human languages suggests a generalization about the human approach apparatus. Human languages presume capacity for thought of objects persisting through time and possessing varying properties, the kind of content organization sketched in Chapter Three. They also presume an understanding of the differing roles of subject and object, which may itself generate artifacts of the approach apparatus. For instance, consider the active feel of the subject in "The picture reminds me of home". What's more, our understanding of the pronoun structure of strings of human utterance longer than individual sentences may presume other sorts of familiar thought organization, for instance certain sorts of stereotyped frames or scripts. Capacity for thought which is unmediated by words and organized in something like these ways seems implied by a capacity to speak a language with the particular syntactical features of human languages.

Of course, we are here close to commitments to content. Indeed, whatever the plausibility of these specific claims, there is always a general point, that the kind of combinatorial syntax we are discussing now seems to be a means by which content and meaning accrues to word-mediated thoughts. We have arrived at our next topic.

2

We will approach a positive account of how meaning accrues to language by considering the attempts of Quine and Kripke's Wittgenstein. As we saw in Chapter Nine, the resources deployed in those attempts underwrite more determinacy of meaning than their authors admit, and I will deploy things quite like those resources. Elements of both accounts can also dramatize the need for thoughts, in what might be unexpected places. Word-meanings, like words, rest on thoughts which are not mediated by words.

Quine's account is an account of a language much simpler than our own, but it is quite clear. So it is worth considering this simple model first, before we go on to the more complicated story told by Kripke's Wittgenstein. Quine's translator works by observing behavior, largely from outside the language community, much as a Martian might observe human activity. The primary behavior which the translator observes is linguistic behavior, the uttering of sentences[18] under various conditions of sensory stimulation, but primarily when that syntax is true. In this way, the translator determines something like truth-conditions for the sentences. The translator also queries the speakers about the sentences, again under various conditions of sensory stimulation, and observes whether they assent or dissent, say "yes" or "no". These behaviors are only a very small subclass of the behaviors which actually provide evidence of our linguistic competence, but it is worth noting that, even in this simplified model of language, thoughts pop up in what Quine might well feel are unwelcome ways.

1) As we've already seen, speakers intentionally utter words, and respond to words which they experience. It is the experience of words heard and motor intentions to utter words which must be linked to sensory stimulations. But that's old news.

2) Quine's translator attempts to fix the meanings of sentences by determining their stimulus meanings, the conditions of sensory stimulation under which they are asserted and denied. One might expect the stimulus meaning of "gavagai" to include rabbits. But in line with the internalism which seems characteristic of behaviorism, Quine says that stimulus meanings involve types of retinal stimulations, not rabbits. It is important to notice that this doesn't yield an intuitive meaning for even the most observational of sentences. Our day to day sentences are about rabbits, not about the stimulation of sensory receptor cells. So if the stimulus meaning of a sentence like "there's a red rabbit" is to provide an intuitive meaning for that sentence, we must modify Quine's internalism. On the other hand, the intuitive meanings of human observation sentences are tied to the sorts of things which we humans *experience*, in the particular guise in which we experience them. If rabbits are not in fact like we humans experience them to be, then even actual rabbits can't underwrite an intuitive meaning for "gavagai". Let's peer once more out beyond the edge of the concrete world deployed in this part. If Galileo was right, if rabbits in fact have no colors, then it won't be how rabbits in fact are, but how we humans experience them to be, which will generate an intuitive meaning for our human sentences. And of course our experiences are thoughts. Let me put it this way: When a human translator translates humans, the translator's own experience of the world can provide a relevant sense of the relevant, intuitive stimulus meanings. But if a Martian translating humans had radically different sense organs and experience, then it would be clear how significant the peculiar experience of the translated is to their proper translation. At least in the case of speech with the intuitive, introspectible content articulated in Part One, speech which can mediate thought of the sort which is our focus, not the world but our experience of the world, not rabbits but our experiences and hence thoughts of rabbits, are the relevant things which trigger assertion.

3) Quine's translator considers not only sensory input, but also at least some sorts of behavioral output. And thoughts are latent in this aspect of Quine's account as well. There's one instance of this that is little different from the point I just made. Just as the way the world actually is may be less relevant to intuitive stimulus meaning than the way the speaker experiences the world to be, so too the behavior which the speaker actually performs may be relevant only to the degree that it reveals to a translator the speaker's understanding of that behavior, the speaker's behavioral intentions. If in fact the world is so very different from the way we humans take it to be that we behave in very different ways than we take ourselves to be behaving, still it is our perhaps false human understanding of our behaviors which is relevant to our translation. The content of our motor intentions is crucial. This worry about our behavior differing from our understanding of it is more than an idle possibility, as we will see in Part Three, but at least for now this worry may seem idiosyncratic. Still, there are other ways to make the point. There are other ways in which thoughts are implicated in the behaviors which Quine's translator consults. For instance, the translator is concerned to record assertion of and assent and dissent to sentences, and one may reasonably suspect that thoughts are crucially involved in the conditions which realize those so-called "behaviors". Because lying is popular, verbal behavior alone is not an infallible guide to genuine assent and sincere assertion, and presumably it is sincere assertion and assent which Quine thinks is relevant to translation. Of course, it would be at best controversial and at worst implausible to claim that all instances of sincere assertion and assent are accompanied by an intention to be sincere. Verbal sincerity seems to be the simple, the primitive, the default case. Truthful assertion and honest assent may be what we do when we lack any ulterior motives. Rather, it is *lying* which more plausibly requires an explicit and contrary thought, distinct from the speech itself, or at least analogous dispositions. Perhaps it is merely the absence of such a contrary thought which makes some utterance sincere in those who are sophisticated enough to be capable of lying. But still the thoughts or dispositions for thoughts a human has or lacks seem relevant to whether they are sincerely assenting or asserting.

The various considerations we have surveyed here and in the last section suggest together that the proper development of Quine's account would note the associations not of real world stimulus and actual behavior, object and word or word and assent, but the interanimation of sensory experiences and motor intentions, of thought and thought. Indeed, there are yet more ways to wring thoughts out of Quine's account. I've already suggested that Quine provides an account of a language which is simpler than our own. The additional complexities of actual languages suggest yet more crucial roles for thoughts.

1) Quine inherited from his positivist ancestors what should seem, after Part One, an inordinate fixation on sensory-stimulation as the fount of all meaning. Experience includes the causal. Also, a quinean web of sentences might contact

at its periphery not merely experience, but also thoughts with abstracted contents or other thoughts unmediated by language. Particularly significant in this role may be thoughts with basic contents which are yet beyond experience. Not merely experience but belief beyond experience may trigger assertion, and of course that too is a thought.

2) Quine holds that concrete content accrues to the web of sentences only at its periphery, only to our complex theory of the world as a whole, a theory which consists of many sentences interrelated by inference. If Frege taught us not to ask about the meaning of a word in isolation, and if Duhem taught us that confirmation accrues only to the entire body of a theory as a whole, this may seem a reasonable stipulation. But in Chapter Five we saw reasons to think that it may be less important to isolate a single basic unit of significance, individual words or sentences or webs of sentences, than many philosophers presume. There is less difference than meets some eyes between the facts expressed by sentences and the objects named by words. Words might name what sentences or theories assert. And we also know that confirmation in immediate experience is not quite as closely connected with meaning as Quine presumes. Belief beyond experience can spur assertion. So Quine's claim may properly seem suspicious. Perhaps content accrues not merely to the entire web of a language along its edge, but also directly to certain sub-theories of the language, and to some sentences, and even to some words. In fact, I believe that in our own languages each of these sorts of linguistic item may carry a vector of content. For instance, certain experiences have a tendency to call forth a complex jumble of words, sentences, and theories. Only some of those linguistic items may come to assertion on any particular occasion, and it may seem a puzzle why some are uttered and others not in the face of the relevant experiences. But if this is a puzzle, it is worth noting that it inhabits Quine's simpler landscape as well. Why is it that a particular sentence internal to the web of sentences is occasioned by a particular sensory stimulation on a particular occasion? Lots of other sentences seem to be equally good candidates. Plausible solutions to this puzzle seem at least sometimes to invoke other psychological states, for instance the presence of other thoughts or dispositions for thoughts, as among the explanations for one explicit utterance rather than another. It may be that these other thoughts are mediated by words, but they are at least characteristically mediated by other words than the thought centrally in question. Of course, if they *are* mediated by words, then it may be a rather suspect liberty for me to call such internal and external utterances or dispositions for such utterances "thoughts" in this context, on the way to showing the importance of thoughts unmediated by words for the realization of meaningful speech. But, in any case, there is this complexity.

3) Quine ignores the inner speech, the speech in the mind's ear and throat, which constitutes some thought, and which involves no external behavior at all. We talk silently, to ourselves. We faintly experience, or quasi-experience, the words we speak to ourselves, which aren't out in the world to be heard. Such

speech seems to have both an "input" and an "output" side. Galileo had some ghost of a motor intention to move his tongue and throat, and then he had some ghost of a sensory experience of their movement and of the appropriate accompanying sound. Here we have a number of interanimated thoughts, belonging to the faculty I will call "the primary imagination". These forms of inner speech seem capable of playing much the same role as words heard or uttered out loud. Inner speech is undoubtedly a parasitic phenomena, something to which we come after explicit speech. But it is important nevertheless. Though there is a lot to be said for the view that some of our thinking is constituted by explicit speech or even things we do on paper, surely this inner speech is one of the most characteristic forms of our thought. And of course inner experience of words is an instance of thought which is not *mediated* by words. The word is the content, not the carrier of the content. Inner experience of more than one sort seems significant to word-mediated thought. We think to ourselves in inner speech, assert in private. But we also can sit and introspect the hypothetical conditions under which we would assert various sentences, and hence come to understand something of what we mean by them, the introspectible content they bear for us. We can perform a kind of radical translation on ourselves, in imagination.

4) Quine ignores many of the ways in which competent speakers respond to language. From Quine's account, one would think that someone might rate as a master of English even if their only behaviors consisted of the assertion of sentences under appropriate sensory stimulations and assenting or dissenting to sentences presented to them. But when we assent to sentences, or hear them from those we trust, we do other appropriate things as well. Crudely put, we perform behaviors which are appropriate to the meaning or the content of those sentences. Someone says, "It's raining", and Galileo takes his hat. He accepts "Gavagai", and buys a rabbit trap. Of course, if Galileo sees a rabbit and then asserts "Gavagai", his experience alone might lead to the appropriate behavior. But if he *infers* to "Gavagai", suddenly utters it with a slap on his head, that may occasion new behavior. We engage with language not only as speakers but as *listeners*. And even speakers react to what they say either to themselves or out loud, though let me ignore that complication for the moment.

In response to language which we hear, we do more than merely utter "yes" and "no". It matters who utters what sentences to us, of course. Different individuals, and the same individual on different occasions, will behave in different ways upon hearing a certain sentence even from the same person. Certainly the behaviors and corresponding motor intentions to which experience of a sentence will lead are very sensitive to lots of factors. In fact, they are quite often sensitive to the presence of other psychological factors, indeed other thoughts. But there also seems to be a more or less stable and characteristic set of tendencies for experience of a certain sentence to call forth various motor intentions under various specific conditions (conditions fixing, say, whether the hearer likes rabbits or is suspicious) and also to call forth other thoughts (say of rabbits). There is a certain "role" of this sort associated with a particular sentence. To determine whether someone is the master of a language, we need to know whether the sentences of that language play the right sorts of roles for them, whether they respond as those who understand the language do. For reasons that are by now familiar, these roles should be underwritten by the interanimation of a speaker's thoughts. Also, the particular behavior which is appropriate on a particular occasion, given the complex role of a particular sentence, may depend crucially on the listener's various thoughts.

5) As we saw in the last chapter, Quine pays too little heed to evidence which would help reveal the web of sentences accepted by speakers, the inferences they would draw from one sentence to the next. There are a number of things to note about this web of sentences. First, it seems to provide another intuitively *semantic* resource, beyond the concrete content which is supposed to accrue to the web only along its edge. The intuitive meaning of a sentence will be in part a matter of its place in such a web. But, second, the web provides reasons supplementary to those we surveyed in section 1 to think that language users must be capable of thinking of their sentences, or more exactly the inscriptions of those sentences. Here's another role for thoughts. As I said in the last chapter, a translator's identification of the form of the web of sentences accepted by someone may depend on the admission of sentences themselves into stimulus-conditions. We assent to certain sentences in the face of sensory evidence only when that evidence itself includes the recognizable utterance of certain other sentences by other speakers of the language, or at least only when one accepts them oneself. I suppose that on Quine's view one accepts a sentence when one is disposed to utter it under certain conditions, and one might wonder what this has to do with thoughts. But both the conditions which release this disposition and the action it is a disposition for will involve thoughts.

A short aside: Can the entire semantic content of a sentence, at least on Quine's simple model, be collapsed into its concrete stimulus meaning? It is intuitive to distinguish, on one hand, the rules for entering and exiting a language, which take us from concrete stimulus conditions to sentences or from sentences to concrete behavior, and on the other hand the rules for operating *within* a language, which for instance tell one to infer from one bunch of sentences to another.[19] But it seems that a translator can determine the inferential web of a speaker when the stimulus conditions of sentences are taken to include other sentences, or at least the speaker's dispositions to utter other sentences. And that suggests that to each sentence there corresponds some characteristic set of stimulus conditions, which determine among other things the sentences from which it is to be inferred.[20] There might seem to be a problem with this, since the same concrete shapes and sounds can legitimately occasion different inferences for speakers of different languages. Consider, for instance, reactions to utterances of "Empedocles liebt" and "Empedocles leaped" by German and

English speakers. And of course Quine's own examples suggest that a given sentence can differ in such a stimulus meaning for different speakers of the same language. But part of what constitutes someone as being a speaker of one language rather than another are quite particular dispositions to react to particular concrete shapes and sounds. And the collateral information one possesses may be relevant to the content if not the meaning of one's word-mediated thoughts.

6) One at least apparent difficulty with Quine's account is that it seems not particularly well-situated for a successful assault on noncognitive meaning. Consider for instance the "yes" and "no" by which speakers indicate their assent or dissent to Quine's translator. What is Quine's account of the meaning of those words? Do they have a place in his web? It may be that Quine intends "yes" to have a stimulus meaning which includes appropriate queries in appropriate conditions of sensory stimulation. It may be that he thinks that assent is a kind of assertion. But this is certainly not obvious. Quine seems simply to ignore anything beyond truth-linked assertion, except to deploy "yes" and "no" when he needs them. Let me address this apparent difficulty of Quine's account by considering the more complicated picture sketched by Kripke's Wittgenstein, who at least walks around a behaviorism of a more complex sort. Wittgenstein himself may suggest an even more complicated variety. These more complex behaviorisms suggest a yet more complex role for thoughts.

The "+" symbol is in fact used in a complex way which involves many activities and behaviors. These include the behavior which Kripke's Wittgenstein explicitly considers--addition, the writing down of sums in a certain canonical form. But additions are at least ordinarily imbedded in a complex web of other human activity, activity of the sort which Wittgenstein himself drew to our attention. For instance, we count three apples. We count two oranges. We utter "there are three apples on the table" and "there are two oranges on the table". We remember that no apple is an orange. And then we infer through $3+2=5$ to "there are five apples or oranges on the table". And that little activity involving the "+" sign is part of a yet larger activity, setting the table. Remember also our worries about Quine's "yes" and "no", and the noncognitive meaning of commands and requests and promises. We do lots of things with words other than merely assent and assert in the narrow quinean ways.

Behaviors other than utterance or immediate response to utterance, other than "linguistic" behaviors, and also linguistic behaviors other than the mere assertions and assents which Quine considers or even the straightforward responses to assertions and assents which we considered above, are among the behaviors which help constitute someone as a competent speaker of a language. All this "use" of words may help constitute their meaning or content. But it is important to distinguish two ways in which use is relevant here. Wittgenstein told us to look to the use, not to the meaning, and Kripke's Wittgenstein suggests that we seek assertibility-conditions rather than truth-conditions for sentences, which presumably does not mean merely appropriate conditions of quinean truth-linked assertion. These seem to be points about the kind of semantic content which linguistic items should be conceived to have. And for that matter, they seem like reasonable points. It does seems that we must in some way go beyond Quine's apparent focus on truth to provide an account of the noncognitive meaning of at least certain terms, for instance of "yes" and "no". But it is also important to see that some sorts of intuitive meaning and content for words is "constituted by their use" in a different sense. The actual behavioral "use" of words, and dispositions to use them, say in scribbled calculations on paper, are crucial resources which help *realize* meaningful speech. And these uses are imbedded in complex behaviors and responses of other sorts, which help give the words their meaning. All these varied behavioral resources plausibly invoke thoughts in crucial ways, just as we saw that Quine's own behaviorism implicated psychological resources. The slogan "meaning is use" is suggestive not only of a kind of meaning words have, but also of a way they get it, and it seems to point us towards thoughts again.

Let me work through some parts of this slowly, and particularly in light of Kripke's Wittgenstein. Imagine a Martian observing not merely those who engage in quinean assertion and assent and even behavioral response to assent and assertion of the sort we have considered, but real people. All sorts of behaviors by humans in their language communities, with and without words, seem relevant to determining what their words mean. Or at least that is so if we conceive the behaviors in the appropriate way, as occasioned by and underwritten by thoughts.

First, let me begin with the obvious: Kripke's Wittgenstein discusses the use of "+", and also dispositions to use it. These are in effect behaviors and dispositions to behave (or perhaps that and a bit more). And we saw in the last chapter that these can take us a lot closer to determinacy of meaning than Kripke's Wittgenstein suggests. After our recent discussion of Quine we know that such "behaviors" plausibly invoke thoughts in a way behaviorists traditionally ignore, that they are initially triggered by experience or some other element of a psychology of thoughts, and are immediately occasioned by motor intentions. What is really crucial here is the interanimation of thought and thought, or perhaps of other more complex psychological phenomena, say of dispositions to affect the interanimation of thoughts. In fact, as the behaviors we perform with words become more complex than mere quinean assertion, there is even more place for thoughts to play a crucial role. Some of the intuitive "assertibility" conditions which trigger commands, for instance, involve desires to obtain certain results.

Second, recall Kripke's Wittgenstein on the normativity of meaning. We saw in the last chapter that a certain down-to-earth understanding of this normativity can help underwrite the determinacy of meaning, can help to constitute the appropriate "use" which gives words their meaning. We correct certain assertions and certain responses to assertion. And the capacity to correct seems rooted in our psychology, in the interanimation of our thoughts: To *correct* behavior is, it seems, at least in part to express acceptance of norms for behavior. While discussion of the acceptance of norms is complex matter for another day,[21] it is pretty likely to involve thoughts of various kinds. All creatures who deploy syntax have reasonably well-entrenched habits mediated by their psychologies, by the interanimation of their thoughts. Among the habits of adult humans are certain metalinguistic habits. We call certain sentences "true" or "false" under certain conditions, where the words "true" and "false" play for us a complicated social and psychological role. And we also engage in correction behaviors which are not mediated by words, but rather by stern looks. This "truth-calling" and correction behavior helps underwrite pretty subtle differences between our sentences, which for instance may express rather than assert good feeling about ice cream. And this correction behavior seems rooted in complex ways in the interanimation of our thoughts. As I've suggested, the corrections one would make seem rooted in one's psychology in the same way that all intentional behaviors are. But, more importantly, when those who accept norms perform behaviors which fall outside of those norms, at least characteristically, at least in simple cases, they feel uncomfortable, or have conflicting motivational states. Feeling or motivation seem involved in the acceptance of norms. And they seem to involve thoughts in my expansive sense.

Third, there may be completely non-linguistic behaviors relevant to fixing the intuitive meaning of someone's words, for instance the activity of setting the table in which counting apples and oranges may be imbedded. If so, then once again the interanimation of stimulus thoughts and intentions to behave becomes, for now familiar reasons, relevant.

So far we have focussed on ways in which Kripke's Wittgenstein suggests yet more roles for thoughts. That's the main point. But there are other resources which he also suggests, which are of a significantly different sort. We saw in the last chapter that there are other resources which help fix the intuitive meaning of a language or the proper "use" of its terms. Recall the distinction between content and meaning. Each speaker may have an idiolect whose content is fixed solely by the actual and potential interanimation of their thoughts. Certain thoughts interanimate others, and other psychological states are complex dispositions for certain interanimations, and all this may fix the content of an idiolect. It is this kind of psychologically rooted content which is most relevant to our concerns, because it is this kind of content which the speaker can introspect and which is most immediately reflected in their behavior. Of course, there are complications. There may well be psychologically associated contents which aren't relevant to the intuitive "content" of words even within an idiolect. For instance, a sentence to which a second sentence is a proper response may not be something the second sentence is about, so even within an idiolect we should make some distinctions. I'll get to some of those distinctions in a moment. But, in any case, these individual psychological resources are probably not enough to fix intuitive meaning. Nor will it be sufficient to include other individual psychological resources, like those that underwrite a speaker's capacities for non-linguistic behaviors. The appropriate use of a piece of syntax in a linguistic community is probably constituted in some way by the nature of the idiolects of *all* the speakers, and perhaps other features of the context of speakers, like who's in authority and what the local water is made of. A Martian translator of humans would have to notice all of this to get intuitive meaning right.

"Social" resources like these may well be important in determining intuitive meaning, but it is also possible to over-stress them. In the same way that some crude correlational accounts of experience fail, by ignoring the behavior relevant to thoughts, so too would some crude socialized accounts of meaning. The meaning of someone's words can't be completely indifferent to the introspectible thoughts reflected in their behavior. It would be very implausible to maintain that *all* that matters to the meaning of the words of a speaker is what other members of his or her linguistic community do with those words. If all a speaker can do is mouth certain words on random occasions, without any sense of the conditions under which it is appropriate to assert them, without any tendency to respond to their utterance in appropriate ways, then we would not attribute to them any thoughts at all in making those utterances. *Some* understanding of a word seems required before social factors can play a significant role in fixing intuitive meaning. And it is that understanding, rooted in the interanimation of our thoughts, which underwrites the complex introspective content of word-mediated thought. It is that introspectible understanding which is our central concern.

We have come by our dialectical discussion of Quine and Kripke's Wittgenstein to a positive although still somewhat abstract picture of the nature of meaning, and the mechanisms by which it is fixed. Let me review the main points, and add a few more of the necessary qualifications:

If a speaker has some prior capacity for thought with a particular content, mediated or unmediated by words, then that content can become part of the content of some new form of words. If we can experience red blood, we can have a word for it. So far word-mediation seems to provide no resources for content extension. But words may collect together content from many different thoughts, gather them together in a bunch whose components have different roles. Words can presume or command such contents, rather than merely possess them as truth-conditions. And words can be related in various ways, say by inference, to other words. In this way, thought content may be extended via the mediation of words, and hence some of our thought may depend crucially on the mediation of language. Words may collect lots of what we might call "associated" contents, but in different ways.

What sorts of linguistic items collect content? It seems that all sorts may--words, phrases, sentences, theories. There is a complex structure of overlapping associated contents, contents tied directly to the words in a sentence, to its phrases, to the sentence as whole, and to the theory in which it is imbedded.

What sorts of contents can be collected? All sorts of contents, for instance those which are abstracted and mediated by other words, can be lumped together by a word or other linguistic item. The truth dependencies among contents suggested in Chapter Three may seem to allow a sort of collapse of associated contents into concrete basic contents. A linguistic item may be conceived to collect merely the range of basic contents which would ground the truth of its associated contents. But this possible economy may only get in the way when we start distinguishing between the roles which contents play for some linguistic item.

Even particular inscriptions of a sentence which is inferentially related to a second sentence become a part of the contents associated with the second. To learn French or Italian is to change some concrete marks in what is for a new speaker an irrevocable way. Try to see the last word of this sentence as just a concrete shape. There are quite distinct and complicated roles which different associated contents may play for a word or phrase which collects them. Not all associated contents are associated in the same way. But to see this, it is best to consider at the same time the mechanisms by which contents are collected by words.

As we have seen, the basic apparatus for the assignment of content to words is the interanimation of thoughts. Thoughts of inscriptions of a word call forth thoughts of elements of its content. Thoughts of those elements call forth thoughts of the word. Or, more exactly, these thoughts have various complex tendencies to call forth one another, tendencies released only under various complex but psychological conditions, and tendencies of greater and lesser strength, which have or more or less probability of being realized and more or less capacity to triumph over competing tendencies. Still more exactly, such thoughts would have those tendencies, if only they occurred. Words found together in a sentence uttered to oneself or to others may more or less immediately dampen out the locally irrelevant associated resonances of one another. They may lead more or less directly to appropriate motor intentions or further introspectible word-mediated thought or thought of intuitive meanings. Or results may be delayed. There may be a time-consuming competition for effects between those words and other words which one is variously disposed to say, or among various associated contents of the original words. Indeed, the very words one uttered may have themselves been the result of such a competition.[22] But it is also important that humans have complex capacities for planning and long range control of action which can play a significant role as well, so that we can engage in quite complicated discourse with ourselves and with one another.

Associated contents are quite an indiscriminate bunch. A word like “red” has as associated contents inscriptions of other color words, a range of phenomenal hues, fire trucks, and for that matter the contents of intentions to say “yes” or pick up certain objects in response to certain utterances in certain situations.

We're still a long way from meaning. But we can get somewhat closer even within the psychology of a speaker:

1) There is a *direction* of interanimation. Experiences with certain contents tend to call forth motor intentions to utter certain words, and experiences of certain words tend to call forth appropriate motor intentions, intentions to "appropriate" behaviors, intentions with appropriate contents. There is, as it were, first incoming associated content, then the word, and then outgoing associated content. There are stimulus conditions,[23] but also appropriate responses. Of course, the stimulus conditions need not merely involve experiences, and the responses motor intentions. Other thoughts may also take part.

The ingoing associated content of a word can encompass all sorts of things, including positive tests for its applicability which it is yet not intuitively about.[24] We will get to resources which help to distinguish between the different roles which this ingoing associated content can play in a moment. And the outgoing associated content of a word seems particularly complex. For instance, the contents of appropriate motor intentions seem to depend significantly on who one experiences a word to be uttered by, not just on the experience of the word itself, and also on whether one thinks they speak German or English. And of course what we do in response to certain sentences depends in complicated ways on our desires and beliefs. But it may be that the primitive and basic case involves a certain sort of fixed response to certain words whoever says them. As people age and are complicated and corrupted and sophisticated by experience and education, this basic tendency may come to be in conflict with other tendencies, or may be deployed as part of more complex tendencies. These complications may suggest still further ways in which the interanimation of thoughts underwrites linguistic behavior. But still there must be some characteristic abstract pattern or regularity present in this interanimation if a person is to be a competent speaker of a particular language. This invokes the next resource:

2) There are certain patterns of stability in the association of words and contents by interanimation. Some persist over time in the psychological life of an individual. But, whether they in fact persist or not, such patterns may be more or less *prone* to persist through time and through various counterfactual courses of experience and education. And there may be various probabilities with which thoughts tend to call forth other thoughts, or various abilities of tendencies to achieve the calling forth in light of conflicting dispositions. These factors may privilege certain associated contents over others, and even in a way a speaker can introspect.

3) A certain *kind* of thought with a particular content, say a belief or desire or intention, may be linked by relevant interanimation to another particular kind.

4) There is a complex background of non-linguistic behavioral dispositions which supports the broad practices in which someone's linguistic behavior is imbedded. This background helps support the content of their speech, and these

dispositions are underwritten by the interanimation of their thoughts. Behavioral dispositions of the relevant sort involve dispositions for various trajectories of thoughts, say from particular experiences to particular motor intentions.

5) At least normal adult speakers accept norms, and intentionally engage in practices of truth-calling and correction. For instance, the word "true", which is said also of thoughts with contents unmediated by words which are thought to match the world, and which meets other constraints suggested by its complex social and psychological role, is bandied about regarding certain sentences in certain conditions and not others. This is one way in which we may come to be able to distinguish between what words presume and what they say, what they are merely associated with and what they are about, and it also adds other sorts of refinement and stability to the content of our speech. One's practice of norm-acceptance and truth-calling is also reflected in one's individual psychology, in the interanimation of one's thoughts, at the very least in the interanimation of experiences of conditions judged and motor intentions to utterance of "true".[25]

6) Nor should we forget generative grammar. The way in which meaning and content accrues in actual human languages is mediated by the combinatorial syntax of those languages. Some of our words are function words like "or", which collect no content of their own which could be a meaning of any intuitive sort. And our capacity to deploy combinatorial syntax, both as speakers and listeners, allows us to formulate and understand word-mediated thoughts of a more complex sort, given a prior capacity to understand the content which accrues to particular words. We have already seen that this also involves the interanimation of thoughts. In particular, it may crucially involve the interanimation of thoughts of sentences which underwrites the inferences we are disposed to make. And we have also already seen that this may provide crucial semantic resources. As Sellars has suggested, perhaps inferential roles of words are crucial in underwriting much of the intuitive content of our language.[26] Certainly other words make up an important part of the ingoing associated content of other words. Generative grammar is not merely crucially dependent on the interanimation of thoughts of sentences. It helps in turn to distinguish between the various roles of contents associated with a word by interanimation.

This and the factors noted in the preceding paragraphs help to fix what we might call the "proper" content of words in one's idiolect. To know whether some sentence is true or not in someone's idiolect, we need to know more than which contents are associated by them with that sentence, and which match the world. We need also to know such things as whether the speaker accepts that they are grounds for calling it true or false. But still the basic mechanism here is interanimation. Still the proper content of the idiom of a speaker is fixed by the interanimation of their thoughts, actual and potential. It is for this reason that at least normal adult humans with a certain level of self-consciousness can come, when they utter sentences out loud or to themselves, to introspect at least much of the content of their words accurately. One can determine even the proper content of one's words from one's armchair, I think, by considering for instance a range of possible imaginary circumstances, how one would speak under those conditions, how one would respond to speech, and perhaps how one would otherwise behave. At least in normal adult humans, the introspectible contents of word-mediated thoughts fix the proper contents of those thoughts.

Given our latent non-objectual interests, it's perhaps worth stressing again that it's the *experience* or other thought of words, not *actual* words, and it's the *experience* of balls and rabbits rather than actual balls and rabbits, which seem absolutely crucial if there is to be word-mediated thought with intuitive content. So there might be word-mediated thought even if there were in fact no words out there in the world, not even written in our brains. All we need is the experience of words, or the quasi-experience we have of words when we speak to ourselves. Again, it's only the interanimation of thoughts which is crucial in the constitution of inner speech with content.

If this be associationism, then let's make the best of it. No other mechanism seems capable of underwriting the introspectible content crucial if there is to be word-mediated thought. And we came to recognize the significance of the interanimation of thoughts by developing what are often thought to be alternative conceptions of the realization of meaningful speech.

Still, as I've admitted, all this interanimation is probably not enough to fix the intuitive meaning of a language, the intuitive meaning which must be preserved in intuitive translation of a speaker. The idiolects of a speaker's fellow speakers, the authority held by some speakers over others, even the configuration of the local water, may help fix the intuitive meaning of that speaker's words. No doubt they only do this within a certain intuitive range of indeterminacy, of the sort we discussed in the last chapter. But they help give meaning what determinacy it has.

On the other hand, let me repeat that the proper content of someone's idiolect is fixed merely by the interanimation of their thoughts, actual and potential. It is this proper content which is the best analogue of the introspectible content of thoughts which are not mediated by words. It is this sort of content of words which is our central concern.

This sketch has exhibited the complex interdependency of human thought and language which I promised. While some thoughts are mediated by language in the way suggested in Part One, meaningful language itself presumes many sorts of capacity for other thoughts.

NOTES

1. "Cause" may unfortunately suggest the kind of robust causal relation between spatio-temporally distinct entities of the sort discussed in Chapter Seven, and this may be a misleading picture of what interanimation involves.

2. See for instance H.P. Grice, "Meaning", *Philosophical Review* 66, 1957, 377-388; "Utterer's Meaning and Intentions", *Philosophical Review* 78, 1969, 147-177; "Utterer's Meaning, Sentence-Meaning, and Word-Meaning", *Foundations of Language* 4, 1968, 225-242. See also David Lewis, *Convention* (Cambridge, MA: Harvard University Press, 1969), and Stephen Schiffer, *Meaning* (Oxford: Oxford University Press, 1972).
3. Ferdinand de Saussure, *Course in General Linguistics*, translated by Roy Harris (London: Duckworth, 1983).
4. Jacques Derrida, *Speech and Phenomena*, 50.
5. Paul Hoffman, "Kripke on Private Language", *Philosophical Studies* 47, 1985, 23-28.
6. Consider this analogue, which can help dramatize the interesting parallel between semantics and syntax to which Hoffman points:

P1) *The position of Kripke's Wittgenstein's requires that there be such a thing as X's responding in one way and not another to a problem such as "57 + 68 = ?"* This is because quadition and addition involve different ways of responding to that problem.

P2) *This requires that certain inscriptions of numerals, say "5" and "5", be of one type, and other inscriptions, say "125" and "125", be of another.*

Any two inscriptions of a numeral will have some different properties, but there must be something which constitutes them as of one type. However,

P3) *The actual past and present use by X of inscriptions of numerals will not serve to determine to what types they belong.* This is because there is an intuitively strange classification of the inscriptions which is consistent with all of their actual past and present use by X, and which deviates from the intuitive classification of the inscriptions in a way similar to the way in which quadition deviates from addition, out beyond actual past and present use. Tomorrow "125" may count as an inscription of the same type as "5" does today.

P4) *But Kripke's Wittgenstein can allow nothing to help fix this typing but actual past and present use.*

Hence Kripke's Wittgenstein's position is inconsistent. Let me be clear. This argument doesn't at all adequately capture Hoffman's criticism, which suggests that finite resources do not determine syntax, rather than merely that actual use does not. And certainly it would require such a generalization to be an appropriate criticism of the argument of Kripke's Wittgenstein, because my P4 is false. That is not merely because Kripke's Wittgenstein makes no explicit claim about the resources available to fix the typing of inscriptions, but also because Kripke's Wittgenstein allows more resources than actual use, for instance dispositions to use, even to help fix meaning. Nevertheless, this argument does draw out what seems an interesting parallel.
7. W.V.O. Quine, "The Problem of Meaning in Linguistics", in *From a Logical Point of View* (Cambridge, MA: Harvard University Press, 1961), 47-64.
8. Edward Becker, "Quine and the Problem of Significance", *Proceedings of the 7th International Wittgenstein Symposium* (Vienna: Holder-Pichler-Tempsky, 1983).
9. This sort of case worries, for instance, Jonathan Bennett. See the beginning of *Linguistic Behavior* (Cambridge: Cambridge University Press, 1976).
10. I owe something like this point to a discussion of Rorty with Thomas Blackburn.
11. It may be that at least humans and sophisticated aliens are capable of speaking a language with sentences too large to utter or experience. But this seems a parasitic and secondary phenomena, to which we will return in a bit.
12. There is some ambiguity about what it is to produce things, say utterances, at will. It seems reasonable to presume that in the first and primitive instance the capacity to utter language cannot be contingent on possession of a stylus or the like. So something like speech seems more plausibly primitive and primary for creatures than a written language. On the other hand, we come to be able to write things, say equations, which we cannot easily pronounce. Writing differs in a number of interesting ways from speech. For instance, under ordinary conditions speech is evanescent in a way that writing is not. It is gone quickly and cannot persist beyond the conditions which give it meaning for its speaker. This may make speech a better analogue of other sorts of thought than writing, but still

the *act* of writing may be a very close analogue as well.
13. The invisible thermal wiggle I mentioned above was thus a different sort of case. We can't so wiggle falsely or to ourselves, and we can't introspect its content.
14. A good introduction is Steven Pinker, *The Language Instinct* (New York: William Morrow and Company, 1994). Two classic texts are N. Chomsky, *Syntactic structures* (The Hague: Mouton, 1957), and N. Chomsky, *Aspects of the theory of syntax* (Cambridge, MA: MIT Press, 1965).
15. M. Aronoff, *Word formation in generative grammar* (Cambridge, MA: MIT Press, 1976). Of course, context may be required to determine what a particular inscription of a homonym means.
16. R. Friedin, *Foundations of generative syntax* (Cambridge, MA: MIT Press, 1992) R.S. Jackendoff, *X-bar syntax: A study of phrase structure* (Cambridge, MA: MIT Press, 1977).
17. Or even which links thoughts of individual words and of their possible continuations, if we allow that the possible continuations of the preceding words may dampen out conflicting interanimations.
18. Perhaps I should say instances of sentences.
19. See Wilfrid Sellars, "Some Reflections on Language Games", in *Science, Perception, and Reality*, 321-358.
20. Of course, we are ignoring the possibility of mistakes, but that is natural given the form of Quine's account. We will soon return to a consideration of mistakes.
21. Allan Gibbard, *Wise Choices, Apt Feelings* (Cambridge, MA: Harvard University Press, 1990) provides one helpful account.
22. This may be one mechanism which reasonably suggests the existence of certain unconscious thoughts, namely those which lose the competition.
23. Recall that quinean stimulus meanings may encompass both positive and negative elements. The conditions which lead one to deny a sentence may be part of its ingoing associated content, though they are presumably not as strongly associated with it as with its denial. The inferential and normative resources noted below play a large role in helping to underwrite the necessary differences in roles of various sorts of ingoing associated content.
24. Two important semantic projects, influenced by Wittgenstein, which deploy tests and verifications as important semantic resources are Dummett's and Shwayder's. See Michael Dummett, *The Seas of Language* (Oxford: Oxford University Press, 1993), and also D.S. Shwayder, *Statement and Referent, Part I* (Dordrecht: Kluwer Academic Publishers, 1992).
25. It may be important to note that to say that meaning involves the acceptance of norms does not at all obviously imply that it involves normative facts, facts about the truth of the norms which are accepted. In fact, at least the appearance is just the opposite.
26. This inferentialist conception of semantics is developed and elaborated in Robert B. Brandom, *Making It Explicit* (Cambridge, MA: Harvard University Press, 1994).

CHAPTER ELEVEN

RESOURCES

In this part, we presume a world which is much as our experience seems to reveal but which incorporates the resources of contemporary neurophysiology, where there are phenomenal colors splashed over things and neurons in our heads. Neurophysiological resources are deployed, along with phenomenal colors, in the coherently conceivable but not ultimately plausible account of the realization of our experience developed in Chapter Twelve. And they are the primary resources deployed in the apparently plausible account of the realization of thought beyond experience developed in Chapter Thirteen, an account which fits not only the coherently conceivable account of experience developed in Chapter Twelve, but also the more plausible accounts pursued in Part Three.

This chapter concerns these neural resources, and how they might realize the interanimation we have already deployed. It has three sections. Section 1 concerns neurons. Section 2 concerns the interanimation of thoughts. Section 3 attempts to fit those two things together, at least in a general way, before we consider the realization of specific kinds of thoughts.

It is easy to see that neurons are likely concrete resources for the realization of our thoughts which are not experiences. While in experience our thought seems to open out into the world, while there may be no obvious objection to the claim that our experience is realized by conditions which include our environment of a moment, still we seem to carry the rest of our thought capacity around with us as we walk about. That capacity seems indifferent to our changing environment. It seems to depend on our relatively stable *internal* states, on what's no further out than skin's end, and no further back in time than a brief moment. Of course, this may be a misleading appearance. As we walk around, we also carry with us our history and our broad social environment, and some may insist that these or similar things play a crucial role in constituting the thought capacities we will consider in Chapter Thirteen. But our internal states of the moment seem at the very least obviously implicated as well. They in the most obvious sense intervene between our sensory input and motor output, as thoughts must. Since our psychology of thoughts mediates between sensory input and motor output, and since we at least seem to be concrete, fleshy beings, what in fact lies in the concrete interstice between our sensation and action seems to be most plausibly what realizes the capacities we will attempt to underwrite in Chapter Thirteen.[1] And we will see that what's so inside us is in fact enough to underwrite our capacities for thoughts beyond experience, at least if we ignore the problem of experience itself. Because other resources are unnecessary, I will ignore other possible resources in Chapter Thirteen. And even an account of the realization of our experience which meshes with the account sketched in Chapter Thirteen can make quite helpful, though not necessarily exclusive, use of what's inside us, between our sensation and action.

The components of that concrete interstice most relevant to the mediation of the effects of our sensory stimulation on our action are *neurons*, the quite concrete living cells which constitute our brains and nervous systems. Neurons make up a vast network of interconnected cells, beginning in sensation and ending in motor output. Along these cells pass electrical impulses, in patterns modulated by the firing of other cells, in patterns responsive to sensation and controlling motor action. We know that different people act in different ways in the same circumstances, depending on their thoughts and perhaps on other features of their psychology entwined with the interanimation of their thoughts. And the concrete mechanisms which apparently so mediate in us are our neurons. Our complex neurophysiology, arrayed between cells responding to sensory stimulation and manipulating muscles, is what plausibly constitutes our capacity for thoughts, or at least for thoughts beyond experience.

Let's leave aside for the moment the traditional galilean understanding of neurons, as purely causal things without phenomenal properties. Let's begin with a naive concrete understanding of neurons, as possessing concrete properties of all the intuitive sorts, colors as well as powers. Let's begin with neurons that might fit into the mundane world we presume in this part. And then let's ask: How could such concrete things root our capacities for thought, especially for thought beyond experience?

1

The components of the nervous system, like the rest of our bodies, are of course living cells. The nervous system includes numerous support cells, for instance "glial cells" which hold things together, and "oligodendroglia" which provide insulation. But its primary functions, as I've suggested, are mediated by cells called "neurons", of which there are something on the order of 100 billion in humans.[2] Let me focus on a rather typical sort of neuron, though by no means the only kind. The cell body of such a typical neuron has a long, slender extension called an "axon". The axon terminates in a large number of small branches, which themselves end in "terminal buttons". The cell's body has another set of shorter, spiny appendages, perhaps typically opposite the axon, called "dendrites".

Neurons "synapse" on others. At a synapse, the terminal buttons of one neuron connect up with another neuron, sometimes by touching but typically with a small intervening gap, and typically at the second neuron's dendritic spines. Neurons affect the neurons on which they synapse. Large numbers of neurons may synapse on a particular neuron, and it may in turn synapse on a large number of other neurons. The number of synapses in humans is vast. Typically, perhaps 5000 cells synapse on a given human neuron, and it synapses on 5000 more.

We will return to the issue of how neurons and synapses function in a bit. First, it will be helpful to get some sense of the overall structure of the human nervous system. Very schematically, that structure is this: Sense organs of various kinds, for instance the eyes, include sensory receptor cells, which are neuron-like cells responsive to sensory stimuli. Certain neurons synapse on muscles, whose action they control. In between such receptor cells and motor neurons is a large and vastly complicated structure of interconnected neurons. The central nervous system, in which those interconnecting neurons are concentrated, has a clear and memorable gross anatomy. The spinal chord bulges at its upper end into the brain stem and lower brain. It is topped and surrounded by the cerebrum, which fills most of the skull, and which is the most characteristically "human" part of the brain. At the back of the brain stem is the cerebellum, which is apparently involved in coordinating balance and motor action. Typically, sensory receptor cells synapse on nerve cells which in turn synapse on other cells so that causal influence rooted in the action of sensory stimuli is passed up though the spinal chord to the lower brain, often particularly the thalamus, from which neurons project out to various surface areas of the cerebrum, various regions of "cerebral cortex". These are apparently dedicated to so-called sensory "processing"[3] of particular kinds. For instance, there is visual cortex at the lower rear of the skull, which seems to be involved in visual recognition. Neurons in such sensory processing areas typically synapse on a complex structure of interconnected neurons which eventually synapse on areas of the cerebral cortex which seem to be involved in initiating motor action of some sort. Chains of neurons involved in motor action, often via the mediation of the cerebellum, project back down the spinal chord and on out to muscles.

That is our very gross neural anatomy, but there is significant small-scale organization of neurons as well. For instance, the cerebral cortex has six layers, with each layer possessing different characteristic kinds of neurons arranged in characteristic ways, for instance projecting widely to other areas of the cortex, or narrowly within a local region. And small regions of the cortex appear to constitute cell assemblies which function more or less as units, at least for a while.

How do the cells and the synapses work? What sort of neural activity intervenes between sensation and action? First of all, neurons fire. Electrical impulses of constant magnitude pass down the length of their axons, away from their cell bodies. To see how this works, first consider a small segment of axon:

First, a pump in the cell wall of the axon expends energy provided by metabolism to pump sodium out of the cell, so that there are relatively many potassium ions and few sodium ions on the inside of the cell at that point, and relatively few potassium ions and many sodium ions on the outside. This chemical difference creates a difference of electrical potential between the inside and outside of the cell, much as in a chemical battery, of 50 to 90 millivolts. Then the wave impulse, to which we will return in a moment, causes a sudden increase in the electrical potential in that segment of cell wall. This causes the cell wall to become locally permeable to sodium. Next, sodium ions rush down their concentration gradient into the cell, and this discharges the electrical potential, creating an electrical current which passes down the axon to its next bit. This current is the wave impulse which causes an increase in electrical potential at the next bit of the axon. This in turn causes *that* bit to become permeable to sodium, and so on, so that an electrical impulse is passed on down the axon.

How does the wave impulse originate? There is a relatively slow, "pacemaker" oscillation of the electrical potential across the cell wall, which is created by the action of potassium and calcium pumps. Such an oscillation may reach an amplitude that fires the cell. Neurons fire in this way "spontaneously", at a more or less regular rate. But the spontaneous firing of a cell is modulated by the firing of cells which synapse on the cell, and, in the case of sensory receptor cells, by sensory stimuli. These may influence the pattern and rate of a cell's firing.

How do the synapses work? There are at least two characteristic sorts of synapses, electrical and chemical. At an electrical synapse, an electrical impulse passes directly from one cell into other neuron which it touches. But the most common sort of synapse is chemical. The stereotypical chemical synapse works in this way: First, the terminal button of a neuron contains tiny vesicles of various chemical "neurotransmitters". When that neuron fires, the neurotransmitters are released into the synaptic cleft between that terminal button and the dendritic spine of a neuron on which the first neuron synapses. Second, the neurotransmitters bind with receptors on those dendritic spines, causing adjustment of the chemical permeability of the second cell's wall, and hence an electrical inhibition or excitation, a "post-synaptic potential". Third, the chemical effects on a neuron, by the various neurons which synapse on it, sum up or cancel out in a way which modulates the spontaneous firing rate of the cell. The firing of some incoming cells is excitatory, of others inhibitory. Finally, neurotransmitters are broken down on receptors and formed again in vesicles, so that this process may reoccur.

Synapses are the site of a lot of important activity. There are different systems of neurons, employing different sorts of neurotransmitters and apparently performing different sorts of roles. Specific drugs act at specific kinds of synapses, as excitatory or inhibitory neurotransmitters, or by blocking receptors. Neurotransmitters of certain specific sorts, affecting certain specific sorts of cells, may become generally distributed via the blood stream as hormones, to work their effects in more global ways than merely at single synapses. But the preceding paragraph may serve as a rough sketch of the most typical action at a synapse.

Of course, the web of one's neurons is imbedded between an active set of sensory receptor cells and muscles aligned in a skeleton. It functions in a crucially important context even within one's body. And it also characteristically functions in a very limited range of "external" background conditions. At the surface of the sun, the light would burn out our eyes, and normal gravity plays a role in supporting our customary behavioral responses. But clearly, the states of our neurons are quite crucial in constituting our various capacities for thought. And among their crucial states seem to be their patterns of firing.

This is an extremely schematic picture of human neurophysiology. For instance, there are a number of somewhat more specific features of brain organization which will provide us with some important resources even in the quite abstract account developed in Chapter Thirteen:

1) There is significant evidence for the existence of various special neural subsystems, which perform specific and identifiable functions in cognitive life. For instance, there are subsystems rooted in the central and lower brain and projecting out to the cortex which appear to modulate wakefulness and sleep, attention, and memory formation, and to be implicated in specific sorts of emotion and arousal and in pain and pleasure.

2) As I briefly noted, even within the cortex there seem to be groups of neurons which receive "input" and emit "output" as a group, and there seems to be also a weaker kind of association of certain neurons or groups of neurons, whose firing is coordinated whatever their other input or output. Synaptic connections between neurons can constitute them as groups which function together on some "processing task", or coordinate their firing even when they don't constitute such a group.

3) Some neural structures are hierarchically organized, in much the way we would expect from our earlier discussions of Llinas and Pellionisz' TNT and connectionist structures like NETtalk. These hierarchical structures are capable of the complex input-output patterns we discussed before. In fact, we just noted structure like this in the six layers of cortex.

4) A typical neuron is affected at once by the firing of thousands of other excitatory and inhibitory neurons, and affects other neurons only in concert with thousands of others. So there may be a kind of statistical competition among neurons, or for that matter among groups of neurons, for effects.[4] When behavior or cognition is the result of such a competition, it is perhaps less likely that specific neurons or even groups of neurons have specific cognitive or behavioral roles. The presence of certain intuitive kinds of psychological state may be a kind of statistical phenomena.

But this point is perhaps best understood in light of the *dynamics* of the brain. A person's neurophysiology does not function merely in a moment, of course. Over time, Galileo's neurophysiology exhibited a quite complex set of changes, and clearly this temporal dynamics was quite crucial, for instance, to the coordinated timing of his actions as he got up smoothly from a table. What sorts of changes occur in someone's neurophysiology over time? Neurons may be firing or not at any given moment, and in fact are each located at a particular point in their firing cycle. And of course, over somewhat longer but still tiny time periods a neuron will exhibit different temporal patterns of firing. What one thinks in a psychological "moment" may depend on the temporal pattern of firing exhibited by one's neurons, so that a psychological "moment" may be more than a moment of physical time. But more than the firing patterns are variable in one's neurophysiology.[5] Neural *connections* also change.

The action at synapses is quite complex. There are chemical changes which can occur in neurons which make them more or less susceptible to influence passed along through particular synapses. Certain connections between neurons can grow weaker or stronger, can make a first neuron more or less able to excite or inhibit a second. And these chemical changes can come about because of patterns of firing over time, for instance as the result of the repeated coordination of firing in a pre- and post-synaptic neuron. A quite complex interaction among various sorts of more or less stable structure hence occurs. The firing patterns of neurons take place in an arena of relatively stable neural connections, and yet over time they affect that arena. And this is not the only complexity. There is also growth and extinction of entire synaptic connections and even of whole neurons. This is itself modulated by the firing of neurons over time.

These different forms of instability and their interactions are quite important. Since neural connections are influenced by firing patterns, neural structures are capable of "learning" of various kinds. We have already seen that the strategy deployed in training NETtalk, in which connection weights are adjusted towards a trained response, can give quite simple neural nets interesting capacities. And Donald Hebb long ago proposed that the strengthening of connections in response to synchronization of activity in pre- and post-synaptic neurons can underwrite learning.[6]

There are other complexities in neural dynamics as well. Recall that there may be kind of competition among many neurons for effects. Hence it may be that the sorts of probabilistic evolution which occur in weather changes or the development of a gene pool are better analogues of what goes on in our brains than are the fixed transitions in an ordinary computer.

We are looking at a very complex situation. So let me pause to review and draw some threads together. Consider Galileo over some brief interval of time, say a second or two. Clearly, how his sensory receptor cells *will* fire in response to *future* sensory stimulation will affect the future states of his brain. But also many of his nervous system's current internal features will also affect its future states.

Galileo has a neural system in a complex of states which possess different degrees of stability. We might distinguish three "layers" of structure. Certain neurons are connected up to certain other neurons, and this may change more or less slowly over time, as neurons grow and die. Less stably, various synapses are more or less potentiated, more or less likely to influence firing. Even less stably, certain neurons are in fact firing at certain rates and in certain patterns. We can distinguish the particular patterns of firing exhibited at a particular time by Galileo's interconnected neurons, and two layers of relatively stable neural structure in which it is imbedded. This alone makes explanation and dynamics in his brain very complex, independent even of the complexity of the sensory input to which he might be subject.

There is a certain level of potentiation of each of the synapses in his structure of neurons. Given that relatively stable context, a certain pattern of firing in the set as a whole, connected up as it is, will in fact lead over time to certain others, perhaps with greater or less certainty. But also, that relatively stable neural structure would make it more or less likely that certain *unrealized* patterns of firing in the set as a whole *would* lead to certain others.

But this is not the only complexity. Even levels of potentiation are only relatively stable. They will change over time. The greater potentiation of certain synapses might in time lead to the greater potentiation of others, given the still more stable background of certain synapses between certain neurons. And even the existence of synapses is not completely stable. And as certain neurons grow synapses or shrink and die, that too may lead to the growth or extinction of other synapses or neurons.

In a sense, smaller-scale phenomena are here imbedded in somewhat more stable larger-scale structures. The various levels of this make things complex enough. But worse, in fact the "levels" interact. For instance, patterns of firing can influence over time the more stable levels of potentiation in which they are imbedded. The "smaller-scale" phenomena are themselves able to influence their larger-scale context.

Also, there is a level of *less* stable structure we shouldn't ignore. We might partition the *global* pattern of firing of the brain and nervous system as a whole into sub-patterns, and consider the dynamics of the set if merely some sub-pattern were absent or modified. We might consider the dynamics of that variation in that particular sub-pattern if we were to hold not merely potentiation and synapses but also other patterns of firing constant. And of course we might consider similar complexities for the other two layers of causal structure discussed in the preceding paragraphs. As I've said, in a structure of this sort all sorts of statistical phenomena may be quite significant. Certain explanatorily-relevant features present in Galileo's brain in the moment may themselves be statistical phenomena. There may be phenomena relevant to the explanation of his neural dynamics which occur when the relative percentages of conflicting patterns of neural firings turn out one way rather than another. Or explanatorily-relevant features may occur in lesser or greater degrees. And the dynamical evolution of relevant features from one moment to the next may be probabilistic in form, so that a given feature only makes another later one more or less probable, even with background context fixed. And there may be a kind of probabilistic competition for effects among relevant features.

Also, it is important to note that there is no guarantee that a relevant feature in such a structure, say a pattern of firing which explains some later pattern, is localized spatially and temporally in the manner presumed by our most ordinary notions of causation. There may be relevant features which exist at a rather abstract level. For instance, it may be that features which play distinct explanatory roles overlap in space, as different waves can overlap between a beach and a pier.[7]

2

The interanimation of thoughts will be one of the central resources deployed in Chapter Thirteen's account of the realization of thoughts beyond experience, for instance word-mediated thoughts. Before we begin, in section 3, to consider how thoughts and their interanimation are realized by the neurophysiological resources we have just surveyed, it will be useful to introduce some direct clarification of thoughts and their interanimation.

First of all, it may be helpful to contrast the interanimation of thoughts with more familiar and not dissimilar resources which have been deployed in the history of the philosophy of mind. For instance, classical empiricism made much of the association of ideas,[8] and this seems similar in certain ways to the interanimation of thoughts. But there are differences. First, to speak of the association of ideas is to invite a confusion between thoughts and their contents, and also to suggest that thoughts and contents are all distinct and separable entities, like pebbles in a bag. My talk of the interanimation of thoughts avoids both these commitments. Second, association was often traditionally held to be a single sort of symmetrical relation of varying strength, whereby one idea called forth another more or less readily. But interanimation is not necessarily symmetric. It may have a direction. And it is a kind of causal or explanatory relation which can take many different forms. Thoughts can interanimate in more than one way, and not simply more or less strongly. For instance, particular thoughts can call forth other thoughts which are specifically motor intentions or specifically mere imaginings, and not merely any old thought with the relevant associated content. Third, there may be interanimation of thoughts with contents which are not intuitively and traditionally associated, which are neither intrinsically similar or dissimilar, nor found in the agent's history of experience together, at a moment or in successive moments. So there are differences between interanimation and the association of ideas, though I admit that they may be rather quibbling. As we saw in the last chapter, behaviorism's favored form of association, the association of stimulus and response, also bears some affinities to the interanimation of thought and thought. But we've already spent enough time on that analogy.

In making much of the causal interanimation of thoughts as a resource which helps realize capacities for certain thoughts, I also invite comparison with functionalism. But we need to be wary of too close an identification of the view being developed here and functionalism, for three reasons. First, functionalism is perhaps most characteristically an account of what thoughts and other mental states *are*.[9] On the traditional functionalist view, to be a thought with a certain content *is* nothing but to play some sort of causal-functional role, which might be realized in a variety of materials but which *must* be played if there is to be such a thought. But I am merely attempting to specify here one way, though a coherently conceivable and plausible way, in which thoughts beyond experience *might* be realized. I am not seeking a specification of conditions which all conceivable thoughts would require for their realization.[10] Second, while we have already seen that interanimation is a crucial resource for the realization of certain thoughts, namely word-mediated thoughts, it is worth noting that it is *another* thought than those which are in the crucial way interanimated which is constituted by that interanimation. This is not the suggestion of functionalism. I have admitted that the *kind* of thought with a particular content which a given thought is, say a desire or a belief, may depend on the causal or explanatory role of that very thought. But still what makes it a thought with that *content* is often independent of that role. Third, the causal-functional role of a thought may specify causes and effects which are not thoughts, but interanimation links only thoughts.

Still, in noting these surface differences between my attempt and functionalism, I don't deny that I am going to deploy some traditional functionalist resources. Even if too close an identification of interanimation with standard functionalist resources would be misleading, still this account is clearly in the functionalist tradition. Thoughts in general mediate between sensory input and motor action; they have as a body that role. I have admitted that the distinction between different kinds of thoughts with a given content, say beliefs and desires with that content, may turn crucially on their causal roles. And certainly some thoughts may have even the content they do largely because of their peculiar causal role. Functionalists usually concede that the specification of the causal-functional role of a state involves not merely a specification of its actual causes and effects, but those it would have under various other conditions. And we will deploy such resources in what follows. After Chapter Eight we know that it is crucial that, unlike some crude correlational accounts, we pay adequate heed to the characteristic role of a thought in leading to behavior or to other thoughts. Fulfilling such a role seems to be a necessary condition for the existence of many thoughts, and that is a kind of functionalist resource.

This suggests that we should face certain classic difficulties which plagued functionalism. One classic worry is that the causal-functional structure of the brain may be indeterminate. Putnam, for instance, has argued that any physical structure which meets certain plausible conditions realizes any causal-functional structure which might intervene between its relevant inputs and outputs.[11] Hence it may seem that any internal causal-functional structure which might help further determine what thoughts we have, beyond the determinacy already provided by traditional behaviorist resources, beyond the determinacy provided by a specification of how we will behave in various conditions of sensory stimulation, would be itself indeterminate. But there is more determinacy of relevant structure than Putnam allows. This is because there are discernible levels of salient and explanatorily-significant physical organization in the brain, relevant to the mediation of sensation and action. Let me elaborate: Even if we didn't know how a living brain was hooked up or what it did, cutting it up alive and examining the detail of its internal operations would suggest some causal-functional descriptions as more antecedently plausible than some others. What's more, we know that brains, insofar as they realize thoughts, are for mediating between sensation and action, and our capacity to introspect thoughts with particular contents puts a further constraint on the kinds of entities which are relevant to the intuitive psychological explanations of our behavior, and hence to the kinds of features which might realize them. Because we know that thoughts have the role of intervening between sensation and behavior and that brains have a certain physical organization and are hooked up to sensory organs and muscles in particular ways, and because we operate with an intuitive sense of how to classify sensations and behaviors for humans into relevant kinds and alternatives, rooted in our capacity to introspect similarities and differences among sorts of sensory and motor experience, and because we can introspect even some of the mediating psychological states, we can discern a more determinate causal-functional structure in the brain than Putnam suggests. Putnam focusses on smaller-scale causal structure than is relevant, microphysical structure rather than neural firing, and then considers various alternative arbitrary ways of abstracting features of that very complex micro-causal structure. But we in fact know not to look down there, as mechanics know in fact not to look too low for structure relevant to fixing a car. On the other hand, as we saw in the last section, the brain does have a complex salient structure with interacting "layers", of a sort not deployed by traditional functionalism. As we will soon see, this introduces a number of complexities. But it does not suggest that there is no determinate causal-explanatory structure of a psychologically-relevant sort.

There is another classic problem for functionalism. It is far from obvious that there is any particular causal-functional role which is characteristic of, say, the belief that there's a red ball falling by a window, which is shared by all people whenever they have that belief. Consider the blind, for whom such belief would not be caused by visual perception in the ordinary way. Consider the crazy, who believe that red balls explode when they fall. How can we get around *this* worry? Part of the solution lies in understanding that causal roles may include more than a specification of actual causes and effects. They may also include a specification of effects under various counterfactual conditions, for instance the presence of disabilities or strange collateral beliefs. But another part lies in the fact that, unlike traditional functionalists, sometimes we will not need to deploy a *characteristic* causal-functional role, invariant between individuals. For instance, a word may collect associated contents of very different kinds for different individuals or over the life of a single individual. And we saw in the last chapter that still there are ways to underwrite an appropriate regularity in intuitive meaning for that word, without requiring that interanimation take the same form for everyone at all times. Nevertheless, we will sometimes need to field some "characteristic" roles. This may be required for a specification of the proper content of a speaker's idiolect, and in any case it is assured by the worries that underwrote the complaint of Chapter Eight, the complaint that some correlational accounts of content ignore the characteristic effects of various sorts of thoughts. No more than traditional functionalists am I very well-placed to actually articulate a particular causal-functional role. But for a thought to fulfill some intuitive causal-functional role is for there to be some relatively stable and abstract pattern in the interanimation of that thought and others, and perhaps in the causal relations of that thought and other things. Since the objection of Chapter Eight is intuitively reasonable, there *are* some characteristic causal-functional roles for certain thoughts, whether it's easy to articulate them or not. And we are well-positioned to underwrite the roles we will need by the resources we will deploy here, for instance by a relatively abstract and stable pattern of interanimation, once somebody figures out exactly what they are.

Even if its relation to traditional associationism and functionalism is clear, interanimation is not yet. I have spoken of thoughts and the interanimation of thoughts, and also of dispositions for thoughts and for trajectories of interanimation, in a rather vague and waffling way. This needs to be cleaned up. It will help if we start by distinguish between various kinds of thoughts, on the way to distinguishing between various kinds of interanimation.

First, as I suggested in Chapter Eight, there are certain clear cases of thoughts. Most clearly, there are thoughts whose contents we are immediately aware of in the manner of experience or the quasi-experience involved in the primary imagination.[12] Remember that, given the expansive conception of experience introduced in Chapter Seven, our experience may include motor intentions.

Second, though this really turns on details of how our thoughts contingently happen to be realized, there may well in fact be other thoughts which are realized in a manner quite like the first set of cases, and yet which have neither contents nor mediating vehicles like words of which we are immediately aware. There may even be some such thoughts which we *cannot* be aware of, in the sense of Freud and not in a sense which requires an expansion of the content theory of Part One. I'll call both these occurrent but unintrospected thoughts and also the introspected thoughts we just discussed "primary thoughts". The next chapter and part of Chapter Thirteen will concern the realization of various sorts of primary thoughts.

Are there other kinds of thoughts as well? I believe that there is a third class of thoughts, which I will call "virtual thoughts". Virtual thoughts are thoughts which it is intuitive for us to ascribe to someone on the basis of i) their primary thoughts, and ii) their dispositions for primary thoughts, and whose content is hence bound as the content of those primary thoughts is bound.[13] That is in a certain sense to say they are not *real* thoughts at all, that they are too merely in the eye of the ascriber. But certainly they are a kind of thought of which common sense talks freely.

Some cases may help make the notion of virtual thoughts clearer, but first let me sketch some necessary background: Dispositions for thoughts, even for thoughts with introspected contents, are of various sorts. Roughly, there is a disposition for something *if* there would be that thing under various specific conditions, conditions which would lead the disposition to be fulfilled. For instance, brittleness is a disposition. And knocking a glass off a table might lead to the fulfillment of the brittleness of the glass. But we might also say that there is a disposition for something when there is merely a certain *probability* that fulfillment would occur under various relevant conditions. For instance, there might merely be a tendency which would have to compete with conflicting tendencies for fulfillment. These "iffy", conditional claims about something are often underwritten by its causal structure. The brittleness of a glass is presumably underwritten by its microphysical constitution. We have already noted some of the complexities which are involved in the causal structures which plausibly realize our thoughts. But there other significant complexities at the intuitive level of the thoughts themselves, in the intuitive explanation and causation of thoughts by thoughts. Here we begin to see some of the complexities which infect the interanimation of thoughts.

Virtual thoughts are to be ascribed, I said, on the basis of primary thoughts and dispositions for primary thoughts. One relevant question about those dispositions is this: What conditions lead to, or make more or less probable, the fulfillment of the relevant dispositions?

Even if all the relevant psychological dispositions are released by other intuitively "psychological" features, those psychological features can be of various sorts. They might be primary thoughts, or dispositions for primary thoughts (so that there is a kind of explanatory interplay among dispositions), or even neural conditions which are entwined with what realizes the rest of our psychology but which aren't themselves primary thoughts or thought-dispositions at all.

And the dispositions can be dispositions *for* various things. Virtual thoughts are rooted in dispositions for primary thoughts, but these can be "indirect" or "direct" dispositions. Direct dispositions for primary thoughts would be immediately fulfilled by those primary thoughts under the relevant conditions, at least if we ignore the probabilistic cases, without the temporal mediation of other primary thoughts. Indirect dispositions are dispositions for changes in the kind of dynamic of interanimated thoughts which *will* occur in the future, or *would* occur under various other hypothetical conditions. They affect the sequences of primary thoughts that will happen, or would happen if we began with certain hypothetical primary thoughts or were influenced in various other hypothetical ways along the way. Or they may even be merely dispositions for changes in dispositions of this kind.

I think that there are virtual thoughts when the dynamics of someone's primary thoughts which would be supported by these various dispositions can be intuitively modeled as underwritten by thoughts which have contents of the sort sketched in Part One, but which are not primary thoughts. I think there are virtual thoughts when we can tell a commonplace psychological story about how such a thought which is not primary could help constitute the relevant dispositions.

Some examples may help make this clearer: First of all, even if Galileo lacks an introspected thought with a certain content, it is sometimes the case that *if* he considered a certain matter then a certain content concerning that matter would come up to awareness in him. If he turned to the issue of the bakery downstairs, then he would think of it in a certain way he would be aware of. In this case, I think it is plausible to say that he has a virtual thought of the shop when he isn't aware of the shop, even if he has then no primary thought of it at all.

Second, there is inference: If Galileo has a firm disposition to infer from A to B, even if he is not aware of anything at all equivalent to "if A then B" or which even makes B likely given A, then there is reason to ascribe to him a virtual thought with a content of roughly that sort, a content which links in some appropriate way the content of the primary thought of A and the content of the primary thought of B. This sort of presumption may be overridden by other considerations, for instance when Galileo cannot introspect the relevant thought when he tries. And there may be borderline cases, for instance the ascription of complex implicit knowledge of principles of generative grammar to speakers of a language. So there may well be some indeterminacy regarding what virtual thoughts someone has, given their dispositions for inferences. But there are, I think, also some intuitively clear cases.

Let me elaborate a bit. Some inferences seem rooted in memory, and memory can involve virtual thoughts in more than one way. One case we've already considered. Galileo may have a disposition for a primary thought of his neighbor, have a disposition for a kind of primary imagination of ways he had once seen her to be. But much of what we call memory may rather be a kind of recognitional capacity, a capacity to categorize or to respond in some other appropriate way, which involves no memory images.[14] Galileo can recognize certain faces even if he can't at will form memory images of them. And he knows how to act if certain situations come up. He has the capacity to respond with some appropriate abstracted or word-mediated recognition, or to form appropriate motor intentions, in the face of certain experiences or primary imaginations. And this capacity may be intuitively modeled by virtual thoughts, virtual memories. It is as if Galileo's psychology is organized hierarchically at a particular moment: The "injection" of a particular experience would lead to all sorts of abstracted or word-mediated thoughts or motor intentions in him. And this sort of transition may be modeled by reference to an unconscious memory, which helps underwrite a capacity for inference, a capacity which is caused by the past experiences which intuitively cause the "memory". Hence we have a virtual thought. It may be worth stressing that into this hierarchical structure may be injected not merely experience but primary imagination of the sort we will discuss in the next chapter, including memory images and fantasy. The latter may hence lead to word-mediated or abstracted thoughts and even motor intentions, but in an appropriately as-if mode, so that Galileo can be quite primed to act in situations he does not currently inhabit.[15]

Here's another example of virtual thought: When Galileo has dispositions such that he is led always to the pursuit of something which he perceives to be candy and then is satisfied and relaxed when he gets it, then it is appropriate to ascribe to him a virtual desire for candy, even when there is no corresponding primary thought. And of course there may analogous but less stable virtual desires. A virtual thought which is a drive or desire may seem to organize the sequence of one's primary thoughts around it.

Another example, which will be relevant later on, might be called "virtual experience". Recall that we have causal experience in the first instance because we do things. But there is another sort of intuitive causal experience, our experience of the causal powers of the objects on which we act. Our expectation regarding the force of objects in our immediate environment is no doubt tied to certain of their properties of which we have phenomenal experience, say phenomenal pressure. But of course their causal powers are not to be identified with their phenomenal properties. Rather, our expectation of their powers is present as a virtual thought around which our action is organized, a kind of virtual experience of the objects.

In effect, I have been suggesting here that those who hold that we have thoughts only as a matter of "interpretation" are right about *virtual* thoughts. But I think that certain specific sorts of evidential grounds, primary thoughts and dispositions for primary thoughts, are the relevant grounds for these "interpretations". Ascriptions of virtual thoughts are plausibly bound by principles of coherence, though not I believe by principles as strong as those Dennett deploys. And there may be several admissible "interpretations", even apparently contradictory ones, which meet all the relevant constraints. We might have had a practice which allowed ascription of all the apparently contradictory thoughts which meet the constraints, but I think that is not our practice. Rather, I think we must accept an indeterminacy among apparently contradictory interpretations which meet all the relevant constraints. There are some thoughts which we determinately have, among them primary thoughts. But certainly many intuitive thoughts are virtual thoughts, and there may in fact be significant indeterminacies about the presence of particular virtual thoughts. People who know all the relevant facts about what realizes Galileo's thoughts may at least in some instances reasonably disagree about what virtual thoughts he is to be ascribed, and there be no fact of the matter which adjudicates between them.

We have primary thoughts of two possible sorts, and virtual thoughts. Are there any other kinds of thoughts? There is at least an intermediate set of cases, which indeed includes some of our clear cases from Chapter Eight. We are not immediately aware of the full range of contents of most word-mediated thoughts, but merely of their vehicles. Thoughts which are mediated by words involve a complex interanimation of thoughts, but what we are directly aware of at the moment of utterance is usually only the words which mediate the thought, and perhaps a bit of their content. We are not aware of most of the content of such a thought, which we only have a tendency to become aware of. Nor need that extra content necessarily be born by any primary thought at the moment of that thought. The word-mediated thought includes as components primary thoughts, but also virtual thoughts, or at the very least conditions of the sort which might lead us to ascribe virtual thoughts. Likewise, thoughts with basic contents which are not seed contents sometimes include a component which is a primary thought of a bit of their content, say of what is present in immediate experience, but also virtual components as well.[16] This mixed type of thought has some affinities with primary thoughts and some with virtual thoughts. And they add complexities of their own to mental dynamics. The mixed sort of thought, and dispositions for them, may lead to the ascription of further virtual thoughts, which for instance may underwrite inferences between word-mediated thoughts.

But all such thoughts should be fixed when primary thoughts and all virtual thoughts, including the virtual thoughts which make up the virtual components of the mixed sort of thought and those which underlie inference among the mixed sort of thoughts, are fixed. All these complications ultimately merely provide psychological explanations of primary thoughts. If Galileo's primary thoughts, and his various dispositions for primary thoughts which I have distinguished, are fixed, then so too are his virtual thoughts and his thoughts of the mixed kind, at least to the degree that there are facts about what those thoughts are. These, I suggest, are all his thoughts.

We might ascribe thoughts to Galileo at some moment on the basis not just of his primary thoughts and dispositions for primary thoughts at that moment, but on the basis of his condition over an extended period of time. It seems to me that common sense sometimes ascribes thoughts in this way. But still it will help provide clarity in what follows if I stipulate that virtual thoughts and thoughts of the mixed kind are to be ascribed to someone at some moment only on the basis of their primary thoughts and dispositions for primary thoughts at that moment, on the basis of what I will call their "primary psychology". Galileo's primary psychology at some moment constitutes his psychology at that moment, even if this involves some revision of common sense.

All this allows me hereafter to largely ignore the realization of virtual thoughts, and focus on the realization of primary thoughts and dispositions for primary thoughts. But I will give thoughts of the mixed sort some special attention in Chapter Thirteen. This is because they introduce new sorts of contents, linked to the contents of primary thoughts but not quite bound by them. Hence they are of special interest to us.

So far I've clarified merely thoughts and dispositions for thoughts, and we need to turn to a consideration of the interanimation of thoughts. In the last chapter, I distinguished between actual and potential interanimation. The actual interanimation of one's thoughts involves the actual temporal sequence of those thoughts. But one also has at any given moment various potentials for various sequences of interanimation, if some experience, or other psychological state, only occurs. This potential interanimation lies curled up in one's psychological dispositions in the moment. There are, we now know, various kinds of thoughts. But if we focus first on the interanimation of *primary* thoughts, then it is evident that their potential interanimation is latent in the various direct and indirect dispositions for primary thoughts which we discussed above.

The instances of interanimation I discussed in the last chapter, and most of those I will discuss in what follows, involve merely the interanimation of primary thoughts. But one may also speak of the interanimation of other sorts of thoughts, and even perhaps of that of other "psychological" states involving features of our neurophysiology which don't constitute thoughts. For instance, one might want to talk about the interanimation of virtual thoughts. So we might wonder if we have the resources to deal with this. One's primary psychology, one's primary thoughts and dispositions for primary thoughts at a particular moment, fix one's entire psychology of thoughts at that moment. The trajectory of one's primary psychology over time will hence fix the trajectory of one's entire psychology of thoughts. But one might well wonder if one's primary psychology at a moment fixes the potential interanimation of one's entire psychology of thoughts.

I believe that it does. Since that primary psychology includes all the complex indirect dispositions for primary thoughts of the sorts we've noted, it captures all of one's present psychological states which are relevant to the psychological explanation of one's future thoughts, and even of those one would have under various hypothetical but psychologically-relevant conditions. Those indirect dispositions help explain not merely one's actual future primary thoughts, but one's future dispositions, and relevantly hypothetical future dispositions, for primary thoughts.

Clearly, however, we are looking at a complex explanatory structure. Psychological dynamics, like neural dynamics, is quite complicated. It seems to me not essential to a psychology that it have this sort of complex and unstable dynamics, but our psychologies do. It is not an accident, I think, that these complexities reflect the parallel complexities of the neural structure which helps realize our thought. Indeed, for a clearer understanding of some of the complexities involved in the interanimation of our thoughts, it may be useful to turn finally to the issue of how our thoughts and their interanimation are rooted in plausible neurophysiological resources.

3

Let me try to pull things together at least a bit. How are the things which are the focus of section 2--thoughts, dispositions for thoughts, and the interanimation of thoughts--rooted in neurophysiological resources of the sort sketched in section 1?

Thoughts are hard to exactly place in such complex structures as our brains. It is not implausible to claim that certain thoughts involve particular patterns of firing, a certain pattern of electrical activity across certain neurons in a particular brain at a particular moment. Perhaps, at least in a particular context of other fixed neural states in a particular person, certain patterns of firing are necessary to help constitute certain thoughts, say certain perceptual beliefs or motor intentions. Such thoughts would be, like the patterns of firing which help constitute them, relatively unstable. On the other hand, it may seem equally plausible to insist that something more stable might constitute a thought, for instance a memory which is retained over a long period of time which encompasses radically different rates and patterns of neural firing in all the different areas of the brain.

Interanimation seems equally difficult to place. At a given moment, in a certain environment provided by other neural states, certain patterns of firing which help constitute a thought might (perhaps more or less probably) quite quickly cause other patterns of firing which would help to constitute other thoughts. That might constitute a kind of interanimation of thought by thought. On the other hand, the firing of certain neurons might lead over time to a relatively slow facilitation and stabilization of certain synapses, which hence facilitate other thoughts. That might be a kind of interanimation too.

So that we can start to clean this up, let me simply assume a hypothesis which seems to be not implausible for all we know now. Let our *primary* thoughts be assumed to be thoughts whose realization conditions include actual patterns and rates of firing of a potentially quite unstable sort.[17] At least when the environment of that neural activity, say its context of other neural states including other neural firing and various connections, is fixed, the loss of such a relatively unstable pattern would constitute the loss of that thought. Such a firing pattern is analogous to a Mackie-style "inus" condition:[18] It is a necessary but possibly insufficient component of a set of conditions which while perhaps unnecessary are jointly sufficient for the existence of a primary thought. Let the primary components of the mixed type of thought also be of this sort.

This is, of course, speculation. But it is not totally unfounded. For instance, experience involves perhaps the clearest set of primary thoughts. And our sensory experience seems correlated to the firing of our sensory receptor cells, which are themselves responsive to environmental stimuli, in such a way that makes it very plausible that firing patterns caused by or involving the firing of sensory receptor cells are involved in the constitution of that experience. It seems antecedently plausible that different patterns of firing would, at least in the relevant context, help constitute a different sort of sensory experience. Analogous things might be said about motor intentions. The differential firing of sensory receptor cells might have effects on the brain other than effects on firing patterns, but effects on firing patterns would be the quickest, and experience seems quite quickly affected by sensory receptor cells. Firing patterns, like experience, seem well positioned for very quick effects on behavior. What's more, there is a good deal of neurophysiological evidence that specific sorts of experience are in fact accompanied by specific forms of firing activity in specific parts of the brain. But, as I said, my speculation is meant only as a hypothesis which is not implausible for all we know now.

The truth of this hypothesis would still leave us with the large ambiguities to unravel, regarding dispositions for and potential interanimation of primary thoughts. For instance, assume that whatever else besides a person's neural states which helps constitute their thoughts is fixed. Then a certain relatively stable pattern of their neural states, say of synaptic strengths, might make it likely that a certain sequence of primary thoughts *would* occur in response to particular initial patterns of firing which helped constitute a particular initial primary thought. There will be primary thoughts which a given stable neural structure in fact helps constitute, and which in fact interanimate other primary thoughts in certain ways, which in fact causally generate conditions which help constitute those others. But there are also other primary thoughts which such a structure *could* instantiate (if the right patterns of firing occurred in it) and which *would* causally generate certain others. So far so good. But neural states may in fact be stable in several different ways. There are several sorts of conditions which might be the "stable" background for certain hypothetical trajectories of interanimated primary thoughts, the background which helps constitute various direct and indirect dispositions for primary thoughts. And they exhibit the complexities of structure we noted in section 1.

Aristotelian terminology may help us a bit in understanding the complexities we face. We might distinguish between the *actuality* of a primary thought, involving an actual pattern of firing which in fact helps constitute the thought; the *first potentiality* for such a thought, had when neurons are connected and synapses weighted *and other neurons firing* so that some pattern of firing in some neurons would constitute the thought (remember that the relevant non-neural context is also assumed to be fixed); the *second potentiality* for such a thought, had when neurons are connected and synapses weighted so that some pattern of firing in such neurons (including those which might merely be a context for that thought) could help constitute such a thought; and the *third and fourth potentialities* for a primary thought, which might only be realized through changes in neural structures, in the first instance through the facilitation of synapses, and in the second instance through the growth of synapses or death of neurons. The distinction between first and second potentiality requires that there be some way to distinguish between patterns of firing that constitute a thought and those which merely constitute its context, and this distinction may be problematic. If such a distinction cannot be made, then my talk of first and second potentials should be collapsed.

We've just distinguished primary thoughts and various potentials and dispositions for primary thoughts. We might similarly distinguish between various types of actual interanimation, and various potentials for interanimation which also constitute certain dispositions for primary thoughts. In the central case, we might say, actual primary thoughts interanimate other primary thoughts which they in fact help causally generate. Continue to call this "actual interanimation". But we might also speak of "a first potential for interanimation" when we mean that the fulfillment of a first potentiality for a primary thought would cause the fulfillment of another first potentiality with no change in the patterns of firing in the relevant neural context required, where the realization of a primary thought for which there is a first potentiality would lead to the realization of another primary thought. And we might speak of "a second potential for interanimation" when the fulfillment of a second potentiality for a primary thought would cause the fulfillment of another second potentiality, with no organic changes in the synapses or neurons required, where the realization of a primary thought for which there is such a second potentiality would lead to the realization of another such. There are clearly other sorts of psychologically relevant interanimation and dispositions for interanimation as well. For instance, if one comes to have a certain second potential, then one may come to have another second potential. The second potentials themselves may be interanimated, if I may be permitted to stretch my own usage and speak that way. Also, there can be dispositions for such an interanimation. And we should remember that there are intuitively cross-level effects, say of firing on synapses and of thoughts on dispositions for thoughts. And since causal relations between even primary thoughts may well be merely probabilistic, with for instance one primary thought making other primary thoughts in a certain context more or less probable, we would probably need also to speak of degrees of interanimation of various kinds, and probabilistic dispositions. And there are yet further complexities. For instance, while we seem to have the capacity for any sort of neural firing which sensory stimulation could give us, it may be that some other firing patterns for which we have the first or second potential in my sense are not in any intuitive way consistent with the limitations of our psychologies. Maybe only some patterns are those for which we have the appropriately characteristic first or second potentials, which can be released by our experience or generated by other of our psychological states. And we should always remember that our dispositions may be for particular kinds of thoughts with a content, and not just any old thought with that content. But let me stop with only this very rough and ready model of the realization of our primary thoughts and of relevant dispositions and of interanimation. That should be more than enough complexity for our purposes.

The next two chapters go some way towards fleshing out this rather rough conception of the neural realization of our thoughts and their interanimation. Chapter Twelve discusses experience, and also the quasi-experience involved in the primary imagination. These are both primary thoughts. Chapter Thirteen will discuss primary thoughts we do not and even perhaps cannot introspect. It will also discuss word-mediated thought, and thoughts with basic contents beyond seed contents. These are cases of our mixed sort.

In the model I pursue here, primary thoughts involve, in the relevant context, particular patterns of firing. This ensures that at least one element deployed by the dominant correlational accounts of content is present: While a particular experience may not require the existence of an object of the sort experienced, it does seem to require a pattern of firing with which, if it did exist, that object might be correlated. This is at least a remote analogue of an inner sentence of Mentalese, an internal representation. It might not be a pattern which is spatially distinct from other relevant patterns in the manner of ordinary sentences, but it is still a specific pattern. Even plausible non-objectual models of our experience must allow this, it seems. And this fact will allow us to construct an account of the realization of our thought beyond experience which fits with a coherently conceivable but not fully plausible objectual account of our experience in this part, and yet which might mesh well with a non-objectual account of our experience of the sort we pursue in the next part. It is a hinge for the rest of the book.

NOTES

1. Note that I say sensation and sensory input, not sensory experience. The point of this distinction will become evident.

2. The following exposition is standard, and underwritten by standard introductions to neurophysiology. Of special interest to philosophers are Patricia Churchland, *Neurophilosophy*, and Patricia Churchland and Terrence Sejnowski, *The Computational Brain* (Cambridge, MA: MIT Press, 1992). Jean-Pierre Changeux, *Neuronal Man* (Oxford: Oxford University Press, 1986) is cheaper. See also Neil Carlson, *Physiology of Behavior* (Boston: Allyn & Bacon, 1977), E.R. Kandel, J.H. Schwartz, and T.M Jessell (editors), *Principles of Neural Science*, third edition (Norwalk, CT: Appleton and Lange, 1991), and C. Koch and J.L. Davis (editors), *Large-Scale Neuronal Theories*

of the Brain (Cambridge, MA: MIT Press, 1994). The September 1992 issue of *Scientific American* is an interesting collection of popular essays by leading figures.

3. The scare quotes are motivated by the worry that it may be a mistake to think that the content of our thoughts, even of our experience, is to identified with any information we "process".

4. See J. Allan Hobson, *The Dreaming Brain* (New York: Basic Books, 1988) and Daniel C. Dennett, *Consciousness Explained* (Boston: Little, Brown and Company, 1991) for discussion of ways in which this sort of mechanism may be important.

5. See Churchland and Sejnowski, *The Computational Brain*, 239-329, for a summary of recent work on neural plasticity.

6. D.O. Hebb, *The Organization of Behavior* (New York: John Wiley & Sons, 1949).

7. For a relevant discussion, see Robert Batterman, "Theories Between Theories", *Synthese* 103, 1995, 171-201.

8. One excellent review of the history of association principles is Geo. Croom Robertson, "Association", in *Encyclopaedia Britannica*, volume II (Chicago: The Werner Company, 1894), 730-734. Classic references include David Hartley, *Observations on Man* (Gainesville: Scholars' Facsimiles & Reprints, 1966), and Sir William Hamilton, Note D** and Note D***, in *The Works of Thomas Reid, D.D.* (Edinburgh: Maclachlan and Stewart, 1852), 889.

9. It will be more efficient if for the moment I ignore the remarks in Chapter Three that certain metaphysical distinctions invoked by this claim are mere artifacts of the approach apparatus.

10. Except for the constraint that thoughts like ours must be rooted in the presence of experience.

11. Hilary Putnam, *Representation and Reality*.

12. Someone might argue, collapsing quasi-experience of the sort we will discuss in the next chapter into experience, that we only have one of these at any moment. However, I think that we have at least some reason to cordon off quasi-experience from experience, in the way suggested in the next chapter, and also cordon off the words we hear in the mind's ear from other sorts of "imaginings".

13. Clearly, if all there was to everyone's psychology was the same function from experience to behavior then thoughts wouldn't be very interesting. Inner experience does differ from person to person depending on their history, even when they are in the "same" situation. We say different things to ourselves, and our hunger differs. But also people are often in intuitively different psychological states when there is no difference in what they are aware of. Occurrent thoughts do not take us all the way we need to go here. Virtual thoughts play, I think, a crucial role.

14. See for instance Gerald Edelman, *Neural Darwinism* (New York: Basic Books, 1987).

15. One puzzle about this is how some of our imaginings are memory images and some mere fantasy. I think there are at least two elements of the difference. We can recognize certain images as memories of certain kinds. But memory images are also less arbitrary than fantasy, less at the command of an arbitrary will.

16. This ignores certain complexities to which we will return in Chapter Thirteen.

17. These primary thoughts are only potentially unstable because firing patterns may persist for long periods.

18. J.L. Mackie, "Causes and Conditions", *American Philosophical Quarterly* 2, 1965, 245-264.

CHAPTER TWELVE

EXPERIENCE AND QUASI-EXPERIENCE

This chapter provides a coherently conceivable account of the realization of our experience, which meshes with the coherently conceivable and apparently plausible account of our capacity for thought beyond experience developed in Chapter Thirteen. It also concerns the realization of what I call "the primary imagination". Section 1 concerns experience, Section 2 the primary imagination.

1

Galileo's momentary experience was a thought, with seed content which matched and exhausted how he experienced things to be in that moment. Or at least that is roughly correct. There are a few complications. Since certain sorts of experience may be realized only by firing patterns which take more than a physical moment to occur, some art would be required to specify exactly how long the relevant "moment" of Galileo's experience lasted. And there may be grounds for worry that his entire experience of a moment encompassed more than a single thought. But we can at least vaguely say that experiences are thoughts, and that each person has a temporal sequence of fleeting experiences, experiences which I will perhaps misleadingly call "moments" of experience. Our concern here is the realization of Galileo's experience, and we can understand that, it seems, if we can understand the realization of each moment of his experience, each moment of its temporal trajectory.

Seed contents, which match and exhaust moments of possible human experience, are a kind of basic content. And coherently conceivable accounts are accounts fleshed out in basic content. So it is immediately evident that *some* coherently conceivable account of the realization of Galileo's momentary experience is possible. Here's a rather ridiculous and solipsistic one: As Galileo watched a red ball drop beneath his window, the entire world consisted solely of those things which he experienced at that particular moment, being just and merely as he experienced them to be.

But we pursue not merely *any* coherently conceivable account of the realization of our experience, but an account which can also mesh with the largely plausible account of our capacities for thought beyond experience developed in the next chapter. This requires that our experience be constituted at least in part by neural resources. It requires that sensory experiences and motor intentions be primary thoughts, which crucially involve particular patterns of neural firing. Also, we seek an account which meshes with the familiar concrete understanding of the world we presume in this part, which surely includes more than a moment's experience. Any even *remotely* plausible account of our experience must explain how there can be misleading artifacts of that experience. These artifacts are the very phenomena which ensure the intensionality of our experience. The world outran Galileo's experience in each moment, both in tiny detail and in spatial extent. The boundaries of his experience hence constituted mere artifacts of that experience. And there were other artifacts as well. For instance, his visual experience exhibited a focus of attention which revealed no plausible feature of the objects he saw. And it incorporated spatial distortions, so that distant objects looked smaller. Clearly, we need an account of the realization of experience which allows for artifacts of experience and which also allows experiences to be primary thoughts which involve firing patterns. We seek here a coherently conceivable account of Galileo's experience which yet meets these two constraints.

Since through our experience our thought opens out into the world, it is not unreasonable to claim that more than neural resources are required to constitute our experience. For instance, it might be claimed that a particular object in the world, which we experience in part through the mediation of a certain pattern of neural firing, may play a crucial role in constituting that pattern of firing to be an experience of an object of that sort. This in fact is the suggestion of the dominant correlational accounts of perceptual thought noted in Chapter Eight. Our obvious strategy is to root around for objects which can be "correlated" with the requisite patterns of neural firing. Since basic contents which capture a mundane world of the sort we presume here do include entities of the sort we experience, certainly objects of those sorts can be deployed in coherently conceivable correlationist accounts of our experience. So, it seems, we can meet one constraint. Experiences can be primary thoughts.

But we need to meet the other constraint as well. We need to explain the intuitive artifacts of our experience. The entire world of a moment is not present in the content of anyone's experience, even if it happens to be correlated in *some* way with the firing of their neurons at that moment. Generally, we need to ensure that the right objects are correlated in the proper way with the particular patterns of firing which constitute our experience, in a manner which underwrites the intuitive introspectible contents of that experience. And there are other artifacts of our experience than its merely leaving some things out, for instance valences of attention in which certain objects of high attention are raised up from the surrounding ground, and these correspond to no obvious object. Hence our initial model requires elaboration.

Let me begin by deploying some hints from Part One. There we saw that the two kinds of elements present in seed contents and our experience, phenomenal and causal elements, might correspond respectively to our capacities to sense and to do various things. Galileo's nervous system begins in sensory receptor cells and ends in motor neurons controlling muscles, and the more or less parallel structure of his thoughts seems to begin in sensory experience and end in motor intentions. His sensory receptor cells and motor neurons, his sense organs and muscles, and what they fairly immediately respond to and push and pull, seem the obvious places to look as we search for conditions in addition to neural firing which help constitute his experience. For instance, such objects as, barring its obvious artifacts, his experience seems to reveal might be the very things he responds to or pushes and pulls. By the very fact that they are the particular things which he more or less immediately responds to and pushes and pulls, they might be the particular things which help constitute his particular experience of the moment, with its peculiar bounds and perhaps its other peculiar artifacts as well.

Still, Part One also suggested that phenomenal and causal experience should be treated in slightly different ways. Galileo's *phenomenal* experience of a falling red apple might be in part constituted by the apple, or at least by the side of it which faced him. We only need to be sure that such things are correlated in the right way with the appropriate patterns of his neural firing. But, on the other hand, Galileo's *causal* experience seems constituted partly by the way in which his patterns of neural firing control his muscles. We begin with the following very abstract account of the realization of experience: The conditions which realize phenomenal experience of type X include objects with phenomenal properties of the sort apparently revealed in that experience, which fix the contents of correlated patterns of neural firing, patterns which might be held to "represent" those objects. The conditions which realize causal experience of type X include motor organs with relevant causal properties "controlled" by correlated patterns of neural firing. Note that there is more than one asymmetry in this. At least in the case of sensations rather than inner feelings, the *phenomenal* content of firing patterns gets fixed by apparently *external* objects which are correlated with those patterns of firing, firing patterns which presumably are causally *responsive* to features of the world. On the other hand, the *causal* content of certain firing patterns gets set by objects *internal* to the body, and in particular by muscles and limbs *controlled* by that firing. In the language of Chapter Eight, these are both *objectual* accounts, but of different types.

Because causal experience is unfamiliar, Chapter Seven provided a relatively detailed sketch of its realization, which deployed not only coherently conceivable but seemingly plausible resources. On that account, it is quite crucial to the powers which we can experience, to the causal contents our motor intentions can exhibit, that we have musculature and joints and motor control systems of certain specific sorts. For instance, we can intend to project a hand into a position and orientation in a familiar space of three dimensions, even while we keep our shoulders straight. These motor intentions control antagonist muscles at three joints which have various degrees of freedom.[1] These muscles allow us to exert a kind of mechanical force in the space we in habit and move through. We can move our limbs with more or less force and speed in various directions, and hence push or pull with more or less force at variously moving and resisting things. Since the forces we experience are exerted in space and over time, and since they cause movement through space in light of other forces, a physics of mechanical force in three spatial dimensions is just what creatures like humans might be expected to develop, after they had become convinced of the illusory nature of their phenomenal experience.[2] If we had other capacities for action, say capacities to change phenomenal colors directly and at will and with different degrees of insistence, and if things in our environment possessed similar powers, then very different sorts of powers would be present in our causal experience.

We will return to these issues and cases in Chapter Sixteen, but this brief sketch clearly meshes well with the neural resources we now deploy, and also provides an explanation of the only obvious artifact of our causal experience, the fact that we don't at a moment experience every causal feature of the world. The content of a motor intention, plausibly a primary thought, is fixed by the bodily movement which it controls, say out at finger's end. That is a very specific and limited thing, certainly only a small bit of the world's full causal structure, and that explains the artifact. There are difficulties which threaten this explanation. One might reasonably object that any firing pattern which controls a limb movement also controls intervening firing in motor neurons, and also various phenomena in the world which result from or are affected by the limb movement. So one may reasonably wonder about the legitimacy of fixing the content of the firing patterns by what happens precisely at skin's end. It may be that the only phenomena with which that pattern is consistently correlated over time are no further out than that.[3] But certainly this can't rule the intervening patterns of firing out of contention. The full response to this objection requires that we deploy introspective resources. One's intention has an introspectible content which ties it to the limb movement in particular. The mechanism of this is much the same as in the phenomenal case. The neural firings which, for instance, control one's explicit utterance about a motor intention are causally responsive to those which help constitute that bit of causal experience. And if the muscles controlled seem suspiciously downline, unlike sensory receptor cells, still galilean explanations of the correlation between the nature of the object, the musculature, which helps constitute the causal experience, and the nature of the firing patterns which control it, are in fact easier to provide than in the case of phenomenal experience. Learning and evolution could serve to link those causal configurations. Still, however helpful the more or less non-objectual resource of these firing patterns may be in helping to fix the introspectible content of one's causal experience, we have seen reason to believe that non-objectual resources are not alone sufficient, at least in any coherently conceivable account. So it is fortunate that skin's end is at least an *intuitive* boundary for resources which help constitute the content of one's causal experience of a moment. There is an intuitively "direct" sense in which one controls one's limbs but not the objects in one's environment or the hidden firings of one's motor neurons. Let's rest, for now, on that point. We will return to these issues in Part Three.

Because of what has come and what will follow, that's enough for the moment on specifically causal experience. But though I will focus in the rest of this chapter primarily on phenomenal experience, one other skein of issues should detain us for a moment. We need to understand the realization of spatio-temporal experience, whether causal or phenomenal.

Some of the spatio-temporal structure present in basic contents is merely causal structure. Though the differences between the chiral orientation of paths of causal connectibility should give us pause, for the most part this sort of spatio-temporal structure need not appear within our experience. If we have a capacity for the conception of the causal, it may seem that we can get spatio-temporal resources automatically. Still, both causal experience and phenomenal experience exhibit spatio-temporal structure of another sort. We need some account of those spatio-temporal features, which are present in our experience. And, in fact, the diremption between our capacity to conceive causally-generated spatio-temporality on the one hand and our capacity for experience of spatio-temporality on the other is probably not in fact as great as appearances may suggest. The capacities which underlie our causal experience and motor action may well play a crucial role in constituting the spatio-temporal structure of all of our experience, phenomenal as well as causal, and there may be important influences which run in the other direction as well. For instance, our capacity to project our limbs through trajectories in space, say to intentionally project our hands out to a particular position in three spatial dimensions and to a particular orientation, accomplished by various degrees of pitch, yaw, and spin, may be quite crucial in constituting our capacity to conceive continuous causal paths. And this is probably entwined with our capacities for even *phenomenal* experience of spatio-temporality.

But, still, the most obvious and crucial resources to deploy in accounts of the spatio-temporal features present in our experience, the second sort of spatio-temporal structure we can conceive, are objectual resources, which are just like the features they help us to conceive. Indeed, in Part Three we will see that objectual resources must be deployed by coherently conceivable accounts of the realization of the spatio-temporal features of our experience. For instance, it is hard to conceive how we might have the experience of temporal change if we did not in fact possess various "moments" of experience which follow one another in time, and correspondingly successive neural states. And the fact that within a moment of experience we can experience the same powers or colors at different places and different concrete properties at the same location, intuitively suggests realizations which involve particular locations in space, for instance spatially-distributed perceived objects and spatially-distributed firing patterns with which they are correlated.

We'll return to these issues. For now, let me focus most on the remaining set of intrinsic properties revealed in our experience, phenomenal properties. In particular let me focus on the phenomenal properties involved in sensation rather than inner feeling, because these two sorts of cases may be handled in a roughly similar way. We will develop in some detail a correlationist objectual account of the experience of intrinsic phenomenal properties, which yet can mesh with neural resources and explain obvious artifacts of phenomenal experience.

Certain phenomenal features of the objects we experience are supposed to be "correlated" with certain patterns of firing. But that formulation hides a lot of complexity and difficulty. First of all, consider all the difficulties which would be involved in determining exactly what the relevant patterns of firings in fact are. We presumed in the last chapter that the patterns of firing are analogous to inus conditions. Only in a particular relatively fixed context is a particular relevant pattern such as to help constitute the appropriate experience. In different background conditions, different patterns of firing would presumably be necessary. Also, we saw there that the relevant "patterns" may not be easily isolated and separated from one another. Second, it may be unclear what particular phenomenal entities or features are to be correlated with particular patterns of firing. Should something which is matched by the entire content of a moment of phenomenal experience be the relevant correlate,[4] or instead what is matched by the contents of what are the intuitively distinct "experiences" which together make up that moment of experience, or instead certain features of such experiences which other experiences can share? And if the latter, which features are the relevant ones? Third, we need a fuller account of what kind of correlation between firing patterns and phenomenal entities or features is required. And there are other complications also. If we are not to duplicate the problems of traditional correlational accounts, then we cannot neglect the characteristic behaviors to which experiences lead. Ordinary adults who have phenomenal experience must be able to verbally characterize that experience in an appropriate way, and to sort things which are experienced on the basis of how they are experienced to be. Hence the correlated firing patterns must be capable of the appropriate effects. They must fulfill appropriate actual and hypothetical causal roles, as well as be properly correlated with phenomenal entities.

Because of the special nature of phenomenal experience, these various difficulties can be met in an intuitive way. We can see this by considering how we would go about finding out what patterns of firing help constitute various forms of phenomenal experience. Some hints about the proper solution of that epistemic problem can provide some guidance regarding the analogous metaphysical problem, the problem about what phenomenal experiences *are*.

At least to a first approximation, it seems intuitively clear that at any given moment Galileo is capable of a certain very wide range of phenomenal experience, the normal human range. And it also seems intuitively clear, at least to a first approximation, that he would have each alternative form of that experience if his senses were stimulated in various alternative ways. While his expectations and various background neural states no doubt to some degree limit the phenomenal experience he would have if the firing in his sensory receptor cells were different than it is, and while firing in sensory receptor cells isn't *causally* influenced in the strict sense introduced by Chapter Seven by the phenomenal and hence non-causal properties of things, at least roughly the following helpful conditions seem to obtain: At any moment, there is at least a rough partition of Galileo's brain states into background conditions on the one hand and "sensory" neural firings on the other, which are immediately responsive to the firing of sensory receptor cells. There is also at least a rough correlation between particular patterns of that "sensory" firing and particular phenomenal features he would experience through the mediation of or in response to such firing. These conditions are what constitute Galileo's sensory experience as being, at least intuitively, environmentally responsive.

Also, recall that the causal *roles* of the firing patterns which constitute Galileo's experience must be appropriate given the introspectible content of that experience. In effect, something like abstraction must underwrite the very constitution of his experience, so that the features of his experience which he can introspect can lead to the appropriate sort of effects on the sequence of his thoughts or his motor responses. There must be elements of his firing patterns, though not necessarily spatio-temporally distinct or stable elements, which help realize his capacity to respond in the appropriate way to each introspectible feature of his phenomenal experience, so that he can sort objects by color or trace their edges.[5]

Hence, there are constraints which push from two directions, in-going and out-going, and which help specify the particular kinds of patterns which are to be correlated with particular phenomenal features to help constitute Galileo's phenomenal experience. These dual constraints are in fact quite like those deployed by neurophysiologists when they search for neural correlates of particular sorts of experience. The wide space of introspectible features that the phenomenal experience of someone might intuitively possess in a moment must be correlated with sensory patterns of firing which they would intuitively suffer in situations which would give them such an experience, and those patterns must be capable of underwriting the causal role appropriate to experience of those features.

It might be that the firing pattern which has a particular role and which correlates with a particular phenomenal feature varies in a significant way from one moment of experience to the next, even in a given person, that the context which helps constitute a particular inus condition as the condition which is relevant on a particular occasion is seriously unstable. But still it seems not implausible, at least for all we know now, to presume otherwise, along with much of current neurophysiology.[6]

There is a problem latent in all this. The causal properties of the objects we experience which causally influence the firing of sensory receptor cells are not their phenomenal properties. On the other hand, they are at least apparently correlated with their apparent phenomenal properties. So perhaps the phenomenal colors of things just happen to be correlated with their causal properties in the right way, or perhaps their causal properties merely generate within us the presence of objects with the requisite phenomenal colors to help constitute the necessary experience. According to the intuitive and commonsense picture of things there is the required correlation between the firing of our sensory receptor cells and phenomenal properties. But, at least since Galileo, this sort of correlation should also seem a mysterious and ultimately fatal element in the commonsense understanding of the world and our experience. It is a kind of correlation which, given our post-galilean conception of the world, is miraculous, too miraculous to be true. Still, we are pledged to ignore this particular difficulty until Part Three. If we ignore it, then the following two-part suggestion seems not implausible, at least for all we know so far:

1) To each intuitively distinct feature which Galileo might introspect his experience to possess, to each feature which might have a particular causal role, which for instance might lead to a characteristic sort of copying behavior, a certain kind of tracing or coloring, there corresponds a particular pattern of firing among his range of possible sensory firings. That is the pattern which is (or would be) present whenever that feature of experience is (or were) present in experience, which is (and would be) absent whenever it is absent. Of course, these "patterns" might be relatively abstractly characterized, or they might be disjunctive patterns, and certain patterns might be subpatterns of others. Note that these correlations might be fixed, by the truth of relevant counterfactuals, in the moment, even if we'd have to investigate over a period of time to figure out what they were.

So far we have picked out the relevant patterns of firing, by considering correlations between those patterns and introspectible features of phenomenal experience. But now we should ask how those patterns can help to constitute the phenomenal experience they do. And this involves another sort of correlation according to the objectual model we are pursuing, a correlation, again perhaps fixed in the moment, between the firing patterns and real phenomenal features of the world. This is the relation that obtains in the world between the firing pattern which helps constitute a certain sort of phenomenal experience and the particular objectual resource which also helps do so. That is the second part of our suggestion:

2) Such a pattern of firing helps (or would help) constitute the kind of experience it does because it is (or would be) correlated in this way with a phenomenal feature in the world which the content of that experience matches.

Let me focus now on some of the difficulties which face this second part of our sketch. Certainly, the counterfactual nature of some of the relevant correlations might present difficulties, but let me focus for the moment on other problems. Clearly, not all of the actual phenomenal features of the world are experienced by Galileo. We need to specify phenomenal objects and a kind of correlation which yield just the right content for his experience. We need to somehow distinguish those phenomenal features of the world which help constitute his experience from those that do not. And we need also to explain the existence of the full range of artifacts of phenomenal experience.

There are various kinds of such artifacts. There are artifacts of omission, when we miss the far side of a table or cat. There are artifacts of commission, as our attention yields a phenomenal valence of attention. And there are artifacts of distortion, as sizes and shapes and colors seem to change as things move away from us. The last two sins of experience seem especially difficult for objectual accounts to explain, but even artifacts of omission present real problems. Consider them first.

Somehow from all the phenomenal features of the world just exactly those we experience at some moment must be picked out as those which correlate in the appropriate manner with our neural firing at that moment. Call these features "present qualia". Once we have picked out the present qualia, then it seems we can adopt something like the following specification of what constitutes phenomenal experience of a particular sort, at least when the relevant context of the relevant firing pattern is fixed. A certain firing pattern which helps constitute a particular kind of phenomenal experience underlies the phenomenal experience of the most inclusive phenomenal feature of the world which meets the following condition: It is (and would be) a present quale for the person in question when and only when that pattern is (or were) also present. In other words, particular firing patterns help constitute the experience of the particular features within present qualia with which they co-vary.

This is still too sketchy in a number of ways. One might wonder again about the modal form of the correlation, which is presumably of some sort which is not a mere artifact of the approach apparatus. And one might wonder if the relevant correlations hold across all people or only some period of a single person's life. But we have other and more important difficulties to face. The central question this formulation leaves unresolved is this: What picks out the present qualia from the other phenomenal features of the world with which it might be that our patterns of neural firing co-vary? Why, for instance, don't we experience the backsides of objects as well as their fronts, if all that matters is co-variation? And there is of course another important question which remains for us as well: How do we handle the artifacts of experience which are not merely artifacts of omission? Let me discuss these two crucial questions at once, and in a somewhat more concrete manner.

It might seem that Galileo's visual experience of a red apple on the window ledge is in part constituted by just such a red apple, an entity which, insofar as it is a raw concrete entity captured in visual experience, consists of a bunch of color microevents standing in spatio-temporal relations to other microevents. Those color microevents possess intrinsic phenomenal hue-shades. But Galileo only experiences the color of the facing surface of apple, even if we ignore niceties like highlights and shadows. And of course as the sun goes down, the apple will look darker than it does at noon, and there are misleading valences of attention which pollute Galileo's visual experience of the apple. So the most obvious objectual accounts of visual experience must deploy a factoring strategy. Some of the features of that experience are, so it seems, plausibly veridical, and may be constituted by phenomenal features of objects out in the world. Those features must be among the relevant present qualia. But other features of that experience are not veridical, are mere artifacts, and not of omission. For different people, different qualia are present. We need some account of this. And a plausible objectual account must also include an account of how artifacts of commission and distortion occur because of the peculiar circumstances of the person who has an experience.

For instance, we might postulate a three-dimensional and third-person color world, consisting of color microevents arranged in such a spatio-temporal structure as objective measuring instruments might seem to reveal to us. And we might claim that the color experience of, say, a cyclops, was in part constituted by the color-microevents without null-colors most immediately facing its eye along each of the relevant geometrical rays emanating from the point at the center of its eye and through its pupil. Only they count as present color qualia. We could claim that the relative size of things in the cyclops' visual experience was controlled, even constituted, by the relative size of the angles subtended by the rays which glance the boundaries of those things, and that valences of attention in that experience were determined by states of attending in the cyclops.

This isn't a terribly plausible model. It implies, for instance, that the color-microevents which help constitute visual experience for the cyclops shift closer in and farther out as the closest color-microevent without a null-color along the relevant ray happens to be closer in or farther out. And it ignores the fact that in the dark the cyclops would have no experience of the color of anything. Also, it is hard to motivate such an account. Why should just those features of the world I've cited be part of a whole which constitutes an experience? Why do the back sides of things get left out, given that things at an equal distance might help constitute color experience if there were nothing else in the way? Perhaps a more rigorous understanding of co-variation could help with some of this, could help underwrite what makes present qualia present. Or perhaps it would help to put the account this way: The first opaque surface facing the cyclops' line of sight through a transparent medium helps to constitute the cyclops' visual experience, and the manner in which it helps is a function of the amount of illumination present. We might also claim that mirrors and lakes have some sort of specific image on their surfaces which our cyclops would see, ignoring for the moment the fact that such things may reflect quite different images to different perceivers.

Such an account of our experience has a kind of immediate appeal. But in fact historical objectual accounts of color developed quite quickly in other directions. It's worth looking at those historical accounts for hints regarding how objectual models which are somewhat more plausible than that we have just sketched might work. One caveat: Since only quite recently have we realized the importance of neural resources and sensory receptor cells, historical accounts could overlook a problem which we now face. It may be that the objectual resources which historical accounts deploy do not fit quite as handily with neural resources as with traditional accounts of the constitution of sense organs. But, nevertheless, we are stuck with neurons and sensory receptor cells. It may also be worth reminding ourselves that neither do the objectual phenomenal resources of the old models mesh very well with the sorts of causal structures affecting sensory receptor cells which we know the world to contain. As I've suggested, and as we will see at length in the next part, objectual accounts of phenomenal experience suffer two debilitating difficulties. There are no phenomenal objects of the sort they deploy. But even if there were, it would be miraculous if they were coordinated in just the right way with our behavior, or our neural firing, or for that matter the causal properties of the objects we experience to have colors. My intention is to ignore these problems in this part, but, even so, we will soon be unable to avoid evidence that the objectual models we are now pursuing present at best a tense and unstable compromise between modern post-galilean neurophysiology and traditional realism about phenomenal properties. Still, I think we shouldn't laugh too quickly at their antiquated elements. The current dominant objectual accounts of color attempt to identify color with properties more acceptable to Galileo himself, with causal powers of a galilean sort. But we know from Part One that causal properties should not be identified with phenomenal properties. They *cannot* constitute them. Hence in fact any physicalist objectual account of *phenomenal* color,[7] involving for instance the causal correlation of post-galilean properties like surface spectral reflectance and the firing of sensory receptor cells, is not coherently conceivable. The old models of color perception at least did better than that. So let me continue to try to mash together those old models and current neurophysiology.

According to *Aristotle's* account of vision, a red ball has a visual form, say the color red in a circle-shaped look, which can also be taken up by someone's visual sense.[8] When that form is not taken up, then it is not experienced. And that form will only be taken up by someone's visual sense under particular conditions. There must be a medium of air between the object sensed and the sense, and that transparent medium must be in the state of activity which is light. Darkness does not transmit the form. So that explains one artifact of our visual experience. We don't see the true colors of objects in the dark.

This is an objectual account of our experience of phenomenal color. Aristotle says that if something is seen as red then *something* is red, though we may be mistaken about what it is. In taking up the form of that thing, our sense gives us the experience. But while he says some useful things, Aristotle does not say enough about artifacts of experience. For instance, he ignores spatial distortion, the fact that more distant objects look smaller. And he is more than a little vague about the actual concrete realization of his rather vague scheme. To approach a more adequate objectual account, it is worth considering the history of post-aristotelian but pre-galilean accounts of visual perception.[9]

Aristotelian theories developed in a number of directions. Most aristotelians held that there was no action at a distance,[10] that color must in some way be transmitted from object to eye by the intervening medium of air. This presents difficulties. If the air itself were to take on the color which is transmitted, then the air between an orange and a perceiver would be orange. But of course another perceiver can look through the same air, say in a direction perpendicular to the first, and see a green object. Surely the air cannot be both green and orange at the relevant points, nor in fact does it look either orange or green to certain perceivers. How, then, is color transmitted by the air? It was often suggested that the air didn't carry actual colors, but rather "species" of colors. But what are species? It might be tempting to interpret them in some post-galilean way, as, for instance, information about phenomenal colors encoded in radiation, which might be decoded by the eye upon receipt. But traditional aristotelians held that the various visual species possessed a much more deeply natural relation to the relevant colors than that, so that no very complicated story about how the perceiver took particular species to encode or represent particular colors was required. Late scholastic authors said that the sensible species were identical in essence to sense qualities. Unfortunately for us, such an identity of essence is not coherently conceivable. *Coherently conceivable* aristotelian accounts, which demand a kind of transmission of color by contact, seem stuck with actual colored media. Perhaps these media are unusual in that they can only be *seen* head on, though they "have the same color" in all directions, and also in that they can pass unimpeded through one another and with effects only in their direction of transmission. This requires that it be possible for there to be the fusion of more than one color microevent at a given location, but perhaps that isn't too much of a stretch beyond coherent conceivability to be reasonable, or perhaps my account of content gets that detail wrong. Or perhaps we ought to deploy action at a distance.

How about perspectival distortion? Many ancient and medieval accounts of visual perception involved "extramission", the emission by the eyes of some sort of physical power towards the object of sight, in something like the manner suggested by Plato's *Timeaus*. Aristotelian accounts rooted solely in the "intromission" of color from objects to eyes sound much more plausible to modern ears. But the extramission theories seemed to the tradition to allow a more reasonable account of perspectival distortion. Euclid provided an early account of perspective, and his speech of geometric rays emanating from the eyes, as they do from the eye of our cyclops, rightly or wrongly suggested to many historical figures that concrete rays of sight emanated outward from subject to object, that extramission theories were correct. Aristotelian accounts seemed to lack a plausible alternative explanation of perspectival distortion. It seemed hard to believe that the visual surface of a red ball managed to emit a form which somehow shrank to just the right diameter and became appropriately flattened, and also somehow made it to the eye of each perceiver of the ball, as an aristotelian account apparently required. *Viable* intromission accounts require a treatment of colored objects as collections of point sources of species, with each point on the colored surface of an orange radiating visual species out in all directions, along for instance euclidean geometrical rays towards a particular perceiver's eye. This treatment was eventually incorporated into the aristotelian tradition by Alhazen, but it created problems of its own. Each point within the pupil of the eye, for instance, receives species from all points on the visible surface of a ball. How then is a coherent visual perception of the ball possible? Some authors suggested that only sensible species received at a perpendicular were sensed, which may fit with the way we just tried to treat sensible species. But it was not until Kepler proposed refraction onto the retina that an aristotelian explanation which people found generally satisfying was available.

Somehow sensible species were supposed to be emitted from objects and refracted onto the retina. There, it seemed, there forms a properly colored image which somehow helps constitute our visual experience. Even if we ignore the details of the retina which make this particular story finally implausible, and to which we will return in Part Three, there are other worries to consider. Retinal "images" are reversed right to left and up and down, and of course there are two distinct retinal images. Historically, this seemed troubling. But perhaps we are to suppose that principles of constitution for our experience could be worked out which patch over these inconvenient details in a reasonably plausible way.

One might wonder, after these convolutions, why these accounts are to be preferred to the more straightforwardly objectual account of the cyclops. But sensible species do seem to promise more plausible accounts of mirrors and reflection on lakes, and also of the fact that objects look differently in the dark. These aristotelian accounts are, like our cyclops theory, objectual accounts. They hold that objects have color, as do images in the retina. So do the species which transmit them, at least if species are to be coherently conceivable, and in any case species were traditionally held to be dependent in existence on their associated qualities. Aristotelian accounts offer, I think, about as much as we can hope for if we are to avoid the intuitive difficulties presented by our cyclops and still have an objectual account.

There is another objectual route we might attempt, which also has historical roots. We might claim that the world at large contains no color, but rather that our momentary experience gets certain special objects exhaustively right. These are sense data, little sensory images in the theater of the mind, perhaps colorful objects under the hat of the person who has the phenomenal experience they help constitute. Such sense data might incorporate all the artifacts of omission and commission and distortion. They would be intensionally transparent objects, captured fully in our experience, as present qualia must be. They are a bit like the entities which traditional aristotelian accounts deploy at the retina itself, but they are caused not by the transmission of sensible species rooted in objective colors of oranges and apples, but by all the galilean machinations which lead to or are caused by the firing of our sensory receptor cells. In fact they might even be caused by the firing of those sensory receptor cells. If one's sense data were under one's hat, if they were like one's muscles within one's skin, or if alternatively they were, like one's own movements, the immediate causal product of one's neurophysiological machinations, then this might provide an intuitive and unified way to distinguish between the objects which help constitute one's experience and those which do not. But unfortunately this model cleaves away from the commonsense notion of the world we are presuming in this section, in which colors are splashed on the concrete objects we experience, for instance balls and tables, and in which there are no ghostly and unfamiliar objects like sense data, or at least no ghostly and unfamiliar objects except sensible species and their concomitants.

I have gestured at a coherently conceivable model of our phenomenal experience, indeed at several distinct coherently conceivable models, which meet the constraints with which we began. Experiences are primary thoughts. The conditions which constitute them include appropriate patterns of neural firing. They also include correlated phenomenal objects, objects with the phenomenal properties we experience. Further, on what seem to be the least implausible and most commonsensical candidates, artifacts of phenomenal experience are explained in one of the traditional pre-galilean ways. Of course, one should wonder about such stories, about how plausible it is that the world contains phenomenal elements of the sorts we have deployed, and how plausible it is that there would be the kind of correlation between those objects and our neural firing and hence behavior which I have presumed. But still these are, at least for the most part, coherently conceivable accounts, and consistent with the two constraints with which we began. And that, for now, is enough.

An objectual story of phenomenal experience must also counter the standard objections to the dominant correlational accounts of perceptual thought, which we reviewed in Chapter Eight. But the stories we have sketched would counter such objections, as a side benefit. In some cases which trouble the currently dominant causal correlational accounts, for instance cases of perceptual error, there are correlated firing patterns without the intuitively appropriate objects of perception. And this presents a puzzle for the dominant accounts. If the relevant correlation is causal correlation, then it is hard to explain why the actual causes of a firing pattern do not count as its content, even in the cases where they intuitively cause a perceptual illusion or other error. And not everything in the chain of causes leading to the firing of some perceptual system counts as its intuitive content, even in cases where there intuitively isn't perceptual error. But the correlational accounts we have sketched here are not causal accounts of this standard form, and hence avoid these difficulties quite easily. All the conditions we have built in to pick out the present qualia from other things in effect solve this problem as well. We can plausibly maintain, with Aristotle and the sense data theorists, that there is no error about present qualia, qualia which inform one's sense or characterize one's sense data. And only present qualia are reflected in the content of someone's experience of a moment.

There is another way to think about how people have thoughts with content which is currently quite popular and which may seem distinct in detail or emphasis from the dominant form of correlational account. It may provide another helpful foil here, and suggest yet another set of objections. In the last chapter's discussion of virtual thoughts, I mentioned those who think that we have thoughts just because we are properly attributed thoughts. Some of these friends of interpretation, perhaps most notably Davidson, have claimed that there is a principle of charity which binds the appropriate "interpretation" of people. People have the thoughts which they are properly interpreted to have, and there are various constraints on their proper interpretation, including the principle of charity. This requires that people be interpreted in such a way that their beliefs come out largely true. It is hence a kind of constitutive constraint on one's having beliefs that they be largely true.

In effect, we are discussing a special variant of that view here. Focus not on beliefs in general but on perceptual thoughts, say sensory experiences and perceptual beliefs. Then one might consider it a constitutive constraint on agency that any agent must have true perceptual thoughts regarding his or her present qualia, must think that they are as they are in fact. This variant on the familiar notion of a principle of charity is made unusually plausible by the traditional recognition that our perceptual thoughts about our present qualia might be a lot less fallible than those about most features of the world. If you are presented with a red round thing, then the principle of charity to present qualia might demand that you think there is something round and red if you are to be attributed thoughts at all, if you are to be a haver of thoughts. Of the variety of possible attributions of thoughts that could be made to a creature with your neural structure, the correct attribution would be among those in which you think that your present qualia are as they are. What were once held to be epistemically basic beliefs or thoughts might be, rather, attributionally or semantically basic. In effect, an "interpretive" model of this kind is just a correlational model as it appears from a different angle, shorn of some modal difficulties. So responses to obvious questions about how such an interpretive model would work may help clarify the kind of account we are pursuing.

First, present phenomenal qualia are entities whose intrinsic properties are phenomenal and not causal. They may play a role in quasi-causal regularities, but don't possess true causal powers of the sort introduced in Chapter Seven. It isn't present phenomenal qualia's nature qua phenomenal qualia to be producers of effects at all. But puzzles then arise: How can present qualia be epistemically accessed and explain behavior, if they have no effects, if they are by their very nature epiphenomenal? The response I suggest is this: Present qualia explain behavior not by causing it, but by as it were constitutively restricting agents to have the thoughts they do, given the principle of charity. On this view, it is one of the things that constitutes a structure of neurons to be a realization of thoughts that it meets the constraint of constituting true perceptual thoughts about the present qualia. The neural structures which help constitute the thoughts cause the behavior. Present qualia are epistemically accessed only in the sense that, given the charity principle, for a neural structure to count as something which realizes thoughts, it must realize true thoughts about the relevant present qualia.

Second, there is the question of what exact form the constitutive charity principle should take. It cannot require that an agent think everything true of his or her present qualia. You cannot be expected to believe that you are experiencing a quale phenomenally identical to one experienced by Galileo's aunt in 1525. You don't perceive *that*. We might restrict consideration to intrinsic facts regarding present qualia, facts fixed by the way the qualia currently are and nothing else. While you might believe that your experience is misleading in certain ways, still that reflective belief would not be your relevant perceptual thought, say your experience. Still there is another problem. There is a puzzle about whether true perceptual thoughts regarding all "intrinsic" features of present qualia can reasonably be ascribed to you. You might well have a present quale of a hen with 137 speckles, and not have any thought regarding the number, or, worse, an incorrect one. So it is not entirely unreasonable to claim that you do not experience the hen as having 137, even though it has 137 in your present qualia. You couldn't introspect that feature of your experience. Still, Moreland Perkins provided us with one hint about how to handle the speckled hen:[11] Present qualia have whatever determinate properties it is necessary that they have to underwrite the discriminations that the percipient can "infallibly" make regarding them. So if there are 137 determinate specks in your present quale, then you can make privileged discriminations rooted in introspectible features of your experience, say discriminations among specks, which would together entail that there are 137 present in your experience, even if you cannot introspect directly that there are 137. You can introspect features of your experience which entail that there are 137 speckles in your experience, even though you can't introspect that directly.

The objectual accounts we have pursued here imply that experience is not *radically* erroneous. Our ordinary experience does commit certain sins of omission and commission and distortion, which any remotely plausible objectual account must explain. But in the basic instance, according to the accounts we have pursued, we experience what we do because it is there. So there is one specific sort of intuitive error which, it may seem, cannot be very easily shrugged off by these accounts. This class of errors includes perceptual illusions, dreams, and hallucinations. In these cases, we sometimes see colors which aren't there to be seen. There are no appropriate qualia to be present. What can we say about such cases? Colorful sense data, though not public aristotelian colors, might be present in these cases as well as in ordinary sensation. They might be present even when we are asleep or have our eyes closed. That may seem to give sense data accounts a leg up, but of course sensible species might be stored up inside us as well as transmitted through the air. In any case, I think that the friend of objectual accounts should adopt another strategy. They should treat these cases however they treat the primary imagination.

2

Our experience of a moment is a thought,[12] with seed content which matches and exhausts that experience. But we also have primary thoughts with seed contents which don't capture what we *do* in fact experience,[13] but rather merely what we *might* experience in a moment. We need some account of our capacity for this "primary imagination".

It is important to distinguish three things: 1) Our capacity for a range of experience at a moment, a range of experience with a range of contents. 2) Our capacity to understand that we can have experiences with that range of contents. 3) Our capacity at a moment for a range of thoughts which are not experiences but which have the very range of contents which our experience *might* have had at that moment. The third thing is our focus here. But, at least to a first approximation, in normal adult humans these three things line up fairly neatly. Certainly there might be creatures capable of a sort of experience whose content they could not, in the absence of that experience, conceive. Certainly creatures can experience things without being capable of explicitly thinking that they can have such experience. But we seem not to be like that, at least to a first approximation. In the absence of a particular experience, we are still capable of a thought with a content which would match that experience, and we realize that we have such a capacity and what its range is.

The primary imagination underlies our capacity for thoughts with the wide range of basic contents beyond those we might exhaustively experience in a moment, and it is also crucially implicated in our capacity for word-mediated thought. The next chapter deploys the primary imagination in crucial ways. Here we will consider it on its own.

If we ignore worries about plausibility, there are a number of axes along which we might organize possible models of our capacity for primary imagination. First of all, primary imagination might involve a special sort of experience, perhaps fainter than actual experience, which except in regards to vividness is captured by seed contents of the sorts we have already characterized. Or it might not involve experience; we might not have any *experience* of what we merely *imagine*. And of course, whether there is some special sort of experience involved in the primary imagination or not, that primary imagination might involve two different sorts of realization conditions, objectual or non-objectual.

For instance, the primary imagination of an apple smashing into the ground might crucially involve a red *object*, perhaps a merely possible red object external to the thinker, located in a strange and ghostly realm of possibilia, or perhaps a red apple-image somehow under the thinker's hat. On the other hand, such an instance of primary imagination might merely be a state of the thinker which crucially involves no red object, no apple or red image, but rather merely grey or colorless neurons firing some way.

I believe that the primary imagination does involve a kind of faint experience, which is most plausibly realized in something like the non-objectual manner we will pursue in the next part. But since we are saddled now with a coherently conceivable *objectual* account of experience, and because imaginary objects or sense data may seem particularly offensive resources to deploy in an objectual account, or at least too far from sufficiently mundane to be a part of the world we presume here, I will pretend for the moment that faint experience is not involved in the primary imagination.[14] But so as not to rule out the possibility which I really favor, I will fudge with the waffling phrase "quasi-experience". Primary imagination involves quasi-experience, which is something a lot like ordinary experience. We can introspect what we quasi-experience in at least roughly the same way as we can introspect what we experience. And this suggests that the primary imagination may be realized in a way which is not *entirely* dissimilar from the way in which our experience is realized, even if we should mix an objectual account of experience with a non-objectual account of the primary imagination. Let me elaborate.

Galileo is capable of primary imagination of how the Tower of Pisa appears from all angles and distances, but at any given moment in which he imagines that tower to himself he does so from a particular angle and distance. Such a thought seems very likely to be a primary thought, positioned, in the manner characteristic of firing patterns, to immediately influence his action and behavior, for instance a drawing he might make. In hallucinations, dreams, memory images,[15] some imaginings, the "experience" of phantom limbs,[16] and speech to ourselves, we have at least sometimes a quasi-experience, in the mind's eye or ear or throat or arm, of certain sorts of things we might also experience. And, at least for all we know now, it is not implausible to assume that this involves particular patterns of firing, in the manner of primary thoughts. This will allow what we say here to mesh with both objectual and non-objectual accounts of our experience, and hence provide our usual hinge between Parts Two and Three.

But how can particular patterns of firing help constitute the requisite primary thoughts? What the realization of the primary imagination requires is a way that there might be a primary thought with a content matching some experience[17] even in the absence of that experience. Languages provide one handy analogy for how this might be achieved. Imagine a language whose meaning is fixed *a la* Quine by dispositions to utter particular words in the presence of concrete experiences of particular kinds and to respond to those words in particular ways. If one could also utter such a word in the absence of such experiences in some special way, say *sotto voce*, it might still retain the meaning it possesses by virtue of the quinean dispositions. While our own primary imagination is not most characteristically mediated by words, something analogous to this quinean language in fact probably does the trick.

Whether or not neural firing alone can constitute experience, we have assumed that there is a particular pattern of firing which is, at least in a particular context, necessary for a certain sort of experience. To each seed content someone might experience at a moment there corresponds a particular pattern of firing which would only occur, in that context, if they had that experience. But there are then a number of ways in which there might be a closely *related* pattern of firing which would, in the relevant context, constitute primary imagination with the same seed content. This pattern would be to the original pattern as *sotto voce* speech is to public speech in our quinean analogy.[18] There might be a question about whether it is proper to call such an account of the primary imagination objectual or non-objectual. The pattern of firing which constitutes primary imagination with a given content is related to that which would constitute the allied experience, and by the account we developed in Section 1 that would only constitute such an experience in the presence of the requisite present qualia. But we also presumed that the firing which constitutes the experience *would* be present only if those qualia *were*. So while there is an object deployed indirectly by this account, it is still appropriately non-objectual, since possibly hypothetical. It doesn't involve the present existence of an object corresponding to the primary imagination, nor even an actual one at any time. It merely requires that if the allied pattern of firing *were* present, so *would* the object.

Let me be more concrete. If, as Chapter Eleven suggested, population phenomena are crucial in our neural lives, and if in particular the outcome of a numerical competition between firing subpatterns found in a particular class of neurons helps to constitute that someone has one experience rather than another, then a statistical model of the primary imagination seems not implausible. A relatively few instances of the firing subpattern which would in large numbers help constitute an experience might help to constitute the corresponding primary imagination. Alternatively, it might be that a slower form of the firing pattern characteristic of a certain sort of experience helps to constitute the corresponding primary imagination. Less likely, it might be that a certain sort of primary imagination involves the same pattern of firing as the corresponding experience, but with its ordinary effects somehow dampened.[19] Or it might be that there is some particular higher-order, upstream firing present whenever the firing which constitutes experience of some sort is present, but which yet can also be present independent of the firing which constitutes that experience.[20]

Primary imagination of a thing must retain something like the causal role of the corresponding experience, but there must be some differences as well, at least if we are not to confuse mere imaginings with actual experience. Population stories might achieve the relevant modification immediately and directly, by the differences in the numbers of competing firings which constitute experience and quasi-experience. A lot of those patterns would lead to an effect characteristic of experience, a few would just lead to the dampened effects characteristic of the associated quasi-experience. Stories which appeal to slower forms of some characteristic pattern might immediately achieve this result in another way. The upstream accounts would require that some of the effects of actual experience be mediated by other than the particular upstream firing they deploy.

Corresponding to the hypothesis about primary thoughts which I adopted in the last chapter, which was merely not implausible for all we know now, let me pretend that primary imagination is constituted as the population stories suggest, that it is a kind of statistical phenomena. In that case, the areas of the brain active in experience of a certain kind are also the location of the corresponding quasi-experience, the venue of the primary imagination. No separate neural systems are required.

We still haven't quite completed our sketch. Any plausible model of the primary imagination must involve a feature I haven't yet noted. The pattern of firing which constitutes a particular primary imagination can, it seems, be called forth more or less at will, under the promptings of the firing which helps constitute a wondering memory or wandering fantasy. It might be that the prompting firing does not itself constitute a primary thought, but merely the activation of some sort of neurally-rooted disposition. In fact, there is some neurophysiological work which bears on how this might occur.[21] But, in some cases, quasi-experience of the phenomenal seems to be "under our control" via motor quasi-intentions, via what stands to motor intentions as phenomenal quasi-experience stands to phenomenal experience, or perhaps via something similar to motor quasi-intentions but with a more abstract content. Motor intentions are on the outgoing side of our psychologies, so it should not be a surprise if we can form similar quasi-intentions "at will". For instance, when we speak to ourselves, we may first quasi-intend a movement in our throat, and then perhaps a quasi-experience of the associated phenomenal sound may occur in our mind's ear. And it may be that at least some memory images are under our control in this word-mediated way, or perhaps in a similar way but without the mediation of a *phenomenal* quasi-experience of the requisite word. We say something to ourselves, and quasi-experience of the thing we are talking about occurs. Sometimes, of course, quasi-experience does not occur "at will", but by a more direct associative train of quasi-experience familiar from the writings of the empiricists and our previous discussions of word meaning, and sometimes it may occur "at will" but not at the behest of a thought of which we are aware. But when it does occur "at will" introspectible motor quasi-intentions are at least sometimes involved.

There are, of course, many differences between various instances of the primary imagination. As I've said, some images are fantasies, and others are memories. The differences between memory and fantasy partly involve various recognitional capacities of the sort we discussed in Chapter Eleven. But some of the differences seem also to lie in the way these kinds of images come forth in the first place, in what underlies our disposition or capacity to form them or activates that disposition or capacity.

But let me leave these particular complexities aside. We have a coherently conceivable and not obviously false model of the way in which the primary imagination might be realized. Patterns which in abundance would be correlated with experience are in scarcity constitutive of the associated primary imagination. Or, I should more precisely say, we have a model which is not obviously false as a first approximation. In actual fact, our capacity for experience, our sense of that capacity, and our capacity for thought of a content matching a possible experience in the absence of that experience, *do* come apart in certain ways. In the absence of certain colors or odors we may retain at best a dim capacity to conceive them via the primary imagination, even though we could experience them. The primary imagination in fact provides us with somewhat abstracted thoughts, which might be filled out in a variety of ways to match a variety of experiences. There are probably many individual differences in our capacities for primary imagination of various kinds, rooted at least in training. Think of painters and wine connoisseurs and the differences in their visual and odoriferous imaginations. So, at best, I have been engaged in some idealization across individual capacities of a moment, though perhaps not across what all normal adult humans would be capable of after the right training in discrimination, a training which would appropriately modify their synaptic connections. Perhaps we have some capacity curled into our psychological dispositions to do this training on our own, without props, but probably we would need to be confronted with real wines.

In any case, words and abstract thoughts clearly do a good deal of work in stabilizing and refining and extending our sense of what we might experience beyond anything the primary imagination provides. We can learn vocabularies for wine-tasting or languages of conceivability that fulfill just such a task, and even ordinary speech provides many helpful resources. So the neurophysiological capacities which underlie our capacity for word-mediated and abstracted thought clearly play a crucial role in extending and stabilizing the capacities rooted in the primary imagination. On the other hand, language alone, for instance, cannot plausibly provide resources to assist the primary imagination unless it itself can possess relevant content, and we have seen that the interanimation of thoughts, including thoughts of the primary imagination, plays a crucial role in the realization of our linguistically-mediated thought.

I have ignored other important individual differences, which in light of my last claim may seem especially relevant. Many people, especially many philosophers, report that they have no visual primary imagination at all, although those I know do report speaking to themselves in their minds' ears. So it may be that the way in which the primary imagination helps realize certain kinds of thoughts, say word-mediated thoughts, is different in different people. It may be that different forms of primary imagination, visual and aural for instance, are underdeveloped or absent in some normal humans, and this may affect how they think what they do. For instance, my discussion in Chapter Ten suggested that inner speech of the word "red" may call forth inner experience of that color, but it may be that in some people it merely calls forth other words. Or it may be that their understanding of the word consists solely in a capacity to respond with the right color word when they do have experience of the color. So it may be that some details of the account I develop in this part are only relevant to how there might be thought in some normal humans, not in all.

There is another complication worth noting. I have spoken of a single faculty of primary imagination, as if for instance what happens in dreams and some memory and the introspection of language-meaning and fantasy are at least roughly the same thing. But one might wonder if these aren't quite distinct faculties. For instance, some philosophers report to me that they dream in visual images but are not able to introspect visual memory images at all.

Still, even though these various matters may require complication of our rather simple model, and even though there are complex imaginative phenomena beyond the primary imagination, none of this suggests that we abandon this account of the primary imagination. Our model provides at least a rough sketch of one coherently conceivable and at least not implausible[22] resource through which our neurophysiology might realize at least the central component of a no doubt very complicated capacity we humans possess, to think thoughts with contents matching experiences which we might have but don't have. That for now is enough.[23]

NOTES

1. Eye-hand coordination which constitutes merely know how, direct feedback, and reflex arcs are also no doubt involved in the execution of motor action.

2. We were lucky that a plausible and coherent theory was there to be adopted, but of course in the end it isn't all that plausible, and up to some point we had good luck with phenomenal colors as well.

3. Shortly we will deploy not correlation over actual time, but a correlation fixed by counterfactual conditions in the moment. But let me ignore this complexity for now.

4. This might lead to special problems. There may be reasonable grounds to maintain that one's entire momentary experience is never exactly duplicated over one's life. This would make correlation especially difficult to chart. Note also that the content of visual experience may well not exactly match anything out in the world in all respects, because of perspectival distortion.

5. Certain features might be subfeatures of others, and hence certain of the corresponding patterns of firing might be subpatterns of others.

6. It may be worth noting that there may be an obvious explanation of the facts i) that we cannot have an experience which consists, say, just of a line without any intrinsic properties, that certain features of experience cannot exhaust the experience of a moment, and ii) that certain features are mutually exclusive in experience. For it may be that the brain must be in some global pattern of firing, but of

course only one, across the whole range of subsystems involved in the constitution of phenomenal experience. Though note that this pattern of firing cannot exclude the presence of the patterns constitutive of the primary imagination.

7. I don't yet mean to dismiss physicalist accounts of the *experience* of phenomenal color.

8. Aristotle, *De Anima*, Bk. II, ch. 5-7.

9. See David C. Lindberg, *Theories of vision from al-Kindi to Kepler* (Chicago: University of Chicago Press, 1976). I am also indebted to discussion with Alison Simmons.

10. William of Ockham was apparently first to suggest action at a distance in color perception.

11. Moreland Perkins, *Sensing the World* (Indianapolis: Hackett, 1983), 295-305.

12. Or set of thoughts.

13. If quasi-experience is to be imbedded in experience, I should put this differently.

14. If faint experience is involved, then we should adjust the account of Part One to admit different degrees of vividness, though that introduces features which are plausibly mere artifacts of our experience. Note also that the content of a quasi-experience which is the imaginary correlate of an actual experience would then fail to match the content of that experience in regards to vividness.

15. At least some memory is probably a capacity for categorization rather than the possession of such memory images, as I suggested in the last chapter. But there are, I think, sometimes such memory images, at least for many of us.

16. Present even in some lacking limbs from birth.

17. Or perhaps matching that experience except in regards to vividness.

18. We still have the problem of accounting for the primary imagination of a certain feature by someone who is incapable of experiencing it, if this is possible, but as always let me focus on the case of normal adult humans.

19. This would require some refinement of the kind of correlation deployed in the last section.

20. For some neurophysiological work which underwrites models roughly like those suggested in this paragraph, and provides some suggestions about the specific brain locations involved, see S.M. Kosslyn, N.M. Alpert, W.L. Thompson, V. Maljkovic, S.B. Weise, C.F. Chabris, S.E. Hamilton, S.L. Rauch, and F.S. Buananno, "Visual mental imagery activates topographically organized visual cortex: PET investigations", *Journal of Cognitive Neuroscience* 5, 1993, 263-287; and H. Damasio, T.J. Grabowski, A. Damasio, D. Tranel, L. Boles-Ponto, G.L. Watkins, and R.D. Hichwa, "Visual recall with eyes closed and covered activates early visual cortices", *Society for Neuroscience Abstracts* 19, 1993, 1603. See Antonio R. Damasio, *Descartes' Error* (New York: Putnam, 1994), 96-108, for a popular sketch by a distinguished neurologist which is in accord with my suggestions.

21. See Damasio, *Descartes' Error*, 102, and the references he notes.

22. In fact, I did deploy somewhat suspicious modal correlations, but non-objectual accounts of a quasi-experience which was included in experience might look roughly like this, and would avoid that resource. The real problem, again, is that we cannot generate coherently conceivable non-objectual accounts of the realization of experience, and that objectual accounts are implausible.

23. One might wonder if the primary imagination is really a distinct faculty from the faculty of experience. Indeed, it might be that we should collapse all the contents of primary imagination into experience of a faint sort, and then treat it in the same way as experience. We might try correlation with correspondingly ghostly objects. Sense data might be useful here. And certainly in the next part we will see that non-objectual accounts of both experience and quasi-experience are probably the most plausible accounts. But surely the most commonsensical *objectual* models involve real colored objects for experience and something else for quasi-experience, neural firing without an object. And even the more plausible non-objectual accounts of the sort we will pursue in Part Three have reason to treat the "quasi-experience" of the primary imagination as a distinct and significant phenomena in its own right, even if in the end it isn't radically distinct from experience.

CHAPTER THIRTEEN

THOUGHT BEYOND EXPERIENCE

Our remaining task in this part is to construct a coherently conceivable account of the realization of thoughts which are not experiences or quasi-experiences. But, for economy, we will attempt an account which is plausible as well, or at least not implausible for all we know so far. We will proceed by pulling several threads together. From Chapter Three, we have a sense of the content generation operations. From Chapter Nine, we know how infinity and normativity provide little obstacle to the concrete realization of our thought. From Chapter Ten, we have a somewhat detailed understanding of how thoughts are mediated by words, and how word-mediated thoughts are rooted in the interanimation of thoughts which are not mediated by words. From Chapter Eleven, we have a sense of how neural resources plausibly underwrite the interanimation of our thoughts. It is because experiences are *primary* thoughts,[1] which involve in particular contexts particular patterns of neural firing, that it is possible to develop an account, not only of quasi-experience but of our other thoughts beyond experience, which can mesh with both objectual and non-objectual accounts of experience. From Chapter Twelve, we have a sense of how quasi-experience might be realized, and a coherently conceivable if finally implausible objectual account of the realization of experience. Finally, we know from Chapter Eleven that there are only two sorts of cases which we need to treat explicitly here. Those sorts are primary thoughts, and thoughts of the mixed sort. Virtual thoughts will take up the slack. In fact, we know that even thoughts of the mixed sort are fixed by primary thoughts and their virtual components, or more exactly by primary thoughts and the kinds of resources which lead us to ascribe virtual thoughts. Still, some important instances of the mixed sort deserve special treatment here. And it will be revealing to give each of the content generation operations some explicit attention in what follows, even if thoughts with any human content might be mediated by words in roughly the manner of the essentially word-mediated contents noted in Chapter Three. Even if thoughts with contents generated by certain operations are not always realized in the particular ways we will discuss, it is useful to explicitly discuss at least one special mechanism for each.

Our question, then, becomes this: Given that various patterns of neural firing in the right contexts help to constitute various sorts of experience and quasi-experience, how are capacities for various other thoughts, thoughts beyond experience and quasi-experience, plausibly realized by a neurophysiology of the sort sketched in Chapter Eleven? In particular, we will consider three cases. First, we will consider certain *primary* thoughts which yet are not quasi-experiences or experiences. They have contents generated by the quasi-logical operations, abstraction, or their vague analogues. The second and third cases we will consider are important examples of the *mixed* sort of thought. On one hand, there are word-mediated thoughts, and also certain similar thoughts which are mediated by metaphors or involve certain artifacts of the approach apparatus. On the other hand, there are thoughts with basic contents which outrun the possible experience of a moment. Each of these three cases occupies one of the following three sections. Our discussion will be sketchy, but sufficient to reveal that thoughts beyond experience provide no problems in principle for coherently conceivable and even apparently plausible accounts of realization. It is experience which is the real rub.

This account of the realization of thoughts, and not just of their content, is empiricist.[2] To explain how it is so may also help explain why it is appropriate to focus on the particular cases I treat here. First and foremost, there are certain thoughts we introspect--experiences and quasi-experiences with quite concrete contents. Two of the cases we consider here, word-mediated thoughts and thoughts of basic contents, are in effect built up out of these experiences and quasi-experiences and their actual and potential interanimation. We have certain sequences of phenomenal experience and quasi-experience "in-going", and motor quasi-experience and experience "out-going". Words that flash through this concrete arena have their content fixed not only by the actual sequence of our introspected experiences and quasi-experiences, but also by the sequences we would or would likely or might undergo if various conditions occurred. But these mixed sorts of thoughts are in some sense constructed out of introspected thoughts, even if the conditions which would release all the relevant dispositions aren't obviously so constructed. So far, except perhaps for the last qualification, this may suggest an introspectionist analogue of behaviorism, in which phenomenal experiences and quasi-experiences replace stimuli, and motor intentions and quasi-intentions replace responses.

But my empiricism is also at least potentially limited. I think there *may* also be other thoughts, even other primary thoughts, which are not built up out of experiences in this way. Experiences and quasi-experiences are primary thoughts. They involve in particular contexts particular patterns of firing. But certainly there are lots of things going on in our brains other than those particular patterns of firing, even things other than the neural context which helps constitute them to be the experiences and quasi-experiences they are. Certainly one might have those same experiences and quasi-experiences, constituted as they are, and yet various different potentialities, various different dispositions, rolled into one's neurons. One's psychology of introspected thoughts is "surrounded" by a vast structure of causally relevant neurophysiology.[3] The word-mediated thoughts and thoughts of basic contents which we will treat here have some content fixed by that structure. But the other sort of primary thought we will treat here would be found entirely there. Let me elaborate. It is customary to think of neurons as information-processing units. But we will see in Part Three that our neurons process little information about our world of the kind we can introspect, that our introspectible content and information about our world have little overlap. Even still, our neurons *might* process information about the real world, about our firing patterns, or about our experience of things as partly constituted by and hence reflected in our firing patterns. Only one thing is clear,[4] that our complex neural structure comprises complex mechanisms which *do* things, which intervene between one firing pattern and another in specific ways. They intervene between the world and our action on the world, between the firing patterns of our sensory receptor cells and those that most directly control our muscles, in a manner that we have every reason to believe provides a complete causal explanation of our behavior. And they intervene between the firing which helps constitute the introspected quasi-experience or experience of one moment and that of another. Certainly we should remember that the firing patterns which help constitute these primary thoughts may not be peripheral, may not be found specifically in the so-called "sensory" or "motor" cortex, may not be localized at all. It may be that these firing patterns overlap all others in our brains like waves at a beach. But, so to speak, "around" the sequence of one's introspected primary thoughts, there are other neural sequences. Some underwrite unrealized potentials and dispositions for sequences of introspected thoughts in a manner that can help constitute thoughts that also have primary components, for instance word-mediated thoughts. But some do other things. For instance, hormones may potentiate certain synapses rather than others, or certain neurons may fire, and a given sequence of introspected thoughts may be granted a range of different effects, and hence constitute a desire rather than a belief. I make no claims here about how all the neural context which surrounds our experiences and quasi-experiences works, except that it underlies the dispositions for interanimation of introspected thoughts which we will need to deploy to constitute word-mediated thoughts and thoughts with basic contents beyond experience, and that it *may* underlie a different sort of primary thought. These other thoughts are at least possible, and may help make up the sequence of one's primary psychology. They are primary thoughts which are constituted not out of the interanimation of introspected thoughts, as are word-mediated thoughts and thoughts with basic contents. Rather they are constituted out of the "interanimation" of i) firing patterns which, outside of that interanimation, would have no content at all, certainly no introspected content of their own as is had even by our experience of words, and ii) firing patterns which do constitute introspected thoughts. These new thoughts are, along with some borderline cases, the primary thoughts with contents generated by the quasi-logical operations, abstraction, and their vague analogues which we consider in section 1. There might be still other thoughts, yet farther removed from introspected thoughts than these, but we will soon see that in our world they would have contents far different from those I sketched in Part One.

Note one more complication before we begin. I will treat the realization of thoughts beyond experience as involving merely internal states of a moment, but this creates certain problems. Many characteristic human activities, for instance walking, may be controlled by regular oscillations in neural states, and such cycles may encompass more than an intuitive moment of a psychology, more than a moment of experience. So it should not be surprising if some human thoughts, for instance those which control such action, require for their realization a longer time than that which might realize a brief moment of experience. Indeed, some cases we will discuss in sections 2 and 3 take some time, at least in their most characteristic form. It takes more than a moment to say a sentence to oneself. But still, at a moment one may have a set of dispositions which will carry one through to the end of that sentence. In a secondary sense, such thoughts are present in the moment, curled up into those dispositions. So I will ignore this complication.

1

Since we are supposing that particular firing patterns in the right context constitute certain primary thoughts, in particular experiences and quasi-experiences, it is relatively easy to conceive other firing patterns which in the same context[5] would constitute primary thoughts with contents generated by abstraction, the quasi-logical operations, and their vague analogues. The mediation of words and virtual thoughts also provide an arena for the operation of these content generation operations, but we should treat some examples explicitly and in their own specific manner.

First, consider conjunction. Someone who has the capacity for a primary thought of A and a primary thought of B seems in a trivial sense capable of a primary thought of A *and* B, at least if they are capable of having the same *types* of such thoughts, say beliefs, at the same time. A conjunctive primary belief that A *and* B could simply consist of the primary belief in A and the primary belief in B. If our only primary thoughts were experiences and quasi-experiences, and we could only have one of each at a moment, then there would be no opportunity for conjunction of this simple sort. But conjunction might link together other primary thoughts which we will soon consider.

Can such a simple story capture all there is to conjunction? It seems to me that there are a number of different "flavors" of what one might reasonably call "conjunction", and that it does suffice for some. But there are certainly stronger flavors. For instance, conjunction of one sort would require that the causal role of the conjunctive thought of A and B somehow tie A and B appropriately together. It might be that the thinker must be disposed to utter a single sentence which can express the sense of both conjuncts at once, or at least be capable of *some* sort of intuitively single action relevant to both conjuncts taken together.

Also, some flavors of conjunctive thought require that the thinker be capable of *inferring* to either conjunct alone, in some explicit way which would not be trivially assured by the simple model we've already presented.[6] So some sort of mental dynamics, or dispositions for a certain sort of mental dynamics, might be required for certain sorts of conjunctive thought. Also, we might hesitate to attribute conjunctive thought in anything like the full sense to someone who lacked a practice incorporating a word which functions at least roughly as our "and" functions, a word which plays an appropriate role in explicit inferences and also is included in utterances in response to intuitively conjunctive situations. We might even demand a capacity for explicit recognition that a content was intuitively conjunctive.

What should we make of all these complications? We should conclude, I think, that the weak conditions which I originally noted are sufficient for conjunctive thought in my perhaps weak and unusual sense. But if you prefer something a bit stronger, there is at least this story: Assume that the relevant context is fixed. Let there be a *distinct* pattern of firing which would occur when and only when there occurred both the patterns of firing which constitute a primary thought of A and a primary thought of B,[7] and let that new pattern have effects distinct from merely the effects of the firing which constitutes thought of A and the firing which constitutes thought of B. Further, let these be effects on neurophysiological states which help constitute primary thoughts or dispositions for primary thoughts,[8] and effects "appropriate" to the conjunctive thought, whatever they happen to be. That would clearly be a primary thought with conjunctive content.[9]

We can treat the remaining cases somewhat more quickly, by ignoring some of the complications to which I just attended. Let me even ignore the fact that we must keep context fixed[10] in order to keep things simple. Consider disjunction and abstraction. If there is an initial specific range of primary thoughts which, were they to occur, would call forth a distinct firing pattern X, and if that firing pattern X will occur when and only when at least one of those primary thoughts occurs, and if that pattern fulfills appropriate necessary causal roles, then we have inclusive disjunction or abstraction of at least one kind, over the range of contents of the initial primary thoughts. And it is easy to specify the analogous structure which would be sufficient for exclusive disjunction. What constitutes the difference between inclusive disjunction and abstraction of these sorts? Presumably the characteristic causal role of the primary thought in question. An abstraction generates or would generate effects characteristic of thought of the particular feature which is abstracted, while a disjunction fulfills a causal role which doesn't focus on one feature,[11] but is still appropriate.

We are also capable of abstracted or disjunctive thought of a second kind, perhaps the most typical and important. We sometimes think of an abstracted content without thinking of anything which would realize that abstraction. So we may have certain primary thoughts which have the kinds of effects or dispositions for effects just noted, characteristic of the role of abstracted or disjunctive thoughts, but which can be present even when no primary thought of any of their abstraction bases or disjuncts occurs or has recently occurred. To meld these two kinds together: Perhaps such a thought would be caused *in one way* only by thoughts of its disjuncts or bases, but can be caused in another way by other conditions.

Chapter Twelve presumed that experiences and quasi-experiences are made up of elements which recur across experiences and quasi-experiences, that they are rooted in recurring firing patterns, so in a sense our first sort of abstracted thought is always present when experience or quasi-experience is present, if we aren't inappropriately restrictive about what "distinct" means in this world where relevant firing patterns may generally overlap. This suggests that some abstracted thoughts may even carry introspected content in the second form we identified, and hence that abstraction is sometimes a rather mixed case in the typography of primary thoughts which I deployed in the introduction. The introspected disjuncts of a disjunction may carry introspected content as well; ditto for conjunction. But the firing pattern that constitutes the disjunction or conjunction does not introduce any unique concrete content of its own.

One basic mechanism which negation might involve is easy to understand. If firing of some sort constitutes a primary thought of A, and there is another firing pattern (which might merely be the absence of firing) which would occur when and only when the first pattern does not occur, then the second might constitute some kind of "negation" of the first. There are many flavors of negation. Some cannot be distinguished from the mere absence of a primary thought with the content which they negate, and at least that is too weak to capture what we need. But differences in the role characteristic of the thought should again suffice to constitute the differences between the different flavors, and a role of the proper sort will be sufficient to generate the kind of negation we seek. For instance, if the primary thought is an *external* negation, true when and only when the content from which it is generated is false, then it will generate, or constitute dispositions for, effects appropriate if and only if the primary thought of A is false. And if it is an *internal* negation, then it will cause, or constitute dispositions for, effects appropriate when and only when both i) the primary thought of A is false and ii) some positive alternative is true.

There are also vague, degreed analogues of the content generation operations which we have just discussed. But their realization is likewise easy to understand. Vague contents are the natural result of a statistical structure like Galileo's brain, where neurons compete with many other neurons for influence, and where transitions from one form of firing to another may take a probabilistic form. Firing patterns can have various probabilities of causing one another, and this can generate the vague analogues.

Clearly, I have ignored a lot of detail. The characteristic role of these various primary thoughts may depend on whether they constitute, for instance, beliefs or desires. Abstraction may occur in-going, *from* sensory experience, or out-going, *to* specific motor intentions. There may be borderline cases with merely some of the characteristic effects and/or causes noted. And while it is plausible that the characteristic effects of these primary thoughts would be exercised most directly on neural states, which might for instance potentiate certain introspected motor intentions, certainly the roles deployed demand more refined treatment. But at least the general mechanisms which allow us these thoughts are clear. They involve the entwining of certain firing patterns with others which help constitute introspected primary thoughts.

All of the structures we have just suggested are quite naturally realized in neural resources explicitly recognized by current neurophysiology and cognitive science. One account of higher-level neural structure which we have already canvassed, TNT, was explicitly designed to model abstraction. And PDP-style neural nets can be trained into the forms required to mediate between the primary thoughts of A and of B and the primary thoughts which are their conjunctions, disjunctions, and negations. Such nets are also well positioned to achieve the complex association of particular "appropriate" effects with primary thoughts, and to provide the capabilities for explicit recognition of particular kinds of contents which some very rich flavors may require.[12]

2

Chapters Nine, Ten, and Eleven provide us the resources for a plausible model of the realization of word-mediated thought, and indeed of the realization of some thoughts whose contents are generated by metaphor and by the approach apparatus. That previous discussion will allow me to be relatively brief here.

We saw in Chapter Ten that word-mediated thought is rooted in the interanimation of thoughts. Those interanimated thoughts seem to be primary thoughts in particular, say Galileo's experience of a stimulus condition, quasi-experience of the appropriate words, and motor intentions occasioned by those words. Of course, word-mediated thought involves more than the actual interanimation of primary thoughts. It also involves their potential interanimation. As Galileo's various tendencies to think of particular bits of the outgoing content collected by an experienced word compete amongst themselves, the losers strive for primary thoughts for which he has perhaps first potentialities. First potentials for interanimation might help ground the content of that word. And his general competence in Italian may be reflected in the relatively stable pattern of his synapses, so that he has second potentialities for thoughts of all the bits of content of all the Italian words that he knows. Hence second potentials for interanimation might be relevant to fixing the content of his idiolect also. All the relevant actual and potential interanimation of primary thoughts might lie curled into Galileo's dispositions of the moment in one of the complex ways sketched in Chapter Eleven, ways we know might be realized in neural resources.

Let me elaborate a bit. If word-mediated content is to provide thoughts with content like other sorts of representational content, that linguistic content must leave its mark on the psychology of the speaker, on the interanimation of their thoughts. In thought mediated by words but which does not involve explicit speech, there is quasi-experience of the words, a primary imagination of the production of the utterance by one's throat and of its sounding in one's ear. These are primary thoughts. Of course, there is explicit speech, and perhaps Galileo even sometimes *thinks* through explicit utterance, through talking out loud, but even then the motor intention which moves his mouth and tongue, and his sensory experience of the uttered word, constitute primary thoughts. It might even be that when we hear someone *else* speaking, or when we read something, something goes on in *us* which is quite like a thought, the thought we immediately and unreflectively understand to be expressed through those words. But, in any case, in all instances of word-mediated thought there are primary thoughts of words. These primary thoughts of words have a somewhat stable potential to interanimate primary thoughts of bits of their contents. That helps to underwrite their "outgoing" content. And the primary thoughts of the words are interanimated by or potentially interanimated by other primary thoughts, relevant to their "incoming" content. Of course, as we saw in Chapter Ten, words may collect contents which aren't concrete in the manner of the experiences and quasi-experiences which we presume here to be primary thoughts, but in the last section we saw that other sorts of primary thoughts with other sorts of content are at least possible. Even if there aren't any thoughts like that, virtual thoughts might constitute crucial bits of the contents accruing to certain words, so that cross-level interanimation would be important.

Of course, there are further complications to consider. We know that the relative stability of certain associations may be relevant to determining what is part of the *proper* content of words, but of course we also have variously stable potentials for neural firing to deploy here. Such associations are further stabilized and refined by the speaker's acceptance of norms for speech, and by their speech about truth and meaning, in particular practices of truth-calling. These practices are linguistic practices, but both they and the acceptance of norms involve certain special resources. If these factors are to be relevant to the introspectible content of a word-mediated thought, then it is plausible that they too must be underwritten by the speaker's primary psychology. The capacities required for norm-acceptance are probably quite complex, but there is no particular reason to think that neural resources constituting the interanimation and potential interanimation of primary thoughts are insufficient to realize them. Our discussion of "normativity" in Chapter Nine was sufficient to remove ambiguities which might underwrite certain objections to this claim. Correction behavior and the acceptance of norms are not mysterious in the way that normative truth is mysterious. Certainly there is some concrete difference in the motor intentions and hence behaviors, and dispositions for motor intentions and hence behaviors, and also in the emotional experience, of those who accept certain norms and those who do not. And those intentions and feelings are plausibly primary thoughts.

So all of the resources which we deployed in Chapter Ten may be underwritten by plausible neural resources in something like the way suggested by Chapter Eleven. The thoughts which are interanimated seem to be, at least largely, primary thoughts, which are constituted in context by particular patterns of firing. And the dispositions for interanimation which are relevant seem to be the various dispositions for primary thoughts which we discussed there, realized by various sorts of neural structure. This is why word-mediated thought is a mixed case.

But let me be at least a little more specific. There is evidence of the existence of special neural systems in the cerebrum dedicated to speech production and understanding, and presumably they help constitute the mechanisms we've considered. Our capacity for truth-calling governed by norms probably requires not only recognitional capacities but also our "higher" cerebral faculties and the special control systems rooted in our midbrains, which mediate arousal and attention, pleasure and pain and emotion. These help give us our capacity to feel guilt or shame or discomfort, or at least contrary motivation, in the face of our violation of norms, and to control and modulate the sequence of our primary thoughts in response to norms accepted.

Still, there are obvious complexities I'm ignoring. The capacity for the form of word-mediated thought which we humans enjoy involves a capacity to utter and write sentences which take quite a while to express. Somehow we are skilled at associating a trajectory of utterance to a complex of content which the form of that trajectory severely constrains. Grammar matters. Also, at least after suitable training, we can be quite skilled at extended discussions, which take up a longer time even than the utterance of a sentence, and which have inferential and narrative structures of various complex kinds. These capacities are important to word-mediated thought at all like our own, and they no doubt depend on our complex capacities for the commission of long motor routines and for planning, as well as certain sorts of content organization. No more than anyone else do I have a complete account of how all this works. But it does seem that at least for now we have no particular reason to believe that such capacities are beyond neural resources and all the complex dispositions for primary thoughts which they underwrite. As we saw in Chapters Nine and Ten, objections from the supposedly infinite nature of human languages are not obviously effective. Any concrete duplicate of Galileo, who not merely exhibits all his neural structure and behavior but also has all the same concrete introspected thoughts and dispositions for concrete introspected thoughts, seems intuitively capable of word-mediated thought like his. If the duplicate weren't, we'd have little reason to believe Galileo was, or that we are.

This picture of the realization of word-mediated thought bears, as I suggested, some affinity to associationism. And it is easy to see how neural resources might underlie an association of primary thoughts. If patterns of firing in two distinct groups of neurons constitute the primary imagination of two different sorts of things, say sensory experiences of two types or quasi-experiences of a word and of a bit of its content, then a specific neural connection between those two groups might underwrite interanimation which in turn underlies something quite like the traditional association of a taste with a smell or a word with a color. The characteristic patterns of firing in one group might call forth the characteristic patterns of firing in the other groups. In Chapter Eleven, we even noted a mechanism which might explain how such associations are learned. This general kind of interanimation yields an important *class* of content extension capacities, including but not exhausted by word-mediation. It underwrites metaphor-mediated thought and also thoughts involving certain artifacts of the approach apparatus as well.

The machinations and artifacts of the approach apparatus are not all realized in the same way. There are artifacts inflicted on other than seed contents, and even the organized elements of seed contents may have certain modal features whose conception requires the mediation of language. But another important sort of artifact is plausibly due to the kind of neural connectivity we have been discussing, and yet does not involve the mediation of language. Consider the way in which the different sensory aspects of some single intuitive object are associated together into that single thing: Galileo blundered into a door, and turned on impact to see the wood against his face. There was a fusion of distinct phenomenal fields in his experience, but there was also a kind of artifact in his thought. Galileo's conception of the *door* in particular invoked a special unity. The door was conceived as a unit, something which had a look, a sound on impact, a certain rough feel against the skin, a power to cause abrasions, but which lacked the feel of the floor below and the look of the sky outside the window. Those other feels and looks were present in Galileo's experience, but they were not conceived by him as part of the *door*. This conception clearly invokes capacities at least much like those required for thought of basic contents beyond experience, with their complex spatio-temporal structure. And in any normal adult human it would not be entirely divorced from capacities for speech about the door. But it also involves something else. It involves a particular *organization* of contents into *objects* which is not merely mediated by words, an organization of which Galileo would be capable independent of his capacity for speech, and which indeed some of his linguistic capacity presumes. Such an approach apparatus allows for a re-identification of something as the same thing, despite the fact that it does not appear in the same guise in two different perceptions of it. It allows him to think "Oh that again, and from another side." And it structures content so that even brief and spare perceptions of an object may invoke thought of the whole object, including features which are not present in immediate perception. Various sorts of experience and quasi-experience seem associated together into the door and dissociated from experience of the floor.[13] So here we have a structure reminiscent of that which underlies word-mediated thought. Primary thought of one aspect of a thing has a tendency to call forth primary thoughts of its other aspects, and this plausibly involves interanimation of certain kinds which neural connections might underwrite, as indeed some neurophysiologists have suggested.[14] All that's required to turn this organization of content into an *artifact* of the approach apparatus is linguistic mediation, the word "true" bandied about in a misleading place. We might well wonder what allows interanimation in *this* case to constitute thought of one object, and in the last case to constitute word-mediated thought. But let me delay consideration of this until all the relevant cases are on the table.

Another instance of this general kind of phenomenon may be found in metaphor-mediated thought. In metaphor-mediated thought, a certain primary thought may be taken not to be true, but to model the truth, to approximate it in useful ways. This involves a capacity to think of the metaphor, but also to take it as a mere model. This second thing might involve merely some modification of the causal-functional role of the thought of the metaphor, but it would be a modification which is appropriate given the semantic relations between the modeling content and the contents which such a content might properly model, semantic relations reflected in the psychology of the possessor of the metaphoric thought. There must, it seems, be some connection in the psychology of the thinker between the modeled and the modeling, the metaphor and what it conveys, so that for instance the thought of the model interanimates or has some potential to interanimate thoughts of the modeled. This might sometimes involve the recognition of an abstract similarity, and such connections between the model and the modeled may be refined by conventions or decisions about how to take the model, including some perhaps crucially mediated by words. But a certain sort of direct interanimation linking thoughts of the model and the modeled seems also to be a crucial resource, not unlike that which links a word to its content, at least if we are to have any genuinely metaphoric content generation. And certainly neural connectivities could underwrite this.

3

Basic contents play an especially important role in the content theory of Part One, and thoughts with basic contents which are not seed contents are plausibly realized in a way which is especially complex. So those thoughts deserve our special attention. They are somewhat different from the cases we have just discussed, but let me begin by noting some similarities.

Some basic contents which are not seed contents have complex details and spatio-temporal structures. Such contents rival in complexity the contents of word-mediated thoughts. They are clearly not often, if ever, the content of a primary thought. Rather, they are characteristically contents of thoughts of the mixed sort. Their realization involves both primary thoughts and the kinds of conditions which lead us to ascribe virtual thoughts.

When there is a thought with a basic content which is not seed content, it is plausible that there is an interanimation of primary thoughts at least somewhat reminiscent of word-mediated thought. One can imagine how the world would look from some vantage point in particular, and then stroll in imagination along a path one might traverse in the world, with one quasi-experience leading to another in time in a way which reflects the spatial structure of the world. Motion links together space and time, and our ability to conceive basic contents which extend out beyond seed contents seems to exploit this linkage. Thoughts of basic contents which extend out beyond what is present involve at least one peculiar and characteristic form of interanimation, which underwrites such an imaginary stroll. To elaborate, I will first discuss the complex basic contents at issue in more detail, before we consider more details of their realization. Note that I will only treat the case of those common humans who have an active visual primary imagination.

Closely associated with a basic content which extends out beyond the experience of a moment are various seed contents which we might call its "segments". They match the experience one might have at a moment if variously located and oriented in such a world. One might at some moment have a primary thought which is either an experience, or a quasi-experience in memory or fantasy, of a particular one of those segments. Call it the "present segment" of the thought in question. Certainly the typical basic content outruns its present segment, is associated with many more segments.

While each segment has in itself a certain complexity of spatial structure, basic contents extend out beyond what we might immediately experience, beyond a present segment, in ways which add still more spatio-temporal complexity. Consider first temporal extensions. Basic contents may include segments associated with earlier and later times than the present segment. These include the sorts of things we might experience if we were in the relative past or future. This temporal feature of basic contents must integrate properly with certain features of our experience of time. We experience the passing of one moment of experience into another. And it may also be, as some writers on time have suggested, that one's experience of the immediate past hangs around afterwards, a reverberating dim artifact, in present experience. But of course basic contents can also include temporal structure out beyond what one might experience even in a lifetime. In fact, some basic contents reach infinitely into the past or future.

Spatial extensions of basic contents out beyond momentary experience are more complex. First of all, there are segments of basic contents which are views from elsewhere, from another position or orientation. Such segments are, in ordinary cases, spatially related to what is present, in the sense that the points from which the world would have the look of those segments are spatially related in some way to the point from which it looks as it does in the present segment. But this feature of basic contents must properly integrate with other spatio-temporal features of our experiences and hence our contents. Recall some things from Part One. The spatial form of the experience of a moment may encode certain spatial information in a disguised or indirect way. Via perspective, the relative size in immediate experience of the visual images of two objects, say of two red balls or planets known to be of the same size, may carry information about their relative distance. More generally, one's immediate visual experience of something has a place in a continuum of the visual experiences of that thing one would have over time if one moved in various ways. From one's knowledge of the spatial structure of the world, one can form on the basis of the experience of a moment an expectation about how that experience would change if one moved about. To each object with a particular shape and size and orientation, and with a particular spatial relation to one, at a certain distance and in a certain direction, there corresponds a series of visual experiences one would have of the object if one moved in various ways, along various paths in the world. This is so even if the object is not within one's immediate experience, assuming that the object itself is stable and unmoving over the relevant temporal internal. And there is a different series of experiences which one would have of the object if it itself were moving along some path. One's sense of the paths which some object, including oneself, might take through the world is, at least in ordinary cases, constituted by two different sorts of things, and the second introduced another sort of rudimentary spatio-temporal relation into basic contents. Such paths of objects through the world may appear in phenomenal experience from various vantage points, as continuous spatial paths traversed by objects over time. But one's sense of such paths is also one's sense of how one or an object would travel if one or it *did* various things (or simply coasted along).[15] For instance, one's sense of a particular path forward, from where one is, is in part one's sense of what would happen if one performed a series of motor operations, running forward and turning slightly left. And this is a sense of a path by which causal influence can pass through the world, of the trajectory an object like a ball or a planet or a light beam might take. The account of content sketched in Part One predicates causal powers of microevents, and speaks of paths by which causal influence propagates, of for instance what a particular power instantiation can immediately act upon, can act upon without causal intermediaries, and also of chains of such immediate influence. In doing so, it is capable of generating more spatial-temporal structure than relations of the sort which appear in experience alone might allow. Indeed, there are still other complexities of spatial structure to consider. We can zoom in close to things and see more details than would otherwise be present in our experience. A spatial structure may not only reach out towards infinity, but have an at least potentially infinite complexity buried within it.

I have so far restricted our consideration to only two aspects of our experience and of basic contents--visual and motor aspects. They can provide us together with a reasonable model of how thoughts with spatio-temporally complex basic contents are realized. But it may be important to remember that of our other senses only hearing, which like vision is a relatively recent evolutionary development, rivals vision in its capacity to capture structure at a distance. In fact, the rather singular nature of visual experience is related to another important fact we should notice explicitly. The visual segments associated with a basic content are not literally parts of that basic content. A visual segment involves not only a selection from but a perspectival distortion of the spatial structure of its associated basic content. Distant objects look smaller in visual experience. Other senses, say touch, do not involve such distortion. This feature of basic contents beyond seed contents helps make them somewhat different from the cases we considered in section 2.

The spatio-temporal complexity of basic contents must infect any capacity to entertain them. How might thought with a content such as we've just sketched be realized? Here's a rather abstract story: i) Take thoughts with the full range of seed contents which might be the experience of a particular bigger basic content from some position and angle or other, which might be its segments. ii) Dampen or suitably transform those features of the seed contents which are mere artifacts of experience, for instance magic boundaries and the fact that distant objects look smaller. iii) Then somehow stitch all that together into the one bigger basic content, but in a structured way, so that some bits, for instance, constitute the pasts of others. Primary imagination gives us the capacity for thoughts with all of the seed contents which (i) requires. And interanimation of various sorts seems plausibly capable of underwriting (ii) and (iii). But now let me try to flesh out this very abstract story in plausible and somewhat more concrete resources. Where might we look for plausible resources?

1) Of course, the primary imagination is itself such a resource. It provides us with a capacity at any moment for primary thoughts with the full range of seed contents (or contents perhaps somewhat abstracted from these). And of course, there is also experience. These things in themselves provide crucial spatio-temporal resources for our thought. The relation of "being after" is present at least in the experience of more than a moment, and there are a variety of spatial relations present in the experience of a moment. Causal experience in particular has spatial structure of an important and familiar kind, since motor intentions must function to move limbs in a world with six degrees of spatial freedom, the three spatial directions plus pitch, yaw, and spin. To move limbs through any complex trajectory takes time, but it is plausible that there are motor intentions at any given moment which control and encompass the entire temporal sequence of one's motor plan for a short action. Such a motor intention may constitute causal experience and be a primary thought.

2) Next, we have word-mediated capacities to extend and refine our sense of what we might experience, and also to delimit the full range of contents of causal restrictions which the full range of basic contents may incorporate. That last phenomena is something to which we'll shortly return, but we have a sense already of the kinds of neural connectivities which can underlie these linguistic capacities. Abstraction unmediated by words may help in similar ways, along perhaps with thoughts mediated by models. Together with the primary imagination, these resources help deliver to us a capacity to conceive the building blocks of all basic contents.

3) The presence of certain word- or metaphor-mediated thoughts or of certain abstracted thoughts, whose realization is or involves primary thoughts, may help to realize our sense of at least the general structure of a particular basic content, a sort of scaffold for that basic content out beyond the experience of a moment. For instance, not only experience but primary imagination may be accompanied by higher-order firing patterns which constitute primary abstracted thoughts. These may be primary thoughts of a certain abstract spatial organization of entities. We may in this way have primary thoughts with the content of at least an abstract map of a very large basic content. At the very least, we can string words together in relevant narrative forms.[16] In addition, no doubt we have certain sorts of neurally-rooted dispositions which constitute our implicit beliefs about things present in such a world. These would generate relevant primary thoughts if they were activated.

4) Basic contents are potentially infinite in various ways. So it is important that we have, as we saw in Chapter Nine, certain "infinite" dispositions, dispositions to repeat some action whatever comes up. This gives us the capacity for thought of things which are potentially infinite, even without the mediation of words. One may have a disposition to walk another step wherever one is, and this gives one a capacity for behavior which may underwrite a thought of the potentially infinite. Only word-mediation can give us the capacity to think of certain complete infinities. But one kind of thought of the infinite does not require the mediation of words.

The plausible neural bases of these resources have already been at least roughly outlined. They involve primary thoughts and dispositions for primary thoughts of sorts with which we are already familiar already. But there are some new "special purpose" mechanisms, special forms of interanimation or of neural connectivity, worth explicitly noting as well.

5) We have some sort of capacity to assess the temporal variation in our experience, to note succession and change in that experience. There has been some neurophysiological work on that capacity. It may be mediated by what Edelman has called "organs of succession". These may for instance reenter patterns of firing characteristic of immediately past experience into the stream of firing characteristic of present experience, so that higher-level neural processing can respond to differences between succeeding experiences.[17] This helps provide

us with a capacity for primary thoughts which abstract not just from a moment's experience but which capture temporal patterns.

6) Most importantly, we have a capacity to understand what transformations would occur in the spatial form of our sensory experiences if we traveled about in an unchanging world in various ways, or if objects themselves moved in the world. This is, I think, a certain sort of know how, rooted in a certain sort of special capacity for the interanimation of primary thoughts. Let me elaborate. Galileo understands how his visual experience would unfold were he to run down the winding stairs and out onto the street. This capacity allows him not only to move *out* in imagination from a particular segment, which constitutes one particular viewpoint on the world, to others which constitute other viewpoints. It also allows him to move *in*, to look at smaller detail. It allows him like a camera to zoom, pan, and rotate about the imaginary world of a basic content. This seems to involve a special kind of interanimation of primary thoughts. Bartlett Mel[18] has shown that a PDP-style neural net utilizing Hebb-style learning rules can come to reflect "the way in which one's view of the surrounding 3-dimensional world would transform as a result of any given shift in one's vantage point."[19] So plausible resources might underwrite this special capacity. In effect, Mel's net learns to associate various motor commands, which move the net in various ways through a stable and unchanging world, with particular changes in the visual perception of the world which accompany such motion. By actually "experiencing" such transformations as occur when it moves about, the net learns how to anticipate and imagine them on its own, in its "primary imagination". Work has begun on the modifications required if such a net is to deal properly with moving objects. Such a net might link motor intentions and visual experiences, and also quasi-intentions and quasi-experiences. Hence it might underwrite the special kind of interanimation of primary thought by primary thought we need here.

One note on how this resource interacts with another: There is more than one infinity which may be present in a basic content, even if we ignore the difficult distinction between dense and continuous contents. There are infinities of extent, as space extends out infinitely, and of detail, as we look down to smaller and smaller structure. Our capacity for conception of either sort of infinite structure involves our capacity to at least potentially imagine infinite series of operations of the sorts we just discussed. We might be disposed to move always farther out in space, or to move always further in, to zoom in closer and see more details. And we might have a capacity rooted in Mel-style resources to understand the resulting visual transformations. In actual fact, when we zoom towards things in the real world we eventually lose resolution or our noses get in the way. But the conception of an infinity of points within something seems to depend on some sort of idealization of these actual capacities.

How might we deploy all these resources together, to constitute a thought with a basic content which outruns what we might experience in a moment? In lots of ways, but let me sketch one. First, primary thoughts: We might experience or entertain via the primary imagination a seed content. Then we might have an abstracted primary thought, or perhaps the primary imagination of words which mediate similar content, which provides the rough structure of a larger basic content of which that original seed content is a segment. Now, some dispositions for primary thoughts: We might have a capacity to recall or imagine the way such a world looks from certain viewpoints. For instance, we might have a specific tendency to the primary imagination of particular things when we utter "Pisa" to ourselves. But we also have relevant but more indirect dispositions. We also "understand" how these various segments would need to be transformed to correspond to the experiences we would have if we moved about in the world of the content. That is because we have a capacity for imagination of that transformation rooted in Mel-style interanimation, because we have a disposition for a certain trajectory of visual quasi-experiences in light of certain motor quasi-intentions. We also have organs of succession which would allow us to recognize the changes in our quasi-experience over time. Our various dispositions might underlie together a sense that after we get to a certain point in the basic content everything is dark from then on out towards infinity and eternity. Basically, we have primary thoughts and dispositions for primary thoughts of certain features of such a basic content, and then a capacity to fill in the detail in a coherent way which is underwritten by a Mel-type neural network, a special faculty which would deliver the requisite segments as we move in imagination up and down and through the world of the basic content. There are limits to the detailed differences between two somewhat similar basic contents which we can actually bear in mind, but we also have a capacity to potentially fill in some undetailed structure which we can actually bear in mind in a number of different ways, by the free exercise of the imagination within the limits set by that general structure.

Thoughts with basic contents which outrun experience may sound somewhat like word-mediated thoughts, and indeed they are also thoughts of our mixed sort. But there is the additional complexity in this particular case that visual segments are not really components of a basic content. They involve distortion by perspective. So the thought which is realized in the already complex way we have sketched so far is perhaps not quite to be identified with the thought of the basic content in itself. It is more like the thought of how that basic content would look from various points of view. Rather, we can project from the thought we have just discussed to something on the order of a second-level virtual thought, which is to be ascribed to us to explain our capacity to understand the transformations in our visual experience which would occur as we moved about in the world at issue. *That* is our thought with the basic content itself. It isn't quite a virtual thought, since its existence is so dependent on the existence of various particular and fleeting primary thoughts, like the primary thought which is the thought of the present segment of the content. But it is like a virtual thought in explaining the primary thoughts and dispositions for primary thoughts noted.

We have so far only discussed the realization of a certain specific sort of basic content by our plausible resources. So we need to go beyond that model in certain ways. But even that model helps explain some actual limitations of our conceptual capacity. For instance, our incapacity to entertain more than mere relative haecceities as possibly characterizing two microevents in a basic content probably rests on our incapacity to entertain a difference between how the world would look when centered on one or the other. We can entertain a sense of how the world would look if we were sitting on one of Max Black's balls, in which the other would be a distinct entity off in the distance. But we cannot entertain any distinct sense of how it would be to be on one rather than the other of the two balls. Also, our incapacity to link segments together in deviant ways to generate basic contents with unfamiliar spatio-temporal structure is probably rooted in our having developed only Mel-style transformation capacities through training in our particular spatio-temporal environments.

But we should also at least briefly consider the ways in which basic contents can extend out beyond what we could conceive merely in the manner so far characterized. The main point is that some basic contents exhibit causal powers we cannot exhibit in motor action. Our capacity to entertain powers is in fact even more complex than I have pretended so far, even in our complex discussion in Chapter Seven. Certain powers we experience via our motor action, by acting in one way rather than another way. But we exhibit these powers in the face of our concrete expectations about the powers exhibited in our environment, which constitute the virtual causal experience introduced in Chapter Eleven. And there are still more complications. Some of the powers exhibited in our environment are mechanical powers like our own. They involve forces governing motion in space and time. But we also seem capable of quite primitive thoughts, say of the power of fire to burn, which involve different sorts of restriction. We clearly associate fire with burning; we think of visual flame and burning feelings together. But we also can come to think of burning as a *power* of flame. It seems to me that this does not require word-mediation, and that it is the conception of a genuine power, not a mere regularity. Because of our capacity to *do* certain things, we have the conception of certain powers. Because of our capacity to "understand" the content of those restrictions in two ways, by exhibiting such powers and by experiencing contents which match their content, we become somehow capable of thoughts of powers we can merely experience, things which can merely happen to us. These are powers we can exhibit only through the manipulation of tools like torches, not directly in the way we can exhibit force of one sort or another, so perhaps our capacity for long-range planning and tool use somehow also underlies our capacity to think of all these things as powers and not as mere regularities. To burn things and to change their colors is something we can *plan* to do, albeit through the mediation of tools, and such a plan does not obviously require the mediation of words. It may be that our understanding of these sorts of powers of the objects in our environment can be reflected to at least a certain degree in our limb movements, along with our understanding of the mechanical powers of those objects, as for instance we run away from things which feel good but have hurtful effects, though on the other hand it may be plausible to insist that the same behavior would be the result of belief in a mere regular association of these "causes" and "effects". There are still more sophisticated sorts of powers, I think, which *can* only be talked about, whose conception requires word-mediation. Perhaps we can act in some way which reveals our belief that the world contains even those powers, but only by exhibiting some word-mediated thought to that effect. In any case, clearly the story I have already told is the mere bare outline of a complete story which needs to be told. But still we seem to have no particular reason to believe that neural resources cannot deliver the goods. If you require assurance, consider again the concrete duplicate of Galileo, with his experience and quasi-experience and embodied neurophysiology. Any causal thought of which Galileo is clearly capable would be within the capacities of that duplicate.

There are other ways in which basic contents extend out beyond what we might conceive on the basis I have so far characterized. For instance, I haven't said anything explicit about the distinction between dense and continuous contents. This involves, I think, a peculiar kind of measure structure which involves the mediation of words. But, as always, I will avoid that labyrinth.

One other feature of the conception of basic contents is worthy of some note. One might have a quasi-experience of a basic content which constitutes a "present segment" of that content. But one need not conceive it *as* present. In fact, it most likely wouldn't be something one would conceive as present in that sense, say if it were a quasi-experience of some far but remembered corner of the real world. Yet we also can entertain basic contents which *are* centered on here and now, and even a hypothetical here and now. They involve at least one kind of presence which isn't a feature of experience. In being capable of conceiving a world which reaches beyond our experience we yet retain a capacity to understand from where in such a world we act. And this capacity is, I think, at least one element which plays a role in constituting thought of genuinely *centered* contents, focussed on a here and now.

Let me now return to the question or objection I dropped like a hot potato in section 2. Interanimation of thought and thought is supposed to constitute the connection between a word and its content, a model and what it models, one aspect of an organized thing and another, and a present segment and other segments of a big basic content. How can one mechanism do such different things?

It is important to remember that there may be different kinds of interanimation, unlike association, which differently link different kinds of thoughts with the same contents. But we can also go at least a long way towards answering this objection by being clear about exactly what contents are involved, and remembering that interanimation has a direction. In fact, the kinds of interanimation we have deployed differ in regard to the kinds of contents they link. To keep discussion manageable, let me simplify. Ignore, among other things, the difference between experience and quasi-experience, certain ways in which causal contents accrue to words and are organized by the approach apparatus, the way the approach apparatus discussed in section 2 has some affinities to the structure deployed in 3, and even metaphoric mediation. Then we might say this: The approach apparatus links the phenomenal experience we might have of a concrete object to another phenomenal experience. Mel's net links a certain intention to move in the world, a world with a certain look, to a certain new visual experience. In word-mediated thought there are two sorts of link, of phenomenal experience to intentions for appropriate utterance, and of phenomenal experience of a word to intentions for appropriate motor response. So here are different conditionals linking different sorts of contents.[20]

4

That completes my too brief sketch of the realization of thought beyond experience. Throughout this part, we have seen that various highfalutin worries about our capacity for thought beyond experience can be dissolved. Some are skeptical about word-mediated thought because of worries about infinity and normativity or other putative features of meaningful speech. And these worries can be met in the way we sketched in Chapter Nine.

But others may be skeptical in another way. Anti-realists have raised various worries about our capacity for thoughts which we cannot confirm or disconfirm, including thoughts about the inaccessible past, and those with certain kinds of quasi-logical and infinite contents.[21] Sometimes anti-realists appear merely to favor a revision of our customary inferential practices. But sometimes they argue that plausible resources cannot realize some of the thoughts we have attempted to realize here. Perhaps some anti-realists favor fewer resources than we have now seen to be plausible, but still some might argue that the resources which I have deployed here are not enough to get what I have claimed to get from them. An anti-realist may attempt to argue that in fact those resources do not suffice to constitute thoughts with the contents I have claimed, as opposed to some anti-realist alternative. They may make a kind of indeterminacy argument, suggested by the parallel between Putnam's argument for anti-realism and Quine's for indeterminacy. Or they may claim that thought with their favored content has a better claim to being realized by the resources I have deployed than thoughts with the content I favor. Such anti-realist arguments fail, I think, but they are a useful foil. If they do fail, it is for a particular reason which will be worth bearing in mind in the next part. Appropriate objectual resources get us out of the jams these anti-realists try to put us into. Non-objectual resources, for instance appropriate but non-objectual causal roles, are also helpful, but they are not sufficient, I think. On the other hand, the objectual resources leave us with significant hostages to fortune. Let's look at some examples.

A rather strange anti-realist might argue that the primary imagination as I have characterized it in fact realizes not thoughts about things which are not present in experience, but rather thoughts about things which are present but faint, about what's present and ghostly rather than what's absent and solid. Our response to this should be, at least in part, an objectual one. There are in fact no things of that sort in the world to be present in our experience, no faint or dream or hallucinatory objects floating around.[22] And certainly they bear no cognitively relevant relation to our primary imagination. So the strange anti-realist has made an improper attribution.

That case runs one way, but the most plausible anti-realist arguments run the other. For instance, one might claim that there is nothing which determines that the resources I deployed here realize thoughts with genuinely infinite contents as opposed to thoughts with contents merely too large for humans to traverse. But remember that the dispositions which I have deployed are themselves in some sense *infinite*; they might be actualized across an infinity of different circumstances. So we can deploy an objectual resource to get around objections like this. It isn't perhaps quite the same kind of objectual resource as we have been discussing, but still we are capable of thought of the infinite only because there is some kind of infinity present in the world, if only of a dispositional variety. Of course, not all basic contents have the particular sort of infinite structure that we might treat in this way, which just keeps iterating more of the same. Some other sorts of infinite basic contents may be conceivable by us only via the mediation of descriptions, which for instance specify a certain pattern of repetition or development, and still others are in fact only capable of being conceived by infinitistic caricatures of human beings, so that some idealization infects my account of basic content. But it isn't the infinite in itself which generates a problem for the realization of our thought. We can have a disposition to perform a potential infinity of Mel-type transformations on one segment to get another, so we can pass in imagination along a street without determinate end.

Consider another case. Someone might argue that the resources we have deployed in this chapter in an attempt to realize thoughts with basic contents which extend even finitely out in space or time, but beyond our capacity to immediately verify or disconfirm, in fact might realize thoughts with lesser or different content. For instance, the organs of succession might help realize thoughts of precession. Or Mel's net might realize a capacity for imagining the swelling and shrinking of seen objects. But again, objectual resources seem to get us out of these problems. The organs of succession respond to differences in sensory input over time, and the temporal direction of that input seems relevant to the content capacities which they help underwrite. We have to go a bit outside of the moment to get these resources, a moment to which we have mostly constrained ourselves in this part, but still they are plausibly available to us. And certainly we should expect the need for an objectual account of temporal experience. What about the other case? Not only does visual experience fuse in various ways with causal experience which possesses depth, but Mel's net itself ties intentions to move to experiences of visual transformation. It doesn't tie intentions to shrink and swell objects to visual experiences in the way the alternative suggests. We might wonder why those intentions *are* intentions to move rather than to exercise powers of shrinking and enlarging objects. But, on the objectual model we have developed, the content of those intentions is fixed by the actions which they control. We have a capacity to move at will and without tools, but not to so shrink and enlarge objects.

So we have developed in this part a deeply objectual account of our thought. But the most obviously problematic feature of this account, we will soon see, is the way it deploys objectual resources in the constitution of our experience. It is the realization of our experience, I think, which generates the most significant and direct problems for this account, not the rather sophisticated features of our thoughts beyond experience. If there were objects of the concrete sort we experience, then we could deliver thoughts with an intuitive range of contents, as we have seen in this part.

Where are we? All of the general capacities beyond experience required for our thoughts beyond experience, not only for quasi-experience but also for thoughts with abstracted contents, contents generated by the quasi-logical operations, vague contents, contents polluted by artifacts of the approach apparatus, contents mediated by metaphors and words, and basic contents which are not seed contents, can be realized by neural resources which are coherently conceivable, and apparently plausible. We are also in possession of coherently conceivable accounts of how our experience might be realized which mesh with the rest of our story. So the task of this part has been at least roughly discharged: We have developed a coherently conceivable sketch of how there might be thoughts with the full range of contents exhibited in Part One. And we seem also to have gone some distance towards discharging even the task of the next part. We have a coherently conceivable and apparently plausible account of all the capacities other than capacities for experience required for the realization of all our thoughts. And even the accounts of experience we have developed look homey and familiar, if a little frayed along the edges.

Galileo's experience of the street is supposed to involve the correlation of his neural firing and the street. His neural states are to constitute his quasi-experience of what looking up would reveal, a tower and then Mars beyond, and also his capacity to conceive how his experience would unfold if he flew out that way. This tale deploys only quite concrete resources of a sort beloved by common sense, but involves an account of experience which is somewhat creaky, though coherently conceivable. So the question that remains for us is this: Can we develop an account of our capacity for experience which is not only coherently conceivable, but also plausible, at least for all we know now?

NOTES

1. At least for the most part. There is also the virtual experience introduced in Chapter Eleven.
2. Antonio R. Damasio, *Descartes' Error* also deploys something like the empiricist elements of this picture.
3. The quote marks indicate that the firing which helps constitute the introspected thoughts may not be spatially localized. And of course the firing patterns constitute the thoughts only given lots of specific context.
4. Barring, of course, the general worries about humanly conceivable things we will face in Chapter Nineteen.
5. "Same context" varies somewhat elastically over what follows.
6. Christopher Peacocke considers such a model. See *A Study of Concepts* (Cambridge, MA: MIT Press, 1992), 6.
7. I am presuming that the thoughts are of the same type, say both beliefs.
8. Or sequences of primary thoughts or dispositions for sequences of primary thoughts.
9. One might reasonably wonder what sort of modal force, if any, governs the co-variation of firing patterns required. But, as before, let me walk by this complication.
10. Though, as I said in the last chapter, we are presuming that in the case of at least experience and quasi-experience the relevant neural context doesn't vary in a quick and interesting way.
11. Since there may be no intuitively single feature shared by all the disjuncts.
12. For an introduction to connectionist resources, see David Rumelhart and James McClelland (editors), *Parallel Distributed Processing*, vol. 1 (Cambridge, MA: MIT Press, 1986).
13. If we have but one experience at a moment, then it might be certain features of experiences, and hence certain sorts of abstracted thought, which are associated together.
14. For one model of this sort see Gerald Edelman, *Neural Darwinism*.
15. This involves some analogue of the persistence of objects, but it is something we can reconstruct without recourse to artifacts of the approach apparatus. When I speak of one's continuing to execute a plan over time, that carries basic content, even if that particular way of speaking also carries some artifacts.
16. Words may be tied to features of present experience which can yet exist outside of that present experience. Ditto for certain features we can abstract. So we can have the thought of those features outside of experience. We can think or speak of temporal relations, which we experience, existing also outside of our experience. There is no great mystery in this. The content of experience is not marked as present within experience.
17. Gerald Edelman, *The Remembered Present* (New York: Basic Books, 1989), especially 119-139.
18. Bartlett W. Mel, "A Connectionist Learning Model for 3-Dimensional Mental Rotation, Zoom, and Pan", *Proceedings of the Eighth Annual Conference of the Cognitive Science Society* (Hillsdale, NJ: Lawrence Erlbaum Associates, 1986), 562-571.
19. Roger Shepherd, "Internal Representation of Universal Regularities", in Nadel, Cooper, Culicover, and Harnish (editors), *Neural Connections, Mental Computation*, 103-134, 127.
20. This issue introduces some interesting complexities. For instance, it may be intuitive to distinguish between intentions to move in the world and to utter certain words simply because the introspected content of intentions to utter is in fact a rather unusually abstracted motor intention, which conceives alternatives phonetically. This may be good grounds to postulate more than one causal field of experience, but, because it involves abstraction, it does not require modification of C.
21. Michael Dummett, "The Reality of the Past", in *Truth and Other Enigmas*, 358-374. John McDowell, "On 'The Reality of the Past'", in C. Hookway and P. Pettit (editors), *Action and Interpretation* (Cambridge: Cambridge University Press, 1978), 127-144. Christopher Peacocke, *Thoughts: An Essay on Content* (Oxford: Blackwell, 1986), 65-85. Crispin Wright, *Realism, Meaning, and Truth* (Oxford: Blackwell, 1987), 85-106.

22. Maybe there are real sense data of unicorns, though no ghostly unicorns. But then in imagination we *would* have experience of those objects.

Part Three

EXPERIENCE AND PLAUSIBILITY

CHAPTER FOURTEEN

PHENOMENAL OBJECTS

In the last part, we sketched a coherently conceivable account, in fact a number of somewhat different coherently conceivable accounts, of the realization of our experience. But while those models met some weak plausibility constraints, they aren't fully plausible when all things are considered. We turn now to a complete survey of the range of ways in which our experience might be realized, in pursuit of an account which is at once fully plausible when all things are considered and coherently conceivable. Chapters Fourteen and Fifteen will concern phenomenal experience, and in particular the characteristic intrinsic phenomenal properties. Chapters Sixteen through Eighteen consider causal experience and spatio-temporality. But this part also traces an historical route. We will replay the development of our science after Galileo, as it progressed from early worries about the reality of phenomenal properties like color to later worries about the reality of even traditional galilean properties, of even spatio-temporal and causal properties. We will see that difficulties which first troubled accounts of our experience of intrinsic phenomenal properties now also threaten accounts of our experience of spatio-temporal structure and causal powers.

As we know, there are two kinds of accounts of the realization of experience. This chapter concerns what I have called "objectual accounts" of our phenomenal experience, according to which the realization conditions of the experience of objects with particular phenomenal properties crucially include things with those very phenomenal properties. The next chapter concerns "non-objectual accounts", which do not include things with such properties in the relevant realization conditions. Both of these types of accounts face difficulties. While there are coherently conceivable objectual accounts, including those we sketched in the last part, no objectual account is fully plausible. On the other hand, while non-objectual accounts of the phenomenal may be more plausible, they are not coherently conceivable. Later in this part, we will see that similar difficulties trouble accounts of our experience of even the spatio-temporal and the causal.

1

The account of the realization of our thought which was sketched in the previous part rooted many features of basic contents in features of the seed contents of experience. These include many phenomenal features of basic contents, including some sorts of spatio-temporal structure and valences of attention. But in this and the following chapter I will focus primarily on the characteristic intrinsic phenomenal properties: phenomenal color and sound and taste and smell and so on. And even within that class, I will focus my discussion in a limited way. Until the last section of this chapter, I will concentrate our discussion on visual experience in particular, on phenomenal color. That is because this case is familiar from the philosophical tradition and has received a highly developed empirical study, and because it involves the full range of issues relevant to other sorts of characteristic intrinsic phenomenal properties.

Objectual accounts of phenomenal experience in general and visual experience in particular divide at least roughly into two classes. On the one hand, there are accounts which hold that the objects with phenomenal properties which help constitute phenomenal experience include such third-person, public objects as that experience seems at first blush to reveal, truly red planets and stars, which can be seen by more than one person at a given time. A single such object, with a single pattern of phenomenal color, can help constitute the experience of many different observers. On the other hand, there are other kinds of objectual accounts, which hold for instance that the only red objects involved in the experience of a planet are inner sense data under our hats, so that different people's visual experiences of a particular red planet involve different red objects.

There may be legitimate questions about the adequacy of this classification scheme, and I will return to that issue. But for now let me consider merely accounts of the first and most traditional and straightforward kind, which I will call "simple" objectual accounts. These crucially deploy a single object with a single pattern of phenomenal colors in the realization of many different people's visual experience of an ordinary material object.

2

Plausible simple objectual accounts of visual experience must distinguish in a reasonable way between mere artifacts of experience on the one hand and objective phenomenal properties of balloons, balls, and planets on the other. Simple objectual accounts maintain that many features of our visual experience are inherited quite directly from the features of the objects out in the world which help constitute that experience. But of course mere artifacts of phenomenal experience cannot reasonably be explained in this same simple way by simple objectual accounts. For instance, if in visual experience distant objects look smaller, that cannot plausibly be because in fact they are smaller. And there are some artifacts of visual experience which involve even intrinsic phenomenal properties, for instance the fact that colors seem to change as objects move into the darkness.

There are various ways to achieve the requisite factorization. Recall, for instance, one simple model of our visual experience sketched in Part Two: We look out at a red planet or star. There is a certain pattern of neural firing in us that correlates in some way with the present phenomenal qualia which help constitute that experience, say the red surface of the planet or of the star, which we might hope is not long dead. The colorful surface of the star or planet counts as a present quale only when certain conditions are met, say when it is the closest surface to the viewer across a transparent medium in the lighted and animated state Aristotle imagined. And the surface appears within someone's experience with the size suggested by Euclid's treatment of perspectival distortion. This account is creaky in more than one way, but let me assume that the factorization could be achieved in *some* plausible way. Still, there are reasons for worry.

It is important to remember that the characteristic intrinsic properties present in visual experience are "colors" in a traditional and non-revisionary sense. They are phenomenal colors of the sort discussed in Chapter Six, which are both i) as they appear in our experience and ii) apparently objective properties of things like planets and stars. They are not causal powers of any sort, not even powers to cause experiences, nor can they be identified or constituted by any of the other sorts of intrinsic properties of microevents introduced in Chapter Six. That is assured by the content theory of Part One, in part by the fact that constitution is a semantic relation. Nothing can constitute *phenomenal* color but phenomenal color.

The plausibility of simple objectual accounts of phenomenal color experience is put in serious doubt by certain traditional arguments, arguments deployed by Galileo but even older, against the presence of phenomenal color on balls and planets and other ordinary "material" objects. This section reviews those traditional arguments against color, in somewhat modern dress. It concludes that phenomenal color is not really a property of material objects, that it is a mere artifact of our experience of those objects. We will see that the proper development of these arguments encompasses the two objections with which we have been flirting since Chapter Eight. There are no objects with phenomenal colors, and even if there were, they wouldn't plausibly mesh with the neural states which explain our behavior and help constitute our experience.

The central case against simple objectual accounts of the experience of phenomenal color rests on "perceptual relativity" arguments like this one:[1]

P1) Different perceivers in different circumstances experience a given object to have different phenomenal colors, even at the same time and on the same bit of its surface.

P2) If P1, then the object has no single true phenomenal color (or pattern of colors).

P3) If an object has no single true phenomenal color (or pattern of colors), then a simple objectual account of our experience of the color of that object is false.

The third premise of such an argument seems unassailable, at least short of a radical modification of traditional commonsense conceptions. Simple objectual accounts require such true phenomenal colors (or patterns of color). The first premise is supported by a variety of commonplace phenomena. One's experience of the color of things varies as one wears variously colored glasses.[2] Those who are color-blind have a different experience of the colors of things than those who are not. As objects recede into the distance, they edge towards an indifferent grey-blue. As illumination varies, so do the colors we experience things to have. But there is a traditional response to this sort of argument which questions the second premise.[3] Traditional simple objectual accounts, incorporating such a response, have all sorts of stories to tell about the distortion of perceptual forms by intervening media and the need for a properly receptive sense organ. Just because different perceivers experience an object to have different colors, that does not mean that the object does not have a single true color, a true color which plays an important role in constituting normal experience. The single true color of an object, so the story goes, is that seen by *normal observers*, people who are not color-blind and who are not wearing colored glasses, *in conditions of standard illumination*, not under red strobes or in darkened rooms.

However, empirical developments in color science have made this response much less plausible than it might once have seemed, as C. L. Hardin has shown philosophers.[4] First of all, the colors we experience something to have can vary quite significantly within the range of intuitively "standard" illumination. Leaving aside obvious differences introduced by fluorescent and incandescent artificial lighting, even variations in the position of the sun during the day can introduce variations in the exact phenomenal colors which balls and balloons are perceived to have.[5] Among the range of illumination which counts as intuitively "normal", it seems that there is no non-arbitrary way to specify one particular sort of illumination, and hence one particular phenomenal color, as privileged, as true. In addition, there are metamers, which appear to have the same color under intuitively standard conditions of illumination but which appear to have different colors under unusual forms of illumination. This suggests that there are different colors which simply do not appear different under "ordinary" conditions of illumination.[6] Similar difficulties infect the notion of a "normal" observer, and some of these difficulties seem decisive. They lead us straight towards both the crippling objections I have been hinting about since Chapter Eight. But for the moment we'll remain with the first objection, the argument that there are no phenomenal colors of material objects.

It is important to note that there are probably significant differences in the phenomenal color experience of intuitively normal color perceivers even under fixed conditions of illumination. For instance, the spectral locus of unique green, the wavelength of light which a subject sees as a green without any other chromatic component, as neither yellowish nor bluish, is identified by a particular subject as the same wavelength from trial to trial with very little variation. But different "normal" observers identify wavelengths which range from 490 to 520 nanometers as the spectral locus of unique green. This is a range which any given subject will see as involving significant differences in phenomenal color, and which I see as ranging from quite yellowish to quite bluish greens.[7] The natural conclusion from this is that different "normal" humans do not really see a given object even in fixed and uniform illumination as possessing exactly the same phenomenal color. It's just that the differences are small enough to escape our ordinary notice. And there seems no reason to privilege one such normal human's color experience as "truer" than another's. So there is no "true" phenomenal color.

There are ways to resist this inference. One might grant that normal human color experience differs in the way suggested, and strain to specify some subset of intuitively normal perceivers as those who get the color right. But this seems terribly ad hoc and implausible. Alternatively, one might maintain that all normal perceivers have the same color experience, but claim that they "draw the line" between bluish and non-bluish green in different stable places, that their color words have slightly different meanings. But the preponderance of evidence on color words now suggests that they are not introduced in quite the arbitrary way which such an objection presumes.[8] For instance, Berlin and Kay's famous cross-cultural work suggests that color words are introduced into distinct languages in the same order and with the same foci.[9] And there is a plausible neurophysiological explanation[10] of the difference in the locus of unique green which further undercuts the claim that the problem is merely a problem about the meaning of color words.

This is a crucial point, so let me approach it quite slowly. First, let's talk a little about the general neurophysiology of color vision. Human color vision seems to be mediated by an "opponent-process" organization in early stages of visual processing, with sensory receptor cells immediately responsive to incoming light feeding into higher-level neurons which are responsive to the kinds of illumination which we see as black and white, or red and green, or blue and yellow, as opposing pairs of colors. A particular neural system seems to respond to so-called "green" and "red" light as in opposition, being active in one case and inhibited in the other. Various kinds of human color-blindness seem to correspond to particular deficiencies in these opponent systems. Some seem blind to the difference between red and green, for instance. And this plausibly reflects some deficiency in the red-green opponent system. There are many other pieces of evidence which suggest that the form of an individual's color experience reflects their peculiar neurophysiology. For instance, there have been cases in which someone who has been hit on the head has lost "color" vision entirely, has come to see everything in greys. But let me focus in particular on the way in which these considerations are relevant to the case immediately at hand, to our experience of unique green.

We have at least pieces of a reasonable *neurophysiological* explanation for the differences in "normal" experience of unique green. The spectral point where the so-called "yellow-blue" opponent system is neutrally balanced and the "green-red" system is tipped toward green might plausibly be identified with the experience of unique green. Unique green is greenish but neither yellowish nor bluish. So differences in individual perceptions of unique green might plausibly reflect small individual differences in the neurophysiology which underlies our color perception, small differences in the particular wavelengths which correspond to the neutral point in the yellow-blue opponent systems of different individuals. This suggests that the form of our color experience in fact reflects our neurophysiology as well as the true properties of the objects we view. The uniqueness of phenomenal colors is an artifact of our phenomenal experience. So there is no true phenomenal color of objects. The structure provided by unique colors is too deeply imbedded in phenomenal color to be factored out and leave a color behind, in fact to leave anything behind which is coherently conceivable, anything sufficiently saturated to be the characteristic intrinsic property of a microevent.

These considerations can be extended to encompass the other objection which we have been tracking since Part Two. I have been arguing that there are in fact no phenomenal properties of the sort deployed by simple objectual accounts. But plausible explanations of our supposedly color-responsive behavior would make them causally redundant in any case, and leave it a miracle that they were correlated with our behavior in the appropriate way. That point is also worth making at some length. This will also help reveal the full force of the considerations we've already deployed.

The neurophysiological differences which seem to explain differences in the experience of unique colors among normal humans, and which cause any differences in our behavior, aren't plausibly the sort of thing which would screen off some but not other normal humans from the true phenomenal colors of things. They seem rather to be differences in the way colorless radiation received at retinas by sensory receptor cells is processed, differences which seem to have nothing to do with the transparent or clouded receipt of true *phenomenal* colors of objects. Even if there were true phenomenal colors, they would play no legitimate explanatory role. Different people may be differentially sensitive to some causal *power* of an object, say to surface spectral reflectance, a disposition of the object to reflect certain sorts of light, but this we know from Part One is not a *phenomenal* color. It may be that some phenomenal similarities which are rooted in the opponent organization of our visual system *map*, are isomorphic to, causal properties, for instance tendencies to reflect various ratios of different sorts of light. But isomorphism alone is not match. Causal properties like surface spectral reflectance cannot constitute phenomenal color, no more than phenomenal sound can constitute phenomenal color. And it is important to note that there are limits even to an isomorphism of our color experience and causal properties of objects. Consider how the traditional color wheel rounds about, from red to purple to blue. Bluish-purple looks quite like reddish-purple. But the spectrum of corresponding wavelengths of light does not round the circle in this way.

If phenomenal color is not to be identified with any of the objective causal properties of objects to which our eyes respond, then phenomenal color seems to play no role in explaining our behaviors, for instance our matching of colored socks or speech about color. The semantic theory of Part One assures that phenomenal colors cannot be identified with powers to reflect light and hence to affect neural firing in visual systems. And according to our empirical color science, these causal properties are the only contribution of the objects we see to our experience of their color.

Let me make the point in a more global way. In part on the basis of arguments of the sort we are now considering, post-galilean science came to privilege certain properties of things, properties like mass and velocity and charge, as their true properties, and to disparage other apparent properties of those things, for instance phenomenal color, as mere artifacts of our experience. As we will see at greater length in Chapter Sixteen, these post-galilean properties are causal and spatio-temporal properties, at least to the degree that they are coherently conceivable. The charge of an electron seems to be its power to move oil drops and the like. And, in any case, since post-galilean science eliminated all phenomenal properties, causal powers were the only coherently conceivable characteristic intrinsic properties that remained to it. We know now that post-galilean science has been spectacularly successful. Galileo's gamble has borne fruit. Post-galilean science has even gone some way towards an adequate explanation of our color experience. And it is an explanation in which phenomenal colors of objects play no role: light of certain wavelengths and intensities is reflected from objects, and received by the eye in a certain environment of other illumination. It hits the retina and variously affects the visual sensory receptor cells--the cones and rods--and these modulate firing in various neurons, which fire other neurons in turn. Somehow this creates our experience of color. Nowhere in this story does the phenomenal color of objects play any role.

The defender of a simple objectual account of color experience can reasonably reply that a post-galilean explanation of our color experience is not really in hand unless the final chapter of this story is filled out in an appropriately post-galilean way, so that we can see for instance how neural firing of some sort can constitute our color experience. And, as such a defender may reasonably insist and we will see in the next chapter, there are grounds to doubt that this is possible. The explanatory work which phenomenal color properties must be deployed to perform, they may claim, is just to close this gap, to explain our phenomenal experience not by causing it but by helping to constitute it.

But even such a defender should admit the well-established part of the post-galilean story, the part which runs from material objects to sensory receptor cells. And that is not consistent with *too* great a role for phenomenal colors of the sort simple objectual accounts deploy. The phenomenal colors of objects, if there are any, don't affect neural firing, and hence don't seem to affect our behavior, not even our speech about color. Perhaps this shouldn't be surprising. Since phenomenal colors cannot be identified with causal powers, they *can't* have in the fullest sense any *causal* effects. They might still play a role in quasi-causal regularities. But there is nothing in the action of neurons or the machinations of particles as currently understood which suggests or leaves any room for such a quasi-causal "effect". Objective phenomenal colors, even if they did exist, would be implausibly epiphenomenal.

Still, the fan of the simple objectual accounts may insist, phenomenal colors may help constitute color experience, experience hence in some of its features bereft of causal effect on our neural firing and behavior. Constituting such an experience, they may insist, is role enough for phenomenal color. We see it, they may say, at least in part because it's there. Its being there is part of what constitutes us, not causes us, to see it. Change the color and the experience would be changed.

But still it would be a miracle if the phenomenal colors of objects lined up with their causal influence on our neurophysiology in just the right way. The phenomenal colors have no effects, and our color-responsive behavior is caused in a post-galilean way. So there is no reason at all to expect that, even if there were phenomenal colors, they would be correlated in the right way with our behavior. The correlation would be miraculous. It would be the kind of miraculous correlation which, since Galileo, our very successful science has eschewed. That's the second sort of objection noted in Chapter Eight.

And there's another point. To see the full force of both our objections, it's worth seeing how they work together. Simple objectual accounts involve the postulation of a true phenomenal color for an object, a color which seems to have no causal effect on neural firing in the visual system, or on our behavior, but which serves merely to help constitute the appropriate phenomenal color experience. But remember that there are *differences* in color experience among different normal observers, even in standard conditions of illumination. Even this is consistent with the existence of a unique and true phenomenal color, of course, but such a color is not very well suited to play the only role in which it is cast for us, the role of helping to constitute the color experience of various normal observers. Plausible simple objectual accounts must give some explanation of the differences in color experience among intuitively normal observers with different loci of unique green, an explanation which yet meshes with some crucial role for the single true phenomenal color of a green object in constituting our visual experience of that object. But it seems quite implausible that one can factor out this artifact of our color experience from possibly veridical features in any plausible way. If we can explain the artifacts of normal human experience of unique green in some other way than by phenomenal colors of planets and balls, and it seems we must, then an alternative explanation of the other features of our experience of green should also be available. And it seems that it would be the more plausible mesh with the requisite explanation of those artifacts. Differences in our experience of unique green show that the artifacts of our color experience are so deeply imbedded in the phenomenal colors which objects seem to us to have that simple objectual accounts of our experience of color are implausible.

Again, if we can explain the differences among normal experiences of unique green without deploying simple objectual resources, and we must, then we should also be able to explain the similarities among normal human color experiences in an analogous way. And even if we had to tell an objectual story about those similarities, it isn't clear what it might be. An abstract but concrete phenomenal color of the sort required, a property of saturated concrete objects which yet fuzzes out the differences among normal experiences of unique colors, is not even coherently conceivable.[11]

I have focussed primarily on normal human color experience. But we should also ask ourselves, given what seems the plausible root in our neurophysiology of the differences in normal human experience of unique green, whether normal human color experience deserves the privileged status which traditional simple objectual accounts presume. As was in fact suggested by our previous discussion of neurophysiology and color-blindness, color-blind humans may not be so much blind as different, with a different form of equally misleading color experience. They cannot sort some objects in some ways that normal humans can, but not even normal humans can sort metamers in standard illumination. And perhaps we should remember that while humans have three kinds of sensory receptor cells responsive to three different ranges of "colors" of light, pigeons have four.

The world does not possess the sort of phenomenal color which normal humans experience it to have. And even if the world could include such a contradictory color, it would play no plausible role in explaining our supposedly color-responsive behaviors and speech. In fact, it would be miraculous if it fit those behaviors and speech. Simple objectual accounts of our experience of phenomenal color are flatly implausible.

That's the main point of this section. But let me do a bit of house-keeping before we move on. Some may be tempted to answer perceptual relativity arguments against simple objectual accounts[12] with the claim that different observers are after all seeing different light, light which might have different objective phenomenal properties. We will return to this sort of response in the next section. An alternative answer would deploy objects with relativized but irreducible phenomenal color properties, so that a planet might be irreducibly unique-green-for-Galileo and slightly-bluish-for-me. But such properties are not coherently conceivable. So we need another route.

Let me stress how shocking this situation is, because philosophers have a long-standing tendency to avert their eyes at exactly this crucial point. The arguments I have given are in essence quite old. They are Galileo's arguments, arguments which in turn took inspiration from arguments of the epicureans. Buttressed by what we know now, by what color science has shown us, they have a great deal of force. But it is important to keep squarely in front of our eyes how radical their conclusion is. Our normal human experience is, at least in one respect, radically misleading. That should be shocking. What, we might wonder, seems more evident to us than that things have colors? If we can't even trust our eyes about that, then what can we trust?

Indeed, as we will see, close analogues of these arguments will suggest that our experience is radically misleading in a myriad of other ways. In effect, this part will several times retrace arguments of just the sort we have reviewed here, as they gradually erase all the features of the world which our experience seems to reveal. Such arguments are radical arguments, no matter how old and familiar they are. But so great is the pressure to believe our eyes that philosophers have been tempted here by what ought to seem obvious and implausible tricks and self-deception. Descartes claimed that experience itself is neither true nor false, as if it did not present objects as being one way or another. And many later philosophers claim that even the ordinary, traditional conception of color rooted in our experience is the notion of a power, a power to cause varying sensory experiences. They not only substitute for the traditional notion of color a revised notion, but they claim that the revised notion *is* the traditional notion. But let's not kid ourselves. The color which we experience balls and planets to have, phenomenal color, color of the sort discussed in Part One, color as traditionally understood, is not out there in the world.

3

There are other objectual accounts than simple ones. The galilean expulsion of phenomenal color from the world of ordinary material objects prompted all sorts of elaborate attempts to put it back somewhere else. Some thought that our experience was infallible. So if we experienced color, then something had a color. Others thought that at least our access to the content of our experience was infallible or at least beyond reasonable doubt, and couldn't see how we could possibly experience color unless something had color. They thought that there had to be some things with phenomenal color to help constitute our experience of color, even if ordinary material objects like trees and balls lacked color. Perhaps these people should have known better, and perhaps we do now. But this section concerns their baroque alternatives.

I will begin by considering the plausibility of accounts of our color experience which crucially employ not red and public planets, but rather private objects, red sense data. I have spoken of sense data as if they were internal, under our hats. But they are instances of a more general sort of object. The accounts in which they figure are examples of a more general sort of account, which we must consider in all its forms. Sense data are what I will call *subjective* objects. The particular sense datum which is involved in constituting the visual experience of a particular thing depends on whose experience it is. A subjective objectual account of our visual experience of one planet postulates *distinct* objects with distinct phenomenal colors, or at least distinct instances of a single phenomenal color, as crucial constituents of the experience of that planet by different people.

Subjective objectual accounts are well-placed to avoid some of the difficulties which face simple objectual accounts. Perceptual relativity arguments are less telling against such accounts, since they can invoke different objects with different colors as constituents of each subject's experience. For instance, they may postulate for each person in each sort of light a different sense datum with a different phenomenal color. Differences in the spectral location of unique green, to pick another example, present little difficulty for such accounts. Indeed, some subjective objectual accounts can attribute all the mere artifacts of our visual experience to features of the relevant subjective objects, objects in which for instance the images of distant objects *are* smaller. So those subjective objectual accounts do not face the hard task of at once factoring out mere artifacts of our color experience from phenomenal reality, and yet integrating an account of the experience of those mere artifacts with an objectual account of the putatively veridical features of phenomenal experience. Subjective objectual accounts clearly have some advantages over simple objectual accounts.

But there are other traditional difficulties which subjective objectual accounts must face and which simple objectual accounts avoid. And they share certain other difficulties with the simple objectual accounts. Together these difficulties show that subjective objectual accounts are pretty implausible.

As I said, we will begin by considering merely one kind of subjective objectual account, involving sense data. Phenomenal sense data, constituted merely by microevents with phenomenal intrinsic properties, may have phenomenal properties like color, but no causal powers. So colorful sense data have no power to affect neurons and hence behavior, even our speech about color or our sorting of objects by color. These sense data are simply objects which play a crucial role in constituting certain firing patterns to be thoughts with particular contents, at least if we cede to neurophysiological states, as plausibility requires, the role they played in Part Two. Sense data are miraculously suited for just their task. And that in fact is just the problem. They are just too miraculous.

Let me elaborate first on their causal inefficacy. One might propose that colorful sense data involve a *fusion* of color microevents with causal microevents, so that different sense data in fact have different causal powers. But if this did happen in an appropriate way, it would be another miraculous correlation. And notice that this would be a kind of fusion which cannot appear within anyone's experience, so hence may not be coherently conceivable. The causal-color fusion which appears within experience is the fusion of the powers of material objects with their colors. And even if this alternative sort of fusion is coherently conceivable, the colors *themselves* are not powers, and have no powers. Of course, phenomenal colors might enter into interesting quasi-causal regularities. But color microevents lack powers in the full sense, powers which seem characteristic of the particles which make up the world according to classical post-galilean conceptions. And our understanding of the causal structure of the world, in which particles exhibit no perturbations which cannot be explained appropriately on the basis of the powers of other particles or other galilean phenomena, seems to exclude any plausible role for sense data in quasi-causal regularities of this kind. They seem epiphenomenal.

That is the first problem with colorful sense data, which is quite like familiar problems suffered by phenomenal colors of public objects. They don't affect our speech about color, or our color-matching behavior. But there is yet another, more characteristic problem as well. Considering that other problem can help us see the full force of the first. Subjective objectual accounts must provide some way to distinguish the particular subjective objects which help constitute the color experience of different subjects, a way for instance to tie the right sense data to the right neurons in the right head. And if a subjective objectual account is to be coherently conceivable, then that tie must be expressible within the resources of C. But C provides quite limited resources. The sort of spatio-temporal coincidence which C can express, of for instance a power with a color and a taste, is not a very helpful resource. Certainly the relation between a colorful sense datum and the neurons which it is supposed to help constitute as a particular thought cannot appear as a fusion within anyone's experience. The subject of the experience doesn't experience the neurons, at least *as* neurons, and some experimenter, having opened the subject's skull, would not experience the sense datum, at least *as* a color sense datum of the right kind. Fusion allows us to coherently conceive neurons with phenomenal colors, but not firing grey neurons which are the experience of red, which are red so to speak "on the inside". Perhaps a particular set of neurons is supposed to *causally* generate the appropriate sense data; perhaps the requisite tie is causal. This is coherently conceivable, but the particular sort of causal powers and connections this requires do not seem plausible. One way to see this is to consider how this objection works together with the last, in the traditional problem of emergence.

If simple objectual accounts of color experience are wrong and planets have no color, if something like a post-galilean picture of non-sentient things, of stars and planets and other things present in the world previous to the evolution of nervous systems, is correct, if such things are constituted by particles with powers and standing in spatio-temporal relations, then the oddity of colorful sense data is straightforward: At a certain point in the evolution of life, life constituted by physical particles of the same sorts which constitute the rocks and stars, suddenly a nervous system, of a certain structural complexity but involving no unfamiliar particles or kinds of spatio-temporal relations among them, exhibits radically unfamiliar causal powers, or at least radically unfamiliar aspects of its causal powers, and secretes colorful sense data. And this wonder is repeated in the growth of each individual up from sperm and egg. These new entities are so radically discontinuous from what came before that basic contents must admit a whole new class of intrinsic properties, phenomenal properties, to match them. But that is only half of the mystery of emergence.

What miraculous entities these sense data are, exactly suited to play the role of fixing a content for the thoughts of the animals which secrete them. The properties of visual sense data in humans exactly match the kind of verbal behaviors and discriminations which the human nervous system causes, without causally influencing that nervous system or those behaviors. Visual-processing is organized in an opponent-process mode, and we find that humans secrete sense data which match that opponent organization, in which there is a phenomenal opposition between red and green and between blue and yellow. People differ in the point at which the blue-yellow opponent system is in a neutral state and the red-green system is tipped towards green, and they secrete sense data which are exactly appropriate to help constitute their varying experiences of unique green.

While these sense data are "appropriate" to our nervous systems, so that for instance we can talk about them in an accurate way despite the fact that they have no causal influence even on our verbal behavior, still that appropriate match-up is not one which suggests a causal dependency of the sense data on the nervous system of an at all familiar or plausible sort. The causal powers of a nervous system which secretes sense data don't arise straightforwardly out of the ordinary powers and spatio-temporal arrangements of the molecules which make it up in the way which we have come to expect. Certainly computers and automobiles and human bodies do things which the ancient Greek philosophers might never have expected ordinary non-living matter to be capable of, but we have come to an understanding of how the ordinary powers of tiny particles in the right arrangements might sum up to such capacities. And the powers which the nervous system exhibits if it secretes just the right sense data are quite different, miraculously and unfamiliarly emergent. They allow firing neurons to generate a radically new kind of stuff, phenomenal stuff, when all our ordinary post-galilean understanding of the world would lead us to expect otherwise. And this new stuff is quite miraculously just the sort of thing which can fix the kinds of contents for thoughts which would be appropriate given our neurophysiology and behavior, even though they have no effect on our neurophysiology and behavior. It is rather as if we found that inscriptions of the word "planet" had the power to cause the existence of planets in some distant galaxy. It is magic, and magic isn't plausible. Subjective objectual accounts of color experience are implausible, at least if they take anything like the form we have so far considered.

There are alternative forms of subjective objectual account which we should consider. If the particular account which we have just considered is implausible, still other forms of subjective objectual account may not be. One traditional response to the argument from emergence is panpsychism, the suggestion that to each entity of the world, not merely to each suitable nervous system, there corresponds at least some primitive sort of phenomenal experience. On this view, it is as much like something to be a planet or ball as to be a bat or a human.

There are different varieties of panpsychism, but we need only consider subjective objectual variations. Let me elaborate such a view:

It's not that causal powers unknown in the history of the world are suddenly released when neurons are arranged in the right way. It's just that the phenomenal "insides" or sense data of things like stars and balloons are ignored in our classical post-galilean conception of those things, in which we treat them as constituted merely by particles with powers and spatio-temporal properties of traditional physical sorts. We see objects to have color on the outside. They don't. But still somehow they have phenomenal properties on the "inside", in their experience, just as we do. And these are real phenomenal properties in the world, if admittedly in odd, unfamiliar, and private corners of the world.

There are a number of difficulties with panpsychism. We still don't have a coherently conceivable account of the "tie" between an entity and its phenomenal "inside", except the causal one we have been considering. And it doesn't make that sort of causation any less implausible to claim that it is widespread. More magic is not more plausible than a little. And there are also special difficulties with the view at hand. The way in which human phenomenal experience is appropriate to the human nervous system and behavior is not easy to project onto balls and balloons.

If we are constrained by coherent conceivability and hence C, the appropriate phenomenal experience of a planet is hard to construe. It seems implausible to claim that it involves any of the particular intrinsic phenomenal properties invoked by C, for instance color or sound or the like, though simple pressure-like experience might represent one remote possibility. We have even less sense of what it might be like to be a planet than we do of what it might be like to be a bat. To take panpsychism seriously is probably to think that C, rooted in *human* experience, cannot capture the whole truth. But then, of course, we fail to coherently conceive what panpsychism demands.

And independent of these worries about coherent conceivability, there are reasons to think that phenomenal experience, which in the familiar human case is reflected in our behavior and neurophysiology in various ways, is especially the province of nervous systems and their close analogues, the physical things which help constitute *ordinary* psychologies. For instance, there seems to be no obvious reason why a planet rather than merely just half a planet or a planet surface or a continent or a particular molecule should possess a unitary phenomenal experience. But this does seem appropriate for a creature which has a single nervous system, which in some recognizable way acts on and responds to things of the sort it experiences as a single unified entity. And remember that we have already seen a number of ways in which our particular phenomenal experience seems appropriate to our particular neurophysiology. The phenomenal opposition of red and green seems to reflect the opponent-process organization of our visual system, and unique green seems to mirror the neutral position of the blue-yellow system. Also, our phenomenal experience seems appropriate to our behavior and judgment, say our color matching and speech about colors, and this behavior and judgment seems in turn constrained by our neural firing. But it is hard to locate specific enough analogues for either neural processing or the action which it controls in a planet. Planets seem plausibly not to possess even particular sense organs or motor organs. Perhaps all they suffer is what they sense, and how they suffer it is their sense organ. Perhaps all they do is their action, and how they do it their motor organ. And perhaps all that intervenes is their analogue of a nervous system. But this generates no obvious constraint at all on the kind of phenomenal experience which might be properly attributed to them. It suggests no particular number of axes along which the phenomenal properties which they experience might differ. At least cars and typewriters possess some stable mechanism which intervenes between an obvious range of specific inputs and specific outputs, but stars and planets and balloons and balls lack even that. Even our understanding of possible bat experience is greater than this; we can at least see that individual bats might plausibly have a single experience, and we understand something of its parameters.

A particular phenomenal experience is no more plausibly attributed to a planet, or cars and typewriters for that matter, than are particular desires. We can insist that a planet has a dull experience without many parameters, corresponding for instance to the pressure it feels, but just as plausibly that it has rather dull desires, to be wherever it is. Certainly the post-galilean conception of material things is more plausible than such an animism.

There are yet other kinds of subjective objectual account, which steer even farther from the traditional post-galilean conception of balls and stars. We should give these at least brief attention. A number of philosophers in this century--Russell and Price among others--suggested a model of balls and balloons and planets in which such "material objects" were collections of subjective objects, one for each of the views some experiencer might have of them.[13] In their standard form, such views are not very plausible. They fly in the face of the wonderful success of post-galilean science, with its causal conception of objects as constituted from particles with locations and powers. But perhaps the post-galilean component of a planet is somehow accompanied by the whole collection of the possible phenomenal views which might be had of it, and the whole complex constitutes the planet. Still, if such a hybrid conception of a planet is to be plausible, then it should probably include not only the views which various humans might have of it, across the full range of possible illuminations and orientations, but also those of tetra-chromatic pigeons and exotic Martians. This would put such an alternative, like a reasonable panpsychism, well beyond the resources of C, well beyond coherent conceivability. And it is far from clear that the principle by which various phenomenal views are agglomerated together with the post-galilean portion of a star is expressible in C, short of a causal tie of another improbable form.

But the most telling objection to such a conception of material objects lies in the now familiar way in which features of our phenomenal experience of a planet reflect *our* neurophysiology, and nothing objective about the planet. Our experience of the planet is appropriate given just the discriminations and judgments which we make and the kind of neurophysiology which we possess. It would be beyond miraculous if the planet itself were handily prepared for our neurophysiology, as well as all other possible nervous systems and analogues, with a neatly cooperating phenomenal view which might help constitute an appropriate experience of itself. These phenomenal guises, according to a plausible post-galilean conception of the world, have no effects, so they certainly didn't affect the evolution of our nervous systems.

The way in which our phenomenal experience is appropriate to our neurophysiology points towards non-objectual accounts. But before we turn to such accounts, we have some final bits of house-keeping. There are objectual accounts of color experience which deploy different resources than we have yet explicitly considered. For instance, some may feel the temptation to advert to the phenomenal color of some medium, say to the color of radiation as it hits a retina or of a ghostly sensible species thrown off by the surface of a colored object. In fact, we have yet to consider in any explicit way the most sophisticated variants of the aristotelian view of visual perception which we discussed in Chapter Twelve. The phenomenal color which was supposed by those accounts to constitute our color experience was arrayed along the surface of the retina, after having traveled from object to eye. Traditional aristotelian accounts are all simple objectual accounts in one sense, because all of those accounts presume that material objects have colors, and indeed that any sensible species which fly off the objects towards our eyes entail the existence of such colors, are dependent in being. But of course there might be variants which avoided these particular commitments.

One problem with accounts which advert to the phenomenal colors of light rays or images on the retina is that there obviously are none, at least if phenomenal color is something which humans can perceive. The light entering the eye and the inside of the retina do not in fact supply the little phenomenal images such accounts presume. But, in any case, it is obvious that these phenomenal images would play no causal role in explaining the action of the sensory receptor cells in the retina, the cones and rods, and those cells seem clearly to mediate the effects of the objects we see on our behaviors and speech. Such accounts require a now familiar but still miraculous coordination between the phenomenal and causal, a coordination which we post-galileans should not take seriously. What's more, these accounts would face grave difficulties in providing an explanation of the differences in our experience of unique green. Perhaps our nervous systems might be supposed in some way to causally affect the phenomenal images on our retinas or entering our eyes. But this again seems massively implausible, even if there are those tiny pictures.

There are other models possible. For instance, some may insist that the traditional way of dividing up perceptual acts into an object, medium, and subject of experience is misleading, so that phenomenal color is not to be located specifically on the object, or in the medium, or somewhere inside the subject of the experience, at the expense of the other locations. But the arguments we have canvassed in this chapter in fact address these possibilities. Either objectual accounts of color experience involve subjective objects, which differ from experiencer to experiencer, or they do not. If they do not, they are implausible because of the perceptual relativity arguments of section 2. And if they do involve subjective objects, then those subjective objects seem to reflect, in the way we have reviewed in this section, properties of our nervous systems, without having any plausible causal commerce with our nervous systems. Objectual accounts of our color experience are not plausible. Objects with phenomenal color are not constituents of plausible basic contents.

4

So far we have only discussed phenomenal colors, the intrinsic phenomenal properties characteristic of visual experience. But there is little grounds for hope that objectual accounts of other characteristic intrinsic phenomenal properties fare any better.

Chapter Six discussed several classes of characteristic intrinsic phenomenal properties: phenomenal sounds, phenomenal tastes, phenomenal smells, phenomenal heat, phenomenal pressure, and the phenomenal properties characteristic of pain and the various emotions and feelings with phenomenal components.

That last class of phenomenal properties is so obviously subject to perceptual relativity arguments, so obviously involves states of the subject of the experience as well as states of "external" material objects like balls and balloons, as to be ignored even in commonsense conceptions of those external things. Such properties cannot help much in plausible accounts of our experience of planets. On the other hand, they might just conceivably help us in developing an objectual account of our experience of our own bodies, though not of our experience of other people's bodies. Consider for instance pain. Might a leg pain I feel be in fact an object, with the property painfulness, located within my body? If so, then it is a very unusual and implausible object. Someone else might thrust their fingers inside my leg and not feel that pain. It must be an object which is only accessible to me. This is implausible. It is as implausible as the subjective objects with phenomenal color we discussed in the last section, and for the same reasons.

The rest of the intrinsic phenomenal properties fall prey to perceptual relativity arguments familiar from Galileo and Berkeley: the phenomenal sounds of things depend on whether they are fast approaching or receding from us, the tastes and smells of things depend on what else we've recently smelled or tasted, the felt temperature of a room goes up when we come in out of the cold, the felt pressure which an object seems to exert depends on what else we've recently lifted. Nor is it plausible to reply that the "true" sounds, tastes, odors, and such are those perceived by normal human observers in certain "standard" circumstances. Even independently of perceptual relativity arguments, we have seen that the intrinsic phenomenal properties are not very plausible constituents of external objects. The form of our experience of these phenomenal properties, like our experience of color, seems obviously rooted in our peculiar human neurophysiology. It reflects our neurophysiology at least as much as any objective properties of the material objects we perceive. Phenomenal properties of objects seem ill-suited to help explain our experience. And phenomenal sense data and similar entities are no more plausible in these cases than in the case of phenomenal color.

We have seen that no objectual account of the experience of the characteristic intrinsic phenomenal properties is plausible, and indeed that true basic contents include no microevents with such properties. Since there are no phenomenal microevents without characteristic intrinsic phenomenal properties, we are left with few coherently conceivable resources for the realization of our color experience, and phenomenal experience generally. Objects with phenomenal intrinsic properties other than colors weren't likely to be of much help in the realization of color experience, anyway. But still, we are down to very few resources. It seems that plausible basic contents consist merely of causal microevents, standing in spatio-temporal relations, and that plausible and coherently conceivable accounts of the realization of our phenomenal experience must make do with those limited resources. Perhaps we can take some comfort from the fact that this is a traditional post-galilean conception of the world.

NOTES

1. One other traditional class of arguments against simple objectual accounts of experience and phenomenal properties on material objects are "arguments from illusion". One sort goes like this:

P1) Simple objectual accounts do not provide plausible explanations of certain obviously illusory experiences of objects with phenomenal properties of type X, say certain phenomenal colors.

P2) But if P1, then simple objectual accounts do not provide plausible explanations of ordinary, apparently veridical experiences of objects with phenomenal properties of type X, for instance colors.

Arguments with this general form are not always convincing. It does not seem to follow from the fact that an actual bent shape is not part of the plausible explanation of how a stick or a rocket looks when it sticks up out of a water-filled canal that a bent shape is never part of the plausible explanation of an ordinary, veridical experience of bent shape. But some arguments of this form do seem to have some force. For instance, someone might reasonably object to my waffling claim in the last part that dreams and hallucinations involve quasi-experience. They might insist that we seem to have the *experience* of color, say the color of a purple planet, in hallucinations and dreams. And it is not plausible to explain this by postulating a realm of dream or hallucinatory ghost-objects, purple planets only the mad or dreaming can see. If hallucinatory experience of purple can be explained in other than a simple objectual way, it may seem plausible that we can and should explain ordinary experience of purple in that same other way. If the primary imagination does in fact involve a kind of faint experience, then it provides a wide class of important examples of this type.

Such a traditional argument is not in itself obviously decisive. One might for instance deny that there really is any dream experience of color. Perhaps higher-order abstracted thought, and not experience *per se*, is what dreams really involve. Or dreams and the primary imagination might involve mere quasi-experience. And even if simple objectual accounts aren't part of an appropriate explanation of the *illusory* experience of some property, still some may insist that they are the appropriate explanation of our ordinary, veridical experience of that property. There are other kinds of argument from illusion, but neither are they obviously decisive against simple objectual accounts of at least our ordinary experience. An argument based on our apparently illusory experience of a colored rainbow, which may be seen by different observers to be in different places, or of the evanescent color on a CD, might be defused by an account which adverts to the phenomenal colors not of a single material rainbow or CD, but rather of light, say as it strikes retinas. An argument rooted in our experience of a dead blue star, long burnt out but far enough away so that its light is still reaching us, might be defused by an account which deploys either the phenomenal color of the light, or even the *past* phenomenal color of the dead star. Alternatively, a friend of simple objectual accounts may insist that these other sorts of illusory experience require no objectual account, but that a simple objectual account of *ordinary* experience is plausible. While arguments from illusion are not decisive, they do suggest that something which fulfills much of the causal-explanatory role of phenomenal experience might exist independently of phenomenal color. The primary imagination involves at least *quasi*-experience. It seems to me that this should at least soften us up for the other set of traditional arguments.

2. Though not quite as much as one might expect.

3. In effect, this response tries to treat perceptual relativity arguments as arguments from illusion.

4. C. L. Hardin, *Color for Philosophers*. Hardin actually deploys these arguments against the identification of phenomenal colors with certain causal properties. But they also can serve well in the role in which they are deployed here.

5. Hardin, 67-77.

6. Hardin, 28.

7. Hardin, 79.

8. Hardin, 155-186.

9. P. Berlin and P. Kay, *Basic Color Terms* (Berkeley: University of California Press, 1969).

10. In light of our discussion in the next chapter, perhaps I should say "partial explanation".

11. If we can coherently conceive fuzzy colors, perhaps because we can see them out of the corner of our eyes, out at the edge of the visual field, then they might possibly be a helpful resource here. But they are not a very plausible one. Even these fuzzy colors wouldn't be so fuzzy as to avoid many of the correlational miracles we have been discussing.

12. In one way some arguments from illusion can be answered.

13. My favorite is H.H. Price, *Perception* (London: Methuen, 1932).

CHAPTER FIFTEEN

MERE PHENOMENAL EXPERIENCE

We are left with few resources in our attempt to construct a plausible account of the realization of our experience. Nothing with the characteristic intrinsic phenomenal properties remains. The only coherently conceivable resources still available are causal microevents, standing in spatio-temporal relations. But that may seem enough. Our post-galilean tradition holds, at least on one natural interpretation, that the true and objective properties and relations of things are those which our physics uncovers, and those properties and relations seem to be causal powers and spatio-temporal relations. The charge of an electron and its mass seem to be capacities to affect other particles in various ways, as the electron moves through space.

There may be worries about this interpretation of our post-galilean heritage, but let me ignore those worries until next chapter. At least on the surface, it seems that plausible basic contents consisting of causal microevents might include post-galilean versions of our nervous systems, with phenomenally colorless neurons which yet possess all of their intuitive electro-chemical properties intact. They might also include states of a planet which Galileo falsely experienced to be red, and of intervening radiative media. These "physicalist" resources are commonly thought sufficient to constitute phenomenal experience.

We know now that a plausible account of the realization of our experience of the characteristic intrinsic phenomenal properties must be a non-objectual account. A non-objectual account of the experience of a planet as phenomenal red might imply, for instance, that a collection of post-galilean particles, which makes up in turn a colorless firing mass of post-galilean neurons, can constitute someone with the experience of such a red planet, just as a collection of objects which includes no Martians can constitute someone who believes in Martians. This chapter concerns the plausibility and coherent conceivability of non-objectual accounts. I will again delay discussion of the spatio-temporal structure of experience, and focus primarily on phenomenal color.

We will soon see reason to deny that non-objectual accounts of our color experience, and indeed any non-objectual account of our experience of any characteristic intrinsic phenomenal property, can be at once plausible and coherently conceivable. The deep problems are problems of conceivability rather than plausibility. Nevertheless, I will begin with traditional objections to the *truth* of non-objectual accounts.

1

There are two classes of traditional arguments against the claim that the experience of phenomenal color might be constituted by the action of the nervous system or other physical structures: arguments from conceivability and arguments from knowledge. Arguments from conceivability are at least as old as Descartes' argument in the sixth *Meditation* for the "real distinction between the mind and the body". They traverse something like these steps:

1) It can be conceived that there is someone with a neurophysiology and physical environment just like Galileo's, but with no phenomenal experience at all, or with a phenomenal experience in which phenomenal colors are *inverted*, say in which phenomenal red and green are transposed relative to their positions in Galileo's own experience and in which there are corresponding and consistent changes throughout the visual spectrum. Things which seem phenomenal red to normal humans would seem phenomenal green to someone with such an inverted form of color experience. But they would have learned to call "red" what they see as phenomenal green. They would behave just like people with normal color experience, right down to their speech about color.

2) But if this is conceivable, then it is possible also.

3) And if it is possible, then Galileo's neurophysiology and physical environment doesn't in fact suffice to constitute his phenomenal experience.

It may seem easy to resist the second and third steps of such an argument. Certainly we can in some sense conceive even the *im*possible. And it doesn't obviously follow from the mere *possibility* that there be a neurophysiology and physical situation just like Galileo's without his particular sort of color experience that *in fact* that doesn't constitute his experience. And recall that the content theory of Part One implies that much modality is a mere artifact of the approach apparatus anyway.

On the other hand, we also possess some resources to reinforce such an argument. For instance, *coherent* conceivability seems a mark of at least one kind of possibility; it seems to reveal a way the world in some sense might be. More generally, if conceivability of some regimented kind does not constitute our access to what is possible, then it is not clear what does.[1] Also, we saw in Part One that constitution must be underwritten by a semantic dependency of the constituted on what constitutes it, and this ensures necessity of a kind, ensures that one *cannot* have in fact what constitutes something without also having it. Still, I won't directly pursue arguments from conceivability here, because the proper understanding of arguments from knowledge can yield a plausible argument against non-objectual accounts of our color experience which also captures the intuitive force behind conceivability arguments. Traditional arguments from knowledge have this rough form:

P1) One can know all the neurophysiological facts about someone, and indeed all the physical facts about them and their world, and yet not know what sort of phenomenal experience they have, in particular what phenomenal colors they experience.

P2) If P1 is true, then all the neurophysiological facts about that person, and indeed all the physical facts about them and their world, do not suffice to constitute them to have the phenomenal experience, and in particular the color experience, they do.

This form of argument also seems open to immediate objection. P1 is ambiguous. There is more than a little obscurity concerning what all the neurophysiological and physical facts about someone are. After all, if they include facts about what phenomenal experiences accompany what neural firings, then the argument is trivially unsound. And P2 also seems questionable. Wouldn't it be possible to know all the detailed inner workings of a calculator and its physical environment and not know that the thing as a whole performed calculations, or of a watch and not know that it kept time, or of a sample of H-O-H and not know that it was water? But we wouldn't take that as evidence that the physical machinations of a calculator do not constitute its calculations, or that watches and water are immaterial things.

However, arguments from knowledge can be reformulated in such a way as to at once remove these objections, deploy some resources provided by the content theory of Part One, and reveal their similarity to traditional arguments from conceivability.

Before I do that, let me review some vivid forms the argument has assumed.[2] Here's Michael Tye's version of Frank Jackson's case: "Suppose that Jones is an extraordinarily brilliant scientist...who has acquired exhaustive knowledge of what goes on in us physically when we see colors and use color words. Suppose also that Jones is congenitally blind...Is there anything that Jones does not know that his fellows with normal color vision do? The natural and obvious response to this question is 'He doesn't know what red, green, blue, and so on look like.' But ex hypothesi he has all the knowledge there is to have about what is going on in the optic nerves, the brain, the central nervous system, and the vocal chords of his fellows when light of various wavelengths strikes their eyes and they respond by saying, 'This is red', 'That is green', 'That is blue.' It follows that there is knowledge of experiential facts that lies beyond the reach of any physicalist theory."[3] Jackson also has another case, in which normal humans try to understand the experience of Fred, who can sharply distinguish between two colors, red_1 and red_2, within the red spectrum: "What kind of experience does Fred have when he sees red_1 and red_2? What is the new colour or colours like? We would dearly like to know but do not; and it seems that no amount of physical information about Fred's brain and optical system tells us. We find out perhaps that Fred's cones respond differentially to certain light waves in the red section of the spectrum that make no difference to ours...and that this leads in Fred to a wider range of those brain states responsible for visual discriminatory behavior. But none of this tells us what we really want to know..."[4] B.D. Farrell and

Thomas Nagel have made us wonder about even more foreign cases, about what humans even with full knowledge of the relevant neurophysiology and physical facts could know about the phenomenal experience of bats, with their quite different sensory systems, or of Martians of some suitably exotic kind.[5] Bats can experience through their sonar details of the world of a complexity it is impossible to imagine hearing in anything like the normal human way, through experience of human phenomenal sound. Our best grasp at what they "hear" is visual, but it is very unlikely that what they hear is what we see, is human phenomenal color. Bats and tetra-chromatic pigeons and Martians experience phenomenal colors or other characteristic intrinsic phenomenal properties of a sort we humans cannot imagine. Traditional inverted and absent spectrum cases generate still other knowledge arguments: One might know all there is to know about Galileo's neurophysiology and his physical environment, even that it was identical to one's own, and still not know that his color experience was not inverted relative to one's own, and still not know even that he had phenomenal experience.[6]

While some details of these cases may raise questions, they do possess a good deal of intuitive force. One way to properly deploy that force is this. Assume that a post-galilean conception of the world is at least roughly correct, so that the traditional physicalist conception of nervous systems and other material objects captures at least much of the truth about such things. And let "BC" be the most detailed true causal basic content, that basic content which i) consists merely of causal and not phenomenal microevents, and ii) captures all the post-galilean features of the world. Then consider this argument against a post-galilean non-objectual account of Galileo's color experience:

P1) *If one knew that BC were true, one would know enough to fix any truth about Galileo's neurophysiology or about anything else which such a non-objectual view could deploy in a coherently conceivable account of Galileo's phenomenal experience.* This premise is underwritten by the content theory of Part One. Any more inclusive true basic content would have to involve phenomenal microevents which are forbidden by the arguments of the last chapter and eschewed by traditional post-galilean non-objectual accounts, or other sorts of elements which are beyond the resources of C and hence which are not coherently conceivable. And BC is a *basic* content. Hence it would fix the truth of the other contents which depend on it, including contents encompassing neurons. If neurons are post-galilean resources, then BC captures what constitutes them. This is a semantic necessity, rooted in the dependency on basic contents of the relatively abstracted and cooked contents which we conceive when we think explicitly of neurons. It is a semantic necessity that such microevents as are present in BC would constitute such a neurophysiology.

P2) *But if one knew that BC were true, one would not know enough to fix all the truth about Galileo's phenomenal experience, in particular that it involved particular phenomenal colors.* This is a premise which the vivid cases just considered seem to establish. P1 is underwritten by the content theory of Part One. And P2 seems supported by the vivid examples we have surveyed. But together they spell trouble for non-objectual accounts, once we note some seemingly obvious facts about content dependency: If the truth of some basic content A suffices to fix the truth of another content B, but does not suffice to fix in its entirety the truth of a third content C, then clearly the truth of B cannot serve to fix the truth of C in its entirety. B is not sufficient to constitute all that C involves. A proper account of everything in C must invoke more resources than B provides. Hence our third premise:

P3) *If P1 and P2, then a post-galilean non-objectual account of our phenomenal experience, and in particular of our color experience, is at best incomplete, and in fact any coherently conceivable non-objectual account is so also.*

Someone might wonder if there is some special detail of post-galilean orthodoxy which creates this difficulty. But no causal and spatio-temporal alternative to post-galilean orthodoxy seems to offer viable help. So we are in a bind. Objectual accounts are implausible, because there are no objects with phenomenal color. But no plausible and coherently conceivable non-objectual account of color experience seems available to us. This bind puts lots of pressure on the knowledge argument. At least if we place the content theory of Part One momentarily beyond the range of criticism, my reformulation seems to locate the major stress at P2. But that is where it belongs. We'll turn to important objections to P2 and to arguments from knowledge in general in the following sections. First a little commentary:

This reformulation reveals the argument from knowledge to be a kind of semantic argument, which places great importance on semantic relations between contents. According to the content theory of Part One, that is just as it should be. We are considering what might *constitute* Galileo's color experience, and constitution is a semantic relation. Recall our discussion in Chapter Five. If some coherently conceivable phenomenon A is to constitute coherently conceivable phenomenon B, then it must be semantically necessary that A suffice for B. Perhaps other things would suffice for B also, but it must be necessary that A do so. This reflects the semantic dependency of the representational content of thought of B on the representational content of thought of A, among perhaps other contents. There might be lots of different things which could serve to constitute something, and it might take a good deal of empirical work to find out which one actually does, but it is a semantic necessity that it would suffice to do so. A only counts as constituting B if it meets the semantic tests required to be called "B".

We are easily misled in these matters by peculiarities of the cases of constitution with which we are most familiar. It took a long time to discover that water was in fact H_2O, and that case is further complicated by the fact that many philosophers treat "water" as an indexical, and also favor an artifact of the approach apparatus which implies that such a substance can only be constituted by what in fact happens to constitute it around here. But if it is to be possible for some specific physical microstructure to constitute something at least suitably *water-like*, something potable, clear, liquid, generally non-reactive, and so on, then that possibility must be underwritten by a semantic necessity ensuring that any situation which included such a specific microstructure would also include something water-like. Only a posteriori discoveries about the world can reveal to us what the water-like substance around here is made of, but still it is a semantic necessity that such a microphysical constitution would count as water-like. It would have been a miraculous coincidence if people in the far past had ever even considered a structure like H-O-H, but still it was within their powers of conception in my sense. And if they had considered it, then they could have seen that it might constitute something water-like. It is a semantic necessity, rooted in the dependency of contents, that any H_2O with its powers and hence relevant laws intact, would be at least water-like. And that is a necessity that our ancestors could assess "a priori".

It is a semantic necessity that a congeries of molecules such as constituted Galileo, arranged just as they were and with just their powers, would make up such a living animal. And if our neurophysiology or physical environment *could* constitute our color experience, then that fact would be underwritten by a corresponding semantic relation. But the argument from knowledge suggests that it is not. This is also the point of the arguments from conceivability, when they are properly formulated. Let me now consider specific *objections* to the argument from knowledge.

2

It will help to focus our critical discussion of the knowledge argument if we consider a particular concrete case, which links together some traditional cases. Imagine a physically omniscient but congenitally blind neurophysiologist studying Galileo. Consider whether that neurophysiologist would know whether Galileo's phenomenal color spectrum was of the normal sort, so that he saw a particular planet and ball as phenomenal red, or inverted in a systematic way, so that he saw them as phenomenal green. It seems intuitive to claim that the blind neurophysiologist would not know this, that the neurophysiologist would learn something about Galileo's color experience in coming somehow to actually experience what Galileo experienced. And this intuitive case seems to underwrite the crucial second premise of our knowledge argument: *If one knew that BC were true, one would not know enough to fix all the truth about Galileo's phenomenal experience, in particular that it involved particular phenomenal colors*.

There are ways to resist this intuitive case and premise. First of all, one might object that a blind neurophysiologist could learn that Galileo experienced the planet and ball as phenomenal red from Galileo's own testimony, or from the testimony of some colleagues with normal color vision. But the issue is precisely whether the congenitally blind neurophysiologist can come to understand the words "red" and "green" in the way which would be required for that testimony to help. I will focus on two other objections. Both are ways of insisting that there is nothing true and relevant about Galileo's phenomenal color experience beyond what is fixed by BC. The first deploys a deflationary conception of phenomenal experience, and is one reading of an ambiguous objection made by a number of philosophers.[7] It is the concern of this section. The next section will concern the other objection.

The first objection runs this way: In coming somehow to experience what Galileo does, the blind neurophysiologist would not learn any new facts, but rather simply come to know a second time old facts already fixed by BC, facts they already know. The blind neurophysiologist would simply come to know the old facts in a new way. To be the subject of a phenomenal color experience is to know one's state of experiencing in a different *way* than a blind neurophysiologist might know it from the outside, but it is to know the same facts. The *facts* are all fixed by BC. It is just that the subject of a phenomenal color experience has a different ability than the blind neurophysiologist, can know their experience in a different way, differs in know how rather than knowledge that.

There is some ambiguity in this objection. First of all, one might wonder if it is supposed to be a fact that Galileo knew his experiencing of the ball and planet in a specific way, a way with certain specific characteristics which Galileo also knew. Presumably, the answer is yes. To claim that there is no fact at all about this is simply implausible, even if BC fixes all the facts. At the very least, BC seems to fix that Galileo knew his experience by having it and that the blind neurophysiologist knew it in some other way. And Galileo knew that he had it. But the main ambiguity remains: There is a question about how much determinacy what I will call this "mode of presentation"[8] is supposed to have, to what degree BC is supposed to fix the mode of presentation of Galileo's experiencing to himself. I will focus primarily not on the issue of whether Galileo can introspect the particular nature of the mode of presentation of his experiencing to himself, but on the prior question of whether there is such a determinate mode of presentation to introspect. And I will consider two options in interpreting this objection along that axis.

Take the question of whether Galileo had normal or inverted color experience, or, to put it in the currently relevant mode, whether his mode of presentation of his experiencing is as in the normal or inverted case. Is the objection at hand supposed to be that the facts about the mode of presentation to Galileo of his experiencings, facts fixed by BC, are sufficient to discriminate between these two options (among others), that for instance BC fixes that the mode of presentation to Galileo of his experiencing is the normal and not the inverted one? If the answer is yes, then this objection simply becomes another form of the objection to P2 and the knowledge argument which we consider in section 3.

If the answer is no, however, then we have an interesting alternative objection. One might put that reading of the objection in the following way: There is a fact about whether Galileo is the subject of his experience or not. The mode of presentation to Galileo of his experiencing is to that degree determinate and fixed by BC. But there is no fact about whether the mode of presentation to him is the normal or the inverted one; there is no fact of the matter between those two apparent options. BC doesn't fix whether Galileo experienced the planet as phenomenal red or as phenomenal green, or to put it in the local idiom, whether he was presented with his experiencing in the manner involving phenomenal red or in the manner involving phenomenal green. But those aren't distinct alternatives. There is no fact of the matter between them.

This form of the objection may seem obviously problematic: If anything like the intuitive theory of human content sketched in Part One is correct, then humans can distinguish between contents involving phenomenal green and phenomenal red balls, and can even introspect the difference between experiences which have those contents. But this response is not completely decisive. The fan of this objection to the knowledge argument may insist that Part One is in error in proposing a content theory which allows a difference between phenomenal red and phenomenal green. Or the fan may admit that there is a semantic difference between the two properties, but insist that the content theory of Part One misconstrues that difference. Perhaps differences between red and green are analogous to the differences introduced by relative haecceities, which can make a difference *within* a content but not between two *different* contents. Perhaps there is a difference between red and green *within* a given person's experience, but not a difference between two *different* people's experiences or one person's different hypothetical forms of experience of the sort which the knowledge argument deploys. Alternatively, the fan may admit that the content theory of Part One captures what humans can think, but insist that the contents we can think create the illusion of a possible difference in truth when there is none. On this view, it is a kind of transcendental illusion created by our contingent constitution that it seems to us that there is a difference between phenomenal green and red and hence between experience of them, and yet there is in fact no difference between normal and inverted experience which BC fails to capture.

But even if this objection isn't *obviously* unworkable, it turns out to be implausible enough in the end. It seems that we have much more certain evidence that there are differences in the experience of red and green of the sort Part One presumed than of anything which might make us doubt it. Of course, if I cannot provide a plausible and coherently conceivable account of the realization of that experience, then that may well put this claim in legitimate doubt. To this issue we will return in the final chapter. But, beyond this, it is important to see what this objection to the knowledge argument gives up. Our attempt here is to develop a plausible and coherently conceivable non-objectual account of our intuitive range of color experience, which can be part of a plausible and coherently conceivable account of an agent who can entertain all the contents allowed by Part One. And this objection to the knowledge argument cedes that this cannot be done.

3

The second and most central objection to our intuitive case and to P2 of the knowledge argument is more straightforward: It is the claim that everything true about Galileo's color experience is fixed by BC, and that this includes its being a normal and not an inverted experience, that it involves a mode of presentation with the requisite degree of determinacy. But again it will be important to eliminate a certain ambiguity in this objection, to pursue the right version of it. There are in effect two readings, which I'll call "the revisionary" and "the heroic". Only the heroic version is really to the point.

We in effect already considered the revisionary reading, in our discussion in Chapter Nine of Paul Churchland's Roger the Crab. The revisionary strategy involves a modification of Part One's intuitive and traditional characterization of normal and inverted color experience. After that modification, there remains a difference between normal and inverted color experience, but it is a difference which can obviously be underwritten by facts fixed by BC. For instance, Churchland has suggested that the phenomenal content associated with a particular sense should be represented by a phase space whose axes represent properties of the environment to which the appropriate receptor cells respond.[9] Let's assume that the properties present in the environment are traditional post-galilean properties. Then in having a normal neurophysiology responding to the objective post-galilean properties of objects, say surface spectral reflectances, Galileo would have a normal and not an inverted color experience. Since on Churchland's view the properties of the environment to which sense organs respond play a crucial role in constituting the content of the corresponding experience, it might even be *impossible* for a creature to have an inverted color experience. According to the revisionary reading of the objection, the knowledge argument fails. Our blind neurophysiologist could easily determine the appropriate phase space for Galileo, and hence his form of phenomenal experience. In fact, they might do the same for a bat.

But that is just the problem. We cannot construct a content theory for a bat *at all* like that proposed in Part One for humans, or at the very least not simply by characterizing its sensory phase space. Such a phase space does not specify how the world would have to be for the bat's thought to match it in anything like the sense introduced in Part One. The revisionary reading is so revisionary that it changes the subject. Churchland might respond that we can know to what features of the world the bat's thought is responsive, so that we can formulate a sense in which the bat's thought is true to its environment. But it is important to see just how different from the sort of thing which we have been pursuing that *this* sort of content and truth would be. Thoughts with phenomenal content of the sort introduced in Part One may be in radical error, just as Galileo held our color experience to be. But even under the conditions which Galileo presumed, still our experience would possess "truth" of the kind Churchland favors. And it is also important to recall to what end we are pursuing here a non-objectual account of our color experience. We are attempting to construct a plausible and coherently conceivable account of our color experience as traditionally conceived, on the way to vindicating thoughts with the traditional contents charted in Part One. If Churchland-style content were all that we required, there'd have been no need for us to retreat to a non-objectual account of experience anyway. The revisionary version of the objection at hand isn't adequate for our peculiar needs.

Consider, then, the heroic reading of the objection: It claims that BC fixes whether Galileo experienced things in the normal or the inverted way, and under the traditional characterization of those ways of experiencing (or those modes of presentation of experiencings). It claims that BC fixes whether Galileo saw the planet as phenomenal green or phenomenal red. There are in effect two classes of proponents of this objection. The first class consists of Bernard Harrison and C.L. Hardin. Harrison has suggested that traditional inverted spectrum arguments ignore the fact that the spectrum of ordinary color experience exhibits asymmetries which make simple inversions impossible.[10] And Hardin has argued that these asymmetries map onto asymmetries in the neurophysiology which underlies color perception.[11] Hence it might be that Galileo's neurophysiology, even independent of his physical environment, in fact fixes whether his color experience is normal or inverted.

Hardin has provided what seems to me to be the best attempt by a physicalist philosopher at an account of the experience of phenomenal color, so let me consider his story at some length. One caveat: Hardin is something of a partisan of the Hering-Jameson-Hurvich opponent-process theory of color vision, and hence to some degree neglects alternative traditions of scientific work, for instance work stemming from Land's famous retinex theory. But still at least the general kinds of considerations which Hardin tries to bring to bear seem exactly the right ones. Hardin suggests the following, partly conjectural, account of how neurophysiology might fix phenomenal color experience:

Step One: It is worth noting that in traditional inverted spectrum cases, such as that we are considering, unique hues are substituted for unique hues, say unique red for unique green and unique yellow for unique blue. No one proposes that unique hues be substituted for binary hues, say unique red for orange. And indeed such a non-traditional inversion seems quite implausible, especially given the way we have already seen that the phenomenon of unique hues seems to plausibly reflect features of our neurophysiology, features which probably cause our talk of some hues being unique and others being binary. The spectral point where the so-called "yellow-blue" opponent system is neutrally balanced and the "green-red" system is tipped one way is plausibly identified with experience of a *unique* hue. At least the fact that unique green is *unique*, neither yellowish nor bluish, seems reflected in the underlying neurophysiology. So there is at least one way in which Galileo's neurophysiology might make some color inversions, though not the traditional one I deployed, implausible.

Hardin's general strategy is to extend this sort of treatment until it tells against traditional inverted spectrum arguments. But first he speculates that the opponent-process organization of our visual system might underwrite certain other asymmetries in our color experience which traditional inverted spectrum arguments also cagily respect.

Step Two: The phenomenal opposition of phenomenal red and green, and of phenomenal blue and yellow, their relative positions across the phenomenal color wheel from one another, may well reflect the opponent-process organization of our visual neurophysiology. Normal human neurophysiology may well impose even that level of structure on our color experience. There are visual processing systems which respond to the radiation we see as blue and yellow, and as red and green, as opposing pairs.

Still, this eliminates none of the traditional inversions, which not only map unique hues to unique hues but preserve the structure of color similarities and differences embodied in the traditional color wheel. Traditional inversions simply give the color wheel a spin, or flip it around. But Hardin has more to say:

Step Three: The so-called "yellow-blue" (and also the "red-green") opponent system is presumably organized so that high or increasing levels of activation in that neural system help generate an experience of one color while low or decreasing levels help generate experience of the opposed color. But this could underwrite another important asymmetry of phenomenal colors. Yellow and red seem to be warm colors, and blue and green seem cool. Perhaps this reflects the fact that yellow and red correspond to high or increasing levels of activation in the relevant opponent-process systems. Hence a spectral inversion of red and green, of a warm with a cool color, might not be plausible.

All of this suggests that a normal neurophysiology might rule out all color inversions except that in which unique red and unique yellow on the one hand, and unique blue and unique green on the other, are interchanged, with corresponding changes all around the color wheel. Hardin suggests that other phenomenal and neurophysiological asymmetries might rule out even this inversion.

Step Four: There is a phenomenal asymmetry between even unique red and unique yellow. The typical unique red is more saturated, more colorful than the typical unique yellow. And there is a neurophysiological asymmetry which this may reflect. The spectral range which normal humans see as yellow is also the range at which achromatic response, response to "white" light, is also at a peak. It is natural that yellows seem more washed out. And it may be relevant that there is no sensory receptor cell responsive to the "color" of radiation, no cone, whose receptivity is at a peak in the range of illumination we see as yellow.

All this suggests that if Galileo had a normal human neurophysiology, then we should expect his color experience to be normal and not inverted. It suggests that BC may well fix phenomenal color experience. If so, P2 is false, and the knowledge argument fails. Hardin's story is in certain respects speculative, and would of course need to be filled out in great detail to exhibit how all the second-order phenomenal properties of phenomenal colors might be rooted in our neurophysiology. But it seems to me to represent the most promising strategy for those who would defend a physicalist account, a post-galilean account, of our color experience. However, it does not really suffice for our purposes. There are several problems.

First of all, some of the asymmetries in our color experience which Hardin exploits seem relatively soft, for instance the relative saturation of typical reds and yellows. We may well be able to conceive, to express in C, and even under unusual conditions to experience,[12] yellows as saturated as reds. It may be that we can coherently conceive an unusual sort of phenomenal color experience which fits normal human neurophysiology as well as the normal sort of experience, even if it is not exactly an *inversion* of that normal experience.

Second, Hardin's strategy is to root higher-order phenomenal relations of phenomenal colors in our neurophysiology, and this is insufficient to fix their complete nature. For instance, the phenomenal difference between unique green and unique blue is not exhausted by the fact that they are in phenomenal opposition to colors which typically have different levels of saturation, nor by other differences in their relational properties. This would be a problem even if differences in saturation *were* a relatively hard feature of red and yellow. Let me elaborate. Hardin's account is objectual in certain respects. The apparent plausibility of his account trades on the apparent sharing of higher-order properties between neural phenomena on the one hand and the forms of phenomenal experience which they are supposed to constitute on the other. Hotter neurons mean hotter colors. But this is problematic in several ways. Some of the supposed shared higher-order properties may be no more than puns. And we will shortly see that maybe Hardin shouldn't be so sanguine about even the objectual resources he does deploy. It may be that these objectual elements of Hardin's account are as suspicious as those which might be deployed in an analogous attempt, by our mythical science of colors revealed by drugs, to account for the experience of phenomenal sound in the machinations of phenomenal color by noting certain shared higher-order structures. But, in any case, even if we ignore these objections, such resources are clearly insufficient. For instance, Hardin trades on differences between the high and low intensity, or perhaps between the increasing and decreasing intensity, of neural firing to underwrite differences between cool and warm colors. But intensity differences like these are presumably common to many sensory processing systems, and hence are insufficient to capture the specific difference that there is between red and green. The full nature of a phenomenal color is not fixed by its relations to other colors of the sort which Hardin attempts to exploit. Its nature as a phenomenal *color* comes to more than the fact that it has a specific place in a structure of other colors, a color-space determined by relations of opposition and the like, a space with a different geometry than sound-space. One way to see this is to consider that even if we knew the *geometry* of the auditory space of a bat, we still wouldn't know what a bat hears.

There may be other reasonable objections to Hardin's account. I think appropriately, he focusses on introspectible features of color experience. But his suggestion is in effect that it is higher-order properties of our neural firing which we introspect. Introspecting thoughts, which we can assume are patterns of neural firing, respond to differences in intensity in the firing of the red-green opponent system, for instance. But recall our second worry from Chapter Eight. The effects of the introspecting thought should be relevant to its *content*. And it seems more the vehicle than the intuitive content of phenomenal experience which gets mirrored according to the picture Hardin presents.

These considerations alone are not, I think, obviously decisive. It might be that further development of Hardin's strategy could help mitigate some. On the other hand, I think they do suggest that it may well be that we need an even more radically non-objectual account than Hardin's. Shared higher-order properties cannot, I think, take us all the way, if they can take us any way at all. But, in any case, there is another criticism of Hardin's strategy. It presses some of the same points I have just made, but in perhaps a more telling way.

Hardin presents the problem he means to solve in this admittedly traditional form: We have a pair of options in assigning color experience to someone, a normal and an inverted assignment. Given that person's neurophysiology, we make our best inference to the most plausible assignment, and it is the normal one. He concedes that it might be *possible* for an inverted spectrum to occur in someone with a normal neurophysiology, but tries to show that that is unlikely, that it is less plausible.

But recall that, at least according to Part One, constitution is a semantic relation. If such and such micro-particles can constitute a neuron, for instance, then it is a kind of semantic necessity that they do so. If BC fixes our color experience by fixing our neurophysiology, then it must be a similar semantic necessity that such a set of neurophysiological states would constitute such an experience. And Hardin's considerations cannot establish anything remotely this strong. It may be that the doctrine of Part One regarding constitution is in error, though I doubt that it is, at least about the coherently conceivable, about coherently conceivable contents linked by coherently conceivable constitution. Certainly if it is in error, then we are owed some alternative account of how things can constitute others, and as far as I know no one has proposed a viable alternative. And, in any case, even if such an escape route is available, it cannot help us in our particular situation. It cannot help us vindicate the content theory of Part One by helping to sketch plausible and coherently conceivable realization conditions for phenomenal experience. The only way to defend Hardin's account is to abandon that intuitive theory of content, at least in some ways.

There are other ways to press this objection, which do not depend so openly on what may seem arguable claims about the semantic nature of constitution. As I said, Hardin's strategy, like the argument he attacks, presumes our prior understanding of two options in phenomenal experience, the normal and the inverted form of color experience. Given that prior understanding and the phenomenal asymmetries it reveals, we are to look for plausible corresponding asymmetries in the underlying neurophysiology. But if P2 and the knowledge argument are to be defeated in all the forms which they might assume, we need to be able to solve things in the other direction. From a complete understanding of Galileo's neurophysiology, we need to be able to project the form of his phenomenal experience. The blind neurophysiologist, who has no prior phenomenal experience of color, must be able to project all the facts about Galileo's color experience. But we have good reason to believe this impossible. Consider a bat, or some exotic Martian. A bat's neurophysiology is presumably accompanied by phenomenal experience, but of no humanly familiar kind. And while we may glean some sense of what the world seems like to a bat from study of its neurophysiology, of how the world would have to be for its thought to match the world, still it seems that we can come to no complete understanding of bat content. We can only go so far as its overlap with human content allows. We cannot construct a content theory for a bat of the type we pursued in Part One. But if Hardin's strategy could succeed, if a blind neurophysiologist could properly understand Galileo's color experience, then a similar strategy would allow us to properly understand a bat's experience. If Hardin's strategy could succeed as a defense of a non-objectual account of color experience, then we could construct a theory of the type of Part One for a bat. And we can't do that.

Twice we have relied on our inability to do this. But perhaps we can do it, it may be objected. We just need to try harder, and modestly remember that we don't know as much about the neurophysiology of vision as we will someday. But this is whistling in the dark. We have somewhat different sense organs than bats, and if our thought is as rooted in our peculiar form of sensory experience as Part One and the long tradition of empiricism suggest, then we cannot bridge the gap. And even if we could bridge the gap, then we humans could entertain basic contents other than those admitted by Part One, beyond the limits of human experience respected by C. Again, Hardin's strategy can provide us with no way to defend a non-objectual account of color experience as part of a vindication of the content theory of Part One.

Still, let me continue to press this objection. Though they have affinities with both the accounts we just considered, we have yet to explicitly consider what are now perhaps the dominant physicalist accounts of phenomenal experience, which imply accounts of even bat experience. Brian Loar and William Lycan have sketched physicalist accounts of what it is for Galileo to have a perceptual experience which imply that a blind neurophysiologist and Galileo could both know his experiencing, but under distinct though very determinate modes of presentation.[13] The physical situation which is Galileo having a particular perceptual experience, according to Loar, might be known by the neurophysiologist and by Galileo via distinct recognitional dispositions, involving distinct concepts with distinct cognitive roles which are yet triggered by the same single physical property. Lycan suggests that these distinct modes of presentation deploy distinct words of Mentalese, with distinct conceptual roles in the different thinkers' conceptual economies, but with the same reference.

To Loar and Lycan it seems a purely contingent matter that these words or concepts overlap in reference, and they buttress this intuition by appeal to the familiar and apparently a posteriori identity of water and H-O-H, of heat and molecular motion, and of Hesperus and Phosphorus. But we know that these cases aren't strictly analogous to that at issue here. Even if in fact our phrase "experience of green" is indexical in the manner that some hold "water" to be, still the metaphysically relevant issue, the issue of concern to us, is whether there can be a suitably experience-like phenomenon constituted out of physical phenomenon. And by the content theory of Part One we know that if this is to be then it must be a semantic necessity, which can be evaluated a priori, in an armchair. It was known only a posteriori what water happened to be made of, but it could have been known a priori that H-O-H would count as water-like.

Loar explicitly denies something resembling the semantic thesis I have deployed. Lycan admits some of the differences between familiar cases of constitution and the physical constitution of experience,[14] but claims that they do not defeat the general considerations in favor of physicalism and the explanation he provides of why there is the appearance that there is a difference between what the blind neurophysiologist and Galileo know. But Loar and Lycan's treatment of this case inappropriately relies on an analogy with familiar cases of identity which we now know to be misleading. And, in any case, it cannot help us in an attempt to develop a coherently conceivable account of the realization of our phenomenal experience which can underwrite the content theory of Part One. It is in conflict with that account.

Let me be quite clear. I think there's a sense in which Loar and Lycan are right. We have not so much been pushed away from non-objectual accounts of our phenomenal experience, as from coherently conceivable non-objectual accounts, which require a semantic necessity linking some post-galilean basic content and the representational content of the claim that there is experience of phenomenal green. Someone might still reasonably claim that we have experience of green, and that *something* plausible and hence non-objectual must constitute it, whether or not we can coherently conceive what or how. In fact, I believe something quite like this. Further, they may say, certain things out in the world can be accessed somehow via the mediation of Galileo's introspective conception of his experience of green and via the neurophysiologist's conception of the allied physical facts. Let me even grant even this for now, though we will soon consider some of the pressures faced by a claim that anything coherently conceivable can be constituted by what is not. Further, they may insist, these things might overlap, so that our concepts of introspectibly green experience and of certain neurophysiological facts have the same reference. This I think might plausibly be denied on the basis of my semantic theory, but let me grant even this possibility. Then there would be a sense in which Loar and Lycan are almost exactly right. But the important point for us now is that the presumably coherently conceivable physical resources which Lycan and Loar deploy do not suffice for the coherently conceivable constitution of what we know after Chapter Twelve to be our coherently conceivable experience. And the familiar examples Loar and Lycan deploy to buttress the plausibility of their view do link the coherently conceivable with the coherently conceivable in a coherently conceivable way, and hence are quite disanalogous.

4

Where are we? There is no at once coherently conceivable and plausible account of our experience of phenomenal color. Objectual accounts are implausible, and there is no coherently conceivable non-objectual account. Part Two deployed all the coherently conceivable resources available to us, and once we eliminate those objectual resources which are clearly implausible, the remaining resources do not suffice to provide a coherently conceivable account of our phenomenal experience. The spatio-temporal and the causal are not enough. What's more, the arguments we have reviewed seem to generalize smoothly to accounts of our experience of all the characteristic intrinsic phenomenal properties. There is no at once coherently conceivable and plausible account of our phenomenal experience.

This fiasco may seem to put intolerable stress on my account of content. Some may hope that we can coherently conceive other resources. My account is rooted in our introspection, but it is not indefeasible. Still, I think, it is more certain than anything which yet leads us to doubt it. How could we be more certain that we can coherently conceive how we in fact experience what we do than that we can introspect what we think? Certainly dogs can't understand some things, for instance the realization of their own experience. How can we be so certain that we are any different?

Alternatively, this situation may seem to put irresistible pressure on the arguments presented in this and the preceding chapter. But again, they seem more certain than anything which might now lead us to doubt them. The arguments we reviewed in Chapter Fourteen still show that objectual accounts of our phenomenal experience are flat out implausible. Those arguments point towards a non-objectual account, not merely because that is the only alternative,[15] but also because of the considerations which Hardin deploys, which suggest that our color experience is appropriate in certain ways to our neurophysiology. The problems which face non-objectual accounts are rather different. They are various problems of conceivability. Perhaps we conceive differences where there are no differences, say between normal and inverted color experience. Perhaps there is a kind of constitution which we cannot coherently conceive but which would aid Hardin. Colin McGinn has suggested that something inconceivable, if added on to our post-galilean neurophysiology, might close the gap between our neurophysiology and our experience.[16] Some conceivability considerations seem to tell against the plausibility of certain non-objectual accounts, but still, if we have phenomenal experience, then it seems there must be some appropriate non-objectual account of it, whether we can coherently conceive that account or not.

In light of what follows, I suggest the following tack, at least if in fact there is phenomenal experience: A non-objectual account of our phenomenal experience is most plausible, but in particular a non-objectual account which we cannot coherently conceive in any detail.[17] It is not merely that something inconceivable must be added on to our coherently conceivable post-galilean neurophysiology. Rather, even our human understanding of our neurophysiology is seriously misleading, despite the fact that Hardin has faced us in at least roughly the right direction. Even traditional post-galilean resources, particles and neurons, are implausible. The most plausible non-objectual account would eschew coherently conceivable resources altogether.

These claims rest in part on considerations which we haven't yet faced. But there is a lot of tension coiled into them, and it may seem too much. For instance, I claim that the sentence "our experience is realized in a non-objectual but not coherently conceivable way" is quite plausible, certainly more plausible than its denial. And yet by my own account of content, such a sentence has no coherent truth-conditions. We will return to these issues in Chapter Nineteen. But for now I can at least say some things which may make you feel a little better about this story.

I can remind you once more of the experience of bats and exotic Martians. It is unlikely that we humans can understand everything in the world. And I can recite again the myth of the true color science. That is the science which Galileo and his cronies might have discovered rather than the one they actually did, in which true phenomenal colors of things, revealed only under certain drugs, allowed the development of a spectacularly successful predictive and explanatory science and an equally fabulous technology, while perceptual relativity arguments still told against the reality of phenomenal sound. If such a genuine color science had developed, we would now face the problem of where the experience of phenomenal sound might fit into the world of color. I doubt we could solve that problem, but we might notice that there was something wrong with its terms. Finally, I can promise that difficulties of the sort we have faced regarding the experience of phenomenal color and the other characteristic intrinsic phenomenal properties will also trouble accounts of even causal and spatio-temporal features of our experience. Objectual stories of the realization of even those features of our experience will fail, and we will have no coherently conceivable non-objectual alternatives. In fact, we will have no coherently conceivable resources remaining.

Our attempt to vindicate our agency and our intuitive thought content, in part by providing a plausible and coherently conceivable account of the realization of our phenomenal experience, has failed. Some may be untroubled by this. Ever since Galileo, phenomenal properties have seemed particularly problematic, perhaps even too shadowy to do semantical work. If there are no phenomenal intrinsic properties in the world or even in our experience and thought, some may think it no big deal. It is a very contingent feature of the historical road we have traveled that this seems at all plausible. But I should admit that the classical physicalist conception of the world does imply that what there is is exhausted by merely causal basic contents, shorn of phenomenal intrinsic properties. So thoughts with merely causal basic contents may seem sufficient to capture all the truth of what we think. If we can plausibly and coherently conceive the realization of our experiences and other thoughts whose contents are merely causal and spatio-temporal, that may seem enough. But this traditional post-galilean position, though it is our natural historical position, is unstable. Perhaps you'll feel better about what I've said about phenomenal experience once I up the ante.

NOTES

1. Stephen Yablo, "Is Conceivability a Guide to Possibility?", *Philosophy and Phenomenological Research* LIII, 1993, 1-42.

2. Leibniz gives what I take to be one early form: "Supposing that there were a machine whose structure produced thought, sensation, and perception, we could conceive of it as increased in size until one was able to enter into its interior, as he could into a mill. Now, on going into it he would find only pieces working upon one another, but never would he find anything to explain Perception." See *Monadology* 17, translated by George Montgomery, revised by H. Chandler, in Leibniz, *Discourse on Metaphysics, Correspondence with Arnauld, Monadology* (La Salle, IL: Open Court, 1902), 254. But some authors hold that there is a distinction between knowledge arguments and arguments from explanation. For instance, see Brian Loar, "Phenomenal States", in James Tomberlin (editor), *Philosophical Perspectives* 4 (Atascadero, CA: Ridgeview, 1990), 81-108.

3. Michael Tye, *The Metaphysics of Mind* (Cambridge: Cambridge University Press, 1989), 138. Frank Jackson, "Epiphenomenal Qualia", *The Philosophical Quarterly* 32, 1982, 127-32.

4. Frank Jackson, "Epiphenomenal Qualia", 129.
5. B.D. Farrell, "Experience", in Vere Chappell (editor), *The Philosophy of Mind* (Englewood Cliffs, NJ: Prentice-Hall, 1962). Thomas Nagel, "What Is It Like To Be a Bat?", *Philosophical Review* 83, 1974, 435-50.
6. For instance, see J. Levine, "Materialism and qualia: The explanatory gap", *Pacific Philosophical Quarterly* 64, 1983, 354-361. But also see note 2.
7. Michael Tye, *The Metaphysics of Mind*, 133-150. Terence Horgan, "Jackson on Physical Information and Qualia," *The Philosophical Quarterly*, 1984, 147-151. David Lewis, Postscript to "Mad Pain and Martian Pain", in *Philosophical Papers*, vol. 1 (New York: Oxford University Press, 1983), 130-132. Sydney Shoemaker, "The Inverted Spectrum", *Journal of Philosophy* 79, 1982, 357-381. L. Nemirow, Review of T. Nagel's *Mortal Questions*, *Philosophical Review* 89, 1980, 473-477.
8. Some authors, for instance Loar, distinguish between the Nemirow-Lewis "ability" response we have been discussing and the "mode of presentation" view proper. But, in any case, what they mean by the latter we discuss in the next section.
9. Paul Churchland, "Some Reductive Strategies in Cognitive Neurobiology", *Mind* 95, 1986, 279-309. This is not the only current of argument in Churchland on this topic. He sometimes deploys the argument we considered in the last section, and it is also important that he views phenomenal properties as confused or unanalyzed versions of the true properties of things. He certainly wouldn't think that everyone can introspect the nature of the phase space which characterizes the form of their experience. See also his "Reduction, Qualia, and the Direct Introspection of Brain States", *Journal of Philosophy* 82, 1985, 8-28; and "Knowing Qualia: A Reply to Jackson", in his *A Neurocomputational Perspective* (Cambridge, MA: MIT Press, 1989), 67-76.
10. Bernard Harrison, *Form & Content* (Oxford: Blackwell, 1973).
11. C. L. Hardin, *Color for Philosophers*, 134-154.
12. See Hardin for the details.
13. Brian Loar, "Phenomenal States", and William G. Lycan, "What is the 'Subjectivity' of the Mental?", in James Tomberlin (editor), *Philosophical Perspectives* 4, 109-130. See also Carolyn McMullen, "'Knowing What It's Like' and the Essential Indexical", *Philosophical Studies* 48, 1985, 211-233.
14. Lycan, 122-123.
15. If we for the moment ignore the possibility that we have no experience of the sort we have been presuming.
16. Colin McGinn, *The Problem of Consciousness*. Sometimes McGinn suggests an inconceivable sort of connection between neurophysiology and experience, which sounds a bit objectual. But he also sometimes suggests something which sounds non-objectual to me.
17. More about that qualification in Chapter Nineteen.

CHAPTER SIXTEEN

CAUSAL EXPERIENCE

This and the following two chapters track the interaction of our immediate interest--the realization of our experience of causal and spatio-temporal structure and the plausibility of various features of basic contents--with three stages in the development of post-galilean science. Traditional galilean orthodoxy, which dominated physics until the beginning of this century and still permeates much contemporary physicalist writing, is the focus of this chapter.

Section 1 sketches the way in which that galilean physics seems to support the plausibility of certain causal basic contents, how traditional galilean physics is coherently conceivable. Later sections concern how a galilean understanding of ourselves might underwrite a seemingly plausible and coherently conceivable objectual account of the realization of our causal and spatio-temporal experience; they add some crucial details to the rough sketch we already possess. They also show that non-objectual accounts of our spatio-temporal and causal experience are not coherently conceivable. When we consider special and general relativity and quantum mechanics in the following two chapters, it will become evident that this implies a situation quite parallel to that we faced in the last two chapters.

1

The traditional galilean conception of the world is coherently conceivable, is expressible in C. Let me explain how. What I will call "causal" basic contents consist solely of causal microevents. These are instantiations of causal powers, restrictions relatively characterizable in C, which stand in spatio-temporal relations of the sort sketched in Part One. In the case of certain causal basic contents, which I will call "paradigmatic" causal contents, these spatio-temporal relations include the three basic spatial relations and the one temporal relation which were introduced in Chapter Six, plus a certain sort of measure structure. That measure structure gives the contents a classical and familiar euclidean form, so that for instance within such contents the pythagorean theorem is true and the sum of the interior angles of a triangle is 180 degrees. This structure requires that paradigmatic basic contents be not only dense but continuous, and that is a rather sophisticated and particular detail. But even if no basic contents were continuous, nor even dense, still a true basic content might approximate the necessary continuous structure to as great a degree as we desired. Still basic contents might be approximately euclidean.

Causal basic contents, and in particular the paradigmatic causal basic contents, include those which Galileo and his immediate successors would have held to be the plausible basic contents. Or, to be more accurate, they include those contents which Galileo and his immediate successors would have held to capture the truth about material objects like balloons and planets and stars, though not perhaps the truth about God and human minds. Galileo and his immediate successors had some dualist tendencies. But we know better. The physics of Galileo and his more or less immediate successors still underwrites much contemporary physicalist writing in the philosophy of mind, which deploys paradigmatic basic contents to constitute everything.[1]

Let me review the confluence between traditional galilean physics and paradigmatic causal basic contents. First of all, all causal basic contents exclude the phenomenal intrinsic properties, which Galileo held to be "mere names". The causal basic contents exclude resources which galileans eschew. Now consider things from the other direction. Some paradigmatic causal contents include properties and relations which are, or which can constitute, the properties and relations which galilean science held to be the true properties and relations of material objects like balloons, balls, and stars. I've claimed this before, but it's time for more adequate explanation and argument.

A ball or star, in the traditional galilean view, lacks phenomenal color. But it has at any moment, as a matter of objective fact, a particular shape and spatial location. And it will change that location over time in a particular objective way, say with a particular velocity.[2] That change in its location is governed by various objective properties of things, say external forces acting on the ball or star and also its inertia and mass.

There are a variety of similarities among the list of traditional galilean properties. For instance, properties like shape seem available through more than one sense, and hence may seem more plausible features of the objective world than do the peculiar deliverances of individual senses. But focus for the moment on one particular set of similarities among the galilean properties: They seem either directly or indirectly spatio-temporal. They include location and shape, which are spatio-temporal properties, and the change in location which is movement. And they also include properties which affect such change. Even the striking mathematization of galilean physics seems rooted in its close connection with spatial geometry, and in particular with the traditional spatial geometry of paradigmatic causal contents. Paradigmatic causal basic contents contain sufficient resources to constitute the requisite positions and shapes and motions of galilean rockets and planets. They are spatio-temporal contents of the right sorts. And the properties of galilean bodies which are not directly spatio-temporal seem to be causal powers, of a sort available within the paradigmatic causal basic contents. In fact, they are powers which are quite like the primitive dynamical powers which are present in the content of our immediate causal experience. The mass and inertia of a rocket or ball are causal powers, by which for instance another ball or projectile might be pushed about, just as our arms might push them about.

Of course, galilean spatio-temporal structure is exhibited even in phenomenal basic contents. And I should admit that causal powers are not involved in certain traditional post-galilean conceptions of the world, because of the hostility of some scientific-minded philosophers to causal powers. Descartes, for one, focussed solely on extension as the mark of the physical. But it is important to recall that the content theory of Part One implies that there are no microevents without characteristic intrinsic properties. There can be nothing concrete to enter into spatio-temporal relations without such properties, and galilean physics eschews phenomenal intrinsic properties, so only causal powers remain as viable galilean candidates. If galilean science is coherently conceivable, then it must invoke causal powers.

We have seen some general reasons to think that there are *galilean* basic contents, basic contents consistent with the truth of galilean science. And we have some general reasons to think that they are among the causal basic contents in particular. Certainly the traditional euclidean spatio-temporal structure deployed in the paradigmatic causal basic contents seems to match well with the presumptions of galilean physics. But let me be a bit more specific, and pursue a somewhat more detailed understanding of the particular galilean basic contents which seemed most plausible to our not very distant ancestors.

The euclidean structure of galilean space and the paradigmatic causal basic contents allows there to be a familiar system of cartesian coordinates for that space. That space may be captured by a system of cartesian coordinates which takes any particular point in the space as its origin, and which has a system of axes which are perpendicular to one other but oriented as a whole in any which way. The distance between any two points in the space is the square root of the sum of the squares of the differences of their respective coordinates. And there are a variety of systems of one-dimensional cartesian coordinates which might capture the temporal relations within such a world. The temporal separation between two events can be captured by any of them.

These systems of spatial and temporal coordinates allow the familiar mathematical expression of galilean physical laws. The galilean conception of the world, though rooted in Galileo's important innovations, finds its classic expression in Newton's mechanics: *Velocity* is the rate of change, with respect to time, of spatial position. (Velocity takes into account the direction of motion, otherwise it would be merely "speed".) *Acceleration* is the rate of change in velocity with respect to time. On the newtonian conception, the world consists of particles moving around over time in a euclidean space, where the acceleration of the particles is determined by the forces acting on them, in accord with Newton's three laws: 1) If no force acts on a body, then it continues to move uniformly in a straight line. 2) If a force acts on a body, then the mass of the body times its consequent acceleration is equal to the force. 3) The force that body A exerts on body B is precisely equal and opposite to the force that B exerts on A.

Newton held that one crucial force in the world is gravitation, which acts attractively between any two particles and whose strength is proportional to the product of the masses of the two particles and to the reciprocal of the square of the distance between them. In accord with the constraints required if Newton's mechanics is to characterize a basic content which yet eschews phenomenal resources, we might think of the mass of a particle as involving causal powers, which constitute among other things the gravitational force which that particle exerts on other particles. The inertial phenomena encompassed in Newton's first law suggest that mass involves other sorts of causal restriction as well. And, on the classical newtonian view, particles rebound off one another in a way which suggests yet another sort of causal restriction.

Note two points about this scheme which will be significant in the next chapter. First point: Newton explained inertial phenomena by motion relative to "absolute" space. Imagine two stationary balls connected by a string in an otherwise empty universe. Now imagine that they are spinning uniformly about the midpoint of the string, and hence tug on it. In the first case there is no tug; in the second there is. But in neither case is there any motion of the balls relative to any material objects in the universe. It seems that the only difference between the two cases is motion relative to some fixed space, and that that difference in "absolute" motion is crucial. And this implies that not any cartesian system of coordinates, say one which spins with the balls, is really as good as any other. According to Newton, the true systems of coordinates are those at rest in "absolute" space. "Absolute space" is a space in which the entire material universe might have a different location or orientation than it in fact does. In the interest of accuracy, let me note that this sort of argument from inertial considerations can at best imply not that the true systems of coordinates are at rest, but rather that they don't spin or accelerate. In fact, such an explanation of inertia doesn't quite require "absolute" space.[3] But that is the traditional newtonian explanation. Absolute space might seem to present a difficulty for C, since C constitutes space out of the spatial relations of microevents, and to say that space is constituted out of the relations of material things is, it seems, to deny the existence of a newtonian absolute space.[4] But note that an empty absolute space might be constituted by relatively "immaterial" causal microevents which together simply cause the persistence of such a space into the next moment and constrain things in certain ways, and particles might be constituted by other causal microevents fused to that space.

Second point: The newtonian scheme involves instantaneous action at a distance between particles, the action of particle on particle by gravitational force without an intervening medium. But there are of course other forces than gravitation. And they led eventually to some important modifications of the classical newtonian picture. Consider for instance electricity and magnetism.

Like gravitation, they fall off as the inverse square of distance, though they may act repulsively rather than attractively. Like gravitation, they seem to create fields of force. For instance, a magnet affects iron filings in a way which suggests the presence of a magnetic field of force in space, with a force of a certain strength and oriented in a particular way exerted at each point in the field. Electricity and magnetism are obviously related, in that moving electrical charges can give rise to magnetic fields, and moving magnetic fields can induce current. Through the work of Faraday and Maxwell, it became plausible to think that electrical and magnetic fields exist as real concrete entities in their own right, which push each other along through empty space, and indeed constitute and explain the features of light. This suggests, at least in the case of electricity and magnetism, that there is a medium by which force acts, rather than mere action at a distance. Maxwell's equations provide a description of the way that electrical and magnetic fields will propagate given a particular distribution of electrical charges and current, where the charges are properties of particles which are plausibly causal, and the currents arise from the motion of particles. There might be similar equations which provide an account of how the velocities of charged particles change owing to the influence of magnetic and electrical fields.

Despite the new features they introduce, the electromagnetic forces seem on the surface well within the reach of a galilean conception of the world, and hence of paradigmatic causal basic contents. But this is in fact a misleading appearance. Important developments in physics following Maxwell were radically at odds with galilean mechanics, and rooted in a realization that electromagnetic phenomena spell trouble for the cozy traditional galilean picture. We will return to this issue in the next chapter.

2

Let's assume for the moment that the world is a galilean world, that it is matched, and indeed exhausted, by a paradigmatic causal content, and in particular by a galilean basic content which includes causal microevents which constitute neurons and balls and planets of a traditional galilean sort. Our question is this: How might our experience of the causal and the spatio-temporal be plausibly realized in such a world? We already know in outline, but we need to consider certain details, to make it clear how important are various resources available in galilean basic contents to the coherently conceivable realization of our causal and spatio-temporal experience.

Note a preliminary point about each of those features of our experience, before we turn to the main action in the next section. First, spatio-temporality: Not only causal experience but also phenomenal experience has a spatio-temporal form, and we have yet to say much about its realization. Since there is no plausible and coherently conceivable galilean account of our experience of the characteristic intrinsic phenomenal properties, there can be no plausible and coherently conceivable account of our phenomenal experience in general. But we might hope for a plausible and coherent account of at least its spatio-temporality, even if this is a galilean world. Still, my strategy will be to focus on the spatio-temporality of causal experience only, and hope that provides us with sufficient clues about the other case so that I can legitimately avoid explicit treatment of it. That isn't an entirely vain hope: In general, we might expect an account of the realization of the spatio-temporality of one sense field to be enlightening regarding the realization of the spatio-temporality of other sense fields, and the causal field of experience is at least a close analogue of a sensory field. We will soon see that *some* spatio-temporal objects must play a role in coherently conceivable accounts of the realization of the spatio-temporality of our causal experience, and in a way which will suggest that objectual resources are probably required by a coherently conceivable account of the realization of the spatio-temporality of our phenomenal experience as well. Indeed, the very same parts of the world which seem important for the realization of the spatio-temporality of our causal experience also seem implicated in the spatio-temporality of phenomenal experience. Partly this is because of the important way in which phenomenal and causal experience interact. For instance, we have discussed ways in which motor intentions controlling limbs through six degrees of freedom probably are a crucial resource in constituting our full sense of spatial structure, a kind of structure with which phenomenal elements can fuse and hence receive a more refined spatial structure than they might otherwise possess. And our discussion of Mel's net also suggested that causal experience and visual experience interact in crucial ways. But also the very same resources that help realize our causal experience may play a direct role in underwriting certain spatial features of our phenomenal experience. For instance, when people put on inverting glasses, glasses which invert their visual input, at first the world looks upside down to them. But over time, presumably as they develop the right interconnections of inverted visual input and ordinary motor output, things come to *look* right side up again, despite the fact that sensory input is still in some sense inverted. Of course, the inverting glasses don't invert all of their senses, but there has been some indication that if the victims of such glasses are unable to engage in movement, then they are unable to adjust to their situation. Maybe motor activity plays merely a causal role here; perhaps it merely causes some adjustments in structures which do not realize motor capacities. But it seems not unreasonable to conclude that our capacities for motor activity are crucial elements in the realization of some spatial features of even phenomenal experience.[5]

That's the first preliminary point, but there's another also. It concerns the realization of our experience of causal powers.[6] Galileans retain, even after their loss of the characteristic intrinsic phenomenal properties, a number of resources which might help constitute our causal experience: First of all, there are still functioning neurons with all their complex electro-chemical properties intact. The apparent phenomenal colors of neurons seem to play no crucial role in the action of those neurons. Second, there are galilean muscles, bones, and tendons, which help to constitute our motor action. Third, there are galilean balls, balloons, and stars, constituted by particles exhibiting causal powers and moving through euclidean three-space, and these might possibly help constitute our causal experience of such balls and balloons and stars. But previous chapters suggested that our causal experience is realized by our neurophysiology and motor capacities in particular. They suggested an objectual account of causal experience, but of a peculiar kind: The causal objects which help constitute our causal experience are those which make up our motor systems, and not the causal balls and balloons on which our motor capacities might be exercised and our thoughts directed, not the ordinary *objects* of our causal experience.

This may seem idiosyncratic. In our particular historical situation, the dominant galilean accounts of our experience of the causal are focussed on sensory input rather than motor output. The causal structures which influence our sense organs are supposed to be the causal contents of our sensory experience. Let me review why this is wrong. We have seen that the kind of *introspectible* content present in our sense experience is phenomenal and not causal. The kinds of behaviors and other psychological effects of that sensory experience are appropriate to phenomenal and not to causal experience. As long as Galileo's phenomenal experience of a planet is the same, it seems, his visual perception of the planet is the same, irrespective of the invisible causal differences. So it seems appropriate to continue to pursue an objectual galilean account of our causal experience along the internalist lines suggested first in Chapter Seven, in which our muscles and skeletons, our motor capacities, play a crucial role. It is in our motor action that our causal experience seems revealed.

But despite this, someone may still insist that externalist resources can be a useful supplement to a motor-based account. They may play a useful role in action even if not in sensation. Our causal experience of a wave may be constituted not merely by our own causal-spatial structure, not merely by our bodies and muscles. It may also be constituted in part by the causal-spatial structure of the wave itself, by the object on which we act.

However, consider a world in which a neurophysiological and muscular-skeletal twin of Galileo, indeed his complete internal galilean twin, faces a wave with a different causal structure. Any wave whose causal powers Galileo or his twin experiences will push one or the other around.[7] Some waves they might experience will push them around in different ways. For instance, if the twin faces a wave of a different size or shape or orientation, that twin will be pushed around in a different way. But that difference will be reflected in the motion of the twin's limbs, and in the neurophysiology which monitors and controls the relative position of those limbs and the success and trajectory of motor action. It may not be merely what Galileo *does* with his limbs, but what *happens* to them also, which matters. But, in any case, a role for the waves themselves in constituting, as opposed merely to causing, the requisite causal experience in Galileo and his twin would require that the spatial-causal difference between the waves not be reflected in some difference in their neurophysiology or skeletal and muscular structure, not in the motion of their limbs nor in their neural firing. Any *relevant* difference in the waves could not involve some difference in the way Galileo and his twin are pushed around. It would have to be finer-grained difference than that. But that sort of difference seems irrelevant to their causal experience, at least if it is characterized in the intuitive way sketched in Part One. The details have to be quite fine-grained to make any difference, and then they are too fine-grained to be relevant. I should be clear that I think that some differences in the ways in which Galileo and his twin are pushed around, say how far through the water they are pushed, may not make any difference to their causal experience, in fact that what they do with their limbs and not what merely happens to their limbs is what really matters. But at the very least the waves themselves play no role.

One might insist that, like a particular phenomenal color, some causal feature of the wave might play a crucial role in constituting Galileo's thought and hence action to possess a particular content, a role in giving his thought greater determinacy of content than it might otherwise possess through what is revealed in his motor action, and that this is role enough. But there is a disanalogy between this and the phenomenal case: Differences in casual thought about a wave, at least at the gross level of content characteristic of our unrefined but crucial causal experience, seem something that might be reflected in the intentional movement of one's limbs, in greater force against a wave thought to be more forceful. But differences in phenomenal color experience don't always have this feature, which is of course just what makes inverted spectrum cases so troubling. It is the direct way in which the causal content of intentions can be reflected in behavior which mitigates here the second standard difficulty of objectual accounts, explaining the integration of behavior and content.

We seem pushed firmly towards an internalist, motor-driven account of Galileo's causal experience of the wave, in which his motor organs help constitute his causal experience. Any feature of the wave itself seems either redundant or irrelevant. But there are other sorts of objectual account worth brief mention. Someone may object that when we are dreaming or hallucinating or paralyzed, or when we are brains in vats, we are still capable of the full range of causal thought, and hence by my own account we must still be capable of the full range of causal experience. Yet our motor organs play no role in such cases. If we feel the need for objectual resources, such an objector may continue, they should be of another kind than those I have proposed. Perhaps causal sense data, or rather motor data, are crucial components of our causal experience. But of course causal motor data of the requisite sorts, even if such things are coherently conceivable, would be no less miraculous than their phenomenal cousins. What's more, cases of illusory causal experience involve something analogous to the primary imagination, and we know that the quasi-experience involved in the primary imagination cannot plausibly be given a simple objectual account. Still, that doesn't entail that veridical experience should not be treated in a simple objectual way. But causal motor data will still be massively implausible even if we turn out to need them for that case.

3

That completes my preliminary points. Now the main action. Even if the internalist, motor-side account of our causal experience we have sketched is our best objectual alternative, someone might wonder about non-objectual accounts. But we are now in position to see that there is no *coherently conceivable* non-objectual account of that experience, indeed of either its spatio-temporal or causal features.

First, consider those spatio-temporal features, which we haven't yet treated in any detail. We will soon see that it may be that some elements of the spatio-temporal structure of our experience can, and indeed must, be given a non-objectual account. But there are severe limits to how far this non-objectual strategy can be pursued, at least in a coherently conceivable account. Galilean neurons and muscles and skeletons can provide the resources we need for a largely objectual account of the spatio-temporality of causal experience, but it is hard to see how we could make do with much less. Let me elaborate.

It is natural to assume, almost without thinking about it, that the neural firing and motor action which constitute some causal experience precedes that which constitutes a second causal experience which is experienced to follow the first. If it weren't realized by temporally related objects, the temporality of our experience would be very hard to understand. It seems that the realization of that experience could not be coherently conceived if objectual resources were not involved. How could some sort of coherently conceivable introspective procedure reveal or constitute such a feature were it not present somewhere?

There are similar spatial examples: Consider Galileo's neurophysiology as he braced for a wave to strike him, or a blast to strike his rocket, from his left to his right. He might have a mirror twin, with the same neurophysiology and body but exactly transposed as in a mirror, left to right and right to left. That twin would hence be bracing for a wave, or a blast, to strike *him* from right to left. This suggests that one's neurophysiology alone underdetermines the spatial form of one's causal experience. Galileo and his twin share a structure of neural connectivity and firing, but not causal experience. The twin's experience is a mirror-inversion of Galileo's. The actual spatial properties of their bodies, the ways in which their neurophysiologies are hooked up to muscles and sense organs with a particular spatial distribution, seem to help determinate the spatial form of their experience. One might object that Galileo and his twin don't really share a neurophysiology, because the mirror twin's *neurons* are spatially inverted. But of course if *that* feature of Galileo's neurophysiology is crucial, then we have an objectual account anyway. Nor will externalist non-objectual resources be of any help here. The whole world might have a mirror twin as easily as Galileo. It doesn't even help to insist that the world has at some deep, say microphysical level, some favored chirality, some favored handedness, and that perhaps this chirality isn't so far removed from the action of the nervous system as to allow a relevant mirror twin of Galileo to be possible in a world at all like ours. For such a chiral microphysics itself has a coherently conceivable mirror inversion which we might deploy in a relevant thought experiment. Any coherently conceivable deep chirality would involve spatial objects in a crucial way.

The spatial structure of Galileo's causal experience might be mapped into a wide range of distinct spaces, for instance preserving certain topological features of the original but with certain regions shrunk or expanded in various ways. In some cases, perhaps two intervals of the same length in his experience might map to intervals of different lengths in the alternative space, and lines which are straight in his experience might map to curved lines in the other space. Of course at question here is the very content of a thought that lines are of the same length or are straight. But still this level of spatial structure does seem present in our experience, and these features of spatial experience are finer than features which our mirror twins show us require objectual realization. We will return to this issue in the next chapter, and see that it may be that these particular elements of the spatiality of our experience, captured in its measure structure, can be given coherently conceivable non-objectual accounts, though I think we should retain some worries about that. But, in any case, there are at least *some* kinds of mapping which present what seem to be insuperable barriers to any coherently conceivable account of the spatio-temporal structure of our experience which yet eschews objectual resources. The chiral, mirror-inversion mapping is one case, but others might include a mapping of the space of an experience into another space which did not preserve the topological features of the original. One might hope to pry the necessary objectual resources, say chirality, away from spatial features. But there is clearly no coherently conceivable way to do that. Any helpful and coherently conceivable chirality is spatial.

In general it seems that, at least in certain respects, the only coherently conceivable accounts of the spatio-temporality of our causal experience, and of our experience generally, are objectual accounts. But what about the causal features of that experience? Previous chapters went some distance towards developing an internalist objectual account of our experience of primitive powers, in which that experience is constituted in part by our motor capacities. And we saw earlier that there are a variety of reasons to prefer this internalist objectual account to externalist objectual alternatives. But we might also wonder about non-objectual alternatives. In fact, we will eventually see that a non-objectual account is probably most plausible. But on the other hand, it will not be coherently conceivable. If the galilean resources we presume in this chapter *were* fully plausible, an objectual account would be desirable. That is because there are crippling difficulties which face any attempt to develop a non-objectual account of our experience of causal powers which is both plausible and coherently conceivable. Let me review and amplify.

First, we have seen that characteristic intrinsic phenomenal properties are implausible. Since the only coherently conceivable resources which now remain to us are microevents with intrinsic causal powers, no *plausible* non-objectual account of the experience of such powers can be coherently conceivable. No plausible and coherently conceivable account of *anything* can eschew causal powers.[8] But that's not the main point, nor a very direct one.

Even if we deploy implausible resources like colors, we cannot develop a coherently conceivable non-objectual account of the particular sort of causal experience which we must vindicate. Remember that we are pursuing an account of the realization of the experience of the particular very primitive intrinsic causal powers characterized in Parts One and Two, the mechanical powers we can exhibit. The peculiar content of such an experience seems to demand an objectual account. Recall the argument of Chapter Seven. The particular causal powers we experience seem dependent on our particular motor capacities, which involve muscles exerting forces. To change our motor capacities in certain ways would be to change the content of our causal experience. If Galileo had a much stronger but neurophysiologically-identical twin in a world which was just like this one except that in that world all forces were doubled, that twin would have a different experience of powers than Galileo's.

Nevertheless, let's consider some non-objectual alternatives. A traditional empiricist account of our ability to conceive powers in the guise of phenomenal regularities is in effect an objectual account of the experience of a certain sort of power or quasi-power, since regularities are deployed in such traditional accounts of the experience of regularities. But whether such an account is objectual or not, we saw in Chapter Seven that it is not an account of the experience of the kinds of primitive powers we pursue, which are intrinsic non-phenomenal properties which can involve different degrees of force. Empiricist accounts rooted in our phenomenal experience of pressure and effort suffer analogous difficulties.

Since causal powers are restrictions which have particular contents, we might hope to provide an account of their realization via the specification of a new sort of content generation operation, which generates the conception of a power from the conception of its content. But we possess no account of how such a content generation operation might be realized, at least none except that which deploys in part causal experience rooted in motor action, none which is relevantly different from the objectual story I have already told. There are no reasonable candidates for conditions which would realize such a new and special-purpose content generation operation. And, in any case, we have our familiar cases and the difficulty they suggest. The most primitive powers, the very dynamical powers of which we have causal experience of an immediate and direct kind, are restrictions with contents which would not be conceivable by us unless we had motor capacities of certain kinds.

The powers we exert with our limbs, the most primitive powers, have a quite specific mechanical form. It is perhaps not an accident that this is the sort of power deployed by galilean physics, despite the fact that we can conceive powers with other contents in the relatively indirect ways we discussed in previous chapters. The galilean powers like mass and force are not only mathematizable, but they are mathematizable in a relatively familiar geometric way. And the primitive powers we directly experience are also geometric. Both classes of powers are tied to motion and acceleration, to movement through space and in time. The primitive powers are properties which may apparently affect the motion of entities with other properties, perhaps paradigmatically visual colors, and galilean powers only affect things without phenomenal properties. But of course the primitive powers might only *directly* affect the galilean properties of things, even if in fact they did have other properties.

It is perhaps noteworthy that though all our fields of phenomenal experience have spatio-temporal structure, still the particular spatio-temporal structure most relevant to galilean physics seems to be the fine spatio-temporal structure revealed by our visual experience. We can move our limbs, but also we can see our limbs move. We can see the motion of things in the world, and see how our moving limbs affect other moving objects. It may also be worthy of note that the primitive powers are also the powers by which we move our bodies through the world, which give us a capacity for locomotion. By moving our limbs, we not only move objects in the world, we move ourselves through the world.

So to some degree the content of our powers is accessible to us through our senses. Our powers are tied to movement, and in particular to a kind of movement which we can experience through our senses. But, of course, it is also important that the content of a primitive power, the content of its restriction, isn't fully available in this way, isn't fully available through our sensory experience. Primitive powers can double in force while yet our visual and other sensory experience remains the same.

To see the ways in which various features of our causal experience reflect various contingent features of our constitution and situation, it is worth considering what our causal experience would be if we had radically different capacities to act. That is the burden of the next section. That section underlines the way in which the peculiarly galilean form of the paradigmatic basic contents is especially suited to underwrite a coherently conceivable account of our particular causal experience.

4

It will be useful to consider a variety of hypothetical cases. First, imagine someone who has all the normal human capacities plus a few more, and in a world generally such as our experience seems to reveal, in which there are for instance phenomenal colors and galilean properties like mass and charge. Let's say that such a humanoid can turn any part of their body any color at will. They don't do this by the mechanical manipulation of tools or blood vessels, but directly, through a "motor" organ which consists in part of a power to create certain color microevents. Imagine that this capacity plays a role in their communication and dance. And let's say that they can affect the color of any object they see in their immediate environment by direct will, by action at a short distance. Here we have somewhat unfamiliar powers. Such a creature has "motor" organs which involve powers of a sort ordinary humans do not possess, indeed powers which are not found in our world at all. But they are powers we can coherently conceive, and indeed powers which are restrictions with contents which the humanoid, and indeed any normal human, can see. *We* don't have causal experience of such powers, but we do have sensory experience of the contents of those restrictions. We can coherently conceive them. Still, the humanoid has a kind of causal experience we lack.

Now let me vary the case a bit, to establish another analogy with our own causal experience. Imagine that objects in the environment of the humanoid possess their colors with differing degrees of "force", and imagine also that the humanoid can will color changes with different degrees of "force". Or it might be that phenomenal colors can be willed and retained with different degrees of "spin", a spin which affects the color which objects end up with as a result of interaction with a color-will. Here, I think, we have causal experience whose content has a feature of which the humanoid cannot have sensory experience, though it is a power which they can coherently conceive. And this case involves a power and a causal experience which *we* to some degree cannot *coherently* conceive.

Still, there is an important disanalogy between the color-powers I have been discussing and our ordinary causal powers. Color-power is not linked to the humanoid's powers of locomotion, unlike the causal powers which ordinary humans exhibit. We manipulate objects in our environment in much the same way as we move our bodies. So let me try to develop a strange case which preserves this linkage.

On Mars, we'll say, there are no galilean particles or colors. There are merely phenomenal sounds, at least to a first approximation. The true basic contents which capture at least that region of the universe are phenomenal contents, whose microevents possess characteristic intrinsic phenomenal sounds which differ in timbre, pitch, and loudness. And those true contents have the familiar three spatial and single temporal dimensions. On Mars there are persisting sound-particulars, say repeating tunes, which migrate about through the local space. There are also quasi-causal regularities of various kinds. The Martians themselves are sound creatures. They consist of phenomenal sound. Like other particulars in their environment, they are tunes. The true account of their phenomenal experience is a very simple objectual one. Their distance from the location of a tune is proportional to how loud that tune sounds in their experience. They also sometimes hear tunes in the distance to be at different locations, in much the same way we may hear an oboe and a horn to be playing at different points in a room.

Now focus on the Martians' form of action and "causal" experience. Each Martian can vary its tune in some respects at will.[9] They can sing in much the way we can move our limbs. Certain aspects of their sound-bodies are their voices. Assume that each Martian can hear its own voice. They have sensory experience of at least some differences in the contents of their "causal" powers. If that resemblance to our own causal experience were lacking, it seems to me that it might well be that the Martians would have no causal experience. And note the scare quotes. I have for the moment deployed only quasi-causal regularities, and not genuine powers, in the realization of the Martians' so-called "causal" experience. Hence, it is really only a kind of quasi-causal experience which they possess, at least as characterized so far.

Remember that we want eventually to link together the Martians' powers of song with their powers of movement, to mirror the way our own powers are linked. So let me assume that the Martians move, and that in particular they move through space depending on how they sing. For instance, let's say that the direction of their motion depends on the nature of one phrase of their song, and its speed determines the speed of their motion. There are quasi-causal regularities linking singing of certain kinds and certain sorts of motion. To preserve another crucial analogy, let's imagine that there is a kind of interaction between the motion and singing of the Martians and the motion and sounding of the various other sound-objects on Mars. For instance, it might be that the quasi-causal regularities on Mars are such that sounds of certain timbres push other sounds out of the way.

This sound world so far involves quasi-causal regularities only. We must move to *powers* for the realization of a genuinely *causal* experience, so that the so-called "restrictions" our Martians perform are genuine *restrictions* and not mere regularities. If we add genuine powers to our sound world, then we can also add a feature analogous to the doubling of forces in our earlier cases. We can give the Martians causal experience of causal powers whose contents include features which they cannot sense. Let's assume that there are different degrees of "force", not to be confused with loudness, with which they can sing. And there are different degrees of "force" with which sound-particulars can sing. And this affects the results of their interaction, the movements that result. So let me specify that in the sound world, on Mars, there are, in addition to phenomenal microevents, causal microevents, but causal microevents which feature only microevents that instantiate causal powers or phenomenal sounds in the contents of their restrictions.

We have succeeded now in linking together the movement of the Martians with their novel powers, but we have done so in a way which might make someone legitimately wonder how different their case is from our own. The differences between their powers and our own may be relatively minor. It's worth working through this to see the kinds of differences which are required for genuinely different sorts of causal experience. The Martians' novel powers work, at least in part, *through* sounds. They don't work only directly on other causal forces in the manner of traditional galilean powers. They work on things which sing. But of course we humans also at least seem to manipulate the world we *see* by the moving limbs we *see*. Prior to Galileo, it might well have seemed that, at least in ordinary cases, only objects with a look and smell and so on move other objects or are moved. Our powers might seem to work through colors in the same way that the Martians work through sounds. If in the sound world I've stripped off the color and smell of things, still phenomenal sound remains, and someone might insist that my description of Mars is closer to the oldest traditional conception of our powers, in which they work through various phenomenal properties, in which for instance only the visible can be pushed, than is even the galilean conception. So perhaps this sound world isn't really that foreign.

Where are we? We have developed a case with a mildly different sort of causal experience, another with radically novel powers which lack the link to motion required for any full analogy with our own, and another case where that linkage is present but the powers aren't all that radically different from our own. Can we do better? Is there a case in which there are radically different powers which are yet linked to motion, a case which is relevantly analogous to our own situation yet in which the powers and causal experience are radically different from our own?

My best shot is this: Let's adjust the dynamical form of the powers, by messing around with spatio-temporality in some way. Then we can retain all the desirable links and analogies, and yet sketch creatures with a genuinely novel form of causal experience. Imagine creatures who experience a different sort of sound world from that we have been discussing, a sound world which Strawson first explored.[10] The world of those creatures is so different from our own that I can't even place them on a planet, and there are significant limits to what I can tell you about the realization of their experience. But they do provide the analogy we need.

Strawson's discussion was a commentary on Kant's alleged "refutation of idealism". Strawson tried to imagine a "no-space" world, in which creatures were able to conceive a difference between their experience of something and that very thing existing outside of their experience. Kant held that this was impossible if a creature had no conception of spatial structure,[11] yet Strawson thought that his "no-space" world has features which would provide the resources for this distinction, features which are analogous in certain ways to spatial structure but which aren't really spatial features. So it may provide us with some analogue of motion which yet isn't motion of our familiar spatial kind.

Strawson imagined that there might be creatures which merely had sensory experience of phenomenal sound. He claimed, wrongly I think, that our experience of phenomenal sound in itself, in my terminology "outside of its fusion with other sensory fields", lacks any spatial structure. But still it is possible, consistent with the nature of basic contents, to specify the content of the sound experience of a creature shrunk to a single spatial point. Strawson's case further requires that there be the fusion of distinct phenomenal sounds in that point of experience, but that is something which C also allows. Strawson suggested that such a creature, as its point of phenomenal sound-experience changed over time, might have the experience of something which is a close analogue of spatiality. Imagine that there is a "master-sound" with a fixed timbre, and which varies in pitch. The creature always hears the master-sound, and yet assume that as the creature "moves" the pitch of the master-sound varies. And imagine that the creature always hears, in the "vicinity" of a given pitch of the master-sound, a certain sort of repeating tune. This tune constitutes a sound-particular, fixed in a particular position in the sound "space". Strawson argued that in such a situation the creature might come to the notion of an unheard sound, and hence of the distinction between its experience and the world. It might form the conception of a tune going on at a particular pitch of the master-sound even when it wasn't "around" to hear it.

This situation certainly has enough structure to provide something we can deploy to our own ends. But first, a bit of commentary and modification. Gareth Evans objected to Strawson's scenario, repeating Berkeley's famous argument that to attempt to imagine an unheard sound is to attempt the impossible, that unheard phenomenal sound is an incoherent notion. He did this in support of one traditional dodge deployed also by fans of the reality of phenomenal color, a dodge which we have discussed briefly.[12] The traditional notion of a sound or color was supposed by Evans to be the notion of a power to cause experiences. But we know that Evans' objection is mistaken. In our experience, phenomenal sound does not present itself as a sound-explicitly-within-experience, any more than it presents itself in Galileo's experience as a sound-within-Galileo's-experience. So no questionable abstraction is required to conceive of unheard sounds just like those we experience. A phenomenal sound presents itself as a pitch, timbre, and loudness at a location, and that is all.[13] Still, we might want to vary Strawson's scenario a bit, to make it a better analogue of our familiar spatio-temporal world. Jonathan Bennett pointed out that if Strawson's creatures "move" through sound "space" in a relatively slow and continuous way, as we move through our own world, then the master sound is not needed to generate an analogue of position.[14] The creatures might figure out their position much as we do, by their relations to stationary objects. And Bennett also proposed that objects in the sound world might move from place to place, if they did so in a relatively slow and continuous way. So let them migrate slowly against a relatively stable background, like things in our own apparently colorful world. It might be important here that the creatures be able to hear sound-particulars at a bit of "distance", perhaps less loudly.

Now consider what sorts of "causal" experience these creatures might have, in a world of the strange sort they experience. It depends of course on what sorts of action they perform. Strawson proposed that the creatures can initiate "motion" through their world, which of course would not be literal spatial motion. Now imagine that there are sound "winds" in that world, which impede their "motion", so that a greater or lesser "force" of motion may be required to achieve the same aural result, the same migration relative to the master-sound, or even to stay "in place" in face of the wind. Strawson supposed that each of the sound creatures had a characteristic voice. Let's say it is a tune with a characteristic timbre which is always heard by those in its "vicinity". This might present another way for the creatures to act into the world other than by "motion" in it. Perhaps they might have sound limbs which they could "extend in space" in various ways, and which at those "points" in the world would affect the local sounds in a particular way. It might be that these effects involved "spatial" displacement, but let me take another tack. Sounds might mix in some interesting way to form a new sounds, rather than merely displace one another. If the result of that mixture of sounds could be affected by a kind of force with which the environment resists what a creature sings and with which the creature sings what it sings at the relevant "points" to which its limbs reach, then we have another analogue of our own powers. So far it seems that we have a split between powers of locomotion and powers to manipulate objects, of a sort we want to bridge. But consider the following complication in our scenario. Assume that the motion of the creatures is a *direct* result of their singing. They sing a tune with a base line which constitutes their location, which is some analogue of the master sound in Strawson's original case. They might will this bass line with greater or lesser force in the face of sound winds of varying force, and also will changes in their bass line with greater or lesser force. And this bass line might be affected by the more or less forceful singing of sound particulars with which it mixes in the way I described above, somewhat as our motion is perturbed by objects in the world.

Here we have, I think, a fairly unusual power which yet has many structural analogies with our own powers, which is linked to some analogue of motion and to other powers in the appropriate way. It is, I think, a power which we cannot *coherently* conceive, though of course we can talk about it. And it is a power which gives our creatures causal experience quite different from our own.

5

We have been pushed towards an internalist objectual account of our causal experience. In general, objectual resources seem crucial for any coherently conceivable account of the causal features of our experience, and of at least certain important spatio-temporal features of our causal and phenomenal experience. And those are the only apparently plausible kinds of resources which remain to us anyway.

As I noted briefly in Part Two, there are problems which face our internalist, motor-side objectual account. The intuitive point we stop as we move out from neurons to muscles to tools to world to fix Galileo's relevant powers, the point I've called "skin's end", may be intuitively defensible, but we may also legitimately worry how much pressure that intuition can withstand. This is in some ways analogous to the second characteristic difficulty of the standard correlational accounts. It seems to me that our introspection of the content of our powers is in fact crucial here, and that this pushes us towards recognizing the importance of non-objectual resources even though, for the reasons we've seen, coherently conceivable non-objectual resources aren't in themselves sufficient.

More important, we will soon see that the first characteristic problem of correlational accounts of sensory experience, the lack of plausible objectual resources, quite seriously afflicts this galilean account of our causal experience. A galilean understanding of the world probably can provide a coherently conceivable objectual account of the realization of our experience of causality and spatio-temporality. But it is questionable whether this is a galilean world, whether the objectual resources we need are in fact available to us.

Section 4 concerned one of the many literatures generated by Kant's *Critique of Pure Reason*. And the picture to which we are forced in what follows is reminiscent of the more radical elements of Kant's transcendental idealism, which some recent commentators suppress. Kant, with one of his voices, says that time and space and causation are mere illusions of our experience. There is, he says, in fact no time, no space, and no causation. What there is, the noumenal, is something we humans cannot coherently conceive. We can't even coherently conceive ourselves, how we think and experience what we do.

It seems to me that this is probably right, but not for Kant's reasons. Our experience is as misleading about space and time and causation as it is about color, but there is no necessity in this of the sort Kant sought. It is quite contingent that we experience things as we do. It is rooted in our contingent nature as humans, not any necessary transcendental preconditions for knowledge.[15] And the world might have helped; it might have matched our experience. But, quite contingently, it didn't.

NOTES

1. With the possible and odd exception of abstract entities.
2. Of course it might have a velocity of 0.
3. John Earman, *World Enough and Space-Time* (Cambridge, MA: MIT Press, 1989), 64.
4. See Lawrence Sklar, *Space, Time, and Spacetime* (Berkeley, CA: University of California Press, 1974) for a good introduction to the debate between "relationalists" and "substantivalists". See also Earman, *World Enough and Space-Time*.
5. The literature on inversions of this sort is complicated and controversial. For an introduction see Ian P. Howard, *Human Visual Orientation* (New York: John Wiley & Sons, 1982), 512-516.
6. I focus here on our genuine, and not our virtual, causal experience.
7. Virtual experience might also include a mere expectation of being pushed around which isn't realized, but let me ignore this complication.
8. At least given where we are now.
9. Perhaps the will of each is some concrete feature of its sound-body which is responsive to the environment and yet also to its needs.
10. P.F. Strawson, *Individuals* (London: Methuen, 1959), 59-86.
11. Or something like that.
12. Gareth Evans, "Things Without the Mind", in *Collected Papers* (Oxford: Oxford University Press, 1985), 249-290. See also "Molyneux's Question", *Collected Papers*, 364-399.
13. Evans also pointed out that any full analogue of space would require that there be the possibility of co-instantiation of the same property at the same time, but we might get this even within the experience of Strawson's creatures by allowing the fusion, within a single point of aural experience, of a particular phenomenal sound with itself. Imagine for instance that a tune which overlaps with another in at least one note migrates slowly across the sound space until it reaches the location of the stationary tune, and that they then sound that shared note together.
14. Jonathan Bennett, *Kant's Analytic* (Cambridge: Cambridge University Press, 1966), 33-39.
15. To be fair, Kant also sometimes seems only to be talking about transcendental preconditions for knowledge for creatures like humans.

CHAPTER SEVENTEEN

RELATIVITY AND CAUSAL EXPERIENCE

This chapter concerns the reformulation of the traditional galilean conception of the world required by Einstein's theories of special and general relativity, and the significance of that reformulation for the truth of basic contents and for the plausible realization of our causal experience. Section 1 is a brief exposition of some crucial features of special and general relativity.[1] Section 4 applies those considerations to the two issues which immediately concern us. Sections 2 and 3 provide a bridging discussion. They concern the concrete significance, the proper interpretation, of relativity, and relativity's explanation of the galilean appearance of the world.

1

Special relativity was born in an attempt to reconcile certain electromagnetic phenomena with what Einstein held to be a crucial and traditional physical principle, the principle of "restricted" or "galilean" relativity. To understand this principle, first imagine Archimedes standing by some straight train tracks, and a uniformly moving train passing by, with Madame Curie seated inside.

There seem to be three-dimensional systems of cartesian coordinates for space which might be centered on each. For instance, there is a system centered on Archimedes and which has one axis running in the direction of motion of the train, a second perpendicular to the ground, and a third axis perpendicular to and out to the right of the direction of motion of the train. And there is a second system characterized in a similar way, except centered on the speeding Curie. The second system of coordinates moves uniformly over time through the space characterized by Archimedes' system. Barring practical difficulties of interpenetration, we might think of these systems of coordinates as realized by three-dimensional grids of metal rods. It also seems that Archimedes and Curie might measure time along the same single cartesian axis, for instance by synchronized clocks at each node of their grids. Intuitively, it seems that we might check the accuracy of the physical realizations of such coordinate systems by moving a rigid rod of unit length among the grids, and a single clock among the nodes. Archimedes' and Curie's systems of coordinates constitute what we'll call two "frames of reference".

Note that certain physical measurements and observations will vary when made in these two frames of reference. For instance, a ball dropped out of the train window by Curie will, in her frame of reference, travel in a straight line to the ground, while in Archimedes' frame its path will be curved. Archimedes and Curie will ascribe different velocities to the ball. However, the *laws* of nature seem invariant between such unaccelerated, uniformly moving reference frames. For instance, each of our two frames exhibits the same dependency of various physical quantities, say of force on mass and acceleration. The choice between such reference frames should, Einstein reasoned, be no more significant physically than the choice between fahrenheit and centigrade.

This may seem in conflict with newtonian mechanics. Recall that absolute velocity, velocity relative to absolute space, is a crucial feature of newtonian mechanics, deployed in explanations of differences in inertia. This might in some sense privilege reference frames at rest in absolute space over others which move uniformly through that space over time. The frames at rest would reveal the true inertias of particles, and their true paths and velocities. But even if we accept this peculiar feature of Newton's view, still the lawful dependency of various physical quantities would be the same in Archimedes' and Curie's frames, according to newtonian mechanics. A Newton-style physics developed in either frame would be the same. Their distinct systems of coordinates still succeed in revealing the same objective spatial distances, and objective temporal intervals, between two events, and those are the crucial fundamental physical relations.

But note that Archimedes' and Curie's frames have a crucial similarity: Not all systems of cartesian coordinates, not all frames of reference, are intuitively equal in the way that Curie's and Archimedes' frames are equal. Not all possible frames of reference exhibit the lawful dependencies characteristic of newtonian physics. For instance, a *spinning* frame of reference would ascribe paths to the "fixed" stars[2] which have the stars violating Newton's first law in a dramatic way.[3] But recall from last chapter that inertial effects, observationally significant differences apparently due to acceleration,[4] will be felt by observers moving with such a spinning frame. An observer spinning with a spinning frame will feel centrifugal force, while this is not the case for Archimedes and Curie in their unaccelerated frames. Archimedes' and Curie's frames, unaccelerated and hence not spinning, moving at uniform rates relative to each other, are called "inertial frames". The spinning frame is not "inertial". The principle of restricted or galilean relativity which Einstein wished to preserve, the traditional physical principle central also to special relativity, is that the *laws* of nature are the same in every *inertial* frame.

One intuitive example: A toy rocket flying down the length of Curie's train car in the direction of motion of the train, traveling at a uniform velocity relative to the car, would seem to have different velocities in Archimedes' and Curie's frames. But in each frame its velocity would be, it seems, the sum of the velocity of the car and the velocity of the toy rocket relative to the car as seen in that frame. A law for the addition of velocities would be invariant between the two inertial frames.

The difficulty which faced Einstein was that the principle of galilean relativity seemed to be in conflict with observed electromagnetic phenomena. The Michelson-Morley experiment and other considerations seemed to suggest that the velocity of light in a vacuum was the same in every inertial frame. But this seemed hard to reconcile with galilean relativity. It seemed hard to understand how the velocity of a light beam shone from the back of Curie's train car towards its front could have the same velocity in Archimedes' and Curie's frames of reference.

Einstein's theory of special relativity is a way to reconcile the constant velocity of light with the principle of galilean relativity. Traditional galilean physics held that the objective spatial distance and temporal interval between two events, for instance between the emission of light from one end of a train car and its receipt at the other end, are invariant between inertial frames. Special relativity denies this, and in so doing modifies the traditional galilean formula for the addition of velocities which seems to ensure that the velocity of the light beam must be less in Curie's frame than in Archimedes'.

Einstein's revision of traditional galilean physics was also underwritten by his critique of the observational significance of the absolute simultaneity of events. Insofar as the simultaneity of spatially separated events is empirically determinable, it seems merely relative to reference frames. Imagine that Curie is situated at the midpoint of her train car, as seen in both her and Archimedes' frames.[5] Imagine also that lightning bolts strike the tracks at both ends of the train, so that the light from the two bolts first reaches Archimedes at what seems to him the same moment, and also the moment at which Curie passes by. Given Archimedes' measurements of the distance between himself and the location of each of the strikes, he would plausibly conclude that the two bolts hit simultaneously. But since Curie is rushing away from the point on the tracks where one bolt struck and towards the other over the time it takes the light from the strikes to reach her, the light from the two strikes will not reach her at the same moment. On the other hand, having previously measured the train and seeing that the bolts strike at the ends of the train, Curie could conclude that those strikes were at the same distance from her. So she could reasonably conclude that the strikes were not simultaneous. One might object that Curie could observe that the light from the two bolts was moving relative to her at different speeds, and hence infer that she was traveling towards one bolt and hence must compensate for her motion in her calculations. But recall that the speed of light is the same when assessed in all inertial frames.

Einstein concluded from all this that there was no objective fact about simultaneity, that simultaneity was relative to reference frames. If simultaneity is relative to reference frames, then this of course implies similar things about the temporal separation of events. Traditional galilean mechanics presumes that any inertial frame will reveal the same temporal and spatial separation for two events. But special relativity implies that the spatial and temporal separation of two events, say of the tick of a clock at one node in a frame of rigid rods and the tick of another clock at another node, will not in general be the same when assessed from two different inertial frames, that it is in fact "relative" to the frame. However, it also implies that when the relative speed of the two frames is low in contrast to that of light, these differences will be fairly insignificant, so that under familiar conditions the old galilean view is roughly correct.

Despite the fact that not only the spatial and temporal coordinates assigned to two events, but also their spatial and temporal separations, differ from inertial frame to inertial frame according to special relativity, still there is a system of equations, the Lorentz transformation, which allows the derivation of measurements made in one frame from the measurements made in the other. And there is a certain function of the temporal *and* spatial coordinates of two events which will have the same value in all inertial frames. However, this "interval" does not break down into spatial and temporal components in the same way in different frames. Rather, special relativity implies that events in fact have positions in a four-dimensional continuum called "Minkowski space-time", which might be captured in various systems of coordinates which correspond to each of the inertial frames, and which when captured in each of these ways exhibits a different segmentation into so-called "spatial" and "temporal" components.

Einstein's revision of the classical galilean conception of space and time required, of course, a significant revision of the newtonian laws and properties which were supposed to govern the motion of particles in space and time. For instance, according to special relativity a particle possesses an energy-momentum 4-vector, which breaks down differently into vector components, one representing energy and three representing momentum, in different inertial frames. And the speed of light in a vacuum becomes, according to special relativity, a kind of maximum finite velocity for the propagation of causal influence through the world, and a velocity to which a particle with mass can be accelerated only by the expenditure of infinite energy.

This maximum finite speed for causal influence, and the relativity of simultaneity as well, seem in conflict with the newtonian conception of gravitation, which involves instantaneous action at a distance. Special relativity seems to demand at least a serious reconception of newtonian gravity.[6] This led Einstein to *general* relativity, which incorporates special relativity as a theory which is approximately correct under special conditions.

Let's begin with a way to refigure the newtonian conception of gravitation, independent of the peculiar demands of special relativity, so that it doesn't demand instantaneous action at a distance.[7] Later on we'll add the constraint of special relativity. Galileo knew, not because he had dropped lead and wooden balls off the Tower of Pisa, but perhaps because he had imagined the effect on two dropping balls of being tied together with a string to form "one" heavier object, that objects of different mass and composition will yet fall in a gravitational field at the same rate.[8] Today, we are familiar with the ways in which acceleration creates similar effects. As a rocket or elevator accelerates upwards, it is as if all the objects in it were in a correspondingly stronger gravitational field.

Einstein reasoned from these facts in this way: If we found ourselves in a spaceship without windows, cut off from observation of the world external to the ship, we wouldn't be able to tell whether we were sitting on a planet in a gravitational field, or out in empty space but accelerated via a rope attached to the roof of the ship. Or, rather, all that might reveal to us that we were in a gravitational field would be tiny tidal effects caused by the non-uniformity of the field across the ship. For instance, particles dropping at opposite sides of the rocket towards the center of a planet would fall in paths that were ever so slightly less than parallel. It's these "tidal" effects of gravity which distinguish it from acceleration, and they are very small within our rocket ship. Acceleration and gravity are *locally*, that is within regions small enough to make tidal effects insignificant, more or less indistinguishable.

So we might refigure the newtonian conception of gravity in the following way: Charged particles have electromagnetic fields, and all particles with mass have gravitational fields, but the gravitational field of a particle is a curvature it induces in space itself. Free particles, whose motion is determined only by their own inertia and not by external forces, move not in straight lines, but on geodesics through curved space. Geodesics are the (locally) shortest distances between two points, and in a curved space geodesics are generally curved. For instance, consider the great circle route between Rome and Chicago.

On this view, the curvature of space itself constitutes gravitation, including its tidal effects. Notice that gravitation acts locally, on a particular particle at its particular location in curved space.[9] And so gravitation on this view requires no instantaneous action at a distance. If we add to this reconfiguration of the newtonian conception of gravity the constraints incorporated in special relativity, we get the theory of general relativity.

In general relativity, not space but space-time is curved, in such a way that it approximates the "flat" Minkowski space-time of special relativity only locally. The more it approximates Minkowski space-time in some region, the less significant are gravitational effects in that region. The curved space-time of general relativity requires a new sort of system of coordinates due to Gauss, a kind of generalization of cartesian coordinates suited to curved spaces (and space-times). Here's a two-dimensional example: For each dimension of a curved 2-dimensional surface, let there be a system of non-intersecting curves covering the surface. Assign to each curve a real number. Two real numbers might then be the "gaussian coordinates" of each point on the surface. Given a particular gaussian system of coordinates for a curved space of any dimensions, there will be for each point of the space a set of gaussian coordinates which consists of as many real numbers as the space has dimensions.

Einstein's field equations, the basic equations of general relativity, presume such a curved space-time arena. According to general relativity, free and electrically uncharged particles move along geodesics in curved space-time, and possess properties represented by energy-momentum 4-vectors. These 4-vectors break down differently into components for energy and momentum in different frames of reference.[10] Electromagnetic fields curve charged particles away from the geodesics they would otherwise follow. An electromagnetic field has 6 independent components at any point in space-time, and in any given inertial frame the field will be seen to consist of separate electric and magnetic fields, though the way it breaks down into these components will depend on the frame in question. When a charged particle is at rest according to a frame, its acceleration is governed only by the electric field at its point in space-time in that frame. When a particle is in motion in a frame it is governed by the magnetic field in that frame as well. Particles also have effects on electromagnetic fields and the curvature of space-time. These effects are assessed differently in different frames of reference, in which the particle is at rest, at motion, or accelerated. While rooted in traditional galilean and newtonian mechanics, this picture clearly involves a significant reformulation of that traditional view.

2

General relativity seems to demand a serious revision of the familiar galilean conception of the world. Even special relativity alone would seem to require that. Both theories seem to imply that the paradigmatic causal basic contents favored by the traditional galilean conception, in which microevents possess the three traditional spatial and one familiar temporal relation, are false. This threatens our coherently conceivable galilean story about the realization of causal experience. But let me approach this point slowly.

It might be tempting to interpret special and general relativity in such a way as to avoid this conflict with the galilean conception. For instance, one might claim that while no inertial frame is privileged by special relativity, that isn't inconsistent with one inertial frame in fact being that in which the true and objective spatial and temporal separations of two events appear, so that measurements in other inertial frames are systematically distorted. But there is no empirical way to determine which inertial frame is supposed to be so privileged. Even if one frame exhibits the true inertias and paths of particles, we can't know which it is, nor can we even get any evidence which makes one frame more likely to be the "true" frame than another. So we don't seem to have sufficient reason to believe there is a privileged frame. On the other hand, the theory of relativity seems to explain observations by postulation of entities beyond our mere experience, and to be more than an instrumentally useful device for calculating the succession of our observations. So it has seemed to most that the natural and plausible interpretation of special relativity is one which requires significant revision of the traditional galilean conception of the world. It has seemed to most, as it did to Einstein, that special relativity and general relativity imply that the world is very different from the way we had formerly taken it to be. This inference seems to me correct.

Special and general relativity seem to provide the resources for perceptual relativity arguments against the existence of certain traditional galilean relations and properties, arguments which parallel the traditional perceptual relativity arguments against the existence of the phenomenal colors of balls and balloons. The arguments are of this largely familiar general form: Different perceivers in different circumstances experience or assess an object to have different galilean properties of some sort. And there is no reason to believe one such perceiver's assessments to be truer than another's. So the object has no single true and objective galilean property of that sort.

Special relativity maintains, in its natural interpretation, that different observers in different inertial frames will differently assess the spatial and temporal separation of two events, and hence that there is no objective temporal interval and spatial distance between those two events. All that objectively separates those events, which are located in Minkowski space-time, is the "interval", represented by a function of spatial and temporal separation which will have the same value when assessed in all inertial frames. Both special and general relativity reveal that different observers in different frames of reference will differently assess various galilean properties, and hence that there is no objective fact among those possibilities.[11]

We might well wonder what the concrete physical realization of the truth of general, or even special relativity, is supposed to be. If relativity is to be taken in the most natural way, then some sort of concrete realization of such things as the interval is required. C is my account of any concrete realization which we can coherently conceive, and it may seem to lack the necessary resources. But this worry is in fact misplaced. Relativity is coherently conceivable. To eventually see this, we'll need to talk a bit more about the concrete significance, the physical interpretation, of special and general relativity.

Special relativity, for instance, posits that events have positions in a 4-dimensional Minkowski space-time. What might concretely realize that? One clue lies in the way that space-time is structured by light: According to special relativity, the speed of light in a vacuum is not merely invariant between inertial frames and hence plausibly an objective feature of the world, but it is also a kind of speed limit for the universe, an upper limit for the velocity at which causal influence can propagate between events. To each event in Minkowski space-time, there corresponds a "future light cone", an ever-expanding sphere (as seen from any inertial frame) of positions which may be reached by light emitted from that event and traveling in a straight line. Similarly, positions from which light might pass to the original event in a straight line are its "past light cone". This provides some objective structure for the world: Events on the light cones of an event are said to have "light-like" separation from that event. Events within the future light cone of an event have a "time-like" separation from that event, and will seem temporally later than that event in all inertial frames. Events within its past light cone seem temporally earlier in all inertial frames. Events outside the light cones of an event have a "space-like" separation from that event, and each will seem simultaneous to that event in some inertial frame. These light cones, and the presence of a time-like or a space-like or a light-like separation between any two events, are objective features of the world, the same in all inertial frames.

The interval is also a crucial feature of Minkowski space-time, and this too has a sort of concrete significance according to special relativity. Recall that moving clocks slow down. If event B has a time-like separation from event A and is within A's future light cone, then the interval from A to B is equal in value to the time interval registered by a clock traveling with an inertial particle from A to B. If two events have a light-like separation, then the intervening particle would have to travel at the speed of light, and the accompanying clock would slow to a stop, so that the interval measured is zero. If event B has a space-like separation from A, then the interval is equal in value to the spatial separation which they have in any inertial frame in which they are seen as simultaneous.[12] This concrete interpretation privileges certain frames of reference, not exactly arbitrarily, but still in a way which doesn't immediately reveal what constitutes the interval objectively and in itself, independently of any reference frame. But all these considerations do point us somewhere:

Light travels at the maximum speed of causal propagation. So the structure provided by light cones, the objective difference between time-like, space-like, and light-like intervals, and the way in which that difference allows a particular concrete realization of the interval in at least some frames, suggest that the causal connectibility of events plays a crucial role in generating the structure of Minkowski space-time. And indeed, both the topologies and metrics of the space-times of special relativity are fixed when it is fixed which pairs of events in such space-times are causally connectible, that is which can be connected by some possible causal path, and in which order.[13]

In general relativity, things are somewhat more complex.[14] For a wide class of cases, causal connectibility fixes topological but not metrical structure. It fixes topology in "strongly causal" space-times, in which there are no "almost closed" light-like or time-like causal curves, in which causal influence cannot loop around to the vicinity of its own source. Fixing continuous causal paths is sufficient to fix topology for an even wider class of space-times. There are space-times consistent with general relativity which fall outside of the class of cases in which such "reductions" succeed, but they seem pathological and implausible. At least in all the *coherently conceivable* space-times consistent with general relativity, continuous causal paths fix topology. What about metrical structure? This might be fixed by a specification of ideal clocks and rigid rods[15] or of the paths taken by light and by free particles. Metrical structure has that concrete significance, which C might capture.

Causal paths or connections seem crucial to any concrete realization of general relativity. Note however that there might be a world and a space-time which is a left to right mirror inversion of that we inhabit, and the same pattern of causal connectibility between physical events would be found in that world and our own. More space-time structure than that provided by mere causal connectibility is needed to capture the difference between these two concrete possibilities, nor would it be enough if we knew which events lay along continuous causal paths. What is the concrete realization of this chirality? One might claim that the chirality, the handedness, of a space-time is fixed by the chirality of the experience (or possible experience) of creatures living in that space-time, or that chirality is a mere artifact of experience.[16] For instance, there might be chiral sense data, or some non-objectual account of chiral experience might be true. But we have seen that there are grounds to doubt that such views can be at once plausible and coherently conceivable. One might claim that the apparent chiral differences between contents are mere illusions created by our contingent nature as cognizers, that there really is no difference in truth which separates our world from its mirror inversion. But the intuitive content theory of Part One demands more. So we seem stuck with the handedness of the world. Space-times, it seems, can possess a chirality. If causal paths are to fix space-time structure, then they must involve causal relations of the special sort introduced in Chapter Seven, which reflect chirality. But at least causal paths in that chiral mode and the other concrete resources we noted above would seem to be sufficient to capture the concrete reality which underlies spatio-temporal relations according to general relativity.

3

Relativity implies that the world has a somewhat strange and unfamiliar spatio-temporal structure. Still, our experience, and the paradigmatic causal contents rooted in that experience, exhibit a more familiar spatio-temporal structure. The world is not galilean in the full traditional sense. But of course different reference frames deliver something at least approximating different galilean measurements, different measurements of temporal interval and spatial distance for instance.

The traditional galilean conception of the world involves a two-level structure. It holds that there is an objective world without phenomenal color. But it also holds that there are various experiences of that objective world, and that in those experiences the world seems to possess phenomenal colors of various sorts. Special and general relativity imply analogous two-level structures: Special relativity holds that there is an objective world of Minkowski space-time, in which there is no objective partition of the interval between two events into spatial distance and temporal interval. But it also holds that there are various inertial frames from which various spatial distances and temporal separations are observed. General relativity holds that the objective world has curved space-time, and that particles have features with no objective partition into traditional galilean properties. But it also holds that there are various frames of reference from which various such partitions do appear.

Nevertheless, there are important disanalogies between the sort of two-level structure relevant to phenomenal color and that relevant to the traditional galilean spatio-temporal properties. In the experience of two different people, even two people occupying the same objective external circumstances, an object can seem to have two different phenomenal colors, as the case of unique green suggests. And even ignoring individual differences, the phenomenal colors humans experience seem specially rooted in human neurophysiology. On the other hand, the temporal interval and spatial distance between two events according to a given reference frame seem to be things which might be captured by *instruments* in that frame, instruments which make measurements regarding which all people in that frame, and even scientifically-inclined bats and Martians, might agree. The peculiarities of individual neurophysiology seem irrelevant.

On the other hand, there are certain contingent features which instruments must possess to register two events as having determinate spatial and temporal separations. Clocks and rigid rods must meet certain conditions to be clocks and rigid rods, and to employ certain scales of measurement. Instruments in special relativity are confined to a particular inertial frame. And general relativity implies that special relativity only approximates the truth in regions which are small enough so that the curvature of space-time is insignificant. Big enough instruments wouldn't register traditional galilean measurements. And of course our capacity to read instruments demands something of our neurophysiology. But still the conditions to which a particular measurement of the spatial distance and temporal interval between two events are relativized seem more public, more open to all, than the neurophysiological conditions to which color experience is plausibly relativized.

There is another significant disanalogy between the case of color and that which faces us now: We saw in preceding chapters that there is no at once plausible and coherently conceivable account of our experience of phenomenal color. In particular, the traditional galilean view, at least when extended into a generalized physicalism, cannot provide a coherently conceivable account of our color experience. But the galilean measurements in some sense discounted by special and general relativity are still explained by those theories.

Special relativity first: It's not merely that special relativity includes a system of equations, the Lorentz transformation, which specifies how an interval between two events which breaks down into a certain spatial distance and temporal interval in one inertial frame will break down in another inertial frame. Special relativity also provides a physical explanation of how and why each particular inertial frame yields its peculiar measurements: 1) There is an objective Minkowski space-time which includes an objective, say time-like, interval between two events. 2) There are objective paths through Minkowski space-time traversed by particular inertial frames, and objective paths of light and other signals from the two events to those frames. The differences between those paths underwrite the differences in measurements made from the frames. 3) The inertial frames include instruments which seem to possess galilean properties, say particular lengths. But that isn't inconsistent with special relativity. Special relativity characterizes the instruments of the frame itself. Events within the frame are objectively related only by the interval, but the instruments in the frame aren't moving very rapidly at all relative to one another and to any observer traveling with the frame. They are for all practical purposes stationary relative to each other. And under such conditions special relativity makes predictions which closely and relevantly approximate those of traditional galilean mechanics. The instruments in the frame are not galilean objects, but they closely approximate galilean objects. And in ordinary cases there is enough limitation in their accuracy to make this close enough.

Similarly, general relativity predicts that a small enough set of instruments, at least when the effects of gravity or acceleration aren't severe, will closely approximate instruments in the flat Minkowski space-time of special relativity. Special and general relativity predict and explain the quasi-galilean form of the measurements made in inertial reference frames.

4

We are now in position to make explicit the implications of relativity for the plausibility of basic contents and the plausible and coherently conceivable realization of our causal experience. At least if we restrict ourselves to the non-pathological space-times suggested in section 2, general relativity implies a concrete world which can be exhaustively matched by basic contents. But it cannot be matched by the paradigmatic causal basic contents characteristic of the traditional galilean conception of the world, basic contents which invoke the familiar three spatial and single temporal dimensions. Let me explain.

Like galilean mechanics, Einstein's mechanics postulates properties of particles and fields which are causal powers of various sorts expressible in C,[17] so the particles and fields of general relativity may be constituted out of causal microevents. These microevents may either help constitute space-time itself or, alternatively, they may be fused to other causal microevents constituting the space-time arena.[18] But these microevents do not stand in the spatial and temporal relations characteristic of the paradigmatic causal contents. Rather their objective spatio-temporal structure is constituted by two kinds of things. First, by causal connectibility and continuous causal paths captured by oriented causal relations between microevents of the sorts introduced in Chapter Seven. Second, by the various other concrete phenomena which help fix metrical structure in general relativity. So relativity suggests that the world is matched by causal basic contents, though by relatively unfamiliar contents. It suggests that the world can be captured by C.

Our ordinary conceptions of balls and balloons no doubt include causal components along with plausibly false phenomenal components, but on the other hand those causal components are of a traditional galilean kind, with familiar spatio-temporal structure of the sort found in *paradigmatic* causal contents. So even the *causal* components of our ordinary conceptions of balls and balloons are false according to special and general relativity. Nevertheless, the unfamiliar causal contents consistent with special and general relativity have some structure which is also present in our ordinary causal conceptions of things in the world. *That* bit of structure, for instance certain sorts of causal connectibility, might obtain even if the paradigmatic causal contents *were* true. So according to special and general relativity the ordinary causal conceptions of things capture some truth, are partly true. It's just that they are also false in some respects.[19]

Even if relativity leaves some causal basic contents true, still it may well leave in doubt the plausibility of the coherently conceivable account of the realization of our spatial and temporal experience we developed earlier. We experience space and time quite differently, and yet there is a real sense in which according to relativity that traditional distinction collapses. It is plausible that general relativity is true, and hence that the traditional galilean conception of our muscles and skeletons and neurons is false in at least some respects. There are, of course, versions of muscles, skeletons, and neurons consistent with general relativity; the existence of those things does not require the truth of traditional galilean physics. But there is a legitimate question about whether relativistic neurons and muscles can provide a coherently conceivable realization of our causal experience, which after all seems to have a traditional galilean form, a particular spatio-temporal structure which the world in fact lacks.

We have already seen that the chirality of our experience demands chiral muscles, skeletons, and neurons for its plausible and coherently conceivable realization. The spatio-temporal structure of such left- or right-handed things cannot be fixed by mere causal connectibility, which would itself suffice to fix many of the features of the space-time of general relativity. But do causal microevents and even chiral causal relations, meeting the constraints of the theory of general relativity and constituting relativistic muscles, neurons, and bones which are yet chirally oriented, suffice to realize our galilean causal experience? Yes, I think, and we've already seen in essence how.

Relativity predicts and explains the quasi-galilean measurements made in frames of reference. The measuring instruments in a particular frame of reference meet certain conditions. They are physical clocks and material rods which move relative to each other only slowly, aren't too big, are unaccelerated (when the relevant frame is inertial), and so forth. Given these conditions, relativity predicts that such instruments, or at least those in approximately inertial frames, will at least closely approximate galilean instruments, galilean instruments with for instance objective lengths and lifetimes. But these conditions are also conditions which Galileo's bones, neurons, and muscles ordinarily meet or approximately meet. For instance, Galileo's limbs are relatively slow moving and small, and he is ordinarily more or less in an inertial frame. Galileo's body is a close analogue of the material rods and clocks and other instruments we've already considered. Galileo isn't a traditional galilean object, according to special and general relativity, but he approximates one closely enough for our purposes.

In fact, so close is the approximation of galilean physics to the relativistic truth under the ordinary conditions of our experience that one might wonder to what degree our causal experience does possess a specifically galilean rather than a relativistic form. Surely we don't see events in our own individual experience from two frames at once, which might reveal that experience as conclusively galilean or not. And while our experience does reveal particular simultaneity relations which aren't relativized within the experience, this might come to seem to us as trivial an artifact of our experience as highlights. At least our visual experience *seems* to have a galilean measure structure and include geodesics which are straight lines. But one might reasonably wonder if that structure appears in our experience with enough accuracy or certainty to constitute the experience as obviously of a traditional galilean sort. In particular, those of us who change thick glasses from time to time might wonder a bit. What reinforces our traditional thought that the world has a traditional galilean structure even down to details like fine measure structure, what stabilizes and refines our ordinary sense of spatio-temporal structure so that it is fully galilean, may not be experience alone. It may be that the way our neurophysiology comes to adjust to the relatively slow-moving and mid-sized objects we ordinarily deal with, the way our higher-order visual and motor processing comes to expect traditional galilean measure structure and straight lines, and the way we come to weave together seed contents into bigger basic contents, are crucial things which underlie our finding galilean structure more familiar. But it also seems at least reasonable to claim that somehow our experience reflects or anticipates this other processing and structure, and hence is in fact specifically *galilean* experience.

If indeed it has some, how might the fine galilean details of our experience, say a traditional measure structure, be realized? We might reasonably hope that higher-order neural activity is capable of constituting that level of spatio-temporal structure, and to constitute resources which would still be legitimately available if a relativistic conception of our neurons and musculature replaced the traditional galilean one. But still there is a chance that this is a vain hope. It may be that any coherently conceivable account of the realization of even the common phenomena of eye-glass distortion must be an objectual account. If so, then relativity may lead us early to the point we reach anyway in the next chapter. Perhaps we should even be able to see from a commonsense observation, that severe distortion of straight lines by strong eye-glasses is temporary, that objectual accounts of these sorts of phenomena are implausible. And perhaps there is an argument which shows that only objectual accounts are coherently conceivable. But I don't possess it.

Even if we ignore worries about fine details like straight lines and measure structure, one may resist the claim that relativistic neurons and muscles can constitute crucial spatio-temporal features of our galilean causal experience. For instance, even special relativity implies that there isn't an objective segmentation of the interval between two events into a particular temporal interval and spatial separation, invariant between frames. Hence it may seem miraculous that, in Galileo's experience or the purview of certain instruments traveling along in a particular reference frame, a difference between space and time can appear. That difference is in a certain sense an illusion.

In the last chapter, it seemed plausible, indeed necessary, to hold that if one causal experience of Galileo's follows another, then they are constituted by sequential neural-muscular events. We seemed forced towards an objectual account of the temporality of our experience. But special relativity may seem in conflict with this claim. In the reference frame in which Galileo travels, his motor neuron firings A, B, and C may be such that B is simultaneous to and spatially distant from A, and C is temporally after. But in another inertial frame those same events may have different sorts of temporal and spatial separation. So how could what is objectively there, what is invariant between frames, help constitute Galileo as having corresponding experiences A', B', and C', such that A' and B' appear simultaneous and C' later at least within Galileo's experience, such that it is an objective fact that he experiences things as so related? It doesn't seem sufficient to claim that Galileo's higher-order neural processing, traveling along in the same frame with the rest of his neurons and his body, might constitute judgments about simultaneity or precedence in his experience which might help constitute that simultaneity or precedence. For even about these higher-order neural events similar questions might plausibly arise. It may seem that if objective spatial and temporal relations play the crucial role in realizing the spatio-temporal form of our experience that the last chapter argued, then special and general relativity spell trouble. If later neural firings and motor action are to constitute later causal experiences, then there must be objectively later neural firings and motor action. And relativity may seem to deny that.

This worry, however, is an illusion. The Minkowski space-time of special relativity, for instance, possesses an objective structure provided by light cones, so that some pairs of events objectively have time-like, or space-like, separations. Two inertial frames may differ about details like the measurement of the temporal interval between two events with a time-like separation, but no inertial frames will assess two events with time-like separation as simultaneous or as in a different temporal order. And this level of objective temporal and spatial structure is all that is obviously required for the coherently conceivable realization of our galilean causal experience. All that seems needed in the case of A and C, say, is that C follow A, and hence C' A', in any inertial frame, and hence in the objective world. This merely requires that C and A have a time-like separation.

What about the experience of *simultaneity*? Any distinct neural events which realize distinct features of our experience (if things work that way) might have space-like separations. But then they would seem to have different temporal orders in different inertial frames. Still, the particular small distances and separations involved in such a case might constitute these differences in temporal order to be insignificant given the resolution allowed by the temporal grain of our experience. The temporal separations involved according to *any* inertial frame might be too short to be significant within the experience in question.

Some features of the spatio-temporality of our experience are rooted in objective spatio-temporal features of the objects which make up the world, and the rest are fine details like measure-structure which are introduced by the pattern of our higher-order neural processing. Or so it seems. There seem to be no barriers in principle to a plausible and coherently conceivable account of our causal experience, at least given the strictures of relativity. That we are capable of such experience is rooted in contingencies of our situation, for instance that we are pretty small and can't move our arms very fast. But those contingencies do underwrite that experience, in a plausible and coherently conceivable way.

Relativity is coherently conceivable, and it allows us to preserve our objectual account of causal experience largely unchanged. So far so good, except perhaps for the difficulties introduced by metrical structure. But things are hanging by a thread. It matters that we aren't a lot bigger than we are. As for Goldilocks, it also matters that we aren't a lot smaller. And the problems which the very small introduces into physics will be more difficult for us to shake off than those which Einstein set.

NOTES

1. I have primarily followed the exposition in Albert Einstein, *Relativity, The Special and General Theory* (New York: Crown, 1961), which is Einstein's popular exposition. But Einstein, *The Meaning of Relativity*, third edition (Princeton: Princeton University Press, 1950), and also the original papers "On the Electrodynamics of Moving Bodies" and "The Foundations of the General Theory of Relativity", collected in H.A. Lorentz, A. Einstein, H. Minkowski, and H. Weyl (editors), *The Principle of Relativity* (London: Methuen and Co., 1923), 35-65 and 111-164, are amazingly clear and accessible. E. Taylor and J. Wheeler, *Spacetime Physics* (San Francisco: W.H. Freeman, 1966) is also very helpful.
2. Stars which we know to move at least approximately in accord with the conditions required by Newton's first law.
3. Archimedes and Curie inhabit a spinning earth, but it spins slowly enough so that we can for most purposes ignore that complication.

4. Velocity has a direction, so a point on the edge of a spinning disk accelerates even as the disk revolves at a uniform speed.
5. This is consistent with special relativity.
6. Another important element of Einstein's thinking was that special relativity seemed to him to lack a necessary generality. It only specifies measurements in inertial frames, and not for instance in accelerated frames, including those fixed to the spinning earth. He reasoned that all of the many arbitrary gaussian systems of coordinates for curved space-time are equally acceptable, that the laws of nature are invariant between all such systems of coordinates, just as the laws of nature were supposed by special relativity to be invariant between inertial frames. Einstein put it this way on page 97 of *Relativity, The Special and General Theory*: "All Gaussian coordinate systems are essentially equivalent for the formulation of the general laws of nature." But Einstein was confused on these issues. See Michael Friedman's discussion in *Foundations of Space-Time Theories* (Princeton: Princeton University Press, 1983). So I will ignore this element of his exposition.
7. This follows Roger Penrose, *The Emperor's New Mind* (Oxford: Oxford University Press, 1989), ch. 5, which in turn follows Cartan.
8. I am, of course, ignoring wind resistance.
9. The fields themselves might be propagated in something analogous to the manner of electromagnetic fields.
10. This follows Taylor and Wheeler, 190-197.
11. One might wonder why no philosophers have arisen to postulate some analogue of colorful sense data to explain our experience of determinate spatial and temporal positions, to hypothesize that *some* events have determinate spatial and temporal separations even if ordinary material events do not. As we will shortly see, there is a significant asymmetry in this respect between relativity's treatment of galilean spatio-temporal relations and galilean physics' treatment of phenomenal color. Relativity in fact implies that we would have the sort of spatio-temporal experience we possess, at least in most details. So there is very little motivation to believe that some things have determinate spatial and temporal separations if ordinary material objects do not. Hence I will presume here that if ordinary material events have no determinate spatial and temporal separations, then nothing does. It may be that this treatment will seem especially problematic for temporal separation, which psychological events may seem clearly to retain. But please bear with me for the moment. We will return to this issue shortly.
12. Penrose, 196-197.
13. Lawrence Sklar, "Facts, Conventions, and Assumptions in the Theory of Spacetime", *Philosophy and Spacetime Physics* (Berkeley: University of California Press, 1985), 73-147.
14. See Sklar, "Facts, Conventions, and Assumptions in the Theory of Spacetime", and also "What Might be Right about the Causal Theory of Time" and "Prospects for a Causal Theory of Spacetime", *Philosophy and Spacetime Physics*, 249-267 and 268-288.
15. In fact just by ideal clocks. See the references in the preceding note.
16. If so, different creatures in the same world might see it as a mirror inversion of the way others see it.
17. They might not be if the spatio-temporal relations of the relevant contents were not also expressible in C. But we will soon see that they are.
18. There is more than a little ambiguity about what the difference between relationalists and substantivalists is. There is in fact more than one relationalist and substantivalist debate. See Lawrence Sklar, *Space, Time, and Spacetime* and *Philosophy and Spacetime Physics*, and John Earman, *World Enough and Space-Time* for a survey of some of the complexities. But certainly there is more than a little reason to identify points of a field with points of space-time, and yet points of a field have obvious causal properties, so at least one of the traditional disputes between substantivalists and relationalists seems now to be otiose. It may be that if there are both fields and particles, then there is fusion of concrete events in the manner suggested in the last chapter in plausible basic contents, but that is available to us if necessary. The other traditional reasons for preferring substantivalism to relationalism seem to me not to cut a great deal of ice. Newton argued that inertial effects involving

rotation, for instance centrifugal force, should by explained by motion relative to absolute space. But, as Sklar has in effect suggested, perhaps following up on a suggestion of Leibniz, it might be that differences in inertia are simply differences in intrinsic powers. Alternatively, entities like Newton's tethered spinning balls in an empty universe, which tug at their string, might be seen to be changing certain sorts of oriented spatial relations over time, which may be a way of following up on certain suggestions of Huygens. Kant argued that relationalists cannot give an account of the difference between a right- and left-handed glove, but we have chirally-oriented relations at our disposal. And, as Sklar has pointed out, any sorts of chiral relations available to orient points in substantival space ought to be available between material bits of the glove as well. But in any case, C has the resources to express most substantivalist conceptions as well as relationalist ones. We might wonder how it can, how humans can think such things. It seems to me not implausible to insist that the various flavors of orientation introduced in Chapters Six and Seven demand objectual accounts of realization, at least if their realization is to be coherently conceivable.

19. In fact, even the features of ordinary, paradigmatic causal contents which fail to match the world might be mapped onto true features of the world in some reasonably systematic way. There's a special kind of systematic isomorphism between those literally false features and features which the world in fact possesses according to general relativity, and this might constitute some analogue of match. But of course much the same thing might be said about the phenomenal features of contents. An analogue of match isn't really match.

CHAPTER EIGHTEEN

CLASSICAL EXPERIENCE AND QUANTUM MECHANICS

Quantum mechanics is the second great watershed of twentieth century physics, and in some ways it involved an even more radical break with galilean orthodoxy than relativity did. But the nature of this second rift is somewhat obscure. That is partly because quantum mechanics has such a radical and unfamiliar form, but it is also partly because the mathematical formalism of quantum mechanics preceded its interpretation to an unusual degree. Physicists were in possession of the mathematical expression of quantum mechanics before they had a good sense of what it said about the world. In fact, to some degree it is still far from clear what that spectacularly successful formalism says about the world.

This chapter applies quantum mechanics to the issues which concern us, in much the way that the last chapter applied special and general relativity. Section 1 provides a brief exposition of key features of quantum mechanics.[1] Section 2 surveys the range of ways in which the mathematical formalism of quantum mechanics has been interpreted, the standard views about what that formalism should be taken to say about the world.[2] It isolates a few reasonably plausible interpretations for further treatment. Sections 3 and 4 concern these reasonable options. They discuss the coherent conceivability of quantum mechanics, and its implications for the coherently conceivable realization of our spatio-temporal and causal experience.

1

Very large examples are naturally featured in discussions of general relativity, for instance planets and stars bending space. Quantum mechanics is in a certain sense the science of the very tiny, or at least of very tiny energies. We need to dive down from the scale of stars to that of individual particles. But let me begin our discussion from another angle:

Just as certain electromagnetic phenomena, in particular the constant finite speed of light in all inertial frames, led to the crisis from which special relativity was born, so too certain electromagnetic phenomena could not be explained by classical physics. What is "classical" physics? Classical physics is post-galilean physics prior to the development of quantum mechanics. It encompasses both Newton's mechanics augmented by Maxwell's account of electromagnetism and Einstein's revisions of that traditional view. What was its explanatory failure? Classical physics faced serious difficulties when attempting to explain the interactions of traditional discrete particles and continuous radiation fields. These difficulties occasioned a crisis which led away from classical conceptions towards quantum mechanics. First problem: "Black body" radiation.[3] Some things absorb radiation better than others. "Black bodies" are maximally effective absorbers of radiation at all frequencies, and hence by classical calculations maximally effective emitters as well. For instance, the inside of a cubical box made of opaque material can be, under certain conditions, a black body. The classically calculated expectation for radiation emission from a black body was the "ultraviolet catastrophe", in which the intensity of emission increases with frequency, increases out at the ultraviolet end of the spectrum, and so the energy within our box becomes infinite. But it is observed that the intensity of emission of a black body falls off at higher frequencies, that the ultraviolet catastrophe does not occur. Second problem: The atom. According to Rutherford's classical conception of the atom, electrons orbit around the nucleus like planets around the sun, bound by electromagnetism rather than gravity. But the classical prediction is that such an orbiting electron would emit electromagnetic radiation of smoothly increasing frequency, and spiral down quickly into the nucleus. And, of course, electrons do not so spiral down. Also, atoms emit light only at specific frequencies, the sharp spectral lines characteristic of each type of atom, and this seems hard to explain in a classical way.

In the face of these and similar puzzles, the first fifteen years of this century saw a series of modifications of classical physics in the direction of quantum mechanics. This is the period of what is called the "old quantum theory", an ancestor of full-blown quantum mechanics. Max Planck proposed in 1900 that electromagnetic radiation is emitted only in discrete "quanta". The energy of these quanta is equivalent to hv, where v is the frequency of the radiation and h is a new constant, "Planck's constant". In this way, Planck was able to explain the observed pattern of black-body radiation. Einstein was able to explain the classically inexplicable photoelectric effect by assuming that light is always, even while traveling through space, found in such discrete quanta, that it consists of particles now called "photons". Traditionally "continuous" radiation was seeming suspiciously discrete and particle-like, and it had momentum. Niels Bohr proposed a modification of the Rutherford model of the atom in which the electrons orbiting a nucleus can possess angular momentum only in integral multiples of $h/2\pi$, where h is again Planck's constant. In the Bohr atom, electrons do not quickly spiral down into the nucleus, and Bohr was able to predict the spectral lines of hydrogen. De Broglie proposed in 1923 that particles generally have wave-like features, that there is a connection between the mass of a particle and an associated wave frequency: $hv=e=mc^2$. Again, Planck's constant played a crucial role. Just as light had come to seem unexpectedly particle-like, so particles were coming to seem suspiciously wave-like.[4]

The old quantum theory of Planck, Einstein, and Bohr had a patchwork look, and it did not succeed in giving an account of the full range of electromagnetic phenomena known at the time. But quantum mechanics itself succeeded, in one spectacular swoop, in providing an account of the wide range of known spectroscopic phenomena, scattering phenomena, and the photoelectric effect. And through Dirac's quantum mechanical account of the electron and Pauli's exclusion principle, it soon led even to a successful explanation of the atomic elements, and hence of the wide range of familiar chemical phenomena. The mathematical formalism of quantum mechanics is a spectacularly successful bit of mathematics. That formalism was born twice over. Heisenberg, in 1925, developed a version known as matrix mechanics. In 1926, Schrödinger developed an apparently different mechanics based on a time-dependent wave-equation, but then soon discovered that his wave mechanics and Heisenberg's matrix mechanics were in fact substantially equivalent. Von Neumann formalized quantum mechanics a few years later as a calculus of Hermitian operators on Hilbert space.[5]

The quantum mechanical formalism captures some very odd features of the world. The "two slit" experiment reveals much of that oddity: Let there be a radiation source, say a light source, which emits radiation through an opaque screen with adjustable slits, towards a second screen beyond. And let the second screen register receipt of the radiation. In particular, let the source be a monochromatic light source, and the receiving screen a photo-sensitive plate which darkens wherever light impinges. And let there be two narrow parallel slits in the middle opaque screen, with the second capable of being opened and closed by a shutter.[6]

When light of low enough intensity is emitted by the source, it is received at the photosensitive plate one photon at a time. A pattern of dark dots, each which registers the receipt of a single packet of light, is built up on the receiving screen. And the pattern is built up one dot at a time, as each photon passes through the apparatus. This reveals the particle-like nature of light. On the other hand, certain wave-like features of light are also revealed by the experiment.

If a single slit in the opaque screen is open, then, as we might expect, the pattern of dark dots on the receiving screen is most dense in a line directly opposite that slit, right in line with the light source and the slit. It shades off in density away from that dark central line. Though the light does seem to spread a bit after it passes through the slit, still that might seem something particles would do, as they glance off the sides of the slit.

But if the second slit is open as well as the first, then something quite remarkable happens. The pattern of dots on the receiving screen is not simply the sum of the patterns each slit alone would generate. Rather the pattern on the receiving screen is wavy. It falls into an interference pattern, with many troughs and peaks, each parallel to the two fuzzy lines which one might otherwise have expected. At some points, there may be a density of dots four times as large as a single slit would have produced over the same time period. At other points, there may be far fewer dots than there would have been had only one slit been open. It's as if the light passed through the two slits as a wave, and the two wave patterns which emerged on the other side of the slitted screen interfered with one another, like ripples on a pond from two falling stones. At some points the troughs of one wave pattern and the peaks of another cancel one another out, and at other points the peaks or troughs reinforce one another, and hence we get the interference effects revealed on the receiving screen. Light seems in this way wave-like.

But the light still registers on the receiving screen in discrete dots. One might think that different photons passing through different slits interfere with one another in some way so as to create the interference pattern, but that wavy pattern appears on the receiving screen even though the light source is so low in intensity that light passes through the apparatus one photon at a time, and hence the dots form on the screen one dot at a time. And it doesn't seem plausible to claim that each individual photon somehow passes through both slits as a wave and then interferes with itself on the other side of the screen, because it does after all always register on the receiving screen at a discrete and single point, as a single dot. In fact, if we put a counter at each slot to register the passage of photons, then only one detector will go off as each photon passes through the slitted screen. But, almost miraculously, when we have the counters in place and hence know through which slit a photon passes, the interference effects disappear.

What are we to make of all this? Here's a wild hypothesis: Somehow light in the two-slit experiment propagates as a wave or set of waves when we aren't registering its location by a receiving screen or a counter, and then when we register its location the wave or waves collapse to a single point. Different bits of light which pass through the apparatus can be, up to the point of registration, in identical states, and yet collapse to different points, though with the points to which they collapse distributed in such a way that the characteristic wave-like pattern is built up on the receiving screen, one dot at a time. Quantum mechanics in fact proposes something quite like this.[7]

In the two-slit experiment, it seems that wave-like things add up and interfere with one another when even a single photon passes through the apparatus. Quantum mechanics characterizes this circumstance as involving the addition of probability amplitudes for alternatives. Unlike ordinary probabilities, probability *amplitudes* may be negative, and may even be complex numbers. Complex numbers are numbers of the form $a+ib$, where i= the square root of -1. b might equal 0, so real numbers are in fact also complex numbers. Hence in fact all the probability amplitudes are complex numbers.

The classical view was that the probability that a particle like a photon would get from the source to a certain point on the receiving screen would be, when two slits were open, the sum of two products. It would be the sum of i) the product of the probability that the photon would get from the source to the first slit, and the probability that it would get from that slit to the receiving point, and

ii) the product of the probability that it would get from the source to the second slit, and the probability that it would get from that slit to the receiving point. In quantum mechanics, however, the probability *amplitude* of that final location is the sum of the products of the probability *amplitudes* for each of those discrete steps. Probability amplitudes, unlike probabilities, may be negative or even complex, and hence they can cancel one another out in much the manner of the troughs and peaks of interfering waves.

We might well wonder what the physical significance of a probability amplitude might be.[8] The clearest link with ordinary physical properties is this: The "squared modulus" of the probability amplitude for a photon to be received at a certain point on the screen is the probability that that event will be observed if the requisite observation is made. What's a squared modulus? Let there be a two-dimensional plane with coordinate axes crossing at 0 and at right angles to each other, with the horizontal axis marked in the customary way by negative and positive numbers, and the vertical axis by negative and positive integer multiples of i (the square root of -1). To each point on that plane there corresponds a complex number. The "modulus" of any complex number (say a probability amplitude) is the distance between its corresponding point and the origin of that plane. The "squared modulus", which yields the probability linking things up with classical properties, is simply the square of the modulus. Probability amplitudes are rather like complex square-roots of probabilities.

At the very least, quantum mechanics *characterizes* the states of particles in a quite different way from traditional classical mechanics. Classical mechanics characterizes a particle at a time by specifying a definite position and momentum. In the standard quantum mechanical characterization of the position of a particle at a moment, every possible position in space is an alternative for the particle, and the characterization of the particle includes a complex weighting of all those alternatives by probability amplitudes. This is called the "psi-" or "wave-function" of the particle. The quantum mechanical analogue of momentum can be recovered from the wave-function by Fourier analysis, a bit of mathematics analogous to the harmonic analysis of musical sounds into pure tones.[9] So the wave-function of a particle in fact determines amplitudes for each momentum the particle might possess, as well as specifying the amplitudes for position. These momentum alternatives are related to the characteristic frequency of the particle, so that the momentum in various directions which such a particle might possess as it evolves over time varies in a wave-like way.

Under ordinary circumstances, the quantum mechanical state of a particle (or collection of particles) will evolve in a deterministic way, governed by Schrödinger's wave equation. But at each point in that evolution, the particle (or collection of particles) will be assigned only amplitudes for locations (or combinations of locations), not locations. But we do seem to observe locations for particles, for instance when they land at particular points on the screen in the two-slit experiment. Here's where the squared modulus comes in. In the orthodox version of quantum mechanics, canonized in von Neumann's formalization, when a measurement of some classical property of a particle, say position, occurs, then a radically new sort of evolution of the quantum mechanical state of the particle occurs. There is a "collapse of the wave packet", and the particle assumes a classical position in accord with probabilities equal to the squared moduli of the relevant probability amplitudes. Immediately upon measurement of a position, the particle is characterized not by a bunch of amplitudes for various positions but by a classical position.

Let me repeat. When unwatched and unmeasured, a quantum mechanical particle is characterized by a wave-function which fixes amplitudes for alternative classical properties like positions, and evolves deterministically according to the Schrödinger equation. When a particle is measured in a certain way, say in regards to its position, a new sort of probabilistic evolution occurs, and the particle becomes characterized by a classical property. For instance, in the two slit experiment, a particular photon has a certain amplitude for passing through one slit and a certain amplitude for passing through another to each position on the receiving screen. When the photon reaches the screen it is measured. Hence the wave packet collapses in a probabilistic way in accord with the rule for turning amplitudes into probabilities, and the photon becomes characterized by a particular classical position.

Notice two non-classical features of quantum mechanics: First, quantum mechanics generally characterizes particles not by determinate classical properties like determinate positions and momentums but by probability amplitudes for alternative classical properties of those sorts. It characterizes the particles by describing a "superposition" of alternative classical states. Second, quantum mechanics speaks of two sorts of evolution of particle states. A particle is governed by the deterministic Schrödinger equation until the time when a certain sort of classical property is measured. Then it undergoes a new sort of probabilistic evolution which yields the result of that measurement.

It is important to realize that this new sort of evolution, evolution in measurement, is triggered by something which apparently cannot be completely characterized quantum mechanically, which cannot be constituted solely by a bunch of quantum mechanical particles characterized merely by wave-functions. For instance, if the photosensitive screen in the two-slit experiment were so constituted, then the complex of a received photon plus the screen would be merely characterized by amplitudes for classical properties like positions, and not by positions themselves. The screen and photon would be in a complex superposition of alternative classical states, of all the alternative ways the particle might have hit and even all the alternative places the particles in the screen might be, rather than in the single state which is observed. Von Neumann showed that it doesn't really matter where in the world this dramatic cut between the quantum mechanical and the classical occurs, where wave packets collapse.[10] It could be at registering screens, at the eyes of observers, or even somewhere in their brains. But the cut must, it seems, occur somewhere.

Understanding all this is clearly a large order. For one thing, it is more than a little difficult to understand what it is that the quantum mechanical characterization of a particle is supposed to say about it. What does it mean to say that a particle is characterized by a bunch of amplitudes for classical properties?

Just as both quantum mechanics and relativity were rooted in the need to account for certain electromagnetic phenomena, so, Heisenberg reasoned, there might also be some quantum mechanical analogue of Einstein's critique of the observational significance of absolute simultaneity. Like its relativistic analogue, that might help point the way towards a proper interpretation of the theory. Heisenberg's "uncertainty relations" seem to provide just such an analogue.[11] Heisenberg's uncertainty relations assert that the product of the uncertainty in measurement of the position of a particle and the uncertainty in measurement of its momentum must be, for any experimental setup, $> h/2\pi$. (Planck's constant again.) The more accurately the position of particle can be determined by a given measuring apparatus, the less accurately can momentum be determined. If position is determined exactly, then momentum is completely uncertain. There is a similar uncertainty relation linking time and energy. Heisenberg motivated the uncertainty relations by semi-classical arguments, which suggested that even if there were determinate classical properties they would be beyond our epistemic access, or more exactly that certain determinate combinations of classical properties couldn't be epistemically accessed. For instance, Heisenberg reasoned that any means of measuring the position of a small particle with some degree of accuracy would give the particle a kick of a sort which would leave its momentum correspondingly uncertain, and likewise that any means of measuring its momentum would leave its position correspondingly uncertain. Motivated in this way, the uncertainty relations may seem merely to express our epistemic difficulties in assessing the objective determinate classical properties of particles, though we should still be troubled by the parallel with Einstein's critique of absolute simultaneity, which has been taken to reveal more than merely our epistemic limitations. And one can argue to the uncertainty relations in another way. They are a direct consequence of the quantum mechanical formalism. The uncertainty relations may be taken to express an objective indeterminacy in the world itself, and not merely in our knowledge of the world. Einstein's observational critique of absolute simultaneity has been generally taken to show not merely that we can't access what the objective facts about absolute simultaneity are, but rather that there are none. So too with the uncertainty relations.

Just as Einstein's critique of the observational significance of absolute simultaneity seems to support the conclusion that there is no fact of the matter about the absolute simultaneity of two events, so too Heisenberg's uncertainty relations may seem to support the claim that a particle cannot in fact have at once a determinate position and momentum. On the other hand, as is in fact suggested by Heisenberg's own concrete semi-classical arguments, this isn't the only way to take the uncertainty relations, and quantum mechanics generally. Or so at first it seemed. At least early in its history, quantum mechanics seemed open to two very different kinds of interpretations. On the one hand, it seemed, one might take a wave-function to characterize in a more or less complete way the state of a particular particle at a given moment. On this view, the particle has a very unusual sort of objective state, which is characterized as a collection of amplitudes for classical properties. On the other hand, it seemed, one might take the quantum mechanical characterization of an individual particle as not really adequately representing its complete objective state. On this view, the same wave-function may equally well characterize particles with different properties, with different exact classical positions and momentums. That is because the wave-function expresses merely our knowledge about the particles, and we may well have the same knowledge about the positions and momentums of objectively different particles. Their representation by the same wave-function is appropriate only because we don't know the exact details about the particles, and because what we do know about them is the same. This second interpretation is the "ensemble interpretation". It holds that quantum mechanics in its standard formulation is not a complete theory about individual particles.

The ensemble interpretation is obviously attractive in many ways. Particles retain their easily comprehensible classical positions and momentums, though the uncertainty relations limit our epistemic access to those properties. Measurement of the classical position of a particle may perturb its classical momentum so that we no longer know what it is, but it still in fact retains a determinate classical momentum. Also there aren't really two sorts of evolution operating in the world itself, a deterministic one when particles are unmeasured and a probabilistic one when they are not. The so-called collapse of the wave packet, on this view, is merely our passage from a state of relative ignorance, regarding say a particle's position, to a state of greater knowledge. Particles evolve deterministically even during measurement, and the probabilities of quantum theory are merely epistemic probabilities, linking our state of knowledge before measurement and the observed results of measurement. Measurement seems to involve no change in the objective state of a particle beyond that required to underwrite the uncertainty relations, and this can be explained classically in the manner suggested by Heisenberg's thought experiments. And there is certainly no difficulty in explaining how a measuring instrument which initiates the so-called collapse of the wave packet isn't exhaustively characterized by a superposition. Nothing is. Certainly, understanding what quantum mechanics says about the world is much more difficult if the wave-function completely characterizes the objective state of a particle.

Einstein, Podolsky, and Rosen formulated an interesting idealized experiment, now dubbed "EPR", in an attempt to demonstrate that quantum mechanics was incomplete, and that the ensemble interpretation was correct.[12] Ironically, it is this very thought experiment which eventually led to the realization that at least the traditional ensemble interpretations of quantum mechanics are incorrect,[13] that quantum mechanics says something radical and non-classical about the world. The simplest EPR-type experiment is probably a later version due to David Bohm.[14] I will follow Penrose' exposition of Mermin's version of a Bohm-style experiment, because this is the most accessible I know.[15] But it requires a bit of background. Bohm's experiment concerns the measurement not of position or momentum, but of spin.

The spin of a particle is some analogue of the classical angular momentum of a large spinning body, but it is odd in various ways. First, the *amount* of spin of a given sort of particle, say an electron, is always the same. Second, the *direction* of the spin varies in a strange way. Choose some arbitrary direction in space. We can determine whether or not the particle has a spin with that particular orientation. And if we immediately repeat the measurement, we will get the same result. But if we vary the direction in space for which we register spin, then there are various probabilities that we will get a positive or a negative registration. If the second measurement is for a direction at right angles to the first orientation in which we registered spin, then there will be a 50% chance of a positive answer, and a 50% chance of a negative answer. If the angle between the two measured directions is acute, then a positive answer is more probable.

Suppose now that an electron and a positron (which is positively charged but otherwise like an electron) are produced by the decay of a spinless particle, and move out in opposite directions in space. Spin, like ordinary angular momentum, must be conserved. If one particle has a spin with one orientation, then the other must have a spin with the opposite orientation. Let the particles travel out until they are a light-year apart. It still follows from the conservation principle that if we measure one particle and register a certain spin, then we can conclude that the other particle has a correlated spin.

Quantum mechanics characterizes the particles, prior to measurement, as being in a superposition of spin states, with various amplitudes for various spins. When we measure a particle and determine its spin in some direction, its wave-function "collapses", and we get a definite result. But when we so measure the spin of one of our two correlated particles, the wave-function for the *other* particle must also collapse in a particular way, instantaneously, despite the fact that the second particle is a light-year away from the first. Otherwise spin would not be conserved. The particles are space-like separated, and relativity has taught us that space-like separations cannot be bridged by causal influence. But yet here we have something that looks like forbidden instantaneous action at a distance. The measurement of one particle seems instantaneously to cause the second to have a determinate spin.

The ensemble interpretation seems capable of drawing the sting from this situation. If a particle's wave-function merely characterizes our *knowledge* of its state, then the collapse of the wave-function of the unmeasured particle isn't a real physical process, but merely our passage from a state of relative ignorance about it to a state of greater knowledge. This involves no instantaneous action at a distance, no violation of the principles of special relativity. But if the ensemble interpretation is incorrect, we seem to be in trouble. If the collapse of the wave packet is an actual physical event, then it seems that there is some kind of instantaneous action at a distance involved in these cases, and this seems in violation of the strictures of relativity. If quantum mechanics is complete, it seems to imply a strange "entanglement" of widely separated particles, out of step with ordinary conceptions of causation and in apparent conflict with special relativity. So we might well be tempted to conclude, with Einstein, that it is incomplete, that there are "hidden variables" of particles which are not captured by their wave-functions.

But to yield to this temptation would be a mistake, at least if the hidden variables are supposed to be of any traditional sort. John Bell's analysis of EPR-type situations showed that at least standard ensemble interpretations cannot be correct.[16] He showed that no non-contextual, local hidden variables can reproduce the quantum mechanical predictions for such situations. Non-contextual hidden variables are those which are not affected by the kind of measurement which is performed on them. Local hidden variables are those which are unaffected by events at space-like separations. Any non-contextual, local hidden variables theory makes predictions which satisfy an inequality now called "Bell's inequality", and quantum mechanics predicts that Bell's inequality will be violated.

Imagine that we have two measuring devices, one located with each particle in our EPR experiment. Each device can measure spin in each of three directions, if given one of three possible settings. It yields a yes or no answer to the question: Does the particle have spin with that orientation? Let the three directions be in a plane and at 120 degrees from each other. Quantum mechanics predicts: i) That if the settings of both of the devices are the same, then they will yield opposite answers. If one yields a yes, then the other will yield a no. ii) That if the settings of the machines vary at random and independently, then the two devices are equally likely to yield the same and to yield opposite answers.

But this prediction cannot be reproduced by any local, non-contextual hidden variables model. Consider for instance a traditional ensemble view of this situation: If such a model is to reproduce prediction (i), then it must hold that each particle carries definite answers to the questions about spin direction which may be posed to it by the devices, and not merely definite probabilities for definite answers. The answers registered by the two devices would not otherwise be always correlated, as quantum mechanics predicts. For instance, if one particle carries the answers (yes, yes, yes) to the questions it can be asked by our devices, then the other must carry the answers (no, no, no) to the same questions. If one particle carries a yes for one question and a no for the other two, then the second must carry a no for the first and a yes for the other two. And so on.

But notice that there is no set of such definite answers carried by the particles which can yield the right percentage of agreement in answers, just exactly 50%, when the settings of the two devices vary randomly and independently. If prediction (i) of quantum mechanics is reproduced by such a hidden variables theory, then (ii) will be violated. It's worth working this through: The setting of the devices occurs randomly, so there is an equal chance that each instrument will have each of the three settings, and hence an equal chance of each possible combination of settings. But there is no set of prepared answers which the particles can carry which will yield the same answer in just 50% of these cases. There are really just two sorts of possibilities we need to consider: If the first particle carries a yes answer to all questions, then the second will carry a no for all, and the devices will always disagree. And if the first carries a yes for two questions and a no for the third, then the second will carry a no for the first two questions and a yes for the third, and the devices will agree 4/9 of the time.[17] As it's easy to see, all the possibilities are of one of these two types. So all possible assignments of definite answers to the particles, all the assignments which meet the conditions required to yield prediction (i), will likewise yield agreement here either never or only 4/9 of the time. None can yield the quantum mechanical prediction, that there will be agreement 50% of the time.

One might be tempted to claim that all this serves to show is that the 50% prediction is a crazy prediction, that quantum mechanics is a crazy theory. But note that the issue between non-contextual, local hidden variables theories and quantum mechanics is placed by Bell's analysis firmly in the experimental realm, that it is open to observation and experiment. The relevant question is what sorts of correlations in fact are observed in EPR-type situations. A number of such experiments have been performed. It is widely accepted that they show as a body that the quantum mechanical predictions are correct. Aspect's experiments in particular seem to clearly reveal correlations that no causal influence traveling at light speed can explain.[18] Quantum mechanics does make very strange predictions, and those predictions are correct. They reveal an unexpected entanglement of widely separated entities in EPR-type situations, at space-like separations.

Does this mean that in fact quantum mechanics is in conflict with relativity, and that relativity is false? Not exactly. At least if we take the quantum mechanical formalism at face value, if for instance there aren't non-classical hidden variables which we can both measure and manipulate in some way apparently forbidden by the uncertainty relations, then one cannot use the quantum mechanical entanglement to send a *signal* from one wing of the EPR experiment to the other at a speed faster than light. This is because the manipulable *setting* of the measuring device in one wing of the experiment does not determine the outcome in the other wing. Rather the non-manipulable *outcome* of the measurement in the first wing determines the outcome in the second. The outcome in the first wing cannot itself be manipulated at will by a would-be signaler. The quantum mechanical entanglement reveals "outcome dependence", but not "parameter independence". It involves, in Shimony's vivid phrase, not action, but passion at a distance.[19]

Given the uncertainty relations, one cannot use the quantum mechanical entanglement to send a signal instantaneously from one wing of an EPR-type experiment to the other which an observer can read, and one cannot use it to synchronize distant clocks or the like in a way which would violate the conditions required by special relativity. So we have a kind of uneasy peace between the observational predictions of quantum mechanics and of relativity. Still, quantum mechanics may reasonably seem to be in serious violation of the spirit of relativity, and to imply quite different things about space and time. We will return to these issues.

2

The most traditional ensemble interpretations of quantum mechanics are eliminated by Bell's analysis. But there are a number of interpretive options which remain. This section surveys these alternatives, and isolates the most plausible for more extensive treatment in the following sections.

Among the interpretations of quantum mechanics which attempt to fathom what that useful formalism says about the world, the most sober and plausible have not received the most press. This may be, as Bell has suggested, because they are not romantic, because they require "mathematical work by theoretical physicists" and do not promise "lessons in philosophy for philosophers" of any direct and sexy variety.[20] But we will see that in fact these sober, plausible, and non-romantic alternatives do in fact have a lot of bite on the quite specific issues which concern us. I will begin, however, by discussing a number of interpretive options which we will not pursue in detail.

2.1

In fact, let me begin with an option which isn't in the strict sense an *interpretive* option at all. It is possible to take a merely instrumentalist or positivist attitude towards quantum mechanics, as towards relativity: The formalism of the theory makes excellent predictions about the course of our experience and the observations registered by our measuring instruments, at least when it is deployed with the taste which physicists have developed, their unformalized sense of when to consider things as in superposition, as pre-measurement, and when as classically determinate, as post-measurement. But it is not to be given some "realist" interpretation, in which amplitudes and wave-packet collapse are taken to correspond to true features of the objective world. Nor should we modify the theory in some way to make it more truthful. Rather, the theory is merely a useful instrument or calculus for prediction, linking observations with observations, measurements with measurements. And that is all we should expect from a theory.

The content theory of Part One certainly implies that theories *can* say more about the world than this view suggests quantum mechanics does say. But of course that content theory does not imply that a scientific theory *cannot* possess merely an instrumentalist or positivist form. Still, *our* interest is in what quantum mechanics can tell us about the world, and the implications of that for the general project at hand. It is not plausible to maintain that the world is constituted merely by our sense observations and instrument readings. There is more to any plausible world than that. The strange phenomena predicted by quantum mechanics plausibly involve something beyond our observations and instruments, and our interest here is in what that something is. So the positivist or instrumentalist attitude towards quantum mechanics, whatever its general status as an account of the meaning which accrues to that scientific theory, simply ignores the issues which we face: What is it that (if not the truth then the usefulness of) quantum mechanics says about the world?

2.2

One standard interpretation of quantum mechanics is Bohr's "complementarity" view. It seems to me that Bohr's articulation of complementarity is not really clear in the ways which philosophers value, but the view probably has three main tenets:[21]

i) *Classical properties, for instance positions and momentums, have a privileged place in our descriptions of the world. If experimental results are to be communicable, for instance, they must be couched in a classical language. In fact, any characterization (at least by us) of a particle must be couched in classical language*. It may well be that something quite like this tenet of complementarity is underwritten by the content theory of Part One. Bohr held that certain sorts of properties have a kind of privileged place in our thought and speech, and indeed these are just the sorts of classical causal and spatio-temporal properties which we might expect to have some privileged place in our physics, given the account of basic content in Part One and the traditional post-galilean hostility towards phenomenal properties.[22] Classical properties are supposed to be privileged. But quantum mechanics apparently reveals serious limitations in the applicability of classical concepts. Hence the next two tenets of complementarity:

ii) *A quantum mechanical particle can be characterized as possessing a determinate classical property of a certain kind, say a determinate position or momentum, only when in interaction with a measuring apparatus which reveals that property*. The particle has that property only as part of that whole. For instance, it has a determinate position only when in interaction with a measuring instrument which reveals that location. Now we seem headed for trouble. Heisenberg's uncertainty relations tell us that if a position is measured in some definite way, then momentum will be correspondingly indefinite. But an indefinite momentum is not a classical property, and the characterization of a particle is supposed to be couched in a classical language. The third tenet of complementarity is a way out of this bind:

iii) *Any characterization of a particle will be incomplete unless the particle is considered at once in interaction with more than one mutually exclusive measuring apparatus*, say one apparatus measuring momentum and another location. Since such measurements are mutually exclusive, any complete characterization of a particle will be in fact an inconsistent one.

One might take the complementarity interpretation in two different ways. On the first reading, it doesn't attempt to tell us the truth about the world which quantum mechanics reveals. It isn't really an interpretation of the sort we pursue. Rather, it is something like an account of our cognitive limitations in understanding what quantum mechanics says about the world. We will soon have reason to consider whether, taken in this first sense, complementarity is correct. But taken in this sense it is not directly relevant to the issue we immediately face. We want to know what truth quantum mechanics reveals about the world. On the other hand, there is another option. We might take the complementarity view to be an interpretation of the sort we seek. On this reading, complementarity is not about our cognitive limitations. Rather it implies that *any* complete characterization of the world (not just by us) must be inconsistent. Either the world itself is incomplete, or it is inconsistent.

On this reading, complementarity is an incoherent view. First of all, if anything like the content theory articulated in Part One is correct, then any truth which is coherently conceivable by humans must be rooted in the match of a consistent basic content to the world. In fact, there must be a single consistent basic content which captures all the coherently conceivable features of that world. If we can coherently conceive what quantum mechanics says about the world, then there is some single consistent and coherent basic content which captures what it says. That's just a point about what we can think, of course. *We* can't reach any truth in the world by this version of Bohr's route. But this reading of complementarity is massively implausible in a still more troubling way. The presumption that *the world itself* is complete in the manner under discussion, and also consistent, surely lies far deeper and is much less defeasible than anything which any scientific theory can give us good reason to question. At the very least, as we will see, certainly there is no reason to think that *quantum mechanics* drives that deep. On no reading, then, is complementarity of much immediate help to us.

2.3

Some have proposed that the interpretative difficulties presented by quantum mechanics would be eased by the adoption of a non-standard logic (or probability calculus), so that the strangeness presented by the interference of probability amplitudes might be shoved up inside the logic incorporated in an interpretation, rather than left to haunt the kinds of concrete properties attributed to particles by that interpretation. For instance, it has sometimes been proposed that modification of the distribution laws or adoption of a three-valued logic might ease our difficulties in understanding what goes on in the two-slit experiment.[23]

Again, there are weak and strong readings of the quantum logical approach. On the one hand, it may simply involve a suggestion about the most perspicacious notation in which to capture, discuss, and reason about the strange phenomena which quantum mechanics reveals. It is, then, simply a proposal that some higher-order theoretical language be governed by a non-standard logic.[24] To this I have no immediate objection, no more than to the non-standard logics which govern arbitrary objects. But on this reading a non-standard quantum logic would tell us nothing direct about the concrete world itself, the world matched by basic contents, just as the non-standard logic for arbitrary objects tells us nothing direct about that world.

On a strong reading, however, a quantum logical interpretation may be taken to imply quite a bit about the concrete world itself, to imply that the concrete world itself is governed by a non-standard logic. To put the issue more sharply, and in our usual terminology: A quantum logical interpretation may be taken to imply that basic contents are governed by a non-standard logic, that they possess three possible truth-values or violate the distribution laws.

But, again, this suggestion is incoherent, and for reasons somewhat like those we just faced. Basic contents are characterized by a language which includes the standard logical connectives, and they either match the world or they don't. Inferences among basic contents are hence properly governed by standard logical principles. While this sort of structure is perhaps not so deeply imbedded in any remotely plausible content theory as that we discussed in regard to the last option, still it lies very deep indeed.

Some may say that the point is not about the logic of basic contents but about the logic of the world. It isn't obvious to me that the notion of a logic of the world makes any sense, but let me assume that it does. Still, if the world is coherently conceivable by us, then the logic of the world and the logic of basic contents cannot be distinguished. And indeed something quite like the logic of basic contents would seem to govern any coherent conception of the world, by Martians or bats as well as humans. Like the radical version of complementarity, the strong reading of the quantum logical approach tries to drive deeper than necessary, and probably too deep for coherence. In any case, on neither reading is the quantum logical approach very helpful in providing us with a coherently conceivable understanding of the concrete world.[25]

We need to consider another sort of interpretation. The remaining few interpretive options do attempt to articulate what quantum mechanics reveals about the world, and they violate none of the standard logical principles governing basic contents. The next two classes of interpretations hold that the standard general scheme for interpreting quantum mechanics, incorporated for instance into von Neumann's formalization, is incorrect or at least misleading in a certain way. That scheme articulates a fundamental difference between deterministic evolution in accord with Schrödinger's equation outside of measurement and the probabilistic collapse of the wave-packet upon measurement. Both of the next two interpretations deny that collapse of the wave-packet ever occurs. They maintain that particles are *always* characterized merely by wave-functions, and *always* evolve in accord with Schrödinger's equation. But they attempt to explain the mere appearance of a collapse of the wave-packet in different ways.

2.4

Everett's "relative state" or "many worlds" interpretation is one interpretation which holds that wave packets never collapse, that all the alternatives mentioned in the quantum mechanical characterization of a particle or collection of particles are in fact realized.[26] If a particle has an amplitude for a range of alternative positions, then it has all of those alternative positions. This claim seems in obvious conflict with our experience, in which for instance a photon shows up at one particular place on the detector screen in the two-slit experiment, not at all the possible alternative places. But the relative state interpretation avoids this conflict with experience in the following way:

According to the relative state interpretation, the universe bifurcates or splits into distinct worlds or branches in which each of the alternatives is realized. From within any given branch it seems as if only one alternative is realized. But all branches are equally real. It's just that one cannot experience things in a branch other than one occupies.

The relative state interpretation suffers from two difficulties which seem quite devastating as a pair. It faces all the serious interpretative difficulties faced by more standard interpretations, and yet it is much more massively implausible on other grounds than those alternatives.

Just as the standard von Neumann scheme for the interpretation of quantum mechanics requires that there be collapse of the wave packet at a certain "location" between the microphysical level of quantum mechanical phenomena and our classical causal experience, so too the relative state interpretation requires that there be a fact about when and where bifurcation occurs. If a relative state theory can provide a plausible and well motivated account of bifurcation, it should suggest a parallel von Neumann-style account of wave packet collapse. Wherever the Everett-style account proposes a bifurcation, an orthodox view could propose a collapse. Any mechanism which explained the first should suggest a parallel mechanism which might explain the second. So at least on the surface, the relative state interpretation seems to have no particular advantages in plausibility over the orthodox von Neumann-style accounts. And it certainly has some relative disadvantages.

The bifurcation of the entire universe is a much more implausible phenomena than even the sudden collapse of a wave packet. Every time there was the sort of branching of the world which the relative state interpretation requires, there would be a massive violation of the conservation principles, and a much more massively implausible sort of non-local causation than orthodox von Neumann-style views themselves seem to require. For instance, when there are a number of alternative locations for a photon on our photosensitive screen, then the entire universe must fission into the relevant number of nearly identical duplicate universes. Of course, all the contents of the universe must bifurcate as well, including even all the conscious beings residing in the Andromeda galaxy, and their patio furniture.[27] This is not plausible.

2.5

There is a second set of views which attempt to explain away the appearance of wave-packet collapse. Such views often go under the rubric "DLP", after Daneri, Loinger, and Prosperi.[28] But their work was rooted in earlier work of Jordan and Ludwig.[29]

Here are two observations which motivate DLP: i) Measuring instruments, in fact anything by which a quantum mechanical particle can leave a humanly observable trace, consist of huge numbers of particles.[30] ii) If a system consists of a huge number of particles, then it may seem as a whole to be governed by very different sorts of laws than those which govern its constituents. This can be seen even in classical examples. For instance, the laws which govern classical particles are such that the evolution of any ensemble of such particles is, at least theoretically, exactly reversible. But the second law of thermodynamics maintains that it is at least very likely that large systems of classical particles evolve towards ever greater entropy, in an irreversible direction. These observations suggest that huge collections of quantum mechanical particles may behave more like classical entities than we at first might imagine.

According to DLP, all particles, and measuring instruments, and complexes of instruments and particles, are characterized by quantum mechanical wave-functions, and evolve solely according to the Schrödinger equation. There is no reduction of the wave packet of a particle immediately upon its interaction with a large measuring apparatus. Rather, after interaction the large collection of quantum mechanical particles which constitutes the measuring instrument gradually settles down into a new state of post-measurement equilibrium. If it settles down in one way, one sort of measurement result is obtained (say a pointer points in one direction), and if it settles down in another way, another result is obtained. While the instrument will, even after measurement has occurred, still be properly characterized by a quantum mechanical wave-function as in a superposition of classical states, the very large numbers of particles in the measuring apparatus will allow, as if by phase cancellation in waves, elimination of some of the characteristic oddities of superpositions. Various amplitudes will cancel out, and we can treat those that remain like classical probabilities for classical properties. DLP argue that the superposition predicted by Schrödinger's equation as the result of evolution in such a large collection of particles, and the probability distribution of measurement outcomes predicted by von Neumann-style accounts of wave packet collapse, are in fact quite similar in the following sense: The superposition of states predicted by the Schrödinger equation, and the collection of outcomes across many instances of such a measurement predicted by von Neumann, are statistically indistinguishable at the observational level. The two accounts will agree in statistical predictions for all observable classical properties.[31]

This is attractive in many ways. But there is a serious problem, which we'll look at from two angles: First of all, we know that two different collections of quantum mechanical particles characterized by the same wave-function, constituting two complexes of two-slit apparatus and yet unmeasured test photon, will likely end up with dots on different places on their screens. But evolution according to the Schrödinger equation would always leave them in the same state. Second, at best DLP show that the *statistical distribution* of dots on the screens in a *large ensemble* of *different* two-slit experiments, different firings of a photon through a two-slit apparatus, will be the same if things evolve solely according to Schrödinger's equation as they will if there is collapse of the wave-packet. But evolution according to the Schrödinger equation alone will not guarantee, for instance, that a particular spot on a screen in a particular experiment will remain in the same place over time, as von Neumann-style accounts predict, and as spots obviously do. It is consistent with the DLP prediction that dots jump around on the various screens in the ensemble of various such experiments in a crazy way, as long as the proper statistical distribution of positions is maintained across the whole ensemble of experiments. And dots don't jump around in this way.[32] DLP may be on to something important, as we will shortly see. But at least in this form their proposal is inadequate. Something at least roughly like collapse of the wave packet does occur.

2.6

The next set of views is the most orthodox. It takes seriously the cut between evolution outside of measurement and within it, which is enshrined in the von Neumann formalization. It holds that there is a special kind of evolution which occurs only in measurement, and which is triggered by things which are not constituted solely by quantum mechanical particles.

Adequate understanding of such a view requires, of course, a proper understanding of the physical states of particles prior to measurement, when they are characterized solely by amplitudes for classical properties. We will return to that issue in a bit. But the special and characteristic difficulty of the orthodox understanding of measurement is its need to place the cut between the two sorts of evolution which it postulates. An orthodox view needs to explain where and when and why the wave packet collapses. It needs to provide a non-arbitrary and plausible location for that collapse, a plausible account of its mechanism, and a plausible account of the particular irreducible entities which initiate it. Von Neumann showed that it doesn't really matter to quantum mechanical predictions where the cut occurs,[33] as long as it is some place before observation. But it should occur somewhere plausible, and in a plausible way.

Wigner's suggestion was that the cut occurs when consciousness gets involved.[34] People's conscious minds are in fact irreducible to the complexes of quantum mechanical particles which might otherwise be thought to constitute people and their environments. And such an irreducible consciousness initiates collapse of wave packets, perhaps when it perceives them or things which they help constitute.

But such an irreducible consciousness, say causally secreted by the collection of quantum mechanical particles which constitutes someone's brain, is no more antecedently plausible than the handy colorful sense data which we dismissed in Chapter Fourteen from plausible explanations of color experience, along with the strange laws which would underwrite their secretion. Just as the views we dismissed in Chapter Fourteen implausibly suggested that color suddenly erupts into the world with the coming of sentient beings, so too the Wigner view implies that there were no determinate classical properties before there were minds, but there were afterwards. But let's face it. We aren't that important.

Wigner's view is not the only von Neumann-style account. Other standard proposals for the location of the cut are at "measuring devices", say eyes or photo-sensitive plates, or more generally at the "macro" level, when collections of particles have sufficient energy to make classical mechanics intuitively appropriate, the familiar level of instrument pointers, dust motes, billiard balls, stars, and other mid- to large-sized objects. According to these proposals, measuring instruments, or macro-objects generally, are not constituted solely by their quantum mechanical parts, and they induce a collapse of the wave packet of a particle with which they interact.

Such views face difficulties which mirror those of Wigner's view: First of all, the mysterious irreducibility of measuring instruments or macro-objects generally to quantum mechanical particles is no more antecedently plausible than the irreducibility of minds. Somewhat like phenomenal colors on external objects, which we dismissed as implausible in preceding chapters, irreducible classical properties of measuring instruments or macro-objects seem awkward and insufficiently motivated grafts onto the traditional physicalist conception of the world, according to which physical things are constituted by their microphysical components. Like objective colors, the irreducible classical properties are postulated merely to bring a theory nicely into line with our experience.[35] They seem terribly ad hoc. There are also special problems of conceivability which threaten this feature of such accounts. For instance, the quantum mechanical particles associated with the macro-object do not suffice to constitute it. But then it is hard to see what coherently conceivable relation there might be between the macro-object and those particles.[36] Also, the collapse of the wave packet by a measuring instrument or macro-object is still an implausible phenomena. "Measuring instrument" is a pretty vague term to be found in a fundamental physical theory. And if it were made precise, it is likely that the view that measuring instruments (rather than macro-objects in general) induce collapse would have quite implausible implications regarding the far past which are quite like those of Wigner's view, and also quite implausible implications regarding the kinds of physical mechanisms which operate in the world. For instance, if measuring instruments are supposed to be instruments that measure for *us*, then we are still supposed to be improbably important. "Macroscopic objects" is pretty vague as well, and it is hard to see what plausible mechanism could underwrite a certain size or energy as the source of wave-packet collapse. Or perhaps it is better to say that any plausible specification of that mechanism would probably involve a serious modification of the traditional view.

There are certain heterodox views which at least roughly fit the von Neumann scheme and which may resolve this difficulty in a roughly plausible way. For instance, Penrose has proposed that collapse of the wave packet occurs for systems of particles large enough for gravitational effects to become significant.[37] But such views involve a significant enough reformulation of quantum mechanics to belong among the interpretive options we have yet to discuss. Any clear and precise specification of what constitutes a macroscopic object and the mechanism by which macroscopic objects generate collapse will involve more physics than the traditional von Neumann scheme delivers. So I will treat such options as among our remaining interpretative alternatives. We can conclude, I think, that none of the orthodox von Neumann-style views, or at least none which do not require extra physics, are sufficiently plausible. We need an option which modifies the traditional scheme at least enough to provide a plausible mechanism for the collapse of the wave packet.

2.7

We have few remaining options. We need to figure out what quantum mechanics says about the world, and respect the completeness and consistency of the world. It isn't enough merely to throw out the orthodox claim that there is collapse of the wave packet, along say with DLP. Nor are the standard von Neumann-style interpretations all that plausible. It is quite implausible that there are special and dramatic physical roles for measuring instruments or human observers in particular.

The only options which are plausible enough to carry over into our final discussion modify the traditional understanding of quantum mechanical evolution so that what goes on inside and outside of measurement is not as dramatically discontinuous as von Neumann's formalization suggests. These options in fact introduce enough modification so that it may seem a bit of a stretch to call them *interpretations* of quantum mechanics at all. They require more physics, not just a bit of philosophy.

There are a variety of ways to organize discussion of these remaining interpretive options. One way for us to proceed would be to distinguish between views which deploy coherently conceivable resources only and those which do not. But I will structure the discussion in a slightly different way, so that I can hold off on introducing the peculiarities of my own view until the last possible moment. This will have some disadvantages, since it will make some of the views in the first class we will discuss rather more like the paradigmatic views in the second class in their peculiar application to our concerns. But nevertheless, it seems the most natural division. So here we go: On the one hand, there are among our remaining interpretive options some which retain classical properties for particles even outside of measurement or measurement-like circumstances. And there are some which do not. These two sets of options are treated in the next two sections.

3

There are a variety of ways to modify traditional quantum mechanics so that particles outside of measurement possess determinate classical properties which on the traditional quantum mechanical view they would lack. For instance, there is a class of views which maintain that the kinds of classical properties of a particle which are determinate, say position or momentum, vary from moment to moment, and depend in particular on the wave-function of the world in general[38] or the history of the dynamical interactions of that particle.[39] But I will focus here on David Bohm's older and simpler view, which holds that the positions of particles are always determinate. I will focus on Bohm's "interpretation" partly because it is simpler and more widely discussed, partly because there are certain difficulties which face the alternatives,[40] partly because some of the alternatives deploy some non-classical features outside of measurement and hence in fact sit astride my simple division, and partly because many of them suffer problems of coherent conceivability of the same sort we face in the next section, so that for our purposes they might as well belong to that second class of views. Bohm's view seems to present the best hope for a coherently conceivable and more or less plausible account of the realization of our causal and spatio-temporal experience.[41]

Quite early in the development of quantum mechanics, Louis de Broglie proposed that both waves and particles are involved in quantum mechanical phenomena, that particles are singularities in fields of waves.[42] And indeed this suggestion represents one sort of interpretative option, a kind of hidden variables view which evades the difficulties for standard hidden variables views revealed by Bell's analysis. Bohm's hidden variables theory is the classic articulation of such an interpretation.[43] Bohm's account in essence is this: All particles have at each moment a determinate classical position. The problem of physics is to understand the forces which shape the evolution of those determinate positions over time. Properties like spin and charge and inertia are construed as forces which affect the evolution of positions. There are classical fields of force, for instance electromagnetic force, which push particles about. But in addition, on Bohm's view, there is a "Schrödinger-" or "psi-field", a field of quantum mechanical force which is characterized by a quantum mechanical wave-function and which evolves according to the Schrödinger equation. That field of quantum mechanical force pushes particles about to explain the odd quantum mechanical predictions. But it does so in such a way that any measurement of the position of a particle is governed by the uncertainty relations. The uncertainty relations survive, on Bohm's view, as epistemic limitations of the sort which Heisenberg's semi-classical motivating arguments may have seemed to suggest.

Let's see how this works in our two familiar cases. In the two-slit experiment, waves in the psi-field carry the particle through one of the slits and then on to a particular point in the screen. Exactly where the particle ends up on the screen will depend on its exact initial position, as it is emitted towards the slitted screen, and on the various fields of force acting on the particle, including the psi-field. Everything happens deterministically. But we cannot ascertain the particle's initial position except within the epistemic limitations set by the uncertainty relations. Very fine measurements of that position will affect the particle's momentum in an unpredictable way. Hence we cannot predict exactly where on the screen it will land.

The EPR experiment reveals a more surprising side of this model, though perhaps it should not be so surprising when we remember Bell's result. Measurement of the spin of the particle in one wing will introduce perturbations of the psi-field which govern the motion of the particle even in the other wing of the experiment, a light year away. And it will do this instantaneously. There is instantaneous action at a distance.

Let me focus on the primary innovation here, the psi-field. One early objection to the physical reality of such a wave field was that a field which corresponds to the wave-function for a complex of n particles is a field in a physically unrealistic 3n-dimensional space. On the other hand, this is presumably just an artifact of the most convenient and traditional mathematical expression of the psi-field.[44] Nevertheless, one important feature of the psi-field is captured by that traditional expression. The states of different particles are represented in an entangled way, by a single point in the 3n-space. Their evolution according to the Schrödinger equation is evolution together. Bohm's account cannot disentangle entangled particles like those in the EPR experiment and yet meet the confirmed predictions of quantum mechanics. There is, according to Bohm's model, instantaneous action at a distance, which explains the entanglement evident in the EPR experiment. But if there is instantaneous action at a distance, then there is absolute simultaneity, which is contrary to relativity. The uncertainty relations prevent any observable signaling from one wing of the experiment to the other, so Bohm's view is consistent with the observational predictions of relativity. But still, contrary to Einstein's view, there is a privileged inertial frame which registers true simultaneity, though we cannot experimentally determine which one it is.

Of course, Bohm's mechanics is not a complete physics. For instance, it must be extended to explain the interaction of electrons and photons in the manner of relativistic quantum field theory. Some of the necessary work has been done by Bohm himself and by Bell,[45] and seems to suggest that the necessary extension of Bohm's account will not be deterministic. But still it seems that the extension will retain the privileged inertial frame characteristic of Bohm's original model.

Bohm explains the quantum mechanical correlations in the EPR experiment *causally*. It is this feature of his account which leads him afoul of the spirit of relativity, if not of its observational predictions. So we might be tempted by a variant. Perhaps the correlations are not to be explained causally at all. To take this route may be to give up the psi-field in anything like the form suggested by the surface of Bohm's formulation, but such an option could be very like Bohm's view in other ways, and attribute determinate classical properties to all particles at all times. Let's look at some sub-options in this set. Some people maintain that the quantum mechanical correlations require no further explanation.[46] The correlations happen, and that's all there is to it. Explanations have to come to a stop somewhere. This is, of course, always an alternative, but it seems at odds with our generally very successful scientific attitude, which seeks to root out explanations of correlations. It seems not to be a particularly plausible strategy. But there are other sub-options. Some have been tempted to say that there are correlations between our brain states and phenomenal experiences, and to explain these otherwise strange physical-phenomenal correlations by postulating not a *causal* linkage of brain states and phenomenal sense data, but an *identity* of the two. Similarly, some might be tempted to postulate some sort of strange identity between what happens in the different wings of the EPR experiment. But of course this sort of identity is not within the expressive resources of C.[47] It is not coherently conceivable. Alternatively, one might propose that the explanation of the correlations between the wings involves some new sort of relation or property, not of any familiar sort. It is neither an identity relation nor a causal relation nor simply the unexplained existence of the correlated results, but it is a real feature of the world. Call this "irreducible correlation". It is a kind of restriction on the world, but not the kind of asymmetric restriction which causal powers involve, which are rooted in a particularly located cause, a particular microevent. Irreducible correlation "explains" the correlation, but in a symmetric way. What happens in neither wing has explanatory primacy, nor is there a common cause with some other location. And yet there is more than just the correlated outcomes; there is something which explains them. The world is such that there must be such a correlation between the outcomes in the two wings. But of course this new feature is not expressible in C. It is not coherently conceivable by us.

There might seem to be a way around this last difficulty; it might seem that irreducible correlation *is* coherently conceivable. The so-called "causal" powers introduced in Chapter Seven, the coherently conceivable restrictions, include things which aren't usually considered causal at all. For instance, the persistence over time of a point-particle is characterized by C in the following way: A microevent constituting one moment of the particle's life restricts the world so that there will be a similar sort of microevent at the next moment. Persistence over time is a restriction in my sense, and it isn't commonly considered a causal power. So it might seem that restrictions expressible in C provide the wherewithal to constitute an appropriately non-causal correlation between the wings of the EPR experiment, despite what I just said. However, the restrictions expressible in C involve an asymmetry between the restricting and restricted events and a particular concrete source, and this leaves them unsuited to capture irreducible correlation.

Given the familiar connection between the identity of two objects and their spatio-temporal coincidence, it may well be that inconceivable irreducible correlation and inconceivable identity are not really distinct options. But if they are, it seems to me that the best alternative of all of those which attribute classical positions to all particles at all times, the most plausible, is that which involves irreducible correlation. But certainly it is not our best shot at a *coherently conceivable* account of what quantum mechanics reveals. So let me continue to pursue the implications of Bohm's causal account in particular.

Bohm's view is coherently conceivable. It deploys coherently conceivable spatio-temporal and causal resources. Let me discuss these features one at a time.

Determinate classical positions like those Bohm deploys are clearly expressible in C. In fact, Bohm's account may seem to be in rather too close accord with *paradigmatic* causal contents in this regard. Even if Bohm's view has, like quantum mechanics itself, an uneasy coexistence with the observational predictions of relativity, Bohm-style views may well seem to threaten our capacity to coherently conceive a world in which relativity is also at least apparently true. Relativity suggested to us in the last chapter that the spatio-temporal structure of plausible causal basic contents was at least primarily constituted by causal connectibility relations, that the more familiar sorts of spatio-temporal relations admissible by C play no role in a plausible world. But if events with space-like separations are causally connectible, then the conditions which allowed for such a causal reduction of spatio-temporal structure seem to break down. And of course that is exactly what the Bohm-style views seem to suggest. Still, causal connectibility *of certain particular sorts*, say of the sorts which allow signaling, can still retain its familiar relativistic form even if Bohm is right about the psi-field, and causal connectibility of those particular sorts may be enough to constitute at least the spatio-temporal structure suggested in the previous chapter. The real problem is that Bohm's view suggests that there is *more* spatio-temporal structure than Einstein's observational critique of simultaneity allows, not that it suggests less. So it seems that if Bohm's account were correct, we could coherently conceive the spatio-temporal structure of the world, even a world with the observable features which relativity predicts.

What about the causal resources which Bohm deploys? Microevents which could sum up to particles must have intrinsic properties as well as determinate spatio-temporal positions and relations, and the particles of Bohm's theory are pretty bare. Still, they seem to possess charge and other familiar classical properties, causal properties which give them some of their characteristic effects.

Let me focus then on the psi-field. What sorts of causal powers does it introduce? Fields in general can be treated by C in two different ways. First of all, a particle may exert a kind of causal power on other particles, directly and at a distance, which mimics the effects of an intervening concrete field. Or such a field may exist as a real concrete entity in its own right, which affects and is affected by particles or other entities. It may consist of microevents which exert substantial powers of their own, and not merely the largely null powers characteristic of the vacuum. In either reading, Bohm's causal view of the machinations of the psi-field is coherently conceivable.[48]

Bohm's account is coherently conceivable, and consistent with the truth of some causal basic contents. That suggests that it also fits well with the objectual account of our spatio-temporal and causal experience towards which we have been forced. But let me note at least one minor worry: Remember that objectual accounts of our causal experience must not merely involve coherently conceivable causal powers, but the primitive powers themselves, the powers we actually experience. As I have indicated, it seems to me that the most plausible of the Bohm-style accounts is a variant in which the quantum mechanical correlations are not explained causally at all, but even if we stick with Bohm's own account it might be that there are some problems of fit with an objectual account of our causal experience. The primitive causal powers involve force as traditionally understood and not action at a distance. This may be a problem. Some elements of the momentum of a particle are quite classical, on Bohm's account, but Bohm's account does attribute at least some features of the momentum of a particle to the action of the psi-field. The concrete realization of the psi-field is not specified determinately enough by Bohm for us to see whether the field itself acts locally on the particle and there is merely action at a distance within the field or on the field, or whether there is direct action at a distance on the particle, but in any case the momentum of the particle in one wing is entangled with that in the other. It is not entirely a classical property. The powers which realize the psi-field are coherently conceivable, but they are rather unusual.

It is, I think, unclear if this yields enough of the form of the primitive causal powers to underwrite an objectual account of our experience of such powers. Since quantum mechanical effects are generally insignificant at the macro-level of our limbs, it may be that the contributions of the psi-field can be ignored, but I am not confident of this. And a proper resolution of this issue would require adequate treatment of difficult questions about the kind of match there can be between basic contents and the world when the former leave out some of the fine detail, issues about how the intrinsic property of a single microevent of such a content can match the distinct intrinsic properties of the smaller bits of the world which it encompasses. So let me admit that there is at least some possibility that this set of interpretive options will not really mesh well enough with our familiar account of the realization of our causal experience.

At least on the surface, though, it seems that Bohm's account is coherently conceivable and underwrites our coherently conceivable objectual account of our causal and spatio-temporal experience. And it is at least more plausible, I think, than the interpretive options we dismissed in the last section. So Bohm's account has a lot of advantages from our perspective. That is why I have spent some time on it.

But there is a real problem with the view. This problem leaves it, I believe, less plausible than the interpretive options we will pursue in the next section.

Bohm's view takes the uncertainty relations in a merely epistemic way. Heisenberg's famous motivating arguments for the uncertainty relations are semi-classical arguments, which may suggest such a reading. But, on the other hand, the relations are a direct consequence of the formalism of quantum mechanics as well. And even Heisenberg's semi-classical arguments are in many ways analogous to those which led Einstein to reject absolute simultaneity, and not merely to conclude that we cannot epistemically access what it is. One might insist that there is a privileged reference frame even though we cannot determine what it is, just as one might insist that particles always have determinate positions even when we cannot determine what they are, or similar true colors. But Einstein's contrary inference has come to seem a paradigm of good inference in physics. Bohm's psi-field is quite analogous to special and otherwise unobservable forces which shrink measuring rods and slow down clocks and hence hide absolute simultaneity from us. Which is to say that it isn't very plausible, that it isn't plausible enough. Of course, Einstein's inference was very fruitful, but so too has Heisenberg's been. The uncertainty relations have been deployed in lots of explanations. And in fact there may be more than a mere analogy here. At least Bohm's particular theory exactly contradicts the conclusion of Einstein's inference. It requires absolute simultaneity and a privileged inertial frame despite the fact that we cannot determine experimentally which frame is privileged.

It seems to me that both Einstein's way of taking his observational critique of absolute simultaneity and the more than merely epistemic way of taking the uncertain relations are more plausible than the alternatives. By the nature of the case, this is not something I can *prove*. But let me cite some relevant evidence. Certainly physicists, even the physicists who have developed it, find the notion of a psi-field a bit uncomfortable, a bit ad hoc and cheap. Certainly a theory which covers up its own mechanism in the style of Bohm's theory bears an uncomfortable analogy to Descartes' hypothesis that our experience is the product of an evil deceiver. Certainly it seems a good maxim not to postulate things like a psi-field and determinate positions without some good reason, and our motivation for wanting determinate classical positions for particles may simply be their familiarity from the quite different and classical realm of our experience, of the balls we bounce and the stars we see. And that doesn't seem like adequate motivation. Certainly we have seen reason in this part to believe that the form of our phenomenal experience is misleading because of our contingent constitution. So why should we expect our causal and spatio-temporal experience to be any less misleading? We may have evolved to throw things, but not to do microphysics. Certainly it is also far from clear that we have any clear and concrete understanding of the psi-field and its peculiar action at a distance. The familiar quantum mechanical formalism which Bohm exploits, for instance, has too many dimensions to characterize a three-dimensional field in any very direct way. Of course, I have no general account of the plausibility of inferences, which explains why Einstein's inference and the more radical way of taking the uncertainty relations is more reasonable.[49] But then again, neither do I have a general account of reasonable inference which answers Hume's problem, which explains why inductive inference is better than counter-inductive inference. And Bohm's account does at least seem less plausible than accounts which take the uncertainty relations more seriously. We need another account.

4

The remaining and apparently most plausible set of interpretive options do take the uncertainty relations more seriously than Bohm's interpretation. According to that remaining set of options, particles outside of measurement are not characterized by determinate classical properties, but rather by something like an orthodox quantum mechanical superposition of classical states. Contrary to the suggestion of the traditional von Neumann-style models, however, there are not two radically discontinuous types of evolution. There is merely one general kind of evolution. Our observations and measurements mandate that there must be something at least closely analogous to collapse of the wave packet. DLP fails. Hence if there is to be but one kind of evolution, then some modification of the Schrödinger equation is required. Some more physics is needed.

This set of views falls into two types, which differ regarding what happens after the analogue of wave packet collapse, after what I will call, for no particularly good reason, "spontaneous collapse". According to the first type, particles assume classical properties, say determinate positions. According to the second type, they do not. Rather, after spontaneous collapse, a particle, while not characterized by a traditional wave-function of the sort which led DLP into trouble, is still non-classical.

Neither of these types of views are at all fully developed. But Ghirardi, Rimini, and Weber, hereafter GRW, have explored one promising direction.[50] GRW propose a single simple modification of the Schrödinger equation.

Let me begin with a slight misrepresentation of GRW's view. Take the "position" of a particle to be characterized by a quantum mechanical wave-function, ascribing various amplitudes for positions. Assume that it evolves most often according to the Schrödinger equation. But allow that there is at each moment a tiny probability that the wave-function for the particle will spontaneously collapse to a determinate position, in a way which mirrors the probabilities for positions involved in orthodox collapse of the wave packet.

Consider now a large measuring apparatus, which registers the microscopic property of a particle, say a position, by the position of something macroscopic, say a pointer. If the measuring apparatus is itself characterized by its traditional quantum mechanical wave-function, and that wave-function evolves exactly according to the Schrödinger equation, then it will be after a measurement interaction in a superposition of pointer states. This is why DLP failed. But if only one of the huge number of particles in that apparatus spontaneously collapses to a definite position in the way GRW propose, then so too will the wave-function of the entire apparatus. That's assured by the way the mathematics works, by the quantum mechanical representation of the ensemble of particles which makes up the apparatus. And of course, the huge number of particles involved in a macroscopic measuring apparatus might make it very likely indeed that one of the particles will collapse within a very brief moment of time. There is a very tiny chance that any particular particle will spontaneously collapse in a short period, but a very large probability that the huge collection of particles which constitute any macroscopic object will collapse within a very tiny period of time.

So far this view sounds like it belongs in the first of our two types. After spontaneous collapse, a particle has a determinate position. But I have in fact ignored an important complication, which puts GRW more in the space of the second type. Because of the uncertainty relations, we know that if the position of a particle is *completely* determinate, then its momentum will be *completely* indeterminate. Spontaneous collapse to determinate positions would have effects which are not observed.[51] Particles don't suddenly jump out of orbit when they localize. So GRW in fact propose not that there is collapse of the wave-function of a particle, of its amplitudes for position, to a single particular point, but rather that the wave-function spontaneously takes the form of a bell-shaped curve centered on a particular position. A particle after spontaneous collapse has something like an almost determinate position. The indeterminacy in a particle's position after spontaneous collapse can be restricted enough so that a macroscopic object consisting of many such particles has almost always a microscopic indeterminacy in position, and yet so that momentums are not too indeterminate.

This is very simple and elegant. Of course, there are a number of problems which attend the proposal.[52] It is intuitive and traditional to represent an intuitively single object, say a measuring apparatus, by a single wave-function, and to represent intuitively distinct objects, say two distinct measuring instruments, by distinct wave-functions in the manner suggested by GRW. It is intuitive that if macroscopic objects collapse, then they do so only as intuitive wholes. But it isn't obvious what physical mechanism underlies this intuition, ensures that the spontaneous collapse of one particle in a measuring instrument will draw just the right other particles along. Further, there remain some violations of the conservation of energy and momentum on GRW's view, even if the amount of non-conservation is small and within observable limits. GRW do allow that for very brief time periods there may well be "monstrous" superpositions of macroscopic states.

GRW's proposal also is quite specifically tied to measurements registered by the positions of macroscopic objects, like pointers, and there is some controversy about whether this is sufficient. Albert for instance has objected that we might register a microphysical position by the fluorescence of certain particles which make up a receiving screen, and that this isn't plausibly connected to the position of anything macroscopic.[53] But F. Aicardi, A. Borsellino, G.C. Ghirardi, and R.

Grassi[54] have argued that at least *human* visual experience of one bit of a screen fluorescing rather than another involves some difference in the macroscopic position of a large collection of brain components. Such a move would not suffice to account for shared and public registrations which are not registrations by macroscopic position, but it may be that there aren't any. In even Bohm's account, position plays a special role, and certainly on the classical galilean conception of the world the only properties which are both observed and objectively real are spatial properties and powers which affect them. Albert's objection to Aicardi, Borsellino, Ghirardi, and Grassi seems, in light of our discussion in this part, insufficient.[55] He suggests that such things as our observation of determinate classical positions should not turn so closely on such fine details of the concrete realization of our mentality. But doesn't this part suggest exactly the opposite?

It seems to me that these are problems of detail, which at most require more work than GRW have done so far. But even if they are not merely problems of detail, still GRW have gone some distance towards developing one instance of the most promising class of interpretations, an instance which take the uncertainty relations very seriously. A spontaneous collapse interpretation which maintains that, after collapse, particles have determinate classical properties would be, it seems, less plausible. It would either run afoul of the uncertainty relations in the way our first sketch of GRW suggested, or at least would fail to take them fully seriously in much the way Bohm's view fails to take them fully seriously. GRW seem at least to be pointing us in the right non-classical direction. In any case, GRW merely have developed a modification of traditional non-relativistic quantum mechanics, and hence some more work is obviously required. Although GRW's proposal is non-relativistic, Bell has shown that even their initial model satisfies a close analogue of Lorentz invariance, which suggests that it may well be developed in a direction which will leave it consistent with the denial of absolute simultaneity.[56]

It seems to me that the real difficulty with GRW's proposal, at present our best instance of the most plausible interpretive direction, is coherent conceivability. Along with orthodox non-reductive views and DLP, this interpretation requires that particles possess strange non-classical states prior to spontaneous collapse. And GRW also suggest a near- but non-classical state even after collapse. We need to ask what all this might concretely mean.

A particle has a kind of strange "tendency" for a variety of determinate positions, in fact some tendency for any position. But it isn't a tendency of any familiar sort. Even after spontaneous collapse, its tendencies are merely centered on a determinate point. This feature of a particle is characterized merely as a probability amplitude or probability or tendency for something which can never occur, which is to say that these characterizations are merely metaphors. Perhaps we are to think that the being of the particle is concentrated after collapse in a certain way, that its being is denser at the center of the bell-curve than at other points. But that too is merely a metaphor. Perhaps we are to think of the indeterminacy of a position as a kind of vagueness. But we saw in Part One that the truth or approximate truth of any vagueness that we understand as such is rooted in the truth of something less vague and coherently conceivable, and we seem to lack a coherent understanding of what that something else might be here.

Notice also that in different wings of the EPR experiment particles will "spontaneously" collapse, but in a coordinated way. What's the concrete mechanism which realizes that? It seems to me that the most plausible inference is that here again we have something like the symmetric irreducible correlation we discussed in the last section, though this time a correlation of "spontaneous" collapses. And that too is not coherently conceivable.

One way to underline these points is to try to work out in detail how GRW's proposal might be realized by causal microevents, which are apparently the only plausible and coherently conceivable resources which remain to us. Single microevents, of course, have no spatio-temporal parts, and that seems a helpful feature. But they also have determinate positions of some kind in a spatio-temporal structure, say of the causal variety developed in the last chapter. And this seems at odds with GRW's understanding of a particle. One might hope to elude this difficulty by maintaining that the world has merely a sort of grainy spatio-temporal structure, without the very fine detail which an exact classical position requires. But quantum mechanics predicts that particles have at least some amplitude for any position whatsoever, even after GRW-style collapse. And that's too grainy.

There are other possibilities. Perhaps tendencies for position are properties of points in space-time itself. On this reading, microevents correspond not to particles but to points of space-time with various tendencies for particles, with many different tendencies for many different particles fused at any given point. But there seem to be no coherently conceivable causal powers which quite fit the role of these tendencies, tendencies which you will recall can never be realized in a determinate position for a particle. And if the distinct points of the field of space-time are to *be* distinct points, then that seems to require that there be a certain level of causal structure present, in which things on the order of particles with distinct positions traverse determinate paths, in which causal influence takes a certain determinate route. In fact, special and general relativity seemed to require just such a structure. What *are* points in a spatio-temporal field (or at least in a field of the sort which post-galileans find plausible) if they are not positions at which something with some causal power can be determinately located?

The proper conclusion, I think, is that the most plausible set of interpretations of quantum mechanics are not coherently conceivable by us. Perhaps this is just what Bohr was telling us all along. Some may take this failure of coherent conceivability to be itself an objection to the plausibility of these interpretations. But it seems to me that this would be a mistake. Haven't we seen lots of reasons to believe that various features of our experience are a reflection of our own nature as much as of the objects out in the world? Why should we expect our spatio-temporal and causal experience to be any less misleading, any less idiosyncratically rooted in our contingent history, than our color experience? And remember that even relativity suggests that the spatio-temporal structure of the world is not what we might have been led to expect on the basis of our immediate experience. When objects with very small energies and very large masses get involved, space and time are not what the familiar realm of our experience suggests, and it is only that familiar realm with which we are evolved to deal. There wasn't any selection pressure in our evolutionary history for success at astrophysics and microphysics.

Quantum mechanics, of course, is not a complete and final physics. Things have progressed since 1925. We might hope to gain some illumination from later developments in physics. Much additional illumination isn't yet obviously available to us, but what light is shed by more recent developments does seem also to point in directions which are not coherently conceivable. The best established more recent physical theory is quantum electrodynamics, which incorporates a quantum mechanical account of electron-photon interaction.[57] But it reproduces in slightly altered form the same interpretational problems set for us by quantum mechanics. It is too continuous with quantum mechanics to add much illumination here. Still, more recent and much more speculative theories may give some additional support to our conclusion that the classical causal and spatio-temporal conception of the world, rooted in our experience, involves a serious misrepresentation.

Over the last decade, there has been a flurry of interest in “superstring” theories, which attempt a unified explanation of the full variety of particles, forces, and interactions.[58] Superstring theories come in a bewildering variety of forms, but one classic example invokes, in place of particles, vibrating strings in a space-time with ten dimensions. Six unfamiliar spatial dimensions are curved and curled up so tightly that they are not observed. But such a space-time is not coherently conceivable, at least if it is to possess oriented axes of the sort we have found it necessary to employ. There is no basic content with that kind of structure. It may be that the six extra spatial dimensions are to be interpreted as a metaphor for something else, but then of course it still isn't obvious that what they are a metaphor for is coherently conceivable.

There have also been attempts to constitute both particles and space-time out of spinors and twistors, unfamiliar structures with spin-like chirality.[59] Such accounts were motivated by a desire to explain how something like a particle might retain something like a specific chirality of spin in a truly empty world, without relations even to a space in which it is oriented. These are radically non-classical views, and may well not be coherently conceivable. Spinors and twistors possess an intrinsic chirality, independent of their relations to an orienting space or other objects, while C seems capable of expressing the chirality of a spin only through relations.[60] So spinor- or twistor-like entities may not be coherently conceivable. And hence larger structures constituted out of such beasts may not be coherently conceivable either.

Some recent work in quantum gravity suggests a modification of general relativity in which the general relativistic interval is split into two distinct elements analogous to position and momentum and subject to quantum uncertainty. And it also suggests that certain quantum gravitational states can loop together to form space-time.[61] Here again, we seem to be pushing beyond coherent conceivability. All these proposals are, while exciting, extremely speculative. But if they point anywhere, it is towards the radically non-classical nature of things.

What then are we to conclude? It seems to me that the most plausible conclusion is that causal powers are not quite what the quantum mechanical correlations involve, and that spatio-temporal positions are not quite what quantum mechanical particles possess. After Chapter Fourteen, only causal and spatio-temporal resources remain to us, but we should conclude that they are not enough. The most plausible set of interpretive options for quantum mechanics push us into territory which is not coherently conceivable.

The primary problem is the absence in quantum mechanics of the spatio-temporal determinacy which any microevent, causal or otherwise, requires. I have focussed here primarily on spatial indeterminacy. One might well wonder if it is legitimate for me to draw similar conclusions about temporal indeterminacy as well. But, in fact, there are indeterminacy relations linking not merely position and momentum but also energy and time. Also, in the last chapter we already noted a collapse of certain sorts of distinction between time and space.

There is another conceivability problem as well. Some quantum mechanical correlations are plausibly not causal. Some causal elements may remain in the quantum mechanical understanding of the world, but perhaps we should conclude that they too are illusory. And even if they are not illusory, it is important to remember that coherently conceivable powers are restrictions with contents which can be relatively characterized in C. If there is no determinate coherently conceivable spatio-temporal structure, then any causal powers which survive are not coherently conceivable.

We experience at least large collections of "particles" to possess determinate classical properties. But the "tiny" constituents of things no more plausibly possess classical causal properties and spatio-temporal structure than they do phenomenal colors. So our experience of classical causal properties and spatio-temporal structure may be as illusory as our experience of the distinction between certain spatial and temporal separations, as illusory as our experience of the phenomenal color of things.

If in fact large, high-energy complexes of particles, say our bodies, retain something at least closely analogous to determinate classical positions and powers, then our old story of the realization of at least our *experience* of causal and spatio-temporal structure might seem to be capable of salvation. If the world has at least some relatively large-scale classical causal structure, so it might seem, then causal basic contents might match the world even if they must miss some of the fine detail of quantum mechanics. There might be enough spatio-temporal and causal structure present to underwrite our familiar coherently conceivable objectual account of our causal and spatio-temporal experience. More than one basic content can match the same world, with some expressing less detail than others. So too it might seem that basic contents may match the world even if none of them gets all the tiny detail of that world right. And a basic content such as that sketched in the last chapter might then capture at least the gross structure of our neurons and muscles in a way which underwrites an objectual account of our classical experience.

But this hope is an illusion. We should remember that, according to the content theory of Part One, constitution and abstraction are semantic relations, rooted in relations between contents. If one basic content can match a world more fully characterized by yet another basic content, then that is only because there is an important semantic relation between the two, with the first in many ways analogous to an abstraction from the second. And we face a situation in which this tale breaks down. The requisite semantic dependency is absent, because one of the contents required as a term for that relation is absent. One may insist that the world may well be matched in part by a basic content even if we cannot coherently conceive some of the world's fine details, say if the world includes objective colors on the third planet of Arcturus which we cannot coherently conceive. But if the "details" infect the spatio-temporal structure of the world as a whole, as in the case we face, even this move won't work. If the position of a particle is infinitely indeterminate, then that is far from a benign and localized problem. Under the conditions we face, the inconceivable details are not isolated from the purportedly conceivable features of the world in the way this stratagem requires.

One may attempt another line of resistance. Perhaps some possible, though not coherently conceivable, creature could be capable of a coherent conception of the quantum mechanical world. And one might hope that it could also conceive our basic contents, and see that there was a semantic relation linking the two. However, even if such a creature told us that there was such a link, we would be unable to clearly understand the creature. And our own familiar basic contents may be beyond the conception of someone capable of a coherent conception of the quantum mechanical. To be capable of the coherent conception of the quantum mechanical may well be to be incapable of our classical experience, and the thoughts which are rooted in it. And a creature which could somehow experience both the quantum mechanical and also what we experience would not hence entertain contents which are dependent on one another in the way which is required. The semantic relation between the contents of those different sorts of experience would be like that between phenomenal color and phenomenal sound, and that isn't the right kind of semantic relation.

So there we are. We experience at least large collections of "particles" to possess determinate classical properties, positions and momentums. But our experience of those classical causal properties and spatio-temporal positions is as illusory as our experience of the distinction between certain spatial and temporal separations, indeed as illusory as our experience of phenomenal color. We lack the resources required for a coherently conceivable objectual account of the realization of our spatio-temporal and causal experience. Without spatio-temporal structure, there is obviously no plausible objectual account of the experience of spatio-temporal structure. Any coherently conceivable objectual account of our spatio-temporal experience must deploy microevents, but there are no microevents. A coherently conceivable account of our causal experience requires not only microevents but the presence of coherently conceivable powers of a certain primitive dynamic sort. But our own so-called "powers" are a reflection to at least some degree of non-causal correlations, and any true powers which remain are not coherently conceivable, let alone primitive. They are restrictions with the wrong contents. So the most plausible account of our spatio-temporal and causal experience must be a non-objectual account.

This is a disaster, though for us a familiar one. We know after Chapter Sixteen that any coherently conceivable account of our spatio-temporal and causal experience must be an objectual account, which deploys objects with causal powers and spatio-temporal relations. But quantum mechanics seems to imply, at least given the content theory sketched in Part One, that there are none of the objectual resources we need. The coherently conceivable objectual accounts of our spatio-temporal and causal experience are as false as the coherently conceivable objectual accounts of our phenomenal experience dismissed in Chapter Fourteen. Somehow entities which lack classical positions and powers conspire to produce our experience of entities which have them. But such a non-objectual realization of our causal and spatio-temporal experience is not coherently conceivable by us. We cannot coherently conceive the actual realization of our causal and spatio-temporal experience.

I've just deployed the first sort of difficulty with objectual accounts of our experience which we have been tracking since Chapter Eight. We lack the objectual resources required. But it may be that there's also a role here for our second sort of objection. The traditional galilean might have told a comforting evolutionary story, a causal history, which seemed to explain why our capacity to conceive our acts in certain ways, say to talk about them to ourselves, and our real actions, would fit nicely together. Now we know, however, that the traditional galilean picture even of our behavior is misleading. The only kind of obvious speech with which we do characterize our acts, speech which we experience at least in the mind's ear, does not reflect the true quantum mechanical characterization of our "behavior". But even if it did, we no longer have what can seem a plausible explanation of how or why it would, since we know that, for instance, actual evolutionary pressures are consistent with the state in which we actually find ourselves. This may seem a bit of a cheat, since in the hypothetical circumstances in which we did perform behaviors in accord with our intuitive characterizations of those behaviors actual evolutionary pressures might suffice. But I see no grounds whatever for confidence about that.

Given all we've seen, we might begin to wonder about the distinction between our behavior and what causes it, or between the content of experience and the effects of that experience. Our nature as cognizers somehow leads us to conceive and to experience two sorts of elements of the world, the passive phenomenal and the active and asymmetric causal, all arranged in a spatio-temporal distribution. Our experience of the phenomenal seems to involve two elements we can model--a passive content and also certain asymmetric restrictions in physical behavior or on other psychological states. These things cannot be held together in a plausible way once we abandon childish pre-galilean stories about what constitutes and explains correlations. So perhaps we should conclude that one unified thing underlies our phenomenal experience, both its having a particular content and its effects. Perhaps the apparently distinct passive phenomenal objects of our experience on the one hand and the correlated effects of our experience on the other constitute our all-too-distorted human access to that one thing. Perhaps we should also conclude that the correlation between spin measurements at space-like separations is another phenomenon of this sort. Perhaps the truth projects into our experience in such a way that it seems to involve implausible correlations between distinct things, while it doesn't in fact.

But this vague mysticism is no real help for us. These suggestions are not coherently conceivable by human beings. Our attempt to make coherently conceivable and plausible sense of our own agency, of the realization of our own thoughts, has failed. Above all, this is because of the problems we face in understanding the realization of our experience. And we have those problems largely because our experience is false. The most immediate problem with the realization of our thoughts is not due to their apparently highfalutin features, their normativity or infinity. It is, rather, terribly mundane.

NOTES

1. One quite accessible introduction to quantum mechanics is Roger Penrose, *The Emperor's New Mind*, chapter 6. Peter Gibbins, *Particles and Paradoxes* (Cambridge: Cambridge University Press, 1987) is also quite useful, as is David Albert, *Quantum Mechanics and Experience* (Cambridge, MA: Harvard University Press, 1992). The classic survey for philosophers, both exhaustive and accessible, is Max Jammer, *The Philosophy of Quantum Mechanics* (New York: John Wiley & Sons, 1974). R.I.G. Hughes, *The Structure and Interpretation of Quantum Mechanics* (Cambridge, MA: Harvard University Press, 1989) is an introduction for philosophers to the formalism of quantum mechanics. Bernard d'Espagnat, *Conceptual Foundations of Quantum Mechanics* (Redwood City, CA: Addison-

Wesley, 1989) is somewhat more difficult, but a classic survey of the interpretation problems for quantum mechanics.
2. See especially Jammer, d'Espagnat, and Albert. J. Wheeler and W. Zurek (editors), *Quantum Theory and Measurement* (Princeton: Princeton University Press, 1983) is a collection of key original papers on the interpretation of quantum mechanics.
3. Gibbins presents this economically and accessibly.
4. The Janus-faced nature at least of light, its having both classically wave-like and particle-like features, was in fact long familiar. Various considerations had led Newton to the hypothesis that light should be understood to consist of discrete particles, though other phenomena like interference effects had led nineteenth century physicists to adopt a wave conception of light, as expressed in Maxwell's field equations.
5. W. Heisenberg, "The interpretation of kinematic and mechanical relationships according to the quantum theory" in G. Ludwig, *Wave Mechanics* (Oxford: Pergamon Press, 1968), 168-182. E. Schrödinger, "Quantization as an eigenvalue problem", in Ludwig, 94-105, and "Über das Verhältnis der Heisenberg-Born-Jordanschen Quantenmechanik zu der meinen", *Annalen der Physik* 79, 1926, 734-756. J. von Neumann, *Mathematical Foundations of Quantum Mechanics*, translated by R. Beyer (Princeton: Princeton University Press, 1955).
6. The frequency of the light, the width of the slits, and the distance between the slits are all relevant. See Penrose for a discussion of this.
7. My exposition follows Penrose, who stays a nice distance from the standard formalism.
8. Let me omit discussion of the normalization of amplitudes and probabilities.
9. On the ordinary post-galilean understanding of these things.
10. Though see Albert.
11. Einstein himself did not agree.
12. A. Einstein, B. Podolsky, and N. Rosen, "Can Quantum-mechanical descriptions of physical reality be considered complete?", in Wheeler and Zurek, 356-368. Einstein may not have favored quite the traditional ensemble interpretation. See Arthur Fine, *The Shaky Game* (Chicago: University of Chicago Press, 1986).
13. There are some non-standard ensemble interpretations which are not ruled out. But they are seriously non-classical.
14. David Bohm, "The Paradox of Einstein, Rosen, and Podolsky", in Wheeler and Zurek, 356-368.
15. David Mermin, "Quantum Mysteries for Anyone", in J. Cushing and E. McMullin (editors), *Philosophical Consequences of Quantum Theory* (South Bend, IN: University of Notre Dame Press, 1989), 49-59. Penrose, 284-285.
16. John S. Bell, "On the Einstein Podolsky Rosen Paradox", in Wheeler and Zurek, 903-908.
17. Add them up: Where the questions are dubbed 1,2,3, the answers + and -, and the first device is represented on the left, the possible combinations are (1+,1-), (1+,2-), (1+,3+), (2+,1-), (2+,2-), (2+,3+), (3-,1-), (3-,2-), (3-,3+). There are four agreements and five disagreements.
18. Aspect, Dalibard, Reger, "Experimental test of Bell's Inequality using time-varying analyzers", *Physical Review Letters* 49, 1982, 460-463. Clauser and Shimony, "Bell's Theorem: Experimental tests and implications", *Reports on Progress in Physics* 41, 1978, 1888-1927. M.L.G. Redhead, *Incompleteness, Nonlocality, and Realism* (Oxford: Oxford University Press, 1987), 108.
19. See the papers collected in Cushing and McMullin.
20. See page 190 of J.S. Bell, "Six possible worlds of quantum mechanics", *Speakable and unspeakable in quantum mechanics* (Cambridge: Cambridge University Press, 1987), 181-195.
21. N. Bohr, "Can Quantum-Mechanical Descriptions of Physical Reality Be Considered Complete?", in Wheeler and Zurek, 148-151, and "The Quantum Postulate and the Recent Development of Atomic Theory", Wheeler and Zurek, 87-126. One book by a philosopher on complementarity is Henry Folse, *The Philosophy of Niels Bohr* (Amsterdam: North-Holland Publishing, 1985).
22. Jim Joyce suggested this.

23. Hilary Putnam, "The logic of quantum mechanics", in *Mathematics, Matter, and Method* (Cambridge: Cambridge University Press, 1979), 174-197. See Jammer for a survey of such accounts, and Gibbins for a good introduction and some wise discussion.
24. See Gibbins.
25. In the end we may not be able to coherently conceive what quantum mechanics tells us about the world, but we shouldn't give up this soon. This isn't a sufficiently instructive place to give up, and the strong reading of this approach which might drive us there relies on the questionable notion of a logic of the world and the even more questionable notion of a non-standard logic of the world.
26. H. Everett III, "'Relative state' formulation of quantum mechanics", in Wheeler and Zurek, 315-323. DeWitt and Graham (editors), *The Many-Worlds Interpretation of Quantum Mechanics* (Princeton: Princeton University Press, 1973).
27. There is a related set of views called the "many minds" interpretation, which is due to B. Loewer and D. Albert. See Albert, 112-133. That class goes something like this: Allow the physical world to be always in a superposition. But allow that minds evolve in such a (probabilistic) way that they always register a particular measurement after a measurement interaction. In the simplest version of this scheme, all but one of the many physical alternatives which are superposed in that measurement are mere "mindless husks", but Albert prefers an alternative in which to each human brain there corresponds an infinity of minds, which register the alternative measurements in the right proportion. This seems to me to give minds or their physical bases an inordinate and implausible significance, much like Wigner's version of the orthodox von-Neumann style views, which we will soon discuss. And each mind is supposed to be governed by implausibly special probabilistic laws, which somehow *ensure* that the development of all the minds corresponding to a particular body will be such that they will end up as a group in the right places and in the right proportions. And of course such a view must deal in implausible infinities of minds for each person, as the only way to avoid perhaps even more implausible mindless hulks. So such views seem implausible.
28. A. Daneri, A. Loinger, G.M. Prosperi, "Quantum theory of measurement and ergodicity conditions", Wheeler and Zurek, 657-679.
29. See Jammer for references and discussion.
30. Some interpretations, of course, deny that they do consist at least solely of such particles. For instance, see the next interpretive option.
31. But see Jammer and d'Espagnat.
32. See page 171 of Nancy Cartwright, "How the Measurement Problem is an Artifact of the Mathematics", in *How the Laws of Physics Lie* (Oxford: Oxford University Press, 1983), 163-216. See also d'Espagnat, 196.
33. Though see Albert.
34. E.P. Wigner, "Remarks on the Mind-Body Question", in Wigner, *Symmetries and Reflections* (Bloomington, IN: Indiana University Press, 1967). See also the earlier article by F. London and E. Bauer, "The theory of observation in quantum mechanics", in Wheeler and Zurek, 217-259.
35. Of course, the objective phenomenal colors fail even in this role, because of perceptual relativity arguments. And at least the determinate classical properties would play some causal role, though it would be merely within the realm of the successive classical properties of things.
36. Perhaps the macro-object only emits its various "components" if it is broken up in some way, and otherwise they don't exist. Or perhaps it is constituted by the particles plus some other strange sort of thing, which yet could not make it up without them. But all this seems pretty dicey.
37. Penrose, 348-373.
38. Richard Healey, *The Philosophy of Quantum Mechanics* (Cambridge: Cambridge University Press, 1989). D. Dieks, "On some alleged difficulties in the interpretation of quantum mechanics", *Synthese* 86, 1991, 77-86.
39. B. van Fraassen, *Quantum Mechanics: An Empiricist View* (Oxford: Oxford University Press, 1989).
40. See Albert, 191-197.

41. Nancy Cartwright has proposed another interpretive direction, which retains classical positions for particles outside of measurement. See Cartwright. Bohm's view is deterministic. Cartwright's alternative is not. Particles possess determinate positions but merely classical probabilities for transitions to various successive states. The primary problem with this is that we are not yet in possession of the sketch of such a view, which will require more than a little modification of traditional quantum mechanics. There may be probabilistic elements in a relativistic version of Bohm's view, as we will soon see, but it seems that Cartwright anticipates that transition probabilities play a role even in non-relativistic quantum mechanics. It is hard to see how such an account could deal with EPR-type correlations without invoking the same sorts of troubling resources which Bohm-style accounts deploy. Also like the Bohm-style accounts, it may fail to give proper respect to the uncertainty relations. So because it has no obvious advantages over the Bohm-style accounts, and hasn't been developed, I will not explicitly discuss it in what follows.
42. L. de Broglie, "Sur la possibilité de relier les phénomènes d'interférence et de diffraction à la théorie des quanta de lumière", *Comptes Rendus* 183, 1926, 447-448.
43. David Bohm, "A suggested interpretation of the quantum theory in terms of 'hidden' variables, I and II", in Wheeler and Zurek, 369-396. See also the papers collected in Bell, *Speakable and unspeakable in quantum mechanics*, and Albert, 134-179.
44. See Jammer, 32. "In the treatment of a macromechanical system the vibrations, which undoubtedly have real existence in three-dimensional space, are most conveniently computed in terms of normal coordinates in the 3n-dimensional space of Lagrangian mechanics."
45. Bohm, "A suggested interpretation of the quantum theory in terms of 'hidden' variables II", appendix. Bell, "Beables for quantum field theory", *Speakable and unspeakable in quantum mechanics*, 173-180.
46. See for instance Fine, *The Shaky Game*.
47. Unlike constitution, it seems, it would need to be.
48. There's another possible advantage of the Bohm account which should be noted. At least its simple, pre-relativistic form involves merely deterministic powers, and they may also represent an advantage. This may seem a misguided worry, since irreducibly probabilistic powers are expressible in C. But while that represents my best judgment about what is coherently conceivable, resistance to that feature of C would not be unreasonable: I didn't provide any story about the realization of our thought of such powers. And perhaps our initial conception of probabilistic powers was of powers which were not *irreducibly* so. Perhaps, in our partial ignorance, we conceived of powers of things which we didn't take as irreducible and basic, but rather to reflect just exactly what little we knew, to ignore deterministic inner detail unknown to us in our ignorance. Perhaps the first sort of probabilities we conceived were mere epistemic probabilities, probabilities given our evidence that things would be such and so rather than probabilities in the world itself. And perhaps we came to the later conception of irreducibly probabilistic powers merely by mouthing the word "irreducible" in the direction of powers we conceived initially to be reducible. So perhaps thought of irreducible causal powers does not really have coherent basic content. If so, it may be that Bohm's account in it least its simple pre-relativistic form scores some advantage over the views we will discuss in the next section.
49. See Lawrence Sklar, "Saving the Noumena", *Philosophy and Spacetime Physics*, 49-72, for a nice articulation of the difficulty here.
50. G.C. Ghirardi, A. Rimini, and T. Weber, "Unified dynamics for microscopic and macroscopic systems", *Physical Review* 1986, D34:470. J.S. Bell, "Are there quantum jumps?", in *Speakable and unspeakable in quantum mechanics*, 201-212. Abner Shimony, "Our Worldview and Microphysics", in Cushing and McMullin, 25-37. Albert, 92-111.
51. See for instance Albert, 97.
52. See for instance Shimony, 35-36, and Albert, 97-111.
53. In the reference just cited.
54. "Dynamical models for the state-vector reduction: do they ensure that measurements have outcomes?", *Foundations of Physics Letters* 4:116.
55. In the reference just cited.

56. Bell, "Are there quantum jumps?".
57. R.P. Feynman, *QED* (Princeton: Princeton University Press, 1985) is a wonderfully lucid and accessible introduction. See also Harvey Brown and Rom Harre (editors), *Philosophical Foundations of Quantum Field Theory* (Oxford: Oxford University Press, 1988).
58. Michael Green, "Superstrings", *Scientific American* 255, 1986, 48-60, and "Unification of forces and particles in superstring theories", *Nature* 314, 1985, 409-414.
59. R. Penrose and W. Rindler, *Spinors and Space-Time* (Cambridge: Cambridge University Press, 1984).
60. We might hope to appeal to merely possible or potential chiral relations here, but that probably defeats the reductive intentions which lie behind the pursuit of spinors and twistors.
61. One easily accessible reference is "Gravity Quantized?", *Scientific American* 270:9, September 1992, 18-20.

CHAPTER NINETEEN

CONCLUSION

Review our situation: Part One developed an account of the contents which human thoughts can have. All human contents are generated from basic contents, which consist of phenomenal or causal microevents standing in certain spatio-temporal relations. And basic contents are basic in truth. They either match the world or fail to match the world, and in so doing ground the truth of contents generated from them. It is for this reason that to make sense of something contingent, to show that we can coherently conceive it, is to flesh it out in basic content, to exhibit basic contents which could ground its truth.

Part Two developed a coherently conceivable account of the realization of our thoughts, a coherent conception of an agent who is capable of the full range of thoughts articulated in Part One. We can in that sense coherently conceive ourselves. If we assume a capacity for phenomenal and causal and spatio-temporal experience, then we can make seemingly plausible and coherently conceivable sense of our capacity for thoughts beyond experience, thoughts with the full range of human contents. And there are coherently conceivable accounts of the realization of our experience, of the objectual sorts discussed in Part Two. Indeed, a familiar concrete world of the sort our experience seems to reveal would provide all the resources required for the existence of our thoughts, despite the worries of some philosophers that concrete resources cannot underwrite alleged highfalutin features of our thoughts like normativity and infinity and precise determinacy of translation.

Nevertheless, the coherently conceivable account developed in Part Two, deploying only familiar resources, isn't true. Part Three has shown that no coherently conceivable account of our phenomenal or causal or spatio-temporal experience is sufficiently plausible. All coherently conceivable accounts of our experience are objectual accounts. And objectual accounts are implausible, largely because our experience is false. We pursued a non-objectual account of our experience which was also coherently conceivable, but we didn't catch one. This difficulty ramifies. Any plausible account of our capacities for thoughts beyond experience must hold them dependent in realization on our capacity for experience. So no coherently conceivable account of the realization of any of our thoughts is plausible in all respects.[1] The project of this book, to vindicate our self-conception by showing it at once plausible and coherently conceivable, has failed. We can coherently conceive that we are capable of thoughts with the full range of contents articulated in Part One. But we cannot make at once plausible and coherent sense of the existence of our thoughts.

Still, I am not a thought skeptic. Still, I think we are in position to provide a certain sort of mitigated vindication of our thoughts. In fact, there may be two routes to some sort of vindication. First of all, the very considerations which show objectual accounts of the realization of our experience to be implausible also show that our thoughts are no worse off, no *more* implausible, than any other contingent thing which we humans can coherently conceive. Nothing which a thought skeptic may hope to privilege over our thoughts deserves that privilege. Remember that all basic contents are rooted in our experience, and that our experience is false. Basic contents are constituted by just the resources which plausible non-objectual accounts of our experience must eschew. Part Three has argued that objectual accounts of our experience are false because the world contains nothing with phenomenal or coherently conceivable causal properties, and nothing standing in the sorts of spatio-temporal relations characteristic of microevents. Hence it has also argued, almost by accident, that all basic contents are false, that none match the world.[2] And remember that the truth of any human thought, or at least of any contingent and positive human thought, is rooted in the match of basic contents to the world. So no such human thought is true.

There are two contingencies which bring us down. Our contingent nature happens to provide us only with a capacity for thoughts of the sorts sketched in Part One. And the contingent world is such that those thoughts happen to be false. None of our positive and coherent conceptions of anything contingent is correct. Our common beliefs that there are balls and balloons and stars are in as serious difficulty as our belief that we have thoughts. Indeed, so are the neurons we deployed in Part Two, along with the objectual resources with which we hoped to augment them. But, to put it the other way around, our thoughts are no worse off than the concrete neurons and balloons and stars which traditional thought skeptics prefer. Objectual accounts of our experience, and hence coherently conceivable accounts of the realization of our thoughts, are more *directly* in doubt than many other human conceptions. That is because they *explicitly* deploy objects of a sort which do not exist, and also a miraculous coordination between some of those objects and the form of our neural firing and behavior. But other human conceptions, if not as directly in doubt, are still equally in doubt. Objects of the sort we experience are not explicitly mentioned, under that very characterization, in the writings of those who study neural firing, unlike the writings of those who proffer objectual accounts of experience. And at least the writings of neurophysiologists do not exhibit the internal tensions which threaten Chapter Twelve's account of experience, with its miraculous correlation of the causal and the phenomenal. But still, coherently conceivable tales of the realization of our thoughts are no more implausible, though they are perhaps more immediately and directly problematic, than neurons.

That is one kind of vindication of thoughts, if I can call it a vindication. The coherently conceivable account of the realization of our thoughts developed in Part Two is a natural human account, and in fact requires just the sort of world which would ground the ordinary range of human claims, the kind of world which we all presume when we are walking around and not thinking too hard about our galilean legacy. It is customary for contemporary philosophers to treat the realization of our thoughts and the introspectible content of our experience as separate problems. Philosophers differ over which problem is more difficult, but the problems seem clearly distinct. This division is natural for post-galilean philosophers, but we have seen here that these problems are at root the same. And both of these problems are linked to another set of traditional difficulties. Our thoughts and our experiences are genuinely problematic for us just because of the radical revolution which post-galilean science has wrought in any legitimate conception of the world. Our thoughts and experience are problematic because they are false. I hope at least to have placed our current difficulties with introspectible experiences and with other thoughts in the proper light, to have shown that they are a reflection of a more general cognitive catastrophe. In that light, thoughts may seem more acceptable. If they are problematic in certain ways, still everything else is problematic in more or less the same ways.

Still, this may seem a cold and shallow vindication. Can we do any better? As we will shortly see, if we are optimistic enough, we might hope for another route. Thoughts may be even better off than fleshy neurons, blood cells, balloons, and stars. We may be able to preserve Descartes' optimistic claim that we have more certainly successful access to our thoughts than to the world outside of us. We will return to a discussion of this optimism in section 2.

In either case, whether or not we can go beyond a cold and shallow vindication of thoughts, we humans are in a situation which is in at least some respects like that which Descartes imagined. Descartes pondered a merely *hypothetical* evil deceiver, manipulating him so that his senses always deceived. But *in fact* our experience, and thought generally, are in radical error. They deceive us about the world. Perhaps Kant thought this, with one of his voices, though our problems are rather more contingent than he foresaw. There are some mitigating differences between our situation and that of someone misled by a cartesian evil genie. We possess evidence which reveals the error of our experience, and we have some comfort in numbers, since all humans share pretty much the same errors as a group. But there may also be some aggravating differences: We can't even coherently imagine the truth. And we have no obviously infallible access even to our own thoughts and experience. There is at least a serious possibility that our conception of our own thoughts and experience is, like all our other positive conceptions of contingent things, a false one.

At the very least, this is a puzzling situation. We'll return to a consideration of its coherence and consistency in a moment. But first I will briefly survey some possible escape routes. Each questions some key element in the argument which has led us to this epistemic disaster. I think that none of these escape routes is plausible enough, and that in fact we have already seen why. But it will be worth reviewing and elaborating the alternatives.

1

Some may hope that the progress of science will deliver us from our impasse. Perhaps the progress of physics will explain away all the strange quantum mechanical phenomena as mere misleading appearances. And perhaps the development of neurophysiology and psychology will provide some as yet unimagined alternative account of the realization of our phenomenal experience, an account which is at once coherently conceivable and plausible. But this is probably a vain hope. The quantum mechanical phenomena seem not only strange but real, and if physics is moving away from quantum mechanics, it seems to be going in an ever more incomprehensible direction. Also, we surveyed the full range of accounts of phenomenal experience, if only in a very abstract way. And we can see even now that none of the coherently conceivable kinds are very plausible.

Some may be tempted to say that any science which led us into such an impasse is suspect. But the suspicion seems properly to fall not on the evidential procedures of science but rather on our own cognitive limitations.[3] Consider one instance in particular of this possible escape route: If science holds out little hope for escape, then some may be tempted by some wild and implausible metaphysics. Some may hope to elude perceptual relativity arguments against the objectivity of phenomenal colors, and arguments that quantum mechanics deals in strange and unfamiliar properties, by the claim that there is no complete and consistent way the world is for all of us, independent of our way of conceiving it. But it is important to be clear about just how radical such a suggestion is. According to arguments presented in Chapter Four and the last chapter, it is of doubtful coherence. And nothing we have so far encountered really suggests anything nearly so radical. Perhaps quantum mechanics suggests that things are so entangled that no part of the world is distinct and separable from anyone's mind, but even then there would be a fact for all about what the entangled states of objects and minds are. Perhaps perceptual relativity suggests to some that we experience private objects, perhaps even private balls and balloons distinct from those seen by our fellows. But such distinct private corners of the world, accessible only by particular individuals, would still be part of one big discontinuous world, and that involves no denial of the completeness and consistency of the world itself. And of course, even such private corners of a single world are beyond anything which the considerations we've faced really suggest. The problem seems not to be a problem with the world, but with ourselves, with our conceptual capacities.

A somewhat more plausible escape might lie in the claim that there is something wrong with the content theory articulated in Part One, that there are more things which we can think and which might be basic in truth than merely the basic contents expressible in C. While the content theory of Part One charts an intuitive sort of content, rooted in introspection, our introspection is not obviously infallible and indefeasible. And the difficulties we have encountered may be sufficient to convince some that such an intuitive content theory should be abandoned. There are several ways in which someone might hope to modify the content theory of Part One and avoid our catastrophe.

For instance, someone might admit that a content which is basic in truth must be rooted in experience, but insist that we can experience a lot more than Part One implies. They might insist that we experience strange and unfamiliar objects in their true and unfamiliar nature. Objectual accounts of experience are popular, so some may be prepared to claim that we in fact experience whatever objects we in fact interact with via sensation and action, and in their actual guise, even if those objects are radically non-traditional quantum mechanical amplitudes or some other strange sort of thing. This alternative implies that our experience is in a certain sense infallible, and that it is radically different from what we have taken it to be, or at least from what the surface of our descriptions suggests we have taken it to be. So this route seems to me quite implausible. But perhaps some are prepared to live with these implications.

There are subtler ways to claim that experience can present to us things on the order of quantum mechanical amplitudes. Some think that our experience is so infested by our theories that long acquaintance with quantum mechanical theorizing can put us into a state in which we can see amplitudes.[4] But this alternative doesn't seem much more plausible than the last. Perceptual illusions persist even in the face of knowledge that they are illusions, and people with very different theories share sense experience.[5] So we should be suspicious of the depth of theoretical infestation of our experience. What's more, there is some difficulty in squaring a significant amount of theoretical infestation with a plausible account of the content of theoretical language. The account of language developed in Chapter Ten suggests that no meaning can accrue to theoretical language except through the ministrations of content, and ultimately concrete content, which is not itself mediated by those words. Our own highly theoretical language for quantum mechanics is in fact rooted in complex and indirect ways in our ordinary concrete experience. That's one of the reasons it took us so long to come up with quantum mechanics, and why anyone has to undergo a long education before there's any plausibility in the claim that quantum mechanics infests their experience. And if scientific study could transform our sensory experience so thoroughly that we *saw* the reality at which quantum mechanics gestures, so that we saw amplitudes, then the conditions required for our understanding of our own human and familiar quantum mechanics, which speaks after all of amplitudes for classical positions, which after all takes a rather tortuous and indirect route to quantum mechanical phenomena, might well be eliminated. We need to try another tack.

Even if basic contents expressible in C exhaust those contents which are immediately rooted in our experience, still, it may seem, contents merely generated from basic contents may also be basic in truth. Those contents which are dependent in generation and realization may match the world, and not through the mediation of the concrete causal and phenomenal elements of some basic content expressible in C. For instance, perhaps abstraction can provide us with quantum mechanical contents which match the world directly, not via the mediation of any more familiar concrete content. And some may be impressed by the fact that we can at least apparently speak of things which are not expressible in C. Perhaps, they may say, the machinations of words which constitute our ordinary belief in quantum mechanical amplitudes can be true, can somehow match the world, even though that truth is not rooted in the match of a concrete content expressible in C.[6]

But these possibilities are really no more plausible now than they were Part One, no matter how much more motivated we are now to find them so. Still the truth of any abstracted or word-mediated content to the world is mediated by the match of basic contents. Still the semantic nature of word-mediated and abstracted contents is determined by their semantic relations to basic contents. They are dependent in generation on basic contents in a way which makes them dependent in truth. To *be* such an abstracted or word-mediated content is to be dependent in truth in the ways we have sketched. And still our human sense of what can make words and abstractions true is our sense of what we can concretely interact with.

But some may persist in their resistance. Isn't quantum mechanics true? Don't we know that it says things which match the world, despite the general considerations I have just noted? So let's look at the specific cases. Quantum mechanics and string theory are expressed to a large degree in mathematical sentences. This is not the place to develop a full account of the meaning of mathematical sentences, but we know that the machinations of mathematical signs might possess content in all sorts of complicated and indirect ways. At the very least, there might be axiomatic systems in which some mathematical sentences are provable and others disprovable. There might be various appropriate inferences among mathematical sentences, and this alone might be sufficient to allow a kind of "truth" to accrue to such sentences. Still, the mathematics in quantum mechanics and string theory is a very special sort of mathematics. It applies to the world. In what does its application consist? At the very least, physicists can apply it in a skillful way to generate observational predictions. But that isn't really enough to tell us what the mechanism of the world which explains those observations is, and that is the particular role in which we have cast quantum mechanics and string theory here. Do quantum mechanics and string theory tell us something true about that mechanism? Only, it seems, if they include or are accompanied by some talk or interpretation which goes beyond their use in observational prediction. Physicists say that space has ten dimensions, or that there are indeterminate positions or non-causal correlations. What is the significance of *that* talk? Can that talk, or the mathematical sentences which it accompanies, match the world? Someone might claim that we know what three spatial dimensions are, and we know what ten apples are, and somehow we can abstract out the notion of a spatial dimension from the first case and the notion of ten from the second case and stick them together, so that we form the conception of a space with ten dimensions which yet can match the world. It follows from the fact that something is a coherently conceivable space, in my particular sense, that it has no more than three spatial dimensions. A ten-dimensional space is not coherently conceivable.[7] And yet, someone might insist, it is conceivable enough to exist. "Coherently conceivable" means in this account, at least roughly, *imaginable*, and this may seem to overrate imaginability. Perhaps from bent sticks we can move to the conception of a bent space which yet exhibits even the sorts of spatio-temporal structure discussed in Chapter Six, and from indeterminate desires to truly indeterminate positions.

And someone may insist on the significance of another sort of case. Just as we can prescind from certain features of our immediate experience to generate the notion of a basic content which consists solely of a single red microevent, they may claim that we can generate the notion of an abstract mathematical structure which can be present not only in experience but also in a world which C cannot express. Such a notion might match the world even if no basic content is true.

Certainly we can maneuver with words and abstract out features in at least roughly these ways, but the crucial question is whether or not these maneuvers can give us new notions which yet can match the world if basic contents are false. To assess this, it's worth considering some other cases. Consider phenomenal sounds which are seen, or a shade of color which is no familiar color, which no human can experience. If our mythical true color science had developed, and then had faced difficulties analogous to those of classical physics, someone might well have proposed colors no human can see. Or consider another pair of cases: Someone might claim that we can form the conception of a shape which is no particular shape, or even of a square circle which can match the world. They might say that we abstract out from a particular square which we can coherently conceive the notion of a very abstract sort of squareness which circles can also possess. And this gives us the notion of a square circle which yet can match the world.

The proper response to these claims, I think, would be the observation that our notion of squareness is rooted too closely in the nature of the squares we can coherently conceive, and our notion of shape in the nature of coherently conceivable particular shapes, for these to be plausible maneuvers. Perhaps we can abstract *something* out from familiar squares which can be found also in circles, but it is seriously misleading to call it squareness. That makes it sound more concrete than it is, more fleshy and contentful than is legitimate. Ditto for shapeless shape. A red microevent presents itself within experience as the sort of thing which might exist alone; not so for abstract shape-in-general. And we are misled if we think that the traditional notion of squareness helps gives us a concrete understanding of what any notion of a so-called square circle which we could generate in this devious and unusual way would say about the world, of what concrete conditions would constitute such a thing. In fact, such a notion captures nothing coherent unless it captures something which can be true of a circle we can coherently conceive.

It seems to me that the last case in particular is closely analogous to the crucial cases we face here, that similar things might be said about our supposedly coherent notions of ten spatial dimensions and truly indeterminate positions. Still, consider some further resistance. One might claim that we have a mathematical formalism which guides our inferences about things in ten-dimensional space, and that it is unlikely that such a thing could be developed to help us with square circles, or unseen colors for that matter. Descartes invented a way to arithmetize ordinary geometry, and this allowed us to extrapolate to spaces with many more dimensions. We just added a few more axes and variables. Mathematics which first was applied within experience guides us out beyond experience, and it allows some concrete significance to be carried up out from the familiar space of basic content to ten-dimensional space.

But this story has a crucial flaw. We might have an axiomization or mathematical model which guided our speech about unfamiliar colors and square circles in something like the same way, and yet that would not succeed in giving a coherent concrete significance to that speech. In such cases, we couldn't transfer concrete significance out beyond experience by mere mathematics in any way which would allow our new notions to *match* the world. Such notions cannot match the world because the kind of concrete content which match requires cannot be transferred into them without making them incoherent. And this seems true in the case of ten-dimensional and phenomenally bent and indeterminate space as well.

Still, one may insist, if our mathematics allows us to reason and infer about these so-called square circles and unseeable colors and ten-dimensional spaces in some controlled and responsible way, then those conceptions at least might *model* something, even if we cannot coherently conceive what it is, even if we can form no thought which can *match* such a structure. But this response in fact brings us to our next escape option.

Maybe something else than the match of contents can root truth. Are there plausible alternative candidates? One candidate can be quickly dismissed. Some hold that the true sentences are the verifiable ones. But we saw in Chapter Four that this is an empty claim unless it is filled out in some more specific way. And we also saw that any way of filling it out which involved the denial of bivalence for the contents which are basic in truth, for the basis of verification, was incoherent. Likewise, an infinite regress of content dependencies seemed impossible. There is a basic set of confirmation conditions, whose truth is not constituted by any distinct evidence. If those confirmation conditions include sensory evidence, then our conception of that sensory evidence should be true to the world. If they involve things written in books, then our conception of those words should be true to the world. It may be that this sort of truth is match, or it may be something else. But a coherent verificationist account of truth must incorporate some other such notion of truth. Are there any real alternatives to match, which can be deployed on their own or within a coherent verificationist conception of truth? The two obvious contenders are isomorphism and reference.

First, consider isomorphism. The mathematics of quantum mechanics may well seem isomorphic to some real features of the world. For two things to be isomorphic is for them to share a structure of some sort. There is a map from elements of one to elements of the other which preserves the pattern of interrelationships of those elements, so that one thing can model the other. Match is in fact a sort of isomorphism, but of a very special and specific kind. If match fails, still we might claim that isomorphism, any old isomorphism, yields a kind of truth. We might claim that a contingent and positive thought is true when it is isomorphic to some truth. There are a variety of ways this might work. Many different things might be thought to possess an isomorphism to the world or some elements of the world. Some may claim that thoughts are true because their *contents* are isomorphic to the world. And others may claim that the important thing is the isomorphism of what realizes a thought to the world. Some may admit that basic contents do ground the truth of all thoughts, but insist that it is the isomorphism and not the match of basic contents which matters. And others may claim that there are some contents which we entertain only via abstraction or the machinations of words which yet possess the requisite isomorphism directly, without the mediation of basic contents. But however we try to root truth in isomorphism, we face what seem to be insuperable difficulties.

Anything bears some isomorphism to anything else. For instance, there is some mapping from a thought existing to anything being anything. The proposal under consideration implies that all contingent, positive thoughts would be true in all possible circumstances. But if there is any constraint on what it is for a thought to be true, it is that not all such thoughts are true in all possible circumstances. Clearly, a plausible account of how truth is rooted in the isomorphism of thought and world must place certain constraints on the kind of isomorphism which is relevant. For instance, only certain kinds of elements of thoughts or the world should be relevant, and perhaps only certain sorts of mappings between them. But this presents a serious problem in the strange circumstances in which we find ourselves, at least if isomorphism is to deliver truth for some of our contingent positive thoughts. This is because the kinds of constraints we can coherently conceive cannot be met by the inconceivable world. One might insist that it is the content of thoughts which must be isomorphic to the world, and that contents do have a kind of structure which we might specify as relevant. But what can we do with the world itself? Even a coherently conceivable world would have no single "true" set of elements and structure. Elements of such a world would include not merely microevents, but also properties and points and regions. Still, if the world were coherently conceivable, then we could specify which elements were relevant. But the world is not coherently conceivable, so we cannot specify the elements which are relevant, at least if there are to be relevant elements, which succeed in grounding truth for our thoughts, which meet the specified constraints.

Match is a specific kind of isomorphism, and of course if we insist that match is required for truth then no positive and contingent thoughts are true. But consider also another particular and popular case, a kind of reference which is not mediated by the match of the thoughts of a referent to the world. It involves a particular kind of isomorphism in which correlated elements of a thought and the world are connected by causal chains.

There are difficulties with this strategy. First of all, this sort of reference can be possessed in any direct way only by real things, things which aren't mere objects of thought. This may mean that contents can't really have references in the most straightforward and primary sense, since they aren't real things, since they are mere objects of thought. But, on the other hand, the thoughts which have contents might have references in the primary sense, and that might constitute some subsidiary sort of reference even for the contents of the thoughts. For instance, we might treat all features of basic contents just as we treated indexical features in Part One, as Janus-faced. Indexical elements in basic contents can either match elements of implausible centered worlds directly, or serve to aim their contents in more plausible uncentered worlds. So too, it might seem, other features of basic contents may have two sorts of possible truth conditions; they may match, or merely aim. When they merely aim, they may in fact be true. And they may be aimed by real causal connections in some way.

So it seems that we could get around the first possible problem with reference. But there is another difficulty with this route, which seems decisive. We saw in Chapter Two that we humans attribute reference only when certain concrete conditions obtain, only when certain conditions which we can coherently conceive are met in the world. "Causal" accounts of reference attempt to articulate these conditions. But this familiar sort of reference is unavailable in the circumstances we actually face. For instance, any familiar and coherently conceivable linguistic reference seems to involve the correlation of spatially and temporally distinct bits of language and of the world, a correlation constituted by familiar sorts of spatio-temporal and causal relations or other real and concrete relations. In particular, reference of the popular sort we are considering now seems to involve particular causal paths through the world. If the world lacks a familiar spatio-temporal and causal structure in the way the last chapter suggested, then there are no referential chains of the sorts deployed in currently popular accounts of reference. Some may be tempted to root reference and truth not in causal chains but in the co-variation of certain features of thoughts and certain features of the world. It seems to me that it would be difficult to pry this notion away from even spatial co-presence, but in any case co-variation of any relevant and coherently conceivable sort seems to involve at least some sort of temporal co-variation. And in fact there isn't such co-variation.

We have seen that both isomorphism and reference face serious difficulties if they are to replace match as a ground of truth in our strange circumstances. Though it may turn out that these difficulties can be met, this seems quite unlikely. And there is another problem for these alternatives as well. Any so-called "truth" rooted merely in reference or isomorphism, any "truth" distinct from match, misses something crucial we expect from truth. When we come to know that a thought or theory is true, we ordinarily take ourselves to have come to some *understanding* of the nature of the world. We take ourselves to have come not to the mere recognition that it has bits which can be correlated with the bits of our theory, but to the fuller recognition that the thought or theory captures those bits as they are. There might be isomorphism and reference of the sorts we have been discussing between our colorful experience and a colorless world, and we want more of our thoughts than merely that.

Let me admit that there is a limit to how much weight this objection can legitimately bear. It is very unlikely that our word "true" is determinate enough in meaning to rule out the possibility that some sort of isomorphism or reference is enough for truth when match is unavailable.[8] It's even unlikely that that meaning is determinate enough to rule against even more homely possibilities, for instance that what all we humans can agree on counts as true, at least in the very unfamiliar circumstances in which we find ourselves, in which things we have taken to go together come apart. But, regardless of the tendency of philosophers to fight over words, it shouldn't really matter all that much what nuances of meaning even an important word like "true" possesses. The *facts* are that there is no match between our thoughts and the world, but that there *may* be isomorphism of lots of kinds, too many kinds. And that's it. We should realize what our situation is, and not obscure it by bandying "true" about as if *that* could solve our problems. I risk over-dramatizing our situation by my claims that basic contents do not match the world and hence that none of our positive conceptions of anything contingent are true. But the facts which underlie this claim are worth some dramatization. Otherwise we'd slip back all too easily into forgetting them. We want match and act like we have it even when we don't, even when we should know better.

Isomorphism and reference are not a plausible route to all that we want from truth. Still, they may be a route to at least a little of what we want, and there may be other such routes as well. To one of these routes we will shortly return.

There is one quite specific assumption of the content theory of Part One which may seem quite idiosyncratic and which led us into trouble. I've held that constitution is a semantic relation, that if something can be constituted by some other things then that fact must be underwritten by a semantic dependency between contents. Twice this blocked our access to an otherwise plausible account of experience. If there were a kind of constitution which was not underwritten by semantic relations, then our primary objection to Hardin's heroic non-objectual account of our phenomenal color experience would fail. Just because no semantic dependency privileges one assignment of color experience to Galileo's neurophysiology over another in the inverted spectrum case, still, some may insist, that neurophysiology may in fact constitute one sort of experience rather than the other.[9] And if there is some kind of non-semantic constitution, then it may be that quantum mechanical particles which cannot be coherently conceived can still constitute our familiar muscles and neurons and waves. Those muscles and waves are things which we can coherently conceive, and they might ground our causal experience.

Non-semantic constitution would be a very helpful resource. But non-semantic constitution is, I think, nothing we understand. And it is not underwritten by any familiar examples. If H-O-H counts as water, then that is because it is something which does what we take water to do, which is at the very least in at least roughly the places we take water to be. Its counting as water is rooted in its meeting the criteria we possess for calling something "water", perhaps not all of them but at least the important ones. And those are semantic criteria. In fact, they are introspectible semantic criteria, which we can flesh out in basic content.

Some may object that for something to meet a semantic criteria for being water does not require that there be the particular kind of semantic dependency I have presumed. For instance, it may be that we should understand "constitution" in some spatio-temporal way, so that whatever the spatio-temporal bits of something are, whether we can coherently conceive them or not, constitute that thing. It seems to me that there couldn't be such a spatio-temporal coincidence without some sort of semantic dependency, but in any case this route is of little help given the problems which face us. We are facing a situation in which there is no clear spatio-temporal relation between what we want to constitute and what we have available to constitute it.

Of course there are other sorts of relation which mimic what I have called "constitution" to one degree or another, for instance things rooted in isomorphism or reference of the sorts discussed above. But these would also face the difficulties we reviewed there. They would not provide enough of what we ordinarily expect of constitution, at least in the strange circumstances in which we find ourselves. Still, we need to remember that it is only coherently conceivable constitution, which links coherently conceivable things in a coherently conceivable way, which we know to be a semantic relation. Some non-objectual account of the realization of our experience which we cannot coherently conceive may be, for all this, true, though there are a number of tensions coiled into that claim which we will need to confront in section 2.

This exhausts the obvious escape routes which question the doctrine of Part One. Part Three presents another opportunity. This final escape route involves some compromise with plausibility, but some may prefer that to the alternative. Let me list some possibilities:

i) The relative state interpretation of quantum mechanics is coherently conceivable in at least most respects, and it seems to fit Chapter Sixteen's account of the realization of our causal experience. We might try something analogous for phenomenal experience as well. We might augment whatever determinacy in color experience is provided by Hardin-style resources in inverted spectrum cases with a resource suggested by Michael Lockwood:[10]

All possible assignments of phenomenal experience to our brain states which meet the Hardin-style constraints are in fact realized, but in different branches of a branching world.

ii) An orthodox, Wigner-style account of the collapse of the wave packet might comport nicely with an account of color experience which postulated colorful sense data as components of physically irreducible souls.

iii) We might claim that there are irreducible macro-physical objects, not constituted by their quantum mechanical "components", and capable of initiating collapse of wave packets. These macro-objects might have objective colors, which are not exactly coherently conceivable, but close. Those objective colors fuzz out the differences between different sorts of normal human color experience, but are sufficiently determinate to resolve inverted spectrum cases which Hardin-style constraints alone can't eliminate. The objective color of a thing somehow injects itself into one's experience of that thing, along with the idiosyncrasies in one's experience due to peculiarities of one's own individual neurophysiology.

iv) We might wed a Bohm-style account of quantum mechanics, with its ad hoc causal psi-field, to something similarly ad hoc and causal, though less plausible: There are special causal powers of particles, and they have an observationally significant effect only under very limited circumstances. When the particles are clumped into human brains, they secrete just the colorful sense data which are appropriate to help constitute experience for those brains.

v) Maybe we should treat different sorts of experience differently. Perhaps something on the order of a Bohm-style view is the correct interpretation of quantum mechanics and roots a plausible and coherently conceivable account of our causal experience. And, if I can be allowed for a moment to deploy resources from another set of escape routes, perhaps the realization of our phenomenal experience is beyond our capacity to coherently conceive, say along the lines considered briefly in Chapter Fifteen: The apparent differences in our phenomenal experience which cannot be rooted in Hardin-style constraints are to be explained away as mere illusion, just like the differences between contents which would be introduced by full-blown non-relative haecceities. Or we might try non-semantic constitution at this point.

vi) We might hope to defuse the oddity of any causal laws governing the generation of phenomenal sense data from brains by the suggestion that the apparently odd form of the laws is merely an artifact of our mistaken ordinary understanding of the spatio-temporal structure of the world. Or we could try some of the alternatives above plus God, or at least the Wizard of Oz or some benevolent alien, who desires that we have determinate thoughts, and hence provides an explanation by design of otherwise pretty implausible laws or configurations. If it's good enough for Descartes... On the other hand, remember that Descartes argued that the existence of at least God was inconsistent with our being deceived in what we are impelled by our nature to believe. And we have just seen that we are deceived in that way.

2

I think that if we are clear-headed and honest with ourselves we will admit that none of these options is very plausible, that none is plausible enough. The appropriate response to our situation is to take it straight. Our phenomenal experience reflects features of our neurophysiology, and perhaps of the objects we see, in a way which suggests a non-objectual account of that experience. But no such account is coherently conceivable. And quantum mechanics suggests a non-objectual account of our classical experience, which is also beyond our capacity to coherently conceive. Our experience is seriously misleading. Basic contents are false, and hence cannot ground the truth of any positive and contingent human thought. Indeed, the very existence of our thoughts is in serious doubt. And there we are.

This may seem to provide more than sufficient material for a dismissive *reductio*. We began, in Chapter One, with transcendental arguments, and they may warrant our attention again. Consider this one: If no human sentence is true, then neither is the antecedent of this conditional. So if the antecedent is true, it is false. So it certainly isn't true. Some human sentence is true. Perhaps the dependencies we noted in Chapter Ten then require that there also be true thoughts, and in any case the inner speech or ordinary utterance of such a sentence would constitute true thought. There are true thoughts.

Of course, the mere presentation of a transcendental argument does not alone suffice to show what is wrong with a skeptical argument, to show which of its premises or inferences is incorrect. And certainly transcendental arguments cannot succeed in showing that we can conceive every strange detail of our world. Nor should we, limited by our evolution as we are, expect otherwise. But still such arguments may seem to show that some of the things we think and say are true. If the truth of such claims cannot plausibly be rooted in basic contents, then not all the truth of our thoughts and sentences is rooted in basic content. Nevertheless, such a transcendental argument is really no more decisive now than when we began. This is partly for familiar reasons: Just as there might be a wonderful behavioral mesh we falsely call "true speech", which is distinct from some less wonderful behavioral mess which we falsely call "false speech", so too there might be wonderful and incomprehensible goings on we (so to speak) falsely call "true thought", and equally incomprehensible but somewhat less wonderful goings on we falsely call "false thought". And the first sort of thing might really be better in some cognitively relevant sense than the second. You'll notice that this response is a bit creaky now, or at least that I've expressed it badly, since I've presumed in the response a kind of reference, a resource which is strictly speaking unavailable to us except perhaps as part of a counter-*reductio*. But we'll try to get closer to the resources a straight response would require in a bit. Still, the main point is something else: There would be a simple misunderstanding embodied in the application of this particular transcendental argument to my particular position. It is important to realize that the cognitive disaster I allege is limited in at least one crucial way, so that the conclusion of this argument is, in fact, irrelevant to my position. Not all human thoughts, but only all *positive* and *contingent* human thoughts, fail to be true. In the context of the content theory of Part One, that means something quite specific.

Even if a transcendental argument cannot establish the truth of some of our thoughts, still I admit that some of our thoughts do seem true even in our radically unfamiliar circumstances, at least if I can assume for the moment that there are such thoughts. Contents generated by external negation, for instance, may be true even if no basic content is true. That is why I have waffled a bit, and said only that certain *positive* conceptions of things are false. That is what I mean by that. Likewise, it might be that there are some "contents" which are analogous to traditional analytic propositions, "contents" whose truth is constituted by content dependencies alone, and hence which can be true even if no basic content is true. If there were bachelors, then they would be unmarried, so all bachelors are unmarried. Red is a color, and it is raining or it is not. That's the reason for the other element in my waffling, the part about *contingency*. Frankly, I am not sure if any of our run-of-the-mill thoughts are like this, if any of our actual ordinary thoughts have contents whose truth does not require the match of some basic content to the world. For instance, I worry that it may well be indeterminate whether our thoughts involve internal or external negation in ordinary contexts. But this is at least one reasonably plausible route to some true thoughts. Only positive human conceptions of contingent circumstances are false. This helps us avoid some transcendental arguments.

There is another related point which is worth noticing. One might well wonder how, if basic contents constitute all we can coherently conceive, that we can even entertain the possibility that basic contents fail to match the world. That would seem to require that we conceive a world which is not captured by basic content at the same time that we can form no such coherent conception. But of course a conception need not be a coherent conception. The most plausible understandings of quantum mechanics, for instance, are not coherent conceptions. And while only coherent conceptions can match the world, still it may be that the machinations of words or abstraction can produce a conception which has in fact more cognitive value than is possessed by our ordinary coherent concrete claims about thoughts and balls and balloons, in the strange and unfamiliar circumstances in which we find ourselves. That last point requires some amplification, but there's another point worth noticing first. Consider the following set of transcendental arguments:

If all our positive and contingent thoughts are false, then so is the thought that there are human thoughts with a certain determinate range of contents. So, for that matter, is the thought that there are human thoughts. The overall conclusion of this book implies that at least one of its central premises is incorrect, or at least that we haven't succeeded in thinking what is expressed in that premise. What's more, the very existence of the sentences of this book, sentences which after all we can think about, implies that some positive and contingent thought of which humans are capable is true.

Once again, it's worth remembering that transcendental arguments alone cannot defeat skeptical arguments. And again, there might still be wonderful things we (so to speak) falsely call "thoughts" or "sentences", even if there are no thoughts. But there may also be a more specific route for us around this particular set of arguments. Besides negative and analytic thoughts and claims, there is another kind of thought and claim whose truth we may well be highly motivated to preserve. And this may provide another opportunity to narrow the scope of our cognitive disaster.

Consider my apparently positive and contingent claims about what our experience is, about what our thoughts in general are, and also my suggestions that in fact some of these thoughts have a positive cognitive value. Isn't this a set of positive and contingent claims? Isn't it a set of claims to whose truth I am committed, whatever I pretend to conclude? And aren't at least these claims in fact a lot more plausibly true than my recent arguments seem to suggest?

There are two ways to respond to this suggestion which are at least reasonable contenders. We might try to make out how it could literally be true that we have the experience and thoughts we do, and how they literally have some positive cognitive value, even if basic contents are false. In that case, our thoughts would be better off than neurons and red balls. Or we might give up on that hope. These are the two sorts of "vindication" of which I spoke earlier.

Let me first sketch what sort of thing we might optimistically hope for, before we talk about whether in fact we can get it. Kant held that all humans experience pretty much the same sort of world, even though that world of experience is in many ways a misrepresentation of the true noumenal world which lies beyond experience. Similarly, we might claim that all humans pretty much share experience of the same sort of more or less illusory world. If we are all deceived, at least it's in roughly the same way. While different individuals experience slightly different colors, the differences aren't large.

If the content of a thought matched the world which all humans more or less experience, whether or not that world is really there, then that would provide some sort of positive cognitive value, some bit of what we ordinarily take truth to be. Assume for the moment there really is human experience such as Part One characterized. In a world such as we all seem to experience, such as our experience seems to reveal, there would be resources to ground the truth of many of our ordinary thoughts about red balloons and balls, and hence resources for an objectual account of our experience itself. And there would thus be resources to ground our beliefs about our thoughts as well. Claims about our thoughts and experiences, such as those made in Part One, could possess at least the same cognitive value as ordinary claims about balls and balloons, via the route sketched in Part Two. In fact, it might be that other sorts of seemingly questionable claims, say about the objective value of things, could be equally well rooted in the consensus of human experience, though that's a story for another day. And still other sorts of claims, say those of quantum mechanics, while rooted less directly in the consensus of human experience, could still have greater cognitive value than the more commonsense claims about pointers and balls which constitute their evidential support.

Let me elaborate: Assume that there is at least a fact about what humans experience, that there is a range of human experience with certain contents. Assume also that there is a fact about what humans *would* experience in various circumstances, if they looked in various places. If all normal humans would have or do have a certain kind of experience in a certain situation, then it might be that we could project from the content of that particular experience to a bit of a third-person content which we might call the "forensic truth", truth for the public forum. If Galileo had been hauled into court to testify, at least other than as an expert witness, he would have said that the ball falling by his window was red. Forensic truth is a truth rooted in the shared consensus of human experience, the experience on the basis of which we act even when we have philosophical doubts about it.

This forensic truth is indeterminate where normal human experience differs. For instance, the forensic truth is a sort of abstraction across all normal human experience of unique green. It isn't, strictly speaking, a basic content. What's more, it is only *human* forensic truth, and ignores even non-normal humans. But still forensic truth captures some component of our normal sense of truth. Common sense doesn't realize that match and forensic truth come apart, so our word "truth" probably implies both. They do come apart, but still forensic truth has a high cognitive value, and captures a lot of what we ordinarily mean by "truth".

In the world of forensic truth, there are concrete things of more or less the sorts we deployed in the account of Part Two. There are red balls and balloons and bloody neurons, and so we have the resources required by Part Two's objectual account of our experience and non-objectual account of thought beyond experience, or at least we have the resources required if we ignore the relatively subtle differences among different ordinary humans' experience of unique green. It may be that there are miraculous elements in the account sketched in Part Two, miraculous coordinations between our behavior and the phenomenal properties of the things we experience, but we are stuck with those concrete coincidences in any case, at least if commonsense claims about colored balls and neural firing are to be underwritten by the forensic truth. The less optimistic vindication is imbedded in this way in the more.

Forensic truth may have significant limitations, even beyond those I've noted. For instance, it is unlikely that except under much too wildly hypothetical conditions we would experience much of the sub-atomic micro-structure which common sense now probably holds the world to contain. But at least forensic truth can deliver the macro-objects with which we are most familiar, and probably even neurons. In the world of forensic truth, there are thoughts and balls and balloons, and our thoughts are at least generally true.

It seems to me that in most contexts, forensic truth is what we should strive for. But there are other positive cognitive values. Of course, there is match. Lacking that, we lack something significant. But there are other sorts of positive cognitive value as well, some of which are even more valuable than forensic truth, though rooted in it. Forensic truth grounds the truth of certain sentences. But sentences are connected by inferential relations. And these relations can lead us out beyond forensic truth. Galileo can reason just as he reasoned to the claim that there is no color, and his argument bears weight. Certainly science is rooted in our experience and in forensic truth, but certainly also it can come reasonably to claim that even our causal and spatio-temporal experience is misleading. It may be that a series of arguments can overturn all the features of forensic truth, and yet each retain the integrity they would possess on their own. That is something like the integrity of a *reductio*. It is a bit as if in Descartes' demon world, the demon had hidden tiny inscriptions under the rocks and inside the cats which Descartes experienced, which said that that world was an illusion. These cases involve only negative claims, but it may even be that we can be led beyond forensic truth to apparently positive sentences with a lot of positive cognitive value, even more positive value than that provided by forensic truth itself. Consider for instance the sentences of quantum mechanics. Cognitive value other than match grows out of forensic truth, I think, but it is not limited to it.

If all this works out, then perhaps there can be a literal truth about our experience and about the forensic truth. In fact we experience what we do, and there is in fact a certain forensic truth, a determinate ground for positive epistemic value. But still we seem to lack some things we need. For instance, we still seem not to *literally* have, as a matter of more than forensic truth, the resources to constitute thoughts beyond experience, including those mediated by words. So far it may seem to be merely a forensic truth what thoughts beyond experience and what sentences there are, and not a literal one. So we might hope for just a little bit more.

Much of the concrete presence of one's thought to oneself, much of what one in fact introspects, including the quasi-experience of words said to oneself and the odd bit of their content which one introspects, might in fact be compressed into one's experience, in a rather shadowy and ghostly way. The distinction between ordinary experience and the kind of quasi-experience which we can have in imagination may merely be a matter of their content, of vividness. And the full range of one's thought might be capable of being at least indirectly present through one's experience and quasi-experience. This may help deliver to us the resources for the literal existence of our thoughts beyond experience.

Let me elaborate. Our most obvious thoughts are directly introspected primary thoughts. They are our experiences and quasi-experiences, which also constitute components of quite obvious word-mediated thoughts and thoughts with basic contents which aren't seed contents. Experiences, quasi-experiences, and the word-mediated thoughts and thoughts with basic contents beyond experience which they help constitute, have contents which are either directly or indirectly introspectible in the ways noted in Chapter Eight, through the direct presentation of the concrete. If there is a fact about what you not only experience but also quasi-experience, and also about what you would concretely experience and quasi-experience were you to turn your consideration in various directions, then it may be that there are facts not only about your experiences and quasi-experiences, but also about your word-mediated thoughts, with their complicated contents, and even about what basic contents you have in mind. In addition, if there are various facts about what you would experience and quasi-experience were you to have certain other hypothetical experiences, then there may be other facts which help to constitute what I called in Chapter Eleven your primary psychology. We then can ascribe to you virtual thoughts on the basis of your various dispositions for various primary thoughts. All we really lack, then, are the rather speculative primary thoughts discussed in section 1 of Chapter Thirteen, and virtual thoughts which would be ascribed in part on the basis of these.

Furthermore, perhaps your quasi-experience can be imbedded in your experience. If we've given up on the ultimate plausibility of objectual accounts of experience, we no longer have strong motivation to treat the realization of the primary imagination differently, at least as a matter of literal truth, from that of our experience.[11] In particular, let's assume that the fact that we can mistake a vividly imagined sound with a faintly experienced sound implies that the degrees of intensity of intrinsic phenomenal properties already provide us with the necessary resources to capture phenomenal primary imagination within experience, at least if we allow that there can generally be the fusing of microevents with the same sort of characteristic phenomenal properties, a perception of red fused to an imagination of green. We need to add a similar axis of intensity for causal experience, which apparently is not captured by the degree of force that can appear within our causal experience.

Let me summarize: Because of the compression of some of our thought into our experience and quasi-experience, and of our quasi-experience into our experience, some claims about our thoughts even beyond experience might literally be true, if we literally have the necessary experience. This maneuver can take us only so far. One's thought is not very likely to be constituted solely by what one introspects. At the very least, we also need various dispositions for actual introspection, the truth of various conditionals. Indeed, as I've suggested, other sorts of conditionals involving experience may be crucial as well. Still, maybe we can have all of that. If all this works out, then thoughts may well be even better off than balls and balloons and neurons, though there would be no literally plausible and coherently conceivable and at all detailed account of their realization. There might literally be all the thoughts we clearly seem to have, and the meaningful sentences we utter to ourselves, and they might generally possess at least forensic truth.

Someone might claim that, if we can get all the hypothetical claims about experience I have suggested, then we have enough for the truth of commonsense claims about balls and neurons. That would be a way of saying that forensic truth is truth. As I've indicated, I think that nothing less than match is enough. But again, there's no point in fighting over a word.

The story I have been telling deploys a variety of resources to generate forensic truth and thoughts. But there is a legitimate question regarding whether those resources are really available to us, even if those resources are enough to deliver our thoughts and forensic truth of some useful sort. As I suggested, there is an optimistic alternative, and a pessimistic one. Let's remain for the moment with optimism.

Option One: The primary resource we need to generate forensic truth is experience. And note both that if there is an experience with a certain content then that does not necessarily imply that the content is true, and that a non-objectual account of experience is merely an account which is not objectual. How might this help us? Consider an analogy. Let p be coherently conceivable, some positive claim expressible in C. The external negation of p is a content whose truth does not require the truth of any basic content. And yet its content in some way comes from p; it is dependent in generation on p. Likewise, it might be that the content of the claim that there is experience with content p might be dependent in generation on p, and yet the truth of that claim might not require the truth of any coherently conceivable content. In effect, this suggests an unfamiliar kind of content generation, mediated by words. Notice also that a non-objectual account of the realization of the experience of p might merely deny that there is a true objectual account. It, like the claim that there is an experience that p, might not be a positive and coherent claim about anything, or at least not the kind of detailed positive "account" which we pursued in Part Two. So perhaps there can be literal facts about the experience of p, and hence about what constitutes forensic truth, even if no basic content is true.

There are a number of serious difficulties which face this happy scenario. First of all, certainly the difference between desiring that p and actually experiencing that p is a positive difference, and it is experience in particular that is relevant to forensic truth. Can we make sense of this without deploying resources which are forbidden to us? I've deployed the traditional empiricist assumption that quasi-experience is less vivid than experience, but still how is a certain state an experience of p rather than a desire *qua* quasi-experience of something more vivid than p? We might try to wiggle out here with the claim that, in the absence of any positive feature which constitutes it as a mere desiring rather than as an experiencing, the state of *x*ing that p can play the role which I have suggested that the experience that p plays in generating forensic truth. *X*ing is a generic attitude towards a content, whose existence requires the truth of no detailed basic content. It is somewhat like an experience with that content, but without the particular positive pre-conditions required by that more familiar state. Perhaps then we can say that it is not experiencing p, but rather desiring it, that is the truly positive and dependent case.

It might seem that there must be positive differences between *x*ings with different contents. Different *x*ings with different contents are different. But so are external negations of different contents. Perhaps neither sort of thing requires the truth of a basic content, so that different *x*ings do not involve the kind of positive and detailed concrete differences which make our genuinely positive conceptions of things problematic. Perhaps we can in some weak sense coherently conceive some particular state of *x*ing because we can coherently conceive its content, even though we can't coherently conceive its realization in any detailed way of the sort we have been pursuing. Perhaps a very nearly empty non-objectual account of the realization of *x*ing, merely the denial of an objectual account, is true. Of course, there does seem to be some intuitively positive difference between the experience of p and of q, but there is also an intuitively positive difference between the external negation of p and of q. Perhaps our allegedly "positive" conception of our experience is not the kind of positive conception which requires the truth of a basic content.

Still, there are other problems. Consider another analogy. We experience primitive powers, which are restrictions with a certain content. Our capacity to conceive other powers is rooted in our capacity to conceive the contents of their restrictions. So there's another instance of an unusual sort of orthogonal content generation, which works through the content of the intensional phenomenon causation. Now consider again the case we're interested in. We can coherently conceive experience with content p. Then apparently by another sort of orthogonal content extension we are supposed to be able to conceive *x*ing that p, a notion rooted in the coherently conceivable p and yet which can be true though no basic content is true. But clearly we want to avoid in this case some features of the analogous case of powers. Our orthogonal conception of powers extends basic contents, but it does not leap beyond them. And we already have the notion of a power from our conception of the primitive powers before we perform any orthogonal extensions, while we get the notion of *x*ing apparently only by some sort of unusual abstraction or word-mediation from the notion of experiencing. That in itself is quite problematic. *X*ing is in effect the kind of experiencing whose realization is not coherently conceivable. We seem to be trying here to move by abstraction beyond what is coherently conceivable. And, at the same time, abstraction is supposed not to yield coherent notions of ten-dimensional spaces or quantum mechanical phenomena which can be true other than by the mediation of a basic content. Somehow the fact that *x*ing that p has a content is supposed to make that case different, and special treatment appropriate. That certainly seems like an awful lot to hope for.

Let's be tremendously optimistic, and assume that all this works, that we can manage to get experience, or at least some close analogue, *x*ing. Is that enough? No. We need more than the fact that there is experience of certain kinds to get the forensic truth, the forensic world.

First of all, we need in some way to distinguish between human experience and other animals' experience, and between normal human experience and other human experience. Only normal human experience matters to the nature of the forensic world. And perhaps we also need to distinguish between the experience of different people, between Galileo's experience and Aristotle's. All these seem like positive differences. But just perhaps we can wring even all of these differences out of the content of the experiences, for instance by exploiting the different perspectival distortions present in different people's experience, and the entire temporal sequence of each person's experience. But still we need more. The forensic truth is not constituted merely by what people actually experience. There must be some sort of projection from the content of various people's experience to the nature of the things which seem to be experienced, which removes all the obvious artifacts of the various individuals' experiences. But perhaps this projection can be generated in some a priori way, which does not depend on contingent and positive facts about the world.

Still, there is another serious problem. The forensic world is constituted not merely by projection from actual normal people's actual experience, but from the experience normal people would have under various hypothetical conditions. Can we get that? Again, perhaps just barely. What we seem to need is the truth of various counterfactual conditionals, various claims of the form "If p, then q" whose antecedents are false. Assume that the content of the antecedent and consequent of the relevant conditionals are, as it were, within the realm of experience. Perhaps it can help to fix the forensic truth if we know that if someone, anyone, hypothetically experienced p, then they would experience q. Certain traditional phenomenalist analyses ran to ground on this assumption, but it may be somewhat helpful that antecedents *we* can deploy include motor experience, which is closely related to the motor action of the subject of the experience. We can consider what sense experience people would have if they initiated various sorts of motor action. And we can also try to build enough into the antecedents to ensure that the right counterfactual possibilities are attached to the right individuals' experiences, in their particular situations.

Even all this is not enough. We need not only forensic truth but thoughts. Here too, as I have already suggested, a certain sort of conditional claim is crucial. Our actual experiences, and the quasi-experiences in imagination which we have presumed they encompass, are not alone enough to constitute our thoughts. But at least a large number of the relevant conditionals might be a kind of internal analogue of the type just suggested, "internal" examples of those we discussed in the previous paragraph. It might be that if a particular person hypothetically had a certain introspectible experience, then they would have another, and conditionals like this might constitute their own primary psychology, at least up to a point. Some of the tricks we've already deployed may help us formulate these as conditionals whose consequents and antecedents make reference merely to sequences of experiences.

Even if we can formulate the relevant conditionals, and even if their antecedents and consequents advert merely to states of *x*ing that don't in themselves involve positive and contingent conditions which we know to be problematic, still they may seem problematic. We need to presume that particular counterfactual conditionals of the form "if *x*ing that p, then *x*ing that q" are true, and others false. These conditionals have contents which seem generated from that of their components, and yet, like the external negation of a component, we have been presuming that their truth does not to imply the truth of any basic content. This may be quite problematic. And the quasi-logical operations can only deliver material implication, not a proper counterfactual conditional. Still, if some positive ground for the truth of the conditionals is required, just perhaps we can root the truth of these counterfactuals in solitary causal microevents, bits of the world which have no definite spatio-temporal relations to any other microevents, which restrict the world so that the relevant counterfactuals are true, so that if something relevant happened, then something else relevant would happen. The arguments we reviewed in this part show that the world lacks any spatio-temporally detailed causal structure. But perhaps that isn't enough to show that there aren't some instantiations of causal powers in the world, some asymmetric restrictions of the sort we need to ground the truth of our various conditionals. Perhaps we didn't really see that all causal basic contents are false, but only those with any spatio-temporal detail, only those which aren't degenerate, only those which might capture what our causal experience seems to reveal.

Note that the forensic truth and various individual psychologies might require the truth of conflicting counterfactuals. My thoughts might run in a different direction than yours if we had various hypothetical experiences, and away from the course of experience which would reveal the world. Just possibly, we can get what we need here out of the contents of the *x*ings in question. For instance, maybe we can distinguish between the counterfactuals relevant to your psychology and those relevant to mine, or between those relevant to two different moments of yours, by building enough of our histories of experience into the antecedents of the requisite conditionals. This may also help us to link various counterfactual claims with various actual histories of individual experience, which we might bind together as temporally extended contents of single *x*ings. And perhaps your *psychology* may often be revealed in the hypothetical course of your causal experience and primary imagination if various phenomenal experiences turned up, and the *world* in various phenomenal experiences which would turn up if you had the causal experience of acting in a certain way, though we know from Chapter Thirteen that there are limits to how cleanly this model can capture the distinction between self and world. If we can't build all these things into the contents of the relevant *x*ings, perhaps we can get some of them in a different way. Perhaps more than one asymmetric causal restriction, more than one causal microevent, exists. Perhaps there is a true basic content which includes a number of causal microevents which have no specific spatio-temporal relations to each other. One spatio-temporally unconnected microevent might capture the counterfactuals necessary to constitute my psychology, or my psychology of a moment. And another might capture yours. And another might help constitute the world. We might worry that irreducible powers out in the world are unlikely to be so directly focussed on human experience, or human *x*ing, and that nothing can constitute something which is coherently conceivable but something which is coherently conceivable. But still it *may* be that such a causal microevent without specific spatio-temporal relations can reasonably exist in a world which has no spatio-temporal parts and where any "constitution" is not by spatio-temporal parts. There are other difficulties. No causal microevents within a basic content which has an explicit and positive spatio-temporal structure can "overlap" others within that content. But even such a restriction may be irrelevant if the causal microevents have no positive spatio-temporal relations within the basic content which captures them. And notice another problem. The content of the relevant restrictions are of a new and unfamiliar sort, that involve the mere experiencing or *x*ing of various things, and this seems to me quite a suspicious element. But if we can get a conception of *x*ing that p, then we should also be able to get the powers necessary to ground the counterfactuals we need.

If all this utterly wild optimism is well-founded, then we can properly hope for a somewhat more robust vindication of our thoughts than I suggested earlier. There would be a literal truth that there is a certain sort of forensic truth. There would literally be forensic truth for the account of the realization of our thoughts provided by Part Two, and for various commonsense claims. And the forensic truth could ground the positive cognitive value of various human claims which lack forensic truth, including certain crucial claims made in this book. What's more, it would be literally true that there are human thoughts, that you exist. It would be literally true that they are realized in the very vague non-objectual way we've just sketched, which is in fact the third account of the realization of our thoughts pursued in this book. Still, we could not coherently conceive the actual realization of our thoughts in any detail, nor indeed the nature of the world generally.

In our peculiarly reduced circumstances, this is an awful lot to hope for. But perhaps we can draw comfort from the fact that, at least if my arguments have been correct, pessimism only *ought* to win if we aren't around to make mistakes anyway. If you don't exist, then you can't make an error. Optimism, anyone?

Still, it seems to me that all this may well be considerably too optimistic. The claim that people have a certain sort of experience seems to be positive enough to require the truth of some basic content, and any claim about the existence of *x*ing we can make seems either not positive enough to do all the work we need to be done or too positive not to be false when basic contents are false. Certainly we might also worry about the various conditional claims I've deployed. And even if we can get them, they may well not be enough to deliver all we need. It may be that all of these claims, for instance the claim that there is mere experience of p, can be made empty enough to be consistent with all basic contents being false and still do the work we need to have done, or perhaps that such cases are sufficiently different from other sorts of content extension beyond basic content, sufficiently special, to allow a kind of match in this instance even when no basic content matches. But, to say the least, there doesn't seem to be reason for much confidence about that.

The second and pessimistic option, the merely cold and shallow vindication of thoughts, may well be more plausible than optimism. Or perhaps the content of the claims we have been recently trying to save doesn't determinately and unambiguously allow that they could be true if no basic content were true. There may then be a kind of indeterminacy in our situation, between the optimistic first option and the pessimistic second one. Or perhaps we can get some of the resources we need for Option One but not all of them. That would still leave us somewhere between pessimism and optimism. In any case, we need to consider the pessimistic alternative, Option Two:

My claims that there are experiences of certain sorts, and thoughts, and sentences, and forensic truth, are positive and contingent human claims, hence they are false. In hard fact, none of the claims or pieces of evidence presented in this book are really true. There aren't really any thoughts or experiences of the sort we've been discussing here. Nor is it even strictly true that there are such claims and such a book. Nor is there a determinate forensic truth which might ground their positive value if they did exist. Thoughts are vindicated only in the weak sense that they are no worse off than anything else positive and contingent which humans can coherently conceive.

This situation *is* coherent, if not coherently conceivable in any positive way. Let me try at least to babble incoherently in the right direction. There aren't in fact such things as we (so to speak) conceive, nor can any of our (so-called) positive and contingent thoughts be true in the strict sense. Still, we might hope that there are things at least remotely analogous to those things which we can (so to speak) conceive, including thoughts. These thought-analogues have some analogue of truth, or at least of forensic truth and the other cognitive virtues rooted in forensic truth. They are (so to speak) "better off" than their denials, though still much that (so-called) "we" (so to speak) "want" is lacking. Of course, even my talk of analogy is wildly optimistic. Maybe it would be a little better to say that there is a world which would be "expressed" in some literally inconceivable way within human experience and forensic truth as I have characterized them, if only there were such experience, or at least if only I had characterized it.

Still, even if you grant me analogy or expression, which you probably shouldn't, it isn't very much. Option Two even in its most optimistic form suggests that what really exists is in fact only some remote analogue of thoughts, as well as of balloons and balls and planets. Strictly speaking, there are no thoughts. Strictly speaking, you and I don't exist. We don't think, nor even have human bodies, therefore we aren't. But at least in the same less than strict sense in which there are red balls and stars and human bodies, there are thoughts and sentences, with the contents characterized in this book. And in that same less than strict sense, those thoughts are true.

Whether Option One or Option Two or something between is appropriate, we can conclude in much the same way. Thoughts are at least as plausibly present in the world as stars and neurons and red balloons. In fact they may be, or at least some of them may be, even more plausible. Our human thoughts are no more in doubt than anything else which is familiar to us. And even our positive and contingent thoughts, if I can pretend or hope for the moment that there really are some, have some analogue of what we ordinarily call truth. But, strictly speaking, not one of them is true.

NOTES

1. In fact, there are problems with the plausibility of neurons as well, problems with even the apparently plausible resources which Part Two deployed. But let me hold off on that point for a moment.
2. This is in fact slightly over-simplified. There is a certain sort of degenerate causal basic content which may well still match the world. We will return to this issue in a bit.
3. One might wonder how these can be distinct. There are some suggestions in section 2.
4. Paul Churchland, *Scientific Realism and the Plasticity of Mind* (Cambridge: Cambridge University Press, 1979).
5. Michael Bishop, "Theory-Ladenness of Perception Arguments".
6. Such a strategy might even help to underwrite the truth of more ordinary speech despite the fact that our experience is seriously false. Perhaps ordinary speech of the spatio-temporal relations of balls and balloons is not so determinate in meaning as to be consistent only with the existence of a classical and continuous spatio-temporal world. Perhaps ordinary speech of the spatial and temporal relations of ordinary concrete objects can be legitimately extended in either a classical or quantum mechanical direction. Perhaps either direction involves some development, but of the kind which led twelfth century talk of addition gradually towards talk of transfinite addition, a development which is a refinement rather than a replacement.
7. At least if it involves chirality.
8. See the discussion of Peter Unger's examples in Chapter Nine.
9. There are other ways in which non-semantic constitution would be helpful to us. Perhaps even our color experience might match the world, if the phenomenal colors of balls and balloons which we experience (or at least the slightly abstracted colors consistent with the perceptions of all normal humans) might be non-semantically constituted by plausibly objective causal properties.
10. Michael Lockwood, *Mind, Brain and the Quantum* (Oxford: Blackwell, 1989).
11. We could, of course, still treat it differently within the realm of forensic truth, in our coherently conceivable and commonsense, but literally false tale of its realization within the world of forensic truth.

INDEX

PHILOSOPHICAL STUDIES SERIES

1. Jay F. Rosenberg, *Linguistic Representation.* 1974 ISBN 90-277-0533-X
2. Wilfrid Sellars, *Essays in Philosophy and Its History.* 1974 ISBN 90-277-0526-7
3. Dickinson S. Miller, *Philosophical Analysis and Human Welfare.* Selected Essays and Chapters from Six Decades. Edited with an Introduction by Lloyd D. Easton. 1975 ISBN 90-277-0566-6
4. Keith Lehrer (ed.), *Analysis and Metaphysics.* Essays in Honor of R. M Chisholm. 1975 ISBN 90-277-0571-2
5. Carl Ginet, *Knowledge, Perception, and Memory.* 1975 ISBN 90-277-0574-7
6. Peter H. Hare and Edward H. Madden. *Causing, Perceiving and Believing.* An Examination of the Philosophy of C. J. Ducasse. 1975 ISBN 90-277-0563-1
7. Hector-Neri Castañeda, *Thinking and Doing.* The Philosophical Foundations of Institutions. 1975 ISBN 90-277-0610-7
8. John L. Pollock, *Subjunctive Reasoning.* 1976 ISBN 90-277-0701-4
9. Bruce Aune, *Reason and Action.* 1977 ISBN 90-277-0805-3
10. George Schlesinger, *Religion and Scientific Method.* 1977 ISBN 90-277-0815-0
11. Yirmiahu Yovel (ed.), *Philosophy of History and Action.* Papers presented at the First Jerusalem Philosophical Encounter (December 1974). 1978 ISBN 90-277-0890-8
12. Joseph C. Pitt (ed.), *The Philosophy of Wilfrid Sellars: Queries and Extensions.* 1978 ISBN 90-277-0903-3
13. Alvin I. Goldman and Jaegwon Kim (eds.), *Values and Morals.* Essays in Honor of William Frankena, Charles Stevenson, and Richard Brandt. 1978 ISBN 90-277-0914-9
14. Michael J. Loux, *Substance and Attribute.* A Study in Ontology. 1978 ISBN 90-277-0926-2
15. Ernest Sosa (ed.), *The Philosophy of Nicholas Rescher.* Discussion and Replies. 1979 ISBN 90-277-0962-9
16. Jeffrie G. Murphy, *Retribution, Justice, and Therapy.* Essays in the Philosophy of Law. 1979 ISBN 90-277-0998-X
17. George S. Pappas (ed.), *Justification and Knowledge.* New Studies in Epistemology. 1979 ISBN 90-277-1023-6
18. James W. Cornman, *Skepticism, Justification, and Explanation.* With a Bibliographic Essay by Walter N. Gregory. 1980 ISBN 90-277-1041-4
19. Peter van Inwagen (ed.), *Time and Cause.* Essays presented to Richard Taylor. 1980 ISBN 90-277-1048-1
20. Donald Nute, *Topics in Conditional Logic.* 1980 ISBN 90-277-1049-X
21. Risto Hilpinen (ed.), *Rationality in Science.* Studies in the Foundations of Science and Ethics. 1980 ISBN 90-277-1112-7
22. Georges Dicker, *Perceptual Knowledge.* An Analytical and Historical Study. 1980 ISBN 90-277-1130-5
23. Jay F. Rosenberg, *One World and Our Knowledge of It.* The Problematic of Realism in Post-Kantian Perspective. 1980 ISBN 90-277-1136-4
24. Keith Lehrer and Carl Wagner, *Rational Consensus in Science and Society.* A Philosophical and Mathematical Study. 1981 ISBN 90-277-1306-5
25. David O'Connor, *The Metaphysics of G. E. Moore.* 1982 ISBN 90-277-1352-9
26. John D. Hodson, *The Ethics of Legal Coercion.* 1983 ISBN 90-277-1494-0
27. Robert J. Richman, *God, Free Will, and Morality.* Prolegomena to a Theory of Practical Reasoning. 1983 ISBN 90-277-1548-3

PHILOSOPHICAL STUDIES SERIES

28. Terence Penelhum, *God and Skepticism.* A Study in Skepticism and Fideism. 1983 ISBN 90-277-1550-5
29. James Bogen and James E. McGuire (eds.), *How Things Are.* Studies in Predication and the History of Philosophy of Science. 1985 ISBN 90-277-1583-1
30. Clement Dore, *Theism.* 1984 ISBN 90-277-1683-8
31. Thomas L. Carson, *The Status of Morality.* 1984 ISBN 90-277-1619-9
32. Michael J. White, *Agency and Integrality.* Philosophical Themes in the Ancient Discussions of Determinism and Responsibility. 1985 ISBN 90-277-1968-3
33. Donald F. Gustafson, *Intention and Agency.* 1986 ISBN 90-277-2009-6
34. Paul K. Moser, *Empirical Justification.* 1985 ISBN 90-277-2041-X
35. Fred Feldman, *Doing the Best We Can.* An Essay in Informal Deontic Logic. 1986 ISBN 90-277-2164-5
36. G. W. Fitch, *Naming and Believing.* 1987 ISBN 90-277-2349-4
37. Terry Penner, *The Ascent from Nominalism.* Some Existence Arguments in Plato's Middle Dialogues. 1987 ISBN 90-277-2427-X
38. Robert G. Meyers, *The Likelihood of Knowledge.* 1988 ISBN 90-277-2671-X
39. David F. Austin (ed.), *Philosophical Analysis.* A Defense by Example. 1988 ISBN 90-277-2674-4
40. Stuart Silvers (ed.), *Rerepresentation.* Essays in the Philosophy of Mental Representation. 1988 ISBN 0-7923-0045-9
41. Michael P. Levine, *Hume and the Problem of Miracles.* A Solution. 1979 ISBN 0-7923-0043-2
42. Melvin Dalgarno and Eric Matthews (eds.), *The Philosophy of Thomas Reid.* 1989 ISBN 0-7923-0190-0
43. Kenneth R. Westphal, *Hegel's Epistemological Realism.* A Study of the Aim and Method of Hegel's *Phenomenology of Spirit.* 1989 ISBN 0-7923-0193-5
44. John W. Bender (ed.), *The Current State of the Coherence Theory.* Critical Essays on the Epistemic Theories of Keith Lehrer and Laurence BonJour, with Replies. 1989 ISBN 0-7923-0220-6
45. Roger D. Gallie, *Thomas Reid and 'The Way of Ideas'.* 1989 ISBN 0-7923-0390-3
46. J-C. Smith (ed.), *Historical Foundations of Cognitive Science.* 1990 ISBN 0-7923-0451-9
47. John Heil (ed.), *Cause, Mind, and Reality.* Essays Honoring C. B. Martin. 1989 ISBN 0-7923-0462-4
48. Michael D. Roth and Glenn Ross (eds.), *Doubting.* Contemporary Perspectives on Skepticism. 1990 ISBN 0-7923-0576-0
49. Rod Bertolet, *What is Said.* A Theory of Indirect Speech Reports. 1990 ISBN 0-7923-0792-5
50. Bruce Russell (ed.), *Freedom, Rights and Pornography.* A Collection of Papers by Fred R. Berger. 1991 ISBN 0-7923-1034-9
51. Kevin Mulligan (ed.), *Language, Truth and Ontology.* 1992 ISBN 0-7923-1509-X
52. Jesús Ezquerro and Jesús M. Larrazabal (eds.), *Cognition, Semantics and Philosophy.* Proceedings of the First International Colloquium on Cognitive Science. 1992 ISBN 0-7923-1538-3
53. O.H. Green, *The Emotions.* A Philosophical Theory. 1992 ISBN 0-7923-1549-9
54. Jeffrie G. Murphy, *Retribution Reconsidered.* More Essays in the Philosophy of Law. 1992 ISBN 0-7923-1815-3

PHILOSOPHICAL STUDIES SERIES

55. Phillip Montague, *In the Interests of Others.* An Essay in Moral Philosophy. 1992 ISBN 0-7923-1856-0
56. Jacques-Paul Dubucs (ed.), *Philosophy of Probability.* 1993 ISBN 0-7923-2385-8
57. Gary S. Rosenkrantz, *Haecceity.* An Ontological Essay. 1993 ISBN 0-7923-2438-2
58. Charles Landesman, *The Eye and the Mind.* Reflections on Perception and the Problem of Knowledge. 1994 ISBN 0-7923-2586-9
59. Paul Weingartner (ed.), *Scientific and Religious Belief.* 1994 ISBN 0-7923-2595-8
60. Michaelis Michael and John O'Leary-Hawthorne (eds.), *Philosophy in Mind.* The Place of Philosophy in the Study of Mind. 1994 ISBN 0-7923-3143-5
61. William H. Shaw, *Moore on Right and Wrong.* The Normative Ethics of G.E. Moore. 1995 ISBN 0-7923-3223-7
62. T.A. Blackson, *Inquiry, Forms, and Substances.* A Study in Plato's Metaphysics and Epistemology. 1995 ISBN 0-7923-3275-X
63. Debra Nails, *Agora, Academy, and the Conduct of Philosophy.* 1995 ISBN 0-7923-3543-0
64. Warren Shibles, *Emotion in Aesthetics.* 1995 ISBN 0-7923-3618-6
65. John Biro and Petr Kotatko (eds.), *Frege: Sense and Reference One Hundred Years Later.* 1995 ISBN 0-7923-3795-6
66. Mary Gore Forrester, *Persons, Animals, and Fetuses.* An Essay in Practical Ethics. 1996 ISBN 0-7923-3918-5
67. K. Lehrer, B.J. Lum, B.A. Slichta and N.D. Smith (eds.): *Knowledge, Teaching and Wisdom.* 1996 ISBN 0-7923-3980-0
68. Herbert Granger: *Aristotle's Idea of the Soul.* 1996 ISBN 0-7923-4033-7
69. Andy Clark, Jesús Ezquerro and Jesús M. Larrazabal (eds.): *Philosophy and Cognitive Science: Categories, Consciousness, and Reasoning.* 1996 ISBN 0-7923-4068-X
70. J. Mendola: *Human Thought.* 1997 ISBN 0-7923-4401-4; pb 0-7923-4402-2

KLUWER ACADEMIC PUBLISHERS – DORDRECHT / BOSTON / LONDON